| APR 2 7 1993 DATE DUE | | | |
|---|---|---|---|
| OCT - 3 1994 | | | |
| | | | |
| | | | |
| | | | |
| | | | |
| | | | |
| | | | |
| | | | |
| | | | |
| | | | |
| | | | |

**SECOND** EDITION

# COGNITION

Arnold Lewis Glass

Rutgers University

Keith James Holyoak

The University of Michigan

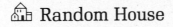 Random House

New York

# COPYRIGHT ACKNOWLEDGMENTS

8    Kroll, N. E. A., T. Parks, S. R., Parkinson, S. L. Bieber, and A. L. Johnson, 1970. Short-term memory while shadowing: recall of visually and aurally presented letters. *Journal of Experimental Psychology* 85: 220–224. Copyright 1970 by the American Psychological Association. Reprinted by permission.

12, 13    Shepard, R. N., and J. Metzler, 1971. Mental rotation of three-dimensional objects. *Science* 171: 701–703. Copyright 1971 by the American Association for the Advancement of Science.

36    Rock, I., and D. Gutman, 1981. The effect of inattention on form perception. *Journal of Experimental Psychology: Human Perception and Performance* 7: 275–285.

49    Estes, W. K., D. H. Allmeyer, and S. M. Reder, 1976. Serial position functions for letter identification at brief and extended exposure durations. *Perception & Psychophysics* 19: 1–15.

50    Yarbus, A. L., 1976. *Eye Movements and Vision.* B. Haigh, (trans.) New York: Plenum Press. Copyright 1967 by Plenum Publishing Corporation. Reprinted by permission.

(*Continued* on page 539)

Second Edition

98765432

Copyright © 1986 by Newbery Award Records, Inc.

**Library of Congress Cataloging in Publication Data**

Glass, Arnold Lewis, 1951–
   Cognition.

   Bibliography: p.
   Includes index.
   1. Cognition.    I. Holyoak, Keith James, 1950–
II. Title.
Bf311.G54   1986f        153        86–2017
ISBN: 0-394-35057-X

This edition is dedicated with affection
to our mentor Gordon Bower
for leaving some questions for us to answer.

# INTRODUCTION

This book is an introduction to cognition, but we must first take a moment to introduce *Cognition* itself. We want both students and instructors to gain some sense of the general orientation of the book and how best to make use of it.

## First Edition and Reactions to It

This book is the second edition of *Cognition,* and we can best introduce it by relating it to its predecessor. This approach may be especially helpful for those instructors who used the first edition, since they will be most susceptible to "proactive interference" (see Chapter 9). We had two interrelated goals in writing the first edition, which appeared in 1979. First, we wished to write a book that would bring together the diverse areas and topics that constitute cognitive psychology. That edition was written at a time when most texts in cognition covered little more than selected aspects of memory and attention. We felt that the study of cognition properly included perception, attention, memory, reasoning, problem solving, and language, and that a book was needed that would integrate this range of topics. Furthermore, we wished to broaden the range of studies presented in the context of these topics. As we remarked in our earlier Introduction, psychology was once criticized for limiting itself to the study of white rats and college sophomores; to an alarming degree cognitive psychology had simply abandoned the rats as well. We combated this trend by adding studies of various other cognitive systems, including children, chimpanzees, and computers. In particular, we took seriously the neuropsychological literature on such clinical syndromes as amnesia and aphasia, even though at that time such research was not easily published in the mainstream journals of experimental psychology.

 The second basic reason that we embarked upon the project was that we felt we had a framework we could use to integrate the range of topics we wished to cover. This framework encompassed several themes that ran through the book, such as the multicode nature of mental representation, the central importance of memory organization, retrieval failure as an explanation of forgetting, and the continuity of simple and complex thought processes. The organization of the book reflected our framework. In order to emphasize the interrelatedness of cognitive processes, we juxtaposed topics that were traditionally treated separately. Because of our emphasis on mental representation and memory organization, we introduced these topics in Chapter 1 and delayed discussion of attention until Chapter 6. In addition, we had been dismayed by conventional treatments of short-term memory. On the one hand, the term was used to refer to a memory store in which an input is supposedly held *prior* to making contact with a matching trace in long-term memory. On the other hand, the experiments presented in this context were related to a verbal-rehearsal buffer for maintaining a representation of the input *after* it has been identified. (Indeed, the term was commonly used in several other senses as well.) It seemed to us that previous textbooks, which had their organization dictated by the central place reserved for one or more chapters devoted to this concept, ended up presenting an inherently contradictory account of human information processing. To avoid this pitfall, we took the radical precaution of writing a textbook on cognition that never referred to short-term memory.

We generally regard with satisfaction the ways in which the field has developed since the appearance of the first edition. Many of the positions we adopted in regard to representation, attention, and memory are now uncontroversially accepted.

For example, we gave minimal space to the concept of sensory registers, such as the icon, often discussed as a kind of very short-term memory. We thus anticipated the proposal made by Haber (1983) that the icon is a misleading concept that should be dropped from cognitive textbooks. In addition, the field has clearly been broadened. To write a text on cognition without covering reasoning and problem solving, for example, would now be unthinkable. The study of populations other than college students is no longer remarkable, and the relevance of data from the study of cognitive pathologies is accepted. We do not claim credit for these changes, but at least we caught the zeitgeist and helped indoctrinate a new generation of students in it. Furthermore, readers generally had only kind things to say about our efforts.

Nonetheless, our vision of what a cognitive psychology text should be was not fully realized by the first edition. Instructors commented that what they liked about the book was that it was eclectic, rather than pushing any particular point of view. This compliment gave us pause, since we had been been trying to present a point of view. Some users understood the reason for the unorthodox chapter order, but others perceived it as more or less random. We have sympathy for the latter view, since we tried alternative chapter sequences when we used the book in our own courses.

Part of the problem was a conflict in our two initial aims. In broadening the data base, we included such a variety of phenomena and results that they did not all fit within a single explicit framework. Also, many topics in the study of cognition are so tightly interrelated that any linear sequencing of them is inadequate. By placing the chapters on memory before the one on attention, we were able to highlight the role of representation in memory. However, in so doing, we broke up the natural continuity of memory, reasoning, and problem solving. Furthermore, we failed to highlight equally important processing concepts, including the key concept of degree of memory activation, which interrelates attention, action, and memory.

## Second Edition

We believe that the second edition is in all respects an improvement upon the first and moves us closer to our original goals. The study of cognition may be naturally divided into five basic topics: perception, attention, memory, thinking, and language. Of these topics perception and language have the greatest conceptual autonomy. Both involve specialized input and output processes, typically covered in separate courses on perception and psycholinguistics, which can be referred to in a central course on cognition without actually being described. However, the topics of attention, memory, and thinking are so intimately intertwined that one of them cannot be satisfactorily discussed without the other two. Furthermore, they can be presented in almost any order if the presentation is sufficiently skillful.

The organization we have arrived at proceeds as follows. We begin in Chapter 1 with an overview of the basic concepts required for describing mental representations and the processes that operate on them. A brief outline of the relationship of structure to process is introduced as a framework for what is to come. The rest of the book fills in this framework. The process of attention is then described. Chapter 2 deals with the selection of inputs, and Chapter 3 deals with the organization and direction of outputs. These chapters illustrate the main levels of representation and the processes that transmit information between them. Next, we examine two forms of representation central to human cognition, the visuospatial code (Chapter 4) and the semantic code that forms the basis of the category system (Chapter 5). Memory is then examined in five chapters, beginning with retrieval (Chapters 6–8) and then turning to learning (Chapters 9 and 10). Thinking is discussed in Chapter 11, on reasoning and decision making, and in Chapter 12, on problem solving and creativity. Chapter 13 focuses on the relationship between hemispheric functioning and language, and the topic of language is further pursued in Chapters 14 and 15.

The second edition of *Cognition* contains an expanded range of topics and increased depth of coverage. In particular, the perspectives offered by work in neuropsychology and artificial intelligence are discussed in relation to a number of topics. As a consequence of the reorganization and expansion, a number of chapters were bifurcated, so that the second edition has three more chapters than did the first.

The one drawback of this abundance is that the book is now too large for all the material in it to be adequately covered in a semester. However, we feel it is preferable to offer too much rather than too little, because an abundance of material allows instructors flexibility in selectively emphasizing the topics they wish to stress. A subset of the chapters can be used as core-reading assignments. Others can be used as secondary readings, especially for students who wish to explore certain topics more broadly.

Of the five major topics of cognitive psychology, we give limited coverage to perception, which is most often covered in a separate course. However, we describe the relationship between perception and attention (Chapter 2), mental representation (Chapter 4), and language (Chapter 13). The other four topics—attention, memory, thinking, and language—receive extensive treatment. We have the following suggestions about how to selectively emphasize particular sets of topics if desired:

1. For a first or only course on general cognition Chapters 10, 13, and 14 can be omitted without substantially disrupting the continuity of the narrative.
2. For a course on attention and memory Chapters 11–15 may be dropped.
3. For a course on memory and reasoning (e.g., psychology of thinking) Chapters 2, 9, 10, and 13–15 are all optional.

Writing this edition was a tremendously exciting experience. As we worked our way through the great mass of research that had accumulated, it became clear that the same basic set of structures and operations were involved, so that everything was coming to fit together within a coherent framework. The basic cognitive experimental paradigms have now been extended to a wonderful multiplicity of phenomena, so a wealth of informative results could be included because these results illustrated some new detail of the basic framework. In the past few years neurospychological research has produced concrete examples of cases in which understanding the functioning of the brain can guide our understanding of the mind. Learning, a venerable but recently rejuvenated topic within cognitive psychology, is much more prominent in the new edition, as it is now discussed in several chapters (Chapters 3, 5, 12, and 14, in addition to 9 and 10).

We believe that a textbook can usefully serve as the focus of an intellectual dialog. Accordingly, we invite readers to send us their questions and comments, which may be addressed to Arnold Glass, Department of Psychology, Rutgers University, New Brunswick, NJ 08903.

Cognitive psychology remains a vibrant, growing science, which can provide intellectual excitement both to those who work in it and to those who are first learning about it. In our presentation we try to provide an organizing framework without allowing it to become a premature straightjacket for a developing field. We hope we have maintained a needed touch of eclecticism. We have tried to provide a balanced treatment of areas of controversy, avoiding both dogmatism and uncritical agnosticism. In a changing field a text should strive not only to illuminate what has already been achieved but also to point the way to accomplishments yet to come. We close this second Introduction to *Cognition* as we did the first, with the hope that students will be inspired by this book to participate in the making of these accomplishments.

*March 1985*                                                                    A. L. G.
                                                                                K. J. H.

# ACKNOWLEDGMENTS

This edition of our textbook has benefited, either directly or indirectly, from the efforts of many people. During a sabbatical leave in 1981–1982, A. Glass learned a great deal about cognition from William Estes of Harvard University and from Nelson Butters, who is now at the San Diego Veterans Administration Medical Center. The sabbatical was made possible in part by a Cattel Fellowship. K. Holyoak was able to devote more time to the project as a result of receiving a Research Scientist Development Award from the National Institute of Mental Health. These opportunites made possible expanded coverage of many areas.

The revision benefited greatly from the expertise of the many reviewers who provided critiques of different chapters. The following people assisted in this capacity:

Mark Altom, AT&T Information Systems

Jonathan Baron, University of Pennsylvania

Irving Biederman, State University of New York at Buffalo

Herman Buschke, Albert Einstein College of Medicine of Yeshiva University

Thomas Carr, Michigan State University

James Chumbley, University of Massachusetts

Mary Gick, University of Toronto at Erindale

Murray Glanzer, New York University

Richard Griggs, University of Florida

John Jonides, University of Michigan

Michael Kubovy, Rutgers University

Morris Moscovitch, University of Toronto at Erindale

Michael Posner, University of Oregon

James Rafferty, Bemidji State University

Irvin Rock, Rutgers University

Per Saugstad, University of Oslo

Eileen Schwab, Indiana University

Marilyn Shatz, University of Michigan

Virginia Valian, Columbia University

Many researchers contributed figures or tables of data, which are evident throughout the book. Our special thanks go to our colleagues Irving Biederman, Albert Biegman, Nelson Butters, Paul D'Agostino, Douglas Detterman, and Gregory Lockhead, who dug into their files and sent us their original figures. Special thanks also goes to Francis Durso and Larry Squire for supplying their original data for figure plotting. Finally, we would like to thank Monika Hellerson for her help in obtaining figures. Michael Flannagan was of tremendous assistance in proofreading and assembling the completed manuscript. Lindsay Oliver assisted in the formidable task of preparing the bibliography. Martha Blanchard did most of the portion of typing done at the University of Michigan. We also thank Barbara Gracia of Woodstock Publishers' Services and our copy editor Carol Beal for their outstanding job of producing the book under trying circumstances. Our publisher, Random House, deserves credit for having faith in the project and providing the time and money needed to create a text of high quality.

Particular thanks are due to a person who shared all of the pain involved in writing the book and little of the reward. As was the case for the first edition, Lynne Glass made the book possible through her constant support of the first author.

# CONTENTS

# CHAPTER **ONE**

# Basic Concepts of Cognitive Psychology

## INTRODUCTION

### What Is Cognitive Psychology?

When most people think about what they know, they probably think about what they studied in school or college. Or perhaps they might consider some specialized kind of knowledge, like how to play the guitar, fly an airplane, or analyze the stock market. They probably will think of knowledge that is a little out of the ordinary or that is valued by other people. What they are likely to neglect is the kind of knowledge that is shared by almost everybody. For example, most of us have at least some memories of our childhood. We know something about our personal history and how we came to be what we now are. Our sense of identity depends on such knowledge. We also know a myriad of facts about the world and the things in it—that wood burns, eagles fly, and water usually flows downhill. We have many other kinds of knowledge as well. We can recall the sounds and smells of the seashore and the face of a friend we haven't seen in years. We know how to speak and understand our native language and how to find our way home from work or school.

We are likely to take our everyday knowledge very much for granted. Yet it adds up to an incredibly complex system that psychologists are only beginning to understand. We can gain respect for our mundane abilities by considering what happens to some unfortunate people who, through accident or disease, suffer various types of damage to their brains. In some cases the behavior and intellectual capabilities of such people remain much as before, yet some particular mental ability is severely impaired. They may lose the ability to speak their language or to recognize faces. Some are unable to remember their doctor from one day to the next or to learn where the bathroom in their house is located. The study of these sad but fascinating cases cannot help but increase our respect for the knowledge that guides our everyday lives.

In addition, the apparent selectivity of impairment raises the intriguing possibility that individual cognitive functions depend on particular parts of the brain.

All our mental abilities—perceiving, remembering, reasoning, and many others—are organized into a complex system, the overall function of which is termed *cognition*. The branch of psychology that studies human cognition is called *cognitive psychology*. Fundamentally, cognitive psychology is the study of knowledge and how people use it. For this reason cognitive psychology is also called *information-processing psychology*. *Information* is a term that we will use essentially as a synonym for *knowledge*. We view a human being (or, indeed, any intelligent cognitive system, including animals and some computer programs) as one who seeks information, remembers it, and uses it to make complex decisions that guide his or her behavior. As you can tell by glancing at the chapter titles, this book is basically about cognitive skills. But in talking about these skills, we'll also be introducing you to some of the ways in which psychologists have been able to study cognition.

### Cognitive Psychology and Related Disciplines

Cognitive psychology is by no means an isolated fragment of the field of psychology. In fact, the study of cognitive processes has had a major impact not only within human experimental psychology but also in related areas such as social psychology, developmental psychology, clinical psychology, animal learning, and neuropsychology. We will point out some of these connections as the book unfolds.

In addition, the study of cognition draws on work in other disciplines besides psychology. Efforts in linguistics, philosophy of the mind, and computer science have important implications for cognitive psychology. To some extent these diverse fields are becoming integrated into a new discipline called *cognitive science*.

An allied research field especially relevant to cognitive psychology is the branch of computer science called *artificial intelligence*, which involves the development of computer programs that display "intelligent" behavior. Modern computers are able to perform many other tasks besides rapid mathematical calculations. In principle, a computer can perform any task that can be described in the form of a computer program—that is, as an explicit set of instructions coded in a computer language. Researchers in artificial intelligence build programs designed to perform such tasks as recognizing visual patterns, processing spoken and written language, and solving complex problems.

Some computers programs (often developed by psychologists) are intended to be *simulations* of human behavior in some task. For example, the program may make errors or take more time in the same kinds of situations that people find difficult. In contrast, general artificial-intelligence programs are not intended to mimic human performance. They are designed to perform cognitive tasks, but they are not explicitly modeled after human cognition. Nevertheless, such programs can be relevant to cognitive psychology. For if a program is able to show how a task might be performed, it may help develop our ideas about how humans actually perform it. Furthermore, humans are so skillful in performing some cognitive tasks that in such cases the best way to design artificial systems may be to actually simulate aspects of human cognition. In addition, it may one day be possible to develop a theory of intelligent systems that will allow us to understand the similarities and differences between human intelligence and other possible varieties. We will occasionally be discussing particular artificial-intelligence programs that seem relevant to understanding human cognition.

## READING: AN EXAMPLE OF HUMAN INFORMATION PROCESSING

Cognitive processing is so much a part of our daily activities that it is easy to overlook the feats of intellectual prowess that the most mundane tasks require. For example, reading a page of a text like this one poses little apparent difficulty for the average college student. But a subjectively easy task may require mechanisms of staggering complexity. As a preliminary to our investigation of cognition, let us take a closer look at the task of reading.

Reading is first and foremost an example of visual perception, so it is useful to begin with an overview of the medium in which reading takes place: the eyes, the neural pathways to the brain, and the brain itself. While reading a page like this one, your eyes move in unison, in brief jumps called *saccades*, from word to word. In between jumps your eyes *fixate* on each word for a period of time, ranging from as short as a fiftieth of a second to as long as 1 second (Just and Carpenter 1980). On the average, your eyes move about four times a second. During each fixation light reflected off the page is focused by the lens of each eye onto its interior surface, called the *retina*. As the light falls on the retina, it activates a pattern of activity among cells embedded there.

The letter patterns must be extracted from the light that falls on the retina. Imagine that you were looking inside your own head and watching your brain processing information as you read. The part of the brain we will be concerned with is the large area called the *cerebrum* (see Figure 1.1). The input from the retina goes through successive transformations as it passes through layers of nerve cells, or *neurons*, and is conducted to various areas deep within the cerebrum. From one of these areas, known as the *lateral geniculate nucleus*, the input is next sent to a particular area on the surface of the cerebrum. The surface of the cerebrum is called the *cortex*, and the area of the cortex at which the visual input first arrives, located at the back of the head,

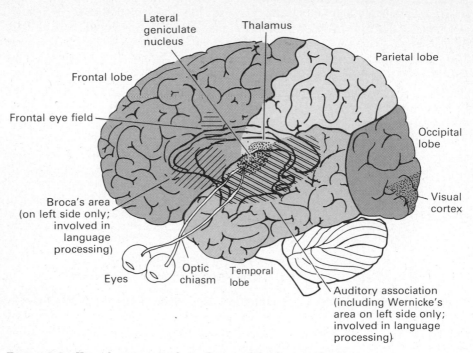

**Figure 1.1**   **Visual system and cerebrum of the human brain.**

is called the *visual cortex* (Levinthal 1979). What happens to the input at each step of its journey is not well understood, but it is believed that it is not until after the input has been processed by the visual cortex that you perceive the letters on the page. All this activity has occurred in less than a tenth of a second, with the greatest portion of the time consumed at the retina itself (Riggs 1971).

As you read, the strings of letters that form words must be matched to traces in memory and identified. At the same time that the visual input is being processed on the cortex, areas deep within the brain (which are known to be involved in memory) are also active. In addition, the meanings of the individual words must be retrieved and combined to form sentences. Sentence construction involves other areas of the cerebrum in addition to those already discussed. Additional areas of the cortex, forward from the visual area, are involved in this task. In particular, large areas of cortex on the left side of the cerebrum are involved in language processing.

But we are not yet done. When you read, the meanings of the successive sentences must be integrated to form the message of the passage. This processing requires the frontal part of the cortex. So, in fact, virtually the entire surface of your brain, as well as many subcortical areas within the cerebrum, are alive with activity while you are reading.

There is much to ponder in this brief survey of the neural events that transpire when we read. All the activities that go into reading are coordinated with such smoothness and proceed with such rapidity that we are hardly aware of more than the message of the passage. Reading is so effortless, and we are unaware of so many steps in the process, that it is easy to overlook the complexity of the mechanism that makes it possible to be aware of the message *without* necessarily being aware of the individual sentences, words, or letters on the page. However, just because an activity seems easy to do does not mean that its underlying mechanism is simple. Consideration of all that must be involved in reading should give you some inkling of the complexity of the mechanism that drives human cognition. We will return to the topic of reading later in this chapter in order to illustrate some of the basic characteristics of human information processing.

## REPRESENTATION AND PROCESSING OF KNOWLEDGE

Cognitive psychology faces two central problems, which are intimately related to each other. First, how is knowledge stored in our memories? Second, how is knowledge actually used to perform particular cognitive tasks? These questions are central because every cognitive skill you might think of depends in some way on using information stored in memory. For example, you don't have to memorize this book in order to use the information in it. But you do need to know how to read, and reading is a skill based on a vast amount of knowledge (e.g., knowing the meanings of thousands of printed words). If you did not have the meanings of these words stored in your memory, or you could not gain access to them rapidly, printed pages would be completely meaningless to you.

As the previous example suggests, knowledge really has two essential aspects, which correspond to the concepts of *representation* and *process*. That is, knowledge must be stored, or represented, in memory, and it must be used, or processed, to perform cognitive tasks. As we will see, these concepts are interconnected, because the form of mental representation determines the kinds of mental processes that can be used.

### Mental Representation

What, then, is a representation? In essence, a representation corresponds to the way in which information is recorded or expressed. A representation stands for the corresponding information. For example, the typescript used in a sentence represents the meaning of a sentence. A photograph represents the scene that was photographed. As these examples suggest, a representation is always a representation *of* something. The psychological question is straightforward: What information do people have, and how is that information represented in their memories? This question can be clarified by making several important distinctions between aspects of mental representations.

**Content vs. code.**   A simple English word like *cat* is a representation. It represents a certain *concept* or idea, namely, the concept of a furry household pet that purrs. Note that this same concept can be represented in many different ways. We could use a picture of a cat to represent the concept. We could translate *cat* into Spanish and represent it by *gato*. We could represent it in Morse code by a series of dots and dashes or in Braille by a certain tactile pattern. Across all these examples the information being represented stays the same. This common information is called the *content* of the representation. Each different way the information can be expressed is called a representational *code*. So the words *cat* and *gato* represent the same content but are in different codes (i.e., written English vs. written Spanish). In contrast, the words *cat* and *lawyer* represent different contents but are in the same code (written English).

Another example of alternative codes is illustrated in Figure 1.2. We might represent this picture by a description in English, such as a "picture of a cup without a handle on a flat saucer." But as Figure 1.2 illustrates, the picture could also be represented by mathematical equations. The saucer can be represented by $x^2 + y^2 = 1$ (the equation of a circle) and the cup by $z = x^2 + y^2$ (the equation of a paraboloid). Most people probably find the English description more intuitive or simpler than the equations. But if you had to find the volume of the cup, the English code *cup* would prove far less useful than the equation $z = x^2 + y^2$. This idea is an important one to remember: While different

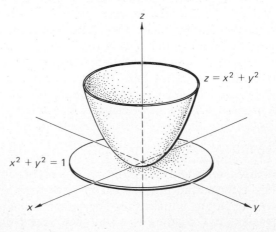

**Figure 1.2   Alternative codes. This cup and saucer can be represented by equations.**

codes can represent the same information, which code is most useful depends on what the information has to be used for—how it needs to be *processed*.

People are able to represent information in many different mental codes, and the memory code can be quite different from the form in which the information was presented. This result was demonstrated in a simple but elegant study performed by Conrad (1964). Conrad presented a group of college students with lists of six written letters (e.g., PHKVCR). The subjects read the letters silently. Then the list disappeared and the subjects had to report the letters in order. The most interesting results concern the errors people made. Sometimes, they would substitute an incorrect letter for one they had seen. If subjects were remembering the letters visually (i.e., in the code in which the letters were presented), we would expect them to substitute letters that looked similar to the actual letters (e.g., X for V). But instead, Conrad's subjects tended to confuse letters with names that sound alike (e.g., they might substitute B for V). So it appears that subjects were *recoding* the letters —changing the visual code into a speech code in order to remember them. This is the kind of mental activity we mean by "information processing."

Conrad's results are interesting because of the questions they raise. For example, why should people recode visual letters into a speech code? Presumably, they do so because they have had a great deal of practice naming letters and find the letter names easy to remember. But then what will happen with people who haven't learned to name the letters? What about deaf people who have never learned to speak? Conrad (1972) found that such deaf subjects tended to make visual rather than auditory substitutions. So the deaf may code letters very differently than do people with hearing.

Another question is whether hearing subjects can also code letters visually if necessary. An experiment performed by Neal Kroll and his colleagues (Kroll, Parks, Parkinson, Bieber, and Johnson 1970) at San Diego State University suggests that the answer is yes. In this experiment subjects heard a list of letters being read in a female voice at a rapid rate, and they had to repeat each letter aloud. This task is called a *shadowing* task, because subjects had to repeat (shadow) what they heard. At some point while they were shadowing, the subjects were presented with one letter that they had to remember. The letter was presented either visually (displayed on a screen for just 0.4 second) or orally (spoken in a male voice to distinguish it from the other letters). The subjects continued shadowing for either 1, 10, or 25 seconds, and then they were asked to recall the critical letter.

You might think that remembering one letter for a few seconds would be so trivial that subjects would never make any mistakes. But as Figure 1.3 shows, mistakes *were* made. Although subjects almost always remembered the letter for 1 second, they made many errors after 10 or 25 seconds. But note that they made fewer errors when the letter was presented visually than when it was spoken. We wouldn't expect this result if the visual letter had

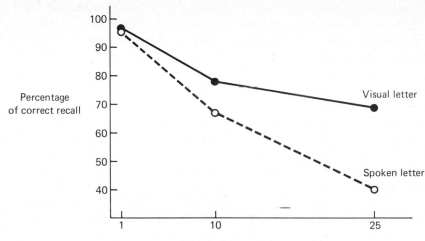

Percentage of correct recall

Delay before recall (in seconds)

**Figure 1.3    Results of shadowing task. Shadowing interferes with the recall of a spoken letter more than it interferes with the recall of a visual letter. (From Kroll, Parks, Parkinson, Bieber, and Johnson 1970.)**

been recoded into a speech code just like the spoken letter. Thus the visual letter was being maintained in memory in something other than a speech code—probably in a visual code. The shadowing task, which involves speaking, interferes less with a visual code than with a speech code.

So apparently, even in the simple task of remembering letters for a few seconds, we can find evidence for multiple memory codes. Furthermore, a comparison of the results of Conrad (1964) and Kroll *et al.* (1970) reveals an important principle that makes selection of a memory code an adaptive process. If two pieces of information are represented in different codes, they will be less confusable and produce less interference in memory. In the Kroll *et al.* study the critical letter was embedded in a context of auditory inputs; accordingly, subjects were able to minimize interference by maintaining a visually presented letter in a visual code.

**Code vs. medium.**    Some people may find this talk of a speech code and a visual memory code surprising. If a psychologist wants to describe how information is represented in a person's head, isn't it necessary to talk about how the brain and nervous system work, as we did in our overview of the process of reading? After all, psychologists generally agree that all information is ultimately represented by electrical and chemical activity in the nervous system. However, cognitive psychologists claim that it is possible—indeed, necessary—to study mental representations without investigating the nervous system directly.

To show why mental representation is conceptually separable from neural activity, we have to make one more distinction. We have already distinguished the content of a representation from its code. Now we must distinguish the code from the *medium* of the representation. An example should make the distinction clear. Listen to someone singing. Then listen to a good recording of the same person singing the same song. The two sounds would probably be virtually identical. Yet the sounds would be produced in very different ways—in one case by human vocal cords, in the other by electronic components. These are two different media for producing the same auditory code.

Also, different codes may be realized in the same medium. For example, the same cassette tapes can be used to record either music or computer programs. These two codes are completely different. Similarly, the different codes in human memory (e.g., both speech and visual codes for letters) may be realized in the same neural medium. But the different patterns of errors that characterize the codes give us concrete evidence that at some level they are distinct ways of representing information. Cognitive psychologists are able to study these codes even though at present they know very little about how the codes are realized in the medium of neuronal interconnections.

There are other reasons why we need to be able to describe codes without talking about neural activity. For example, suppose that we were able to construct a computer like the various imaginary ones that have starred in science fiction movies. Then we might carry on conversations with the computer in English (a possibility that still remains no more than science fiction). We would want to be able to describe the information we and the hypothetical computer were sharing. But we couldn't describe this information in terms of the underlying medium, because this medium would be vastly different for people and the computer. In one case the medium would be biological; in the other case it would be electronic. But even though the representational media would differ, both human and computer would be representing information in a common code—English. So even if we knew everything about the nervous system, we would still want to be able to describe information and its representation at a more abstract level. For reasons such as these, cognitive psychologists primarily study codes rather than media.

We do not mean to imply, however, that cognitive psychologists can simply ignore the neural bases of cognition. After all, a record is different from a cassette tape, although they both can store music; and a brain is different from a computer, although they both may be able to add numbers. If we want to know about human cognition, at some point the human brain must be studied. Furthermore, a careful examination of the brain may provide valuable clues about how cognition takes place. The burgeoning research field of *neuropsychology* is concerned with the relationship between the nervous system and cognition. We will be discussing what is known about the neural underpinnings of cognition at various points throughout this book.

**Levels of representation.**    Mechanical devices for processing information may use several different representations of the same content in performing their functions. Consider the telephone. A person's voice initially causes a diaphragm in the transmitter to vibrate. The voice is thus initially represented by the vibrations of the diaphragm. These vibrations then cause an electric signal to be generated along the wire. The medium of this representation is quite different from the first. Finally, at the receiver the electric impulses are turned back into vibrations.

An electronic calculator also makes use of different representations. The initial representation of the input is a sequence of key presses at different spatial locations on the surface of the device. These key presses activate a pattern of electric impulses within the calculator and transform that pattern in various ways. Clearly, both the medium and the code of the internal representation of the numbers are different from the spatial and temporal pattern of button presses used to control it. Finally, the internal electrical pattern controls a visual display. Again, this visual display is a very different representation in both its medium and code from the electrical pattern on which the arithmetic operations are performed.

What both the telephone and calculator illustrate is that an information-processing device typically makes use of a sequence of interconnected representations. There is a *central* representation, and there are also *peripheral* representations. The peripheral representations are used to perform *input* and *output* operations. That is, they are used for communicating with the rest of the world. The central representation is the one that best serves to do whatever it is that the device does. In the case of the telephone, for example, it is convenient to turn a voice into a pattern of electric signals in order to move it rapidly from one place to another.

The human information-processing system also makes use of levels of representation. Indeed, the human information-processing system is much more complex and makes use of many more levels of representation than any mechanical information-processing device. Information is *recoded* from one representation to another, beginning with initial sensory detection and registration, and often ending with a code for initiating and guiding motor movements. The core of cognition involves the central codes used to store information in memory, to reason, and to solve problems. Accordingly, whereas we will only touch briefly on more peripheral codes, we will discuss central codes in considerable detail in later chapters.

## Mental Procedures

If your knowledge remained passively stored in memory, it would be completely useless to you. In order to use your knowledge, you must execute a *procedure*. A procedure is a purposeful sequence of overt actions or mental operations. For example, in order to add two single-digit numbers on a calculator, you would perform the following simple procedure:

**A-1.** Press a number key.

**A-2.** Press the + key.

**A-3.** Press another number key.

**A-4.** Press the = key.

Each key you press is an instruction to the calculator to perform a particular action. So in response the calculator performs the following procedure:

**B-1.** Read the number from the keyboard into memory position 1 (number key).

**B-2.** Read the number from the keyboard into memory position 2 (number key).

**B-3.** Add the contents of memory position 2 to the contents of memory position 1 ( + ).

**B-4.** Write the contents of memory position 1 on the liquid crystal display ( = ).

(The key press initiating each action is shown in parentheses. Notice that the calculator actually performs the task in a different order from the order of the directions given.)

Each step in a procedure performs one of two kinds of actions. A *recoding operation* transforms information from one code to another. Statements B–1, B–2, and B–4 in the example procedure are recoding operations. The first two steps transfer information from the keyboard to the calculator's memory, and the last step transfers it from the memory to the visual display. Thus the content was transformed from a position code (i.e., a location on the keyboard) to a binary code (i.e., a string of ones and zeros) to a digital code. In contrast to recoding operations, *intracode operations* change the content *within* a code in some way. For example, statement B-3 performs the intracode operation of addition.

In the example the calculator transformed not only the code of the information but its medium as well. Many appliances important in our lives are simply ways of transforming information into a medium that is especially convenient for some purpose. As noted earlier, the telephone is a mechanical device that performs a procedure for transforming sound waves into electricity and back again, because electricity can be quickly transmitted over long distances. However, transforming information across codes does not necessarily involve a change of medium. For example, as you read, the visual input is transformed through many different codes that all exist within a relatively homogeneous neural medium. In this case the content is transformed to a code that is convenient for some purpose. The act of reading is essentially an elaborate recoding procedure in which the visual patterns on a page activate memories and operations within the brain. It is akin to, though vastly more complicated than, steps B–1 and B–2, which activate memories within a calculator.

**Mental rotation.**  Human beings are not merely recording devices, and the whole purpose of recoding some input is to make use of it in some way. This use often involves performing some intracode operation on it that creates a new content and hence new knowledge. For example, examine the drawings of three-dimensional objects in Figure 1.4. Are the two objects in Figure 1.4(a) identical, except for their orientation? What about the pairs in Figures 1.4(b) and 1.4(c)? You can probably see that the pairs in Figures 1.4(a) and 1.4(b), but not in Figure 1.4(c), are identical. But since the two objects of each pair are at different orientations, you had to perform some procedure involving operations on your mental representation of the pair to determine whether the objects were identical.

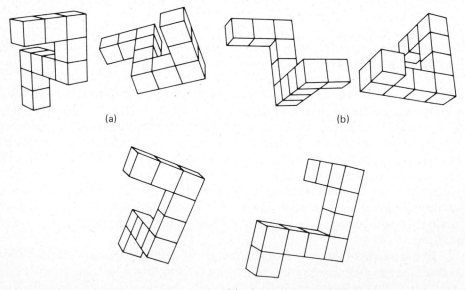

(a)                                                    (b)

(c)

Figure 1.4   Examples of pairs of patterns used for shape comparisons: (a) A same pair that differs by an 80-degree rotation in the picture plane; (b) a same pair that differs by an 80-degree rotation in depth; (c) a different pair that cannot be matched by any rotation. (From Shepard and Metzler 1971.)

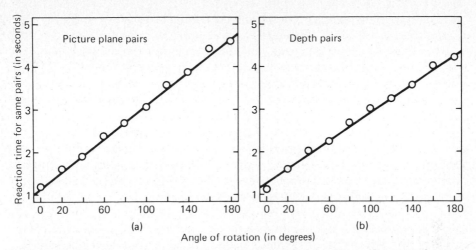

**Figure 1.5    Reaction time to judge that two pictured objects have the same three-dimensional shape:(a) Pairs that differ by a rotation in the picture plane; (b) pairs that differ by a rotation in depth. (From Shepard and Metzler 1971.)**

We can study the nature of the code that comprises a mental representation and the kind of operations and procedures that can be performed on it. Roger Shepard and his colleagues at Stanford University (Cooper and Shepard 1973; Shepard and Metzler 1971) asked college students to respond, as quickly as possible, whether the members of a pair were the same. They found that the greater the difference in orientation of the pair members, the longer it took the subjects to make a decision, as shown in Figure 1.5. From this result they concluded that the way the students determined whether the two forms were identical was to apply a procedure to their mental representation of one of the forms that transformed it into a representation of what the object would look like if it was in the same orientation as the other form. The students then checked whether both mental representations were identical. Shepard's results suggested that this procedure, which they termed *mental rotation*, was analogous to a physical rotation in that the greater the difference in the initial orientations of the forms, the longer it took the procedure to bring them into congruence.

These studies illustrate a very important general point about the study of mental procedures. Even though mental procedures are not directly observable, they take *time* to perform. By measuring the time people require to perform procedures, psychologists can make inferences about what internal representations and operations are like.

Another question that has been asked about the same-different judgment task is whether the rotation procedure can only be applied to a visual code or whether it can be applied to a more general spatial code. In one study (Carpenter and Eisenberg 1978) congenitally blind subjects judged whether a letter was normal or a mirror image on the basis of touch. As in the case of sighted subjects and visual forms, the time to make the judgment increased as the angle of the letter departed farther from the upright position. It is highly unlikely that mental rotation could be based on visual imagery for such blind subjects. Because of such evidence, we describe the code used for mental rotation as *visuospatial* rather than simply visual (see Chapter 4).

The evidence from these studies of shape comparisons should make our general point clear. A particular code, such as a visuospatial code, permits particular operations and procedures, such as mental rotation. The code and the procedures jointly determine people's performance on cognitive tasks.

**Complex procedures.** Human intelligence depends on our ability to construct complex procedures for performing tasks. Complex procedures can be constructed from simpler ones. Mental rotation, for example, is a relatively simple procedure. More complex procedures for transforming visuospatial representations might be built by organizing a sequence of rotations.

Shepard and Feng (1972) provided evidence for this possibility by having subjects perform a task that involved mental paper folding. Their subjects were shown displays of six squares, such as those illustrated in Figure 1.6. Each pattern represented an unfolding of a cube. The gray square represented the base of the cube. Subjects had to decide as quickly as possible

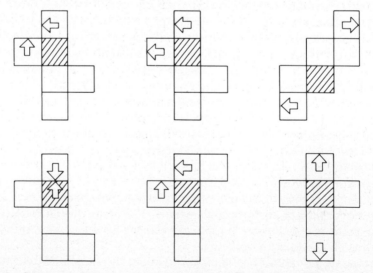

**Figure 1.6   Some examples of mental-folding problems. (From Shepard and Feng 1972.)**

whether or not the arrows on two of the squares could be made to meet by folding. Reaction time increased linearly with the number of mental folds required to reach a decision, as would be expected if subjects were using a procedure based on a sequence of 90-degree mental rotations of the squares.

## CHARACTERISTICS OF HUMAN INFORMATION PROCESSING

Several characteristics of human information processing are so pervasive that they deserve to be discussed at the outset. We will be returning to these central concepts repeatedly throughout this book. Here we will introduce four of these concepts—feature analysis, hierarchical organization, bottom-up versus top-down processing, and parallel processing—in the context of reading. As we pointed out earlier, reading is an excellent example of human information processing, since it calls into play virtually every aspect of the cognitive processes that we will be exploring in this book. Reading involves the perception and recognition of words, retrieval and use of the rules of language, storing information in memory, and complex types of reasoning.

### Feature Analysis

A printed word, such as *cat,* can be perceived as a single pattern or as three smaller patterns side by side: the letters *c, a,* and *t.* As a further alternative, the printed word can be perceived as five, still smaller, interconnected patterns. The *c* could be perceived as (1) a half circle; the *a* as (2) a circle and (3) a hooked line tangent to the circle on its right; and the *t* as (4) another hooked line that bisects (5) a horizontal line, intersecting it one-third of the distance from its top. We can apply this sort of geometric analysis to any visual display and describe it in terms of the simple geometric elements, such as lines and curves, that compose it. The simple geometric elements used in the construction of more complex patterns are called *features.* How, then, does the visual system process a word? Does it process the entire pattern *holistically*—i.e., as a single unit corresponding to the overall shape of the word? Or does it construct a representation of it from simpler features? The latter possibility—constructing a representation from more elementary features—is usually called *feature analysis.*

Holistic processing and feature analysis require very different mechanisms. Suppose that a word such as *cat* was only processed holistically. Then at some point that pattern would have to be identified as the word *cat.* That identification would be done by comparison of the input pattern with patterns corresponding to every single word in memory—every word the person knows—until an exact match was found (see Figure 1.7). Such a process is called *template matching.*

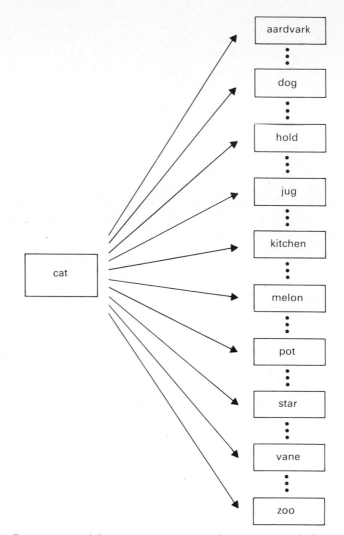

**Figure 1.7    Comparison of the input to every word in memory in holistic template matching.**

The comparison of the input pattern to the word patterns in memory could not be done *serially*; i.e., the input could not be compared with the patterns in memory one at a time. A typical college student probably has a reading vocabulary of more than 25,000 words (Francis and Kučera 1982). Since it takes 1 millisecond for a neuron to transmit information, the absolute minimum time that a comparison could take is 1 millisecond. (In fact, many neurons are involved in a comparison, so the true minimum time is much longer.) On the average, you can expect to get about halfway through the list before you find a match; so you can expect to make an average of about 12,500 comparisons for each word. If you make 12,500 comparisons, one at a time, for each word, and each comparison takes just 1 millisecond, then you would need an average of 12.5 seconds to find the meaning of each word as you read. Clearly, you can read much faster than this rate. Therefore if you processed each word holistically, you would have to compare every word you read in *parallel* to many thousands of patterns in memory.

A feature analysis mechanism would operate quite differently. The processing of *cat* by such a mechanism is shown in Figure 1.8. Initially, your representation of the input pattern consists of a curve, some straight lines, and a circle. Each of these simple patterns is compared with the patterns defining the shapes of the twenty-six letters of the alphabet, and three matches are found. Once you have identified three letter patterns, you could take advantage of the alphabetic structure of writing to identify the word efficient-

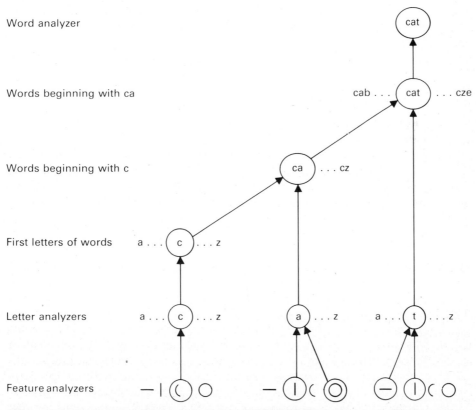

**Figure 1.8   Feature analysis model of word identification. Arrows indicate comparisons, and circled characters indicate the results of matches.**

ly. Suppose that your knowledge of words is organized alphabetically, like the dictionary. The main word list is divided into twenty-six sublists, each containing words beginning with a different letter of the alphabet. Furthermore, these twenty-six sublists are in turn each organized into at most twenty-six sub-sublists by their second letter, etc. The result would be a *hierarchy* of lists based on letters, as illustrated in Figure 1.8.

A word could then be identified by a procedure such as that shown in Figure 1.8. First, the first letter of the input word is compared with the first letter of the first word on each first-letter sublist until a match is found. So *c* is first compared with *a*, then *b*, then *c*, at which point a match is found. Next, the second letter of the input word is compared with the second letter of words that begin with *c*. So *a* is compared with *a* on the sublist of words beginning with *c*. Next, the third letter of the input word is compared with the third letter of words on the sub-sublist of words beginning *ca*. Eventually, *c*, *a*, and *t* will be matched, and *cat* will be identified. This identification process requires on the average only $n \times 13.5$ comparisons to identify the letters, plus $n \times 13.5$ comparisons in which the letters are used to identify the word, where *n* is the number of letters in the input word. Hence identifying a three-letter word requires an average of only 81 comparisons, in contrast to the thousands of comparisons that holistic processing would require.

## Hierarchical Organization

In fact, the visual-processing system is a feature analysis procedure, although one that is more complex than the hypothetical system based on an alphabetical organization. The procedure initially encodes the input as simple patterns, such as lines and circles, and then combines these patterns to construct the more complex patterns, such as letters and words, that you perceive. Hence the visual feature analysis procedure consists of several levels of representation, arranged *hierarchically,* so that the output of each level serves as the input for its successor. The most peripheral level of representation is called the lowest level, and each successive representation is one level higher. Thus the line and circle representation is lower than the letter representation, which in turn is lower than the word representation.

Hierarchical organization is an essential aspect of human language. When we read, we do not simply identify individual words. Rather, the words are in turn integrated into higher-order linguistic units, called *syntactic categories.* Figure 1.9 depicts the hierarchical organization of a simple English sentence. The individual words (nouns, verbs, etc.) are organized into groups corresponding to higher-order units or *constituents,* such as noun phrases, prepositional phrases, and verb phrases. The constituents are in turn organized into the overall sentence. In fact, the hierarchy need not end there. The sentence might in turn serve as a constituent in some still larger linguistic unit, such as a story.

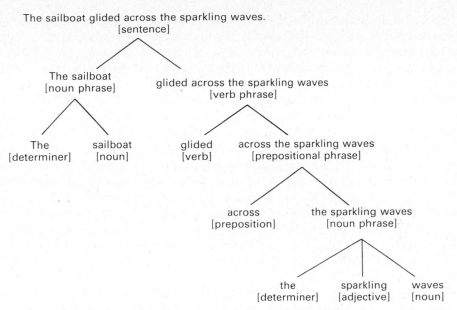

**Figure 1.9   Hierarchical structure of a simple English sentence.**

Hierarchical organization is a fundamental aspect of all of cognition, and we will encounter the concept in virtually every chapter of this book. For example, motor skills are procedures based on hierarchically organized movements; memory retrieval depends on the hierarchical structure of concepts; and complex problems can only be solved by decomposing the overall goal into constituent subgoals.

## Evidence of Hierarchical Feature Analysis in Reading

Experiments done by Alice Healy (1981) provide evidence of hierarchical feature analysis during reading. College students were asked to read passages at their normal reading speed but to mark any spelling errors they noticed while reading. She created the spelling errors by substituting one letter for another in the passage. For example, c was substituted for e, creating *studcnts*, and s was substituted for o, creating *absut*. According to the feature analysis hypothesis, c and e differ by only a single feature, the horizontal line that is present in the e but not in the c. However, s and o differ by more than one feature. Suppose people process letters as bundles of features. In normal reading at the letter level they might not process every feature of every letter in order to identify it but just enough to be reasonably sure what letter it was. In this case people might sometimes misread a c as an e and hence fail to detect the substitution. But they should less often misread an s as an o, since these letters share fewer features. This result is what Healy (1981) found. The students failed to notice 60 percent of the *c*-for-*e* substitutions but failed to notice only 5 percent of the *s*-for-*o* substitutions. More generally, Healy found that if the substitution maintained the outer configuration of the original, as in *c* for *e* or *C* for *G*, the student was more likely to fail to detect the substitution than if the outer configuration was changed.

Healy's (1981) result suggests that individual letters are composed of simple visual features. But her finding does not mean that when a person reads, the feature analysis process always begins with all of the simplest features and exhaustively constructs every letter of every word from them. Rather, the results of other experiments show that people can use their knowledge of their language to infer the identity of a word after having examined only some of its features. (See the discussion of top-down processing that follows.) Furthermore, it may be that for common words more complex holistic representations are formed, and the printed input is matched directly to these representations without ever being analyzed as a bundle of simple features of all.

This hypothesis suggests that you may be able to read a common word without ever being aware of some of its visual features, or even of some of the letters it contains. Healy (1980) tested this hypothesis by instructing college students to read a prose passage at their normal reading speed and to encircle all the *t*'s they came across. The students missed more *t*'s in common words like *fact* than in rare words like *pact*. Similarly, function words are more frequent than content words, and Schindler (1978) found more letter detection errors on function words than content words. The most common word of all in the English language is *the*. In one passage Healy (1980) found that students missed *t*'s in 38 percent of the *the*'s but only in 20 percent of the other words containing *t* (see also Corcoran 1966; Healy 1976).

If students do not read common words letter by letter but use some holistic representation, any change in the printed word that alters this holistic representation should be detectable while they are reading. In contrast, changes that do not influence its holistic representation should not be detected. We have already seen that the outer configuration is an important part of the representation of an individual letter. Haber and Schindler (1981) showed that shape is an important part of the representation of a word. They found that misspellings that changed the overall shape of a word were more likely to be detected than ones that did not. The difference was greater for function words (which are the most common words in a language) than for content words. Hence it appeared as if the students were identifying the function words on the basis of their overall shape, while doing a letter-by-letter analysis of many of the content words (see also Holbrook 1978).

The visual-processing system is thus quite flexible. Your perception of a word may be at the level of features, letters, or the entire word. When you read, some words may be identified holistically, while others may be identified by a letter-by-letter matching. You may perceive the same word holistically when you read, as a sequence of letters when you look it up in the dictionary, and as a sequence of interconnected lines and circles when you print it. Inputs from the other receptor modalities besides the visual also undergo feature analysis. In fact, *phonetic features*—the features for the sounds of words—also play a role in reading (Corcoran 1966, 1967; Corcoran and Weening 1968). For example, a phonetically compatible word substitution such as *werk* for *work* will be less likely to be noticed than a phonetically incompatible substitution such as *wark* for *work* (MacKay 1968).

### Bottom-up vs. Top-down Procedures

The flexibility of the overall reading procedure is the result of the interplay of two kinds of analysis procedures that exist at different levels of the hierarchy. Their names are based on the metaphorical conception of information processing as involving hierarchical layers of recoding, with sensory analysis of the input at the bottom of the hierarchy and abstract semantic representations at the top. Hence the two complementary kinds of processing are called *bottom-up* and *top-down*.

To illustrate what *bottom-up* means, let us consider a hypothetical bottom-up process for perceiving the letters in a word such as *birthday*. Such a process is illustrated in Figure 1.10. As indicated in the figure, a bottom-up process consists of a series of successive processing steps, in which the output of

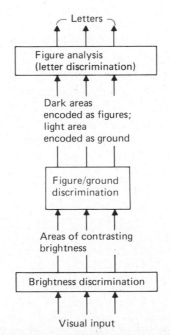

**Figure 1.10  Hypothetical bottom-up model of letter discrimination.**

each step serves as the input for the step that follows it. In our hypothetical model we first discriminate between the light and dark areas on the page. Second, the dark areas are encoded as characters and the light areas as the background by the feature analyzers. Finally, the individual letter shapes are identified. At still higher levels the letters might be used to access a representation of the word.

A bottom-up process like this one begins with the visual input and ends up with a representation of it. We can order the steps from lower to higher on the basis of the order in which they transform the visual input. The lowest step (brightness discrimination in Figure 1.10) operates directly on the visual input. The highest step (figure analysis in Figure 1.10) produces the perceptual representation. The defining property of a strictly bottom-up process is that *the outcome of a lower step is never affected by a higher step in the process.* For example, according to our hypothetical model, the result of figure analysis plays no role in the initial discrimination of light from dark.

To illustrate top-down processing, consider a rather different reading task. Suppose you come across the word *porcine* while reading and don't know what the word means. Furthermore, let's assume that rather than go to a dictionary to look it up, you try to figure it out. The subsequent process is illustrated in Figure 1.11. First, you may try to think of words that sound like

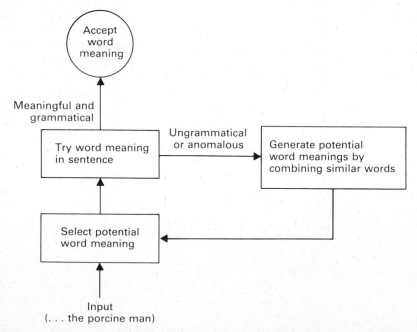

**Figure 1.11    Top-down procedure for figuring out the meaning of an unknown word.**

*porcine. Porcelain, porch, port,* and *pork* all begin the same way, and *ravine* and *bovine* end the same way. Are any of these words similar enough to *porcine* for you to guess its meaning? Perhaps not. However, you may be able to use the context in which the word appeared to help narrow down the possibilities. Suppose the sentence it appears in is, "When he opened the door, he faced a porcine man." So *porcine* must be an adjective, which would seem to eliminate *porcelain, porch, port,* and *ravine* as potential models. *The pork man* would be grammatical but doesn't make much sense. However, *the bovine man* does make sense, assuming you know that *bovine* means "cowlike." Since *pork* suggests another kind of animal, the best guess is that *porcine* means "piglike," which is in fact correct.

In the process of finding the meaning of an unfamiliar word like *porcine,* the sequence of generating a potential meaning and trying it in the sentence may have to be repeated several times. Thus as Figure 1.11 indicates, the output of a lower step (i.e., the selection of a potential meaning of the unknown word) is influenced by the outcomes of higher steps (i.e., whether the potential meaning fits in the sentence, and what similar words are generated). A procedure in which the output of a lower step is influenced by a higher one is called top-down.

## Parallel Processing

In reading, as discussed previously, common words may be identified holistically, whereas rare words are identified by analyzing them into smaller units, all the way down to their individual letters. Suppose the reading procedure could only initiate one identification procedure at a time. When a string of letters had to be identified, with what should they be compared first: a holistic representation or to a list of individual letters? Neither solution is satisfactory. If the letter string is first compared with representations of common words, the time needed to identify rare words will increase. But if every letter is first analyzed into its individual letters, the time needed to identify most common words will increase. A procedure that can perform only one action at a time to a single input is called a *serial procedure.* A procedure that can perform more than one act on an input at a time is called a *parallel procedure.* The reading procedure frequently performs parallel actions on an input. For example, visual input is analyzed at both the letter and the word level at the same time.

Parallel processing can involve not only multiple procedures applied simultaneously to a single input but also multiple procedures that operate on multiple inputs. Consider the many actions involved in reading. You have to focus your eyes on a particular location on the page, identify the visual input as a word, retrieve the word's meaning, and fit it into a sentence. If each of these steps was performed one at a time, reading would be a slower and more tedious process than it actually is. If we did not move our eyes to the next word on the page until the previous word was fit into the sentence, the reading process would be like reading a set of words printed on individual cards that were presented one at a time. There would be perceptible dead time between the moments that the meaning of each word became available for integration with the rest of the sentence. But when we read, we do not process individual words in this serial manner. Rather, the eyes have already moved to the next location on the page before the previous word's meaning has been retrieved. That is why the act of reading appears to be a continuous process. Several different procedures required for reading—including movement of the eyes, visual identification, and sentence construction—are coordinated so that they all occur at the same time but for different parts of the input.

Much of the brain's ability to process information efficiently stems from its ability to coordinate several procedures that occur in parallel. Its very structure suggests a parallel-processing device, since in the brain each neuron does not receive signals from only one neuron but from thousands and in turn transmits its output to thousands of other neurons. As a result, information can be transmitted in parallel circuits to many neurons, and hence to many parts of the brain, at the same time.

## MODELS OF WORD RECOGNITION

In order to illustrate how the characteristics of human information processing discussed in the previous section can be described by a cognitive model, let us examine several models that have been proposed in the area of reading.

### Logogen Model

The *logogen model* developed by John Morton (1969, 1979) has been an influential conception of the process of word recognition. This model, a modified version of which is sketched in Figure 1.12, provides a nice synthesis of several of the ideas we have just been discussing. The heart of the model is the *logogen system*. *Logogens* (derived from the Latin *logos,* or "word," and *genus,* or "birth") are the permanent memory representations corresponding to the words in a person's vocabulary. Every word the person knows has a corresponding logogen. Each logogen consists of a *feature list,* comprised of features that identify the word, and a *criterion,* which specifies the number of matches that must be found between the features of an input and the features of the logogen before the logogen is accepted as the correct identification of the input.

Here is how the recognition process operates. Suppose a person sees a word, such as *stupor.* This word is the input in Figure 1.12. A process of visual analysis begins at once, extracting visual features of the word (e.g., letter

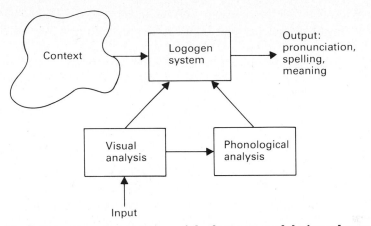

**Figure 1.12    Schematic representation of the logogen model of word recognition.**

shapes, shape of the whole word). These visual features feed into the logogen system. In addition, the visual features may be passed along for *phonological analysis*—a process of deciding the word's pronunciation. Phonological analysis is often not necessary for skilled readers; nonetheless, it can certainly help identify some words. For example, *stupor* may *look* unfamiliar to a reader, but if its pronunciation (*stoo'-per*) can be derived, it may seem more familiar (especially if the word has been heard more often than read). In any case both visual and phonological features of the input are passed to the logogen system. In addition, the *context* can also pass information to the logogen system. For example, if the person has just read, "For years the mental patient had sat rigidly in his chair in a catatonic. . . ," the logogen for *stupor* would tend to be activated.

An important property of the logogen model is that all of these activities—visual analysis, phonological analysis, and use of context—can proceed at least partially in parallel. Furthermore, the results obtained from each of the three information sources are matched simultaneously against all the logogens in the logogen system. The process continues until one of the logogens finds enough features matching its representation to satisfy its criterion. At this point the successful logogen signals that the input has been identified, and it makes available the various kinds of information about the word that are associated with the logogen (e.g., its pronunciation, spelling, and meaning).

**Hierarchical Models and the Word Superiority Effect**

The logogen model thus uses both feature analysis and parallel processing. However, the model depicted in Figure 1.12 does not clearly illustrate the hierarchical aspects of the representations of words in memory, since all sources of information flow directly into the logogen at the word level. Other, similar models have been proposed that share most of the central characteristics of the logogen model but are hierarchical in nature.

The earliest such model was the Pandemonium model outlined by Selfridge and Neisser (1960). A more recent version is the hierarchical model of Johnston and McClelland (1980), sketched in Figure 1.13. The arrows in Figure 1.13 represent pathways by which processing at the various representa-

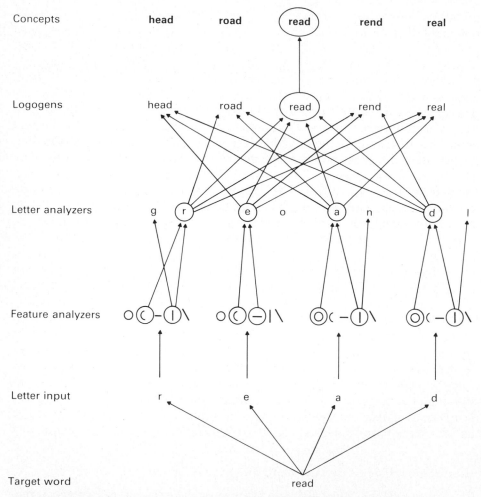

**Figure 1.13   Schematic diagram of a fragment of the analyzer network hypothesized to mediate word and letter identifications. A possible set of active analyzers after presentation of target word *read* is circled. (After Johnston and McClelland 1980.)**

tional levels influence each other. In the hierarchical model representations of lower-level components of words, such as letters and visual features, operate much like minilogogens. Johnston and McClelland were able to apply this model to account for one of the most interesting phenomena observed in studies of word recognition: the *word superiority effect* for letter recognition.

The word superiority effect was first noted in a brief comment by Cattel (1886), but its significance was not appreciated until the careful work of Reicher (1969) and Wheeler (1970). Under certain circumstances a briefly presented letter can be identified more accurately when it is presented as part of a word than when it is presented alone or as part of a letter string. Conditions sufficient for generating the effect are shown in Figure 1.14. The sequence of displays for the letter condition is shown in the top row. First, a fixation point is presented, which indicates about where the target letters will appear. Then the letter itself appears for a brief duration, say 60 milliseconds. Immediately following is a *pattern mask* in the same location. A pattern mask is made up of lines and simple shapes that activate the visual feature detectors of the brain. The purpose of the mask is to terminate the processing of the preceding target letter by giving the visual system something else to process. Finally, two letters appear just above and below the target's location, and the observer must select which letter was just presented.

The letter string condition is identical, except that in the target display the target letter is part of a string of four letters. The word condition is identical to the letter string condition, except that the four letters form a word. In the forced-choice test that follows in the word condition, both alternatives form a

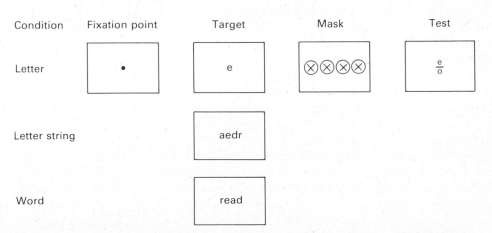

**Figure 1.14   Sequence of displays presented in a letter identification task that produces a word superiority effect.**

word with the sequence presented (e.g., *read* versus *road*). Reicher (1969) varied the duration that the target display was presented and obtained the same result for three different durations: Accuracy was about 10 percent better in the word condition than in either the letter string or individual-letter condition. For example, at the longest duration the observers selected the correct alternative 90 percent of the time in the word condition but only 80 percent of the time in the letter or letter string conditions. Their accuracy in the word condition could not be due to their guessing the critical letter from the other letters in the sequence, because both alternatives formed words. Accordingly, the result implies that the letter was better perceived when it was part of a word than when it was presented alone, and that a four-letter word was more accurately perceived than its individual letters.

The key to the word superiority effect turned out to be the use of a pattern mask to terminate processing of the letter string. When another kind of mask, such as a brightness mask (i.e., a brightly illuminated visual field), was used to terminate the processing of the string, observers were slightly more accurate at reporting letters presented alone rather than embedded in words (Johnston and McClelland 1973). Pattern masking apparently causes the word superiority effect because the pattern mask ends awareness of the individual letters faster than it ends awareness of the entire word.

The longer a subject is aware of a briefly presented letter or word, the more likely he or she is to report it accurately. According to the Johnston and McClelland model, awareness requires the continued activation of a corresponding analyzer. A subject is thus aware of a letter only for as long as its letter analyzer is active and is aware of a word only for as long as its logogen is active. In the letter and letter string conditions the pattern mask terminates the activity of the letter analyzers when it first comes on, so that a letter is only glimpsed for about 60 milliseconds. In the word condition the pattern mask again terminates the activity of the letter analyzers as soon as it comes on, but it takes longer to inhibit the activity of the logogens at the next higher level of the hierarchy. Accordingly, the observer perceives the entire word longer than the letter, even though they were both presented for the same amount of time. This theory makes the interesting, and correct, prediction that an observer will be able to read a briefly presented word followed by a pattern mask without being able to report what the letters looked like—i.e., their type font or case (Adams 1979)—because that information was obliterated by the mask before it was apprehended.

The word superiority effect dramatically illustrates an aspect of human information processing that is related to many phenomena discussed in this book. A single input may activate several representations at different levels of the information-processing system, and the different representations enter awareness for different durations. The observer may never be aware of some low-level representations, such as those corresponding to visual features.

The logogen model and such similar proposals as the hierarchical model of Johnston and McClelland provide good first approximations to an account of how skilled reading is possible. And as we will see in the next chapter when we discuss attention, the general principles illustrated by the logogen model pervade many other cognitive skills besides reading.

This point is illustrated even more dramatically by experiments reported by Marcel (1983). In one experiment Marcel took advantage of the fact (to be discussed in Chapter 2) that people can determine that a letter string is a word (a *lexical decision* judgment) more quickly when it is preceded by a priming word that is related in meaning than when it is preceded by an unrelated word (e.g., people can decide that *dog* is a word more rapidly if it follows *cat* rather than *rock*). In Marcel's experiment a word is presented for only 10 milliseconds before being replaced by a mask, so observers are uncertain whether they saw a word at all. Nevertheless, the "unseen" word apparently activates its meaning sufficiently during that brief presentation to prime the identification of a word that follows it. Marcel's remarkable results must still be considered preliminary (Fowler, Wolford, Slade, and Tassinary 1981); however, they suggest that even a brief presentation of a word can activate the meaning of a related word, and a mask that terminates processing at the perceptual level leaves the activation of the concept analyzer (see Figure 1.13) intact.

## SUMMARY

In this chapter we discussed many of the most basic concepts of cognitive psychology. Cognition is based on mental *representations* of knowledge and *processes* that operate on these representations. A representation has three important aspects: *content* (what is being represented), *code* (the format of the representation), and *medium* (the physical realization of the code). Information processing involves successive *recodings* of inputs from peripheral to more central codes. The central codes used for memory storage and reasoning will be the central concern of this book.

The code is intimately related to the *procedures* that can be performed on it. A procedure is a sequence of purposeful actions. There are two kinds of actions, *recoding operations* and *intracode operations*. A recoding operation transforms some content from one code to another. An intracode operation alters the content within a code. For example, the procedure causing mental rotation can be performed on the *visuospatial code*.

Skilled reading provides a good illustration of many important concepts. Reading is based on the analysis of *features* of the input and involves a great deal of *parallel*, or simultaneous, processing. The act of reading consists of successive recoding of the input through *hierarchically organized levels* of representation. It involves both *bottom-up procedures,* based directly on the sensory input, and *top-down procedures*, which use higher-level information such as expectations generated by the context. The *logogen model* of word recognition and such similar but more elaborate models as the hierarchical model of Johnston and McClelland provide examples of how these characteristics of information processing can be theoretically integrated.


## RECOMMENDED READINGS

This section and similar sections at the end of the subsequent chapters are intended as guides for students seeking additional readings to further explore topics in cognitive psychology. Our list of possibilities is by no means exhaustive, but it does include a selection of classics in the field, major theoretical books, textbooks, and journals. Several general textbooks in the field of human experimental psychology were so well written that they have become classics in the field and still make interesting reading. If you are interested in the origins of the science, these texts include James's *Principles of Psychology* (1890) and Woodworth's *Experimental Psychology* (1938). Also very interesting is the second edition of *Experimental Psychology* by Woodworth and Schlosberg, which appeared in 1954.

In the 1960s two books were published that led to the creation of the modern field of cognitive psychology. *Plans and the Structure of Behavior* (1960) by Miller, Galanter, and Pribram was influential in the development of the information-processing framework. This book set the stage for the book that gave the field its name, Ulric Neisser's *Cognitive Psychology* (1967). If you wish to study the field in more detail, we can think of no better way to begin than by reading this book. For a more up-to-date picture Lachman, Lachman, and Butterfield have written a thorough survey of the history of recent models in cognitive psychology, entitled *Cognitive Psychology and Information Processing: An Introduction* (1980).

If you become very interested in a topic, and you don't mind difficult reading material, then you should turn to journals that publish reports of the results of new experiments and new theoretical contributions. Two journals attempt to cover all of psychology and devote a large number of pages to cognitive psychology: *Psychological Review* publishes theoretical contributions, and *Psychological Bulletin* publishes articles surveying areas of research.

Quite a few journals cover the entire field of cognitive psychology. *Cognitive Psychology* tends to publish long articles of both theoretical and experimental interest. That is, the author may marshal a number of new results in support of a new theoretical position. The *Journal of Experimental Psychology: General, Journal of Experimental Psychology: Learning, Memory, and Cognition, Journal of Experimental Psychology: Human Perception and Perfor-*

mance, *Journal of Memory and Language* (formerly *Journal of Verbal Learning and Verbal Behavior*), and the *Quarterly Journal of Experimental Psychology* all publish many important experimental contributions. *Cognition* tends to publish articles with a philosophical and linguistic orientation, and *Cognitive Science* emphasizes papers related to computer simulation and artificial intelligence. *Brain and Behavioral Science* publishes major position papers on cognitive topics, accompanied by comments by other researchers in the area. Another source to consult for surveys of recent work on major research areas is the continuing series *Annual Reviews of Psychology*. The major journals in the related field of neuropsychology are *Neuropsychologia, Cortex,* and *Brain and Language,* and in the field of artificial intelligence the major journal is *Artificial Intelligence.*

For an overview of the broader field of cognitive science, in which cognitive psychology plays a major role, a good initial source is *The Universe Within* (1982) by Morton Hunt. This book is written for a popular audience, but it does a good job of highlighting many of the most currently active areas of research. Margaret Boden's very well-written *Artificial Intelligence and Natural Man* (1977) provides a good introduction to artificial intelligence and computer simulation, with an emphasis on psychological implications. Elaine Rich (1983), John Sowa (1983), and Patrick Winston (1984) have written good general textbooks on artificial intelligence. An in-depth survey of artificial intelligence is provided by the three-volume *Handbook of Artificial Intelligence* (Barr and Feigenbaum 1981, 1982; Cohen and Feigenbaum 1982).

Ned Block (1981) has edited a book that contains a number of papers arguing opposing theoretical positions regarding mental representation, especially concerning the nature of the visuospatial code. Roger Shepard and Lynn Cooper have published a collection of their papers, including several on mental rotation, entitled *Mental Images and Their Transformations* (1982). (Also see the Recommended Readings for Chapter 4.)

On the topic of reading a good introduction is *The Psychology of Reading* (1982) by Robert Crowder. Crowder's book provides many excellent suggestions regarding further sources at the ends of its chapters, so his book is a good guide for exploring a topic about which an enormous amount has been written.

# CHAPTER **TWO**

# Attention

## INTRODUCTION

The study of attention begins with the problem of information reduction. Every second of the day our bodies are being bombarded with all kinds of energy, including light, heat, and sound. Furthermore, our bodies are generating signals of their own to indicate hunger, weariness, and many other internal states. We know that the human information-processing system has a *limited capacity*—there is only so much it can do at one time. As a result, the sheer quantity of information that is available at a given moment makes it impossible for us to perceive and encode everything. The best we can do is choose the important things and ignore the rest. Thus the core of the topic of attention is our ability to perform *selective analysis* of inputs. (*Analysis* is used as a cover term for all the processes involved in the perception of inputs and the encoding of representations of them into memory.) The idea of viewing attention as the result of the way a limited-capacity, information-processing system operates was first proposed by Donald Broadbent (1958) and has since been extended by the many investigators mentioned in this chapter.

In order to understand the central problem of attention, consider how you distribute your analyzing capacity while reading this book. The inputs that are impinging on you while reading may be roughly divided into two categories: the ones that you are aware of, and all the others that you are not aware of. Hopefully, the input that you are aware of is the meaning of the words on this page. In contrast, you are not aware of auditory, tactile, temperature, and extraneous visual inputs. Yet if you shift your attention, you will find that you can become aware of the surrounding sounds or temperature rather than the visual information from this page. It is normally quite satisfactory not to be aware of such inputs, since they are usually not very important. In fact, these extraneous signals receive so little attention that we are tempted to believe that they are not processed at all. However, the complete failure to process such inputs could have disastrous consequences. For example, if you were not processing the temperature, and the room suddenly became very hot, you might be trapped in a fire. If sounds were being totally ignored, then an explosion would bring no response. It would also be inconvenient if you did not hear your name when addressed unexpectedly. The central problem of attention, then, is how to monitor the environment sufficiently to detect unexpected but important events, without unduly interfering with the processing of whatever input is currently most important to the person.

This chapter and the next will be concerned with the solution to that problem. In this chapter we will examine the process of attention from the bottom up, as we follow the processing of inputs from the points at which they are detected to the points at which the response to each input is determined. We will see that initially many different inputs are processed in parallel and analyzed to a rudimentary degree. From this pool successively smaller sets are selected for finer analysis. Your level of awareness of an input reflects the degree of analysis that it receives. (We will use *awareness* and *consciousness* as synonyms.) For example, when you read, you are clearly more conscious of the meanings of the words than of the shapes of the letters or the pressure of the book on your hand. But if you are reading, you must also be processing the letter shapes, even though you are unaware of these shapes while reading. And to turn a page, you must process the weight of the book and page, although again with little consciousness of these aspects of the environment.

At a given moment you are usually aware of only one of the many inputs that are impinging on your body. (Later in the chapter we will discuss how the attended input is defined by the information-processing system.) This input is the one to which you are *paying attention*. The act of paying attention selects one input out of many and brings it into consciousness. This input receives the greatest degree of analysis. The ability to select an input for detailed analysis gives you enormous control over your environment, because you can process whatever inputs are relevant to a task you want to perform. Hence one minute from now you might decide to stop reading this book and get something to eat. With no effort at all you can shift your attention away from the page to whatever task you choose to undertake next.

In the next chapter we will examine the process of attention from the top down and describe how actions are initiated in response to inputs. We will see that at the highest level you can select from a wide variety of actions in response to consciously processed inputs. However, at lower levels of analysis the ability to respond to an input is limited to the initiation of a preset action.

## ATTENTION AND INFORMATION PROCESSING

By far the most fruitful technique for studying what attracts attention has been to force people to attend to a particular input and then to determine what other types of information break through to consciousness. For example, in a shadowing task (described in Chapter 1) people are asked to listen to a message played through an earphone to one ear. As a guarantee that they are attending to the message, they are asked to repeat each word as it is heard. If you are ever in a shadowing task, you will find that it requires considerable effort to perform without making errors.

### Awareness of Unattended Inputs

Now suppose you are shadowing a message played to your right ear. What do you think would happen if a different message was played to the left ear at the same time? How much do you think you would remember of the message played to the unattended ear?

In the original experiment by E. Colin Cherry (1953), people were presented with spoken passages in the right ear for shadowing, while what was presented to the left ear always began and ended with normal English spoken in a male voice. However, the middle portion of the left ear's input either remained the same or changed to English spoken in a higher-pitched female voice, to reversed male speech (e.g., a segment of tape-recorded speech played backward), or to a single tone. In no case in which normal human speech was used did the person fail to identify it as speech; but no person was ever able to remember any word or phrase heard in the rejected ear; furthermore, people were unable to definitely state that the language had been English. The reversed speech was remembered as having "something queer about it" by a few listeners, but it was thought to have been normal speech by others. In contrast, the change of voice from male to female or the introduction of a tone was almost always noticed.

Cherry's experiment suggested that people do not notice much of the unattended message. However, in his experiment the participants were asked to recall information about the unattended message only after they had finished shadowing. Possibly, the participants had been briefly aware of much of the unattended message when it was presented but were unable to recall it later because the shadowing task had prevented them from using a mnemonic strategy to encode it.

Cherry's original conclusion, though, has been supported by a series of landmark experiments performed by Anne Treisman and her collaborators (Treisman and Geffen 1967; Treisman and Riley 1969). In a typical experiment Treisman and Riley (1969) presented students with two lists of digits, one to each ear. The students had to repeat one of the two lists. Occasionally, a letter was presented along with the digits. The students were told that when they heard a letter in either ear, they should stop shadowing at once and tap their desk with a ruler. If the students were equally aware of both the attended and unattended message, they should have detected the letter equally often for both ears. In fact, when the letters were spoken in a different voice from the voice used for the digits, the students detected nearly all the letters presented to both ears. Hence Cherry's finding that gross perceptual changes in the unattended and attended message are almost always noticed was replicated. However, when the letters were spoken in the same voice as the voice used for the digits, subjects detected about 75 percent of the letters presented to the attended ear and only about 33 percent presented to the unattended ear. Thus Cherry's conclusion that fewer details of an unattended message are noticed was also supported.

### Attention and Memory

Irvin Rock and his colleagues (e.g., Rock and Gutman 1981; Rock, Halper, and Clayton 1972) obtained similar results for the visual modality. For example, Rock and Gutman (1981) showed Rutgers University college students cards that contained two novel shapes, one superimposed on top of the other, as shown in Figure 2.1. One shape was red and the other was green. They were told that the experiment was concerned with aesthetic judgment under conditions of distraction. For each card half the students were asked to rate how pleasing the green form was, and the other half were asked to rate the red form. After the rating task was completed, the students received a surprise recognition task in which they were asked to identify all the shapes they had seen from a list. They were unable to recognize any of the unattended shapes, doing no better than they would by guessing. But they identified nearly a third more of the forms for which they had made pleasantness judgments than they could have identified by guessing (see also Hoffman and Nelson 1981).

Apparently, then, fewer details of an unattended input than of an attended input are capable of evoking a voluntary response or of later being recalled. However, an unattended input might have an unconscious effect on conscious processing. We will return later to the difficult question of how unattended inputs influence memory and consciousness. But first, let us examine in more detail how attention is allocated to inputs.

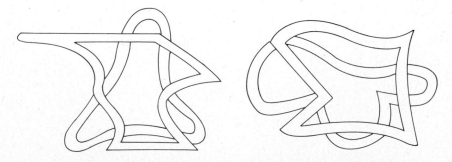

Figure 2.1   Examples of the figures used by Rock and Gutman (1981). (The overlapping figures were colored red and green within the outlines shown here.)

### Mechanisms for Rapid Response

In order to survive, you must be able to detect and respond rapidly to changes in the environment. A fundamental limitation on how fast you can respond is the speed at which a signal can be transmitted from one neuron to the next. Transmission speed varies with the kind and size of the neuron. The fastest time is about 1 millisecond (Kolb and Wishaw 1980, p. 37). One millisecond may seem like a very short period of time, but in terms of environmental necessity for a rapid response, 1 millisecond can be quite slow. For example, suppose you step on a nail. A 1-millisecond transmission speed for that signal if it passed through a chain of a thousand neurons would mean that you would have the nail stuck in your foot for at least a second before you could initiate a response.

One way to view attentional processes is as mechanisms that produce rapid and appropriate responses despite the inherent limitations imposed by the time required for the neural mechanism to operate. Let us consider two basic ways in which these limitations are overcome: reflex arcs and neural parallelism.

**Reflex arcs.**   The first type of solution is to generate responses on the basis of a very short, serial chain of neural connections. In the case of a nail piercing the skin, nothing like a thousand neurons are required to produce a response. In fact, a single neuron transmits the signal to the spinal cord, where four *interneurons* both transmit the signal up the spinal cord to the brain, where it is eventually perceived as pain, and simultaneously activate motor neurons that cause the injured limb to withdraw from the painful stimulus. The whole circuit from the foot to the spinal cord and back again involves a chain of about five neurons and takes less than 10 milliseconds. This particular reflex is called a *flexor reflex* (Afifi and Bergman 1980).

Reflex arcs help minimize the possibility of injury from sudden and unexpected contact with sharp or hot things in the environment. More generally, they permit rapid responses to changes in the environment and, in particular, to changes that might be important. For example, some reflexes keep the eyes focused on a changing light source, and some turn the head toward a sudden noise.

**Neural parallelism.**   Three or four neurons may be enough for responding to a nail, but they are not enough for reading a page. Accordingly, a very different and vastly more sophisticated approach to the generation of responses has evolved. To perform tasks that require complex and flexible responses, we have developed brains consisting of 140 billion cells, of which 20 billion are directly engaged in information processing, each with up to 15,000 connections with other cells (Kolb and Wishaw 1980, p. 4). Thus the nervous system overcomes a slow interneuron transmission speed by simultaneously activating a huge number of neurons that process an input in parallel.

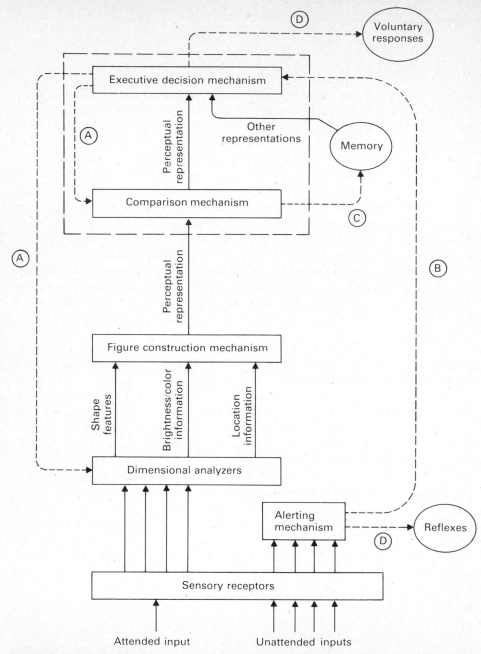

**Figure 2.2  Overview of attention. Mechanisms are shown as solid rectangles. The dashed rectangle encloses mechanisms that operate on representations in awareness. Solid arrows indicate an input's representations. Dotted arrows indicate control processes. (A) controls operation of a mechanism; (B) signals another mechanism; (C) activates representations; (D) generates actions.**

## Model of Attention

Figure 2.2 presents an overall model of attention, which includes both simple reflexes and parallel analysis of inputs. A hierarchy of mechanisms controls the allocation of attention. In Figure 2.2 the paths taken by information about inputs are represented by solid arrows, and the communication and control links among mechanisms and actions are represented by dotted arrows.

As Figure 2.2 indicates, all inputs are processed by the sensory receptors. Beyond that point a single privileged input has its further processing directed by the *executive decision mechanism* (or simply executive), which is so named because, like the executive of an organization, it directs the operation of the other mechanisms that constitute the information-processing system. We will see in Chapter 3 that the executive can be flexibly programmed to execute many different procedures. As we will describe in more detail later, sensory information about whatever input the executive is processing passes through a *dimensional-analysis mechanism,* which yields representations in terms of perceptual dimensions. Figure 2.2 indicates the three visual dimensions (shape, brightness/color, and location).

Next, the *figure construction mechanism* integrates the dimensional values to yield a perceptual representation of a definite pattern. The perceptual representation enters awareness at the level of a *comparison mechanism,* which, as its name implies, compares the perceptual representation of the attended input with representations stored in memory. A match with a representation in memory brings additional information about the input into awareness. On the basis of this information, the executive can select from any one of a large array of actions at any given moment of time. The input from the environment influences the action to be taken but does not determine it. For example, you choose the moment that you stop reading. We may influence that decision by how interesting or boring we have made this book, but other factors, such as hunger, tiredness, and the closeness of an exam, will all influence your decision.

We will refer to the hierarchy of processing that leads to the comparison and executive mechanisms as *preconscious,* because it is directed toward bringing information about the attended input into consciousness. In contrast, sensory information about the unattended inputs is given more superficial processing by *alerting mechanisms.* As we will discuss later, the alerting mechanisms can generate simple reflexes and also signal the executive to shift attention, making some unattended input the new attended input.

## Neurological Organization and Attention

**Anatomical correlates of attentional mechanisms.**   Figure 2.3 is a simplified cutaway view of the interior of the brain. (Some important parts, such as the cerebellum, that are not relevant to the discussion here have been omitted.)

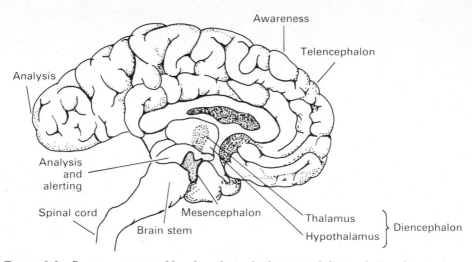

**Figure 2.3  Some anatomical landmarks in the brain and their relationship to attention.**

This figure provides approximate anatomical correlates for the functional model sketched in Figure 2.2.

The various inputs are initially processed by the sensory receptors. Projecting up from the bottom of Figure 2.3, the *spinal cord* carries inputs from the peripheral nervous system in all parts of the body. The spinal cord merges into the brain stem. The topmost portion of the brain stem is called the *mesencephalon,* or *midbrain.* At this level inputs are represented by values along single dimensions. Alerting mechanisms are based in this area. Reflexes can be elicited throughout the area from the spinal cord up to the mesencephalon (Afifi and Bergman 1980).

Just in front of the mesencephalon is the evolutionarily newer and larger *diencephalon.* Wrapped around and dwarfing it in size is the still newer *telencephalon.* The diencephalon and telencephalon have many reciprocal connections. The diencephalon accepts inputs from the mesencephalon–spinal cord system below and also accepts inputs from the eyes and ears that have not passed through the mesencephalon. In particular, the part of the diencephalon called the *thalamus* is a major way station for inputs from the eyes and ears, passing those inputs on to the cortex. Some inputs pass through the periphery of the nervous system and undergo increasingly refined analysis, so that they are no longer single values but pattern representations containing many values. For example, a visual input would correspond to a representation of a definite shape. Eventually, these inputs reach the cerebrum, where they are compared with representations in memory. Somewhere in this vast region is the biological basis of memory, and here comparisons between memory representations and new inputs take place (see Figure 2.2).

**Hemispheric organization.**    Our survey of the brain is still incomplete, for we have not yet mentioned one of its most striking aspects. The cerebrum is divided into two halves, called the *left* and *right hemispheres* (see Figure 2.4). So complete is the division between the hemispheres that it appears that we have two identical cortices, joined at their base, rather than just one. This impression is strengthened by a further examination of the neural organization. As a general principle, the main connections of each hemisphere are to muscles and sensory receptors on the opposite (*contralateral*) side of the body from the hemisphere. For example, Figure 2.4 shows that nerve fibers extending down from the left hemisphere, through the spinal cord, ultimately terminate at the right arm and leg, whereas nerve fibers extending from the right hemisphere ultimately reach the left arm and leg.

The principle of contralaterality also applies to information transmitted from the eyes and ears, but in a more complex way. If you look straight ahead, light from the left side (the left visual field) falls on the right half of the retinas of *both* eyes. Similarly, light from the right visual field falls on the left half of each retina. As Figure 2.4 illustrates, half the fibers from each retina cross at the point called the *optic chiasm*. From this point the group of nerve fibers carrying the input from the left visual field (to both eyes) proceeds to the right

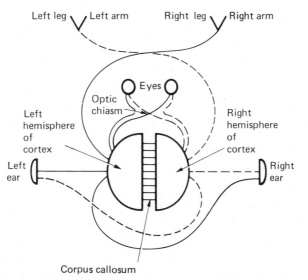

**Figure 2.4   Schematic representation of neurological organization.**

half of the *lateral geniculate nucleus* in the thalamus and hence to the visual cortex in the right hemisphere, and the fibers carrying the right visual input travel to the left lateral geniculate nucleus and visual cortex. Similarly, fibers from each ear connect to both hemispheres. Again, the fibers go first to a part of the thalamus (this time it is the *medial geniculate nucleus*) and then to the cortex—more specifically, to an area close to the ear called the auditory cortex. Though each ear is connected to both hemispheres, the contralateral connections appear stronger (Levinthal 1979).

This anatomical structure is not merely a curiosity. It has an important influence on how the brain functions. The *left* hemisphere of the brain has primary responsibility for processing visual and tactile information from the *right* side of space and the control of movements of the right arm and leg. Conversely, the *right* hemisphere has primary responsibility for processing visual and tactile information from the *left* side and control of movements of the left arm and leg. As a result, damage to one hemisphere often affects only one side of the body. For example, as shown in Figure 2.5, damage to certain parts of

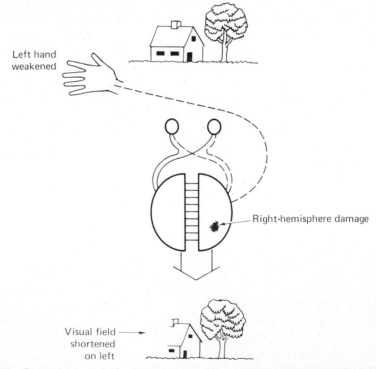

**Figure 2.5  Damage to right hemisphere, causing effects to the opposite side of the body.**

the right hemisphere may result in an inability to see objects in the left visual field and paralysis of the left side of the body. Damage to the left hemisphere may affect the right visual field and the right side of the body in the same way.

The division of labor between the hemispheres provides an interesting problem for the brain as a whole. The world around you is continuous, which is how you perceive it. A thick bundle of nerve fibers, called the *corpus callosum* (see Figure 2.4), connects the hemispheres and facilitates communication between them. Thus at some point their two separate representations of the world are combined into one, and at the same time motor commands to each side of the body are coordinated.

## ALERTING

As we have seen, the process of attention has two basic components. First, automatic alerting mechanisms detect gross changes in the environment. Second, the executive devotes most of the resources of the brain to analyzing and responding to a single input. This system is designed to select from the environment the inputs that require responses from the organism. Keeping this general framework in mind, let us begin to look in detail at how the attention system operates, beginning with the alerting mechanisms.

The function of an alerting mechanism is to rapidly detect a large change in the perceptible magnitude of the stimulus to some sense modality (i.e., audition, smell, taste, touch, and vision). For example, if someone knocks at your door while you are reading this book, your auditory alerting mechanism will detect that the sound of the knock differs from the previous quiet and you will become consciously aware of the knock. This type of reaction is innate. Even newborn infants will produce a startle response to a loud noise. Similarly, a child who leans against a very hot radiator will react instantaneously by jumping away from the unexpected source of pain.

### Dual-Process Model of Alerting

Similar mechanisms to those innate ones that alert us to changes in the environment surely exist in other species. One way to study alerting mechanisms, then, is to study the behavior of animals other than humans. This approach has both advantages and disadvantages. One advantage is that we can use techniques, such as implanting electrodes deep within the nervous system of an animal, to obtain response measures that we cannot obtain with humans. A disadvantage is that animals are limited to relatively gross behavioral and physiological responses. They cannot give us verbal reports of what they are aware of. And obviously, any generalization from whether a cat emits a response to a tone to whether a human being would be aware of that tone is extremely tenuous. Yet in spite of these problems animal research has generated a good deal of information about the physiological mechanisms of attention.

Groves and Thompson's (1970) dual-process model is based on their work with animals. They investigated how certain neurons respond to various inputs. As we have noted, each neuron is connected to many others. A neuron does not transmit the information it receives unchanged but, rather, alters it in some way. Neurons transmit information in the form of discrete pulses. Typically, on the basis of the input it receives from other neurons, a neuron will increase or decrease the rate at which it fires, hence altering the strength of the signal transmitted to other neurons. Groves and Thompson found that if the same input (e.g., a tone of a particular loudness or a light of a particular brightness) was repeated, the rate of firing of certain neurons gradually increased. They called the increase in firing that resulted from repeating the same input *sensitization*. Groves and Thompson also found that when an input was repeated, other neurons, presumed to be involved in the processing of that particular input, would respond less strongly each time the input was repeated. They called the decrease in firing that resulted from a repeated input *habituation*. Groves and Thompson concluded that the strength of an organism's response to an input is the sum of the sensitization and habituation effects. They called this model the *dual-process model*, where the processes referred to are sensitization and habituation.

The key to understanding the dual-process model is to realize that the sensitization of the nervous system is a *general* effect resulting from all inputs, whereas habituation is *specific* to a single input. As an analogy, suppose the nervous system corresponded to a balloon, with two hand pumps attached to it. The amount of air in the balloon corresponds to the sensitization of the nervous system, and the amount of air left in a pump as its compression chamber is closed by a single stroke corresponds to its habituation level (less air corresponds to greater habituation). The depression of a pump handle corresponds to an input to the system. Two boys, called Al and Bob, each take hold of one of the pumps. As Al depresses one of the pump handles, the balloon fills with air (i.e., its sensitization increases) but also the pump empties of air (i.e., its habituation increases). So only so much air can be pumped into the balloon by a single stroke of a single pump before the input "habituates" that pump. However, if there is a different input to the system—e.g., if Bob depresses *his* pump handle—then more air will enter the balloon, possibly bursting it so that Bob calls attention to himself.

To restate the analogy in the terms of the dual-process model, consider the effect of repeating a tone of a certain pitch (tone A, for Al). On the one hand, certain neurons become sensitized and maintain a moderate level of firing. On the other hand, other neurons especially involved in the processing of that particular input, pitch A, habituate. As a result, at some point the total level of firing, summed across both kinds of neurons, does not increase. Now suppose a tone at a different pitch (tone B, for Bob) is presented. This new tone will be processed by different, *unhabituated* neurons. When their stronger responses are added to the responses of the other already sensitized neurons (which respond to any input), the result will be a stronger signal to the new tone B than to the old tone A.

The dual-process model provides a good account of the details of many experiments on the effects of input intensity and repetition on neuronal firings in a variety of animals, including monkeys (Pribram and McGuinness 1975). In general terms it explains why cannon fire is more noticeable than grass growing (greater sensitization) and why repetitions of an input become less and less noticeable (habituation increases). It manages to account for all these facts without ever assuming that an input is matched to a memory representation. Instead, it derives most of its predictions from basic facts about the nervous system—in particular, the fact that inputs differing on basic physical dimensions such as frequency and amplitude maximally stimulate, and hence habituate, different neurons. As a result, the nervous system does not have to do extensive processing of unattended inputs to detect those that are grossly distinct.

### Responses of Alerting Mechanisms

To summarize, alerting mechanisms such as the dual-process model direct your attention to any gross change. This simple, bottom-up model takes us just above the level of the simple reflex arc, so that gross changes in the environment and direct invasions of the self can be detected and responded to rapidly. It describes a nervous system that hardly needs a brain at all but just a few extra cells that become generally sensitized to inputs in the environment. The dual-process model can account for your ability to detect many different kinds of inputs from the sensory receptors by assuming that inputs from different sensory receptors are each processed by a different set of neurons in the nervous system. Different sensory inputs are thus processed in parallel.

When a change in the environment is detected, your attention is directed to it. Michael Posner (1982) and others have carefully examined what happens when an alerting mechanism signals the detection of an unexpected input. When a visual input is detected, two events occur. First, the ongoing input analysis is inhibited, and the executive (see Figure 2.2) begins to analyze input from the location where the change was detected. Second, the eyes move and fixate on the input's location. Note that these events are two separate acts. That is, your eyes can fixate one location in the visual field, and at the same time your attention can be directed at another location (Posner 1980). In fact, Remington (1980) found that attention shifted to a new location 150 milliseconds before the eyes moved. This lag may reflect the fact that it takes the motor system 250 milliseconds to execute an eye movement command. The speed at which attention is shifted to a novel visual input suggests that it may be initiated by a relatively simple alerting procedure associated with the part of the brain called the *superior colliculus*, an area known to be involved in visual processing (Goldberg and Wurtz 1972).

We have stressed the very low-level alerting mechanisms that operate directly on information from the sensory receptors. However, information at higher levels may also be directed to more sophisticated alerting mechanisms. In any case once a change in the environment is detected, its analysis is no longer automatic. Control passes to the executive, which directs processing of the attended input.


## PRECONSCIOUS PROCESSING

The executive performs many functions, which, in turn, have many consequences. In this chapter we will examine how the executive attends to inputs. In later chapters we will examine how it responds to them and how a memory trace is created.

Awareness is the product of several mechanisms for preconscious and conscious processing that are arranged hierarchically under the control of the executive. The early mechanisms in the hierarchy operate automatically to construct a representation of some object or event in the environment. For example, the input from the eyes might be used to construct a representation of a tree, or the input from the ears might be used to construct a representation of a tune.

The preconscious mechanisms operate in a strictly bottom-up manner. They are uninfluenced by the results of the comparison and decision mechanisms that follow them. The only control the executive has over the preconscious mechanisms is to direct them to a particular input (thus defining the attended input). As shown in Figure 2.2, there are two levels of mechanisms above the level of sensory receptors. At the lower level, which performs dimensional analysis, inputs to the nervous system are analyzed as single values on perceptual dimensions. When the executive specifies a value on a particular dimension, such as a location in space or a particular color (indicated by the dotted arrow from the executive to the dimensional-analysis mechanism), the input that has that location or that color will be subjected to further processing by the figure construction mechanism, which constructs a complete, multidimensional representation of the input. The resulting perceptual representation corresponds to your awareness of the attended input. The mechanisms that operate on the perceptual representation are shown within a dotted box in Figure 2.2 to indicate that they operate on the representation that corresponds to your awareness of the world.

The perceptual representation produced by the preconscious mechanisms is compared with items in memory by the comparison mechanism. Finally, the executive initiates some action on the basis of the identification of the input and according to some guiding plan. The executive exerts considerable control over the operation of the comparison mechanism, as indicated by the dotted arrow from one to the other. This control will be discussed later in this and subsequent chapters.

## Focusing Attention

Your attention may be directed to some place in the environment in two ways. One way occurs when your attention is drawn by some sudden change, as when you turn toward a sudden noise or flash of light. In such cases the executive is directed to the input by an alerting mechanism, as discussed above. The second way in which your attention may be directed to some place occurs when you consciously direct it there, usually because you are looking for something. For example, when you wake up in the morning and look around, you may be looking for the clock, or the sun, or a way out of bed. But whatever it is you are looking for, you started with a plan, embodied in your executive, to do something that required identifying some object, called the *target,* in the environment. A representation of that object was retrieved from memory and is now guiding the search for it. The visual system will be used to illustrate how an input is consciously selected.

As Figure 2.2 indicates, an input is initially analyzed by several mechanisms before it reaches the comparison stage. First, the eye serves as the initial sensory receptor. It turns light energy into a pattern of active neurons. At this first level each neuron or group of neurons represents a value along a brightness dimension. Different groups of neurons encode information from different, small areas of the visual field. At the second level, dimensional analysis, the brightness information available from the peripheral level is automatically used to encode separate representations of the input in three different perceptual codes: shape, brightness/color, and location. Processing at this level occurs in parallel over the entire visual field (Biederman and Checkosky 1970; Dykes 1981; Shiffrin and Gardner 1972; Treisman and Gelade 1980). At the third and final level of preconscious processing, the representations in the separate codes are combined to construct a unified representation in the *visuospatial* code (to be discussed in Chapter 4) by the automatic, bottom-up, figure construction mechanism. At the subsequent comparison stage this representation of the input is compared with representations in memory.

How the various preconscious mechanisms ultimately construct a representation of the environment from the sensory input will be described in more detail in Chapter 4. For now the important point is that when you search for or direct attention to something, you are directing attention to a particular representation at a particular level of analysis. The decision mechanism can direct attention to a representation in terms of any one of the three dimensions identified by the dimensional-analysis mechanism or to a representation at the comparison level. For example, you can direct your attention to the brightest star in the sky (brightness/color representation), to the star at zenith (location representation), or to a particular constellation (integrated perceptual representation).

**Analysis at the peripheral level.**   The selection process for visual inputs begins at the very lowest level of analysis. The closer to the center of the retina (the *fovea*) an input falls, the more detailed is its analysis. As a result, whatever you are fixating on and looking at is analyzed in more detail than the surrounding environment. In other words, the closer something is to the center of vision, the more clearly it can be seen.

Let us now move beyond the fovea. If the eyes fixate on a detailed pattern, they may transmit a wealth of detail that overwhelms the ability of the analyzers at the next level to encode it in a single glance. Capturing, through introspection, just how much detail can be encoded from the visual field in a glance is difficult, because when you examine something your eyes move several times a second. However, with special equipment William Estes and his colleagues have overcome the problem of the impulse to move the eyes and studied how much can be processed in an extended glance. Estes, Allmeyer, and Reder (1976) presented both single letters and four-letter strings to observers for 2.4 seconds while monitoring their eye movements. The observers learned to hold their eyes on the fixation point even though the letter string was presented either one or four spaces from the fixation point on the left or right. On some trials the observers simply rated the clarity with which they saw the letter string. On other trials they had to report the letters that appeared.

The letters in this experiment were presented close enough to the center of vision to be seen clearly when presented individually. From 99 to 97 percent of the letters were reported accurately, with the slight decline occurring for the letters furthest from the fixation point. However, although 2.4 seconds is obviously plenty of time to read four letters, the observers reported that they could not see them clearly and made a substantial number of errors in reporting them, as indicated by the solid lines in Figure 2.6(a). In fact, they were only slightly more accurate at reporting the identities of the letters at 2.4-second exposures than they were when the strings were presented for 150 milliseconds, as indicated by the dotted lines in Figure 2.6(a).

Two other results shown in Figure 2.6 are worthy of mention. First, overall, a letter string presented closer to the fixation point was perceived more clearly than a letter string presented further away (Figure 2.6b). In addition, within a letter string some letters were perceived more clearly than others. For the letter strings close to the fixation point, the two end letters were per-

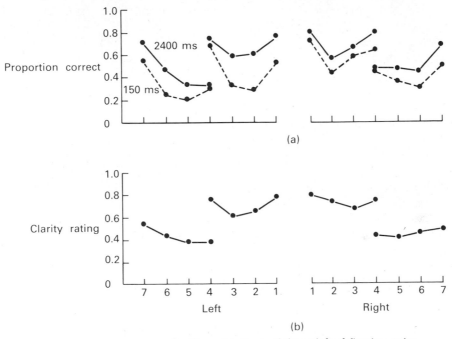

(a)

(b)

Position of letter to right or left of fixation point

**Figure 2.6    Serial position curves for four-letter strings observed for 2400 or 150 milliseconds without an eye movement: (a) For identification; (b) for clarity. (After Estes, Allmeyer, and Reder 1976.)**

ceived more clearly than the letters in the interior positions. For the letter strings further from the fixation point, the end letter furthest from the fixation point was the best perceived, which is the opposite result from that for the letter string as a whole. Why is the world perceived more clearly at the fixation point? Estes (1972, 1982) has proposed that the dimensional analyzers that contribute to the construction of shape and location representations receive inputs from specific points on the retina and that the density of analyzers is greater for inputs from the center of the fovea, so a central input receives more detailed analysis. Furthermore, Estes's results show that when the input is too detailed to be fully analyzed, details at the ends, particularly the peripheral end, receive more analysis than inner details.

The visual system compensates for the scarcity of analyzers by moving the eyes about three or four times a second so that a different portion of the visual field receives the most detailed processing. Although you are unaware of it, your eyes are constantly moving from one fixation point to another. Furthermore, the eyes do not fixate randomly but move to points of contrast, which

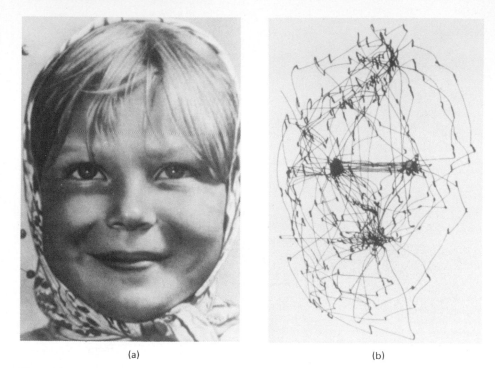

(a)                                              (b)

**Figure 2.7   Eye movements: (a) Picture observed; (b) record of eye movements made in the continuous observation of picture in (a). (From Yarbus 1967.)**

are likely to add some new detail to the input's representation. As Figure 2.7 demonstrates, a person's gaze tends to fixate on the same point and to traverse the same paths. Furthermore, the longer a person stares, the more stereotyped this fixation pattern becomes. This stereotyped fixation pattern is exactly what one would expect if eye fixations were controlled by automatic mechanisms that repeatedly moved them to the same points of high contrast and hence high information density.

**Evidence for representations of separate dimensions.**   At the level of dimensional-analysis mechanisms, visual inputs are first described in terms of brightness, then shape, and finally location. Figure 2.8 expands the description of this level, originally shown in Figure 2.2. At the lowest level contrast detectors distinguish the borders of light and dark areas. At the middle level inputs from groups of contrast detectors activate the basic feature detectors, which encode shape information. Also, a sequence of interrelated location detectors map the areas where shapes have been encoded. Finally, information from all three levels is combined to form the perceptual representation. As mentioned in Chapter 1, the perceptual representation for vision will be called

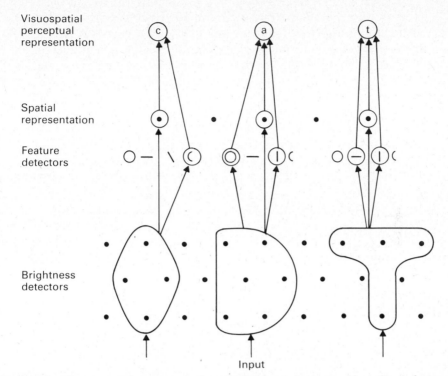

**Figure 2.8    Visuospatial representation. Brightness, shape, and location informa-tion is first encoded separately and then combined.**

the *visuospatial representation*, to indicate that it contains both visual (e.g., brightness, color, shape) and spatial information.

Of course, when you look at something, a perceptual representation is automatically constructed. Even if you are only interested in the input's color, you are also aware of its shape and location. It therefore requires experimental ingenuity to reveal the initial separateness of the representations of different dimensions. One way to produce evidence of the separate dimensions is to limit processing in some way. Evidence for the separation of the shape and location dimensions comes from the study by Estes *et al.* (1976), which compared the processing of more and less central visual inputs without eye movements. They found that for the two middle positions of the four-letter strings observers sometimes reported the correct letters but in the wrong positions. Wrong positions may have been reported because feature detectors are more densely packed than their corresponding location detectors, so a shape can be detected while its position remains uncertain. Comparable evidence for separable auditory dimensions was reported by Cutting (1976) and Efron and Yund (1974).

Another study has shown that a person can respond with great accuracy about whether a target letter was present in a display yet not be able to report whether one or more than one target appeared (Shiffrin and Schneider 1977). A person can thus detect a general shape in a visual display without being aware of such details as its color, its location, or the number of times the shape occurred.

We should note that the brain has two anatomically distinct visual systems. The functions of each system have been investigated by an examination of the performance of animals and humans with lesions in one system or the other (Kolb and Wishaw 1980, p. 190). The *geniculostriate system* consists of neuronal pathways from the retina to a portion of the diencephalon (the lateral geniculate nucleus), from there to the occipital lobe, and from there to other areas of the cortex, including the temporal lobe. This system is primarily responsible for shape and color perception. The *tectopulvinar system* consists of pathways from the retina to the mesencephalon, then to a different portion of the diencephalon, and finally to the temporal lobe, where it meets the geniculostriate system. This system is responsible for locating objects, particularly moving objects, in space. We are therefore tempted to identify the representations of separate dimensions with these separate systems. However, as yet, no clear evidence indicates that the tectopulvinar system is associated with the conscious perception of an object's location. It may act simply as an alerting mechanism that orients the eyes toward an input.

**Selective attention.**    A *selective-attention task* is one in which you are trying to pay attention to one input (the target) in the presence of others. Many daily activities require selective attention. When you focus attention on other cars, traffic signals, and traffic signs while driving, when you attend to a single voice in the presence of many while carrying on a conversation in a noisy room, or when you search for particular products in the supermarket, you are performing a selective-attention task.

Anne Treisman and her colleagues (Treisman 1977, 1982; Treisman and Gelade 1980) have shown that a model in which the executive selects an input (or inputs) that has a particular value on the brightness, shape, or location dimensions gives a good account of the situations in which selective attention to a single input is easy and situations in which it is difficult. When the target differs from other inputs at the level of separate dimensions (e.g., a visual target that differs from its neighbors in shape, color or brightness, or location), then selective attention will be easy. Hence we can easily pick out the white circle from the black ones in Figure 2.9, which differ from it in color, and pick it out from the vertical bars in Figure 2.10, which differ from it in shape. However, when the target does not differ from all its neighbors on any single dimension, and hence must be discriminated at the comparison level, selective attention is relatively slow and difficult to carry out. Thus picking out the white circle

**Figure 2.9  Target that can be effortlessly selected on the basis of color.**

from both the white bars and dark circles in Figure 2.11 is more difficult than selecting it from either kind of distractor in Figures 2.9 and 2.10.

In Figure 2.11 the target cannot be distinguished from the distractors on the basis of shape or color alone. If the executive selects elements of the display on the basis of color, it will encode a pattern of white elements, undifferentiated as to shape. If the executive selects elements on the basis of shape, it will encode a pattern of similar-colored circles, because the representation the shape analyzers operate on has already been organized by color. As a result, the executive will fail to detect the differently colored target circle. The target can therefore only be found by constructing complete perceptual representations of individual elements, conjoining the location, shape, and color of each and comparing each representation with the target representation in memory, as indicated in Figure 2.2.

Note that the level at which a target can be selected depends initially on the similarity of the distractors. In all three of the above cases (Figures 2.9–2.11), the target (white circle) is nominally defined by values on *two* dimensions. However, in both Figures 2.9 and 2.10 it can, in fact, be selected on a *single* perceptual dimension, because its value on one dimension is sufficient to discriminate it from all distractors. Only in Figure 2.11 is it necessary to select the target on the basis of multiple dimensions, hence delaying selection

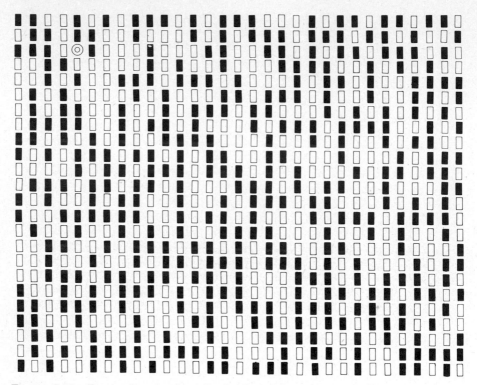

**Figure 2.10   Target that can be effortlessly selected on the basis of shape.**

until an integrated perceptual representation is formed by the figure construction mechanism.

The result for Figure 2.11 is a slower and more effortful selection of the target for three reasons. First, two additional steps, requiring the figure construction and the comparison mechanisms, are added to the selection process, and each takes an increment of time. Second, only a few elements can be compared simultaneously with elements in memory. The number is uncertain but variously estimated at between three and seven. Consequently, the comparison with memory must be done in a partly serial fashion, as successive small groups of elements are compared with the target representation in memory. This serial comparison adds additional increments of time. Third, the executive must perform two kinds of actions to proceed with the search. It must move the dimensional analyzers from location to location in the display, and it must reject all the distractors that are detected by the comparison mechanism until the target is found. Actions of the executive require effort (Kahneman 1973), so it is this sequence of executive actions that makes the search seem effortful.

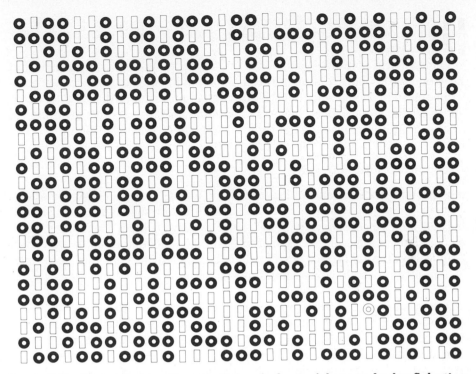

**Figure 2.11    Target that must be selected on the basis of shape and color. Selecting this target requires effort.**

You normally experience no difficulty with selection because the particular target you are interested in differs from all others on one or more of the basic dimensions defined at the level of separate dimensions. For example, you can easily have a conversation with one friend in the midst of a party. You do not consider it amazing that you are able to ignore a loud band and pick out a single person's speech from the fifty or so voices all around. But the task seems so easy only because there are differences between the target and distractors on several dimensions, any one of which can guide your selection. For instance, you know the person's location, and for that matter, you can see the person's lips moving. You are also aware of the pitch, loudness, and speech style of the person's voice. While your ability to focus attention on a single input is impressive, the apparent effortlessness with which you can distinguish between such a discriminable target and background inputs is largely a function of the natural diversity of the environment. If the conversation to which you were listening came from exactly the same location as a second conversation and was spoken in exactly the same voice, you would find it much more difficult or even impossible to attend to it alone (Cherry 1953; Treisman 1964).

The general point to remember is that selection is easy to the extent that the executive is able to define the attended input in terms of a single perceptual dimension in such a way that the attended input includes the target and excludes all distractors. But when it is impossible for the executive to define the input so that it excludes the distractors, selection becomes difficult.

### Detection of Multiple Targets

Suppose that you were shown Figure 2.9 and asked to detect *either* something white *or* something triangular. As Treisman and her colleagues have shown, this task is extremely easy. In fact, it is just as easy to detect "something white or something triangular" as "something white." Selection remains easy even if multiple potential targets must be detected, as long as *each* can be defined by a value on a single perceptual dimension.

**Simultaneous detection within a modality.**   As mentioned above, the only time the detection of a target that differs from all the distractors by a value on a single dimension is impaired is when two (or more) similar targets appear simultaneously (or nearly simultaneously). A number of experiments have investigated simultaneous detection (Moray and Fitter 1973; Moray, Fitter, Ostry, Favreau, and Nagy 1976; Pohlman and Sorkin 1976; Shiffrin and Grantham 1974; Sorkin, Pohlman, and Gilliam 1973). In a typical experiment by Moray the subjects' task was to press a key when a tone was heard that was either higher or louder than others in the series. The critical test occurred when two different streams of tones were presented in two different spatial locations. The observer had to press one key when a different tone appeared in one location and another key when a different tone appeared in the other location. If you cannot attend to two targets at the same instant in time, then detection should be poorer when two different tones are presented simultaneously in the two locations than when only one such tone is presented.

When the two tone detection tasks were different, i.e., when one tone differed in pitch and the other in loudness, persons could detect both tones as accurately as they could detect them separately. When both detection tasks were performed on the basis of loudness and both tones were quite loud, two tones could still be detected as easily as one. However, if the loudness of the two tones was reduced, even if the tones were still easily perceived, two tones no longer were as accurately detected as one. Moray *et al.* (1976) found that when a response was made to one location, the likelihood of detecting a tone in the other location was slightly reduced. Earlier, Moray and Fitter (1973) had shown that such differences remained stable with up to three years of practice.

These results suggest that there are innate perceptual limitations on the kinds of targets we can detect simultaneously. Duncan (1980) reviewed a large number of detection studies and found that the same result held for all sensory modalities and under a variety of conditions. When two similar targets occur simultaneously, there is often a greater likelihood of failing to detect one or the other than of failing to detect a single target. The more similar the targets are, the more likely it is that one will not be detected.

When two simultaneous targets are similar, they are detected largely by the same analyzers, signaling the detection of a *single* target. To detect both targets, we must complete both perceptual representations so that the target's appearance at both locations is encoded. When the target duration is brief, we have insufficient time for this processing step.

**Cross-modality detection.**    Because target dissimilarity increases the probability of simultaneous detection, it is sometimes easier to divide attention between two inputs in different modalities than it is to divide attention between two inputs in the same modality (Treisman and Davis 1973). Eijkman and Vendrik (1965), Moore and Massaro (1973), and Tulving and Lindsay (1967) all found little or no decrement in people's accuracy in detecting a simultaneous tone and light pair, in comparison with their accuracy in detecting only a single target. Gescheider, Sager, and Ruffolo (1975) found a similar result when using tones and brief vibrations as inputs.

**Visual dominance.**    However, even when simultaneous targets are defined in terms of different modalities, responses are, in fact, less than perfect. As we just mentioned, a person presented with two inputs in different modalities simultaneously is as likely to *detect* both of them as the person is to detect just one if only one had been presented. However, the two inputs are not perceived as having occurred simultaneously. If, for example, a light and a tone are presented simultaneously, the light is likely to be detected first (Colavita 1974; Egeth and Sager 1977). This phenomenon is called *visual dominance,* and it occurs in a variety of situations (Posner, Nissen, and Klein 1976). Furthermore, tactile targets dominate over auditory targets in the same way that visual targets do (Gescheider *et al.* 1975). These results generally run contrary to introspection and have therefore been as surprising to psychologists as to anyone else.

Most researchers agree that the cause of this effect is the inability of the executive to continuously process inputs from both the visual and auditory modalities (see Hochberg 1970; Kristofferson 1967; and Shiffrin and Grantham 1974; in addition to the references cited above). Instead, most people appear to have a natural tendency to give priority to the visual modality at the decision level. In fact, if subjects are given special instructions stressing that they should attend to the auditory input, the difference in the time it takes them to detect the visual and auditory targets is virtually eliminated (Egeth and Sagar 1977). Thus the dominance phenomenon arises from competition between inputs at the executive decision level rather than at the earlier selection levels discussed previously.

It turns out that this difficulty in dividing attention between vision and audition has actually been known for centuries. Eighteenth-century astronomers used the ticks of a metronome to time the transits of stars they were observing. It was they who first noticed and recorded the fact that simultaneously occurring visual and auditory targets (a star crossing and a tick) were not perceived as having occurred simultaneously. This observation was confirmed by Wilhelm Wundt, one of the first experimental psychologists, and by 1908 it appeared in a textbook (Titchener 1908) as the "law of prior entry." However, the phenomenon was later neglected by psychologists, who only recently have reconfirmed its existence (Sternberg, Knoll, and Gates 1971).

Experiments on divided attention appear to provide a challenge to our introspections about how we perceive simultaneous events. For example, an umpire must both watch for the exact instant a runner touches the base and listen for the sound of the ball hitting the fielder's glove. Unfortunately for the fairness of baseball, if the player and the ball arrive simultaneously, and if the executive is set to first process the visual input, the umpire will see the runner touch base first. The reverse will be true if the executive is set to process the auditory input.

## COMPARISON LEVEL

Once a unified representation of an input has been constructed, completing the initial preconscious processing, that representation is compared with other representations in memory in order to identify it. The comparison process itself was described in Chapter 1. As shown in Figure 1.13, representations are hierarchically organized in memory so that simple representations are connected to more detailed representations that contain them. Each representation is associated with a criterion that specifies how many of its features must match the input for it to signal a match. As also shown in Figure 1.13, the features of the input representation activate representations in memory that match them. As the matching criterion for each of these simple feature representations is met, they signal more complex representations containing them. Successively more complex representations are thus activated, until the most detailed representation that matches the input representation signals the executive of a match. As a result of this match, other representations associated with the matched representation are also activated. For example, a printed word automatically activates representations of its pronunciation and meaning (Shaffer and LaBerge 1979). The activation of representations by a match will be examined in detail in subsequent chapters.

## Comparison-Level Bottleneck

Often more representations of inputs are constructed than can be compared with representations in memory. As a result, the comparison level is frequently a bottleneck in the human information-processing system. Many inputs are never identified or are only partially identified, because the human brain lacks the capacity to compare with memory all the inputs that it can detect. The comparison-level bottleneck is another instance of the central problem of attention, i.e., the need to keep track of all potentially important changes in the environment.

As a result of the comparison-level bottleneck, you can sometimes have the feeling that you have seen more than you can report (e.g., if you are asked to describe an accident you have witnessed). In a classic experiment George Sperling (1960) showed that this impression is exactly correct. You do perceive more than you can identify and report.

Sperling asked people to report a part of a visual display, with the cue being presented at varying intervals *after* the display had disappeared. In a typical experiment a display of up to twelve letters, such as shown in Figure 2.12, was flashed at a person for only 50 milliseconds. The display always consisted of three rows of letters. In the *whole-* (or *full-*) *report condition* the person was simply told to report as many letters as could be recalled. As shown in Figure 2.13, no matter how many letters were presented in the display, people in the whole-report condition were unable to correctly report more than four or five letters on the average.

In the *partial-report condition,* immediately after the display was terminated, the person heard a high tone, a medium tone, or a low tone. The tone indicated which row of letters had to be reported—high for top, medium for middle, and low for bottom. The person never knew which row was to be reported until after the display was terminated. Thus Sperling could use the number of letters reported correctly for the cued row to calculate the *total number* of letters available to the subject at the time the cue was presented. (Actually, the number is a lower-bound estimate, because some time is needed to process the tone.) The number of letters available is easy to calculate. For

TDRX<br>
SVNB<br>
FZLQ

**Figure 2.12   Kind of display used by Sperling (1960).**

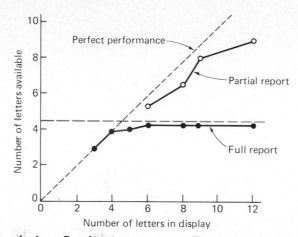

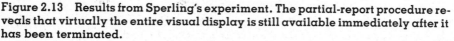

**Figure 2.13    Results from Sperling's experiment. The partial-report procedure reveals that virtually the entire visual display is still available immediately after it has been terminated.**

example, suppose there are four letters in each row, the second row is cued, and the subject is able to report three of the four letters. Since there were three rows in the display, and the subject presumably could have reported three letters from any one of them, the total number of letters available must have been 3 × 3 = 9. In other words, if the subject could report three out of four letters in one row, we can reasonably assume that nine of the twelve letters in the display were available at the time of the cue.

As illustrated in Figure 2.14, Sperling's partial-report procedure revealed that immediately after the display was terminated, subjects had more letters available than the whole-report procedure had indicated. In fact, the subjects reported that they still could "see" the display, even though it was no longer there.

The reason that only four or five letters could be reported in the whole-report condition was presumably that the rest of the display had faded from consciousness by the time the names of four or five letters were spoken. This hypothesis was tested by varying the delay at which the tone followed the visual display. When the tone followed the display by up to about a second, more letters were available in the partial-report condition (Figure 2.14). But if the cue was delayed for longer than a second, the advantage of the partial-report condition disappeared. So by this point the visual input had faded from awareness.

Neville Moray and colleagues (Moray, Bates, and Barnett 1965) performed an experiment very similar to Sperling's, but they used auditory materials. In their experiment people heard three short lists of digits that were presented simultaneously in three different spatial locations. It sounded to the subject as if one list were being read by someone on the right, another by

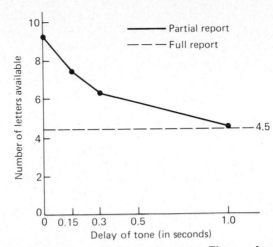

**Figure 2.14   Number of letters available versus time. The number of letters avail-
able for the partial-report condition decreases with delay of the cue tone.**

someone on the left, and the third by someone directly ahead. Three lights
were used as partial-report cues. After 1 second a light would come on, cuing
the subject to report either the left, the forward, or the right digit list. The person reported only the list corresponding to the light. In the full-report condition the subject had to report all three lists. The results closely resembled
those Sperling had obtained with visual materials. More digits were available
for partial report than could be recalled in the full-report condition. In
addition to the results for vision and audition, similar results have been
obtained for touch (e.g., Gilson and Baddeley 1969).

These experiments demonstrate two points. First, more inputs can be
perceived than can be identified. Second, an input may be perceived for a period of time longer than the period it is actually present in the environment.
Even though Sperling (1960) presented visual displays for only 50 milliseconds, people viewing the displays appeared to be able to see them for a full
second when they were dark-adapted. The length of persistence of a visual
input turns out to be influenced by several variables, including the nature of
the inputs that precede and follow it. Estimates of its duration have varied
with the technique used to measure it, from 250 milliseconds to about a second
(Averbach and Coriell 1961; Long 1980; Mewhort, Campbell, Marchetti, and
Campbell 1981). Estimates of auditory persistence have proven even more
variable, ranging from 1 to 5 seconds (Darwin, Turvey, and Crowder 1972;
Glucksberg and Cowen 1970; Guttman and Julesz 1963; Kubovy and Howard
1976; Norman 1969). The persistence of a visual input has come to be called
an *icon,* and the persistence of an auditory input is called an *echo* (Neisser
1967).

The awareness of visual and auditory persistence led to an important improvement in experimental methodology. When a psychologist wants to present a visual display, such as a string of letters, so that it is only seen for 50 milliseconds, the letter string is immediately followed by a second display, called a *mask*. That is, the letter string would be presented for 50 milliseconds; then it would be replaced with the masking string (e.g., a string of X's) that would appear in exactly the same locations as the letters. As we discussed in connection with the word superiority effect (Chapter 1), a mask has the effect of terminating the processing of the input that preceded it. At various places throughout this book where we refer to a visual display being presented for a specific period of time, the display was usually followed by a mask.

## Activation of Multiple Representations

The use of masks has revealed hidden levels in the processing of inputs. In particular, it has revealed that a single input activates multiple representations because, as we saw in Chapter 1, a mask may interfere with the representation of a briefly presented word at one level while leaving its representation at another level intact (Adams 1979; Johnston and McClelland 1980; Marcel 1983). Printed words automatically activate multiple representations so rapidly that one can create unusual gaps in awareness by limiting, through masking, the executive's access to some of the representations. For example, Lawrence (1971) flashed successive words at observers at the rate of twenty words a minute, so that each word appeared for 50 milliseconds before it was masked by its successor. All the words but one were in lowercase, and the observer had to report the uppercase word. Frequently, the word *following* the uppercase word was reported. Apparently, by the time the executive detected the target case at the letter level and then switched to the word-level representation, the word had already been replaced by its successor.

## Automatic Activation

How rapidly a memory representation signals a match with an input depends on three factors: the similarity between the input and the memory representations, the signal criterion, and the initial activation levels of the features that directly match the input representation.

Every time a feature matches an input, its activation level increases and then gradually subsides. The higher its initial activation level, the more rapidly it signals when a matching input further activates it. Hence if the same input is repeated after only a few seconds, the second presentation is processed faster than the first. In this situation the first presentation is said to *prime* the second.

Proctor (1981) showed that priming influences the time required to decide whether two inputs are the same or different. For example, suppose an observer has to decide whether the second of two successively presented letters (the *probe*) is the same as the first (the *standard*). Thus A–A should elicit a "same" response and A–B a "different" response. "Same" responses are made more quickly than "different" responses (Posner 1969), because when the same input is presented twice, the first presentation primes the processing of the probe. Similarly, "same" responses based on physical identity (e.g., A–A) are made more quickly than those based on identical names (e.g., A–a), because A primes all the features of itself but only the auditory features of the name of a (see also Proctor and Rao 1983).

## Conscious Inhibition

As we discussed in Chapter 1, recognition may be influenced by both bottom-up and top-down processes. The process by which an input is compared with memory items is basically bottom-up. However, the executive can influence the process from the top down by altering the signal criterion associated with a particular representation. When an input is identified by a match to a memory representation, other information associated with its perceptual representation is also activated. For example, when the visual pattern that comprises a word input is matched, a representation of its meaning is automatically activated. In response, the executive may block the signaling of other representations by raising the threshold of their criteria for signaling a match. Thus an input can either facilitate or inhibit the processing of subsequent inputs, depending on how the executive alters signal criteria in response to it (Posner and Snyder 1975).

James Neely (1977) developed a clever task for separating the effects of the bottom-up activation process and the top-down selection procedure. People were asked to determine, as rapidly as possible, whether a string of letters was a word (e.g., *robin*) or a nonword (e.g., *rokin*). The letter string was sometimes preceded by a priming word (e.g., *BIRD*). When *BIRD* appeared, the people in the experiment knew that two-thirds of the time the word that followed (if the string was, in fact, a word) would be a body part (e.g., *arm*) and that only one-sixth of the time would it be a bird name. Hence the people were not expecting a bird name.

However, as shown in Figure 2.15, when the word followed the prime by only 250 milliseconds, bird names were identified faster than body parts, because 250 milliseconds was all the time that was needed for the match of the prime *BIRD* to automatically activate logogens for bird names. In contrast,

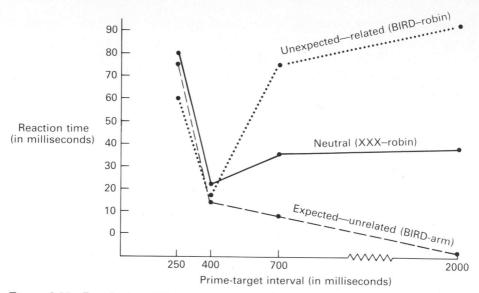

**Figure 2.15   Results from Neely's experiment. As an observer's expectations come to influence the processing of an input, the processing of expected targets is facilitated and of unexpected targets is delayed. (After Neely 1975.)**

when the word followed the prime by 700 milliseconds, body parts were identified faster than birds. The 700 milliseconds provided time for a person's expectations to operate. It provided a sufficient interval for the executive to facilitate activation of the logogens for body parts by lowering their match criterion. In addition, it provided time for the executive to *inhibit* the logogens for birds by setting their criterion for a signal very high; so when a bird name was presented, the signal of a match was delayed. Because of this conscious inhibition of bird logogens, after 700 milliseconds bird names were identified as words even more slowly than words totally unrelated to the priming word, such as tree names. [See Becker (1980) and Neill (1979) for further analysis of facilitation versus inhibition.]

Though in Neely's (1977) study the onset of the prime preceded the target by 250 milliseconds, activation, in fact, spreads so fast that two words presented simultaneously prime each other. This finding was first made by Meyer and Schvaneveldt (1973). They presented undergraduates with pairs of letter strings, and the students had to indicate, as quickly as possible, whether both letter strings were words by pressing either a yes or a no button. Pairs of associated words (e.g., doctor-nurse) were responded to faster than unassociated pairs (table-nurse). In a subsequent study Fischler (1977a) found that pairs of words related in meaning were also identified faster (e.g., wife-nurse), even if they weren't associated (also see Kiger and Glass 1983).

### Executive Selection as Inhibition

Earlier, we described how the executive could inhibit a logogen (or other memory representation) from signaling a match by setting its signal criterion very high. Also, we described how the executive could select inputs on the basis of a value on a single dimension. In fact, both these processes are different descriptions of the same process. The executive selects a memory representation by inhibiting signals from all the other representations. Similarly, it selects a value on a dimension by inhibiting detectors for all other values. Hence, as shown in Figure 2.2, the executive can inhibit signals from both low-level dimensional analyzers and higher-level analyzers involving memory representations.

Up to this point we have used Morton's (1969) analogy of raising a criterion to describe the inhibition process. However, this analogy is somewhat misleading because inhibition is a transient process. The executive does not inhibit the signal from a detector or representation in advance of an input but only in response to another detector or representation that has become active. Furthermore, the inhibition is only temporary. The executive inhibits production of an immediate signal but does not permanently change a criterion. Thus in Neely's (1977) experiment the participants were not permanently inhibited from recognizing bird names. However, as we will see, when the executive repeatedly makes the same response to a stimulus, the sequence eventually becomes automatized, so the response to the stimulus occurs automatically without executive initiation. For this reason, when a target is repeatedly presented in the presence of the same distractors, it comes to inhibit them automatically.

### Processing of Unattended Inputs

In the model of attention outlined in Figure 2.2, only attended inputs (including inputs to which an alerting mechanism directs the executive) are ever processed at the comparison level. This model would suggest that unattended inputs are never processed to the level of being matched to memory representations and identified. It might be possible, however, for some unattended inputs to also be processed at the comparison level. Here we will assess the relevant evidence.

**Conscious detection of unattended inputs.**   Some evidence suggests the possibility that some unattended inputs are recognized and enter awareness. Moray (1959) demonstrated that a person's name does sometimes reach awareness even when attention is directed elsewhere. Moray's experiment involved the usual sort of shadowing task. Participants had to shadow a message presented to one ear and ignore a message presented to the other. Recall that when Treisman and Riley (1969) performed this experiment, they found that people were aware of practically nothing from the unattended ear other than the pitch of the sound perceived in it. However, when Moray included the listener's own name within the unattended message, he found that some of the people would occasionally notice their names in the unattended message.

This result might be interpreted as evidence of an alerting mechanism that operates at the level of meaning. However, we should emphasize that people noticed their names in the unattended message only infrequently. Possibly, the executive occasionally strays in its attempt to focus attention and momentarily attends to the wrong message. If an extremely familiar and hence easily recognized input is presented during such a brief lapse, it may be identified and enter awareness. Thus Moray's (1959) result certainly does not demonstrate that all unattended inputs are processed at the comparison level.

**Unconscious influences of unattended inputs.**    What about all the times Moray's (1959) subjects failed to notice their names in the unattended message? Is it possible that the names were detected at an *unconscious* level? And is it possible for an input that has been detected only at an *unconscious* level to have an influence on *conscious* processing?

Ever since Freud (1904) first proposed his detailed theory of the relationship between the unconscious and the conscious, the effect of the unconscious on conscious acts has been an area of great controversy. Experimental research in this area has tended to come into and fall out of fashion. For instance, the 1950s saw a wave of interest in the question of whether an input could be detected unconsciously [see Erdelyi (1974) for a review]. The most extravagant claim of this type was that an input (e.g., a soda bottle) flashed at a person so briefly that the person was unaware of having seen anything would influence the person's desires (e.g., the desire to drink soda). This response was called *subliminal perception* (Packard 1957). This line of research eventually foundered for two reasons. First, some of the more dramatic results, like subliminal perception, could not be consistently replicated. Second, and more importantly, devising techniques that would accurately test the predictions of the hypotheses then being proposed was extremely difficult.

Research on the role of the unconscious has never died out entirely, and psychologists have addressed the problem with ever more sophisticated methods. A great deal of evidence now suggests that *attended* inputs can be processed to the level of meaning even if their perceptual representation is masked extremely quickly so that the observer cannot report seeing the input (e.g., Marcel 1983, discussed in Chapter 1). However, in such experiments the observer is clearly attending to the location of the briefly presented input. Accordingly, such results do not indicate high-level processing of *unattended* inputs.

A variety of studies have attempted to demonstrate unconscious influences of unattended inputs. Lewis (1970) and MacKay (1973) found that an unattended word influenced the processing of an attended word to which it was related in meaning. They inserted words in the unattended message that were related in meaning to the words the person was shadowing. Lewis found that even when people were not aware of the unattended words, those words made the shadowing task more difficult. MacKay found that the unattended words influenced the shadower's interpretation of what was being shadowed. For example, shadowers who were presented with *water* in the unattended ear would identify the meaning of the sentence *They threw stones toward the bank yesterday* as "They threw stones toward the side of the river yesterday." Shadowers who were presented with *money* in the unattended ear would identify the meaning of the same sentence as "They threw stones toward the savings and loan association yesterday." But this result only occurs when subjects have some difficulty discriminating attended from unattended words. When they are able to do it more easily, the effect of the unattended on the attended words disappears (Johnston and Heinz 1979; Johnston and Wilson 1980; Treisman, Squire, and Green 1974; Underwood 1976). Accordingly, such effects are more likely to be due to lapses of attention than to actual high-level processing of unattended inputs.

Corteen and Wood (1972) performed an experiment in which a list of words was associated with an electric shock. Later, when the subjects were performing a shadowing task, words that had been associated with the shock were inserted in the unattended message. When such a word was presented, the shadowers usually registered a change in *galvanic skin response* (GSR), even though the shadowers reported that they had not noticed the word. However, subsequent studies of this phenomenon were dogged by inconsistent results (Corteen and Dunn 1974; Forster and Govier 1978; vs. Wardlaw and Kroll 1976; also see Dawson and Schell 1982). The GSR studies thus do not yield any firm conclusions. At present, then, no convincing evidence indicates that truly unattended inputs are processed at the comparison level when the executive is performing a demanding task on the basis of the attended input.

## Capacity and the Maintenance of Attention

In the previous section we suggested that unattended inputs are processed at the comparison level only when the executive fails to maintain attention on the attended input. In the related experiments the executive was set to perform a very demanding task, such as shadowing. In general, we can think of the attended and the unattended inputs as competing for shared processing capacity at the comparison level (Kahneman 1973; Norman and Bobrow 1975). In a shadowing task the executive typically uses virtually all the capacity of the system to perform the task. Accordingly, as Cherry (1953) and Treisman and Riley (1969) found, little or no capacity remains that could be devoted to comparison-level processing of unattended inputs.

However, not all tasks set by the executive demand all the system's capacity. Furthermore, the amount of capacity assigned to a task seems to be limited by the demands of the task itself. Daniel Kahneman (1973) put it this way (p. 14):

> First, try to mentally multiply 83 × 27. Having completed this task, imagine that you are going to be given four numbers, and that your life depends on your ability to retain them for ten seconds. The numbers are seven, two, five, nine. Having completed the second task, it may appear believable that, even to save one's life, one *cannot* work as hard in retaining four digits as one must work to complete a mental multiplication of two-digit numbers.

An interesting consequence of the impact of task difficulty on the allocation of capacity is that a difficult task will be less vulnerable to interruption by unattended inputs. If the executive uses most of the available capacity to process a very complicated input, little capacity will be left over for processing of unattended inputs. Accordingly, the latter will be less likely to find a match in memory and interrupt the executive's processing of the attended input.

An experiment by Zelniker (1971) demonstrated this principle. Zelniker used a very distracting input called *delayed auditory feedback* (DAF). People spoke into microphones, and their own speech was played back to them through earphones two-thirds of a second later. The DAF is so distracting that people usually stutter and stop when they try to speak under these conditions. Zelniker subjected people to DAF while they were performing an easy task and while they were performing a difficult task. The easy task was essentially to repeat a string of numbers they heard; the difficult task was to repeat one string of numbers while at the same time listening for and remembering a second string. The speech of the participants was much more filled with stutters and stops when they were performing the easy task than when they were performing the difficult one.

The principle that interruptions from unattended inputs can be blocked by conscious concentration on a task has important practical implications. For example, in the Lamaze method of natural childbirth controlled-breathing techniques are used to divert attention from the pain of labor. The breathing techniques serve other purposes as well, but pain reduction is the most important one. In using this method, the woman takes over conscious control of what is usually an unconscious activity—breathing. Because awareness is directed to the task of breathing in a carefully controlled way, attention is less likely to be diverted to the strong pain signals being generated by the contractions of labor.

## AUTOMATIZATION OF ATTENTION

**Effect of Practice**

Modern work on the effect of experience on attention was begun when Neisser (1963a) examined the effect of practice on the search of visual displays. This work has been carried forward by many investigators, including Schneider and Shiffrin (1977; Shiffrin and Schneider 1977). They asked participants to search through a visual display consisting of several characters for some target (e.g., the letter L). Some participants performed the task according to a *fixed-set procedure,* whereas others performed it according to a *varied-set procedure.* The results of the fixed-set procedure will be described first.

The fixed-set procedure uses a fixed set of target characters such that whenever one of these characters appears in a visual display, it is the target the observer has been told to look for. Hence, if 2 is in the target set, then on no trial in which the observer is searching for, say, a 3 does a 2 appear among the items in the display. Initially, the experimental results indicated that people scanned the visual display serially, as depicted by the upper line in Figure 2.16.

After the subjects had fourteen days of practice searching for the same targets, in which over four thousand searches had been conducted, the relationship between display size and reaction time had flattened. The number of characters in the display no longer influenced the searcher's target detection time, as depicted by the lower line in Figure 2.16. Poltrock, Lansman, and Hunt (1982) obtained essentially the same result for an auditory-detection task.

The improvement in detection was the result of two factors. First, the executive had come to discriminate the target at the optimal level, the level at which its representation discriminated it from the distractors. The target representation became the pattern of features activated at the shape analysis level (see Figure 2.8) rather than the complete perceptual representation, be-

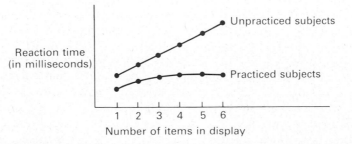

**Figure 2.16**   **Performance on an item recognition task for one or more items from a fixed set as a function of display set size.**

cause the location of the target was irrelevant to its detection. Second, when this representation was activated, it rapidly inhibited the processing of the other inputs. So when the target was present, it was detected prior to the distractors and did not have to be discriminated from them.

As impressive as it is, the ability to automatically detect a target among similar distractors is a fragile one that requires a great deal of practice and dissipates without it. This ability only develops when the target is so important to the person that every time it is detected, it brings forth the same response. When a detection task is altered slightly so that on some trials a particular character is used as a target and must be detected, while on other trials it is used as a distractor and hence must be ignored (Shiffrin and Schneider's varied-set procedure), automatic detection of the input does not develop. Few inputs in the environment are so important that they always call forth a response and so frequent that automatic detection develops.

The value of this restriction on the development of automatic processing is apparent from one of the tasks in Shiffrin and Schneider's (1977) study. After the subjects had had months of practice with a fixed set, Shiffrin and Schneider changed the task so that the characters that were formerly the targets were included in the displays that were searched for other characters. The participants found that they could not ignore the familiar items—the former targets kept intruding on their awareness when they tried to search for other items. Two of the great advantages of human cognition are the abilities to select what to attend to and to select what response to make. This flexibility is impaired if an automatic mechanism always selects the same letter from a display for conscious processing, as occurred in Shiffrin and Schneider's study.

## Stroop Effect

A cleverly devised task demonstrates a related kind of interference with words, the *Stroop effect*, named for the psychologist J. Ridley Stroop, who systematically demonstrated it in 1935. In Stroop's (1935) original experiment he showed people a list of color names that were printed in color in ink. Each color name was printed in a color different from the color it named. For example, the word *red* might be printed in blue ink and the word *blue* in green ink. Seventy college students had to read a second list printed in black ink. Stroop found little difference in the reading times for the two lists. Apparently, the students could largely ignore ink color while reading.

A second group of 100 students named the colors of the inks that the color words were printed in and also named the colors of a list of color patches. Stroop found that students required an average of 63 seconds to identify colors on the color patch list but an average of 110 seconds to identify the ink colors on the word list. Apparently, the students could not avoid reading the words when they tried to name their ink colors, and the conflict between the name and the ink color slowed down their responses. The conflict arises because when the person tries to say aloud the name of the ink color, there are two color names in consciousness. One is the ink color, which is the correct response. The other is the word that is automatically read. Hence if the person does not have to make a verbal response but, rather, indicates in some other way what color the ink is, the interference is greatly reduced (Dyer 1973; Flowers, Warner, and Polansky 1979; Klein 1964).

Recent research has focused on using the Stroop effect to study the relationship between automatically and consciously activated representations. Stroop-like interference has been demonstrated in a variety of tasks. Lupker (1979) and Smith and Magee (1980) showed that interference occurred if a printed word was superimposed on a picture that a person was trying to name. This interference is greater when the picture and word are related than when they are unrelated (Lupker and Katz 1981). As an experiment, try to read aloud, as fast as you can, the number of characters in each row of Figure 2.17. You will find it difficult to ignore the names of the characters in each row (Flowers *et al.* 1979). Reisberg, Baron, and Kemler (1980) report that after subjects have practiced, the names of the numbers interfere less and less with their ability to report the number of characters in each row. However, the loss in interference is highly specific. Practice in ignoring the numbers *2* and *4* does not improve performance on rows containing *1* and *3* (see also Neill 1977).

**Figure 2.17    Stroop effect. Say aloud the number of characters in each row as fast as you can.**

## POSTERIOR CORTICAL INJURY AND THE
## NEGLECT SYNDROME

Recall that inputs travel from the sensory receptors to the diencephalon and thence to the cortex. The surface of the cortex is bunched together in thick folds separated by deep fissures. The largest fissures are used as anatomical landmarks to divide each hemisphere into four areas called *lobes.* The frontal, parietal, temporal, and occipital lobes of the right hemisphere are shown in Figure 2.18. (The left hemisphere is similarly divided.)

In general, any injury of sufficient severity to the posterior portion of the cortex (comprised of the parietal, temporal, and occipital lobes) will cause some defect in the detection or perception of an input (i.e., the operation of the bottom-up mechanisms is impaired). The nature of the defect depends on the location of the injury. For example, damage to the visual cortex, which is in the occipital lobe, impairs the perception of forms, and damage to the auditory cortex in the temporal lobe impairs some aspect of auditory perception. The effect of parietal damage is more subtle. In a routine social interaction a person with parietal damage may appear normal, but the person may be unable to draw the simplest picture of a daisy, a house, or the face of a clock (Goodglass and Kaplan 1972). Such a person is also likely to suffer a defect in spatial orientation, so they do not know left from right, get lost when trying to get from one room to the next in an unfamiliar place, and have difficulty putting their clothes on.

Recall that each hemisphere initially processes the inputs from one side of the environment. The *unilateral neglect syndrome* results from a severe injury

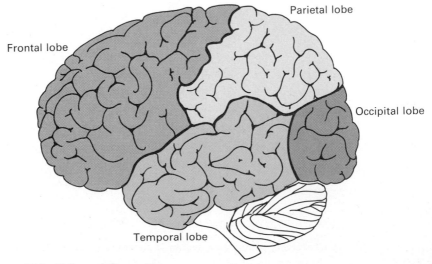

**Figure 2.18   Lobes of the cortex.**

to the lower parietal or temporoparietal region of the cortex. In this bizarre disorder inputs from one side of the body are ignored (Heilman and Watson 1977). In the most severe form of the syndrome the person has no awareness of the deficit. As a result, the person does not try to compensate for the limited field of vision by moving his or her head from side to side. As is dramatically apparent in the self-portraits shown in Figure 2.19, the neglect is most severe immediately after the injury, and then it tends to lessen in severity. During its most acute stage a person will wash, shave, and comb one side of his or her face and head, eat the food off one side of the plate, etc. The person

**Figure 2.19    Self-portraits of the painter Anton Räderscheidt before and after he suffered a right-hemisphere stroke in October 1967: (a) Self-portrait in 1965; (b) December 1967; (c) January 1968; (d) March 1968; (e) April 1968; (f) June 1968. (From R. Jung. Neurophysiologie and psychiatrie. In H. W. Kisker, J. E. Meyer, C. Müller, and E. Strömgren (Eds.), *Psychiatrie der gegenwert* (2nd ed.), pp. 753–1103. Berlin, Heidelberg, New York: Springer, 1980.**

also is only aware of sounds from the side of the environment to which he or she can visually attend. In the mild form of the syndrome a person can attend to a single input presented to either the left or the right. But when two inputs are presented simultaneously on different sides of the body, the inputs on one side are always neglected.

The severe form of the neglect syndrome seems to result from disruption of processing at two levels. First, the orienting responses controlled by the midbrain, at the initial level of analysis, are no longer directing processing capacity, or causing the eyes and head to move, toward the location of an input when it occurs on one side of the body. Second, damage to the cortex disrupts the executive so that the person is unaware of the problem. As always, when the executive processes an input, it inhibits the processing of all others until the task is completed or is interrupted by an alerting mechanism. But since the executive is not receiving inputs from one side of the environment, there is no stimulation to counteract the flow of inhibition to its orienting mechanisms.

Left-side neglect is far more common than right-side neglect. The reason for this asymmetry is not known, although it is certainly related to the special functions unique to each of the two cerebral hemispheres, to be discussed in Chapter 13.

## SUMMARY

The central issue of attention is how the information-processing system copes with the vast quantities of information arriving at a given moment. Because the system is limited in its capacity to process information, analysis of inputs must be *selective*. The *dual-process model* of alerting describes how gross changes in the environment are detected.

Processing of inputs is controlled by an *executive decision mechanism*. Attended inputs receive preconscious processing from a *dimensional-analysis mechanism,* which forms representations of separate perceptual dimensions, and from a *figure construction mechanism,* which produces an integrated perceptual representation of which the person is aware. The *comparison mechanism* then compares the perceptual representation with representations in memory. A match results in identification of the input and triggers further processing, including both automatic activation of related representations and conscious inhibition of other inputs. Because the number of perceptual representations that can be simultaneously compared with memory items is limited, the comparison stage is a bottleneck that limits the number of inputs that can be identified. Unattended inputs do not appear to be processed at the level of meaning except when lapses of attention occur or when the task being performed by the executive does not exhaust the capacity of the system.

Attention is modified by experience. For example, the *Stroop effect* illustrates the inability of skilled readers to suppress reading of words. Abilities related to perceptual attention are impaired by injury to the posterior portion of the cortex. A particularly dramatic example is the *neglect syndrome,* in which inputs from one side of the environment (usually the left side) are ignored.

## RECOMMENDED READINGS

The classic that revived the study of attention after nearly a half century of neglect was Donald Broadbent's *Perception and Communication* (1958). Many reports of experiments on aspects of attention are published in the *Journal of Experimental Psychology: Human Perception and Performance.* This source is also a fruitful one for reports relevant to topics in Chapters 3 and 4. Other important papers appear in the continuing series of edited volumes entitled *Attention and Performance.*

A good source for learning more about the neuropsychological basis of cognition is *Fundamentals of Neuropsychology* (1980) by Bryan Kolb and Ian Wishaw. Howard Gardner's *Shattered Mind* (1976) provides the best introductory descriptions of a variety of neuropsychological disorders. The leading journals in neuropsychology are *Neuropsychologia* and *Cortex. Advances in Neurology,* volume 18 (1977), edited by Friedland and Weinstein, is a collection of papers on the neglect syndrome.

# CHAPTER **THREE**

# Action and Control

## INTRODUCTION

It is quite possible to teach a fish to strike a particular key whenever a red light comes on. The ability to perform such a task does not appear to require anything like conscious awareness. All an animal needs in order to learn such a task is a perceptual system for detecting the input, a movement control system for executing the response, and a memory that can store an association between a representation of the input and the response so that the former activates the latter. Many creatures far less cognitively sophisticated than humans can learn such stimulus-response associations.

If the task is changed, however, so that a particular key must be pressed only when two lights of the same color come on in succession, then the fish may fail to learn the task. This more complex task requires that the animal's information-processing system, in addition to including the basic perceptual, memory, and response components, must be able to maintain a representation of the first light in an active state until the second light appears and can be compared with it. Many animals, including monkeys, dogs, and pigeons, can perform a matching task to some degree, but no creature's performance approaches that of a human.

The performance of infrahumans on matching tasks is severely limited by the duration of the interval between the initial input and the subsequent probe, the presence of irrelevant stimulation during the retention interval, and the complexity of the input that must be maintained. The best nonhuman performance is observed in dolphins (Thompson and Herman 1981) and primates. After extensive training, monkeys can match simple shapes at durations of 3 minutes (D'Amato 1973). In contrast, humans can maintain a simple visual or auditory input indefinitely even in the presence of irrelevant stimulation.

A representation of an input may be retained during a matching task in two basic ways. First, after the input is no longer present in the environment, its representation may be kept in awareness, as mentioned above. In humans examples of such active maintenance include visual and auditory imagery (see Chapter 4) and rehearsal of a verbal input (Chapter 10). This method of maintaining an input, useful though it is, has serious limitations. Because the amount of information that can be in awareness is limited, the continued activation of past inputs may interfere with processing current environmental inputs. Maintaining a visual image, for example, interferes with detection of visual inputs, whereas maintaining an auditory input interferes with detecting an auditory input (Segal and Fusella 1970). Conversely, if a new input sufficiently stimulates an alerting mechanism, directing attention to itself, the representations of past inputs may be deactivated and lost. For example, Reitman (1974) demonstrated that if a person is prevented from rehearsing an auditory input, its representation rapidly decays.

The second basic way of maintaining an input avoids these difficulties. A representation may be stored in memory after being tagged with associated cues that can later be used to retrieve it. When a probe appears, it will serve as a cue to reactivate the stored representation and make a comparison. When you go to the grocery store, for example, you do not have to continually keep in mind the things you want from the moment you leave until you sight them in the store. In humans the semantic code (Chapter 5) is especially important for this mode of information maintenance.

The relationship between memory, activation, and awareness is illustrated in Figure 3.1. Memory is a single system comprised of a vast number of representations. As we mentioned in Chapters 1 and 2, the memory representa-

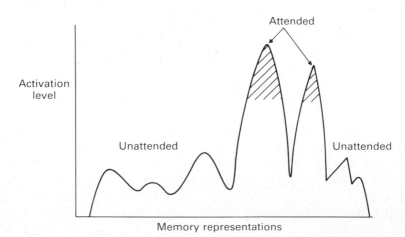

**Figure 3.1    Hypothetical distribution of activation over memory representations at a given moment. The shaded peaks indicate the representations in awareness.**

tions form a complex network of associations, and each representation may receive activation from inputs or from some of its neighbors and may transmit activation to others. Hence each representation is also called an analyzer, or a logogen if it is a word representation. The abscissa of Figure 3.1 corresponds to the set of memory representations. Each memory representation has some degree of activation. As Figure 3.1 illustrates, at any given moment the vast majority of memory representations are at some relatively low level of activation. Some representations, however, are the focus of current processing activity and hence are highly active. These active representations—the "mountains" in Figure 3.1—are currently receiving activation either from input representations being compared with memory items or from associated active representations.

Once the source of activation for a memory representation ceases its activation level decays. Thus as the executive shifts the focus of attention from one input to another, the pattern of activation over the memory system quickly changes. Hence if we could show an illustration like Figure 3.1 over time, the mountains of high activation would be dynamically rising and falling over relatively brief periods of time.

As we saw in Chapter 2, the number of inputs that can be in awareness simultaneously is severely limited. Only the most active representations are in awareness, as indicated by the shaded peaks in Figure 3.1.

As we will see in later chapters, once memory representations are established, they remain in the system indefinitely (although they may not be easily accessed). Accordingly, the overall memory system is sometimes called *long-term memory*. The set of representations that are currently most active and hence are in awareness are sometimes called *active memory*. Of course, as Figure 3.1 makes clear, active memory is not something separate from the overall memory system but simply the currently most active portion of it.

To the extent that an animal has awareness, the contents of its awareness are largely determined by its environment. That is why an animal's ability to perform a delayed matching task is limited. Once the input is no longer present, its representation fades from the animal's awareness and no longer determines its actions. But humans are relatively free from such environmental control. In a human the executive itself can initiate actions that maintain the activation of a representation and hence maintain it in consciousness. As we have mentioned, when you activate a representation, you may experience visual or auditory imagery. Furthermore, while a representation is being maintained in consciousness, procedures can be applied to it that alter it in various ways, such as the mental rotation procedure mentioned in Chapter 1. As we will describe in Chapters 11 and 12, the ability to perform these alterations allows you to solve a variety of difficult tasks. For this reason those representations in consciousness are sometimes said to comprise *working memory.* Finally, as we will discuss in Chapters 9 and 10, the longer an input's representation is maintained in consciousness, the more likely it is to be stored in a form that will permit the executive to reactivate it whenever it is needed. Hence the ability to maintain a representation in consciousness is at the center of your ability to control your actions independently of the environment. In this chapter we will examine how this ability has evolved and how it is used.

## ACTIONS

We begin our study of conscious control in a surprising place: the execution of simple motor movements. However, as we trace the initiation of action up through the nervous system, we will find that our path leads to the locus of awareness, the executive, from which all actions are ultimately directed.

### Reflexes

The simplest form of action is the *unconditioned reflex* (Chapter 1). A reflex is a *ballistic* movement that is stimulated by an innately specified input. A ballistic movement is one that, once initiated, is not under the continued control of the nervous system. A reflex can involve as little as two neurons: the neuron that detects the stimulus and the motor neuron that initiates the motor response to it.

Reflexes, as noted in the previous chapter, activate rapid, simple movements away from potentially harmful inputs and toward interesting ones. In addition, a reflex can be *conditioned* so that it is elicited by a slightly wider range of stimuli than the innately specified one. If another input (the *conditioned stimulus*) that activates an interneuron connected to the motor neuron of a reflex is repeatedly presented about a half second before the innate (*unconditioned*) stimulus (in some cases simultaneous presentation also works), then eventually the conditioned stimulus will also activate the response. For example, a puff of air (or any light pressure) on the eye causes the eye to blink. A click before the puff will also come to cause the eye to blink (Reynolds 1945). Some psychologists have believed that conditioning is a precursor of learning, and it has been studied intensively since the famous experiments of Ivan Pavlov (1927). However, conditioning is quite different from what we normally mean by learning because its effect is transient. When the conditioned stimulus is no longer paired with the unconditioned stimulus, the response to it undergoes *extinction.* That is, after a number of unpaired trials the unconditioned stimulus no longer elicits the response. The only role that reflexes are known to play in the information-processing system is their role in alerting, which has already been described.

### Discrete Motor Movements

The same ballistic movements that are initiated as parts of reflexes can also be performed voluntarily. Hence you can open and close your eyes when you choose. Also, ballistic movements like finger presses can be aimed accurately (Zelaznik, Shapiro, and McColsky 1981). Nevertheless, a ballistic movement, by its nature, is an extremely primitive way of interacting with the environment, and pure ballistic movements play an extremely limited role in cognition. Their study by psychologists has been desultory, mostly in the form of specialized skills such as telegraphy (Bryan and Harter 1899) and typewriting.

Here we make several points. First, even though a ballistic movement is not under control *during* the movement, the perceptual system usually detects the result of the movement. This information on a movement's accuracy is called *feedback*. The two most frequent kinds of feedback are visual feedback and *proprioceptive feedback* from sensory detectors in your joints, which is used to keep track of your arms, legs, and fingers as you move them. Adams (1968, 1971) proposed that the executive makes use of feedback to aim subsequent movements. He called a system in which feedback is used to guide actions a *closed-loop system*. A large number of experimental results show that actions are generated by a closed-loop system. For example, West (1967) showed that experienced typists detected 50 percent of their errors even when they could not see what they were typing. Rabbitt (1967, 1968) reported even higher error detection rates for a simpler key-pressing task.

If the executive always initiates the same action in response to an input, eventually an automatic procedure consisting of the sequence of actions taken in response to the input is formed so that the input comes to elicit the response without conscious effort. An automatic procedure for a sequence of actions is called a *motor program*. For example, the typing program consists of a set of letter–finger movement correspondences. An *automatic procedure* is a procedure that is completely self-contained; so if the appropriate input initiates it, its sequence of steps is run off from beginning to end without interruption.

The advantage of an automatic procedure is its speed. For example, consider what it is like to type, a skill that one of the authors has painfully achieved to a moderate degree of proficiency. When you have acquired the skill of typing, you do not, as you identify each letter, consciously recall which key it is and then consciously press it. Rather, as you notice each letter, your finger finds its own way. All the letter-key information is contained within the motor program, and so no time need be spent in memory retrieval during typing once the program is activated. This description, of course, does not mean that a conditioned response has been established. A typist's fingers do not jerk inappropriately when he or she is reading a book or eating a bowl of alphabet soup. The responses only occur when the executive has initiated the typing motor program. The disadvantage of a motor program is its inflexibility. Thus if the letters on the keyboard are rearranged, a new program has to be learned.

An important question is the role feedback plays in the motor program. According to Adams's (1971) hypothesis, the feedback from each action activates the next one in the sequence, so feedback plays an essential role. The alternative view is that when a motor program is formed, the entire sequence of movements is executed by the program without the guidance of feedback. The latter hypothesis predicts that a skilled performer will be less dependent on feedback. Adams, Goetz, and Marshall (1972) provided evidence against this hypothesis by showing that reducing feedback was even more disruptive to skilled performers than to unskilled performers. In fact, the circumstances under which the skill is learned appear to influence the kind and amount of feedback incorporated in the motor program. For example, Notterman and Tufano (1980) showed that a repetitive motion learned under visual control required less proprioceptive feedback than a comparable voluntary motion.

In addition, the role of feedback in the performance of very fast motor sequences is still unclear because it is not clear whether the feedback from each action in the sequence can reach the brain in time to influence the aiming of its successor. A pianist's fingers can execute movements only 60 milliseconds apart. This speed is too fast for individual movements to be under visual control, because Carlton (1981) found that it takes about 135 milliseconds for visual feedback to correct a movement. However, Adams (1976, p. 215) cites a variety of results indicating that proprioceptive feedback can reach the brain from a variety of muscles in less than 25 milliseconds and from tongue and eye muscles in only 4–6 milliseconds. Measurements for more muscles are needed before the general role of proprioceptive feedback in motor programs is known.

Another important aspect of discrete motor skills is the way a motor program operates. For the typing example it does not translate letters into keystrokes one at a time. Rather, the executive inputs several letters to the typing motor program, which converts them all into keystroke commands. The sequence of keystroke commands is then passed to a lower-level motor program, which activates the entire sequence of muscle motions described by the commands. This brief example illustrates three pervasive aspects of the control of human action: It is top-down, it is hierarchical, and the fundamental unit is the action sequence (Rosenbaum 1984).

Recently, how sequences of keystrokes are executed has been studied intensively. Rumelhart and Norman (1982) have described a detailed hierarchical computer simulation of typing that models many of the keystroke latencies and errors that are observed. Also, Sternberg, Knoll, and Wright (1978) found evidence that subprograms for sequences of keystrokes are retrieved and then executed during rapid typing. They found that when prespecified sequences of different lengths had to be typed to a signal, the latency from the signal to the first stroke increased with the length of the sequence. The model they propose, though also hierarchical, is quite different from that of Rumelhart and Norman. So many details of the typing process remain controversial.

The memory trace of a motor program for discrete movements is much more permanent than that of a conditioned reflex. Once a skill is well learned, people retain such skills throughout their lives. However, discrete skills are susceptible to forgetting from two sources. The first is interference from the learning of another program that re-pairs the same stimuli and responses differently. For example, if you learned to type on a keyboard with a new arrangement of letters, you would be somewhat slower when you returned to the first. Skilled performers rarely have to learn such conflicting responses, so this source of forgetting plays only a small role in daily life. The second source of forgetting is disuse. When a skill such as typing is not used, the speed and accuracy of its performance decreases over time (Baddeley 1976, p. 255).

## Continuous Perceptual Motor Skills

We now turn to actions that are clearly made under the control of feedback. Only short, fast motions, like a key press, are ballistic. For longer or slower motions feedback is used during the execution of the motion to guide it to its goal (Christina, Lambert, Fischman, and Anson 1982). Acts made under the control of feedback include almost every important voluntary action you take, from standing up, to walking, to scratching your nose, to chewing your food, to reaching for a pencil, picking it up, and writing a few lines. It includes driving a car, swinging a bat, and humming "Swanee River." These movements are sometimes called *continuous* because they are under control continuously from initiation to termination, rather than just at initiation, like ballistic movements. They are also sometimes called *perceptual motor skills* because the movements are guided by perceptual feedback from a variety of sensory systems. Like a discrete ballistic movement, a perceptual motor skill can be combined with some other movement (either another perceptual motor skill or a ballistic motion) into a sequence controlled by a motor program.

The primary sources of feedback are the kinesthetic and vestibular perceptual systems, which are controlled from the *cerebellum*, a portion of the rhombencephalon of the brain that until now we have ignored. The *kinesthetic system* makes use of proprioceptive feedback from sensory detectors in the joints to keep track of where your arms, legs, and fingers are as you move them. All of this information is used to construct a constantly updated representation of the orientation of the limbs. In addition, the vestibular system, which relies on sensory detectors in the inner ear, keeps track of the orientation of your body with respect to gravity.

Together, the kinesthetic and vestibular systems construct a complete perceptual representation of your own body. This representation complements the representation of your environment constructed by the external perceptual systems of vision, touch, and audition. Because the two systems are interconnected, you can effectively move about in and act on the environment. People unfortunate enough to lose a limb are surprised to discover that they can still feel a phantom limb in its place. Though the physical limb has been lost, it takes some time before the body representation containing it in the brain is modified accordingly.

You may not have considered the importance of feedback in action before because most movements are made so effortlessly. When you pluck a grape, you do not grasp it too lightly, so that it slips through your fingers, nor too hard, so that it is crushed between them. Rather, you adjust the pressure you exert to just match the resistance you receive. Furthermore, the feedback is used to calibrate future motions. For example, standing up and walking is a learned skill. Learning to balance on your own legs is no different from learning how to balance on a bicycle or on a pair of stilts. Initially, the motions are under conscious control. On the basis of vestibular feedback you become more and more accurate in initiating muscle changes in response to changes in body position. From constant repetition these procedures become automatized. It is worth mentioning in passing that psychologists have established that feedback from some perceptual system is necessary for the learning of a continuous motor skill. Without feedback no learning occurs (Moates and Schumacher 1980, p. 311).

Motor skill learning has several extremely useful characteristics. The first is that the kind of feedback that can be used to calibrate the motor commands during learning is extremely diverse. Visual as well as proprioceptive feedback can be used. The use of visual feedback is extremely important because the visual system often provides a second source of information that speeds the learning of certain skills and because many skills require the integration of visual and motor information. One of the most basic skills is reaching to grab something that can be seen. This action requires an infant, say, to calibrate visual and kinesthetic information (i.e., where its hand appears to be and where it feels to be) in order to predict where the hand will feel to be if moved to the location of the desired object.

In fact, the motor system is so flexible that it can even accommodate visual information that conflicts with proprioceptive information. Perhaps you remember how difficult it was the first time you tried to comb your hair while looking in the mirror. However, after a few attempts you presumably became sufficiently calibrated that it seemed less disturbing to see your hand move away from you as you moved it away from the mirror. Stratton (1897) demonstrated just how far the motor system was willing to go to accommodate the visual when he wore an inverting lens over one eye (the other eye was patched); with this lens down appeared up and right appeared left. The visual field never reversed itself, but over a period of days the motor system recalibrated itself so that he could reach for objects and move about normally.

A second useful aspect of perceptual motor skills is that the perceptual representation formed on the basis of feedback used to calibrate actions can extend beyond the body. A novice carpenter feels the hammer handle in his hand when he strikes a nail, whereas a journeyman feels the head strike the nail. Clearly, this feeling is an illusion, but it is also an essential part of the skill related to the calibration of the visual and motor systems. Once the hammer feels as if it were part of your hand, so that you feel it where you see it, you are that much more accurate at striking the nail, just as feeling your hand to be where you see it is important for accurate reaching. Another example is the feel of the road that a driver gets. One does not feel the steering wheel vibrating and the seat bouncing; rather, one has the illusion of feeling the road through them. Again, this illusion exists because a driver makes use of this information in controlling the speed and direction of the car.

The motor program itself is quite abstract, so the same skill can be performed a variety of ways. People can write equally well on a paper by moving their wrists or on a chalkboard by moving their arms. They can even trace letters with their toes. There is one barrier, however. Right-handed people who learn a skill with their right hand cannot then perform it well with their left hand. However, the skill can be relearned separately with the left hand. Unlike perceptual inputs, motor representations are apparently not transferable across the corpus callosum.

Another useful aspect of perceptual motor skills is that once one is learned, it is never forgotten. The familiar example is that no one ever forgets how to ride a bicycle. Although we don't know of anyone who has tested bicycle riding after decades of disuse, a variety of other continuous motor skills have been tested over retention intervals of up to several years, and no forgetting has been found (Bilodeau and Bilodeau 1961; Fleishman and Parker 1962; Hammerton 1963).

## Skill Learning

As discussed previously, when the same sequence of motor acts is performed over and over, a motor program is formed so that when the program is initiated, the entire sequence is run off from beginning to end automatically. Virtually every motor skill we have, from grasping, to walking, to talking, to driving a car, is under the control of a motor program.

**Alternative ways to learn skills.**   How are these programs acquired in the first place? In some cases the environmental contingencies are such that the same action is performed over and over so that it become automatized. Grasping undoubtedly falls into this category. Many objects in an infant's visual field excite its curiosity, so it encounters many occasions in which it tries to grasp an object.

Another reason a motor sequence may be repeated is in imitation of another person in the environment or under the active encouragement and instruction of another person. Walking falls into this category. Toddlers are constantly in the presence of walking role models and are frequently lifted to their feet and encouraged to balance themselves.

Finally, most skills, from speaking to typing, are not learned by mimicking a model that is under observation but, rather, are learned under the guidance of either a representation of the model in consciousness or a representation of the sequence of acts to be performed. When children learn to speak, they do not attempt to produce speech sounds simultaneously with an adult model so that their utterance matches that of the adult. Rather, they attempt to utter sounds they *remember* hearing. Hence the acquisition of speech is dependent on children having the ability to bring into consciousness a representation of the sounds that they want to produce in the absence of the perceptual input. Thus self-activated auditory representations serve as the models for the learning of some skills, and self-activated visual representations are the basis of others. A child can learn to dial a phone by observing an adult and then trying it herself. She does not have to perform the act simultaneously with the model.

Language is a powerful tool for encoding information and activating it from memory. Once language is acquired, a person has a new way of constructing a model from which to learn a skill. For example, when a person first learns to swing a bat or a tennis racket, to dance a waltz, or to shift gears on a standard automobile transmission, he initially performs the sequence under self-generated verbal commands. As you took your first, tentative movements, you surely can remember saying to yourself, "Shoulders back, wrists together, eye on the ball." "Step, together, step." "Press clutch, shift stick, release clutch."

**Three phases of skill learning.**   The ability to self-generate a set of instructions makes the learning of long and complicated motor sequences practical. Such learning goes through three phases, as control of the motor sequence evolves from a sequence of verbal commands to a motor program. In a study of the learning of Morse code William Bryan and Noble Harter (1899) were the first to describe skill learning as a sequence of phases. Details of these phases were studied over the next half century. Fitts and Posner (1967) described three phases in the learning of a skill: the cognitive phase, the associative phase, and the autonomous phase.

During the *cognitive phase* the learner must consciously make each movement in response to a verbal command and then observe the consequences to ascertain whether the movement met the specifications of the command. One must therefore attend to inputs that later go unnoticed. For example, in learning a dance step, one first attends to visual and then to kinesthetic information about the feet. Some instructors report that one of the most difficult things for beginners to learn is to process information concerning their own limbs. Later, the kinesthetic information will be encoded automatically, and the visual information will not be used at all.

During the *associative phase* conscious memory search is no longer required to recall the steps of the activity. Frequent repetitions have formed associations from one action to the next, so feedback from each action automatically cues the next action in the chain. As the associations between the separate actions become stronger, one need no longer consciously initiate each individual action. Instead, a single decision initiates a chain of actions that then proceed automatically, one following the other. Eventually, all the steps are assembled into a single motor program.

During the *autonomous phase* the entire sequence of actions is under the control of a single motor program, which, once initiated, carries out the entire sequence automatically. As a result, the executive can carry out other activities while a motor program is executing its sequence of actions. Thus a well-practiced task like walking may not interfere with talking. However, even during the autonomous phase practice on a skill will continue to improve skilled performance for years. The classic study in this field is Crossman's (1959) study of cigar rollers. The time to operate a cigar-rolling machine decreased for four years, at which time a person reached the mechanical operating limit of the machine.

## THE EXECUTIVE

So far, we have considered sequences of actions intended to affect the environment. However, some actions influence the processing of information as well. For example, when you close your eyelids, they shut off the flow of visual information. The evolution of the ability to initiate actions that influence perceptual processes was an important development, because it gave the organism more control over its interaction with the environment. For the first time what was processed was under the control of the organism to some degree; hence for the first time it could selectively attend to one target or another. As we saw in Figure 2.2, in humans actions that regulate a variety of information-processing mechanisms are under the control of the executive mechanism atop the information-processing hierarchy. The executive can perform four kinds of actions. First, it can regulate perception through the selective inhibition of the outputs of perceptual mechanisms. Second, it can both inhibit representations from entering consciousness and perform actions that activate representations so that they are likely to enter consciousness and perform operations that modify those representations. Third, it can initiate motor programs or individual motor responses. Finally, it can initiate a procedure that takes control of the executive mechanism itself.

Just as the executive can execute a sequence of motor acts in the form of a motor procedure to perform some complex action, it can execute a procedure that causes a sequence of perceptual mechanisms to perform some mental activity essential to a task, as when a person engages in visual imagery to retain a target that will have to be matched to a subsequent probe. Through such perceptual control procedures people attain much greater control over their perceptions and actions than animals have.

Unlike lower mechanisms, which execute only fixed procedures, the executive is flexible. The executive mechanism is analogous to a computer, which can be programmed to execute an indefinitely large variety of procedures. At any given time some particular procedure, which we term a *schema*, has control of the executive mechanism. Thus when we refer to what the executive is doing, you should understand that we are referring to the procedure specified by the schema that currently controls the executive mechanism.

### Schemas

A schema does more than specify a sequence of operations that are run off from beginning to end without alteration, as other procedures do. Rather, a schema consists of a sequence of *if-then rules*. An if-then rule makes the initiation of an operation contingent on the presence of some input or signal; i.e., *if* the appropriate input is detected, *then* a certain operation is performed. An executive schema may thus select any one of a variety of actions, depending on the situation and internal status of the person.

Schemas vary from the simple to the complex. For example, only a very simple schema is necessary to perform a two-choice discrimination task in which a right-hand switch is pressed when a red light appears and a left-hand switch is pressed when a green light appears. Such a schema consists of only two if-then rules: "If input is red, press right," and "if input is green, press left." At the other end of the complexity scale people may possess, say, a restaurant schema, which specifies the behaviors required for restaurants, cafeterias, and fast-food outlets. How such complex schemas are formed and what form they may take will be discussed in subsequent chapters.

A schema does not necessarily run through a sequence of operations once and then terminate. Rather, a schema may continue to operate until an input triggers a rule that, as its action, activates another schema to replace the current one. For example, a person in a discrimination task may continue to respond to red and green lights until the experimenter says the experiment is over. The restaurant schema usually does not give up control of the executive until a meal has been ordered and consumed and a check has been received and paid. One does not usually leave a restaurant before the food arrives or before the check is paid. Of course, sometimes an alerting signal prematurely terminates a particular schema. One does not continue to sit in a restaurant in which a fire has broken out.

Schemas can be arranged in a hierarchy in which a higher-level schema activates a lower-level one, which at some point reactivates the higher one. For example, the general schema for maintaining well-being may activate the schema for planning the day, which in turn sequentially activates the schemas for dealing with the daily situations as they are encountered. Hence during most of the day activities are being conducted by a schema that is at least two levels down from the top, such as the schema for getting and eating breakfast. When this schema has run through to completion, it reactivates the schema above it, which selects the next daily activity and initiates the appropriate schema for accomplishing it.

Thus conscious thought and action is under the constant direction of a schema. The ability of people to cope with various tasks and situations is largely determined by the demands the task places on the executive to process task-relevant information and on the schema controlling it. Let us examine some tasks that have been used to find the limits of the executive's capacity.

## Divided Attention

The world contains some situations in which it is imperative that you attend to multiple inputs. For example, in driving a car, you must divide attention between the gas pedal, steering wheel, speedometer, windshield, sideview mirror, rearview mirror, and possibly even the radio. Also, in such a situation you are not in control of the rate of environmental change that must be dealt with—cars go whizzing by, traffic lights change, the road curves, and unwary pedestrians step into the street. When attention is viewed from the perspective created by this type of situation, the critical question concerns how much information you can consciously become aware of in a limited amount of time.

One way to measure the speed of the executive is to determine the number of rapidly presented sequential elements a person can count or identify (Woodworth and Schlosberg 1954, p. 100). Unfortunately, at a rapid rate of presentation visual flashes perceptually run together because of positive afterimages (Woodworth and Schlosberg 1954, p. 396). The fastest rate at which they can be counted without error is just two per second (Taubman 1950). In comparison, as many as ten tones per second can be counted without error.

To put these results in another perspective, the highest estimate of the rate at which a sequence of targets can elicit separate responses is obtained from the task of counting sequentially presented tones. This rate is ten items per second, which is not a particularly fast pace. Thus when individual targets, which require separate responses, assault the executive at a rate faster than ten per second, the executive becomes a bottleneck in the information-processing system. We saw in the last chapter that a person can monitor the environment for two or more targets, each requiring a separate response. When two targets are detected in rapid succession, the response to one or both of them is delayed because the executive can initiate only one action at a time (Klapp 1979, 1981). The period during which two responses interfere with each other is called the *psychological refractory period.*

Of course, we do not mean that two or more actions cannot be performed simultaneously. However, as we have discussed, two or more coordinated simultaneous actions are under the control of a single motor program, while multiple independent actions are under the control of separate motor programs operating in parallel. So when the executive must achieve a very high

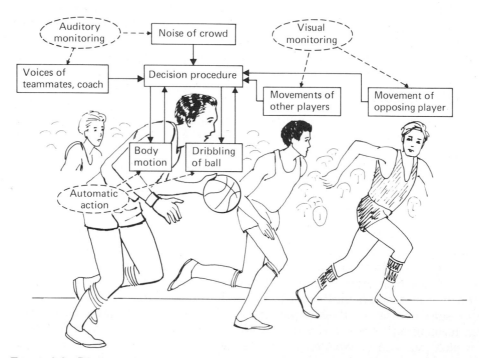

**Figure 3.2    Division of attention, which requires both automatic and conscious processing.**

response rate, as much of the input as possible is assigned to automatic procedures and to motor programs that initiate sequences of actions. Each automatic procedure and program can then be initiated by a single executive command. As Klapp (1979, 1981) demonstrated, response sequences can only be automated when they are predictable so that a program can be set up to repeatedly execute one action after another at specified temporal intervals. This repeated temporal-action sequence is perceived as a *rhythm*. When the interval between responses is not fixed, so that they cannot be coordinated, interference between closely spaced responses occurs.

Figure 3.2 presents a model of how attention may be divided, using the example of a basketball player in action. As the figure illustrates, each input and action is controlled by a separate mechanism. The player is dividing attention between several visual and auditory targets (e.g., an opposing player, the voice of the coach) as well as dribbling the ball. The executive receives information about each of the targets. On the basis of the information received, a variety of actions are taken—moving, passing, shooting, etc. Some actions are initiated by the executive, whereas other actions may be preplanned and executed automatically when a certain input is identified.

## Monitoring

Often, once an attended input has been analyzed and identified, the executive need only detect an unexpected *change* in the input. Detecting a change provides efficient use of processing capacity, since the executive does not need to fully reanalyze the input at each moment in time. Instead, it can devote the bulk of its efforts to processing novel inputs rather than those it had recently identified. For example, when you first walk into a room in which a clock is ticking loudly, you will notice and attend to its sound. Soon, however, you will scarcely notice the ticking at all. But if the clock were to suddenly *stop* ticking, you might notice the change.

This continued processing of previously attended inputs is called *monitoring*. One influential theory of monitoring is the *matching model* proposed by Sokolov (1969). In order to monitor inputs, the executive constructs a representation of the current environment, which it continually updates. This internal representation can be viewed as a chart that provides a set of expectations about the immediate future. For example, the tick of the clock will be entered on the chart at regular intervals. At each moment the chart is compared with current environmental inputs. If the expected tick is matched at the appropriate time, no further processing is required. But if the tick doesn't occur, the resulting mismatch between the environment and the monitoring chart will cause a signal to be sent to the executive, bringing attention to the source of the mismatch.

**Orientation reaction.**   Testing the matching model has required subtle methods, because what is of interest is how observers process inputs they are not presently aware of. One approach is to place a person in a controlled environment, record a variety of physiological responses, and then introduce a change in the environment. A person who detects a change in the environment typically exhibits several detectable physiological changes. These changes include pupil dilation, contraction of blood vessels in the limbs (*vasocontraction*), and dilation of blood vessels in the head (*vasodilation*). Also, the galvanic skin response changes. Finally, a change in the electrical activity of the brain occurs, as measured by an *electroencephalogram* (EEG). When a person is alert but resting, so that close attention is not being paid to any input in particular, large groups of neurons fire in unison at regular intervals, producing a characteristic pattern of electrical activity that can be detected by electrodes placed against the scalp. This pattern of activity is called the *alpha pattern*. The regular alpha pattern momentarily gives way to an irregular pattern when a change is detected. Collectively, these changes are referred to as the *orientation reaction* (OR).

In a typical OR experiment a person is exposed to some continuous sequence of events, like a flashing light or a beeping tone. Usually, the first and perhaps the second presentation elicits an OR, after which there is no measurable response. If a louder beep or a brighter flash is inserted, the OR returns. So far, these results can be explained by the dual-process model of alerting, discussed in Chapter 2. However, *omitting* a flash also causes an OR (Sokolov 1969). The dual-process model does not explain this result, because according to it, the nervous system only responds to stimuli that impinge on it—it does not respond to nothing. However, the matching model can explain the result: The environment failed to match the chart generated by the executive—i.e., the next tone in the sequence did not occur on time. Even more abstract changes than a missing tone can elicit an OR. When Unger (1964) presented a series of numbers in ascending order, he observed an OR to a number out of sequence (e.g., 11, 12, 13, 17). This result is strong evidence for the matching model because the detection of a number out of sequence requires an identification in memory.

Since the matching model assumes that inputs are continually matched to representations, it requires a fully developed cerebral mechanism with reciprocal connections so that a higher level can influence a lower level. In fact, when Pribram and McGuinness (1975) examined neural-firing patterns to see whether they corresponded to the dual-process model or the matching model, they found that at lower levels of the brain the firing patterns were consistent with the dual-process model. However, at higher levels the results corresponded to those predicted by the matching model.

We should note that a monitoring procedure, like other high-level processing of inputs, competes for capacity with ongoing conscious processing. Thus monitoring occurs when the person is performing a relatively easy task, such as knitting a sock or waiting for a bus, and is sharply curtailed when the central task is difficult.

**Lie detection.**   We mention in passing that another well-known use of the components of the OR is to detect lies. Lie detection is a case of pseudopsychology run amok. The theory behind the lie detector, or *polygraph,* is that when a person tells a lie, they feel sufficient anxiety to cause a detectable OR. First, anyone who has ever had the choice between admitting an unpleasant truth or covering up with a convenient falsehood may question whether veracity or mendacity causes more anxiety and therefore whether the theory makes any sense. Second, years of testing (Ben-Shakhar, Lieblich, and Bar-Hillel 1982; Kleimuntz and Szucko 1982; Lykken 1981) have clearly shown that as a practical tool for telling truth from falsehood, the lie detector is useless. Nevertheless, lie detectors are still used in business and government.

## Vigilance

Suppose you operate the sonar device on a submarine. Your job is to watch a screen for a blip that would indicate a ship on the surface. This task requires *vigilance.* Suppose the screen remains absolutely blank for hours; then, suddenly, a blip appears for a few seconds. Are you any less likely to notice the blip after a few hours than after a few minutes or a few seconds of observation? The answer is no (Elliot 1957; Martz and Harris 1961). No matter how little conscious attention you are paying, an alerting mechanism will cause you to notice a sufficiently large and bright blip. This result follows from the dual-process model of alerting (Chapter 2).

Now suppose that the sonar screen is a little more active. About every 5 minutes, on the average, a blip appears on the screen. A small blip indicates a school of fish, while a large blip indicates a ship. Your task is to alert the rest of the crew every time you see a large blip. Will the likelihood that you will detect a blip larger than the others change as the time you spend staring at the screen increases? It will, indeed (Broadbent 1956; Mackworth 1948). After a half hour there will be a measurable decrease in the likelihood of your noticing the larger blip.

The second task is much like the task a sonar operator had during World War II, which is why interest was stimulated for the problem. However, modern research on the reasons that attention deteriorates did not begin until after the war. The seminal study was reported in 1948 by Norman Mackworth. Research since then indicates that a multifaceted explanation for vigilance deterioration is required (Davies and Tune 1969; Mackie 1977; Stroh 1971).

In the second task, where a larger blip must be detected, alerting mechanisms alone cannot discriminate a target from the distractors, because the mere detection of a blip is insufficient. That is, the operator must detect a blip that is somewhat larger than all the others. Determining whether the blip is larger requires that it be compared with memory. However, as time passes, changes in the human information-processing system reduce the probability of the comparison occurring.

In a vigilance task a person is trying to maintain attention to a sensory channel in which nothing of importance is usually happening. In that case little or no capacity is being used to compare inputs from that channel with memory items. Hence surplus capacity is available to process unattended inputs. If any of these inputs happen to be matched, they draw attention—and hence capacity—away from the attended channel. Of course, one way to reduce the likelihood of unattended inputs capturing attention is to place the observer in a comfortable, quiet location with no distractions. But a person cannot be isolated from his or her own thoughts, and in the absence of anything else to do, the executive generates its own distractions. The mind wanders from the task at hand as the observer begins to think of different things, and so the likelihood of missing a target increases.

Placing a person in a quiet, comfortable environment reduces the possibility of external distraction. But this environment is likely to quickly make the person bored and drowsy (Bakan 1957; Davies and Krokovic 1965). This condition apparently decreases the likelihood that an unattended input will be matched to memory. For example, the closer you are to being asleep, the less likely you are to notice that one blip is slightly larger than the others. That a decrease in external stimulation puts a person to sleep is something that most people know intuitively. After all, what do you do when you want to go to sleep? Probably, you decrease external stimulation (noise, lights, etc.). The role of external stimulation will be discussed further when the relationship between arousal and attention is described later in this chapter.

To summarize, an input may be detected in two different ways: It can activate an alerting mechanism, or it can be compared with memory to find a match. The conditions under which a vigilance task are performed rule out the use of an alerting mechanism and cause the sensitivity of the comparison mechanisms to deteriorate over time. Hence as time passes, the activity of maintaining attention to the part of the environment where a target may occur becomes increasingly effortful. How long a time passes before the decrement in performance becomes noticeable depends on a host of task variables, environmental variables, and subject variables (Davies and Tune 1969; Mackie 1977; Stroh 1977). Under certain conditions a decrement occurs within 10 minutes of the task's onset (Jerison 1977; Mackworth 1964). As the vigilance activity becomes more effortful, the motivation of the subject becomes more important. For example, paying monetary rewards (Bergum and Lehr 1964) or telling subjects that the task is a selection task for a high-paying job (Nachreiner 1977) delays the onset of the decrement in performance.

## VARIATIONS IN EXECUTIVE CONTROL

The capability of the executive to control cognitive processes varies both within an individual across time and from one person to the next. We will first consider some special states involving an extremely high degree of executive control, and then we will consider changes in control that occur with age.

### Hypnosis and Meditation

**Hypnosis.**  Hypnosis is a fascinating topic, partly because the perceptual and cognitive phenomena involved are unusually mysterious and partly because the phenomena are wrapped in a lurid net of popular mythology.

A hypnotic trance is not something that one person (i.e., the hypnotist) induces in the other but, rather, a state of consciousness that some people are able to voluntarily attain. People develop no special abilities under hypnosis that they do not have when they are not hypnotized (Barber 1969; Orne 1959). Rather, hypnotizable individuals are highly susceptible to suggestion. In fact, a hypnotizable individual will be compliant with a hypnotist's requests whether or not the individual is told he or she is undergoing hypnosis (Orne 1966).

In a test of hypnotic susceptibility a person is given a set of suggestions, such as that his arm is growing heavy, his eyelids are glued shut, or there is a fly buzzing about. The more suggestions the person translates into a perceptual experience, the more hypnotically susceptible the person is said to be. There are three standardized tests of hypnotic susceptibility. The Stanford Hypnotic Susceptibility Scale (Weitzenhoffer and Hilgard 1959, 1962) and the Barber Suggestibility Scale (Barber and Glass 1962) must be administered to individuals. The Harvard Group Scale of Hypnotic Susceptibility (Shor and Orne 1962) may be administered to groups. Perhaps 15 percent of all people respond to nearly all the test items and hence are highly susceptible to hypnosis.

What distinguishes the hypnotic state is the kind of perceptual and cognitive experiences the hypnotized individual is capable of having (Orne 1977). A hypnotized individual may not feel pain from an input that would cause an unhypnotized individual to feel pain (Hilgard and Hilgard 1975). (Lack of pain is called *analgesia*.) A hypnotized individual may not be able to remember something she has been told to forget (Kihlstrom 1977). Also, a hypnotized individual may be susceptible to perceptual distortions and even hallucinations (Graham 1977). Such cognitions are unusual, if not downright mysterious. Their cause—in fact, their very existence—is still hotly debated. For example, some theorists find it easier to believe that a hypnotized subject can be induced to *say* that they are experiencing a perceptual illusion than to believe that the illusion is actually being experienced (Barber 1969; Sarbin and Coe

1972). We will certainly not attempt a definitive account of hypnosis here. However, we may make some tentative hypotheses about it on the basis of the best-documented phenomena.

The hypnotic state seems to be an extremely effective form of selective attention, which apparently accounts for the phenomenon of analgesia. The person in the hypnotic state is able to direct so much of his or her processing capacity to some other input that the signal from the pain-causing input fails to reach the level of conscious awareness. This response is an extension of a use of selective attention that all people possess to some degree. As we noted in Chapter 2, the Lamaze child-bearing technique relies on selective attention to a distractor to reduce pain, and this method can be practiced by anyone.

Hypnotically induced amnesia is a more impressive feat of selective attention. If someone asks you who the president of the United States is, the answer seems to enter consciousness immediately, without any effort on your part. Certainly, there seems to be no way you can suppress the answer. Similarly, if you hear a list of words and are then asked later what you remember, usually at least some of the words spontaneously come to mind. However, try to imagine what it would be like if you were asked to recall the words while you were deeply engrossed in watching a television show, reading a book, or listening to a record. In this case, with so much of your attention taken up and directed elsewhere, none of the words might spontaneously occur to you. You might just barely understand the query, and after responding with a vague "What?" you might feel the effort of consciously directing your attention from whatever you were doing to the task of retrieving the words. Apparently, when asked to forget something, a hypnotized subject directs his or her attention to some other input. The person may thus succeed in blocking the automatic retrieval of the "forgotten" information when a request for it is made.

Of course, suppressing something so that you do not remember it requires a lot of effort, as does suppressing pain. Yet the hypnotized subject claims to be attempting to comply with the request to supply the information rather than actively suppressing it. Thus, somehow, the subject is able to be of "two minds" regarding the task, repressing the information and trying to retrieve it at the same time. Of course, if researchers could show that some people really can divide their consciousness in the way that hypnotized people appear to be able to do, this result would have tremendous implications for our understanding of human consciousness and personality, since it would imply that a person can do something and at the same time block out knowledge of what he or she is doing. So the reality of hypnosis is potentially as fascinating as the legends that surround it.

**Meditation.**   We have mentioned how various physiological indices (e.g., pupil size, heart rate, EEG, GSR) related to the orientation reaction (OR) change when a person directs attention toward processing an input. The various physiological measures that make up the OR are indices of a person's *level of arousal.* A person's arousal level seems to reflect the amount of stress that the environment or a task places on the body (Kahneman 1973). For example, a loud noise, a hot room, or a difficult exam will cause an increase in arousal.

One question that has been answered is whether, through meditation, people can gain increased control over their level of arousal. While the primary purpose of meditation is spiritual, it involves several exercises in concentrating on a single input. In particular, certain exercises are supposed to help a person gain control over those muscular and nervous activities usually associated with arousal. However, meditation apparently has no physiological effects beyond facilitating relaxation. When Holmes (1984) reviewed all the experimental studies that had then been done on meditation, he found no evidence that people using meditation techniques had more influence over their arousal level than control subjects who were simply told to relax.

## Changes in Control with Age

**Development.**   In general, the ability to focus attention on a particular input improves all through childhood, peaks in early adulthood, somewhere between the ages of twenty and thirty, then gradually declines with increasing age. In childhood, performance on both tasks that require automatic bottom-up procedures and tasks that require voluntary top-down procedures show improvement with age. For example, the number of characters reported from a briefly presented display increases (Arnett and DiLollo 1979; DiLollo, Arnett, and Krunk 1982), indicating that identification time per character decreases with practice.

Performance also changes on a selective-attention task (Lane 1980). The amount of task-relevant and task-irrelevant information remembered after completion of a selective-attention task has been used to measure what was attended to during the task. As age increases from childhood to adulthood, people recall more of the inputs they are told to attend to and fewer of the inputs they are told to ignore. For children, performance on attended and ignored inputs is positively correlated. The more attended inputs that are recalled, the more unattended inputs are recalled as well. This result implies that children are not selectively attending to the targets but, rather, are indiscriminately encoding every input they fix on. In contrast, for college students memory for attended and unattended inputs is *negatively* correlated. The more targets that are recalled, the fewer distractors are recalled. In fact, high school and college students remember fewer distractors than elementary school children (Druker and Hagen 1969; Hagen, Meacham, and Mesibov 1970; Wagner 1974).

**Decline.**   Once a person passes his or her third decade, the ability to divide attention between multiple inputs begins a slow, but measurable, decline. As a person ages, a representation in memory, activated by either a match or by the executive, declines in activation more quickly. As a result, when faced with multiple inputs, the executive must refresh needed representations more often and hence can distribute processing among a smaller number (DiLollo *et al.* 1982).

## DISORDERS OF CONTROL

We have seen that the ability to respond appropriately and effectively to a situation depends on the appropriate schema being in control of the executive and the executive being able to effectively carry out its commands. In this section we describe how damage to the executive can disrupt the conscious control of perception and action.

### Frontal Injury

Frontal injury can be the result of a tumor, of an operation to remove a tumor, of an occluded or burst blood vessel (i.e., a stroke), or of a blow to the head. People who choose not to wear seat belts—and hence in an accident are thrown forward and receive a blow to the front of the head—are a particularly fruitful source of subjects for this type of research. Luckily, the brain is robust enough to sustain some localized injuries without obvious loss of function. An injury localized in just the left or right frontal lobe may not impair a person's daily activities. However, the effects of bilateral damage are typically severe (Benton 1968).

The procedures that organize, initiate, and terminate voluntary responses appear to be frontally located. For example, one symptom of bifrontal injury is a tendency to repeat responses, called *perseveration*. For example, when a patient tries to say as many different words as possible, the same word is repeated. In trying to tell a story, the patient may repeat the same incident. Or if you ask the patient to define a list of words, and you come to a word the patient does not know, you may hear the exact definition, verbatim, of a word the patient defined earlier. Perseverations are as common with nonverbal responses, involving drawing and various motor tasks, as they are with language.

Apparently, at least two components are involved in the production of perseverations. The first problem is in inhibiting a response once it has begun. For example, try to copy the loops shown in Figure 3.3, first with one hand and then with the other. This task is quite easy. However, a frontally injured pa-

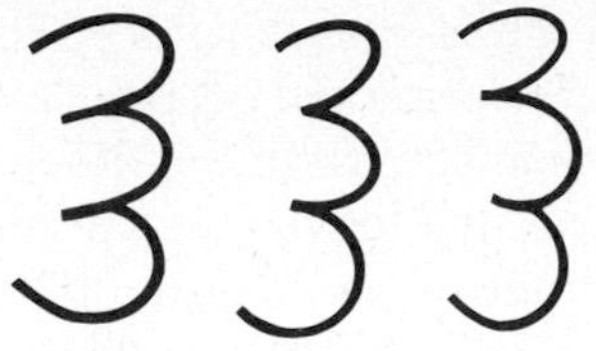

**Figure 3.3    Test for perseveration. Try to copy the loops with your right hand and then with your left hand.**

tient is likely to produce one or more quadruple loops. The second component of perseverations is a difficulty in keeping track of the responses that have already been made. For example, frontally injured patients were unable to carry out a task in which they had to touch once every one of several different figures on a piece of paper. Unlike normal individuals, they would lose track and touch the same figure more than once (Petrides and Milner 1982).

The frontal lobes are involved in diverse cognitive processes, and other common effects of bifrontal injury are unrelated to selective attention. For instance, large areas are involved in the execution of motor programs. So impaired motor performance accompanies even a unilateral injury. Also, dramatic changes may occur in the individual's personality. One aspect is a mild euphoria, in which normal concern is not shown by the patient about his or her injury. Subtle changes in memory and reasoning are also evident on systematic testing. Patients with bifrontal injuries show impaired performance in a task that requires learning to associate pairs of words (Benton 1968). Also, when asked the time of day, the day of the week, the day of the month, and the month of the year, patients with bilateral damage are likely to make small errors that normal individuals never make on these easy questions. Finally, bilateral frontal damage severely impairs abstract thought. For example, patients make errors when asked to select the correct meaning of a proverb, such as "Don't cross that bridge until you get to it," from among several alternatives. Why bifrontal damage causes these changes in memory and reasoning is not known.

## Split-Brain Patients

*Split-brain patients* undergo a surgical procedure that relieves them from life-threatening epileptic seizures. Most cases of epilepsy can be controlled by medication. However, in some cases the fits become so violent that they cannot be controlled by medication and eventually threaten the life of the sufferer. Such a seizure starts in a specific portion of one hemisphere of the brain. A chain reaction then develops in which the seizure spreads to the entire hemisphere and then across the corpus callosum, where it sets off the other hemisphere as well. Severing the corpus callosum prevents the seizure from spreading from one hemisphere to the other. This operation greatly reduces the size of the seizures and leaves the patients with their intellects and personalities relatively intact. In fact, only upon careful testing, begun by Roger Sperry and continued by him and his collaborators, Michael Gazzaniga and Jerre Levy, were the cognitive effects of the operation discovered.

Split-brain patients appear to be normal at the level of daily social intercourse. However, they generally have accomplished less with their lives than might be expected of a perfectly normal individual. On close examination they show strange anomalies of concentration even on tasks not likely to impose undue stress or a vigilance burden on them. For example, patients were given a test of motor proficiency. After the patients had performed well on a task for 5 or 6 minutes, they often stopped and asked, "How do I continue?" or "What do I do now?" even though the task had not changed, it had been performed perfectly well, and there was no extrinsic reason for the patient stopping (Dimond 1977).

Dimond (1977) used a vigilance task to study these lapses of consciousness. The patient was required to keep looking at a central fixation point but had to respond to four lights in a display. These lights ordinarily remained on, but as a signal, one and only one of the lights would flash off for a period of 300 milliseconds. The patient had to spot when one of the lights had flashed off

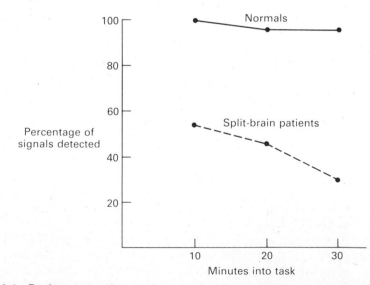

**Figure 3.4   Performance of normals and split-brain patients on a vigilance task. (After Dimond 1977.)**

and respond by pressing the correct key. Signals of this sort occurred, on average, every 30 seconds. If a patient missed a signal, the same signal would flash again at intervals of 1 1/2 seconds until the patient spotted it or until ten signals had been given. The task lasted a half hour.

The performance of six split-brain patients was compared with that of a group of normal controls. The results are shown in Figure 3.4. The normals detected nearly all the signals throughout the half-hour session. In contrast, the split-brain patients only detected half of the signals presented in the first 10 minutes, and their performance became progressively worse. Also, the normal individuals averaged less than one response when a signal did not occur for the entire session. The split-brain patients averaged seven such false alarms.

The poor performance of the split-brain patients was reflected in large gaps in their performance during which they failed to respond to multiple presentations of a signal. As many as five signals in a row (a total of 7.5 seconds) were repeatedly missed in the left visual field, and all ten signals (a duration of 15 seconds) were repeatedly missed in the right visual field.

The performance of the split-brain patients is further evidence that sustaining attention to a task requires effort. Apparently, the operation of the executive requires some resource that is transmitted between the hemispheres. If the flow of this resource is interrupted, then attention lags.

## AROUSAL

We have seen that a schema can control a variety of information-processing mechanisms both by direct action and by initiating other, automatic procedures. We now turn to the question of how a particular schema becomes activated and takes control of the executive in the first place. The answer is that schemas are activated in response to signals indicating certain internal states of the organism or inputs from the environment. Winding their way up from the spinal cord, through the mesencephalon and the diencephalon and projecting to all parts of the cerebrum, but in particular toward the front of it, are tracts of nerve fibers that have come to be called the *reticular activating system* (named for a group of cells in the brain stem called the *reticular formation,* which are at the base of the system). This complicated, barely understood network of nerve fibers is known to control sleep and wakefulness and to be involved in alertness and awareness (Stroh 1971).

The summation of nervous system activation caused by changes internal and external to the organism is called *arousal.* The activation and efficient functioning of a schema depends on the arousal level of the nervous system. For most of this section we will be concerned with the general question of how a schema becomes activated. First, we examine how both transient and daily changes in arousal affect executive functioning. Next, we discuss disorders caused by chronic defects in arousal. Finally, we briefly examine how a particular schema is selected.

### Yerkes-Dodson Law

On easy tasks such as vigilance, performance may actually be improved by the presence of irrelevant stimulation. Also, when you are extremely tired, an irrelevant input (e.g., the radio playing, even a loud noise) may improve performance on a task.

Let us take a person's arousal level as our (admittedly indirect) measure of the amount of stimulation impinging on him or her. The relationship between arousal and task performance is shown in Figure 3.5. This relationship is known as the *Yerkes-Dodson law*. Notice that each task has an optimal level of arousal at which performance is best. The optimal level is not the lowest level of arousal but some level between the highest and the lowest. Hence if a person's performance on a task is measured at various levels of arousal, performance first increases and then decreases as the level of arousal increases. Accordng to the Yerkes-Dodson law, the optimal level of arousal is lower for difficult tasks than it is for easy tasks, as also shown in Figure 3.5. As a result, the best level of performance on a more difficult task, like reading this book, will be achieved in quiet and comfortable surroundings, where you feel relaxed and undisturbed. In contrast, the best performance on an easy task, like watching for a flash of light, will actually be achieved in noisy and uncomfortable surroundings in which you feel stimulated and aroused. For example,

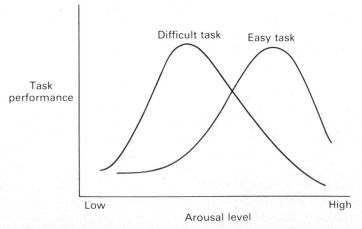

**Figure 3.5    The Yerkes-Dodson law. Performance on easy tasks peaks at a higher arousal level than performance on difficult tasks.**

performance on a vigilance task can often be improved by adding a source of stress to the environment (Poulton 1977).

Why does stimulation improve performance on easy tasks? Easterbrook (1959) suggested that as a person's arousal level increases, she is able to analyze fewer and fewer inputs. An easy task, such as a vigilance task, requires that the person attend to only a few, or even one, input. So reducing the number of inputs that she can attend to is actually an advantage, since it tends to reduce the number of distracting inputs that are being processed. But more difficult tasks are more difficult in part because the person has to attend to more inputs as well as to more complex inputs. The arousal level that may be suitable for an easy task may so restrict the person's processing capacity that she will fail to process certain features of task-relevant inputs or miss inputs altogether when attempting to perform a more difficult task. As a result, task performance suffers. Consistent with Easterbrook's hypothesis, Hockey (1970) found that when arousal was increased by a loud noise, performance on a primary task improved and performance on centrally located signals of a secondary task also improved, but performance on detecting peripheral signals of the secondary task deteriorated.

Level of arousal has an important effect on how people perform in a dangerous environment, as was pointed out by Alan Baddeley (1972). Baddeley was initially interested in the performance of deep-sea divers. The original aim of the experiments was to study the effects of nitrogen narcosis on diver performance; nitrogen narcosis is the intoxication that occurs when air is breathed at high pressure. Discrepancies between open-sea results and pressure chamber simulation occurred, and Baddeley subsequently found that the degree of danger was a crucial variable affecting performance. Baddeley was stimulated to review findings on people's performance in dangerous environments, including deep-sea divers, soldiers in combat, army parachutists, and soldiers subjected to extremely realistic, simulated, life-threatening emergencies (see also Weltman, Smith, and Egstrom 1971). He found that a dangerous situation tends to increase level of arousal, which, in turn, as Easterbrook's (1959) hypothesis predicts, focuses the person's attention more narrowly on those aspects of the situation he considers most important. If the task being performed is regarded as most important, then performance will tend to improve; but if it is regarded as peripheral to some other activity, such as saving one's life, then performance will deteriorate.

## Changes in Consciousness During the Daily Life Cycle

The most obvious indication that conscious decision making uses up some resource of the brain is the change in awareness that occurs between sleep and wakefulness. Everyone falls asleep during some part of almost every 24-hour period. When someone tries to stay awake beyond her normal retiring time, she finds it increasingly difficult to remain conscious as time passes. During a successful attempt to set the world wakefulness record, a seventeen-year-old high school student experienced concentration difficulty and memory lapses. His brain's EEG pattern began to resemble that of a sleeping person's, even though he was still awake (Johnson, Slye, and Dement 1965). After 264 hours of wakefulness, he slept for 14 ½ hours.

In recent years careful testing of cognitive performance at different times has accumulated evidence that the sleep/wakefulness cycle has subtle effects on cognitive processing throughout the day. For example, Folkard (1979) found that men and women of various ages, from twenty-two to sixty-two years old, tended to attend more to the sounds of words at 10 A.M. but more to their meanings at 7 P.M. Perhaps this work will someday tell us what time is the best time to study and, more generally, how a person can optimally organize a daily routine.

In addition to the 24-hour sleep/wakefulness cycle, there is a shorter, 90-minute cycle of brain activity. During your waking hours the ordinary cognitive activity of daily life makes the cycle difficult to observe; it was first discovered during sleep. When arousal was monitored during sleep, researchers found two distinct sleep states that alternated about every 90 to 100 minutes. When a person first falls asleep, his EEG recordings are very different from what they are during wakefulness. The person has few, if any, eye movements and relatively few dreams. This phase is called *quiet sleep.* About 80 minutes after the person falls asleep, *active sleep* occurs, during which the EEG pattern more closely resembles wakefulness, the eyes move rapidly, and vivid dreams are likely to occur. In addition to these differences, quiet sleep and active sleep differ on all the standard measures of arousal, including respiration, heart rate, blood pressure, and galvanic skin response (Levinthal 1979). The cycle repeats throughout the night.

Kleitman (1963) proposed that the quiet/active cycle observed during sleep was part of a basic rest/activity cycle that continues throughout the day and on which the sleep/wakefulness cycle is imposed. Broughton (1975) proposed that the apparent rest/activity cycle actually reflected an alternation in the relative activation of the two hemispheres, with the right hemisphere being most active during the peak of the active part of the sleep cycle, and that, as Kleitman suggested, this alternation in activity occurred throughout the day.

Klein and Armitage (1979) tested Broughton's (1975) hypothesis. They made use of the fact that the two hemispheres cannot process all inputs equally well. As we will see in Chapter 13, the left hemisphere is superior for verbal tasks, and the right hemisphere is better for visuospatial tasks. Klein and Armitage chose two matching tasks that could be performed better by one hemisphere than the other. The verbal task was to decide whether pairs of letters, one uppercase and one lowercase, had the same name, and the visuospatial task was to decide whether pairs of seven-dot random patterns were identical. Participants in the experiment were given a booklet filled with pairs of items and had to make decisions about as many pairs as possible within a 3-minute period. They were tested every 15 minutes over an 8-hour period beginning at 9 A.M. Eight young adults participated in the task.

The variable measured was the number of pairs correctly matched on each task in each 3-minute test period. As Broughton's (1975) hypothesis predicted, there was a 96-minute cyclical fluctuation in performance throughout the day. Furthermore, performances on the verbal task and the shape task were opposite in phase. When a person matched the greatest number of verbal pairs, she also matched the fewest shape pairs, and vice versa. (In addition, there was an unexpected cycle lasting 4 hours, and another lasting 37 minutes. These cycles have yet to be explained.)

Apparently, our ability to consciously attend to something does not remain constant throughout the day but is subject to at least two cyclical fluctuations. The sleep/waking cycle is controlled by the reticular activation system. Damage to this system puts an animal to sleep permanently. The 90-minute cycle is controlled by entirely different anatomical structures and may reflect fluctuations in activity levels between the hemispheres.

We are embarrassed to state that despite all the work in this area, no one knows why these cycles exist or why sleep occurs at all. This significant aspect of human existence remains to be explained.

## Defects in Arousal

**Attention deficits in schizophrenia.**   Other patients have an entirely different problem with attention. These patients are people who have been diagnosed as schizophrenic (Shean 1978). In 1961 McGhie and Chapman published the self-reports of individuals who had been diagnosed as being in the early stages of schizophrenia. Here are some samples of what they said (pp. 104–105):

> Patient 13: My concentration is very poor. I jump from one thing to another. If I am talking to someone, they only need to cross their legs or scratch their heads and I am distracted and forget what I was saying. I think I would concentrate better with my eyes shut.

> Patient 6: I am easily put off what I am doing or even what I am talking about. If something else is going on somewhere, even just a noise, it interrupts my thoughts and they get lost. If I am somewhere there is a lot going on, I am swinging from one thing to another instead of concentrating on one thing and getting it done.

> Patient 10: Have you ever had wax in your ears for a while and then had them syringed? That's what it's like now, as if I have been deaf before. Everything is much noisier and it excites me.

As you would expect, the patients also reported difficulty in paying attention to any one conversation or in maintaining a chain of thoughts on any one topic, since anything would interrupt them. Here are some examples (McGhie and Chapman 1961, pp. 106, 108):

> Patient 22: When people are talking, I just get scraps of it. If it is just one person who is speaking, that's not so bad, but if others join in, then I can't pick it up at all. I just can't get into tune with that conversation. It makes me feel open—as if things are closing in on me and I have lost control.

> Patient 15: It's the same with listening. You only hear snatches of conversation and you can't fit them together.

> Patient 20: My trouble is that I've got too many thoughts. You might think about something, let's say that ashtray and just think, oh yes, that's for putting my cigarette in, but I would think of it and then I would think of a dozen different things connected with it at the same time.

> Patient 21: My mind's away. I have lost control. There are too many things coming into my head at once and I can't sort them out.

Some researchers speculate that many other symptoms of schizophrenia (e.g., inability to complete tasks, paranoia, inappropriate emotional responses, withdrawal) are responses to the flood of stimulation that schizophrenics report. For example, Broen (1973) and Brown and Herrnstein (1975, p. 654) have suggested that paranoid schizophrenics conclude that they are being watched and followed because they are aware of background details and sounds that normally would not enter consciousness. Broen (1973) suggests that chronic schizophrenics respond to the flood of information by ignoring most of it, just as you would ignore a TV set if it brought in all the stations on a single channel. After all, what's the point in trying to process any particular target if you are going to be interrupted before you complete the processing?

This hypothesis has led psychologists to begin to study the selective attention of schizophrenics. Schizophrenic performance has been compared with normal performance on many of the tasks described in this and the previous chapter [see Chapman and Chapman (1973) and Oltmanns and Neale (1975) for reviews and critiques]. It is still too early to draw conclusions about how schizophrenic attention differs from that of normals or to say whether their attention problems are a cause or a symptom of schizophrenia. However, the results of these cognitive studies dovetail with a biochemical hypothesis about the physiological cause of schizophrenia. The chemical dopamine is important in facilitating the transmission of signals from one neuron to the next. Snyder (1974) suggests that schizophrenics have an excess of dopamine in their neurons. As a result, to put it in terms of the dual-process model, they are overly sensitized and cannot shut off the flood of stimulation. This theory explains why abuse of amphetamines, which increase the availability of dopamine, produces symptoms indistinguishable from schizophrenia. This research may someday be an important chapter in our understanding of normal and disturbed attention.

**Parkinson's disease.** Just as too much arousal floods consciousness with unwanted stimulation, too little arousal makes it difficult to respond at all to any stimulation. A malady characterized by chronic low arousal is *Parkinson's disease*. It is apparently caused by a decrease in the amount of dopamine in certain brain cells. A person with Parkinson's disease might first appear to a naive observer to be suffering from muscle damage. The patient exhibits pronounced slowness of all voluntary movements (Merck 1972, p. 330) and walks with slow, short, shuffling steps, arms flexed and held stiffly at sides, and trunk bent forward. In advanced cases the patient may be confined to a wheelchair.

But it is not the muscles that have been damaged in Parkinson's disease (reflexes remain normal). Rather, the person's arousal level is too low to activate voluntary movement. However, an occasional input that is extremely significant or extremely familiar to the person can generate a response, either because the signal is so strong that it briefly causes the activation level to rise dramatically or because the response it evokes is so overlearned that it requires only a low level of arousal to initiate it. The classic story is of the grandmother with Parkinson's disease who is sitting in a rocking chair, with her grandchild in a crib beside her. No one else is around. Suddenly, the room catches on fire. For the first time in ten years the grandmother rises from her chair, grabs the infant, runs outside to safety, and collapses, again unable to move a muscle. Another story is of a former baseball player confined to a wheelchair in a hospital. One day, unexpectedly, a doctor throws a baseball toward him but over his head. In a single fluid motion the player leaps from the chair, catches the ball in his outstretched hand, pegs it back to the doctor, and collapses back into the chair.

Stories like these would be considered totally apocryphal if similar effects were not generated with animals in laboratories. For example, Levitt and Teitelbaum (1975) produced lethargic behavior in rats by damaging a part of the animals' brains believed to control their arousal level. When an injured rat was placed in tepid water (neither warm nor cool), the rat sank to the bottom without making an effort to keep afloat. However, if the water was markedly colder, it elicited a vigorous swimming response from the injured rat. In one instance the animal leapt from the water and scampered halfway across the laboratory floor before it again collapsed in an inert heap.

It turns out that the same things that stimulate other people sometimes have a beneficial effect on Parkinson's patients. For example, amphetamines sometimes lead to improved performance.

## Drives and Motives

Every organism has a hierarchy of needs that begins with the necessities of life: food, water, and rest. As the body becomes depleted of these resources, hunger, thirst, and fatigue are perceived. These perceptions of internal states are sometimes called *drive states*. The most basic executive schemas are activated by these drive states and carry out operations designed to eliminate these unpleasant perceptions by satisfying the body's basic needs. In the hierarchy of needs, once the basic needs are satisfied, others come into play. Thus once the basic survival needs are satisfied, sexual and social needs become important. These social needs are perceived as emotions such as fear, love, and loneliness.

People in our culture live in an extremely complex social environment in which the satisfaction of basic needs, such as obtaining food, is usually easy; so, in practice, conscious activity is largely governed by a many-layered hierarchy of schemas directed toward social needs. Schemas affect the balance of internal and external states so as to increase the activation of positive emotions and decrease the activation of negative emotions. For example, at the top may be a schema that initiates other procedures designed to preserve a basic sense of well-being. It may initiate a schema for getting through the school day. The latter schema consists of a sequence of actions—getting up, eating, practicing, going to class—that are performed throughout the day. It, in turn, initiates schemas to perform the sequence of actions that operate in each of these specific situations.

The schemas that control information processing make up what we call an individual's personality. The study of personality is, of course, a fascinating topic in its own right. However, we will not pursue it here; instead, we will return to the basic information-processing mechanisms themselves.

## SUMMARY

Physical actions range from simple *unconditioned* and *conditioned reflexes*, to automatic *motor programs*, to complex *perceptual motor skills*. The acquisition of skills involves three phases: *cognitive*, *associative*, and *autonomous*. A fully developed skill is assembled into a single motor program.

The executive mechanism is at all times under the control of a particular *schema*. A schema specifies a particular procedure, which can be described by *if-then rules*. Hierarchically organized schemas serve to regulate perception, alter memory representations, initiate overt actions, and pass control to other schemas. The executive controls complex tasks requiring divided attention by using automatic motor programs and *monitoring* procedures. It is difficult for the executive to maintain control of perception in tasks that require *vigilance* for occasional inputs over extended periods of time.

*Hypnosis* seems to be an extremely effective form of selective attention governed by executive control. The ability to perform tasks requiring selective and divided attention varies with age. People who suffer damage to the *frontal lobes* are impaired in their ability to initiate and control actions. *Split-brain patients* have difficulty sustaining attention.

The activation and efficient functioning of a schema depend on the *arousal level* of the nervous system. The optimal level of arousal is lower for difficult tasks than it is for easy tasks. Schizophrenia appears to involve over-sensitization to inputs that leads to excessive arousal.

## RECOMMENDED READINGS

*Consciousness and Behavior* (1983) by Wallace and Fisher provides a brief, simple introduction to some of the topics discussed in this chapter. *Schizophrenia* (1978) by Shean offers an introduction to research on that disorder. Kahneman's *Attention and Effort* (1973) provides a detailed discussion of major theories of attention and consciousness.

*Human Vigilance Performance* (1969) by Davies and Tune and *Vigilance: The Problem of Sustained Attention* (1971) by Stroh provide good introductions to this topic. Though it first appeared in 1967, *Human Performance* by Fitts and Posner is still an excellent introduction to human action.

# CHAPTER **FOUR**

# Visuospatial Representation

## IMPAIRED PERCEPTION: A CASE STUDY

In November 1966 a twenty-five-year-old soldier home on leave accidentally suffered carbon monoxide poisoning from leaking gas fumes. This accident was a serious one, since exposure to carbon monoxide can cause brain damage and death. Following resuscitation, the soldier was able at first to converse with relatives. But the next day he lapsed into a coma from which he recovered only slowly. In a month he was alert and talkative again; however, he experienced severe visual problems.

Seven months after the accident the soldier was admitted to Boston Veterans Administration Hospital for extensive tests. Most of his cognitive abilities, such as language use and memory, appeared normal. Most of his perceptual system was also intact. He could readily identify and name things through their feel, smell, or sound. In addition, his most elementary visual abilities were also preserved. He was able to identify colors, discriminate between lights of different intensities, and tell in what direction an object was moving. Nevertheless, the soldier's visual perception was severely impaired. He was unable to recognize objects, letters, or people when he saw them. His impairment was so severe that on one occasion he identified his own reflection in a mirror as the face of his doctor!

A common factor in these recognition failures appeared to be the inability to identify any visual shape or form. To test this hypothesis, two neurologists, D. Frank Benson and John P. Greenberg (1969), gave the soldier a variety of tests in which he had to verbally identify a pattern, copy a pattern, select which two of several patterns were the same, or simply say whether two patterns were the same or different. The results of a typical task are shown in Figure 4.1. In this task the soldier had to mark one of four comparison patterns that was the same as a standard pattern on the left. He was unable to match any of them correctly. All of the results from this and similar tests were equally dismal. The soldier was simply unable to distinguish visual shapes from one another. He could not even tell a circle from a square.

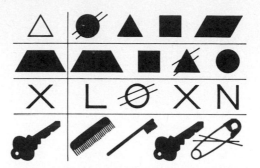

**Figure 4.1    Matching task. The soldier who suffered from carbon monoxide poisoning was unable to mark the appropriate matching figure in any of these examples. (From Benson and Greenberg 1969.)**

What was wrong with this soldier, and what does his disorder tell us about pattern perception? The second question is easier to answer than the first. The soldier's disorder dramatically demonstrates that pattern perception requires much more than the eye's ability to detect a beam of light. A great deal of cognitive processing is required in order for the person to figure out whether that light beam was reflected off a square object or a round one. As we will see in this chapter, pattern perception is a complex ability. The perceptual process has many steps, any one of which might have been impaired so as to produce the soldier's disorder.

When an input from the environment is detected by one of your sense organs, it comes to be represented at many places in the nervous system, as was shown in Figure 2.2. The major levels are sensory reception, separate dimensions, unified perceptual representation, and comparison with memory. In visual and tactile dimensions the eventual result of perception is usually a representation of an object in the surrounding environment. For auditory information it may be a representation of the sounds of a spoken message. Clearly, the soldier was either unable to construct a unified representation of visual objects or unable to make use of that representation to identify them. Since the representation of the input at the comparison level corresponds to a person's perception of the world, he was unable to perceive the world in much detail.

## VISUAL PERCEPTION

### Retinal-Image Theory

We have good reason to believe that we usually perceive the world accurately. If you look out your window and see a tree, quite likely a tree is really there. This fact is so unremarkable that we hardly ever stop to think about it. Yet the

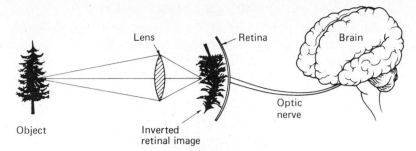

Figure 4.2  Schematic diagram of the visual system.

task is quite a formidable one. How do we go about determining the shapes and locations of objects through vision alone? For example, when you see a square, how do you know that it is a square and not a rectangle, a parallelogram, or a trapezoid?

The first step toward answering this question is to realize that the answer is not obvious. That is, we don't simply see the square as a square because that's its shape. For this reason we presented the case study of the soldier. His disability demonstrates that perceiving light is not equivalent to perceiving shapes of objects.

To demonstrate why pattern perception is not a simple process, we will briefly examine the reasons that one apparently simple explanation—*retinal-image theory*—is very clearly wrong. Figure 4.2 presents a highly schematic outline of the visual system. When we look at an object, the light reflecting from the object passes through the lens of the eye, which focuses an upside-down image on the *retina* at the back of the eyeball. The retina is a curved surface containing light-sensitive cells that transmit signals along the optic nerve to the brain. According to the retinal-image theory of pattern recognition, when we look at an object like a square, the retinal image is transmitted to the brain, where it is turned right-side up and recognized immediately.

The problem with this simple theory is that unless you are looking at the square head-on in absolutely even illumination (which is practically impossible to obtain), the image of a square does not fall on your retina. Instead, the image will most likely be of some trapezoidal shape (see Figure 4.3). Often the shape will be even less squarelike, since the square will be broken into light and dark areas by glare and shadow.

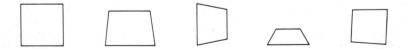

Figure 4.3  How a square may actually appear when viewed from different perspectives.

When we turn from this artificial example of viewing a single simple shape to the everyday perception of the environment, the problems of a retinal-image theory of perception increase a thousandfold. Consider what we see when we look around a room. Perhaps we see walls, tables, chairs (all with rectangular surfaces), a round clock on the wall, a picture, and a tree through a window. But if we stop to analyze what the retinal image must be like, we realize that no shape in the retinal image is actually as we perceive it. The right angles we see everywhere as parts of walls, tables, etc., are almost all acute or oblique angles when they fall on our retinas. Similarly, that round clock is likely to be an ellipse in the retinal image.

Colors and sizes also differ between the retinal image and our perception. A shadow falls across an orange couch, yet the entire couch appears to be the same color. One chair of two is closer to us, yet both appear to be the same size. We can easily tell the difference between the picture and the window, though the images they present to our retinas are very similar. The most remarkable aspect of the discrepancies between the retinal image and perception is that usually it is perception, not our retinal sensation, that is veridical. Our eyes lie, but our mind tells us the truth!

## Cues for Visual Perception

If our perception does not correspond to the retinal image, how, then, do we perceive the world? The answer is that even though the retinal image is by no means an exact copy of the environment, our eyes do detect a great deal of information about the environment. Several different kinds of information might be used.

Gibson (1957, 1966) and his co-workers have shown that when a three-dimensional object is moved through space, certain characteristics of the two-dimensional retinal image will either remain the same or change in some regular way that corresponds to the true shape of the object. For example, no matter how we rotate a square, we will almost always see four corners (the only exception is if the square is held perfectly flat so that we are looking directly at an edge). Accordingly, the four corners constitute an invariant *cue* corresponding to a square (also see Todd 1982).

## Perception as a Constructive Process

We see, then, that the retinal image does not directly correspond to our perception of the environment. However, the visual input does provide many cues that convey information about the environment. Three-dimensional visuospatial representations are *constructed* on the basis of visual cues. It is this constructed representation that corresponds to your perceptual experience.

We thus perceive the world as three-dimensional because its representation in our visuospatial code is three-dimensional. Our perception depends on the ability to integrate multiple sources of information into a single representation. Consider what would happen if you took several pictures of a statue from different perspectives. The pictures would contain all the information needed to construct a three-dimensional representation. Nevertheless, all you would have is a stack of two-dimensional pictures. Similarly, no matter how many different perspectives of an object your eyes recorded, you would not perceive it as three-dimensional if the perceptual system did not construct a three-dimensional representation of it.

In this chapter we will examine a small part of the constructive process of perception. [For more extended discussions, see Hochberg (1971) and Rock (1983).] Because our purpose is to convey the flavor of what is meant by *constructive process*, only the perception of some simple two-dimensional patterns will be examined.

## Visuospatial Subcodes

As we discussed in Chapter 2, the visuospatial code is comprised of three modular subcodes: a color code, a shape code, and a location code. (The color code includes all brightness information, so according to our terminology, black, white, and shades of gray are colors.) Modular subcodes are those subcodes that can have an existence separate from the supercode of which they are part. For example, when you look at an apple, you perceive its shape and color together. But when you feel the apple, you encode a representation of its shape that contains no information about its color at all. Accordingly, shape and color information must be independent of each other. Now, think of a point in space a foot beyond your nose. Probably nothing is there, no shape and no color, yet you can mark that location perfectly well. So location information is separate from shape and color information. The fact that you can treat color, shape, and location as separate dimensions, attend to each, and think about each separately suggests that their underlying codes are separate from each other.

**Selective attention.**    Recall from Chapter 2 that a unidimensional representation of a target can be compared with a memory representation before the integrated perceptual representation is formed. Similarly, the representations of two elements of a visual display can be compared with each other along a single dimension before their complete perceptual representations are constructed. So the detection of a difference between them on one dimension will not be influenced by a difference on another dimension.

For example, suppose a person is presented with a series of visual displays and must press a button every time a display contains a red target. Each display also contains green distractors. In the *neutral condition* all the display items are circles. In the *correlated condition* the target is always a circle and the distractors are always ovals. In the *uncorrelated condition*, the target and the distractors are sometimes circles and sometimes ovals. In this task and with practice, people can detect the target equally fast in all three conditions (Garner 1970). This result indicates that people can selectively attend to the representation of a visual input in one of the codes while ignoring its representations in the other codes.

**Integrating subcodes.**   The information from the modular subcodes must be combined to form an integrated visuospatial representation of the input. The degree of perceived *similarity* between two inputs is directly related to their similarity on the underlying subcodes. Similarity is an extremely important concept that we will encounter repeatedly throughout this book, and we will discuss it in detail in Chapter 5.

One technique for representing similarity that is especially useful for understanding the manner in which perceptual subcodes are integrated is *multidimensional scaling.* Multidimensional scaling, developed by Shepard (1962a, 1962b, 1964, 1974, 1980) and others (e.g., Caroll and Arabie 1980; Jorgerson 1965; Kruskal 1964a, 1964b), assumes that inputs' similarity to each other can be decomposed into a representation of a finite number of independent dimensions. The representation of each input is then equivalent to a point in the resulting *multidimensional space.* For example, suppose the pattern is a red circle. Then your perception of it might consist of your perception of its shape and of its color, which could be represented as shown in Figure 4.4. The per-

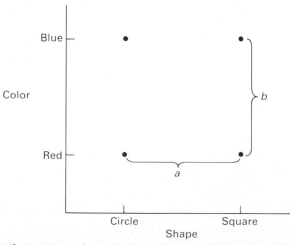

**Figure 4.4   Similarity space for colored geometric shapes. The dissimilarity of the red circle to the blue square is $a + b$.**

ceptual space for visual patterns shown in the display consists of the two dimensions shape and color. The red circle has the value "circle" on the shape dimension, as shown in Figure 4.4. Thus "red circle" is described as a point in a two-dimensional space.

Different patterns can be represented as different points in a visual space. For example, Figure 4.4 also represents a blue square, a blue circle, and a red square. This space was constructed from people's ratings of the similarity of the four inputs to each other. Multidimensional-scaling techniques derive a spatial representation from similarity ratings by assuming that the distance between two points increases as the rated similarity between the corresponding inputs decreases. Furthermore, as Figure 4.4 illustrates, the overall distance between two points can be derived from their distances along the various dimensions on which they differ. For example, the distance from the red circle to the blue square in the similarity space is related to the distance from red to blue along the color dimension and the distance from circle to square along the shape dimension.

Note that although Figure 4.4 represents shape and color as single dimensions, this representation is a considerable oversimplification. In fact, the three visuospatial subcodes can *each* be represented as a multidimensional space. For example, location has three dimensions corresponding to height, width, and depth. Shape, the most complex of the three subcodes, involves a number of component dimensions that are not fully understood.

## Perception of Form

The black heart shown in Figure 4.5(a) is a simple example of figure perception. We will examine only a single step in the process shown earlier in Figure 2.2. This step is the construction of a shape representation on the basis of brightness information. When you look around, you see distinct objects, or figures, against the background. For example, most people perceive the pattern

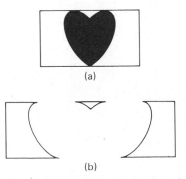

(a)

(b)

**Figure 4.5   Figure perception: (a) A black heart; (b) the white components of the black heart.**

in Figure 4.5(a) as a black heart on a white background. However, the pattern could also be perceived as three white shapes against a black background, as illustrated in Figure 4.5(b). Why do you see the pattern one way and not the other? More generally, what characteristics of a pattern determine which parts of it are encoded as the figure (e.g., the black heart) and which parts of it are encoded as the ground (e.g., the white areas in Figure 4.5a)?

A more complicated and hence much more impressive example of figure perception is shown in Figures 4.6(a) and 4.6(b). First, look at the pattern in Figure 4.6(b). You will probably agree that this pattern is perceived as a symmetrical black pattern on a white background. Although the black heart in Figure 4.5(a) consists of a solid black area, whereas the pattern in Figure 4.6(b) consists of many small unconnected black areas, the black parts of both patterns are perceived as a *gestalt,* i.e., as an organized whole. When the perceived shape is simple, as in Figure 4.5(a), it is usually called a figure. When the perceived shape is complicated and discontinuous, as in Figure 4.6(b), it is usually called a pattern. However, in both cases the same step in the visual-input-processing sequence is invoked. In this step some areas of the visual display are connected together in a single representation of a definite shape.

Figure 4.6(a) illustrates what the visual world looks like when the input does not correspond to any of the patterns that the visual system detects. In this case no definite shape emerges, and the input appears to be random noise. This pattern may represent how the world tended to appear to that unfortunate soldier described at the beginning of the chapter. To him, the patterns in Figures 4.6(a) and 4.6(b) probably would both have looked like random noise.

**Figure 4.6**  Complicated figure perception: (a) Repetition pattern, which is difficult to perceive; (b) symmetry pattern, which is somewhat easy to perceive. (From Julesz 1975.)

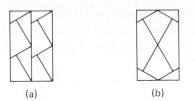

(a)                              (b)

**Figure 4.7    Letter patterns: (a) The letter *K* repeated four times; (b) the letter *K* repeated four times, symmetrically.**

You may be surprised to learn, however, that in fact Figure 4.6(a) contains a pattern just as well organized as the pattern that is apparent in Figure 4.6(b). Bela Julesz (1975) developed this striking illustration of how people see some patterns and not others. To understand what Julesz did, examine the simple patterns in Figure 4.7. Notice that both Figures 4.7(a) and 4.7(b) contain the letter K in the upper left quadrant. (This pattern is not so easy to see in Figure 4.7(b). To find the K more easily, cover the rest of the pattern.) Both Figures 4.7(a) and 4.7(b) were generated by repeating the letter K four times. The pattern in Figure 4.7(a) is simply the letter K in each of the four quadrants. The pattern in Figure 4.7(b) was created by reflecting the K in the upper left quadrant across the vertical axis so that the upper right quadrant is its mirror image. Similarly, the lower half of Figure 4.7(b) is the mirror image of the top half. Hence the pattern in Figure 4.7(a) is repetitive, while the pattern in Figure 4.7(b) is symmetrical.

Now, return to Figures 4.6(a) and 4.6(b). These patterns were generated in exactly the same ways as Figures 4.7(a) and 4.7(b), respectively. But in this case the generating pattern in the upper left quadrant was a 50 × 50 matrix randomly filled with dots. As you can see, when the pattern is simply repeated four times, as in Figure 4.6(a), you cannot perceive the repetition. The array looks entirely random. In contrast, the symmetrical pattern in Figure 4.6(b) is immediately apparent (see also Fisher and Bornstein 1982).

The demonstration provided by Figure 4.6 has important implications for an understanding of perception. Shape/figure/pattern perception must be more than the perception, as a gestalt, of all parts of the visual display that have the same brightness. If perception were this simple, then Figures 4.6(a) and 4.6(b) would provide equally good gestalts. But as the contrast between Figures 4.6(a) and 4.6(b) illustrates, only particular configurations of areas of similar brightness are perceived. Thus some mechanism of the visual-processing system must accept, as input, areas of similar brightness and then attempt to combine the areas into a single representation. This mechanism succeeds for Figure 4.6(b) but not for Figure 4.6(a). Why does it succeed only for Figure 4.6(b)? In Figure 4.6(b), along the central vertical and horizontal axes where the four reflections meet, a contiguous symmetrical pattern is formed. When these axes are combined with the areas on either side of them, the entire symmetrical pattern emerges. In contrast, for organization of Figure 4.6(a), areas far apart from each other must be combined into a single representation. Apparently, only contiguous areas are automatically combined into patterns.

If this mechanism were not part of your visual-information-processing system, you would be overwhelmed by the complicated, ever-changing patterns of light and dark that your eyes detect. You would be as blind to patterns as the soldier described at the beginning of this chapter. Since the days of the Gestalt psychologists (Rubin 1915; Wertheimer 1923), the task of those psychologists studying the perception of form has been to identify patterns that people can and cannot perceive and to try to use this information to analyze the mechanisms people use to organize visual perception.

**Feature detectors.**   The output of the initial level of analysis produces the division of the visual field into areas of light and dark. That is, the visual input is segmented into areas that have similar values on the brightness/color dimension. Figure 4.8(b) shows the output of this mechanism when the input is Figure 4.8(a). Notice that the only information encoded at this level is the number of different shades of gray (three) and the number of different contiguous areas (five). Next, those areas that might correspond to the *boundaries,* or *edges,* of objects are categorized into different features, as shown in Figure

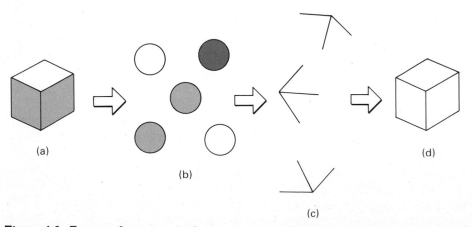

(a)

(b)

(c)

(d)

**Figure 4.8   Feature detection: (a) Input, (b) areas of common brightness segmented (initial analysis), (c) features extracted (next analysis), and (d) percept constructed.**

4.8(c). In Figure 4.8(a) the darkest portions of the input are the edges. Finally, the features are connected by the figure construction mechanism to form the representation of some two- or three-dimensional forms, as shown in Figure 4.8(d).

Features are categorized into three types, which we call *lines, corners,* and *shapes.* An example of each feature is shown in Figure 4.9. A line feature (Figure 4.9a) is a straight or slightly curved line. A corner (Figure 4.9b) is made up of two or more lines meeting at a single point. A shape (Figure 4.9b) is any continuous border enclosing any convex area.

The edge features are used by the figure construction mechanism at an unconscious level, and you certainly don't perceive them when you look at the world. So it took considerable experimental work to discover what they are (e.g., Beck 1966, 1967, 1972; Olson and Attneave 1970; Pomerantz, Sager, and Stoever 1977). After many studies the features were finally described by James Pomerantz (1981).

The basic method used was to present a visual display containing multiple tokens of the same pattern. In one quadrant of the display the patterns were altered so that they uniformly differed from those in the other three (as shown in the two displays of Figure 4.9). The observer's task was to determine, as rapidly as possible, which quadrant was different. Pomerantz reasoned that if all four quadrants contained patterns composed of the same feature or features, then the different quadrant could only be detected at the comparison level. But if the different quadrant had a different feature, this difference would be detected earlier, using the shape code at the level of independent dimensions. As we have seen, difference detections based on a single dimension

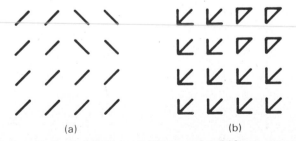

(a)                    (b)

**Figure 4.9**   **Lines, corners, and shapes: (a) Lines only; (b) lines, corners, and shapes. The upper right quadrant is different in both parts. The different quadrant takes longer to detect in (a) than in (b) because in (a) all four quadrants contain the same feature (lines), whereas in (b) the different quadrant contains shapes while the other quadrants contain corners. (From Pomerantz 1981.)**

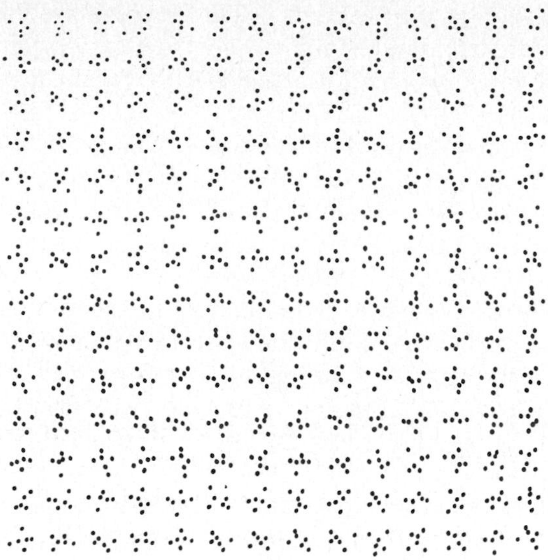

(a)

(b)

**Figure 4.10    Julesz's experiment: (a) All corner feature; (b) corner feature versus shape feature. (From Julesz 1981.)**

are made faster than those based on complete patterns, because they are made at an earlier level of analysis. So Pomerantz used different patterns that could be detected unusually fast in order to isolate critical features. He eventually discovered the line, corner, and shape features shown in Figure 4.9.

Julesz (1981) developed a sensitive test of feature detection that provided strong support for Pomerantz's features. Julesz constructed visual displays that consisted of many small dots. The density of dots across the display was uniform, so the brightness level across the display also was uniform. Consequently, the display could not be segmented into different areas on the basis of brightness at the initial level of analysis. That is, if visual perception were this simple, the display would appear to be an unbroken field.

However, without disturbing the overall uniform density, Julesz organized small groups of dots into specific micropatterns. When the micropatterns were all instances of the same feature, the entire display was perceived as homogeneous (Figure 4.10a). But when the two micropatterns were instances of different features, then the areas containing difficult micropatterns appeared different from each other (Figure 4.10b).

**Figure construction mechanism.**  The process of integrating feature information to identify objects is highly complex. First, a judgment about shape requires a judgment about orientation, so information from both the shape and the location dimensions is required. Second, in many scenes, forms are partially occluded by other forms, and the visual system must "guess" in order to complete them. Figure 4.11 illustrates this point. You see this display as one circle partially occluded by another. The striking thing is that this interpretation seems like the only natural one, even though there are many other possibilities. A few of the alternative completions are depicted in Figure 4.12. In each case the occluded portion of the left figure is represented by a dotted line. Figure 4.12(a) represents the natural interpretation of Figure 4.11 as overlapping circles. But as Figure 4.12(b) shows, Figure 4.11 might simply be perceived as a chippod circle adjacent to a complete one. Furthermore, as Figures 4.12(c) and 4.12(d) indicate, the occluded portion of the left figure might have a noncircular completion.

The visual system must construct a representation of the input according to some rule that chooses among all the possible alternatives. It is *because* the visual system constructs the representation illustrated by Figure 4.12(a) that

**Figure 4.11   Overlapping circles?**

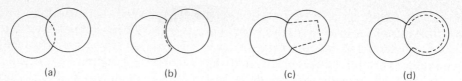

(a)                    (b)                    (c)                    (d)

**Figure 4.12    Potential completions of Figure 4.11: (a) Natural completion; (b) chipped circle on left; (c) light bulb shape on left; (d) dumbbell shape on left.**

you perceive one circle occluded by another. This perceptual effect is called *closure,* because you perceive what is physically only a semicircle as a part of a closed figure. You literally fill in a place of the representation that is not provided by the sensory input. For a still more striking example of closure, examine Figure 4.13. You probably cannot see a pattern here. Now look at Figure 4.14. Here the pattern (the letter *B*) is obvious.

**Figure 4.13    Fragments without a pattern, since there is no information for occlusion.**

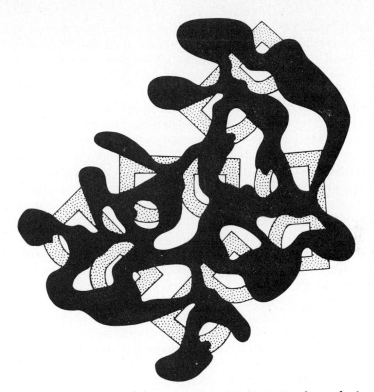

**Figure 4.14    Fragments shown in Figure 4.13 with information for occlusions added. Here the fragments on the boundaries of the occluding form can easily be grouped. (From Bregman 1981.)**

The closure phenomenon is a particularly convincing demonstration that your perception is guided by general principles for constructing representations. The question of how the visual system completes a figure has not yet been definitely answered. For a discussion and some data, see Buffart, Leeuwenberg, and Restle (1981) and Calis and Leeuwenberg (1981).

### Bottom-up and Top-down Processing in Visual Perception

Only a few details of the figure construction process have been sketched. The complete process is an extremely elaborate sequence of bottom-up mechanisms that rapidly produce a single stable vision of the world. It succeeds because the typical visual input from the normal three-dimensional environment is such a rich source of information about the environment. When enough information provided by brightness gradients, including edges and shadows, is taken into account, typically only one three-dimensional representation of the world is consistent with all of it. The number of cases in which you misperceive the visual world are few, and these visual illusions inevitably involve situations where a source of information the visual system normally uses has been eliminated.

A second effect of the automatic, bottom-up, figure construction process is that seeing a three-dimensional scene in more than one way is very difficult or impossible. If you look at a rectangular picture on the wall, no matter how hard you try, you will probably never see it as a trapezoid, although visualizing a trapezoid may not be absolutely impossible. We saw in Chapter 2 that people, with practice, can focus on lower levels of representation. Perhaps if you were an artist and had practiced looking at the relations of objects in space, you would be able to see the picture as a trapezoid. But such a perception, if possible at all, is very difficult to achieve.

When the sources of information in the environment are reduced sufficiently, the figure construction mechanism no longer has enough information to construct a single representation of the input. In such a case two or more possible representations are constructed, and the executive can choose between them. An input that produces more than one possible representation is perceived as *ambiguous*. Whenever the figure construction mechanism produces multiple representations, one representation may be selected at the comparison level because it matches the representation of a familiar object. Hence a top-down mechanism comes into play. For example, under normal illumination you have no difficulty detecting the different sizes of a real chair and of a much smaller toy chair. Each object is automatically assigned a size by a bottom-up mechanism. But if the visual information is reduced, size judgments become more difficult, and a toy chair may appear to be the size of a real one (Franklin and Erickson 1969; Schiffman 1967; Slack 1956).

When we turn to flat drawings, the sources of information are much reduced, and demonstrating ambiguity, illusion, and the operation of the comparison stage becomes easy. Take a look at Figure 4.15 (without peeking at the labels in the caption), which contains some degraded pictures of familiar objects, pictures that are difficult to identify. The problem is that the bottom-up mechanism can carry perception only so far. The pictures have been so degraded that their individual components cannot be combined into a single recognizable pattern.

Now look at the label identifying each picture. Once you read the label, you can recognize each picture. The label influences the perception of the picture by causing you to reorganize the elements of the pattern into a different representation. Instead of seeing many unconnected elements, you perceive a few connected areas, comprised of many individual elements, that match the contours stored with a representation activated by the label. In such cases perception is a product of both bottom-up and top-down processes.

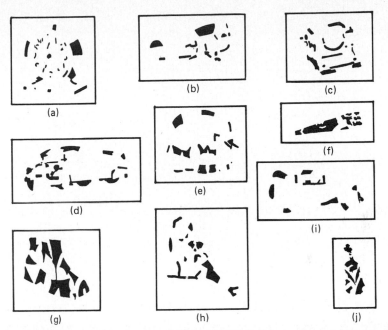

**Figure 4.15   Figures used by Leeper (1935): (a) Clock; (b) airplane; (c) typewriter; (d) bus; (e) elephant; (f) saw; (g) shoe; (h) boy with dog; (i) roadster; (j) violin.**

## Artificial Intelligence and Vision

As we discussed briefly in Chapter 1, computer programs designed to exhibit artificial intelligence can sometimes shed light on potential mechanisms for human cognition. Some progress has been made by computer scientists who have written programs to analyze visual scenes. In doing so, they faced the same problems that the human visual system has already solved.

Several early computer vision programs were written to analyze various kinds of scenes depicting block worlds, such as the one shown in Figure 4.16. A person will naturally interpret such complex, two-dimensional line drawings as representing a collection of three-dimensional objects. Notice that many of the objects appear to be hidden behind other objects. Could a computer program make any sense out of this jumble?

One program that analyzes block worlds such as the one depicted in Figure 4.16 is called SEE (Guzman 1968). SEE has a fairly limited goal. It does not attempt to classify the objects' shapes as "cubical" or "triangular" or anything of that nature. The program simply attempts to discover how many objects are represented in the scene. However, this task is not a trivial one for a scene as complex as the scene in Figure 4.16.

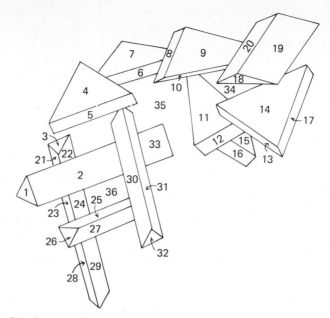

**Figure 4.16   Block scene. The program SEE can divide this scene into separate three-dimensional objects. (From Grasselli 1969.)**

SEE operates almost entirely in a bottom-up manner. The basic features that it uses are the various ways in which two or more lines can intersect. Figure 4.17 illustrates four important types of intersections, with the names Guzman gave them. It turns out that the type of intersection can provide a great deal of information about how the lines should be linked together to form three-dimensional objects. For example, an arrow often represents the outside corner of an object. Note, for instance, that an arrow is formed at the top of the intersection between the regions labeled 19 and 20 in Figure 4.16.

SEE began to analyze a scene after an earlier program divided the picture into regions (numbered in Figure 4.16) and decided which regions were parts of objects and which were background. SEE then processed the object regions in two steps. First, it looked at each intersection and decided whether it pro-

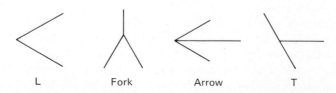

**Figure 4.17   Four types of line intersections SEE uses to identify objects.**

vided evidence for (or against) linking regions as surfaces of a single object. For example, the arrow rule would link regions 19 and 20 at this point. Second, the program identified those regions that had been linked by at least two different rules. For example, regions 19 and 20 would be linked with each other and also with region 18, because there is a fork at the intersection where these three regions meet. Such clearly joined regions were used as the nuclei of objects, and the program attempted to attach each remaining region onto one of these nuclei. When this task was done, the program listed how the regions were grouped to form objects.

While Guzman's program is quite successful in dealing with block world scenes, it also has clear limitations. Its rules for interpreting intersections are simply inadequate for many types of figures, such as objects with holes. Also, the pictures SEE deals with are cleaner in many ways than more realistic scenes would be. For example, compare the two versions of a block scene depicted in Figure 4.18. Figure 4.18(a) is the kind of scene Guzman's program could work with. Figure 4.18(b) introduces shadows, which we would expect to find if the scene were illuminated from a particular direction. SEE could not deal with this version at all, because it has no way of distinguishing regions of shadow from the shaded regions of objects.

SEE is not the only vision program with this type of limitation; in fact, most have the same problem (Boden 1977). Some programs actually begin by trying to clean up the scene, finding shadows and then ignoring them. But shadows may provide useful information about objects. In a block scene like the scene in Figure 4.18(b), the shadows indicate that the objects are resting on a surface rather than being suspended in midair. Waltz (1975) found that by using shadow information, his program could interpret line intersections more efficiently than was otherwise possible. His program was able to correctly analyze scenes like the one in Figure 4.18(b). Furthermore, the program would assign the same interpretation to the scene even if the direction of illumination (and hence the shadows) were changed.

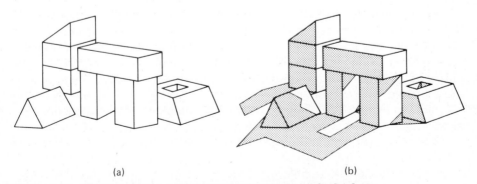

(a)                                        (b)

**Figure 4.18    Block scene: (a) Without shadows; (b) with shadows.**

The programs of Guzman and Waltz are only a sample of the work that has been done on computer vision. Unlike their programs, which basically use bottom-up processes, other programs have used a mixture of bottom-up and top-down mechanisms for scene perception (Hanson and Riseman 1978; Tenenbaum and Barrow 1977). Many computer vision programs have been limited in that they can only process *static scenes,* whereas humans and other animals use many cues provided by motion. However, some vision programs can operate on scenes that move (Ullman 1979).

McArthur (1982) provides a review of work on computer vision and a discussion of its relevance to psychological theories. At a global level artificial-intelligence work seems to support the kind of constructive approach to visual perception that we emphasized when discussing human perception. That is, in computer vision programs features of the visual input, sometimes together with knowledge about what objects usually look like, are used to construct a representation of the input. In addition, work in artificial intelligence has helped to identify specific features that may guide perception.

## Intermodal Conflict

**Vision vs. touch.**   If you visually examined an object, such as a toy block, before it was thrown into a bag with several blocks of other shapes, you would have no difficulty reaching into the bag and selecting the one that you had seen. The visuospatial code receives inputs from the tactile organs in the skin as well as from the eyes. Accordingly, the shape representation of each tactile input could be compared with the shape representation of the visual input. In order for the comparison mechanism to find the correct match, the visual and tactile sensory modalities must be calibrated so that the same representation of the shape of an object is constructed on the basis of either visual or tactile information. Of course, for most people information from the visual and tactile modalities are very well calibrated, which is what makes the task described above so easy. But how does information from the different senses come to be calibrated? Do things look the way they feel, or do they feel the way they look?

A classic experiment answered this question by placing information from the visual and tactile modalities in conflict. Rock and Victor (1964) asked students to grasp a square while simultaneously examining it through a lens that contracted its visual width to half its original size. The hands of the observers were covered with a cloth, so they could not see their fingers and were unaware of the distortion. Following the examination period, the students were asked to pick a match, visually or tactually, from an array of undistorted similar items or else to draw the standard. The students selected or drew a square that was the size that it had appeared visually, rather than its actual size. Thus vision dominated completely over touch—the square felt the way it looked.

Very strong or complete visual dominance over touch has been demonstrated many times in a variety of perceptual tasks, including judgments of size (Kinney and Luria 1970; Miller 1972), curvature (Easton and Moran 1978), length (Teghtsoonian and Teghtsoonian 1970), depth (Singer and Day 1969), spatial location (Hay, Pick, and Ikeda 1965; Pick, Warren, and Hay 1969; Warren and Cleaves 1971; Warren and Pick 1970), and texture (Lederman and Abbott 1981). The results of these studies indicate that vision completely predominates over touch in the perception of form. When there is a conflict between vision and a body sense with regard to spatial location, as when an observer views her hand through a prism that displaces its location, vision again dominates completely. However, perceived location is a compromise between what would be seen and what would be felt. And when there is a conflict between vision and touch with regard to texture, the perceived roughness of the surface is an even compromise between vision and touch. Thus the degree of visual domination depends on the nature of the task. If the conflicting information is a kind that is usually obtained visually, such as shape information, vision dominates completely. But if the conflicting information is of a kind usually obtained tactually, such as texture information, then tactile information also strongly influences the perception.

**Temporal conflict.**    The dominance of vision over touch does not extend to all modalities or to all representations. When James Walker and Karen Scott (1981) investigated the perception of duration, they found a different pattern of results. A tone or a light was presented to students for 0.5 second (500 milliseconds), 1 second (1000 milliseconds), or 1.5 seconds (1500 milliseconds). Immediately following the presentation of the input, the students held down a button for as long as they thought the input had occurred. For the light the students' perceived durations were 578, 991, and 1333 milliseconds, respectively. For the tone the perceived durations were 582, 1140, and 1510 milliseconds, respectively. Thus the students perceived the lights as shorter than the tones. Hence, at least for short inputs, temporal perception of visual and auditory inputs is imperfectly calibrated.

Walker and Scott (1981) next presented the lights and tones together. The students perceived the lights and tones occurring together for exactly as long as they had perceived tones occurring alone. Audition thus completely dominated over vision. Walker and Scott suggested three reasons for these results. First, whenever auditory and visual information is in conflict in the representation of a temporal interval, the visual information may be ignored. Second, the input with the longer perceived duration may dominate over the input with the shorter perceived duration. Third, the input that is perceived as more *salient* may dominate over the input that is perceived as less salient. For instance, tones are usually more noticeable than lights, even when both inputs are intense enough to make detection certain. In one further experiment

Walker and Scott reduced the intensity of the tone. This tone was perceived as shorter than a light at 500 milliseconds, and in this one condition the perceived duration of the light dominated over the tone. Thus some evidence supports the longer duration and salience hypotheses. However, more research must be done before the perception of duration will be understood.

## MENTAL IMAGERY

Visuospatial representation, as we have described it so far, is the direct product of perception. However, you can also activate perceptionlike representations from memory. People can form images corresponding to many different sense modalities. Can you imagine the sight of your mother's face? The sound of a bugle? The feel of coarse sandpaper? The smell of bacon? The taste of strawberries? All of these images are kinds of *mental imagery* that we can form without the physical presence of the imaged objects, using top-down mechanisms based on knowledge stored in memory. Since vision is the richest sense for most people, most of the research we will discuss involves visual imagery (more precisely, as we will see later, *visuospatial imagery*).

### Properties of Mental Imagery

Almost everyone is introspectively aware of experiencing visual images. In fact, simple demonstrations offer convincing evidence that images not only exist but are used to perform various question-answering and reasoning tasks. For example, suppose you are asked with which hand the Statue of Liberty holds aloft the torch. You might answer this question by imaging the Statue of Liberty and noting that she is holding the torch in her right hand. Images seem to make it possible to read perceptual properties of objects. A great deal of research has gone beyond such intuitive demonstrations and served to clarify the nature of mental imagery.

**Selective interference.**    Perhaps the most central characteristic of imagery is that it is somehow similar to actual perception (Shepard and Podgorny 1978). A visual image should resemble seeing, and an auditory image should resemble hearing. For example, Podgorny and Shepard (1978) presented college students with five-by-five grids on which a pattern, such as a block letter *F*, was either actually imposed or imagined. Then a probe (a blue dot) was presented in one of the cells of the grid, and subjects had to decide as quickly as possible whether the probe fell on or off the figure and to press a corresponding button. Podgorny and Shepard found that subjects' reaction times varied systematically with the relationship between the probe's position and the structure of

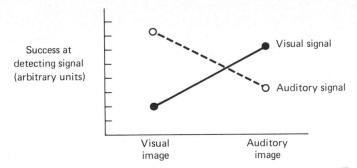

Success at detecting signal (arbitrary units)

Visual signal

Auditory signal

Visual image

Auditory image

**Figure 4.19    Selective interference between imagery and perception. (From Segal and Fusella 1970.)**

the figure. For example, reaction time was faster for simpler figures. For probes that were in fact off the figure, reaction time decreased as the distance of the probe from the figure increased. The most important result, however, was that the reaction time pattern was essentially the same regardless of whether the figure was actually perceived or imaged.

As discussed in Chapter 2, the representations that can be in awareness at one time are limited, and two representations from the same code will interfere with each other more than two representations from different codes will. So we would expect that imagery might actually *interfere* with perception in the same-sense modality. For example, because visual imagery results from the activation of a visuospatial representation, forming a visual image should make it more difficult to perceive a visual target. This prediction was tested by Segal and Fusella (1970). They asked subjects to form either a visual image (e.g., the appearance of a tree) or an auditory image (e.g., the sound of a telephone ringing). Then either a faint visual signal or a faint auditory signal was presented, which the subject had to detect. The results are depicted in Figure 4.19. When subjects formed a visual image, they were poorer at detecting visual signals; but when subjects formed an auditory image, they were poorer at detecting auditory signals. This pattern of results is called *selective interference*, because forming an image selectively interferes with perception in the same-sense modality. Brooks (1968) and Byrne (1974) have also found selective interference effects with imagery.

**Image space.**    Imagery emanates from the same representation used to encode the perceptual representations of environmental space. So it should have many of the same properties as perception. These properties have been examined at length by Stephen Kosslyn (1975, 1980, 1981). For example, just as the size of the perceptual representation that can be in awareness is limited, so is the size of the imaginal representation.

Rabbit beside an elephant                    Rabbit beside a fly

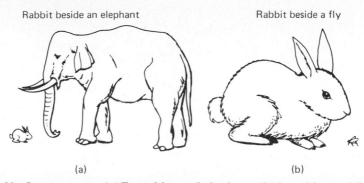

(a)                                          (b)

**Figure 4.20    Image space: (a) For rabbit and elephant; (b) for rabbit and fly. Because image space is limited, a rabbit is imaged at a smaller size when it is beside an elephant than when it is beside a fly.**

In one study Kosslyn (1975) demonstrated that the size of the image space is limited. He asked college students to image one animal standing next to another one, and then he timed them as they verified a statement about one of the animals by consulting the image. For example, they might be asked to respond true or false to "A rabbit has ears" when the rabbit was standing next to either an elephant or a fly. As Figure 4.20 illustrates, the limited size of the image space should force the subject to image the rabbit at a smaller size when it is beside an elephant than when it is beside a fly. Kosslyn hypothe-

**Figure 4.21    Fictional map used by Kosslyn, Ball, and Reiser (1978).**

sized that a property would be more difficult to "see" on a small image than on a large image. Accordingly, the decision should be made more quickly when the rabbit is imaged next to an elephant rather than a fly. The results supported this prediction.

Just as attention can be shifted from one location to another in environmental space, it can be shifted to different locations in image space. Kosslyn, Ball, and Reiser (1978) had subjects memorize the map of an imaginary island (Figure 4.21). The map contained seven objects. After the subjects had memorized the map, they performed a reaction time task. One location was named, and then a second word was presented. Subjects were told to mentally scan from the first named location to the second and press a button. All possible pairs of locations were included in the experiment, making a total of twenty-one different distances. As Figure 4.22 indicates, mean reaction time was directly proportional to interpoint distance: The longer the distance to be scanned, the more time the subjects required.

We should note that a number of investigators (e.g., Intons-Peterson 1983; Mitchell and Richman 1980) have argued that results such as those found by Kosslyn *et al.* are due not to image scanning but to demand characteristics of the experimental situation. They suggest that subjects simply produce times proportional to distance because that is what they believe the experimenter wants them to do. However, as we will see shortly, strong evidence indicates that demand characteristics cannot explain a variety of other imagery-related phenomena (see Kosslyn 1980).

Another source of evidence for an image space is the work on mental rotation (Shepard and Cooper 1982; Shepard and Metzler 1971), which we

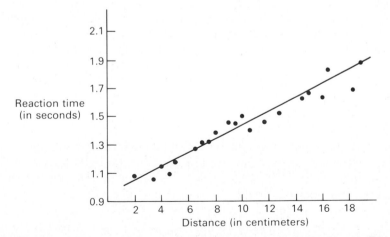

**Figure 4.22    Time to scan between all pairs of locations on imaged map. (From Kosslyn *et al.* 1978.)**

discussed in Chapter 1. The central result from these studies is that the time needed to compare shapes increases with their difference in orientation, as if one form had to be rotated through an internal space to bring it into congruence with the other.

**Imagery and the third dimension.**   Most of the research discussed so far indicates that images depict only two-dimensional forms. In fact, however, visual images can represent the shapes of objects in *three* dimensions as well. For example, Shepard and Metzler (1971) found that people can rotate line drawings of three-dimensional objects in depth as well as in the picture plane.

  More recently, Pinker (1980) adapted the scanning paradigm of Kosslyn *et al.* (1978) to investigate three-dimensional imagery. In Pinker's study subjects first memorized the locations of several objects suspended in space (analogous to the map presented to Kosslyn and colleagues' subjects). Afterward, the subjects were timed as they scanned from one object to another for all possible pairs of objects. Reaction time increased linearly with the three-dimensional distances between the objects. Image space may thus be more analogous to a three-dimensional model, such as a hologram, than to a two-dimensional display (see also Pinker and Finke 1980).

**Spatial nature of imagery.**   In much of our discussion we have spoken of imagery as if it were basically visual. However, most of the evidence we have reviewed primarily indicates that imagery preserves *spatial* information rather than purely visual information. Mental imagery, like the visuospatial representations of perception, can be constructed on the basis of tactile, auditory, and other kinds of information, in addition to visual information per se. In fact, congenitally blind subjects perform many imagery tasks, such as mental rotation (Carpenter and Eisenberg 1978; Marmor and Zabeck 1976) and image scanning (Kerr 1983), in a manner qualitatively similar to sighted subjects (see also Zimler and Keenan 1983). The images of the blind thus represent spatial shapes and distances. Mental images, like perceptual representations, are more aptly described as visuospatial than as simply visual.

## Imagery and Perception

In 1883 Galton became interested in mental imagery. He made up a questionnaire about the vividness of their images and distributed it to 100 people in a variety of walks of life. To his surprise, he found an enormous range in the degree of imagery reported. To this day, individual differences in reported imagery have plagued imagery research. Some individuals report such vivid images that they can literally see an imaged object or scene before their eyes, while other individuals report no imagery at all. Their differences are so extreme that at one time psychologists believed that extremely realistic images were produced by a special neural mechanism and called them *eidetic images.* However, today such vivid images are viewed as one end of an imagery continuum, and though *eidetic* is still sometimes used as an adjective to describe a particularly vivid or stable image, it no longer implies a special mechanism (Gray and Gummerman 1975).

The surprising aspect of individual differences in reported imagery is not merely that they exist but that there are so few functional consequences. People who experience vivid visual images do not necessarily encode more detailed visuospatial representations and are not necessarily more adept at performing tasks requiring visuospatial operations. A vivid image may be as inaccurate a description of a remembered object as a vague one (Baddeley 1976, p. 222). Psychologists have been driven to more and more specialized tests to discover functional consequences of differences in reported imagery.

**Imaginal illusions.**    Another kind of parallel between imagery and perception has been observed in many studies indicating that various perceptual illusions can also be produced by imagery [see Finke (1980) for a review]. For example, Figure 4.23 shows two well-known visual illusions. In the Wundt illusion (Figure 4.23a) the horizontal lines appear to bow outward, and in the Hering illusion (Figure 4.23b) they appear to bow inward. In fact, the lines are parallel in both figures, just as are the two isolated lines in Figure 4.23(c).

Wallace (1984) selected subjects who were either high or low in the vividness of their imagery as measured by a standard questionnaire. All subjects were shown the two horizontal lines alone (Figure 4.23c) and asked to image either the Wundt or the Hering diagonals superimposed on the horizontal lines. (The diagonals were shown alone in advance so that subjects would know what to image.) None of the subjects had any prior experience with the two illusions. Wallace found that all of the high-imagery subjects were able to induce the illusions by imagery and correctly report the direction of the apparent bow in the horizontal lines. However, the low-imagery subjects not only

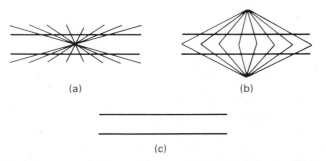

(a)                              (b)

(c)

**Figure 4.23    Two illusions and the reality: (a) Wundt illusion; (b) Hering illusion; (c) parallel lines.**

failed to produce the illusion but reported being unable to image the diagonal lines.

The existence of large individual differences in imagery ability may account for the fact that despite the overwhelming evidence that has established the visuospatial nature of mental imagery, various theorists have resisted this conclusion (Anderson 1978; Pylyshyn 1973, 1981; and in rebuttal, Kosslyn 1981; Kosslyn and Pomerantz 1977). Those who do not experience clear visual imagery are not easily convinced by empirical evidence that others do.

**Left-side neglect in images.**   A particularly intriguing link between imagery and perception involves the unilateral neglect syndrome, discussed in Chapter 2. Recall that patients who suffer damage to the right hemisphere of their brains tend not to attend to the left side of visual space. A group of researchers in Italy (Bisiach, Capitani, Luzzatti, and Perani 1981) identified a similar type of neglect in a memory task that required visual imagery. They asked patients with right-hemisphere lesions to describe a location familiar to them: the cathedral square in Milan. The patients first described the features of the square from a vantage point facing the cathedral from the opposite side of the square. Then the patients were asked to describe the square again, this time imagining their vantage point to be the central entrance to the cathedral looking out onto the square.

The researchers found that a group of patients who showed visual-field defects and left-side neglect in perceptual tests exhibited left-side neglect in the memory task as well. These patients were able to correctly report more details on the right of the square than on the left. Since this pattern was obtained for both perspectives, it implies that a patient who remembered a visual feature when it was on the right might well fail to report that same feature when the perspective was reversed so the feature was on the left. As is the case for the perceptual neglect syndrome, left-side neglect in imagery appears to reflect difficulty in attending to a portion of space. But in the latter case the "space" is not the external environment but an internal image space.

As suggested earlier, a likely explanation of the neglect syndrome is that damage to the right hemisphere impairs the figure construction mechanism. Because the same figure-construction mechanism operates on both perceptual and memory representations, damage produces neglect of the same region of both perceptual and imagined space.

**Mental abacus.**   A possible reason for such varied reports of the degree of imagery, and so few functional consequences, is that in Western culture no tasks require vivid imagery and relatively few require detailed visuospatial representation. The development of these abilities is therefore a hit-or-miss proposition. To test this hypothesis, psychologists have looked at the visuospatial skills and imagery of people in other cultures (e.g., Gardner 1980; Stratton 1917). Along the way they have discovered some fascinating skills requiring imagery.

Of all the skills that depend on mental imagery, probably none is more spectacular than that associated with the use of the *abacus,* a device for mathematical calculations, which is commonplace in modern Asian cultures. Numbers are represented with beads on parallel rods. Figure 4.24 depicts the digits 1 through 9 (i.e., the number 123,456,789) as they would appear on a Japanese abacus. The rightmost rod represents units, the next rod tens, the next hundreds, etc. Each rod has two sections, with one bead on the top and four on the bottom. When the top bead is *down,* it represents a sum of 5 (or 50, 500, etc.). Each bottom bead that is *up* represents a single unit. The digit 7, for example, is represented when the top bead is down and two of the bottom beads are up.

By entering successive numbers onto the abacus in accord with a specified set of rules for manipulating beads, people can perform arithmetic calculations quickly and accurately. Indeed, the abacus survives in Asian cultures despite the advent of the electronic calculator because people trained in use of the abacus can do calculations on the abacus more quickly than they can key numbers into a calculator. What is truly astounding, however, is that expert users of the abacus dispense with the physical device and perform the calculations mentally. They claim to visualize an abacus, then mentally move the beads just as they would on a real abacus, and read off the answer. In fact, experts find that actually moving the beads of a real abacus is too slow— imagined beads can be moved more quickly. In Taiwan, for example, many eleven-year-old children trained in mental abacus can perform such feats as finding the product of two five-digit numbers in under 10 seconds and adding five three-digit numbers in under 3 seconds.

A skeptical psychologist might wonder whether such performance actually involves mental imagery. Stigler (1984) performed several experiments that support the introspective claims of the abacus experts. He found

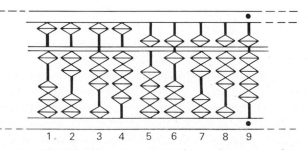

**Figure 4.24   Number 123,456,789 as represented on a Japanese abacus.**

that experts could readily identify intermediate states in calculations that were unique to abacus addition, and that the time to make such judgments increased the further along the state occurred in the sequence of moves required to solve the problem. Furthermore, the errors made in addition problems were predictable from an analysis of the operations required on the abacus and were quite different from the kinds of mental-arithmetic errors made by subjects untrained in abacus use. Stigler's results provide detailed evidence that the internal operations used in mental abacus are in fact analogous to the external operations that would be required to manipulate a real abacus. Skill in mental abacus thus appears to depend on imagery that is visuospatial or perhaps motoric in nature. (We will discuss other methods of rapid mental calculation in Chapter 10.)

## SPATIAL COGNITION

One of the most important functions of visuospatial representation is to encode knowledge about the spatial layout of the environment. Such knowledge is essential to our ability to navigate through the world. We share this basic function of the visuospatial code with many other creatures. Even rats, which rely on the visuospatial representation for recognition less than humans do, have a highly developed sense of spatial location. Indeed, most early research on the acquisition of geographical knowledge was performed with rats.

The term *cognitive map* was first used by Tolman (1948) to describe the spatial knowledge that seemed to be acquired by rats in a maze. In a typical experiment a group of rats was trained to go down a particular path to reach food in a goal box. When the original path was later blocked, many of the rats selected another path that led in the direction of the goal. They had learned more than just a sequence of responses that would lead to the goal; they had learned *where* the goal was located relative to the starting position.

### Route and Survey Knowledge

Many theorists have suggested that two kinds of spatial knowledge can be usefully distinguished (see Thorndyke and Hayes-Roth 1982). *Route knowledge,* as its name implies, is closely tied to particular known routes through the environment, such as the route you follow from home to school or work. Route knowledge may take the form of a series of actions associated with landmarks (e.g., "turn right at the Student Union Building"). *Survey knowledge,* on the other hand, is more maplike in that it conveys the global relations between locations. Tolman's rats that were able to discover detours were exhibiting survey knowledge.

The most direct way for a human to acquire survey knowledge is simply to study a map. Thorndyke and Hayes-Roth (1982) tested the spatial knowledge that people acquired about a large office building on the basis of either map learning or direct navigational experience. They found that subjects who studied a map of the building for just 20 minutes were able to make judgments of distances and relative location as accurately as secretaries who had worked in the building for two years. However, one disadvantage of map learning was that people trained with maps had difficulty changing their perspective to make orientation judgments (also see Evans and Pezdek 1980). Extensive navigational experience can produce more flexible spatial knowledge than map learning tends to produce.

An important question, which has yet to be clearly answered, is how navigational experience can eventually lead to a transition from route to survey knowledge. Part of the answer may lie in the role of landmarks or salient reference locations with respect to which other locations tend to be encoded. Sadalla, Burroughs, and Staplin (1980) identified reference locations by asking Arizona State University students which campus building locations they knew well, visited often, and thought were important. When students were told to imagine themselves at a particular location and asked whether a particular building was close by, the proximity of a reference point was verified faster than the proximity of a nonreference point. Also, students verified the direction they would have to go from a reference point to another building more quickly than the direction from a nonreference point to another building. People may remember familiar routes in terms of landmarks. Then as they learn intersecting routes, with common reference locations, they could begin to form a survey representation.

## Distortions in Geographical Knowledge

Although geographical knowledge, at least in its survey form, is encoded as a visuospatial representation, such knowledge is by no means entirely accurate. The fact that geographical knowledge is error-prone will come as no surprise to anyone who has found themselves disoriented in an environment they thought they knew. In fact, the errors that people make are highly systematic.

**Alignment and rotation.** Barbara Tversky (1981) performed a series of experiments on people's memory for real and artificial maps, local environments, and visual patterns. The results indicated that errors arise from the strategies people employ to remember the locations of figures. For instance, a location on a map, such as a state, is represented as a figure against a background. Because remembering the absolute location of figures is difficult, people encode locations *relative* to other locations or natural directions. This

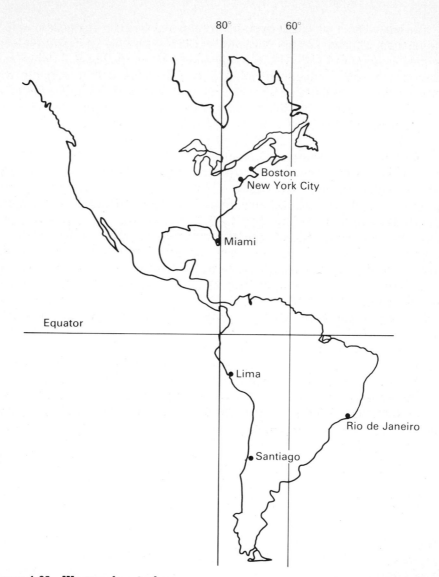

**Figure 4.25    Western hemisphere.**

technique can lead to distortions if the relative encoding is made more regular than, in fact, it is. For example, look at the map of North and South America in Figure 4.25. Most people are surprised that Miami, a city on the east coast of North America, is actually *west* of Lima, a city on the west coast of South America. People tend to mentally *align* the two continents on a north-south axis, so they mistakenly think that South America is directly south of North America.

The tendency to regularize geographical locations manifests itself in other related ways. For example, people tend to remember street intersections as being closer to right angles than they really are. A closely related bias observed by Tversky is that subjects *rotate* the edge of a geographical line so that it corresponds more closely to a natural axis. For example, she found that students at Stanford University believed that San Francisco Bay runs due south from San Francisco to San Jose, when in fact it runs markedly southeast.

**Geographical superordinates.**    Geographical regions are commonly viewed as hierarchical structures. Thus a building is in a city, which is in a state, which is in a country, etc. Because we know that the location of a superordinate constrains the location of all the regions within it, any distortions caused by biases such as rotation and alignment will be inherited by the subordinate locations. For example, try answering the following question: Which is farther east, Los Angeles or Reno? Most people who are asked to draw a map of California and Nevada place Los Angeles considerably west of Reno. This location is illustrated in the distorted map of Figure 4.26(a). But as the accurate map in Figure 4.26(b) shows, Los Angeles is actually *east* of Reno. We think of California as west of Nevada, and so we tend to straighten the border in an attempt to put *all* of California west of all of Nevada.

Here's another question that would fool many people in Michigan: If you travel due south from Detroit, what is the first foreign country you would come to? The answer, as the map in Figure 4.27(a) shows, is Canada.

People are very prone to make such errors based on superordinate locations (Stevens and Coupe 1978). As another example, most people believe that the Pacific terminus of the Panama Canal is west of the Atlantic terminus. But as the map in Figure 4.27(b) reveals, the reverse is true. In this case many peo-

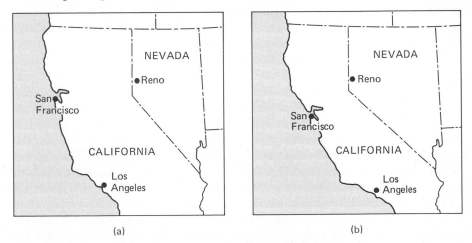

(a)                                          (b)

**Figure 4.26   Geographical distortion: (a) Mental location of Reno as east of Los Angeles; (b) actual location of Reno — west of Los Angeles.**

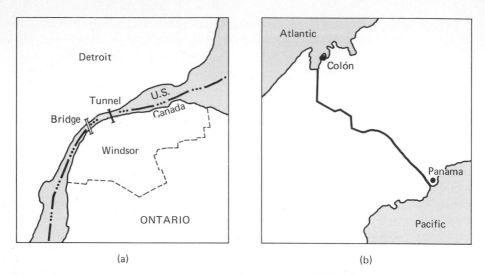

(a)                                          (b)

**Figure 4.27**  **Geographical locations easily confused: (a) the first foreign country south of Detroit being Canada; (b) the Pacific end of the Panama Canal being east of the Atlantic end.**

ple may simply not have a visuospatial representation of the local area near the Panama Canal. However, they may reason approximately as follows: "I know the Pacific is west of the Atlantic, so the Pacific end of the Panama Canal *must* be west of the Atlantic end." As this example illustrates, geographical information may be derived in other ways besides accessing a direct visuospatial representation.

**Spatial inconsistency.**   Although the studies cited in the previous subsection and many other studies illustrate systematic errors in geographical knowledge, they do not demonstrate that such knowledge could not be represented in a single maplike structure. For example, the map in Figure 4.26(a) is perfectly consistent, even though it is wrong. However, other evidence reveals distortions that could not be captured in *any* single, consistent map. Thus Moar and Bower (1983) had residents in Cambridge, England, estimate the angles formed by each of the three street intersections depicted in Figure 4.28. They found that the estimates were all biased toward 90 degrees, as would be expected as the result of the tendency to regularize. The consequence, however, is that the sum of the three angles exceeded 180 degrees, which would be an impossible triangle. In another experiment Moar and Bower had American subjects estimate the relative orientation of pairs of U.S. cities in both directions. For several pairs of cities, including New York and Chicago, the subjects were inconsistent in that the estimated direction from one city to the second was not equivalent to the estimated reverse direction from the second city to the first.

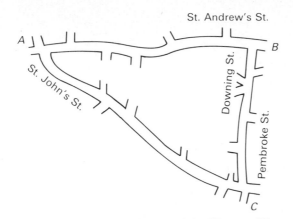

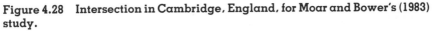

**Figure 4.28     Intersection in Cambridge, England, for Moar and Bower's (1983) study.**

Such spatial inconsistencies suggest that geographical knowledge is often represented in several small mental maps rather than one large map of the entire environment. Because the maps overlap, the environment can be navigated by switching from map to map. Familiar reference locations that appear in many maps can be used to piece together a route from one unfamiliar location to another. For example, a student might not have a mental map containing both the chemistry building and the psychology building, but she might have a map containing the dormitory and the chemistry building and another containing the dormitory and the psychology building. By using the dormitory as a reference point and using both maps that contain it, she could trace a route from the chemistry building to the psychology building. This kind of piecemeal representation may foster the transition from route to survey knowledge.

## VISUOSPATIAL REPRESENTATION AND THE BRAIN

Damage to the cortex may cause a defect in the visuospatial code. Recall that most of the input from the eyes first reaches the cortex at the visual cortex, in the occipital lobe in the rear of the brain. Not surprisingly, then, a visuospatial defect is more likely to result from a posterior injury to the cortex than an anterior injury, because posterior injury is more likely to cut the pathway that a visual input follows to other parts of the brain and hence interrupt its processing. When Benton (1980) examined a group of patients with head injuries sufficiently severe to cause a visual deficit, he found that only 12.5 percent of the patients with anterior injuries were impaired on a visual matching task, whereas 50 percent of the patients with posterior injuries were impaired on the task.

**Figure 4.29   Drawings indicating parietal injury: (a) A clock with the hands set at 10 past 11; (b) a daisy.**

The specific location of a posterior injury influences the nature of the resulting deficit. Damage to the occipital lobe generally results in a deficit in form and/or color perception, which is revealed by discrimination and matching tasks. The deficit in form perception may vary from severe, as discussed at the beginning of this chapter, to mild, depending on the extent of the injury. In the mildest form that is a noticeable impairment, the patient is able to perceive and recognize most common forms except faces. This apparently idiosyncratic disorder, called *prosopagnosia,* arises because more details must be encoded for face recognition than for any other familiar object, so even a mild encoding deficit impairs it.

Damage to the parietal lobe may result in any one or a combination of several different deficits involving the visuospatial representation. The unilateral neglect syndrome (described in Chapter 2 and in this chapter) may result. Another effect of parietal damage is spatial confusion (Benton 1980; Kolb and Whishaw 1980). In mild cases persons may only get the left and the right confused. For example, they might make an error when asked by an examiner facing them to point with their right hand to the examiner's right eye. In more severe cases persons may have difficulty in putting on their clothes and be unable to find their way about.

Parietal lobe damage also seems to result in impairment or loss of the ability to mentally rotate an object (Butters and Barton 1970; Butters, Barton, and Brody 1970). Another common finding is an impairment in the retention of a visual image in active memory. A revealing task is to show people a simple pattern for 10 seconds and then immediately ask them to draw it from memory (Wechsler 1945). Visuospatial deficits caused by parietal lobe damage may also be detected by having a person do some simple drawings, like the face of a clock or a daisy (Goodglass and Kaplan 1972). Patients produce badly distorted drawings such as those shown in Figure 4.29. Notice that these drawings are distorted on the left. A common finding is that when artwork is distorted as a result of brain injury, the distortion is worse on one side. This effect is reminiscent of the unilateral neglect syndrome. As with the neglect syndrome, the reason for the asymmetry in the distortion is not known.

In another experiment involving parietal lobe damage, Butters, Samuels, Goodglass, and Brody (1970) showed a patient a geometric pattern for 0.5 second; then from 0 to 18 seconds later the patient had to select it from a display containing nine patterns. Parietal patients were less accurate in performing this task than patients with frontal lesions (as well as normal controls) at all study-test intervals. Butters *et al.* (1970) suggested that the visual-retention deficit is the cause of the failure to perform mental rotations, the poor drawing ability, and the confusion of left and right, because all these tasks require a degree of imagery ability that the patient with parietal injury no longer possesses.

## SUMMARY

Visual perception is based on the construction of a visuospatial representation of inputs. The visuospatial code is composed of three subcodes representing *brightness/color, shape,* and *location.* A bottom-up *figure construction mechanism* constructs an integrated representation on the basis of the three visual subcodes plus tactile and auditory information. The construction mechanisms for visual and tactile inputs are calibrated so that an object will yield the same visuospatial representation whether examined visually or by touch. When visual information and tactile information are placed in conflict, the tactile representation is recalibrated to conform to the visual. The relative durations of brief lights and sounds are less well calibrated. Vision programs developed in artificial intelligence illustrate a variety of constructive mechanisms, both bottom-up and top-down.

*Mental imagery* is an abstract type of memory code closely related to the visuospatial code for perception. Images are formed by top-down mechanisms on the basis of knowledge stored in memory. The *selective-interference paradigm* provides evidence for the close link between imagery and perception. Visuospatial imagery can represent three-dimensional space from different perspectives. Imagery is closely tied to perception, and good imagers can even produce perceptual illusions by imagining the appropriate patterns. Since even the congenitally blind appear to have access to spatial imagery, such imagery does not seem to be necessarily tied to vision. Brain damage that produces deficits in visual perception can also produce left-side neglect of visual images.

Geographical knowledge can be represented as *route information* about particular paths through the environment or as *survey information* about the global spatial layout. Survey information can be acquired most readily by studying a map, but information acquired from direct navigational experience can potentially be more flexible. People's geographical knowledge is often distorted in accord with systematic biases such as *alignment* and *rotation,* which regularize the relative locations of figures with respect to each other and natural axes. The known relative location of superordinate units, such as states, can influence judgments about the relative location of subordinate units, such as cities. Sometimes, people's distance and direction judgments are internally inconsistent, suggesting that they are using multiple, overlapping mental maps based on shared reference points rather than a unitary representation.

A great part of the posterior portion of the cortex is involved in visuospatial representation, and damage across any portion of this wide area is likely to result in a detectable visuospatial deficit. In particular, damage to the *parietal lobe* causes failure to perform mental rotation, poor drawing ability, and confusion of the left and the right. All of these deficits may result from impairment of imagery ability.


## RECOMMENDED READINGS

Irvin Rock's *Perception* (1984) is a beautiful introduction to the topic by a master of the field. As mentioned earlier, Gardner's *Shattered Mind* (1976) and Kolb and Whishaw's *Fundamentals of Human Neuropsychology* (1980) are good texts for learning more about the effects of brain damage on cognition.

# CHAPTER **FIVE**

# Categorization

## INTRODUCTION

The tendency to divide the world into categories is a pervasive aspect of human thought. Categorization is a fundamental cognitive process because every experience is in some sense unique. For example, no two apples are entirely alike. However, if each experience were given a unique mental representation, we would be quickly overwhelmed by the sheer complexity, and we could not apply what we had already learned to deal with new situations. By encoding experiences into an organized system of categories, we are able to recognize significant commonalities in different experiences. A category system allows us to derive further information about an object that has been assigned to a category. For example, if you have categorized some object as an apple, you can infer how it is expected to taste, that it has a core, and that it can be used to fill a pie.

Note that the possible inferences extend to properties that are not immediately observable. A study by Gelman and Markman (1983) demonstrates that children as young as four years old rely heavily on categorization to direct their inference processes. Children were presented with triads of pictures such as the triad shown in Figure 5.1. For this example the experimenter first told the child, "This bird gives its baby mashed-up food" (pointing at the flamingo), and "This bat gives its baby milk" (pointing at the bat). Then the child was asked, "Does this bird (indicating the blackbird) give its baby mashed-up food or milk?"

Even though the critical instance was always more similar perceptually to the out-of-category instance (the bat), about 85 percent of the children selected the answer corresponding to the instance of the same category (i.e., they claimed that the new bird would feed its babies mashed-up food). In contrast, control subjects who were asked the question without seeing any prior instances responded at the chance level, with about 50 percent selecting each of the two possible alternatives. Thus even four-year-olds know that instances

**Figure 5.1    Examples of test pictures used by Gelman and Markman (1983).**

of the same categories are likely to share properties that are not readily observable.

The category system serves to organize information stored in long-term memory. Many inferences follow directly from the categorization of an input. For example, imagine that you arrive home and are greeted by a four-legged furry friend. As well as identifying him as good old Rufus, you might be able to classify him as a living creature, an animal, a mammal, a canine, a dog, a pet, or a mongrel. Some categories *overlap*, as in this example. Others are *mutually exclusive*. Since the categories *dog* and *pet* overlap, there is no contradiction in thinking of Rufus as a dog as well as a pet. But since *dog* and *cat* are mutually exclusive, he certainly cannot be both a dog and a cat. Knowing the category to which something belongs thus provides us with a great deal of information about it. By knowing the category of an object (e.g., *dog*), we can derive some other categories the object must be in (e.g., *animal*), some it might be in (e.g., *pet*), and some it can't be in (e.g., *cat*). Such derivations are what make categorization such a powerful tool for organizing memory and thought.

Categories are such a ubiquitous part of the way we view the world that imagining what the world would be like without them is difficult. For example, imagine that you are shown a set of pictures of common objects, spread out in a random order on a table. These pictures may be of such items as a cow, a rose, a desk, a horse, a pansy, and a table. If you were asked to group the pictures into sets of items that go together, you would undoubtedly divide them into categories such as furniture, animals, and flowers. That is, you would use the semantic categories of English to perform the task.

But certain types of brain damage can deprive a person of these natural categories, and in this case the obviousness of these categories disappears. When Shanon (1978) asked such a brain-damaged patient to sort pictures, he appeared unable to use the obvious categories. Rather, he divided up the pictures according to various idiosyncratic criteria. For example, during one test he put all the flowers in a category with domestic animals, justifying his classification of the flowers by noting that "these are small, and are around the house. Therefore, they are domestic animals. They cannot be wild." Such failures to appreciate natural categories do not occur in isolation. Rather, they form part of a general, severe disturbance of the person's ability to understand and produce language. We will discuss disorders of language more fully in Chapter 15.

Categorization is an essential function of the cognitive system, one that is vital to memory, reasoning, problem solving, and language. This chapter will therefore set the stage for the chapters that follow. Let us begin by examining the ways in which categories can be represented in memory.

## REPRESENTATION OF CATEGORIES

When we consider the varied nature of categories, such as *alphabetic character, dog, winter,* and *tropical vacation,* we clearly see that different kinds of categories have different kinds of representations in memory. Representations of semantic categories are termed *definitions.* A definition, as we will use the term here, corresponds to information stored with a category concept that can be used to determine whether any instance is a member of the category. This usage of the term is quite different from the standard usage associated with a dictionary definition.

### Enumeration

The simplest kind of definition is *enumeration.* For example, we really have no way to define what constitutes a letter of the English alphabet other than to list all twenty-six of them. Anything on the list, like *E*, is an English letter; anything not on the list, like < , is not. Another way of enumerating category instances, besides listing them, is to define a rule (see Chapter 3) for enumerating category members. For example, when you learn how to count, you learn a rule for enumerating all the positive integers. By learning the rule, you learn how to generate all the instances of a category of infinite size.

A rule for enumerating the instances of a category is represented by a type of schema (see Chapter 3) called a *generative schema.* A generative schema begins with an initial representation or representations and generates a sequence of items by repeatedly applying some operation or operations to the representation created by a previous application of the operations. For example, you can produce the notes of a scale by starting with an initial note and repeatedly raising it by a fixed increment. Some generative schemas, like the scale, generate only a finite number of items, whereas other schemas, such as counting, can generate an indefinitely large number of items. Whenever one would say that a sequence is being generated by a rule, the underlying procedure constitutes a generative schema.

Generative schemas for enumeration rules are very important because even though memory can contain only a finite number of concepts, a generative schema allows you to deal with the infinite variety of nature by creating new concept nodes as needed. You can use your ability to enumerate things to place them in more than one category. For example, *I* can be both a letter and a Roman numeral. Similarly, you can divide large categories into smaller ones and combine small ones into larger ones. For example, C is a consonant, a member of the alphabet, and a written character. The ability to enumerate is essentially the ability to give a *name* to anything. When you name something, you place it in a category with all the other things that have the same name.

Clearly, you can use this ability to place *anything* in the same category. If you wanted to, you could classify every object in the world as belonging to the same category by simply giving each object the same name. An arbitrary name is called a *symbol*. Using logical symbols, such as *A, B,* and *C,* you can reason and deduce properties that will be true of all categories. For example, logically, if all *A*'s are *B*'s, and all *B*'s are *C*'s, then all *A*'s must be *C*'s. Since *A, B,* and *C* can be the names of *any* categories of objects, we know this conclusion will be true regardless of what the specific categories are.

The ability to perform this kind of abstract thought (which we will discuss in more detail in Chapter 11) is clearly one of the glories of reason. But, in fact, the vast majority of everyday categories consist of instances that have much in common. For example, objects may be categorized on the basis of similar appearance (e.g., *birds, cats, dogs*), similar functions (e.g., *furniture, tools*), or similar roles (e.g., *citizens*). Let us see how such categories are defined in terms of different types of similarities.

## Definition by Properties

Many categories include a visuospatial representation and/or some other perceptual representation that may be compared with an input representation. Any object that adequately matches the representation is then an instance of the category. Most concepts corresponding to concrete objects (e.g., *cat, tree,* and *rock*) are basically defined by perceptual representations. We will discuss such concepts in detail in a later section when we examine natural categories.

**Functional and relational definitions.**    Other categories are defined by their characteristic *functions*, or uses. A *weapon*, for example, is anything that can serve to inflict injury. Other categories defined at least in part by function are *tools, furniture,* and *jewelry*. A *functional definition* is represented in memory by some schema that represents how a category instance is used. That is, you need weapons, tools, etc., to *do* certain things. These categories with functional definitions are well entrenched; i.e., they are familiar concepts corresponding to single words, which people use in many contexts.

However, functional definitions are also a primary source of what Barsalou (1983) has termed *ad hoc* categories—i.e., categories that may be created for use on a particular occasion. For example, consider the following situation (Barsalou 1983, p. 215):

> Roy was in big trouble. The Mafia had a contract out on him for double-crossing them. He knew he couldn't continue living in Las Vegas or he'd be dead in a week. So he started thinking quickly about alternatives.

This scenario leads to an *ad hoc* functional category, *ways to escape from the Mafia*. Instances of this category might include *sail around the world, go to Mexico,* and *become a drunk in Detroit*. An indefinitely large number of diverse exemplars of this category are possible to imagine. What these instances have in common is their function—they are all potential solutions to the problem of escaping from the Mafia.

In general, useful functional categories are often defined as "potential means of achieving a certain type of goal." The creation of new functional categories is thus closely tied to the process of problem solving, which we will discuss in Chapter 12. Although many such categories will simply be used in a particular context and then discarded, those categories relevant to general and recurring goals may be stored in memory and perhaps *lexicalized*, i.e., tagged with a single-word name. For example, *agriculture* is a category roughly defined as "ways to cultivate food."

*Relational definitions* are similar to functional ones. A category may be defined by the relationships between its instances and some other concept in memory. An *orphan*, for example, is "a child whose parents are dead." Kinship terms, such as *mother, father, uncle,* and *niece,* all have relational definitions. So do occupation names such as *employer* or *servant*.

Words for relational categories are frequently invented and added to the language. Often a verb is turned into a noun; thus someone who writes, as an occupation, can be called a *writer*. Novel categories can readily be created and understood. For example, you can probably form a good idea of what a *coconut polisher* might be (though it might be either a tool or an occupation). Note that once a new category term arises, its definition can become more specific. For instance, just being able to write doesn't make you a writer;

you have to write as a serious professional or creative enterprise (e.g., filling out your income tax form isn't enough).

**Mixed definitions.**    These different types of definitions are not mutually exclusive. Many categories are defined by a mixture of perceptual and functional or relational features. For example, the basic definition of *doctor* is relational: "a person who practices medicine." But we also know what doctors typically look like.

Other good examples of categories defined by both perceptual representations and functional procedures are container terms, such as *glass, cup, vase,* and *bowl.* All of these terms are in part defined functionally. That is, any instance of a container must be shaped so that it can hold something inside it; e.g., a container requires a solid bottom, solid sides, and an opening at the top. The perceptual features of a container are therefore in part dictated by its function. But what determines the particular category that a container falls into? A *glass,* for example, used to always be made of glass. But now a glass is often made of some other material, like plastic. You might suspect that a *cup* is always distinguished by having a handle. But a Chinese teacup, for example, has no handle; neither does a Styrofoam cup. Also, glasses tend to be used for cold liquids, cups for hot. But a "typical" cup (like a coffee cup) is still a cup even if you use it to drink cold lemonade.

Actually, an object can be a certain type of container if it has *either* the right perceptual representation *or* the right functional properties. This concept was nicely demonstrated in experiments by William Labov (1973). He showed college students pictures of containers like the pictures in Figure 5.2. All of these drawings resemble cups to some degree, but some objects are rather strange. The cups numbered 10 through 19 illustrate a variety of shapes: cylindrical (10–12), conical (13–15), square (18), and triangular (19). Some of these objects might not always be called *cup.* Object 17, for example, with its long stem, might be referred to as a *goblet.* The cups of particular interest are numbered 1 through 9. Moving across the top from cup 1 to cup 4, the ratio of the width to the depth increases. The wider cups look more like bowls (with handles) than like cups. Similarly, the ratio of depth to width increases from cup 1 down the left column to cup 9. Here the taller cups look more and more like vases.

Labov set out to answer two questions: (1) How will these shape variations influence the names people use? (2) Will the function of the objects also influence naming? To answer these questions, he presented each of the drawings to his subjects in a random order and asked the subjects to name each object. He did this experiment a number of times for each subject, and each time he varied the instructions slightly. Thus in the neutral context subjects were told to simply imagine the object in someone's hand. In the food context subjects were asked to imagine the object sitting on a dinner table and filled with

**Figure 5.2  Series of cuplike objects. (From Labov 1973.)**

mashed potatoes. Finally, in the flowers context they were told to imagine the object on a shelf, with cut flowers in it.

    Figure 5.3 shows the results for one group of eleven subjects. Figure 5.3(a) gives the frequencies with which the drawings were called *cup* or *bowl* as the relative width increased. In the neutral context (solid lines) the most frequent name was *cup*, except for the very widest object. But the pattern was very different for the food context (dashed line). The frequencies for *cup* were quite a bit lower, while *bowl* was a frequent response for objects of medium or large

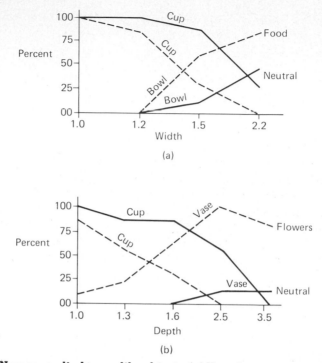

**Figure 5.3    Names applied to cuplike objects: (a) Use of names *cup* and *bowl* in food and neutral contexts; (b) use of names *cup* (or *mug*) and *vase* in flowers and neutral contexts. (From Labov 1973.)**

width. Note that the very "best" cup (width-to-depth ratio of 1.0) was always called *cup*, even in the food context. But the names for the wider objects were heavily influenced by their imagined function.

Figure 5.3(b) shows that similar results were obtained for the use of *cup* versus *vase* in the neutral and flowers contexts. When subjects imagined the objects holding flowers, use of the name *cup* (actually either *cup* or *mug*) greatly diminished, while use of the name *vase* greatly increased. But, again, the effect of context was much more pronounced for the relatively strange-looking objects (i.e., the deepest ones), while the normal-shaped object was usually called a *cup* even if it held flowers.

Labov's results clearly show that *both* perceptual representations (like shape) and functions (such as being used for eating food or displaying flowers) influence the way people categorize objects. His work also shows that no single part of the concept need *always* be present to make an object a satisfactory category member. For example, something may be called a cup *either* if it looks like a standard cup *or* if it has an unusual shape and is used to drink coffee. This situation, in which there may be little in common to all members of a category, has important theoretical consequences, which we will discuss in some detail later in the chapter.

## Categories and Memory Organization

So far, we have discussed the kinds of information that constitute definitions of individual categories. However, we must also consider how the entire category system is represented in memory. Categorization depends on the organization of human memory. Each of us has an incredible amount of information stored in our memory. Yet by and large, we can find the information that we need in a very efficient fashion. Thus if you are given a simple problem like, "Name an animal that purrs," you don't find yourself searching through what you know about the history of Greece. Rather, you immediately start checking what you know about types of animals. How do you find the right information in memory?

The answer involves the way memory is organized. Recall our discussion in Chapter 1, in which we gave the example of a dictionary. Because the words in a dictionary are organized alphabetically, you can use your knowledge of the order of the alphabet to find the exact place where a particular definition will be. Similarly, we saw that human memory is indexed by the features that make up the perceptual representation of the input, and that activation from these features converges on and activates the memory representation most similar to that of the input. The perceptual-feature organization described in Chapter 2 is only one of two levels of the organization used to locate a representation. Right now we will take our first look at the other major level: the organization of the semantic code.

## Organization of the Semantic Code

**Simple associative network.**    Figure 5.4 shows how a tiny fragment of categorical information might be organized in memory. The figure shows representations in the auditory and visual perceptual codes, illustrated by words between slashes and by pictures, respectively, as well as a fragment of the semantic code. Let us first consider the *semantic code*. This code is shown in the form of a *network* of associations. In an associative network pieces of information are represented at *nodes* (the boldface words in Figure 5.4) connected by *arcs* (the lines in the figure). We emphasize that an associative network is simply a graphical means of representing the knowledge that a person has about a category system. People do not literally have such networks in their heads.

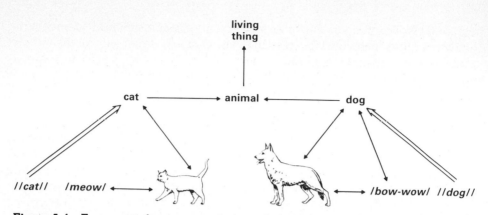

**Figure 5.4    Fragment of a conceptual network showing how words, semantic nodes, and perceptual information are associated.**

Suppose a child is shown a cat for the first time and told that it is called *cat*. How could this information be represented in a network? First, a node representing the *concept* of a cat would be created in the semantic code. In Figure 5.4 concept nodes are represented by words in boldface. The word *cat* is then established as the name for the concept. Speech sounds encoded in an auditory code are represented by the words (in boldface and italic) between double slashes (//***cat***//). The double arrows (⇒) represent the relation "is the name of." So //***cat***// ⇒ **cat** means that //***cat***// is the name of the concept **cat.**

Now we have a name attached to a concept node. But the concept has no meaning until it is connected to some information in memory. The lines with double-headed arrows (↔) in the figure associate representations in different codes. The **cat** node in the category system is associated with both visuospatial representations (represented by a picture) and sound representations (represented by a word between single slashes). In addition, the visuospatial and sound representations are directly associated, so seeing a cat will remind the child of its sound.

The child may also learn that a cat is an animal. This information is a connection between two concepts in the semantic code. In the figure this relation is represented by an arrow (→) that means "is a." The arrow signifies the direction of the relation (i.e., a cat is an animal, not vice versa). The ability to relate one concept to another is a fundamental human capacity.

Figure 5.4 also represents information about the concept of a dog. Notice that the concepts **cat** and **dog** converge at **animal.** The representation therefore contains the information that both dogs and cats are animals. The concept **animal** is connected to **living thing.** Since the "is a" relation is a transitive one, we could use the network to answer the question, "Is a cat a living thing?" (A cat is an animal, and an animal is a living thing; therefore a cat is a living thing.) Notice that some abstract concepts, like **living thing,** will not be connected directly to any perceptual information.

As shown in Figure 5.4, most concepts that humans use involve more than one code. Different types of codes are integrated into a network of associations. Because of this network, you can become aware of the entire concept of **cat** when you see or hear one of its associated features. A major property of human memory is its *multicomponent nature* (Bower 1967). The semantic code provides the basic organization into which all the different kinds of representations are integrated.

**Elaborated networks and propositions.**    The network depicted in Figure 5.4 is oversimplified in many respects. First, an additional node is needed to describe the appearance of the written word *cat.* Also, the word *cat* is attached to only one concept node in the figure. But a person might use the word *cat* to refer to domestic cats, all felines including jaguars and lions, a kind of whip (cat-o'-nine-tails), or a Caterpillar tractor. In an expanded network each of these different meanings of the word *cat* would be represented by a separate concept node.

Not only can one word correspond to several concepts, but also some concepts may have no corresponding word. For example, we have no familiar word in English for the concept corresponding to *either an uncle or an aunt.* But there still might be a node corresponding to that concept in the memory network. These examples show that while concepts are associated with words, they are not the same thing. So it is not correct to say that we always "think in words."

Another limitation of Figure 5.4 is that it represents only the "is a" relation between concepts. This relation is very important because it corresponds to our ability to classify concepts into hierarchical categories (e.g., both dogs and cats are members of the category *animal*). However, there are also many other relations between concepts. For example, we would also want to be able to represent the information that some dogs *chase* cats. A representation in the semantic code that expresses a particular relationship between two or more concepts is called a *propositional representation,* or simply a *proposition.*

As this example suggests, a proposition can be thought of as the representation of the meaning of a simple sentence. We noted earlier that an associative network is simply one way of representing a category system. Theorists often use other types of notation to represent propositions. One common convention is to place the arguments in parentheses preceded by the relation. Thus the proposition "dogs chase cats" would simply be written as follows: chase (dogs, cats). Similarly, the fact that a cat is an animal, which we represented graphically in Figure 5.4, might be represented as the following simple proposition: is (cat, animal).

Because a proposition is based solely on the semantic code, it is an abstract type of representation that does not include visuospatial or other perceptual codes. The propositional code corresponds to the relational links within the semantic code plus the nodes representing concepts. Much work has been done on how propositions are represented in memory (Anderson 1983; Anderson and Bower 1973; Kintsch 1974; Norman and Rumelhart 1975), but we will not describe representations of such complexity here.

Another serious limitation of the simple representation in Figure 5.4 is that it does not contain information about specific cats, such as your girlfriend's cat, your grandmother's cat, and Garfield the cat. If a concept such as those shown in Figure 5.4 can apply to more than one entity in the world, it is called a *category* or *type*. If a concept contains a visuospatial representation that can only apply to a single entity in the world, it is called an *instance* or *token*. The information defining instance concepts includes the category concepts of which they are instances. Thus instances and categories are stored together in the same associative network. As we will see, evidence suggests that comparison processes use instances both to make categorization judgments and to learn new categories.

## NATURAL CATEGORIES

In the previous section we described how category definitions can be based on enumeration, appearance, functions, or relations. In this section we will describe in more detail how *natural categories* are defined and used. The term *natural categories* refers to the categories used by people in everyday life. Most research on categories has concentrated on categories of objects, and that will be our focus here. However, we will also touch on the representation of categories of attributes, actions, and events.

Natural categories are defined in terms of perceptual similarity. Let us begin by considering a set of categories that are defined along a basic perceptual dimension—color terms.

### Structure of Color Categories

The first thing you need to know about color categories is that perceived color (more specifically, hue) is primarily a function of the wavelength of light. As wavelength increases, the color of light moves through the categories *violet, blue, green, yellow, orange,* and *red,* in that order. But as you might imagine, the boundaries of the color categories are usually difficult to judge. You would probably have trouble deciding whether some hues are better described as *orange* or *red.* And anthropologists have found that speakers of different languages have different color boundaries. In fact, languages vary considerably in the number of major color categories they have. Whereas English has eleven, the Dani tribe of New Guinea has only two.

Color terminology was first studied in the context of investigations of what is known as the *Sapir-Whorf hypothesis* (Sapir 1944; Whorf 1956). The Sapir-Whorf hypothesis states that the way people perceive and organize the world is heavily influenced by the categories of their language. Researchers have examined the relation between the verbal codes for colors and memory for them. For instance, Brown and Lenneberg (1954) demonstrated that people are better able to recognize colors previously shown to them if the colors are highly *codable*. Codability is really a composite of several variables, of which agreement in naming is a major one. That is, if a color has one name used by almost all speakers of the language (e.g., *pure red*), it is easy to remember and recognize. But if people disagree on what to call it (one calls it *rusty orange*, another *desert red*, another *dried orange peel*, etc.), then recognition memory is poor. These results were consistent with the Sapir-Whorf hypothesis, since an aspect of language (codability) appeared to influence a cognitive process (recognition memory).

However, the view that color cognition is mainly determined by the categories afforded by language was challenged by two anthropologists, Berlin and Kay (1969). They began by identifying the *basic color terms* in ninety-eight languages. To be classified as basic, a color term has to satisfy four criteria:

1. It must be expressed as one *morpheme*, or meaning-bearing lexical unit. This criterion rules out compounds like *salmon-colored*.

2. Its meaning cannot be included in that of another term. This criterion rules out *crimson*, which is included in *red*.

3. It must not be restricted to a small class of objects. This criterion rules out *blond*, which applies only to hair and perhaps furniture.

4. It must be a common term, like *purple*, rather than *magenta*.

Berlin and Kay then proceeded to map out the domain of the basic color terms in twenty languages by interviewing native speakers of each language. They showed each subject a set of 329 different-colored chips and asked the subject to answer two questions about each basic color term in his or her language:

1. What chips would you be at all willing to call by this term?
2. What chips are the best, most typical examples of the term?

The first question was designed to determine the boundaries of the color categories, while the second was designed to pick out the most central example, the *focal color*.

The results were quite remarkable. People were not at all consistent in drawing boundaries between the basic terms. In contrast, speakers of different languages were very consistent in selecting the focal colors (i.e., the best red, green, blue, etc.). Even though the boundaries of color categories varied from language to language, the focal colors were universal. In fact, speakers of the same language showed just as much variability in their placement of focal colors as did speakers of different languages. In addition, by matching focal colors across languages, Berlin and Kay discovered that all languages draw their basic color terms from a set of eleven. In English (which has all of them) these terms are *black, white, red, green, yellow, blue, brown, purple, pink, orange,* and *gray.*

So apparently, the focal exemplars of color categories are *not* determined by the specific language someone speaks. But can focal colors influence cognition even if they do not correspond to linguistic categories? To answer this question, one would like to find people who speak a language that has no basic color terms. Would they nevertheless show superior memory for focal colors? While no language seems to be altogether lacking in color terms, the Dani of New Guinea speak a language that comes close. As mentioned earlier, they have only two basic color terms: *mili* (roughly "dark") and *mola* (roughly "light"). Rosch (formerly Heider) performed a number of experiments to investigate the Dani memory for colors. In experiments very much like those of Brown and Lenneberg, she showed that the Dani remember focal colors better than nonfocal ones (Heider 1972). The Dani could also *learn* names for the focal colors more quickly than they could for nonfocal colors (Rosch 1973). Furthermore, the Dani judge the similarity of colors in very much the same way as English speakers do (Heider and Olivier 1972).

Rosch's results appeared to demonstrate that focal colors are primary in a way that does not depend on language. However, Lucy and Schweder (1979) examined the set of color chips that Rosch had used in her experiments with the Dani and found that the nonfocal chips were less easily discriminated from others in the set than were focal chips, even when memory was not involved. Thus while focal colors appear to have a special status as the central examples of color categories, as evidenced by the work of Berlin and Kay (1969), whether focality has a direct impact on memorability remains unclear.

However, focal colors do apparently determine color categories, not vice versa. But what determines which colors are focal? The answer lies in the physiology of human color perception. The *opponent process theory* of color vision (DeValois and Jacobs 1968; Hering 1920; Jameson and Hurvich 1955) postulates three types of color detectors: one for brightness (black vs. white) and two for hue (red vs. green and yellow vs. blue). This system has six points of maximal response, corresponding to six of the eleven basic color terms: *black, white, red, green, yellow,* and *blue.* In the first months of life infants only respond to differences among these broad color categories (Bornstein 1976).

These six terms are also especially prominent in the historical development of languages. After looking at almost a hundred languages, Berlin and Kay (1969) discovered that color terms follow a clear sequence, which is as follows:

$$
\begin{bmatrix} \text{white} \\ \text{black} \end{bmatrix} \quad \text{then} \quad [\text{red}] \quad \text{then} \quad \begin{bmatrix} \text{green} \\ \text{yellow} \\ \text{blue} \end{bmatrix} \quad \text{then} \quad [\text{brown}] \quad \text{then} \quad \begin{bmatrix} \text{purple} \\ \text{pink} \\ \text{orange} \\ \text{gray} \end{bmatrix}
$$

In other words, if a language (like Dani) has only two color terms, they correspond to *white* and *black*. If a language has three terms, they always correspond to *white, black,* and *red.* If a language has four color terms, the fourth will correspond to either *green, yellow,* or *blue.* Note that the first six terms to appear are always the six primary colors of the visual system.

We still are left with the question of where the remaining five basic color terms come from. An elegant explanation of the development of the later terms has been suggested by Kay and McDaniel (1978). [The theory in terms of which Kay and McDaniel couch their explanation has been criticized by Mervis and Roth (1981), but their critique does not affect the account as it is described here.] Kay and McDaniel's explanation is illustrated in Figure 5.5. Figure 5.5(a) graphs the hypothetical goodness of the terms *yellow* and *red* when they are applied to a range of wavelengths. Each term applies best to its focal color (the peaks of the bell-shaped curves), and it applies less and less well to colors farther from the focal point.

Now if this hypothetical language could add one more color category, where would be the most useful place to put the new focal point? Clearly, it is right in the middle of the "valley" between *yellow* and *red.* With only *yellow* and *red* in the color vocabulary the language has no term that applies well in this region, and speakers would be unsure about what term to use. This situation is remedied in Figure 5.5(b) with the addition of *orange* to the language. The new focal point is placed so that *orange* applies best at the very point where *yellow* and *red* apply worst. Note that *orange* is a relatively narrow category, one that fills the gap between *yellow* and *red* without competing in the regions in which *yellow* or else *red* applies well.

Kay and McDaniel argue that the five later basic colors emerge in this way to fill gaps in the regions in which the first six terms do not apply well. But why only eleven basic terms in all? Actually, this number may only be a kind of accident of the present moment in linguistic history. More basic color terms may yet emerge as languages continue to evolve. In fact, Russian may be developing a twelfth basic term, *goluboy* ("light blue"). In English, conceivably, a word like *turquoise* may one day acquire the status of a basic term, filling a

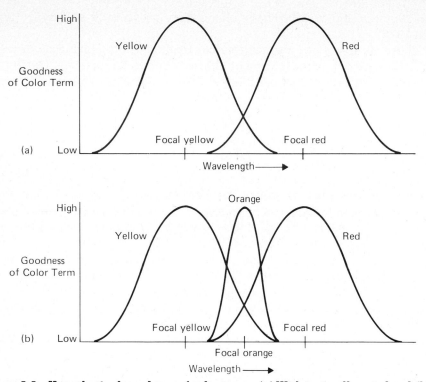

**Figure 5.5  Hypothetical goodness of color terms: (a) With just *yellow* and *red;* (b) with the addition of *orange*.**

gap between *blue* and *green*. As you can see, the study of color categories has brought together work in anthropology, linguistics, cognitive psychology, and sensory psychology in an extremely fruitful way—even producing predictions about the future evolution of language.

## From Focal Colors to Focal Instances

Are categories other than color organized around focal instances? We have already suggested that they are. For example, Labov's cup with a width-to-depth ratio of 1.0 (cup 1 in Figure 5.2) appeared to be the best example of a cup. It might be termed the *focal instance* of the category *cup.* Of course, the focal instance of *cup* is probably not as directly linked to the physiology of vision as are the focal colors.

What kind of evidence indicates that natural categories have focal instances? Three major lines of research support this interpretation:

1. People reliably rate some category members as more typical than others (Rips, Shoben, and Smith 1973; Rosch 1973). For example, people rate robins as more typical than geese for the category *bird*.

2. When people are asked to list instances of a category, they reliably produce some items both earlier and more frequently than others (Battig and Montague 1969). Furthermore, items that are produced most readily tend to be those that people also consider most typical of the category (Rosch 1973).

3. Both of these measures (typicality ratings and frequency of production) predict the speed with which people classify instances as members of a category. For example, people can verify the truth of the sentence *A robin is a bird* more quickly than they can verify *A goose is a bird* (Glass, Holyoak, and O'Dell 1974; Rips *et al.* 1973; Rosch 1973; Wilkins 1971).

In the case of color categories we saw that focal instances appear to be independent of differences in language and culture. Color categories are independent because they are closely tied to the physiology of vision. Also, evidence indicates that symmetrical geometric forms are universal focal instances (Rosch 1973), again as a result of how the process of perception operates (see Chapter 4). Are all focal instances the product of bottom-up perceptual processes, and are they independent of language and culture? Surely not. The structure of most categories is undoubtedly influenced by the instances actually encountered. For example, an Indian living in the Amazon forest, who is familiar with a toucan but has never heard of a robin, will have a different focal instance for *bird* than you do. Later in this chapter we will discuss how category representations can be learned from experience with exemplars.

## From Focal Instances to Prototypes

One hypothesis about category representation is that people are able to abstract a *prototype* of a category from the instances that they see. A prototype is a concept that shares many properties with most or all of the instances, so it reflects the central tendency of the category. For example, a prototypical bird for most of us would probably be one about the size of a robin that had feathers and wings, flew, ate worms, built a nest, laid eggs, lived in trees, etc.

According to the prototype hypothesis, a representation of an instance is compared with the prototype of a category to determine whether the instance is a member of the category. If the instance has a sufficient degree of similarity to the prototype, it will be judged to be a member of the category. This proposal explains how degrees of typicality arise. For example, a robin is a more typical bird than an ostrich because it is more similar to the *bird* prototype.

Note that a prototype, unlike a focal instance, need not correspond to any actual instance of the category. Rather, it is a kind of average of the category instances.

## Basic-Level Categories

The prototype hypothesis was motivated by the belief that the categorization of familiar objects in the environment ultimately depends on basic, bottom-up, perceptual processes. After all, most natural categories include instances that are similar in shape and hence look alike. Thus similarity within the visuospatial code is a major way of defining categories. If a group of instances have visuospatial representations that are more similar to each other than to those of any other instances, then perhaps a category is formed either directly from these focal instances or by extracting a prototype from them.

One implication of this view is that there is a *basic level* at which people naturally divide the world into alternative categories (Rosch, Mervis, Gray, Johnson, and Boyes-Braem 1976). This level maximizes the perceptual similarities *among* instances of the same category as well as maximizing the differences *between* instances of different categories. For example, consider the hierarchical sequence *kitchen table, table,* and *furniture. Furniture* is a relatively abstract category, one that cannot be defined by a single prototypical visuospatial representation common to all instances. *Table,* on the other hand, has a clear perceptual representation ("flat top," "usually four legs," etc.) in the shape subcode. Also, instances of *table* are quite distinct from instances of related categories, like *chair.* What about *kitchen table?* It also has a clear perceptual representation, but one that is very similar to the representation of close alternatives, like *living room table.* In some sense, then, *table* is a basic-level category. It is the concrete-category level with a representation maximally distinguishable from alternative categories within a perceptual code.

Rosch *et al.* found that people can classify pictures most quickly into basic-level categories. For example, suppose subjects are shown a photograph of a kitchen table. They can classify the photograph as a *table* faster than they can classify it as either *kitchen table* or *furniture.* This result suggests that basic-level categories correspond to categories that people use in the recognition of objects. Rosch *et al.* also noted that basic-level categories are the earliest that children use to name or sort objects.

Murphy and Smith (1982) replicated Rosch and her colleagues' (1976) natural-category results with artificial categories for four basic kinds of unusual tools, which were invented especially for the experiment. They confirmed that people use visuospatial representations to categorize instances. In their experiments they varied the level at which a single visuospatial representation of the category best discriminated it from its alternatives, and they found that their pictures of tools were categorized most rapidly at this level.

If pictures of instances are categorized on the basis of their visuospatial representations, then an instance will be categorized most quickly at the basic level only if its perceptual representation is sufficiently similar to the proto-type. In fact, whereas typical instances are classified most quickly as members of the basic-level category, atypical instances are often classified more readily into subordinate categories. For example, although people can catego-rize a picture of a robin more quickly as a bird than as a robin, they can cate-gorize a picture of an ostrich more quickly as an ostrich than as a bird (Jolicoeur, Gluck, and Kosslyn 1984). The basic level thus seems to serve as the entry point into the category system only for typical instances.

### Family Resemblances

As we pointed out earlier, categories can have mixed definitions, so instances can be classified either on the basis of their appearance or on the basis of the functions they have or the roles they serve. For example, a tool specifically designed for pounding objects is called a *hammer*. Objects that satisfy this definition may differ widely in appearance (e.g., from clawhammers to jack-hammers). However, even when a category is functionally defined, typical category members often have a characteristic appearance, as in the case of cups and bowls. Also, most people would probably agree that a clawhammer is a more typical hammer than a jackhammer.

But as functional categories become broader (e.g., *tool, vehicle, toy*), there is no longer a single prototype for the entire category. For categories involving mixed definitions, instance *A* may be quite similar to *B* in appearance but not in function. Instance *C* may be similar to *B* in function but not in appearance. Therefore such a category may include instances that are quite dissimilar and for which the properties sufficient for defining the category are not obvious.

The philosopher Ludwig Wittgenstein (1953) demonstrated this point by raising a deceptively simple question: "What is the definition of *game?*" This question is difficult to answer. Is there really *anything* in common across such diverse games as professional football, amateur golf, Monopoly, tag, chess, and solitaire? You might say that all have rules of some sort, but that really isn't enough to define *game*. Not only, in turn, is defining *rule* difficult, but not everything with rules is a game. After all, mathematics has rules, but solving calculus problems isn't usually considered a game.

Wittgenstein argued that no necessary and sufficient features define *game*. Nor does there seem to be an obvious *game* prototype. But then what makes all the various games fall into one category? Wittgenstein proposed that the instances of the category *game* are tied together by a principle of *fam-*

*ily resemblance.* Members of a family often look alike in various ways. For example, Susan may look a bit like her brother Jeff and may also look a bit like her cousin Mary. But Jeff and Mary may not really look alike at all. What makes a family resemblance is *successive overlap* in the features of instances; e.g., Jeff looks like Susan, and Susan looks like Mary, although *in a different way.*

So it seems to be with games. Professional sports resemble amateur sports; team sports resemble team bridge; bridge resembles solitaire; solitaire is perhaps a bit like golf (or at least like putting practice). The properties of games overlap, even though no property is necessarily common to all games. If we let letters represent properties, then the following four concepts illustrate a simple family resemblance structure: *AB, BC, CD, DA.* Other broad functional categories besides *game,* such as *tool* and *toy,* may also be defined by the family resemblance principle.

Other categories that have mixed definitions are category terms that are associated with both prototype definitions and *technical definitions.* The latter constitute core definitions that may involve necessary and sufficient features. For example, if a *bird* is defined as a warm-blooded, egg-laying animal with feathers, then every animal that meets this criterion will be a bird, and those that do not meet it will not be. So if a geneticist developed a featherless chicken tomorrow, it would not be a bird by this definition. Technical definitions allow us to categorize the world in ways that are not possible on the basis of perceptual similarity alone. For example, the taxonomic categories used by biologists are based on anatomical similarities not apparent to the casual observer. Thus even though whales are more similar to the prototypical fish than to the prototypical mammal, in terms of technical definitions whales are classified as mammals rather than fish.

As we will see, many everyday categorization judgments are based on prototype definitions. But since educated people also are aware of the technical definitions, they can use such definitions to evaluate borderline instances, such as bats and whales. Of course, children and others who have never learned about technical definitions will think that a whale is a fish.

## Abstract Concepts

Even though superordinate categories such as *game* are relatively abstract, their instances are nonetheless physical objects and events. Natural categorization is apparently closely tied to the perception of the physical world. In fact, concepts that do *not* refer to physical objects—*abstract concepts* such as *beauty, truth,* and *liberty*—tend not to have clear instances and are extremely difficult to define. When Herrmann and Kay (1977) asked a group of college students to generate category terms, very few of the words they listed were abstract concepts. Such terms have no real perceptual representations, and most seem extremely vague. For example, try to make up a sentence that definitely sounds false by using only abstract concepts. With concrete concepts this task is easy; e.g., *Dogs are cats* is patently false. But with abstract concepts almost anything goes: *Truth is beauty, Beauty is truth, Love is anarchy* —all sound at least plausible (Glass, Eddy, and Schwanenflugel 1980).

So far, psychologists have generally had little to say about how abstract categories are represented. We do know that they are relatively difficult to comprehend and remember (see Chapter 7). However, political writers such as Stuart Chase (1938) and George Orwell (1949) have pointed out that abstract concepts *can* be used as categories and are powerful tools for manipulating human thought. As we will see in later chapters, category terms are important recall cues, and our interpretation of new information is strongly influenced by our recall of old information. As a result, our interpretation of an event may be heavily influenced by how it is categorized. For example, your attitude toward a guerrilla war you read about in the newspaper may differ a great deal depending on whether the guerrillas are described as "terrorists" or as "freedom fighters." Similarly, you will get one impression if you read that South Africa deters the native black population from migrating from tribal homelands. You will get a different impression if you read that the black population is confined in concentration camps.

A pleasant way of describing an unpleasant reality is called a *euphemism*. Many euphemisms are harmless (e.g., calling a janitor a *sanitary engineer*). People eventually come to see through euphemisms. For example, *disease* was originally a euphemism for *sickness*—literally, it meant "ill at ease." But it has since come to mean simply the underlying cause of a sickness. However, in the realm of politics the use of euphemisms is often simply an insidious way of lying. A common device is to use an innocuous-sounding abstraction to disguise reality. For example, in describing the fate of a South Korean passenger jet that flew over Soviet territory in 1983, initial Russian reports were that "the flight was terminated." This abstract phrase was chosen to suggest such possibilities as an unanticipated landing and thus obscure the cold reality—that a Soviet fighter plane had shot the airliner out of the sky.

## INDUCTION OF VISUAL CATEGORIES

The notion of mixed definitions raises the possibility that different components of a definition play different roles. Smith and Medin (1981) distinguish between the *core* of the category and the *identification procedure.* The core of the category is its definition. The identification procedure is the procedure by which the representation of an instance is categorized. In the categorization of an instance the identification procedure may make use of only parts of the conceptual representation that defines the category. For example, although a category node may be associated to both a prototype and to instance representations, only one or the other may be used to identify particular instances as belonging to the category. In this section we examine the contributions of prototype and instance representations to the identification of category members. Researchers have studied this topic by teaching observers an artificial category and then examining the speed and confidence with which they classify new instances as members.

### Investigations of the Prototype Hypothesis

Much of the work on category induction has been motivated by the hypothesis that people are able to abstract a prototype or central tendency of a category from presented instances. In prototype-learning experiments a common standard form or prototype is created, from which all category members are then derived by performing some transformation or distortion. The first major study of prototype learning was done by Attneave (1957). He showed that subjects could perform a memory task involving variants of a visual form more accurately if they had prior experience with the standard form. Attneave anticipated the main conclusions of later work, suggesting that observers learn three characteristics of a category: (1) its central tendency; (2) the dimensions along which its members differ; and (3) the degree of variability among the category members.

In a series of experiments Posner and Keele (1968, 1970) provided more direct evidence for prototype abstraction. The inputs used in their experiments were designed to be extremely unfamiliar to subjects—randomly constructed dot patterns. Five sample dot patterns are shown in Figure 5.6. To

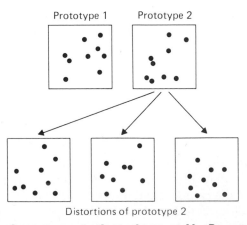

**Figure 5.6   Random dot patterns similar to those used by Posner and Keele (1968, 1970).**

construct a perceptual category, Posner and Keele began by choosing a pattern containing nine dots. This pattern was the category prototype. Each category member was then formed by randomly "jiggling" the dots in the prototype pattern, i.e., moving each dot some distance away from its position in the prototype pattern. Posner and Keele manipulated the variability of the categories by varying the distance that the dots were moved. If the dots were jiggled only a little to form each distorted pattern, the resulting category would be "tight" (low variability among instances); if the dots were jiggled quite a bit, the resulting category would be "loose" (high variability among instances). In Figure 5.6 the two top patterns are prototypes, and the three bottom patterns are possible distortions of the prototype at the top right.

In a typical experiment Posner and Keele (1970) had fifty college students learn sets of four distortions of each of four prototypes. The students were allowed to view the patterns until they were sure they had learned them all. Then they were given a new set of inputs to classify. The new set included seven patterns from each category: two old distortions that the student had seen before; two new distortions close to the prototype (small distortions); two new distortions far from the prototype (large distortions); and the prototype itself. The students were told to classify each pattern as rapidly as possible, and they were not told whether or not they were correct in their decisions.

The results of this experiment are shown in Table 5.1. Note that for the new patterns both reaction time and error rate increased with distance from the prototype. That is, the prototype itself was easiest to classify correctly, followed by the small distortions, with the large distortions being the most difficult. Also, while the old patterns were the very easiest to classify, the differ-

**TABLE 5.1** Error Percentage and Reaction Time of Correct Classifications When Test Was Immediate or After a One-Week Delay

| Test measure | Test time | Pattern type | | | |
| --- | --- | --- | --- | --- | --- |
| | | Old distortion | Prototype (new) | New small distortion | New large distortion |
| Percent error | Immediate | 20 | 32 | 44 | 56 |
| | One-week delay | 29 | 34 | 46 | 58 |
| Reaction time (in seconds) | Immediate | 2.88 | 2.93 | 3.62 | 3.75 |
| | One-week delay | 2.76 | 2.92 | 3.20 | 3.52 |

*Source:* From Posner and Keele (1970).

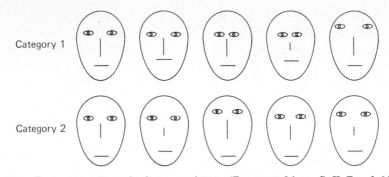

**Figure 5.7    Two categories of schematic faces. (Reprinted from S. K. Reed, 1972. Pattern recognition and categorization.** *Cognitive Psychology* **3: 382–407.)**

ence in accuracy between the old patterns and the prototype decreased after a one-week delay. These results suggest that the prototype, which was never seen during training, was less subject to forgetting than were the specific patterns originally learned.

Reed (1972) obtained similar results with simple schematic faces. In one experiment he first showed his subjects five faces labeled "category 1" and another five faces labeled "category 2" (Figure 5.7). Then the subjects saw twenty-five new faces, one at a time, and had to classify each face into one of the two categories. Subjects were given 12 seconds to make each decision. Reed was interested in what kinds of information subjects would use to classify the new faces. He compared several alternative mathematical models of how people classified the new faces, models that were derived from different hypotheses. In particular, he compared models derived from the prototype and focal-instance hypotheses. The model that best described the subjects' classifications, as well as their introspections, was a kind of prototype model. Subjects seemed to abstract an idea of what the prototypical face was like for each category and then to classify each face into the category with the more similar prototype.

Rosch, Simpson, and Miller (1976) demonstrated that prototype learning will produce all the major phenomena that we cited earlier as evidence for the internal structure of natural categories. In their experiments subjects learned to classify three types of patterns (dot patterns, stick figures, and consonant/digit strings) into categories. As in the earlier work, the patterns that belonged in each category were derived from a common prototype. After subjects had learned the categories, they performed three additional tasks: (1) They rated the typicality of the instances; (2) they tried to reproduce as many of the instances as possible; and (3) they classified the instances into categories as rapidly as possible. Rosch *et al.* found that performance in all these tasks was determined by similarity to the prototype. Just as with natural categories, the most prototypical instances were rated most typical, reproduced most frequently, and classified most quickly.

## Challenges to the Prototype Hypothesis

At this point you may feel that the hypothesis that people use prototypes to categorize new instances is firmly established. In fact, however, substantial evidence indicates that in many situations observers classify an exemplar by comparing it with an instance rather than with a prototype.

Recall that a prototype is a representation of the central tendency of category instances. The first problem for prototype theory is that people clearly know *more* than just the central tendency. As noted above, Attneave (1957) hypothesized that people learn the degree of *variability* among category exemplars. Posner and Keele (1968) found that categories based on more variable instances are initially harder to learn than categories based on less variable instances, but that observers are subsequently more likely to classify new inputs (especially highly distorted ones) as category members if the initial training instance is more variable (also see Homa and Vosburgh 1976). Fried and Holyoak (1984) had subjects learn two categories of complex perceptual forms, one based on low-variability instances and one based on high-variability instances. In a subsequent transfer test subjects were more likely to classify novel instances into the high-variability category, even for some patterns that were actually more similar to the prototype of the low-variability category.

A second problem for prototype theory hinges on its assumption that the prototype is based on an average of the presented instances. When groups of instances differ widely from each other, obviously a single prototype will not suffice as an adequate representation. In some experiments people have been presented with categories in which the most *frequent* feature values are not the same as the *average* values (in statistical terms the *mode* is different from the *mean*). For example, suppose people view instances of a category of faces in which the noses tend to be either very long or very short but seldom average-sized. A simple prototype model would predict that people would nonetheless average the presented instances and subsequently respond most favorably to novel faces with average-sized noses. In some experiments of this sort, however, people have tended to classify as category members novel instances with the frequent extreme feature values more often than the supposed prototype (Neumann 1977).

An alternative to prototype theory is that people base category judgments directly on remembered instances (Brooks 1978; Medin and Schaffer 1978).

According to this view, people do not use presented instances to abstract a summary category-level representation at all (or if they do, it plays little or no role in categorization). Instead, they simply memorize instances; a novel input is then classified into the category with remembered instances most similar to the novel one. People may not memorize all the instances, and their memory for individual instances may not be completely accurate, but some instances will be remembered to some degree. Focal instances, according to instance models, are not remembered better than any other instances. However, since in experiments such as those of Posner and Keele (1968) the pattern corresponding to the prototype was relatively similar to several presented instances—whereas an atypical novel instance was similar to few, if any, presented instances—the prototype will be classified more accurately.

Because the presented instances obviously provide detailed information about the structure of the category, instance models can account for all the evidence we have presented as support for prototype models. We noted earlier that Reed (1972) reported evidence that seemed to favor a prototype model over instance models. However, Medin and Schaffer's (1978) instance model differs from any of those that Reed considered with respect to the assumption that it makes about how the features of instances are combined to assess similarity. Essentially, Medin and Schaffer assume that a single bad mismatch greatly diminishes similarity. Suppose we consider instances that can

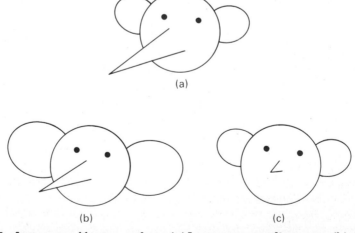

**Figure 5.8    Instances of feature values: (a) Large nose, medium ears; (b) medium nose, large ears; (c) small nose, medium ears. Face (a) differs from face (b) on two features (its ears are smaller and its nose is larger), and it differs from face (c) on only one feature (its nose). Yet face (a) looks more similar to face (b).**

be represented by two feature values, as in Figure 5.8. If face (a) is moderately similar to face (b) on both features, whereas it is highly similar to face (c) on one feature and highly dissimilar to face (c) on the other, then Medin and Schaffer's model predicts that people will judge face (a) to be more similar overall to face (b) than to face (c). If faces (b) and (c) are stored in memory as instances of different categories, and if face (a) is a novel input, then face (a) will tend to be classified into the same category as face (b).

It may well be the case that *both* category-level descriptions and stored instances play roles in categorization (Elio and Anderson 1981; Fried and Holyoak 1984). Remembered instances may play a direct role in classification decisions, especially early in learning. As learning proceeds, people may also tend to memorize as individuals not *any* category instance [as Medin and Schaffer (1978) assume] nor focal instances (which match the prototype well) but, rather, *atypical* instances, which represent significant deviations from the category schema. In fact, Light, Kayra-Stuart, and Hollander (1979) demonstrated that people are better able to recognize unusual faces rather than typical faces. Remembered atypical instances will be useful in classification because they provide information about a category that is not readily available from a prototype. Thus a person might conclude that a novel porpoiselike creature is a mammal just *because* it is similar to a porpoise (an atypical mammal) rather than because it has been successfully compared with a mammal prototype. The most reasonable synthesis of work on categorization, then, appears to be that people will use whatever part of a category's representation is most useful to identify an exemplar.

## RETRIEVAL AND COMPARISON OF CATEGORIES

A concept consists of a semantic node associated to other semantic nodes as well as to perceptual representations. In the previous section we saw that one identification procedure for an instance concept is to compare its perceptual representation with a category. Another procedure is to check whether the concept node of the instance is associated by an "is a" relation to the concept node of the category (see Figure 5.4). The identification of an instance through the comparison of its representation with a category will be called the *comparison process*. The identification of an instance by retrieving a category concept node from the instance concept node will be called the *retrieval process*.

Both identification procedures have been demonstrated in experiments on *sentence verification*. In a typical study of this sort a simple sentence such as *A lion is an animal* is presented to a subject in a tachistoscope or on a computer screen, and the experimenter measures how long the subject takes to decide whether the sentence is true or false. Such decisions usually take less than 2 seconds and are highly accurate. Because the decisions are made so quickly, people seldom have clear intuitions about what mental operations they use to make their judgments. However, the patterns of reaction times for different types of sentences afford some clues.

Theories of sentence verification have differed in their emphasis on retrieval versus comparison as the primary determinants of reaction time to verify sentences (Smith 1978). According to the retrieval view, people verify sentences by retrieving specific semantic relations (Collins and Quillian 1969; Glass and Holyoak 1975). For example, a person could verify that *A lion is an animal* by retrieving the "is a" relation that links *lion* and *animal* in the conceptual network. In contrast, the comparison view holds that verification hinges on a comparison of the properties included in the perceptual and other representations associated with each concept (McCloskey and Glucksberg 1979; Schaffer and Wallace 1970; Smith, Shoben, and Rips 1974). Thus a person could verify *A lion is an animal* by retrieving the properties associated with the typical lion and the typical animal and, by comparison, determining that the properties of *lion* include most of those associated with *animal* (e.g., "has a tail," "moves," etc.).

## Evidence for the Comparison Process

The comparison view is directly related to the prototype hypothesis, and it explains a major finding of studies of sentence verification: "True" decisions are made more quickly when the concepts are closely related, whereas some "false" decisions are made more slowly when the concepts are related. We have already discussed the prototype explanation of why people are faster to verify category statements for typical instances. Prototypes share more properties with typical instances than with atypical instances (Smith *et al.* 1974). For example, *robin* has characteristic bird properties such as small size and the ability to fly; *ostrich* does not. Prototype comparison operates by summing up the evidence indicating that the sentence is either true or false. So if the instance is typical, as in *A robin is a bird*, many shared properties will be found so that positive evidence will quickly accumulate until the criterion for a "true" decision is reached. But if the instance is atypical, as in *An ostrich is a bird*, less positive evidence will be found and the subject will consequently require more time to conclude that the sentence is true.

Similar mechanisms could explain the pattern often seen for "false" reaction times. For example, subjects take more time to conclude that *A bat is a bird* is false than to conclude that *A chair is a bird* is false. The reason, according to the comparison view, is that bats share many properties with the prototypical bird; chairs share virtually none. As a result, for *A chair is a bird* multiple mismatches between the properties of *chair* and *bird* will quickly accumulate and lead to a "false" response. But for *A bat is a bird* the subject will encounter a good deal of misleading positive evidence (e.g., bats and birds both fly).

## Evidence for the Retrieval Process

Comparison theories of sentence verification thus have much to commend them. However, other evidence indicates that their basic assumption—that all semantic relations are computed from an overall comparison of property relations—is too restrictive. Rather, other relations also appear to be retrieved and used to verify sentences. The comparison view implies that some atypical instances could never be classified correctly. For example, most college students know that a porpoise is a mammal rather than a fish. But porpoises are visually similar to the prototype of fish. So if decisions were based solely on comparisons with a visual prototype, subjects would never be able to decide that *A porpoise is a fish* is a false sentence. One way a person could decide that a porpoise is actually not a fish is by using a technical definition, as we discussed earlier. Also, a person could have simply stored "is a mammal" as an explicit fact about porpoises and realize that an animal cannot be both a mammal and a fish.

A possible falsification strategy is thus to determine that two concepts are mutually exclusive instances of the same superordinate category; if they are, one of the concepts cannot be an instance of the other. If such a *contradiction strategy* were used, "false" decisions would be made relatively quickly if the two concepts shared a highly related superordinate (e.g., *A dog is a cat*). Holyoak and Glass (1975) found that such sentences, with highly related but clearly contradictory concepts, are rejected relatively quickly even though the concepts are highly similar in meaning. Other examples include *Valleys are mountains* and *Fruits are vegetables*. In all of these cases the two concepts are semantically opposites; i.e., *fruit* and *vegetable* are alternative types of edible plant.

Sentences containing direct semantic opposites, such as *Brothers are sisters* or *Boys are girls*, provide particularly clear examples. Such sentences are rejected more quickly than others in which the terms are paired again to make the contrast less direct, as in *Brothers are girls* or *Boys are sisters* (Glass, Holyoak, and Kiger 1979). For a sentence like *Brothers are sisters*, the salient contradiction between the meanings of the two words is detected relatively rapidly. These results and others (Glass *et al.* 1974; Lorch 1978, 1981; Schvaneveldt, Durso, and Mukherji 1982), which indicate that a high degree of relatedness can sometimes facilitate rather than hinder "false" decisions, suggest that a pure comparison model is inadequate as an explanation of sentence verification.

Another type of specific relation that can be retrieved and used to evaluate the truth of a sentence is the inverse of the "is a" relation—the relationship between a category and its subordinate instances. Holyoak and Glass (1975) provided evidence that instances can be used as *counterexamples* to disconfirm false generalizations such as *All birds are robins* (also see Lorch 1978). Such sentences can be rejected by retrieving an instance of the subject category that is not an instance of the predicate category. For example, a person could retrieve the fact that some birds are canaries; since canaries aren't robins, *canary* is a counterexample to the claim *All birds are robins*. If the sentence were changed to *Some birds are robins,* the counterexample would no longer be relevant. Counterexamples can also be used to reject some false sentences about properties. For example, you could decide that *All roses are red* is false by thinking of a yellow rose. Note that counterexamples can include personal experience. Remembering a particular yellow rose you saw last week would be enough to falsify the general claim that all roses are red.

## Synthesis of the Comparison and Retrieval Views

Such evidence for the role of retrieval of specific relations in sentence verification by no means implies that the comparison view is entirely incorrect. Collins and Loftus (1975) argued that *both* retrieval and comparison processes are used to verify sentences, and Lorch (1978) has provided experimental evidence in favor of such an integrated approach. In addition, Lorch

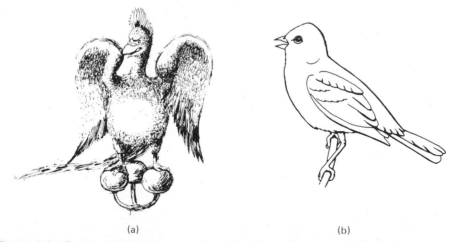

(a)                                              (b)

**Figure 5.9   Comparison process: (a) Novel instance; (b) prototype. The novel instance may be compared with the prototype in a decision to determine whether it is a member of the category.**

(1981) demonstrated that people can strategically vary their degree of reliance on retrieval of specific relations versus property comparisons.

In view of what we know about human memory and learning, this kind of flexibility is only to be expected. That is, property comparisons may be used to initially categorize new entities; but once the entity is familiar and an entry for it has been made in the person's semantic network, category relations may then simply be retrieved rather than recomputed on each occasion by comparison processes. For example, suppose you go to the zoo and see the strange new animal depicted in Figure 5.9(a). Someone asks you if it is a bird. In this case you cannot simply retrieve the answer from memory. Instead, you must compare the perceptual representations of the novel instance with those of typical birds or with a *bird* prototype (Figure 5.9b). Comparison processes are thus critical in evaluating novel instances and, as we saw earlier, in using instances to learn category representations in the first place.

## SUMMARY

Categorization is basic to human thought. Semantic categories are organized in a complex *associative network* that facilitates *retrieval* and *comparison* of concepts. Categories can be defined by *enumeration* or in terms of *features*, including perceptual, functional, and relational features. Natural categories have clear central tendencies and vague boundaries. The central tendency of a category may correspond to a set of *focal instances* or a more abstract *prototype*. A *basic level* of category structure maximizes similarity among instances of the same category while minimizing similarity among instances of different categories. Superordinate categories, which are more abstract than the basic level, are often defined by a principle of *family resemblance*.

Many categories are learned by *induction* from presented instances. Early studies of the induction of novel visual categories by adults provided support for the hypothesis that people abstract prototypes from instances. However, other evidence is problematic for simple versions of the prototype hypothesis and has been used to support alternative *instance models*. Apparently, categorization is based on elaborated prototypes plus some remembered instances. People evaluate the truth of sentences involving category relations on the basis of both retrieval and comparison processes.

## RECOMMENDED READINGS

The classic study of categories and categorization is *A Study of Thinking* (1956) by Bruner, Goodnow, and Austin. The first three chapters of this book provide an intuitive and insightful introduction to the topic. However, the experiments presented in later chapters began a research tradition in which categorization was viewed as a process of identifying necessary and sufficient features. As we have seen, this assumption has now been discredited. More current views of categorization are presented in several papers in *Cognition and Categorization* (1978), edited by Rosch and Lloyd. *Categories and Concepts* (1981) by Smith and Medin provides a theoretical analysis of alternative models of category representation. Smith and Medin have also reviewed recent research in a chapter in the *Annual Reviews of Psychology* (1984).

Semantic networks and propositional representations have been discussed extensively in the philosophical, linguistic, and artificial-intelligence literature, as well as in the psychological sources cited in the text. In the philosophical literature a work of particular interest to psychologists is Jerrold Katz's *Semantic Theory* (1972), which is a detailed presentation of his theory. Overviews of the artificial-intelligence literature can be found in textbooks such as those by Winston (1984) and by Rich (1983).

In this chapter we dealt entirely with categorization by humans. A good reference to begin investigating research on animal categorization is a chapter by Herrnstein and de Villiers (1980).

# CHAPTER **SIX**

# Process of Recognition

## INTRODUCTION

In the previous chapter we sketched the organization of human conceptual memory. In this chapter and the two following chapters we will describe how information stored in memory is subsequently retrieved. It may seem odd that the retrieval of information from memory is being presented before we discuss how information is stored in memory (the topic of Chapters 9 and 10). After all, a representation must be stored in memory before it can be retrieved. But recall from Chapters 2 and 5 that after the representation of an input is constructed, it is compared with representations in memory. The comparison procedure thus requires the retrieval of old representations from memory, and this retrieval occurs before the new representation is stored. Therefore retrieval of the old actually precedes storage of the new. In fact, as we will see in subsequent chapters, what is stored about an input depends heavily on what information about it is first retrieved.

The mere fact that people have memories, which seem to break down the barriers of physics and effortlessly link the present to the past, is a source of wonder. But we usually perform the mental feat of memory retrieval so effortlessly that we can easily overlook what a feat it is, until we consider how we do it. For example, when you remember something, how do you know that you have remembered it and not imagined it? So you think you know your name? How do you know that you didn't think you had a different name five days ago or five minutes ago? The act of retrieval involves precise and subtle judgments that vary with the circumstances. To illustrate, let us play Watson and analyze the facets of retrieval revealed in an interview between Sherlock Holmes and a new client, Mr. Green.

HOLMES: What can I do for you, Mr. Green?

GREEN: Mr. Holmes, I am so glad that you could see me. I am an assistant manager at a bank. This morning I went next door to the post office to pick up the mail. As always, I took with me a black satchel in which to carry it. When I identified myself to the postal clerk, he removed the mail from our box and placed it in the satchel. I noticed as he placed the mail in the satchel that it contained a letter from our foreign representative, a letter that we had been expecting. The letter was to contain information about the soundness of certain securities we plan to purchase. I immediately closed the satchel and returned to my manager's office. He opened the satchel and took the mail from it. As he did so, I noticed the letter was gone.

HOLMES:  I assume that you want me to recover the letter before anyone is aware that it is missing. To do so, I must know everything that happened from the moment you entered the post office. To begin, how many people were there, and did you know them?

GREEN:  I remember seeing three people. There was Harry, the postal clerk I usually pick up my mail from. Just as I entered someone already in the post office stepped up to his window, so I moved to the window next to Harry's. I remember that the fellow bought some stamps from Harry and that he looked very familiar, but I didn't know who he was. I felt embarrassed, and wondered whether he was a bank customer. Then, of course, there was the clerk who put the mail in my satchel. He was totally unfamiliar. I had never seen him before in my life.

HOLMES:  An odd coincidence, Mr. Green, that the first time a new clerk gives you the mail, a letter disappears. Tell me, did anything at all happen, no matter how trivial, at the exact moment the clerk placed the letters in the satchel?

GREEN:  Now, that you mention it, I did sneeze.

HOLMES:  Of course! It is impossible to sneeze without closing your eyes. At that instant, the letter was lifted back out of the satchel. The clerk is our man.

## BASIC RETRIEVAL MODEL

Let us apply what we already know about human information processing to Mr. Green's story and see how memory operates. First, information is accessed automatically at the comparison level. Hence Mr. Green recognized his friend Harry and the foreign letter when he saw them. However, information that is not directly related to any input immediately present in the environment can also be accessed by the executive. In Holmes's apartment Mr. Green was able to tell the detective all about his day's activities in response to the quite vague cue, "What can I do for you, Mr. Green?"

Next, consider the outcomes of the comparison mechanism finding a match. One result is the *identification* of the input. That is, additional information about the input is retrieved. As we just noted, for example, Mr. Green knew his friend and his letter when he saw them. The other result is that the input is perceived to have a degree of *familiarity*. Most familiar things are easily identified, so the two outcomes are fused into one brief phenomenal experience.

However, the two outcomes are distinct, and we all have had occasions on which identification and familiarity were experienced separately. In the post office Mr. Green had the experience we have all had at one time or another of seeing a person who looked familiar but being unable to identify him. Yet Mr. Green identified the foreign letter, although, of course, he could not have seen that particular envelope before. Again, virtually all of us have had the experience of waiting to greet someone we have never met before, or entering a strange house we have heard of but not seen before, or shopping for a new car or appliance. When the new input is perceived for the first time, we get that feeling of newness or strangeness that is the opposite of familiarity. We know that we have not seen that particular thing before, but we can nevertheless identify it.

## Recognition and Recall

The comparison mechanism and the executive are both involved in almost every effort to retrieve information from memory. But some tasks make use of one procedure much more than the other. In particular, recognition tasks usually only require the comparison procedure to retrieve information, but recall tasks more often require that the executive retrieve information. For example, suppose you are asked whether your phone number is 932–1766. In this case you simply have to say yes or no, depending on whether you recognize 932–1766 as your phone number. The critical thing that defines a *recognition task* is that one is given a *copy* of the information one needs to find in memory. In order to respond, one compares the representation of the perceptual input with representations stored in memory.

In contrast, suppose you are asked what your phone number is. Here your task is to *recall* a piece of information stored in memory, given the question as a cue. In order to respond, you must access representations quite different from that of the question. Recognition tasks are often used to study the role of the comparison mechanism in memory, whereas recall tasks are frequently used to study the role of the executive.

Of course, a difficult recognition task sometimes involves the executive, and an easy recall task sometimes only requires the comparison mechanism (Mandler 1972; Rabinowitz, Mandler, and Patterson 1977). If you have to answer a difficult multiple-choice question on an exam, you may have to recall additional information beyond the alternatives presented, even though a multiple-choice exam satisfies the definition of a recognition task. In contrast, when you are asked the first name of the president whose last name was Lincoln, the strong association between the names causes the answer to be activated at the comparison level, even though recall is nominally required. However, for the most part recognition tasks provide a convenient way of studying the activation of memory by the comparison mechanism. Accordingly, we will begin by using studies of recognition tasks to illustrate the workings of the comparison mechanism. In the next chapter recall tasks will be used to examine the executive's role in retrieval.

## How Recognition Operates

Figure 6.1 illustrates how the comparison and decision procedures operate together to produce recognition for the word *dog*. First, the input is encoded into a perceptual representation, as discussed in Chapter 4. The recognition pro-

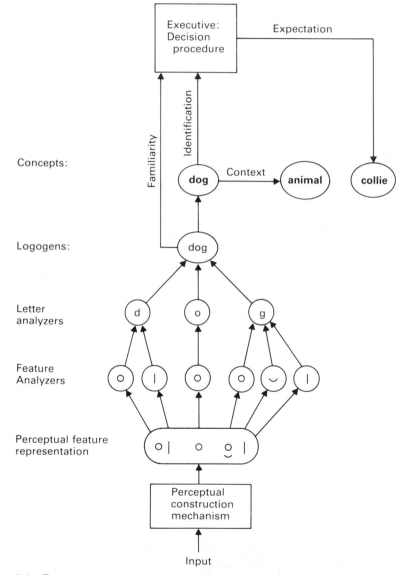

**Figure 6.1    Recognition process for the word *dog*.**

cess operates in much the same way for visual, tactile, and auditory representations, so we will not distinguish among them for the time being, although most of our examples will involve visual recognition.

Second, the input representation is compared with representations in memory, and memory representations are activated until the memory representation most similar to it is found. As we saw in Chapter 1, the human information-processing system represents each input as a set of features and organizes the representations in memory by the features they contain. For example, suppose the representations of words are arranged in memory alphabetically, somewhat as they are in a dictionary. When you look a word up in the dictionary, you do not open it to the first page and begin comparing the word with every entry until you find a match. Instead, you open the dictionary to the part where you expect to find entries beginning with the same letter, and then you move back and forth over several pages as you successively match the second, third, and fourth letters of the word to entries, until after a very few comparisons you find a match.

Human memory has an organization similar to that of a dictionary, although the organizing features are much more general than letters of the alphabet. Consequently, each feature match leads to the retrieval of those representations containing all of the features already matched, so the comparison process is rapidly narrowed to those representations most similar to the target. This process is so efficient that a familiar object can be recognized from a picture in no more than a tenth of a second (Intraub 1980).

However, the activation of memory representations is not solely determined by feature overlap. As Figure 6.1 indicates, the recognition process is also influenced by the person's expectations and the context in which the input occurs. A well-known example illustrating this point is the ambiguous drawing shown in Figure 6.2 *(Bugelski and Alampay 1961)*. If you look at the

**Figure 6.2   Ambiguous drawing. Man or rat?**

picture carefully, you will see that it can be interpreted either as a rat or as a man's face. When the rat-man picture is presented in the context of a series of unambiguous animal pictures, most people see it as a rat. Without a special context most people see it as a man. The *animal* context influences which memory representation ultimately receives the most activation.

The products of a match between an input and a memory representation are an identification and a perception of some degree of familiarity. The identification occurs when the input representation matches the critical features of an instance or category representation stored in memory and activates its node in the semantic code. The familiarity judgment depends on the total number of matching features between the input and memory representation. For example, suppose you are trying to recognize the face of a casual acquaintance. Some features, like the shape of the nose and mouth, may be critical for distinguishing your acquaintance from other persons, so matching those features is central to identification. A match of other features, such as the eyes and hairstyle, may add to perceived familiarity without influencing identification.

The features producing identification and familiarity are sometimes sufficiently different so that familiarity is sometimes perceived without identification and vice versa. On the one hand, you may perceive someone as familiar but not know who they are. On the other hand, you still may be able to identify an acquaintance not seen in years who now looks unfamiliar. So both familiarity and identification are separate outcomes of the comparison mechanism.

Both results produced by the comparison mechanism go to the executive. It is the executive that recognizes the input. In fact, the word *recognition* is used for three different kinds of judgments. One kind of judgment is a category judgment, as when you recognize an object as a chair, a knife, or an instance of some other category. Familiarity plays a relatively minor role in this kind of judgment. Another kind of judgment is an *old judgment.* That is, you feel you have seen that particular instance before. This kind of judgment makes use of familiarity. The more familiar the object appears, the more likely it is to be called "old." Finally, a recognition judgment can be a judgment about whether an object was seen at a particular place or time. Such a judgment may be made on the basis of either identification, familiarity, or both.

## MEMORY COMPARISONS AND RECOGNITION

We will begin our examination of the recognition process with the factors that influence the comparison mechanism. In subsequent sections we will examine the outcomes of a match and how the executive evaluates the outcomes of a match.

## Role of Similarity

The comparison mechanism ultimately matches the perceptual representation of the input to the memory representation most similar to it. But what determines similarity? In the case of a unidimensional input, such as a color patch, similarity is easily determined (Nilsson and Nelson 1981). But in the case of a complex input, such as a shape or pattern, the determination of similarity is more complex, as we saw in Chapter 4. A shape is represented by the figure construction mechanism as a set of features in particular locations (see Chapter 4). The comparison mechanism ultimately matches the shape input to the memory representation containing the greatest number of shared features in those locations.

One experiment demonstrating the role of perceptual features in recognition was performed by Bower and Glass (1976). They investigated the ability of college students to recognize patterns such as those depicted in Figure 6.3. Target patterns like that in Figure 6.3 were first presented to the students. A week later the target was presented along with one of the two distractor patterns shown in Figure 6.3. The subject simply had to choose which of the two patterns had been presented a week earlier. This task is called a forced-choice recognition procedure, because the subject is forced to choose one of the alternative test items as the one that had been previously presented.

To understand the logic of the Bower and Glass experiment, look carefully at the target pattern in Figure 6.3. What are the features of the pattern? Because of the way the figure construction mechanism integrates its features, most people see this pattern as an open triangle atop a right angle. Now look at the two distractor patterns. In each case they differ from the target by the removal of one horizontal line, which is the same length in both cases. So *objectively*, the two distractors are equally similar to the target. But if you look at the patterns carefully, you will probably agree with us that the middle pattern seems more similar to the target than does the pattern on the right.

Why do we think this way? Notice that even after the top horizontal line has been removed, the top of the similar distractor can be interpreted as an incomplete triangle. As a result, the two features of the target are still intact. In contrast, the bottom horizontal line removed to form the dissimilar distractor

Target          Similar          Dissimilar
                distractor       distractor

**Figure 6.3   Examples of the patterns used in a recognition test by Bower and Glass (1976).**

turned the right angle into a straight line, which is a different feature entirely. So most people perceive the right pattern as less similar to the target than the middle pattern is.

The results of the recognition test performed by Bower and Glass showed a striking effect of distractor similarity. The students erroneously selected a similar distractor instead of the target four times as often as they selected a dissimilar distractor. In addition, nineteen of the twenty students were more confident in choosing between a target and a dissimilar distractor than in choosing between a target and a similar distractor. These results show that the features of perceptual representations are also the critical features for recognition.

Another way to demonstrate the role of features in determining similarity is to camouflage a familiar pattern by embedding it in a larger pattern. Then the figure construction mechanism will not produce a unitary feature representation of the embedded pattern but, instead, include its parts in a feature representation of the combined pattern. In this case the embedded pattern will no longer match its unembedded representation in memory and will no longer be recognized. If you try the exercise in Figure 6.4, you will see that the strange symbols are camouflaging some familiar patterns.

The Bower and Glass results also highlight an extremely important fact about recognition performance: In a forced-choice test accurate recognition is largely determined by the difficulty of the distractor items. In general, if the distractors are similar to the original input, many confusions will result. If the distractors are dissimilar, recognition accuracy will increase. For example, suppose that Mr. Green, the assistant bank manager in the dialog presented at the beginning of the chapter, had been asked to pick the postal clerk out of a police lineup. If the distractors in the lineup were Sherlock Holmes, a middle-

**Figure 6.4   Camouflaging experiment. Cover the left-hand side of all symbols and you should find some familiar patterns.**

aged woman, and an elderly skid row bum, no doubt the assistant manager would have singled out the suspect. However, we would not be very confident that he had really recognized the clerk. He might have identified any man in business clothes as the clerk in this situation. But suppose, instead, that the other people in the lineup were three men who looked something like the suspect. If the assistant manager was able to identify the suspect in the context of these similar distractors, we would be much more likely to believe that he had actually seen the clerk.

As this example suggests, we can make any recognition test as difficult as we want simply by making the distractors extremely similar to an actual input. For example, if you are shown a shade of red and later asked to recognize it, you will have trouble if the correct alternative is mixed up with other very similar shades of red. Also, the more dimensions the targets and distractors differ on, the easier they will be to discriminate. For example, targets and distractors that differ in color, shape, and location will be easier to discriminate than probes that differ on just one or two of these dimensions.

Note that a forced-choice recognition test will be difficult if the distractor is highly similar to *any* input item, even if it is not similar to the target with which it is actually paired. Thus if you are first shown a shade of red and a shade of green, you will subsequently have great difficulty choosing the old item if the test pair consists of the red target and a shade of green very similar to the green presented initially.

Tulving (1981) demonstrated that if the distractor item is extremely similar to one of a set of potential targets, recognition performance will be better if the distractor is actually paired with the similar target rather than with a dissimilar target. To construct similar target-distractor pairs, Tulving divided photographs of complex scenes into left and right halves, presented one half as an input item, and then used the remaining half as a distractor on the subsequent forced-choice test. Matched and unmatched test pairs were constructed as illustrated in Figure 6.5. In these examples the scene on the left in each pair is a target item included in the input list. In Figure 6.5(a) the target is paired with its extremely similar distractor. In Figure 6.5(b) the target is paired with a distractor similar to a *different* potential target. Tulving found that subjects were more accurate in correctly choosing the target when the pairs were matched rather than mismatched.

Why was the target easier to recognize when paired with its most similar distractor? When the pairs were presented side by side, an observer was better able to ignore those features common to both, which would increase the familiarity of the distractor, and concentrate on matching the critical distinctive features of the target to its memory representation. Hence Tulving (1981) showed that the context in which a target is perceived can influence the features used in its identification. Let us now examine the effect of context on recognition in more detail.

Target          Distractor          Target          Distractor

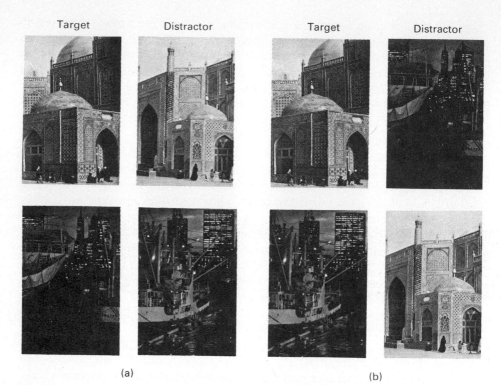

(a)                                              (b)

**Figure 6.5    Examples of target-distractor pairs in which the distractor is extremely similar to an input item: (a) Matched pairs; (b) mismatched pairs. (From Tulving 1981.)**

### Effects of Context

To recapitulate, a perceptual construction mechanism first constructs a feature representation of the input, and then the representation is matched by the comparison mechanism to the memory representation to which it is most similar. The comparison mechanism is therefore guided by a memory organization based on perceptual similarity. That is, each successive memory representation compared with the input representation contains all the features that have been matched in the preceding comparison.

However, perceptual organization has its limits. Consider the case of the phone book. Imagine what it would be like to look up a number in a book that contained the names of everyone in the United States who had a phone. Obviously, the lookup process is greatly speeded by having different phone books for different localities. The comparison of an input is facilitated in a similar way. As discussed in Chapter 5, sets of perceptual representations are associated with different categories. For example, perceptual representations of rats are associated with the category *rat,* and perceptual representations of men are associated with the category *man.* When a category is activated, the activation levels of the representations associated with it are also raised. Suppose, then, that an input is ambiguous and hence matches more than one memory representation. If the category associated with one of the candidate representations has also been activated, then that representation will usually have the greater total activation. For this reason Figure 6.2 was perceived as a rat rather than a man when the context *animal* activated the category *rat.*

In this section we will examine three examples illustrating three basic ways in which the context can influence recognition. For unambiguous inputs the context can shorten the recognition time. For ambiguous inputs the context can determine which interpretation of the input is perceived. For degraded or disguised inputs the context may be necessary for recognition of the input at all.

**Scene recognition.**    A striking example of how context influences recognition involves the identification of an object in a briefly presented picture. In one such experiment (Biederman, Mezzanotte, and Rabinowitz 1982), before each trial an observer was told the name of the target, e.g., *sofa.* A fixation point, presented for 500 milliseconds, was followed by a 150-millisecond presentation of a scene, which, in turn, was followed by a cue marking some position in the scene that had just been presented. The observer had to report whether the target had appeared in the location marked by the cue. The question of interest was whether an object that in some way did not fit with the rest of the scenes (its context) would be more difficult to detect.

Figure 6.6(a) shows a normal scene in which the target is the fire hydrant. The other three scenes in Figure 6.6 have contextual violations. In Figure 6.6(b) the fire hydrant is out of position. In Figure 6.6(c) the hydrant is an improbable object in such a scene. And in Figure 6.6(d) the sofa is both out of position and improbable. Observers failed to detect the target in an appropriate context, such as in Figure 6.6(a), only 28 percent of the time; they missed it 40 percent of the time when it was involved in a single violation, as in Figures 6.6(b) or 6.6(c); and they missed it over 50 percent of the time when it was involved in multiple violations, as in Figure 6.6(d). Thus within a very brief period of time, less than a fifth of a second, representations of objects in a scene interact to facilitate each other's recognition.

**Lexical context and recognition.**    The context can also influence the recognition judgment itself (Hunt and Ellis 1974; Light and Carter-Sobell 1970), as well as the speed with which the judgment is made. In Figure 6.7 the appropriate representation for an ambiguous figure is activated by the other figures in the display. In this case the ambiguity and the effect of context are obvious.

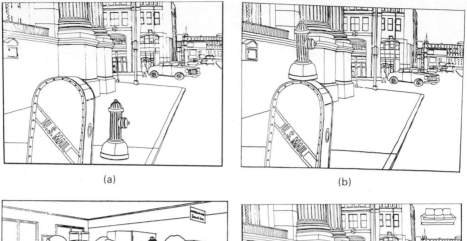

**Figure 6.6  Scene recognition: (a) The target (hydrant) appropriately positioned in a probable context; (b) the target (hydrant) in a position violation; (c) the target (hydrant) in a probability violation; (d) the target (sofa) in both a position and probability violation. (After Biederman, Mezzanotte, and Rabinowitz 1982.)**

However, even when the ambiguity is not obvious, it can still interact with context to influence recognition.

In a typical experiment (Hunt and Ellis 1974) students were asked to study a list of word pairs such as (folder FILE). Later they were tested on their

(a) A B C

(b) 12 13 14

**Figure 6.7  Lexical context: (a) Letters; (b) numbers. The same pattern is identified as B in row (a) and as 13 in row (b).**

ability to recognize the capitalized words that had been presented. These words appeared in a variety of different contexts: (1) with the original context (folder FILE); (2) alone (FILE); (3) with a word biasing a different meaning (smooth FILE); and (4) with a new word biasing the same meaning (cabinet FILE). The students were most accurate in recognizing the capitalized word when the context word was the same during both study and test. Performance was poorest when the text context biased a different meaning, but even a new context biasing the same meaning hindered recognition.

Notice that in this task the students were not merely judging whether FILE was a word but whether it had appeared in the previously presented list. In general, the more difficult the discrimination that is required for recognition, the more likely it is that the context will influence the judgment. Change of context is thus a factor that can make classroom exams difficult. People perform much better on recognition tests if the material is tested in the same order as it was originally presented (Jacoby 1972; Jacoby and Hendricks 1973). If you study a set of questions in a particular order, random order on the exam will make the test more difficult because it breaks the context in which you originally learned the material.

**Degraded and disguised inputs.**   What happens if the feature representation of the input is not similar to any memory representation? There are three possibilities. First, the input may simply be accepted as novel. Second, the executive may try to construct a new feature representation for the input. Recall from Chapter 4 that often many alternative feature representations may be constructed from the same input, along with the one that is constructed automatically. However, conscious construction of different feature representations for the same input is a slow and tedious process and therefore often will not be attempted.

The third possibility is that the input representation will be compared with a representation that has been activated in some other way, which it possibly might match. We saw in Chapter 2 that representations can become activated in two ways. Either the match of one memory representation automatically activates associated representations (see Figure 6.7), or the person develops a conscious expectation of an input, which causes its representation to be activated (see Figure 6.2). In either case the memory representation is used as a guide for reconstructing the feature representation of the input so that it matches the memory representation as closely as possible. For example, once the appropriate memory representations for the patterns in Figure 6.4 are activated, reconstructing the representations of the inputs is easy. With somewhat greater difficulty one can construct the appropriate feature representations for the pictures in Figure 4.5 once the names of the degraded objects activate the feature representations needed.

## DECISION PROCESSES IN RECOGNITION

The outputs of the comparison procedure, identification and familiarity, must be processed by a decision procedure in the executive in order to make a recognition judgment. In this section we will examine how these two outcomes can be used to generate decisions.

### Identification and Recall

In many cases the matching of a few critical features is sufficient to activate a category and produce identification; however, this result is not apparent until you try to recall what you can recognize. For example, try closing this book and drawing from memory each letter of the alphabet exactly as it is printed in this book. How many letters can you reproduce correctly, down to the last line or stroke? Probably not many. Yet you have seen these printed letters many times in this book. If the letter task was too difficult, try drawing the face of a telephone dial. See if you can put all the letters and numbers in their correct places. Then compare your drawing with an actual dial. If you are like most people, you probably cannot do a very good job of reproducing a printed alphabet or a telephone dial, in spite of countless pages you have read and the telephones you have dialed.

Nickerson and Adams (1979) examined the ability of American college students to recognize and recall the appearance of an object they were extremely familiar with—the head side of a penny. They found that the students were quite poor in selecting the correct version of the coin, depicted in Figure 6.8(a), when it was presented along with fourteen distractors in which various

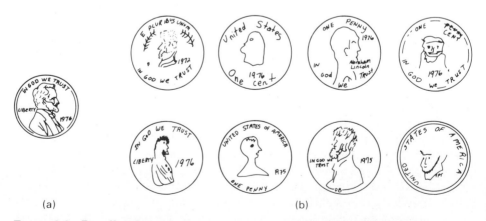

(a)                                    (b)

**Figure 6.8    Recall task: (a) An American penny; (b) examples of drawings obtained from students who tried to reproduce a penny from memory. (From Nickerson and Adams 1979.)**

features were omitted or altered. Subjects had even more difficulty when asked to draw the coin. Some of their rather lamentable efforts are displayed in Figure 6.8(b).

You have the impression that your representations are so detailed because the detail is fine enough for what you use it for—reading a page, dialing a phone number, or selecting a penny out of a few coins of various values. Actually, you usually need many fewer features to recognize something than to form a clear mental image of it. These features are the critical features that define the focal instances or prototype and that most instances have in common (see Chapter 5). Indeed, Rubin and Kontis (1983) found evidence that people base their recall of coins on a schematic representation. Figure 6.9(a)

(a)                    (b)

**Figure 6.9   Recall task: (a) Actual American coins; (b) coins constructed from most frequent features used in drawing each coin. (From Rubin and Kontis 1983.)**

shows the American coins in use at the time of their study, and Figure 6.9(b) shows versions based on the most frequent features subjects used in drawing each one. The striking result is that all the reconstructed coins tended to be the same except for the identity of the president depicted on each. The subject appeared to know little about the specific details of each type of coin (except for its size and color, presumably), but they did seem to have a clear notion of what coins in general are like. We will encounter much more evidence of such reconstruction in Chapter 8.

### Familiarity

The degree of the feeling of familiarity that accompanies the perception of an input can vary more or less continuously from very low, to moderate, to extremely high. As demonstrated by Jacoby and Dallas (1981), familiarity corresponds to awareness of the rapidity and completeness with which an input is matched to a representation in memory. If the comparison process is rapid and complete, familiarity will be relatively high; if the process is slow and incomplete, familiarity will be relatively low. Recall from Chapter 2 that as an input is repeated, the analysis and comparison procedure for it becomes increasingly automatized, so the time required to find a match in memory is reduced. The familiarity of an input is thus influenced by both the recency and the frequency of its repetition. If while lost, for example, you ride around a block and come again upon a house you passed moments before, it probably will appear more familiar than houses that you have not seen before. Similarly, if you return to a house that you lived in while a child, it will look more familiar than a house you have never seen at all.

Atkinson, Herrmann, and Wescourt (1974) made use of the finding that a repeated input is processed faster the second time to show that a rapid match increases familiarity. In their task students had to recognize words that had been on a list they had learned. The experimenter made use of some of these words in giving the students their instructions. Though the students were unaware that they had heard some of the list words as part of the instructions, they recognized these words more quickly (see also Scarborough, Gerard, and Cortese 1979).

Moreover, a person can arrive at a feeling of familiarity without being conscious of exactly what features of the input matched or mismatched the features of a memory representation. This result helps to explain some very curious memory phenomena. For instance, you may have had the experience of meeting a friend who had just shaved off his beard. Your first reaction may have been that *something* about him was different, even though you couldn't say exactly what. What probably happens in such cases is that the person seems less familiar than usual because the match to a representation in memory is no longer perfect. However, you may not be aware of exactly what feature fails to match correctly. The result will be a rather unsettling feeling that the person has changed in some unknown way.

If both familiarity and identification are products of feature matches, then why can one of these outcomes sometimes be experienced without the other? Perhaps, while the identification of an input requires that its representation match exactly the critical features of a relatively abstract representation, the perception of familiarity is the product of the total number of feature matches, whether or not they are critical.

This conception of familiarity provides an explanation for the experience of déjà vu ("already seen"). This experience occurs when a person comes across a place or situation that seems familiar but that the person has never encountered before. What may be happening is that the novel input is similar to one or more representations in memory. For example, the person may not have previously visited the town that seems familiar but may have visited a similar town. If the novel input achieves a fairly complete match with a memory representation, but the memory representation is not identified, then the person will have an unexplained (to him or her) feeling of familiarity, which may be labeled "déjà vu."

## Determinants of Recognition Decisions

To separate their effects, we have considered recognition tasks in which judgments based on either identification or familiarity predominate. But many judgments are based on both kinds of knowledge (Mandler 1980). Of course, people are rarely aware that they are relying on one or the other kind of information. Rather, they are usually only aware of some global judgment that the input is something that was seen before in the specified context. For example, if I ask you if one of the authors of this book is Keith Holyoak, how do you know this information? Does the name sound familiar, or do you remember seeing it on the cover?

We will now describe some experiments that demonstrate the role of familiarity in tasks that logically could be performed solely through identification and others that demonstrate the role of identification in a task that logically could be performed solely on the basis of familiarity.

**Recognizing list members.**   Studies of repetition effects when students recognize lists of words they have learned suggest that people base their decisions on a mixture of familiarity judgments and identification (Atkinson and Juola 1974; Mandler and Boeck 1974). The familiarity model makes two predictions about how reaction times will change when test words are repeated. The first prediction is straightforward. When a target is repeated, you should be able to make a positive response more quickly with more repetitions. The familiarity of the word will increase with each repetition, and responding yes to words that are very familiar will become easier.

However, exactly the same logic leads to a very different and counterintuitive prediction for words that are not on the list. Initially, these distractors will seem quite unfamiliar, so responding no will be easy. But as the distractors are repeated, they will become more familiar, and hence they will become harder to discriminate from the targets. As a result, distractors should produce *slower* response times when they are repeated.

Both of these predictions were supported when this experiment was first performed (Atkinson and Juola 1974). Since then, the first prediction has been replicated many times. As mentioned above, a repetition even facilitates when it occurs outside the list context (Atkinson and Juola 1974). However, the second finding, that repetition slows the rejection of distractors, has proven more difficult to replicate (Juola, Taylor, and Young 1974).

**Frequency judgments.**    Suppose you are asked how many times you saw a particular friend in the last 24 hours, or you are asked which of two friends you had seen more often. Logically, the most certain answer would be obtained by thinking of every time you saw the friend and counting the instances. At a minimum this task would involve accessing detailed information through the identification process and might even involve the active generation of information, as in a recall task. However, a simpler basis for a judgment is to translate the perceived familiarity of the friend into a frequency estimate.

Considerable research has investigated how people make frequency estimates. In such experiments the subject typically sees a sequence of words and then must state how often each word has appeared in the sequence. Some results suggest that people sometimes do count up each occurrence they can recall (Hintzman and Block 1971). However, more often people appear to base their frequency judgment on a feeling of familiarity (Harris, Begg, and Mitterer 1980). Hasher and Chromiak (1977) found that students in the second, fourth, and sixth grades and in college were only slightly more accurate at estimating the frequencies of words that appeared in a sequence when they were told they would have to make frequency judgments before viewing the sequence, suggesting that frequency information was accumulated in either case. Greene (1984) found that frequency judgments by college students were equally accurate regardless of whether the subjects were led to expect they would have to make frequency judgments about words or simply that they would be given an unspecified memory test. Hence when people attend to inputs sufficiently to increase their familiarity, they will perceive those inputs as more familiar. However, a third group of subjects who did not expect to be tested about the words at all, and were distracted from attending to them by an additional memory task, were less accurate in their frequency judgments.

**Role of recall in recognition.**    Sometimes, a task in which a person has to decide which items had been presented before is based solely on a judgment of which items are more familiar. However, when the targets and distractors are perceptually similar, and hence similar in familiarity, a person will have to rely more on identification and will actively try to recall the last context in which each item was seen. In fact, as Tulving (1968) has shown, if the recognition task is made sufficiently difficult, people may fail to recognize words that they are subsequently able to recall. The generation of items thus plays a significant role in the recognition task (Jones 1980; Rabinowitz, Mandler, and Barsalou 1979).

In fairness, we should point out that the cause of such recognition failure is controversial, and Begg (1979) and Flexser and Tulving (1978) would disagree that generation played a role. Despite the controversy over these experiments, no one would disagree with the statement that a judgment that something had been seen before often involves more than a pure familiarity judgment, and probably no one would disagree that generation may sometimes play a role in what is nominally a recognition task.

Accordingly, although we could devise extreme versions of a task that would cause people to rely heavily on the output of one process or the other, we would be wrong in thinking of recognition and recall as relying on different processes in everyday life. All the retrieval mechanisms operate in every retrieval task, and the decision procedure makes use of whatever seems to provide the most accurate answer for that input.

## Sensitivity and Criterion in Recognition Judgments

**Setting a decision criterion.**    The perception of familiarity is a matter of degree, but recognition tasks frequently force a choice between two responses: old or new. As a result, a decision procedure must set a familiarity criterion so that every input more familiar than the criterion is called "old" and every input less familiar than the input is called "new." If the least familiar old input is more familiar than the most familiar new input, then one can set a criterion such that no errors are made. However, if the least familiar old input is perceived as less familiar than the most familiar new input, then no matter where the criterion is set, some errors will be made. For example, suppose I give you a list of names that I culled from your junior high school yearbook intermixed with names from another yearbook, and I ask you which of these people you know. Inevitably, you will make some errors because the familiarity values of the names of the people you have and haven't met will overlap. If you set the familiarity criterion at a high level, you will *miss* some people you do know. Alternatively, if you set the criterion at a low level, you will *false-alarm* to the names of some people you do not know.

Both the environmental context and the person's expectations influence the level where the criterion is set. For example, if you are simply given a set of index cards with names on them and asked to pick out the people you know, you will probably use a relatively high criterion. However, if you are handed your yearbook and asked to pick out familiar names, your criterion will be much lower, and you will identify more names as those of people you know. After all, you already know that you know many of these people.

The effect of context on the decision criterion creates a knotty measurement problem for psychologists. We have also seen that context affects the comparison procedure. So when a change in context causes a change in performance, how do we know whether the comparison procedure or the decision procedure (or both) has been affected? For example, perhaps when you see a name in your yearbook, the context of the yearbook causes more features to be activated by the comparison procedure, which increases the familiarity of familiar names. The result would be an increase in the familiarity differences between the names of people you know and the names of those you don't know. Such an increase in your *sensitivity* to the distinction between known and unknown names would allow you to report more names of people you know. The problem is to distinguish changes in sensitivity from shifts in criterion level that might also result in more correct responses to known names.

**Signal detection theory.**    The solution to the problem is to measure not only a person's *hit rate*—the number of targets reported as old—but also the *false-alarm rate*—the number of distractors reported as old. If observers have altered their decision criterion, then inevitably both the hit and the false-alarm rates will change in the same direction. Using the elegant mathematical *theory of signal detection* (Banks 1970; Swets, Tanner, and Birdsall 1961), researchers can partition a change in performance due to context and attribute part of it to a change in criterion and the rest to changes in the output of other procedures that affect the familiarity values assigned to targets and distractors. A change in the value a mechanism assigns to an input is called a change in its *sensitivity*.

Figure 6.10 illustrates a signal detection analysis of two possible effects of providing a supporting context on the task of distinguishing known and unknown names. Figure 6.10(a) shows the distributions of familiarity values for unknown and known names in a test without a supporting context. In accord with most applications of signal detection theory, we assume that both distributions are of the bell-shaped normal form (a form that will be familiar to you if you have had a statistics course). The familiarity distribution for known names is largely to the right of that for unknown names, since known names will, of course, tend to be more familiar. However, the two distributions overlap, indicating that some unknown names will actually seem more familiar than some known names.

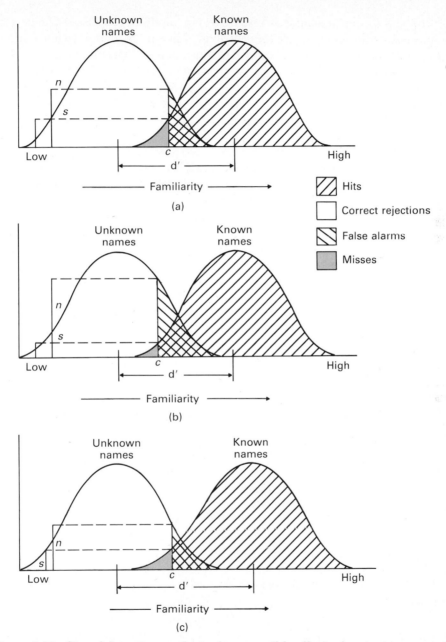

Figure 6.10    Signal detection analysis of two possible effects of context on recognition: (a) No supporting context; (b) a criterion shift; (c) an increase in similarity.

In this situation perfect performance is impossible. Suppose subjects set a familiarity criterion at point $c$ and respond "known" to all names more familiar than the criterion and "unknown" to those that are less familiar. The shadings in Figure 6.10(a) indicate the proportion of responses that will be of the four types logically possible: *hits* (correct responses to known names), *correct rejections* (correct responses to unknown names), *misses* (erroneous responses to known names), and *false alarms* (erroneous responses to unknown names).

Figures 6.10(b) and 6.10(c) illustrate two possible ways that providing a supporting context might increase the proportion of hits. Figure 6.10(b) depicts a pure criterion shift. The familiarity distributions are unchanged from those in Figure 6.10(a), but the criterion $c$ has been shifted to a lower level on the familiarity continuum. The result is an increase in hits but also in false alarms. In contrast, Figure 6.10(c) illustrates a pure change in sensitivity. The criterion $c$ is set at the same point as in Figure 6.10(a), but the familiarity distribution for known names has been shifted to the right, indicating that they seem more familiar when a context is provided. As a result, the proportion of hits increases *without* any accompanying increase in false alarms.

In signal detection theory sensitivity is measured by the distance between the means of the two distributions, which is termed $d'$. When the signal and the noise distributions are both normal, then the distance of the criterion from the mean of the noise distribution can be calculated from the false-alarm rate, and its distance from the mean of the signal distribution can be calculated from the hit rate (actually, these calculations were performed long ago, and the answer can be looked up in any table describing the normal distribution). Adding these two distances gives the distance from one mean to the other.

The location of the criterion is measured in signal detection theory by the ratio of the height $s$ of the signal distribution to the height $n$ of the noise distribution at the criterion, a ratio that is called $\beta$ (Greek letter beta). Again, when the signal and the noise distributions are normal, and if the hit and false-alarm rates are known, the height of each distribution can be found in a table describing the normal distribution with these values. So by measuring the hit rate and false-alarm rate in a recognition task, and applying the mathematical procedures provided by signal detection theory, we can derive separate estimates of both sensitivity and the decision criterion. Signal detection theory thus provides an extremely valuable tool for investigating recognition performance.

## HUMAN RECOGNITION CAPACITIES

Human beings have a phenomenal capacity to recognize perceptual inputs that they have previously experienced. Our visual recognition is exceptional, people can identify thousands upon thousands of different words and objects. Similarly, our auditory recognition capacity is also impressive. Consider our ability to recognize speech sounds, not to mention different speakers and the sounds of various animals and machines. However, we know less about our recognition abilities in the domains of touch, smell, and taste. In this section we will examine recognition memory for different sense modalities.

## Visual Recognition

Experimental studies of picture recognition memory have revealed our remarkable capacities. For example, Shepard (1967) presented 612 pictures of common scenes to college students. The pictures were displayed one at a time for a few seconds. Afterward, the students were tested on their ability to recognize the pictures. Shepard's test consisted of showing pairs of pictures and asking the students to pick the one picture from each pair that they had seen before. The students were exceptionally accurate; they were correct 97 percent of the time when the test immediately followed presentation of the set of pictures. This performance declined to 87 percent after a delay of one week and to 58 percent after four months.

In order to expand this finding, Standing, Conezio, and Haber (1970) first demonstrated that both subjects and experimenters have a great deal of stamina by showing subjects 2500 pictures. Can you imagine how blurry eyed you would be after watching slides four hours a day for four days? At the end of this ordeal subjects were able to recognize correctly 91 percent of the pictures that were tested. Finally, Standing (1973) proceeded to demonstrate that a few stalwart subjects were 73 percent accurate after viewing 10,000 pictures. The fact that accuracy decreases somewhat with such a large number of inputs can easily be accounted for by assuming lapses of attention due to boredom. Seemingly, the major limit on people's capacity to recognize pictures is the size of the experimenter's slide collection.

Superior picture recognition is not restricted to college students. Brown and Scott (1971) showed four-year-old children a series of 100 colored pictures that they had cut from a variety of children's books. The four-year-olds correctly recognized 98 percent of the pictures on an immediate test and about 90 percent when tested seven days later. Their performance dropped to 67 percent after 28 days.

Recognition experiments have even been done with infants only three to four months old. This type of experiment requires considerable ingenuity. One approach, invented by Fantz (1964), is to record the time that an infant looks at a picture. Fantz found that infants spend much more time looking at new pictures than they do at pictures they have previously seen. (Presumably, they become bored with the old pictures.) With pictures of faces Fagan (1973) was able to show that infants look at new pictures longer than at old pictures even after a retention interval of two weeks. Presumably, the old pictures still seemed familiar to the infants. Furthermore, spaced repetitions of a picture improve an infant's memory for it, just as they improve adult memory (Cornell 1980). These results show that an infant can already encode and recognize inputs shortly after birth. [For reviews of work on infant memory, see Olson (1976, 1984).]

People's word recognition is also very good. Shepard (1967) showed people a sequence of 540 words and then tested them on sixty pairs of words in which one member of each pair had been shown in the inspection series. The subjects selected the target 88 percent of the time. However, there is a dissociation between recognition of words and pictures when individual differences in performance are examined. Woodhead and Baddeley (1981) selected people who had done well (the good recognizers) or badly (the poor recognizers) on a facial recognition task and then gave them three more recognition tests: another involving faces, one involving paintings, and one involving visually presented words. The good recognizers performed better than the poor recognizers on the faces and paintings, but there was no difference between them on the words.

### Other Sense Modalities

Most of the work on recognition memory has focused on our visual capabilities, but we have every reason to believe that we are quite good at recognition in other sensory domains. For example, Lawrence and Banks (1973) demonstrated a fairly impressive memory for common sounds. They had subjects listen to tape recordings of 194 common sounds (babies crying, dogs barking, a car starting, etc.). Their subjects were 89 percent accurate in recognizing the sounds that had been presented from a set including similar sounds that had not been presented.

So far, no one has come up with such large-scale capacity demonstrations of memory for smell. This deficiency may be partly due to the fact that most psychologists do not have ready access to a collection of odors. One large collection of smells is at Brown University, which has more than a hundred bottles of different odors ranging from the smell of whiskey to essence of skunk. An experiment from this laboratory (Engen and Ross 1973) found that recognition of smells was only fair. Students in this experiment sat at a table and sniffed forty-eight cotton balls that were presented one at a time. Each of the forty-eight cotton balls contained a different odor. After all of this sniffing the students were tested on their ability to recognize the smells that had been presented. The test consisted of giving the students pairs of cotton balls and asking them to pick the one from each pair that they had previously smelled. Their performance on this task (69 percent correct) was not nearly as spectacular as the demonstrations of picture recognition.

However, there is one other interesting difference between our memory for smells and our memory for pictures. Memory for smell exhibits virtually no decline over fairly long time periods. In the Engen and Ross experiment students were 69 percent correct if the test was immediate, 70 percent correct if the test was a week later, and 68 percent correct if the test was given a month later. In fact, a similar experiment showed roughly the same level of performance when the test was given three months after the students sniffed the odors. Our recognition of odors may not be quite so accurate initially as is our recognition of pictures, but it certainly is persistent. Subsequent studies using more familiar odors have obtained better initial recognition performance than Engen and Ross did and confirmed the slow decline in performance over long retention intervals (Lawless and Cain 1975; Rabin and Cain 1984).

Of course, trying to compare recognition performance across different sense modalities, or even trying to establish some absolute measure of recognition capacity for a single sense modality, is very tricky. We have seen that recognition performance is heavily influenced by how similar the distractors are to the targets and also by how familiar the targets are to the person making the judgment. These factors are difficult to control in the kinds of experiments we have been discussing here. Nevertheless, these studies clearly show that our recognition capacities are very impressive indeed.

## SUMMARY

A recognition task is one in which a person is given a copy of the information that must be found in memory. When the comparison mechanism finds a match between the input and a representation in memory, the outcome is a degree of *familiarity* associated with the input and possibly some kind of *identification* of it. One basic factor that influences the comparison process is the *similarity* of the input to a memory representation. A target will be difficult to recognize if it is presented along with distractors that are highly similar to a potential target stored in memory. A second basic factor that operates is the *context* of recognition, which also influences the activation of the memory representations that are compared with the input.

An input is often identified on the basis of a few critical features, and hence the memory representations even of familiar objects may not be highly detailed. Recognition judgments are based on a mixture of familiarity and identification. Difficult recognition judgments may involve active attempts to recall the original encoding context. In such cases a target will be difficult to recognize if it is presented in a context that differs substantially from that in which it was previously encoded. Recognition performance will change either if the person alters a *decision criterion* or if *sensitivity* to the familiarity differences between old and new inputs changes. These two factors can be measured separately by using methods based on *signal detection theory*.

People show very high levels of recognition performance with visual stimuli such as photographs and with naturalistic sounds. Recognition of smells is particularly notable for the absence of any serious decline over long retention intervals.

## RECOMMENDED READINGS

As we have already mentioned, journals in which research on memory can be found are *Cognitive Psychology*; *Journal of Experimental Psychology: General*; *Journal of Experimental Psychology: Learning, Memory and Cognition*; *Journal of Memory and Language*; and *Memory and Cognition*. The readings listed at the ends of Chapters 7 and 8 are also relevant to Chapter 6.

# CHAPTER **SEVEN**

# Process of Recall

## INTRODUCTION

Who was president during World War II? Name all the states in the United States. What are the primary symptoms of schizophrenia? Can you give directions from where you live to the nearest McDonald's Restaurant? Who are the authors of this book? Each of these queries is a request to *recall* some information from memory.

A recall task taps the same basic process of accessing information in memory as does a recognition task. However, a recall task requires an additional processing step that is usually not required in a recognition task. In a recognition task the person is presented with a copy of the information to be found in memory. For example, when you recognize the word *Utah*, the input is automatically matched to a memory representation, and the match automatically activates additional representations, including a categorical representation that identifies Utah as a state. But in a recall task you are not given a copy of the information to be found in memory. Therefore you must begin by *generating* possible candidate concepts, using the information provided by the question. After each candidate concept is generated, an attempt is made to identify it. For example, suppose you are asked to recall an American state that begins with the letter *U*. You might begin by generating words that begin with *U* (e.g., *Ulysses, Uganda, Utah*), and then you check each word to determine whether it is a state. Or (as is more likely) you might attempt to generate the names of states (e.g., *Wyoming, Virginia, Indiana, Utah*), and then you check whether any of the candidates begins with *U*.

The processing steps required by a recall task are summarized in Figure 7.1. As the figure indicates, the request that initiates the recall operation contains the information that specifies the goal. Each piece of information that helps to guide the recall process is called a *cue*. In our example the recall cues are the letter *U* and the word *state*. The concept (or concepts) specified by the cues will again be called the *target* (see Chapter 2). *Utah* is the target in this example. Next, the person has to decide which of the potential targets (e.g.,

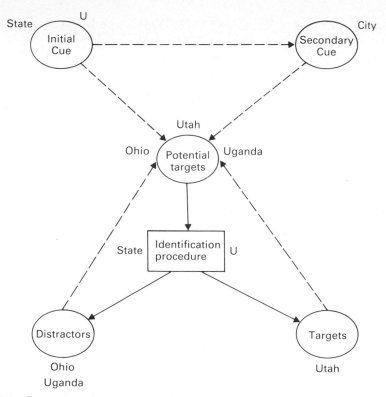

**Figure 7.1    Steps in performing a recall task. The dotted arrows indicate generation steps; the solid arrows indicate identification steps.**

*Ohio, Utah, Uganda)* is the actual one. The process of selecting the actual target is essentially the same as the identification process involved in recognition.

Notice, according to this model, that cues play two roles in a recall task. First, one or more cues are used to generate a set of potential targets. Second, all the cues are used to help identify which, if any, of the generated concepts is the actual target. In essence, then, recall usually involves a two-step process often called either *generate and identify* or *generate and recognize*. That is, when we recall something, we generate possible answers and choose among them in much the same way as we would if the alternatives were presented as part of a multiple-choice recognition test.

The generate-and-recognize model has a long history in the psychology of memory, going back at least to the German psychologist Müller (1913). It is, in fact, a special case of a general problem-solving strategy people use called the generate-and-test strategy (see Chapter 12). To this day, the model has its critics (e.g., Broadbent and Broadbent 1977; Watkins and Gardiner 1979), who wonder how good an approximation it is of what people do when they try to remember something. But as we will show, a great deal of data supports the model (Bahrick 1970), which indicates that it is a good approximation of the process of human recall.

Much of the data has been collected by George Mandler and his students. For example, they have shown that generating possible targets and then trying to recognize the correct one is a strategy that students can use effectively when instructed to do so. In one study (Rabinowitz, Mandler, and Patterson 1977) two groups of college students were presented with a list of fifty words drawn from five different semantic categories (e.g., types of animals or furniture). Afterward, both groups of students were asked to recall as many words as possible. One group of students was explicitly instructed to use the generate-and-recognize method; i.e., they were to think of members of each category and check whether each possible target had actually been presented on the list. The other group was not told to use the generate-and-recognize method. On an immediate-recall test the subjects given generate-and-recognize instructions were able to recall more words than the students in the other group. When the recall test was delayed a week, the advantage of the generate-and-recognize group was reduced. Presumably, the difference in familiarity between presented and unpresented category members diminished with time. As a result, after one week the students would often be unable to recognize target items even after generating them.

In this chapter we will examine a wide variety of recall tasks. We will begin by considering simple recall tasks, such as recalling the names of states or lists of words, which shed light on the generation process. In Chapter 8 we will proceed to more complicated recall tasks, such as recalling a story or describing details of an accident, in which the third step goes beyond mere identification and requires the construction of the target. There we will examine how you retrieve information about yourself, including who you are, where you live, and what you have done.

## GENERATION OF RESPONSES

### Associations and Concept Activation

Figure 7.2 shows fragments of the semantic and visuospatial codes for the states. Recall from Chapter 5 that each node in the semantic code may have associations emanating from it to other nodes and to perceptual representations. A node is said to *dominate* all the other nodes and representations its associations access. A *concept* consists of all the nodes and perceptual representations that a particular node dominates. Each state concept is shown as

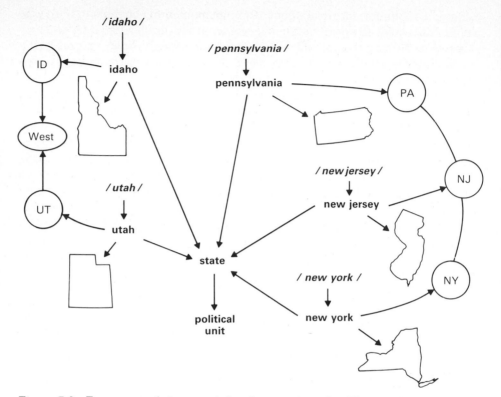

**Figure 7.2    Fragments of visuospatial and semantic codes. The concept *state* is associated with the concepts of individual states. Boldface words are semantic nodes, and pictures and circles are their shape and location representations in the visuospatial code.**

containing three additional kinds of information: category information, shape information, and location information. Though only a few concepts are shown in Figure 7.2, there are fifty state concepts, one for every state. The different state concepts are interconnected in two ways. First, as shown in Figure 7.2, all fifty state concepts dominate the concept **state,** which in turn dominates the concept **political unit.** Second, some state concepts dominate the same perceptual representations. For example, the concepts for New York, New Jersey, and Pennsylvania are shown to dominate the same location representation, which marks their locations relative to each other.

Each concept in memory has a certain level of activation. When the activation of a concept exceeds a certain threshold, the concept enters consciousness (see the discussion of the logogen model in Chapter 1). However, a person cannot bring many associated concepts into consciousness simultaneously (as discussed in Chapters 2 and 3). The maximum number of concepts that may be in consciousness is uncertain: It may be as great as seven (Graesser and Mandler 1978) or as small as three (Gruenewald and Lockhead 1980).

How is this limited set selected? The answer is that those concepts with the highest levels of activation are the most likely to enter consciousness. As you would expect, two major determinants of the activation of a concept are the recency and the frequency of its access. Every time a concept is accessed, its activation is greatly increased, but then a steep decline immediately begins, as shown in Figure 7.3. Also, as we saw in Chapter 2, a concept's activation level is raised by the processing of a related concept as well (Fischler 1977b; Meyer and Schvaneveldt 1973; Neely 1977).

Let us consider how someone might generate the names of states in the United States. In our example the semantic category node of each state concept acts as an analyzer (see Figure 6.1), and the concepts with the highest levels of activation are the ones to enter consciousness. A person can take advantage of the associations that link concepts to raise the activation of concepts related to the recall cue so that they pass the threshold of awareness. Suppose a person from New Jersey is asked to recall the names of states. A priori, the state concept with the highest level of activation is **New Jersey.** So if the recall cue *state* increases the activation of all fifty state concepts by an equal amount, the activation of **New Jersey** will still be the highest, and it will be the first to cross the threshold of activation necessary to enter consciousness. Once **New Jersey** enters consciousness and is identified as a state, then

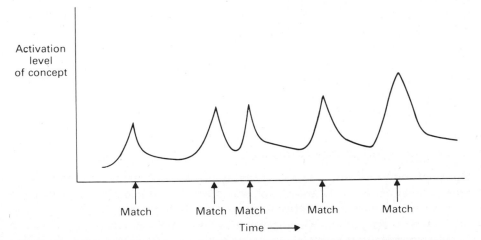

**Figure 7.3    Activation level vs. time. The activation level of a concept increases every time one of its representations matches an input and then immediately begins to decrease.**

additional activation will flow from its concept to additional concepts that share overlapping representations with it.

Of course, all states will have some associative links with New Jersey, but some states will be more strongly associated than others. The more features another state concept shares with New Jersey, the more activation it will receive (Lorch 1982) and the more likely it is to enter consciousness (Bruce 1980; Ross and Bower 1981). For example, as shown in Figure 7.2, adjacent states share a common location feature. Hence on the heels of **New Jersey**, **New York** and **Pennsylvania** are likely to enter consciousness as well. Consequently, an attempt to generate the names of states will produce *clusters* of three, four, or five related states. This clustering effect is a ubiquitous aspect of the free recall of items (Bousfield and Sedgewick 1944). (A *free-recall task* is one in which the person may recall a list or category of items in any order.)

Consider once again the case of someone attempting to think of the names of the states. First, the person attempts to generate the names of states by using the concept **state** as a retrieval cue. Again, assume the person is a New Jersey resident, so the most numerous, high-probability associations are among New Jersey, New York, and Pennsylvania, causing these state names to enter consciousness. Next, the person attempts to generate more names by tracing more associations from the concept **state.** But the activation levels of New Jersey, New York, and Pennsylvania are now higher than those of the other state concepts, so that another attempt to generate state names from the concept **state** is most likely to result in retrieval of the same three state names. Each successive attempt to traverse the associations emanating from **state** only maintains the high activation levels of those names already generated—or drives them even higher. In short, after a single use, subsequent attempts to access additional state names from the concept **state** are likely to fail.

How, then, does the person generate more state names? (We obviously can recall more than three states at one time.) The answer is that the person uses concepts other than **state** as recall cues. But before we discuss this strategy, let us examine in more detail the evidence that the number of concepts that can be generated from a single recall cue is limited.

### Forgetting in the Distractor Paradigm

One source of evidence regarding the ability to generate multiple concepts from a single cue comes from experiments in which a person is prevented from forming associations between a new target item and concepts already in memory. This kind of experiment is called a *distractor paradigm* because the subject is prevented or distracted from fully encoding the target. It is also sometimes called the Brown-Peterson paradigm, after the first investigators to perform this type of experiment (Brown 1958; Peterson and Peterson 1959).

The task is performed as follows: A subject is presented with a consonant trigram, such as *QBF*. The person repeats it once and at the same time is presented with a three-digit number, such as *687*. The person then has to immediately start counting backward by 3s. The only purpose of the counting task is to prevent the person from rehearsing the trigram (i.e., repeating it to himself or herself) or using any other strategy to consciously try to remember it. The counting task distracts the person from learning the trigram. After a specified period of time, which is usually 3–18 seconds, the person is permitted to stop counting and is asked to recall the trigram. The series of events from the presentation of the consonant trigram until the subject is asked to recall it constitutes a single trial. A single experiment consists of many trials, with a different consonant trigram being presented on each one.

**Cue overload.**   The results of this experiment must be analyzed very carefully, because a person's performance changes from trial to trial. The change in performance over trials was first demonstrated by Keppel and Underwood in 1962. Their results are shown in Figure 7.4 (see also Loess 1964). Consider how people performed on the very first trial in the experiment, shown by the point farthest to the left in the figure. As the figure shows, on the very first trial a person was almost certain to recall the trigram no matter how long he or she first counted backward. Virtually everyone who had counted backward for 3, 9, or 18 seconds recalled their first trigram correctly. But look what happens on the second and third trial. The performance of people begins to deteriorate on these trials, and performance is poorer the longer people have to count backward before recalling the trigram. In fact, if the experiment is continued for six trials, correct recall of the trigram averages less than 50 percent after 18 seconds of counting backward.

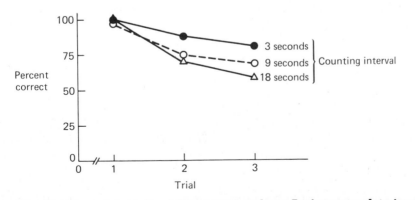

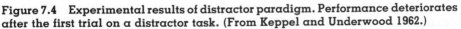

**Figure 7.4   Experimental results of distractor paradigm. Performance deteriorates after the first trial on a distractor task. (From Keppel and Underwood 1962.)**

Before we consider why performance drops off so markedly when a person has to count backward for more than 3 seconds, let us consider what a really remarkable result this is. After all, three consonants are not very much information to remember. For example, memorizing someone's phone number, which contains seven digits, is quite easy. But the results in the distractor paradigm demonstrate that a relatively brief period of interference right at the time when a target would normally be associated to other concepts in memory has a very detrimental effect on later recall.

Why does performance deteriorate so dramatically over successive trials? One explanation is that the distractor task prevents a subject from forming associations between the target and other concepts in memory that could serve as retrieval cues. So when the subject is asked to recall the target at the end of the first trial, probably only one fact serves as a cue for the target—namely, that it was a consonant trigram. However, since this association is recent and therefore strong, this one cue will probably be sufficient to generate the target. The memory structure on the first trial is depicted in Figure 7.5(a).

Now consider the situation at the end of the second trial, when the subject has to recall the most recently presented trigram. The subject again only has a single cue, that a consonant trigram has been presented. But now the cue is associated to two recently presented trigrams, as shown in Figure 7.5(b). As a result, there is a significant probability that when the subject tries to use the cue to generate the trigram presented on the second trial, the trigram presented on the first trial will be generated instead. The retrieval cue has been overloaded.

Even if the subject succeeds in generating both trigrams, he or she will still be faced with the task of selecting the more recent of the two. In general, the more recent trigram will seem more familiar. But here the length of the interval spent counting backward will have an effect. If this interval is relatively long, say 18 seconds, the familiarity of the more recent trigram may have already diminished enough so that it is difficult to discriminate from the earlier trigram. As the number of trials continues to increase, the subject's problems will be further compounded. As Figure 7.5(c) indicates, the recall cue will become associated to more and more trigrams, so the cue becomes increasingly

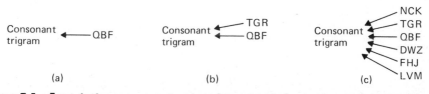

**Figure 7.5   Associative memory structure for presented consonant trigrams: (a) After one trial; (b) after two trials; (c) after six trials.**

useless. With each additional trial both generating and recognizing the most recently presented trigram become more difficult. The contribution of each of these steps to the amount of forgetting has been an issue of controversy among psychologists (Crowder 1976, Chapter 7), but this controversy does not detract from the point made here—that generation does become more difficult.

**Effect of a category shift.**   Psychologists have found one way to dramatically improve recall in a distractor task. If after several trials a new type of input is presented, recall on that trial will increase substantially. This result was first demonstrated in 1963 by Wickens, Born, and Allen. In their experiment subjects first went through three trials with consonant trigrams, with the usual deterioration in recall performance over trials. Then on the fourth trial half the subjects were given a digit trigram (e.g., 549) to recall. Figure 7.6 presents an idealized depiction of the results. As the figure shows, those subjects who were given a consonant trigram on the fourth trial continued to perform poorly. But the subjects given a digit trigram performed virtually as well as they had on the very first trial. Wickens and colleagues obtained the same result when they first presented digit trigrams and then shifted to consonants, and

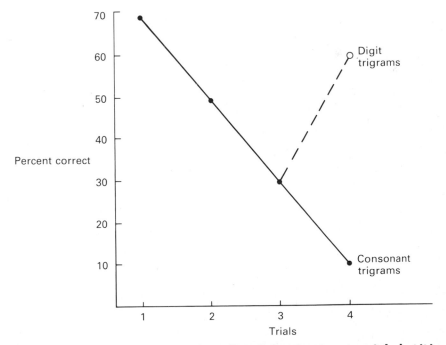

**Figure 7.6   Recall in distractor paradigm. Recall deteriorates over trials, but it increases when the category of the input is changed. (After Wickens, Born, and Allen 1963.)**

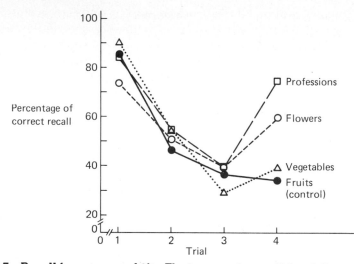

**Figure 7.7    Recall for category shifts. The increase in recall that follows a category shift is greater if the new category is very dissimilar from the first category. (From Wickens 1972.)**

whether the shift occurred on the fourth, seventh, or tenth trial. Performance always returned to the initial level of recall on the shift trial.

In many later studies Wickens showed that this effect is obtained with a wide variety of different shifts in inputs (Wickens 1972). In fact, the degree of increase in recall that follows a shift in category can provide an index of how similar the two input categories are. For example, Figure 7.7 presents the results of a study in which subjects were presented with the names of three fruits to recall on each of the first three trials. Then on the fourth trial the inputs to be recalled were names of fruits, vegetables, flowers, or professions. As Figure 7.7 shows, recall was poorest when the fruit category was used for a fourth time and best when the category was shifted to professions. In general, the more dissimilar the new category of targets is from the original category, the more recall improves.

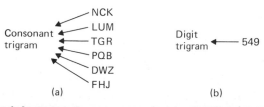

**Figure 7.8    Effect of changing the category of input: (a) Multiple category members associated with a single cue; (b) new retrieval cue introduced by a member of a different category.**

What is the reason for the increase in recall performance that follows a category shift? Figure 7.8 illustrates why performance would increase in the case of a shift from consonant trigrams to digit trigrams. After the first six trials the memory structure would be as in Figure 7.8(a)—six consonant trigrams all associated with a single cue. As a result, this cue would not be at all effective in generating the last input presented. But on the seventh trial the digit trigram will be associated to an entirely different cue, as shown in Figure 7.8(b). Since only one target will be associated with the cue *digit trigram*, that cue will be very effective when the person tries to recall the target.

We have suggested that the reason recall improves so dramatically when the target category is shifted is that the subject then has an effective retrieval cue. However, you might wonder whether the critical factor is that the subject notices that the input is different when it is first presented. But this factor is not the critical one. Gardiner, Craik, and Birtwistle (1972) demonstrated this result by changing the target in a very subtle way and alerting the subject to the change at recall. For example, if students are presented with a series of trials on which the items are cultivated flowers (e.g., *rose, carnation*), followed by a critical trial on which the items are wildflowers (e.g., *dandelion*), recall will not improve. The students simply do not note the subtle shift in category. But if the experimenter tells the student at the time of recall that the items on the last trial were wildflowers, performance will be more accurate. Therefore the critical factor causing improvement in recall seems to be the introduction of a new retrieval cue. [For further evidence supporting this conclusion, see Loftus and Patterson (1975) and Watkins and Watkins (1975).]

## ROLE OF CUES IN GENERATION

The influence of differential concept activation levels on recall was demonstrated in an experiment on free recall performed by J. Brown (1968). (As we will see, no less than four psychologists named Brown have worked in this area.) He required two groups of subjects to recall as many of the fifty states as they could. For one group he first read the names of twenty-five of the fifty states. This group naturally recalled more of the names of the twenty-five states that had been read aloud than did the group that had not heard the list. However, the former group of subjects recalled *fewer* of the twenty-five states that had *not* been read aloud than did the group that had no prior cuing. Thus the use of cues in recall has costs as well as benefits. For example, if New Jersey is associated to both New York and New Mexico, then generating *New York* will make it difficult to generate *New Mexico*.

This property of memory, which limits the number of responses that can be generated from a single cue, often places a limit on the number of similar targets that can be recalled at one time. For example, Battig and Montague (1969) asked college students to generate instances of fifty-six different categories (e.g., *flowers, diseases, ships, metals, toys*). The students had 30 seconds to generate instances for each category. Each student was usually able to generate only five or six instances for a category within the 30 seconds. The greatest average number (11) of instances produced was for the category *human body parts*, and the smallest average number (4) of instances was for the category *building of religious services*. Yet many of the categories obviously had more than a hundred familiar instances (e.g., *female names, male names, cities*).

## Secondary Recall Cues

Is there any way to circumvent the limit on the number of targets that can be generated from a single cue? How can a person succeed in generating large numbers of concepts, especially those that have few strong associates? As an example, let us consider once more how someone might try to generate the names of states. One strategy might be to form a mental image of the map of the United States. Then the person could mentally scan the imaginary map and name each state as its location was encountered. Another strategy might be for the person to think of all the places he or she had visited. What both these strategies have in common is that potential targets are generated in a systematic fashion that prevents the person from generating the same concepts again and again. The map of the United States in the first strategy and the person's own life experiences in the second strategy form the backbone of a chain of associations that prevents the person from getting trapped into repeating the same path.

There are many possible generation strategies for every recall task. Since different people know different things, the choice of strategy is fundamentally idiosyncratic. Thus a sports fan may use the names of sports franchises to cue the states that they are located in. A meteorologist may use the climate type of the region as a cue for the state's name. What cue is effective will depend on how the individual's knowledge is organized. And many different strategies for generating cues may be effective. What is important is that the person must find some strategy or combination of strategies for generating additional recall cues. These additional recall cues, generated from the original recall cue (e.g., *state*) in the hope that they will be associated to the target, are called *secondary recall cues*. In fact, only in the most trivial cases is the target closely associated to the original recall cue (e.g., "Who was the first president of the United States?"). Usually, the person has to generate additional cues in order to perform the recall task successfully. The person's skill at generating secondary recall cues may often be what determines whether the target information is recalled.

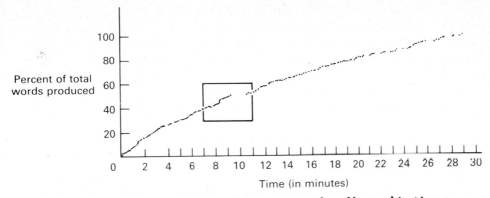

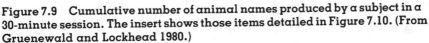

**Figure 7.9    Cumulative number of animal names produced by a subject in a 30-minute session. The insert shows those items detailed in Figure 7.10. (From Gruenewald and Lockhead 1980.)**

The effect of the secondary recall cue strategy on free recall is shown in Figures 7.9, 7.10, and 7.11. Following Bousfield and Sedgewick (1944), Gruenewald and Lockhead (1980) gave students either 15 or 30 minutes to generate all the instances of a category. The three figures illustrate ubiquitous aspects of human performance in the task. Figure 7.9 shows that a continuous effort yields a lower and lower rate of category production (i.e., the curve increases less rapidly as the recall attempt progresses). Figure 7.10 shows that the instances are produced in clusters, as mentioned above, and Figure 7.11 shows the distribution of cluster sizes. As shown in Figures 7.10 and 7.11, most clusters contain only one or two instances, and cluster size drops off rapidly. But a few very large clusters, even clusters containing more than ten instances, are observed. Let us return again to Figure 7.9; the reason the rate of instance production declines with time is that the rate of cluster production declines with time. Average cluster size remains constant.

Gruenewald and Lockhead (1980) show that these results can be completely described by the following model. Suppose, say, a person has 150 animal names stored in memory and embarks on a strategy of first generating secondary recall cues and then using them to generate animal clusters. Furthermore, the secondary recall cues are produced at a constant rate. At the beginning, when virtually no animal names have been generated, the probability of a secondary recall cue adding new animal names will be high, and hence new clusters will be rapidly added. However, as more and more animal names are produced, the probability of a secondary recall cue producing new names decreases, and the person must generate more and more secondary recall cues before a new cluster is produced. As a result, the time between new clusters increases. Therefore if what you know is poorly organized, then the results of an extended recall effort will inevitably diminish with time.

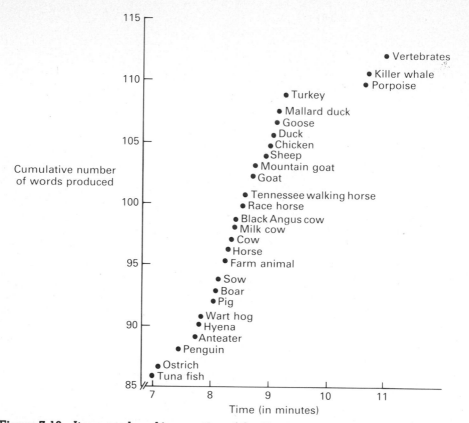

**Figure 7.10    Items produced in a portion of the 30-minute animal-recall task. (From Gruenewald and Lockhead 1980.)**

**Inhibitory effects of semantic cues.**    We have seen that each recall cue has a dual effect on the recall of a set of targets, such as the members of a category or a list of words. The cue first has a potentially facilitatory effect. It may activate new targets sufficiently for them to enter consciousness. However, once the targets have been activated, the cue has an inhibitory effect because its use has increased its activation level, so it is easily reactivated by other cues. That is, a new cue similar to both the old cue and to a new target will be more likely to reactivate the old one because of the old cue's higher activation level. Thus cues, targets, and distractors all come to block the retrieval of new targets once they have been activated.

For example, A. Brown (1981) found that when students had to name members of a particular category that each began with a particular letter (e.g., for *g-animal* one answer is *giraffe*), students took a longer time to produce each successive member. Similarly, when naming a sequence of pictures of mem-

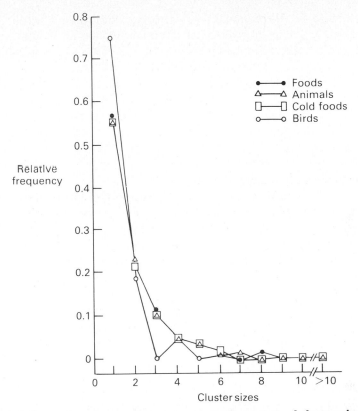

**Figure 7.11   Relative frequency of occurrence of different-sized clusters for the free recall of four categories. (From Gruenewald and Lockhead 1980.)**

bers of a category, after three or four items students took a longer time to name each successive picture.

Blaxton and Neely (1983) added an important qualification to this result. In order for one category member to inhibit the retrieval of its successor, the predecessor must itself be actively retrieved, as in Brown's task. Blaxton and Neely found that merely reading other category names did not sufficiently activate them so that they slowed down the retrieval of the name of another member that began with a particular letter (see also Neely, Schmidt, and Roediger 1983).

If we examine these dual effects from the perspective of an individual cue, then whether that cue facilitates or inhibits recall depends on whether it activates or inhibits more new targets. We have just considered the facilitatory effects of cues. Now we will examine situations where, on balance, the effect of the cue is inhibitory. When Roediger and Neely (1982) reviewed the topic, they found a wide variety of situations in which inhibition occurred. We will describe the most often studied situations here.

In Brown's study students were shown a word followed by a definition and had to decide whether the two matched. If they did not, the students were to generate the word that matched the definition. When the word (i.e., the lexical cue) did not match the definition, then it was related to the target in one of three ways. Suppose the definition was, "to eat greedily" and the target was *gobble*. Either the cue was semantically similar to the target (*cram*), was orthographically similar, by virtue of having the same first letter and number of syllables, to the target (*goggle*), or was unrelated to it (*feud*). The results of two experiments are shown in Table 7.1.

Notice that the orthographic cue facilitated the retrieval of the correct word. The orthographic cue activated the visual representation of the target word by partially matching it. Only the target was a close match to *both* the orthographic cue and its own definition, so the target's total activation was more than the cue's; and on balance target retrieval was facilitated in comparison with retrieval for the unrelated cue.

However, Table 7.1 also shows that retrieval of the correct word was more difficult with the semantic cue than with the unrelated cue. The semantic cue partially matched the definition of the target. So when subjects tried to use its definition to generate the target, they sometimes regenerated the semantic cue instead, because of its high activation from having just been presented. However, in an important qualification on this result Roediger, Neely, and Blaxton (1983) showed that the semantic cue inhibited only when subjects thought it might be the target and tested it against the definition. When subjects knew that the semantic cue would not be the target, they could reject it as well as an unrelated cue. Roediger and his colleagues' result provides a clue to why the experience of being unable to retrieve something you know is as rare as it is. Apparently, only if you are initially misled into fully processing an alluring distractor do all its components receive sufficient activation to block the target.

**TABLE 7.1** Effect of Cue Relation on the Retrieval of a Word to Fit a Definition

| Cue | Experiment 1: Percent correct | Experiment 2 Percent correct | Experiment 2 Time (in seconds) |
|---|---|---|---|
| Semantic | 3 | 86 | 7.4 |
| Orthographic | 12 | 93 | 4.6 |
| Unrelated | 8 | 89 | 5.6 |

*Source:* From Brown (1979).

**Tip-of-the-tongue phenomenon.**   When the phenomenon Brown (1979) demonstrated occurs naturally, it is called the *tip-of-the-tongue (TOT) phenomenon*. We have all had the experience of knowing that we know something without being able to produce it. For example, you might come upon an old acquaintance and be able to remember everything about the person except his or her name. Even five-year-olds can suffer the frustration of knowing they know something they cannot remember (Wellman 1977).

A number of psychologists (R. Brown and McNeill 1966; Hart 1965) have studied the TOT experience. The basic experiment consists of asking a large number of students a long list of questions. The students are then asked how certain they are that they in fact know the answers to those questions they were initially unable to answer. Next, the students are encouraged to guess and give partial answers, if possible. Finally, the students are given cues to help them come up with the answers.

For example, Brown and McNeill's (1966) experiment consisted of reading to students a large number of dictionary definitions, such as "an instrument used by navigators to measure the angle between a heavenly body and a horizon." Then after reading each definition, they asked the students to indicate their ability to recall the defined word. Most students either recalled the word or were certain that they had no idea what the word might be. Brown and McNeill were not interested in either of these groups; instead, they focused on the few students that were left. These students indicated that they were certain they knew the word but could not quite recall it. They expressed the feeling that the word was on the tips of their tongues.

Whenever a student suggested that they were in a TOT state, Brown and McNeill proceeded to ask a variety of questions, such as, "What is the first letter? How many letters does the word contain? How many syllables? Can you tell me what the word sounds like?" They found that students in the TOT state could often answer such questions quite accurately. For instance, they might know that the first letter was an *s*, that the word had two syllables, even that it had seven letters, but they still were unable to produce the name *sextant*. Instead, they might produce soundalikes, like *secant* or *sextet*. Consistent with Brown's (1979) results, if a researcher supplies a perceptual cue that activates the target by a different route, such as the first letter of the word (Freedman and Landauer 1966; Gruneberg and Monk 1974) or a rhyming word (Kozlowski 1977), it sometimes helps the person remember the word.

**Part-list cues.**   As mentioned above, a target itself, once activated, will block the retrieval of other related targets. Recall that J. Brown (1968) showed that giving students the names of some states blocked the retrieval of other states. Slamecka (1968, 1969) introduced the *part-list cuing paradigm* for studying this effect systematically. In this paradigm subjects study a list of words and are then given some of the list words and told to use them as cues to recall the remainder of the list. Fewer list words not used as cues are recalled in this condition than in the condition when subjects are not given any cues and simply told to freely recall the entire list (also see Roediger 1978).

Rundus (1973) showed that the inhibitory part-list cuing effects could be explained by a model quite similar to what has been described here (though his terminology is different). In Rundus's model, presenting some targets as cues increases their activation so much that on subsequent generation attempts they are likely to be retrieved over and over in preference to the other unpresented targets.

## Fluctuations in Recall

If on two separate occasions a person selects somewhat different secondary recall cues when trying to recall the same set of targets, somewhat different targets may be recalled. W. Brown (1923) gave his college students two chances to recall all the states they could in 5 minutes. The two recall trials were half an hour apart. On their second try the students recalled about five states they had failed to recall on the first trial, but they also failed to recall about two states they had recalled previously.

Herman Buschke (1974) observed similar fluctuations in the recall of randomly selected words. Suppose the subject is asked to recall a list of words once, and then a few minutes later the subject is asked to recall the list again. On the second trial the subject will usually recall some new words that were not recalled on the first trial. However, success in recalling new words will be partially canceled out by the failure to recall some words on the second trial that had been recalled on the first trial. Since the number of new words recalled is usually greater than the number of old words forgotten, recall gradually improves. This increase in recall is not what you might expect. You might think that if I read a list of twenty words, and you spend 5 minutes attempting to recall them, any word that you do not recall in the first 5 minutes would never be recalled. However, as Buschke found, further effort uncovers different cues and thus leads to increased recall.

The precise items recalled at any one time depends on the amount of overlap between them, the strength of their associations, their momentary activation levels, and the generation strategy the person adopts. Consequently, deriving a general quantitative model from this qualitative account that predicts *how much* will be recalled in a variety of tasks is difficult. A recent attempt to simulate recall with a ten-parameter computer model (Raaijmakers and Shiffrin 1981) suggested that the initial cues and generation strategy may be quite important, but the complexity of the model makes it difficult to test. Nevertheless, a variety of fairly successful quantitative models of different parameters affecting recall have been proposed (e.g., Jones 1978; Ross and Bower 1981; Rotondo 1979).

The effects of frequency and recency of access on the organization and activation levels of concepts, and hence on their ease of generation and ultimate recallability, have many important consequences for human thinking. As we will see in Chapter 12, the tendency for human memory to move in well-worn grooves can be a block to creative problem solving. This property of memory may also be involved in certain neuroses. A person may continually dwell on some disturbing thought so that it becomes more and more readily retrieved. In addition, the thought may eventually become associated to almost every possible cue in the person's environment. At this point the unwanted thought will have become an obsession that may darken the person's every waking moment.

## CONTEXTUAL EFFECTS ON RECALL

So far, we have discussed only cues that a person consciously uses during recall. But a concept has many different components, and the input cannot be entirely separated from the context in which it appears. When an input is encoded, some aspects of the physical environment in which it is encoded influence the representation it receives. If the retrieval attempt takes place in the same environment, then those same aspects are likely to influence the representation in the same way and hence facilitate retrieval. We have already seen how other inputs directly related to the target can influence its recognition. The effect of context on recall is even more dramatic. Experiments have demonstrated that even aspects of the environment that the person does not consciously associate with the target influence its recall.

### Context-Dependent Recall

In a typical experiment (Godden and Baddeley 1975) sixteen divers learned a list of forty unrelated words either on the shore or 20 feet under the sea. They were subsequently asked to recall the words in either the same or the alternative environment. Mean free-recall scores were as shown in Figure 7.12. As the figure shows, words were recalled more accurately in the environment in which they were originally learned.

Godden and Baddeley performed a further experiment in which they tested divers' recognition of words in different environments. A change in environmental context had no effect on recognition performance, so apparently the environment acts primarily as a generation cue, though a person is usually not aware of it (also see Smith, Glenberg, and Bjork 1978). However, when people placed in a new environment are instructed to recall the original learning environment just prior to free recall of the list, their recall is as good in the new environment as in the original learning environment (Smith 1979). So

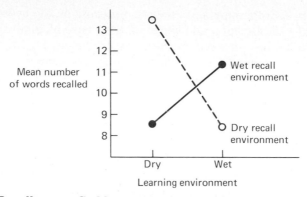

**Figure 7.12   Recall scores. Godden and Baddeley (1975) found that word lists were recalled better in the same environment in which they were learned than they were in a different environment.**

when people are made aware of the learning context, they can deliberately use it as a secondary recall cue to help generate potential targets.

## State-Dependent Memory

A phenomenon that is related to context-dependent memory is *state-dependent memory*. This term originally was used to describe the casual observation that heavy drinkers, when sober, were unable to find money or alcohol they had hidden while drunk, but they remembered the hiding places when they were drunk again. To explain this result, researchers assumed that the physiological state of the person acted as a cue for the hiding place. The existence of this phenomenon was unclear until a thoughtful review by James Eich (1980) showed that the tasks for which pharmacological-state-dependent retrieval is observed are the same as for context-dependent retrieval. That is, state-dependent retrieval is generally observed with free recall but not with cued recall or recognition. Apparently, in the latter cases the effects of the more salient retrieval cues obscure the effect of the state cue.

The effect of a person's emotional state on memory has also been studied. Clinicians have noticed that happy people seem to remember happy experiences and sad people seem to remember sad experiences. Gordon Bower and his colleagues (Bower 1981; Bower, Gilligan, and Monteiro 1981; Bower, Monteiro, and Gilligan 1978), in attempting to confirm this basic observation, found a surprisingly mild and uncertain effect of mood state at recall for word lists and stories. However, two aspects of this project may have reduced the impact of mood state. First, the subjects were Stanford University undergraduates and recent graduates. Mood may have a smaller effect on the memories of healthy young adults than on memories of persons in other age groups. Second, the mood state was hypnotically induced. Perhaps these mock moods do not have the same intensity and effect as genuine emotional states.

## Discriminating Targets from Distractors

We have seen that when people try to recall all the instances of a category (e.g., states, animals), they do not recall them all (Gruenewald and Lockhead 1980). The same result is often obtained for lists of twenty words or more (Tulving 1967). There are at least two reasons why overall recall of a randomly selected word list does not reach perfection with multiple recall attempts. The first reason, which has already been pointed out for category free recall, is that after awhile generating words that haven't been generated before becomes difficult. A vicious circle is established so that the same targets are reactivated over and over (Roediger 1974; Roediger and Schmidt 1980).

The second reason, which is unique to list free recall, is that on successive trials discriminating list words from nonlist words on the basis of familiarity becomes increasingly difficult. On the first recall trial familiarity is a good indicator of whether the word was on the list, since all list words will have just been seen. But on later trials the subject will no longer be able to accurately discriminate target words from distractors. The more detailed the representations of the targets, the more discriminable they usually are. For this reason more items are recalled from lists consisting of pictures of objects (e.g., shoe, telephone) than from lists consisting of the names of the same objects (Durso and Johnson 1980; Paivio 1974; Paivio and Csapo 1973). We will examine visual recall in more detail later in the chapter.

## Summary of Factors Influencing Recall

Apparently, then, two factors influence the recallability of a set of items: the number of potential targets that can be generated and the number of targets that can be recognized.

The number of targets that can be generated is, in turn, influenced by two more basic factors. The first basic factor is the discriminability of the targets from each other. If the targets are too similar to each other, so that a unique recall cue cannot be found for each one, then the generation of some targets will inevitably block the generation of others. The second basic factor influencing generation is the conceptual organization of the targets. If the target concepts are organized in the semantic code so that each one has a unique cue associated with it, then generating all the targets may be possible. Ideally, each target is a unique recall cue for another target; so by generating the first target, one can sequentially generate all the targets (e.g., $A \rightarrow B \rightarrow C \rightarrow \ldots$).

The better the targets are organized in memory, the more targets one will be able to recall. For example, one generally cannot recall even fifty items at a time from one category (e.g., states, girls' names, animals). However, if the words naming the items form sentences, and the sentences form paragraphs, and the paragraphs form a story, people can recall scores of details from a story they have heard once. Given a sufficient degree of organization, there is no limit on the number of concepts that can be recalled upon request.

The number of targets that can be recognized is, in turn, influenced by the discriminability of the targets vs. the distractors. If the targets are too similar to distractors, then some distractors will be generated by the cues that generate the targets, and it will not be possible to discriminate them during recognition. The more detailed the representations of the targets, the more discriminable they usually are.

The interaction between ease of generation and discriminability can be quite complex, because some inputs that are easily generated may be less discriminable than other inputs that are generated with more difficulty. For example, as a result of the procedures usually employed in list-learning tasks, the common words on the list are usually more easily generated at recall, whereas rare words are often more discriminable (for a variety of reasons that need not concern us here). Consequently, common words are often better recalled (Deese 1961; Hall 1954), but rare words are better recognized (Jacoby, Craik, and Begg 1979; Shepard 1967). As psychologists have come to understand these factors, they have been able to manipulate the recallability of words by manipulating their ease of generation (Dunlap and Dunlap 1979) and discriminability. We will examine this interaction further when we compare the recall of a picture and the word that names it.

## VISUAL RECALL

All our examples so far have involved the recall of words. Let us now consider the recall of visual patterns. As we will see, in a free-recall task people generate visual targets in much the same way as they generate verbal targets—by using secondary cues to activate the concepts of which they are components. However, when the cue is a part of the visual pattern, the target is activated more directly. The comparison procedure matches the visual cue to a part of the target representation, and the match activates the entire target.

### Visual Cues

We have already discussed the idea that the representation of a pattern consists of a set of intersecting features. For example, consider the pattern shown in Figure 7.13(a). Most people perceive the features of this pattern as orga-

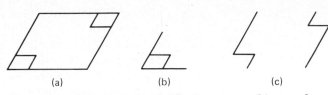
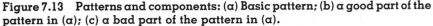

Figure 7.13   Patterns and components: (a) Basic pattern; (b) a good part of the
pattern in (a); (c) a bad part of the pattern in (a).

nized into three subpatterns, which in turn form the entire figure. That is, they
perceive this pattern as a parallelogram with boxes in the lower left and
upper right corners. A complete subpattern will be called a *good part*. So the
part of the pattern shown in Figure 7.13(b) is a good part of the pattern, whereas the part shown in Figure 7.13(c) is not. This result is true even though objectively both Figures 7.13(b) and 7.13(c) contain equally large pieces of the pattern in Figure 7.13(a).

Can a good part serve as a cue for generating the rest of the pattern, just
as one word from a list can serve as a cue for generating other list words? The
answer is yes. Bower and Glass (1976) showed a group of undergraduates a
series of patterns like the one shown in Figure 7.13(a). The students were then
given a piece of each pattern as a cue and asked to draw the complete patterns. If the cue was a good part of the pattern, then the students were able to
recall the entire pattern about 90 percent of the time. But if the part of the pattern presented as a cue was not a good part of the pattern, the pattern was
recalled only about 20 percent of the time.

There are other kinds of evidence for the role of feature organization in
visual recall. For example, Figure 7.14(a) depicts three separate objects,
whereas Figure 7.14(b) shows the same three objects in a single integrated
representation. Studies show that both adults (Wollen, Weber, and Lowry
1972) and children (Reese 1965) are better at remembering integrated patterns than separate pictures.

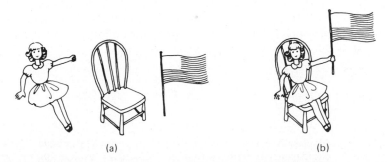

Figure 7.14   Visual representations: (a) Separate; (b) integrated.

## Free Recall

If a person is not given a part of the pattern as a cue for recall but must recall the entire pattern from memory, then the same generate-and-recognize strategy is used for visual patterns as is used for words. The person activates the concept of which the target is a part through self-generated secondary cues. This procedure makes the person vulnerable to producing a distractor pattern that is associated to the same category as the target.

An early experiment demonstrating this result was conducted by Carmichael, Hogan, and Walters (1932). They showed subjects a pattern like the one in the center of Figure 7.15 and described it as either *eyeglasses* or *dumbbell*. Later, the subjects were asked to draw from memory what they had seen. People who had been told the pattern was eyeglasses produced drawings like the one on the left in Figure 7.15, whereas people who had been told it was a dumbbell produced drawings like the one on the right in Figure 7.15. This result suggests that when the subjects attempted to recall the pattern, they had difficulty distinguishing between the representation of the pattern they had seen in the experiment and a similar representation of the concept aroused by the verbal label associated with it. That is, they had difficulty distinguishing between what they had seen and what they had heard. Bower and Holyoak (1973) showed that verbal labels influence the recognition of ambiguous sounds in a similar manner.

### Differences Between Verbal and Visual Memory

**Organization and discriminability.**   The recall of both words and pictures can be explained by the generate-and-recognize model, and the same factors influence the recall of both kinds of targets. However, different factors usually *limit* the recall of words vs. pictures. In general, nouns (and other linguistic targets) are better organized for generation than are pictures. On the other hand, pictures generally access more detailed representations and hence are more discriminable from one another than words are. Consequently, the generation step frequently limits the recall of pictures, whereas the recognition step limits the recall of words. To overcome the different limitations on the recall of these different kinds of targets, people employ two complementary

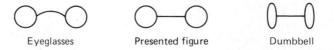

Eyeglasses          Presented figure          Dumbbell

**Figure 7.15   Visual classifications. The way a visual pattern (stimulus figure) is classified influences the way in which subjects later draw it from memory. (From Carmichael, Hogan, and Walters 1932.)**

strategies. People appear to routinely name pictures in order to help generate the pictures during recall. Also, people often tend to visualize the referents of words to make them more discriminable during recognition. Let us look at some of the evidence demonstrating these limitations on the recall of words and pictures and how people compensate for them.

Cohen and Granstrom (1970) performed a series of experiments indicating that people use the generate-and-recognize strategy to recall visual as well as verbal materials, and that the cues they use to generate visual materials are primarily verbal. In one experiment people were presented with irregular visual patterns that they later had to either recognize or reproduce. The subjects were also asked to describe the forms in words. Cohen and Granstrom found that the patterns that could be described most accurately were most likely to be reproduced accurately. However, the describability of the form had no influence on recognition performance. This result is exactly what we would expect if the verbal descriptions were used as cues for generating the forms during recall.

In another experiment people were shown a pattern and then asked to either recognize or reproduce it after a 7-second delay. During the delay interval either three names or three faces were presented, which the subject also had to remember. The names interfered more with the reproduction task than with the recognition task, suggesting that reproduction was more dependent on a verbal code. In contrast, the faces interfered more with the recognition task, suggesting that recognition depended more on a visual memory code.

Seemingly, then, pictures that are easily named or described are the easiest to recall. Also, words like *dog* or *chair* that refer to imageable objects are much more easily recalled than words like *justice* or *belief* that do not refer to imageable objects (Paivio 1971, p. 199). What, then, is the most easily recalled type of target, imageable words or nameable pictures? If the targets are presented as a randomly ordered list, recall appears to be better for the pictures than for the words (Erdelyi and Becker 1974).

**Increased recall during repeated retrieval.** A very striking phenomenon is sometimes observed if people are asked to repeatedly try to recall the items on a list. This task was investigated extensively by Matthew Erdelyi and his colleagues. In one experiment, Erdelyi and Kleinbard (1978) presented subjects with sixty pictures of common objects (e.g., watch, fish, feather) or with the names of the objects. Each target was presented for 5 seconds. Afterward, the subjects were asked to recall the list (always by writing the object names). The subjects then continued to try to recall the list, again and again over a period of a week. Figure 7.16 presents the average number of items recalled over time. When the items had been presented as words, average recall stayed fairly constant after the first hour. But when the items were presented as pictures, recall continued to go up for about four days.

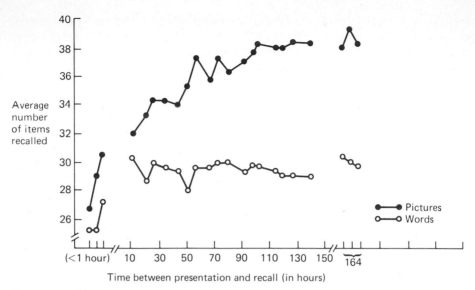

Figure 7.16    **Multiple recall attempts. The number of items recalled increases for a longer period of time for pictures than for words. (From Erdelyi and Kleinbard 1978.)**

Why should the recall of pictures increase for a longer period of time than the recall of words? The generate-recognize model of recall suggests a possible explanation (Erdelyi and Becker 1974). As we pointed out earlier, over successive recall trials the distribution of familiarity values of the new targets that are generated will come to overlap that of the distractors more and more. So discriminating actual list words from other words that had been generated as possible targets on previous recall trials will become increasingly difficult. As a result, on later trials some targets will not be sufficiently familiar to exceed the recognition criterion and hence will be generated but not recognized as list members. But as we saw in the previous chapter, pictures are recognized more accurately than words, presumably because pictures are more discriminable from one another. People will therefore have less trouble discriminating list pictures from nonlist pictures after many recall trials. Because the memory searches conducted on each recall trial will continue to generate the images and names of additional list pictures, the net result will be an increase in the total number of pictures recalled with multiple recall attempts.

We should point out, however, that such differences between memory performance with pictures and words depend on the strategies people use to encode the inputs, which will be discussed in more detail in Chapter 9. For example, if subjects are told to form a visual image of each object as its name is presented, recall over trials will increase in much the same way as it does when pictures are presented (Erdelyi, Finkelstein, Herrell, Miller, and Thomas 1976). Instructions that focus attention on the meaning of the words produce similar effects when the words are easy to image (Roediger and Thorpe 1978) but not when the words are abstract and hence difficult to image (Belmore 1981).

**Reminiscence.**   An even more striking increase in recall with time is observed with children. Ballard (1913) discovered that a partially learned poem studied by twelve-year-old London schoolchildren was not recalled as well immediately after the learning as it was a day or two later. Ballard named this phenomenon *reminiscence,* which was defined as the opposite of forgetting, that is, as an improvement in the memory for a target over time. Since then, reminiscence has been observed many times with children, but it is not obtained with adults (Woodworth and Schlosberg 1954, p. 794). Kasper (1983) obtained reminiscence in a paired-associate learning task in which twelve-year-old Brooklyn schoolchildren studied pairs of Spanish words and their English translations and then had to recall its translation when presented with the Spanish word.

   Though reminiscence is still encountered, it is not much studied, and its cause is not known. In Kasper's (1983) study the children were given the same strong cues for the targets in all recall tests, so it is unlikely that reminiscence results from children finding better secondary cues at longer study-test intervals. The most common and most likely explanation of reminiscence is that some factor depresses the child's immediate recall. One possibility is that a child adopts a very high criterion for recognizing targets during immediate recall, so some targets that are generated are not reported. One and two days later, the child adopts a more lenient recognition criterion and hence reports more targets. For example, in Kasper's study the children made fewer errors of omission during the recall test a day after learning the pairs, when reminiscence was observed.

## SUMMARY

The *generate-and-recognize model* of recall involves two steps: (1) generating potential recall targets and (2) recognizing actual targets. The generation of targets depends on the activation of concepts associated in memory. Activating a concept typically facilitates the recall of associated targets but interferes with the recall of other targets. Research on recall in a *distractor paradigm* indicates that when successive targets are associated with the same *retrieval cue* in memory, recall performance declines. If a further input can be associated with a different cue (e.g., a new category), recall of the new input will improve. The number of targets recalled can be increased by strategically using *secondary recall cues,* which are cues generated from the original cue provided by the query. In certain cases, however, an unfelicitous secondary cue can impair recall. Sometimes, people find themselves in a *tip-of-the-tongue state* in which they are sure they know the answer to a question but are unable to recall it. Over repeated recall attempts the particular targets recalled will fluctuate.

Recall is *context-dependent;* i.e., performance is impaired when the context is altered between the original encoding and the retrieval attempt. Similarly, recall is *state-dependent,* varying with the similarity of the person's physiological and emotional state between encoding and the retrieval attempt. Recall performance with visual inputs such as pictures is also in accord with the generate-and-recognize model. In general, verbal material is better organized for generation than are pictures, whereas pictures are more discriminable than words. The greater discriminability of information stored in a visuospatial code leads to increases in the amount of concrete material that can be recalled over extended recall attempts.

## RECOMMENDED READINGS

A detailed summary of memory research up to 1954 is found in the great classic *Experimental Psychology* by Robert S. Woodworth and Harold Schlosberg. This story is carried up to 1976 in *The Psychology of Memory* by Alan Baddeley, and up to 1981 by Wingfield and Byrnes's *Psychology of Human Memory.*

# CHAPTER **EIGHT**

# Reconstruction
# of Episodes

## INTRODUCTION

Up to this point, we have been treating all recall tasks as essentially the same. However, distinguishing between *episodic* and *nonepisodic recall targets* is useful. This distinction, as we will use it here, is similar to that introduced by Tulving (1972). (Tulving used the term *semantic* for nonepisodic knowledge. But since *semantic* is used in other ways, and since nonepisodic knowledge is extremely diverse, we will use the more neutral term.) The contrast is best illustrated by examples. Suppose you are asked what you had for dinner yesterday. This question is about a specific event in your life that took place at a specific time. The recall target is therefore episodic. In contrast, suppose you are asked who the first president was. This question does not ask anything about your own life; rather, it asks about a fact you might have learned at any point in time. This question involves a nonepisodic recall target. Episodic targets, then, are facts about your personal experiences, whereas nonepisodic targets are facts you may know that are not tied to any particular episode in your own life.

Most of the research we discussed in the previous chapter involved simple types of episodic recall. For example, if you recall that the word *chair* appeared on a list presented to you by an experimenter, you are actually recalling a certain episode (the presentation of the word *chair* at a certain time), not simply the fact that *chair* is an English word (which would be nonepisodic). The distinction between episodic and nonepisodic knowledge is not a sharp one. For example, a story you hear will not contain episodes of your life, yet it will have an episodic structure. Similar mental processes are involved in remembering both events in one's own life and other events, real or imaginary. We will therefore discuss story recall in this chapter.

## RECONSTRUCTION AND RECALL

### Reconstruction vs. Search

Suppose you are asked what your sister looks like (assuming you have one). You might search through a collection of cards and pictures in your wallet until you found one. Or you might draw a picture of her. These two responses provide models for how the generation step of a recall task might proceed. The generation of a concept might mean the activation of a complete representation, like the photograph. Or it might mean the construction of a representation from its parts, as in the case of the sketch.

In fact, both search and reconstruction play a role in generation. The generation of a single, very familiar concept usually does not involve construction. For example, if asked who is president, you certainly do not have the impression that you are constructing the name a syllable at a time. However, as the target becomes more complicated, the constructive aspect of recall becomes apparent. For example, when asked to tell a joke, you choose your words carefully and put the sentences in just the right sequence to maximize the impact of the punch line. As we will see, reconstruction is especially important in the recall of complex episodes.

### Use of Rules in Recall

The use of rules is central to the construction process. Recall from Chapter 5 that a rule is represented by a generative schema, which creates a new representation by applying a sequence of operations to an existing representation or representations. For example, suppose you are asked to give the sum of 32 + 49. Now, you probably never memorized the sum of these two numbers. In fact, you may never have added those two numbers before. Therefore you would not say that "32 + 49 = " was a cue for the target "81." Rather, you would say that you used the rules of addition to compute your answer.

The use of rules in certain situations is so easy and spontaneous that you probably do not realize what you are doing. Suppose someone stops you on your way to school and asks you how to get to the psychology building. You may never have given directions from that exact spot before, yet you will probably find it easy to describe how to get there. Without even trying very hard, you will be able to locate both yourself and the psychology building on a mental map of the campus and translate a pathway between the two points into a set of verbal instructions. This task requires recalling not only a mental representation of the campus but also rules for using the information in the representation to construct the target response.

Rules aid recall in other ways. Even when a rule does not generate the target response, it may at least be useful in generating a set of potential responses. For example, suppose you are asked to describe a football game you saw in which the winning team scored nine points. Further, suppose that you really can't immediately recall how the points were scored. You might remember that there are only four possible ways a team could score nine points: three field goals; a touchdown and a field goal; a touchdown, an extra point, and a safety; or three safeties and a field goal. From this relatively small set of possible scoring combinations, you might then be able to recognize the correct one and use it to cue further details of the game.

Games are not the only things with rules. The world is filled with rules, principles, conventions, and traditions that aid in the generation of responses, such as "The sun comes up in the morning and goes down in the evening"; "We are young before we are old." Whenever recall of an extended description is attempted, whether it is a story or an eyewitness report, rules play an important role in cuing and ordering the output.

If we take a still closer look at the role rules play in recall, we can find further evidence of their influence. In our example of the football game, suppose you remember the winning team having scored a touchdown and an extra point. Thus the only way the team could have scored the other two points needed to make a total of nine was by a safety. Another nice thing about rules is that when the same rules are known to the speaker and the listener, a succinct account can communicate a great deal of information. Hence in stating that one team led 7–0 after a touchdown, one usually does not explicitly mention that after crossing the goal line for six points, the team made a placement kick for the seventh.

As this example suggests, we can use our knowledge of rules to notice gaps in recall and then fill them in. However, the use of rules to fill in gaps in recall causes an important problem in determining the veracity of the information we recall. Does the person describing both the touchdown and the safety really recall both scores, or is one score being described because the person knows it must have taken place, rather than because it was really remembered? We are usually very confident when we try to recall something that we are recalling it accurately. So you might expect that the generation of false memories is relatively rare. However, this task is one in which our intuitions sometimes mislead us. Sometimes, our reconstruction of a story we have heard or an accident we have witnessed is as accurate as we feel it is, but sometimes it is not. Let us consider how we reconstruct one particular kind of input: how we recall and retell stories.

## STORY RECALL

We have seen that various operations may be performed on a set of representations. The outcome of an operation that involves two or more representations defines a *relation* that exists between them. For example, if two representations are compared and they match each other exactly, then the *identity* relation holds between them. The semantic code contains nodes that are activated by the outcomes of various procedures, and these nodes define various relations. The semantic code contains sequences of category nodes and relations that encode relations between particular categories. For example, the sequence *dog is an animal* encodes the category relation (described in Chapter 5). These sequences are called *propositions*. A set of propositions can be used to describe a particular event or episode. A temporally ordered sequence of episodes that relate to a common character may form a story (Kintsch, Mandel, and Kozminsky 1977).

## Story Hierarchies

Table 8.1 presents a simple story called "Circle Island," used by Dawes (1964), Thorndyke (1977), and Buschke and Schaier (1979) to study story recall. The numbers in Table 8.1 indicate how the story breaks down into a series of propositions. This structure is presented in Figure 8.1. You do not need to understand every detail in this figure. It is the overall organization that is

**TABLE 8.1** "Circle Island"

(1) Circle Island is located in the middle of the Atlantic Ocean, (2) north of Ronald Island. (3) The main occupations on the island are farming and ranching. (4) Circle Island has good soil, (5) but few rivers and (6) hence a shortage of water. (7) The Island is run democratically. (8) All issues are decided by a majority vote of the islanders. (9) The governing body is a senate, (10) whose job is to carry out the will of the majority. (11) Recently, an island scientist discovered a cheap method (12) of converting salt water into fresh water. (13) As a result, the island farmers wanted (14) to build a canal across the island, (15) so that they could use water from the canal (16) to cultivate the island's central region. (17) Therefore, the farmers formed a pro-canal association (18) and persuaded a few senators (19) to join. (20) The pro-canal association brought the construction idea to a vote. (21) All the islanders voted. (22) The majority voted in favor of construction. (23) The senate, however, decided that (24) the farmers' proposed canal was ecologically unsound. (25) The senators agreed (26) to build a smaller canal (27) that was two feet wide and one foot deep. (28) After starting construction on the smaller canal, (29) the islanders discovered that (30) no water would flow into it. (31) Thus the project was abandoned. (32) The farmers were angry (33) because of the failure of the canal project. (34) Civil war appeared inevitable.

*Source:* From Dawes (1964).

*Note:* Numbers correspond to locations in the conceptual structure shown in Figure 8.1. The story was written by Dawes (1964) and used by Thorndyke (1977) to test memory for story structure.

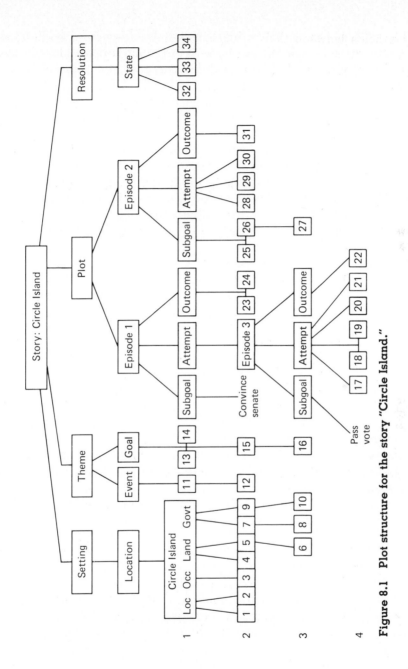

**Figure 8.1  Plot structure for the story "Circle Island."**

239

important. This organization is hierarchical—more general levels of structure divide into more specific levels, until the actual propositions of the story (represented by the numbers from Table 8.1) appear at the lower levels of the hierarchy.

At the top level of the hierarchy shown in Figure 8.1, the story divides into a setting (where the story takes place), a theme (the basic topic of the story), a plot (the sequence of events that is described), and a resolution (the eventual outcome). Each of these major aspects of the story leads to more specific information that fills in the details. For example, the plot consists of several episodes, each of which can be described in terms of a subgoal (a specific goal), an attempt to reach the goal, and an outcome. We will see in Chapter 12 that problem-solving behavior can be described in a similar way. This similarity is not surprising, since stories are generally written about problems (Black and Bower 1980).

Focusing on episode 2, we see that the subgoal of this episode is specified by the information in propositions 25 and 26 of the story; that is, "The senators agreed to build a smaller canal." The attempt to accomplish this goal is specified by propositions 28, 29, and 30: "After starting construction on the smaller canal, the islanders discovered that no water would flow into it." Finally, the outcome of this episode is specified by proposition 31: "The project was abandoned."

The hierarchical story structure shown in Figure 8.1 has important implications for the way people who hear the "Circle Island" story will remember it. To recall a story, one must do more than recall the individual sentences. One must also recall how the individual propositions relate to one another. Without these relationships there would be no story. For instance, suppose someone took all the sentences of the story, wrote them on index cards, and then shuffled the cards. We certainly would not say that someone reading those index cards was reading the story.

How would a person go about trying to recall a story? By now it should come as no surprise that recall will depend on the way the story is organized in memory. A person generally cannot simply find the beginning of the story and then generate every detail in the order in which it occurred, any more than a person can generate every item of a hundred-word list in the original order. There is no guarantee that all details of the story will be generated, or that all the ideas generated will actually be from the story. Someone trying to recall a story will have to decide which ideas were from the story and how they should be combined to reconstruct the conceptual structure of the original story.

How do we go about selecting and ordering the ideas in a story we are trying to recall? This area is where the hierarchical story organization becomes critical. Note that in Figure 8.1 the individual propositions (represented by numbers) in the "Circle Island" story fall at four levels in the hierarchy. Suppose someone is asked to recall "Circle Island." The person will use his or her general knowledge of stories, encoded in a general story schema, to generate general concepts like **setting** and **plot.** These concepts, along with the specific cue "Circle Island," will be used to activate propositions at the top level of the "Circle Island" hierarchy. The propositions at higher levels will then be used to cue propositions at lower levels. At lower levels the higher-level propositions are combined with the basic goal-attempt-outcome sequence generated by the story schema to generate the story's propositions in the appropriate order.

Notice that story recall is not self-limiting like the free recall of a list or a category (see Chapter 7). Each higher-level proposition provides a unique cue for the small set of propositions immediately below it in the hierarchy, so there is relatively little cue overload. Also, the sequence of concepts generated by the story schema, e.g., goal-attempt-outcomes, provides a framework that reveals any important gaps in the recall and provides cues for filling those gaps. So unlike the recall of category and list members, which, as we have seen, approaches an asymptote after only a few minutes of effort, the recall of a story has no limit. That is, there is no known limit to the length of a story that can be recalled in a single attempt. However, as mentioned above, people telling a story rarely report every detail they can recall. Rather, they summarize the story at the level of the hierarchy that is appropriate for the listener.

If people actually use the hierarchical story structure in this way to cue information, then clusters of concepts that correspond to clusters of propositions in the story hierarchy (e.g., 1 and 2; 9 and 10; 28, 29, 30) should be recalled together. This clustering is what Buschke and Schaier (1979) found. Furthermore, a higher percentage of propositions high in the hierarchy than propositions low in the hierarchy should be recalled, because the recall of propositions low in the hierarchy is dependent on the prior recall of the propositions that dominate them. For example, proposition 6 should not be recalled until proposition 5 is first recalled and used as a cue to generate it. But the recall of proposition 5 is not dependent on the recall of proposition 6. Consistent with this prediction, Thorndyke (1977) found that the percentage of propositions recalled at each level of the hierarchy decreased monotonically from level 1 to level 4 (also see Rumelhart 1977).

## Verbatim vs. Gist Recall

When someone tells a story, story construction is accomplished by using the story's hierarchical structure to generate its episodes in order. And as each episode is generated, the language production procedure translates it into words. Since there are many ways of saying the same thing, the person does not recall the exact words that he or she heard, only the same concepts. Memory for the same concepts is called memory for *gist*. Memory for the exact words is called *verbatim memory*. Constructive processes produce memory for gist.

Lynne Reder (1982) contrasted verbatim and gist memory and showed, as one would expect, that people are much better at recalling the gist than the exact words of a story they've heard. Students had to read ten stories and then had to respond, as quickly as possible, whether certain sentences had either appeared in the story (verbatim recall) or seemed true given the story (gist recall). The recall task occurred either immediately after, 20 minutes after, or two days after the stories were read. Judgments about whether sentences had appeared were always less accurate than judgments about whether they were true. Furthermore, the accuracy of the appearance judgments deteriorated considerably at the 20-minute delay and again two days later, while the truth judgments declined only slightly in accuracy. The reaction time data told a slightly different story. At delays of 20 minutes and two days truth judgments were much faster than appearance judgments. But both kinds of judgments were faster for sentences that actually had appeared than sentences that had not. This result suggests that the surface forms of the story sentences were encoded in memory; however only their underlying propositional representations were used to make the truth and appearance judgments.

## Distortions in Story Recall

The most famous experiment on reconstruction in story recall was reported in 1932 by the late British psychologist Sir Frederic Bartlett. He presented Oxford University students with a legend that originates with a Pacific Northwest Indian culture, and he then asked the students after varying intervals to recall the story. By comparing the recall protocol to the original, Bartlett was able to examine how the story was reconstructed. Table 8.2 presents the original legend, "The War of the Ghosts," and Table 8.3 presents the recall protocol of a 1977 Rutgers undergraduate, taken five days after hearing the story.

The important thing to note in comparing the two versions of the story is not just how much was not recalled but how much was invented to fill in the gaps around the material that was left out. Details like the names of places were omitted. But other details, like the shooting of bows and arrows during the fight, were added. The remarkable thing is that the recall protocol is quite a logical story, with a beginning, a simple plot, and a conclusion. In some ways it seems more logical than the original Indian legend, which comes from a culture very different from our own. But note, too, that the recall protocol is really a different story. The ghosts have even become men. The person was unable to distinguish the logical connections that were in the story from those that were not. [For a detailed analysis of the structure of "The War of the Ghosts" and other stories, as well as a discussion of Bartlett's results, see Mandler and Johnson (1977).]

**TABLE 8.2** Original Version of "The War of the Ghosts"

One night two young men from Egulac went down to the river to hunt seals, and while they were there it became foggy and calm. Then they heard war-cries, and they thought: "Maybe this is a war party." They escaped to the shore, and hid behind a log. Now canoes came up, and they heard the noise of paddles, and saw one canoe coming up to them. There were five men in the canoe, and they said:

"What do you think? We wish to take you along. We are going up to the river to make war on the people."

One of the young men said: "I have no arrows."

"Arrows are in the canoe," they said.

"I will not go along. I might be killed. My relatives do not know where I have gone. But you," he said, turning to the other, "may go with them."

So one of the young men went, but the other returned home.

And the warriors went on up the river to a town on the other side of Kalama. The people came down to the water, and they began to fight, and many were killed. But presently the young man heard one of the warriors say: "Quick, let us go home: that Indian has been hit." Now he thought: "Oh, they are ghosts." He did not feel sick, but they said he had been shot.

So the canoes went back to Egulac, and the young man went ashore to his house, and made a fire. And he told everybody and said: "Behold I accompanied the ghosts, and we went to fight. Many of our fellows were killed, and many of those who attacked us were killed. They said I was hit, and I did not feel sick."

He told it all, and then he became quiet. When the sun rose he fell down. Something black came out of his mouth. His face became contorted. The people jumped up and cried.

He was dead.

*Source:* From Bartlett (1932).

**TABLE 8.3** Recall Protocol of a Rutgers Undergraduate Taken Five Days After Hearing the Story

Two young men were by a river when they saw a canoe coming downstream. They hid behind a log but were still seen by the people in the canoe. They asked the two men if they wanted to come along. The one replied that he couldn't because none of his family knew where he was, but he told the other man to go ahead, while he went home. The men in the canoe said they were going to war. When they reached the village they shot their bows and arrows till one man said "We've got the Indian." Then they turned around to go back home. When the young man got home everyone was there. Even though he thought he had been shot, he wasn't dead. The next morning something black came out of his mouth and his body became contorted. He was dead.

## RECONSTRUCTION OF LIFE EXPERIENCES

### Constructing Perceptual Memories

Construction is not just something that happens in recounting stories. Rather, it is involved in every report that we make of our life experiences. Such a construction task may involve constructing a sequence of perceptual representations as well as an accompanying narrative, and as we have seen, both kinds of constructions are susceptible to distortion. The degree of distortion in eyewitness testimony is of particular importance, since the fairness of our justice system depends in large part on its accuracy.

Some studies have shown that eyewitness reports are often inaccurate in certain respects (Brown 1935; Buckhout 1974). In addition, misleading questions can influence reports. For example, Loftus and Palmer (1974) showed students a film of a collision between two cars. Later the students were asked one of two questions: "About how fast were the cars going when they hit each other?" or "About how fast were the cars going when they smashed into each other?" Subjects gave higher estimates of the speed when the question contained the word *smashed* instead of *hit*. In addition, after a one-week delay the subjects who had been asked the question containing *smashed* showed a greater tendency to report erroneously that there had been broken glass at the accident scene. In this case the question itself influenced how the person reconstructed a description of the original event.

### Recall of Personal Episodes

When you recall an episode in your life, you often reconstruct it in much the same way as you would reconstruct an episode in a story. However, your own life story is much richer and contains many more details important to you than any story you might read. So you need a much finer system of cues and rules to reconstruct your life than to construct a story. After all, in a very large measure your personal identity depends on what you can recall of your past.

One cue is familiarity. In general, recent episodes seem more familiar than episodes in the distant past. For example, the name "Ronald Reagan" is probably more familiar to you than the name "Gerald Ford." This cue is one that a person could use to decide who was president more recently.

A second kind of cue includes knowledge of rules of development and of specific facts about the world that can be used as landmarks. For example, you know that you attended high school before college and elementary school before high school. This knowledge provides you with a rule that can be used to order all kinds of events associated with these institutions. Key events, like obtaining a driver's license and graduating from high school, become landmarks around which other events connected to them can be organized. Another kind of landmark is an event that was unexpected but was extremely important and evoked a strong emotional response, an event such as the death of a parent. For example, most Americans who are old enough to remember the event remember the time, place, and circumstances under which they heard that President Kennedy was shot (Brown and Kulik 1977).

The reconstructive aspect of recall becomes more obvious as the task becomes more difficult. If you are simply asked what you were generally doing two years ago, you probably will not be conscious of using rules and landmarks to reconstruct the answer. But now suppose you were asked to describe what you were doing and wearing at noon on January 7, 1984. Your initial response might be, "Are you crazy? That was a long time ago." But if you persist, you might begin to think along the following lines:

> January 7, 1984, let's see, that was during Christmas break, so I suppose I was at home. No, wait a minute, that year Christmas break ended January 6, that was before we switched schedules. So, let's see, I must have been back at school. In fact, that was review week, so I assume I was in a class. Let's see, we came back on a Monday, so the seventh would have been a Tuesday. What classes was I taking that term? Renaissance poetry, physics—wait, I must have been in statistics because it met over the noon hour on Tuesdays and Thursdays. Now I remember the review session. Dr. Shaw was having trouble with all the nervous students, demanding to know if they were responsible for this or that particular piece of information.

Looking back at this hypothetical recall example, we see a lot of recall activity that resembles logical problem solving. A person figures out the context in trying to deduce what might have happened. All of this activity is setting the stage—trying to establish enough context to make contact with a specific memory. If the problem-solving effort is successful, it leads to an actual memory of the experience, not simply a reconstruction of a possible experience.

The first constructive process to influence recall was finding an appropriate landmark to cue the experience (Christmas break). How might this construction of a recall cue influence a person's eventual recall? Possibly, the constructive deductions used to find the cue are incorrect (or use information that is itself misremembered). For example, you might have been wrong about Christmas break ending on January 6; perhaps it really ended on January 8. In this case your recall will be completely incorrect. You may well have located some memory, but it would be of the wrong day or perhaps the wrong year. (January 7, 1984, was a Saturday.)

Let us assume that you have succeeded at the first constructive step and managed to locate the correct record of experience in memory. What further influence does the reconstructive process have? In most cases when we do manage to locate the representation of an experience, we still find that we no longer have a sufficient cue structure to access many of the details. Consider "The War of the Ghosts" story again. Try to recall it to yourself. You will probably find that much of the story is already lost. But you will probably still have pieces of it—some of the general structure and a few very particular phrases. As you begin recalling, you will also construct plausible connections between the specific things you remember. Sometimes, these constructions will again produce sufficient context to serve as a cue to recall (and recognize) another specific detail from the experience. At other times the constructions will seem correct, but they might not lead to that warm secure feeling of clearly remembering (recognizing) the original input.

In general, whenever a person is asked to recall a story or experience, he or she will produce a mixture of actual memories and logical fabrications that might or might not be correct. This second type of construction in recall is simply the result of trying to glue together the fragments of memory in the best way possible. This reconstruction within an episode is fundamentally the same process as the earlier reconstruction of cues to locate the episode in memory. It is just that the constructions within the episode tend to be included in the recall product, whereas the constructions that allow one to locate the memory in the first place are usually not explicitly recalled.

## Temporal Memory

**Temporal landmarks.**   People also use local landmarks in situations in which the response is produced so rapidly that they do not notice their use at all. A fascinating illustration is provided by the simple task of answering the question, "What day is today?" (Koriat and Fischoff 1974; Shanon 1979). In one study Ben Shanon asked students in the Cambridge, Massachusetts, area to respond, as rapidly as possible, to the question of what day of the week it was (the *today* question). As Figure 8.2 shows, this question was answered most quickly on the weekends and most slowly in the middle of the week. This result suggests that students use the weekend as a landmark for keeping track of the days. The days in the middle of the week are probably less distinct from each other than are the days of the weekend.

The landmarks that are most salient and familiar are constantly changing. Concepts are activated by events and by the goals and plans embedded in the procedure directing the executive (Chapter 3). So as new events occur and a person's goals and plans change, new concepts become available as recall cues. This dynamic aspect of episodic memory was also demonstrated in Shanon's study. He asked people two other questions besides the *today* question: "What day of the week was yesterday?" (the *yesterday* question), and "What day of the week will it be tomorrow?" (the *tomorrow* question). Shanon was interested in how long people took to answer these three questions at different times of the day and week.

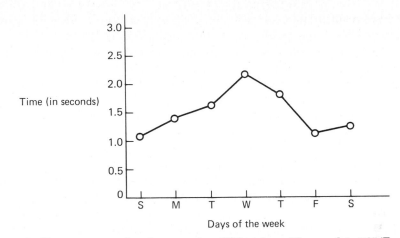

**Figure 8.2    Time to respond to the question, "What day of the week is it?" (From Shanon 1979.)**

As you might expect, at any time the *today* question was answered more rapidly than the *yesterday* and *tomorrow* questions. The times for answering the latter two questions showed a very interesting pattern. In the afternoon the *tomorrow* question was answered more rapidly than the *yesterday* question; but in the morning the *yesterday* question was answered more rapidly than the *tomorrow* question. Shanon suggested that this result occurred because in the morning we are still reflecting on yesterday's events, while by the afternoon we are already planning tomorrow's activities.

But what about the questions asked at noon? These results are especially interesting. In the first part of the week the *yesterday* question was answered more quickly than the *tomorrow* question; but in the later part of the week the reverse was true. Shanon suggested that a similar explanation applies here. At the beginning of the week we are preoccupied with the recent past. On Monday we still vividly recall the weekend; on Tuesday, we recall the start of the new school week or workweek on Monday. In contrast, at the end of the week we are preoccupied with the near future. On Thursday we look forward to Friday. On Friday we look forward to the weekend. Therefore recall of the days of the week is seemingly heavily influenced by recall and anticipation of the weekend. This interpretation is supported by Shanon's finding that all three questions are answered most rapidly on the weekends and most slowly on Wednesday. The idea that the weekend serves as a temporal landmark also fits in with anecdotal reports from people who move to a different country in which the weekend falls on different days. They report finding it very difficult to keep track of what day it is.

Salient temporal landmarks are important cues for reconstructing the time of events. People have a general bias to report events as having occurred more recently than they in fact did occur. This bias is termed *forward telescoping*. Loftus and Marburger (1983) demonstrated that this bias can be attenuated by using temporal landmarks as retrieval cues. They tested subjects in Washington State exactly six months after the first eruption of Mount Saint Helens, which occurred on May 18, 1980. The subjects were asked several questions about either what had happened in "the last six months" or "since the first major eruption of Mount Saint Helens." For example, the subjects were asked whether a failed attempt to rescue American hostages in Iran had occurred during this period. Loftus and Marburger found that many more subjects correctly answered no (the failed attempt actually occurred a few weeks prior to the reference period) when the period was defined in terms of the landmark volcanic eruption rather than simply in terms of "the last six months."

   The research on time questions provides an interesting picture of how our memories are constantly being updated. The principle that more recently accessed concepts are more accessible plays an important role in the recall of information about the present and the recent past. It plays an equal role in recall of the distant past. When people are asked to recall things or events from throughout their lives, a greater number of recent events are recalled (Crovitz and Quina-Holland 1976; Crovitz and Schiffman 1974; Franklin and Holding 1977; Squire and Slater 1975; Warrington and Sanders 1971; Whitten and Leonard 1981). Different cues are most effective for memories of different ages (Robinson 1976; Rubin 1982), and apparently few cues are immediately available for older memories. Furthermore, when Whitten and Leonard (1981) asked college students to name teachers from each of grades one through twelve, more students who were told to search backward from grades twelve to one completed the task than students who were told to search forward from grades one to twelve. Thus older memories can be recovered best through a secondary cuing strategy that successively activates older and older memories.

**Estimates of duration.**    We use cues not only to place episodes in order but also to estimate the length of durations (Ornstein 1969). Sometimes, when you wait for a bus, it seems as if the bus comes in 2 minutes, and at other times it seems as if the bus comes in 20 minutes, even though objectively the wait may have been the same length in both cases. What are the cues that control the perception of the passage of time? One basic rule is that the greater the number of events that occur, the longer the interval feels. For example, a piece of music that contains 40 events per minute is experienced as shorter than one with 120 events per minute. Furthermore, the more complex the sequence of sounds, the longer it will seem.

   Ornstein used his findings to explain some of our basic intuitions about the passage of time. For example, suppose that during winter break you go to Fort Lauderdale for ten days. On the last day of vacation, you feel as though you've been in Florida for a long time. At this point you can think of many specific events that occurred over the past ten days. Yet a month later back at school, your Florida vacation seems to have come and gone in a flash. Now you no longer easily recall many distinct events. The entire episode has been recoded as "a week in Florida," and as a result, its duration is perceived as shorter. Therefore recall cues not only determine how we recall events but also how we remember the duration of episodes in our lives.

## Memory for Actions, Intentions, and Opinions

**Confusion between intentions and actions.**     An important part of your life story is what your intentions were and what you actually did. There is one important difference between memory for intentions and memory for life events. Discriminating between things that actually happened to you and things that you imagined, expected, or hoped would happen to you is easy. Memories of imaginings are less detailed and less well integrated with other memories than memories of perceptions (Johnson and Raye 1981). For example, students are rarely confused about whether they actually got an A on a paper or imagined that they got an A. On the other hand, discriminating between a memory of what you actually did and what you only intended to do is much more difficult. For example, students are often confused between what they intended to write in a paper and what they actually wrote. Other examples are remembering that you intended to mail a letter, lock the door, or turn out the lights but not remembering whether you did it.

When you prepare to do something, or you imagine doing something, you may mentally run through the sequence of operations that the motor system would execute. But the actual execution of the motor system is largely unconscious. As a result, the memory of an intended action and of one actually carried out may be identical. Marcia Johnson and her colleagues (Johnson and Foley 1984; Johnson and Raye 1981) report that discriminating between having thought about saying something and actually having said something (i.e., discriminating between an intention and an action) is more difficult than distinguishing between having said something and having heard something (i.e., distinguishing between an action and a perception).

A person's own actions (and intentions) are very salient temporal landmarks, which are effective recall cues for events related to those intentions and actions. Hence people's memory for what happened is influenced (and in some cases distorted) by their memory of what they did. Raye, Johnson, and Taylor (1980) found that students were more accurate at estimating the frequencies with which they had generated words than at estimating the frequencies with which they had studied words. Furthermore, judgments of internally generated words impaired estimates of environmental word frequency more than environmental frequency impaired judgments of internally generated words.

**Effect of point of view.**   Each person thus seems to recall life from his or her own point of view. An especially clear demonstration of the effect of point of view on episodic recall was provided by a study by Anderson and Pichert (1978). They had college undergraduates read a story about two boys playing hooky from school at one of their homes. The subjects were instructed to take the perspective of either a burglar or a person interested in buying a home. All subjects then recalled the story. Some of the information in the story was particularly relevant to a would-be burglar, whereas other information was particularly relevant to a home buyer. As Figure 8.3 indicates, the subjects were able to recall more of each type of information if they had taken the matching point of view when they read the story. That is, those subjects who had taken the burglar perspective recalled more burglar information, whereas those who had taken the home buyer perspective recalled more home buyer information.

Anderson and Pichert's study also demonstrated the impact of a change in point of view *after* the original encoding. Subjects were asked to recall the story a second time. Some were told to maintain the same point of view, whereas others were now told to shift (e.g., taking the perspective of a home buyer instead of a burglar). Those subjects who changed perspective on the second recall attempt recalled an additional 7 percent of the information related to their new point of view and 7 percent less of the information related to their former view. A shift in perspective appeared to alter the retrieval cues

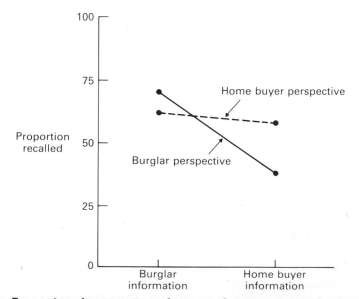

**Figure 8.3   Proportion of perspective-relevant and perspective-irrelevant information recalled on the first test. (From Anderson and Pichert 1978.)**

available for accessing the story information and hence systematically altered the ease of recalling different aspects of the story. Similarly, we would expect a changed perspective on one's own life to affect the recallability of past events, actions, and beliefs.

**Consistency with current beliefs.**   Of course, each person constructs an event sequence that is consistent with their recollection of what they said and did. So if you are mistaken about what you said or did, the error is propogated throughout the recall of the sequence of events that must be made consistent with the initial error. Moreover, when one is attempting to recall past thoughts and intentions, recalling the thoughts most consistent with current beliefs is easier. This result is an inevitable consequence of the structure of memory. Current thoughts and beliefs will have the highest levels of activation. As a result, your past thoughts and actions will seem to you to be more consistent with your current beliefs than they actually were (Greenwald 1980). For example, when attitude change was induced in students by having them write an essay in favor of the opposing side, they remembered their old opinion as having been consistent with their new one (Bem and McConnell 1970; Wixon and Laird 1976).

These results raise the possibility that, whether consciously or unconsciously, unpleasant events will be forgotten more readily than other events. This question is no longer being studied experimentally because of ethical considerations. However, some evidence indicates that the hypothesis is true. Glucksberg and King (1967) taught students a list of words and then, while presenting an additional list, paired the presentation of remote associates of some of the original list words with electric shocks. On a subsequent recall trial more words with associates that had been paired with shocks were forgotten.

## RETRIEVAL DISORDERS

All of our stored knowledge, both episodic and nonepisodic, ultimately depends on the functioning of the brain and the nervous system. The interior of the temporal lobes envelop the diencephalon, and at the place where they come together are several complex anatomical structures. When certain structures in this region are damaged, some sort of memory deficit, or *amnesia*, results. Interestingly enough, this portion of the brain is also important in the generation of emotion. (Recall the connection between memory and mood, discussed in Chapter 7.) Luckily, rather extensive bilateral damage is required for a permanent, severe memory deficit. Thus an injury to one side of the head leaves a person's ability to learn and remember relatively intact. Not much was known about memory disorders until the 1960s. Since then, several types of disorders have been described.

There are two basic types of amnesia (both of which are present in some amnesic syndromes). *Retrograde amnesia* refers to the loss of information acquired prior to the onset of the memory disorder; *anterograde amnesia* refers to the loss of the ability to remember information presented after the onset. Retrograde amnesia is a retrieval disorder and therefore will be discussed here; anterograde amnesia is primarily an encoding disorder and therefore will be discussed in the next chapter.

Retrograde amnesia can be either permanent or temporary. We will examine several disorders that are known to occur as the result of different kinds of injuries. Each of these disorders reveals something different about the structure of memory.

## Temporary Amnesia

If a person receives some kind of shock to the brain, such as a severe blow, he or she may forget events that occurred during some time period leading up to the moment of the trauma. Such loss of memory for events prior to the trauma constitutes retrograde amnesia. In general, the more severe the shock, the longer is the time period that is forgotten. Thus football players who are stunned by a hard tackle may forget a few seconds of their lives. But a patient who receives electroconvulsive shock treatment (ECT) in a mental hospital or a survivor of a severe auto accident with a major skull injury may forget months or even years.

Temporal gaps have been studied by Larry Squire and his colleagues (Squire and Slater 1975; Squire, Slater, and Chace 1975). For example, in the first half of 1974 they gave depressed patients a multiple-choice recognition test for television shows that had been on for only one season between 1957 and 1972; the tests were given before and after electroconvulsive shock was administered. The results are shown in Figure 8.4. Before ECT the patients showed the normal recency effect: The most recent shows were the best remembered. After ECT recognition of shows seen two years previously was severely depressed, but recognition of older shows remained unchanged.

You might suppose that retrograde amnesia would be due to memories actually being destroyed, the way a manuscript is destroyed when it is burned. But memories do not generally seem to be destroyed. Rather, the memories can no longer be retrieved and are like a manuscript that has been misplaced. The evidence for a retrieval failure explanation is twofold.

First, retrograde amnesia, even in many severe cases, frequently clears up. After a few hours or days amnesics can apparently remember all, or nearly all, that they could before the accident. If most memories are recoverable, then they could not have been destroyed by the shock.

Second, evidence suggests that immediately after the shock some memories that will later be lost are still available. In one interesting study Lynch

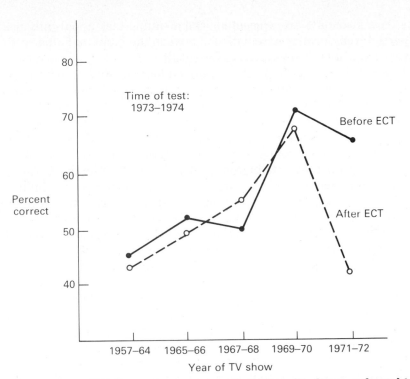

**Figure 8.4    Results of TV show questionnaire administered to depressed psychiatric patients receiving a course of bilateral ECT. Testing was conducted before the first treatment and 1 hour after the fifth treatment. (After Squire, Slater, and Chace 1975.)**

and Yarnell (1973) attended football practices and games in the hopes that they would be in attendance when players received minor head impacts. When players appeared dazed, Lynch and Yarnell would immediately ask them the play they had just run. Players could usually recall the play at this point, but 3 to 20 minutes later they usually could not. Retrograde amnesia therefore seems to develop after a blow, but it does not appear to be an instantaneous consequence of the blow.

What, then, is the cause of retrograde amnesia? There is no certain answer to this question. But we can offer a speculative hypothesis on the basis of what is known about recall. Consider a relatively mild case of retrograde amnesia, as for football players who forget the play on which they got banged on the head. We have considered another situation in which people forget something we might have expected them to remember. In a distractor task, as discussed in Chapter 7, we can prevent someone from recalling something as simple as three consonants by having the person count backward by 3s after the consonants are presented. The counting task apparently prevents the person from forming associations between the input and other concepts, so few cues will later be available for recall.

Now consider what happens to stunned football players. The shock they receive puts them in a dazed state during which they do not associate any of the events that have just occurred with the rest of their conceptual system. As a result, they later have no effective cues for recalling the event. In other words, we are suggesting that a shock acts in much the same way as a distractor task. As we mentioned earlier, different cues are most effective for recent and remote events (Robinson 1976; Rubin 1982). The shock disturbs the cues for recent events while leaving the cues for remote events intact.

When we discussed the distractor paradigm, we saw that if a cue was presented at recall that was strongly associated only to the target—e.g., *wildflower* in the Gardiner, Craik, and Birtwistle (1972) experiment—the target would often then be recalled. The same phenomenon can occur with retrograde amnesia. For example, a soldier who does not remember how he was injured may suddenly recall it while watching a war movie. The movie has provided the cue that the soldier was unable to generate himself.

But what about more severe cases of retrograde amnesia, where a person forgets the two or three years preceding the injury? Examination of a person suffering from severe retrograde amnesia reveals that the person is abnormal in other respects besides loss of memory. As we will see in the next section, evidence clearly shows that the person remains in a dazed state throughout the period of the amnesia and suffers from an encoding deficit as well.

## Permanent Amnesia

In some cases the patient never entirely recovers lost memories. We will describe three different syndromes in which amnesia is permanent.

**Temporal gaps.**    As we noted above, the amnesia resulting from ECT is usually temporary. When the memories of a person suffering from severe retrograde amnesia begin to return, the pattern in which they do so is quite disorganized. At first only a few memories are recovered, and the person may be unable to place them in the right temporal order. Two separate events may be combined into one. As more and more events are recalled, the person is able to create islands of remembering; that is, a series of related events may be placed together in their correct chronological order. As more events are recalled, the islands become bigger and the gaps between them smaller, until finally the islands merge and the complete episodic record is restored.

In rare cases a large temporal gap never closes, and the person in effect loses a few years from his or her life. Permanent temporal gaps may be induced by ECT, stroke, encephalitis, or trauma. A particularly striking case, in which a large temporal gap occurred in the absence of other cognitive deficits, was reported by Goldberg, Antin, Bilder, Gerstman, Hughes, and Mattis (1981). A thirty-six-year-old, college-educated man suffered a skull fracture that initially caused severe impairments in motor movements, language, learning, and memory. In particular, he could only remember something for a few minutes, so he could not recall where he was. The patient maintained that he was sixteen to eighteen years old and mentioned his parents' address as his address. He revealed no knowledge of his subsequent life history, his marriage, children, or past employment. His command of general information was equally impaired.

During the next two years the motor, linguistic, and learning deficits virtually disappeared. The patient again began orienting to the world and became aware of events since the injury from newspapers and television. However, he had no parallel recovery from the twenty-year-deep retrograde amnesia. Though told about his past, he did not remember it. He also failed to recall anything he had learned during the period within the gap. He could not answer questions like "Who wrote *Hamlet*?" or "What is the capital of France?"

This disorder suggests that episodic memories are stored adjacent to each other in the brain in the sequence in which they were encoded, like books on a shelf. Consequently, an injury that damages that particular part of the brain wipes out a particular period of time.

**Korsakoff's syndrome.**   The most interesting decline in recall is associated with *Korsakoff's syndrome,* and it is also the least well understood. Korsakoff's syndrome is the result of bilateral damage to the diencephalon, which extends to both parts of the hippocampus. Such damage can be caused by a physical injury, a disease, or a stroke. But by far the most common cause is severe alcoholism.

In a typical case years of chronic alcoholism end in a final binge that leaves the person severely confused, with difficulties in moving and seeing. Some patients may even die during this acute phase of the syndrome. But if they survive the first few weeks, patients will recover most of their physical and mental abilities. However, in certain respects the patient during the chronic phase of Korsakoff's syndrome is a changed person. One striking reversal is the loss of the chronic craving for alcohol. But the most serious change is a profound amnesia. The person usually forgets events prior to the trauma. Worst of all, the person suffers from a chronic inability to learn anything new. This aspect of the disorder will be examined in the next chapter. Here we will only be concerned with the forgetting aspect.

Albert, Butters, and Levin (1979) demonstrated that patients with alcoholic Korsakoff's syndrome exhibit a gradient in the degree of amnesia for past events, with older memories being better preserved. This effect, of course, is the exact opposite of the recency effect obtained in normal memory. They gave both 60-year-old patients with Korsakoff's disease and normal controls three different memory tests. One hundred photographs of famous individuals from the 1920s to the 1970s were used in a test of facial recognition. A questionnaire was administered that consisted of 132 questions about public events and people famous from 1920 to 1975. Finally, a 132-item, multiple-choice recognition test was given for events in the same period.

The results for patients with alcoholic-Korsakoff's syndrome and for normal subjects on the faces and the verbal-recall tests are shown in Figure 8.5. (The tests were scaled so that normal individuals would achieve equal recall scores for all decades.) A similar but milder gradient was observed for the recognition task. Alcoholics (non-Korsakoff's) are also impaired on facial and verbal recall in comparison with normal controls, and they also exhibit a mild gradient (Albert, Butters, and Brandt 1981a).

This reversal from the normal pattern was so surprising that psychologists have been hard-pressed to explain it. One possibility that occurred to researchers was that as alcoholics became more concerned with drinking, they paid less attention to the world around them. So the apparent retrograde amnesia was the result of having never learned about those events and people in the first place. This hypothesis was disproved by the careful study by But-

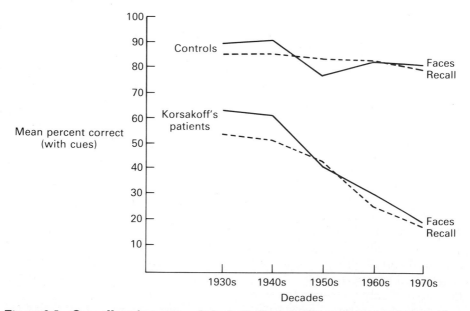

**Figure 8.5   Overall performance of alcoholic Korsakoff's syndrome patients and normal controls on famous-faces test and verbal-recall questionnaire. (From Albert, Butters, and Levin 1979.)**

ters and Cermak of an individual whose learning history was known in detail
(Butters 1984). This patient (P. Z.), an eminent scientist and university professor who developed alcoholic Korsakoff's syndrome at the age of sixty-five, had
written several hundred research papers and numerous books and book chapters, including an extensive autobiography written three years prior to the
acute onset of the disorder in 1982.

P. Z.'s amnesia was assessed through the construction of two special
tasks: a famous-scientists test and an autobiographical-information test. The
famous-scientists test consisted of the names of seventy-five famous investigators and scholars in P. Z.'s scientific speciality, all of whom should have been
well known to P. Z. The vast majority of these names were mentioned

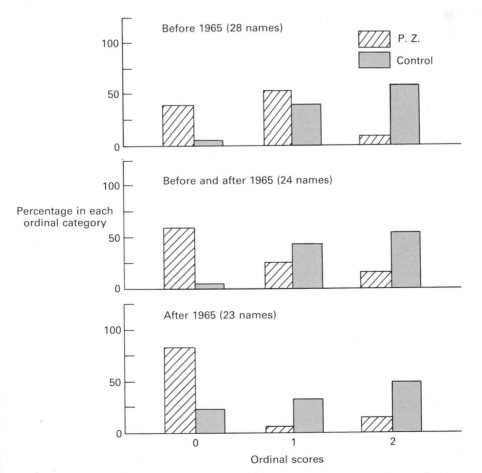

**Figure 8.6    Recall of P. Z. and of other scholars for prominent scientists in their
field. (From Butters 1984.)**

prominently in one or more of P. Z.'s books or major scholarly papers. Other names were chosen because of their documented professional interactions with P. Z. Twenty-eight of these scholars were prominent before 1965, twenty-four made major contributions before and after 1965, and twenty-three attained visibility after 1965.

P. Z. was presented with each name and asked to describe the scholar's area of interest and major contribution. Responses were scored on a three-point (0, 1, 2) scale. Recall of the person's major contribution rated a 2, recall of the person's area of interest rated a 1, while failure to recognize the individual was scored as 0. Another prominent scholar in P. Z.'s area of speciality was also administered the test. The results are shown in Figure 8.6. As the figure shows, the other scholar's distribution of scores for the three groups of scientists hardly changes at all, while P. Z.'s recognition failure rate doubled from about 40 to 80 percent from pre-1965 to post-1965.

The autobiographical-information test consisted of questions about relatives, colleagues, collaborators, conferences, research assistants, research reports, and books mentioned prominently in P. Z.'s autobiography. The results, shown in Figure 8.7, show a steeply graded retrograde amnesia, which cannot be the result of a failure of original learning. The fact that all questions were drawn from P. Z.'s autobiography eliminates the possibility that the information was never acquired. Just three years prior to the onset of the

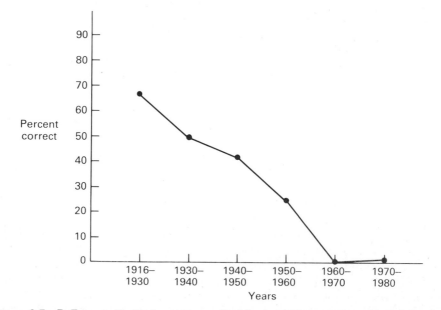

Figure 8.7   P. Z.'s recall of information culled from autobiography. (From Butters 1984.)

Korsakoff's syndrome, P. Z. could retrieve this information and considered it to be important in professional and personal life.

**General decline.**   As one of their advancing symptoms, several diseases that destroy the brain produce a general decline in the ability to recall information and past events. So recall of both recent and remote events is equally impaired. Prominent among these diseases is Alzheimer's disease, which occasionally strikes middle-aged people but more frequently afflicts the elderly. Its cause is unknown. The same pattern is observed with the hereditary degeneration known as Huntington's disease (Albert, Butters, and Brandt 1981b). The decline in recall is associated with a general loss of cognitive function, which includes the person's learning, reasoning, and verbal and visuospatial abilities—in short, everything that is discussed in this book. This general deterioration is called *dementia*.

Also, profound depression in an elderly person may produce a *pseudo-dementia* (Wells 1979) in which there is again a generalized loss in the abilities to learn, recall, comprehend, and reason. In pseudodementia the cognitive loss may be even more obvious than in the early stage of dementia, and the loss of both recent and remote memories—hence producing a uniform decline in recall—may be even more pronounced. Therefore distinguishing pseudodementia from true dementia is very difficult. However, if the depression of the pseudodemented patient is relieved, there is a complete recovery of cognitive function. Why depression can cause such severe cognitive loss in the elderly is a complete mystery. The disorder hints at a connection between emotion and cognition that has yet to be explored.

## SUMMARY

An *episodic recall target* involves an event that took place at a specific time. The most complex types of episodic recall involve the retrieval of life experiences. The recall of episodes involves the generation and *reconstruction* of the target information on the basis of *rules* of various sorts. Reconstructive memory is evident in the recall of stories. Stories are organized hierarchically in memory, and this hierarchical structure guides subsequent retrieval. People are much better at recalling the *gist*, or general meaning, of a passage than at recalling the precise words, which is called *verbatim memory*. If a story or event is structured in a highly unfamiliar way, systematic distortions will be introduced when it is reconstructed.

The reconstruction of personal experiences is heavily guided by rules and temporal landmarks. Often recall of episodes resembles problem-solving activity. People have considerable difficulty discriminating between actual actions they performed in the past and *intentions* to do so and between their current and past beliefs. Recall of episodes is affected by the person's *point of view*.

The complex retrieval system used to recall information can be disturbed if the person receives some kind of shock to the brain. The resulting memory loss is called *amnesia*. *Retrograde amnesia* is the loss of memory for events prior to the trauma; *anterograde amnesia* is the loss of memory for events occurring after the trauma. Retrograde amnesia is primarily a retrieval disorder, and it can be either temporary or permanent. Temporary retrograde amnesia may be due to factors similar to those that cause forgetting in the distractor paradigm. Permanent amnesia can involve irrecoverable *temporal gaps* in the memory of a trauma victim. *Korsakoff's syndrome* typically produces a temporal gradient of recall, with recall performance declining for events earlier in time. Other brain diseases produce a general decline in the ability to recall both recent and remote events.

## RECOMMENDED READINGS

Bartlett's *Remembering* (1932) provides a discussion of story recall in particular and episodic recall in general, and it is still a good introduction to those phenomena. Again, Gardner (1976) provides a good introduction to dementia and to memory loss. Elizabeth Loftus's *Memory* (1980) provides an entertaining and illuminating introduction to many factors known to influence episodic memory. A. R. Luria's account of a Russian soldier's recovery from traumatic amnesia, *The Man with the Shattered World* (1972), provides a fascinating introduction to this topic. Finally, Neisser's *Memory Observed* (1982) and Seamon's *Human Memory* (1980) are excellent collections of stimulating articles on most of the topics of this chapter. Also see the books and journals listed in the previous two chapters.

# CHAPTER **NINE**

# Incidental Learning

## INTRODUCTION

In your daily life you perceive the world, try to understand it, and try to respond in appropriate ways. In doing so, you store information in memory as a by-product of cognitive processing (Craik and Tulving 1975). Suppose, for example, that as you return from class, a cat runs across your path. Back in your room, you may casually remember the cat. The acquisition of such memories is called *incidental learning,* because the learning was incidental to some other purpose. But the importance of incidental learning belies its modest name, for most of the memories of your own life are the result of incidental learning that takes place during the living of it. Incidental learning gives you a great storehouse of information about how to successfully interact with your environment.

The importance of learning is so obvious to us that we engage in *intentional learning* as well. Apparently, however, simply intending to learn, in and of itself, is not the key to successful learning (Mandler 1967). Rather, what is critical is how the information is processed. As we will see in the next chapter, intentional learning can be improved by the use of well-designed strategies. In this chapter we will examine the more basic encoding processes that do not depend on the use of conscious strategies. Although our focus will be on incidental learning, we will refer to some evidence from experiments in which the subjects were trying to learn the material to be remembered. In all such cases we have reason to suppose that essentially the same principles govern both intentional and incidental approaches to the task.

In this chapter we first present what is known about the basic encoding process. When an input is processed, it can alter a representation in either or both of the two basic types of memory codes. That is, it can alter a perceptual representation, and it can cause a new node to become activated in the semantic code. The alteration of a representation in a perceptual code is called *perceptual learning,* and the modification of the semantic network is called *conceptual learning.* Perceptual learning underlies the acquisition of many specialized skills, including reading; conceptual learning allows us to generate concepts and to recall information.

Together, perceptual and conceptual learning contribute to the sum of skills and knowledge that you acquire in the course of living. In this chapter we will also examine how your episodic memory is continually updated and altered. Finally, at the end of the chapter we will describe the most severe of all learning disorders, anterograde amnesia.

## PERCEPTUAL LEARNING

The construction of an input's representation may alter a perceptual code in two ways. First, the activation of a matching representation may be increased. Second, a new perceptual representation may be formed. We will consider each of these effects, in turn.

### Automatic Activation

As we have seen, the activation from an input occurs before the input enters consciousness, so even an input that never enters consciousness can cause activation to occur (Marcel 1983). As we stated in our discussion of identification (Chapter 6), the higher the activation of a memory representation, the less additional activation it needs from a match before it enters consciousness. This fact can be exploited to make an observer aware of a briefly presented, subliminal input by simply repeating the input until the activation from successive presentations increases to the point where even a briefly presented input adds sufficient activation to enter awareness (Chastain 1977; Haber and Hershenson 1965). Suppose a seven-letter word is flashed at you for 10–20 milliseconds. All you will probably see the first time is a few letters or no letters at all. But if the same word is repeatedly flashed at you, once every few seconds, and you keep trying to see it, a striking thing will happen. More and more letters will gradually emerge, until on a single flash you may see the whole word distinctly. Scarborough, Cortese, and Scarborough (1977) showed that if the presentation of an input is long enough so that its representation enters awareness, then the increase in the presentation's activation is high enough to influence the processing of a subsequent input days later. They had students decide whether strings of letters were words. When a word was repeated, even days later, it was identified faster than it had been before.

Recall from Chapter 6 that many people make use of an input's familiarity to judge the frequency with which they've encountered it. Because every occurrence of an input automatically influences the activation level of its representation, which in turn influences its familiarity, the accuracy of a frequency judgment should not depend on whether a person consciously intended to encode it. In fact, Hasher and Zacks (1979) reviewed a large number of studies that demonstrate that frequency information is a by-product of perception and the accuracy of frequency judgments is relatively unaffected by conscious learning strategies.

### Bootstrap Model

The first time a complex visual input is processed, the representation that is ultimately retained in memory is considerably simpler than its perceptual representation. For example, often the first time you meet a person, visit a new location, or see a new picture in a book or art museum, you later can conjure up only a vague image of what you saw, though of course you perceived it perfectly clearly at the time. On subsequent occasions when you see the same person, picture, or locale again, its perceptual representation reactivates the representations from previous exposures. And each time an additional, slightly more detailed representation, with a few more features, is retained in memory. So a succession of exposures to the same input leads to a whole set of similar, successively more detailed representations of it in memory, until at some point there may be no new features to add.

An important consequence of this model is that on successive presentations, as more details about the target are encoded, discriminating it more accurately from similar alternatives is possible. People who are involved in special trades that provide them with a great deal of experience with a particular kind of input become able to categorize those inputs extremely rapidly and accurately. For example, farmers can sort newborn chicks by sex extremely rapidly and accurately, whereas a layperson cannot tell the difference between male and female chicks at all. Here we will consider a kind of input that everyone has a great deal of practice recognizing—faces.

### Face Recognition

As we discussed in Chapter 6, any recognition task that requires a target to be selected from similar distractors will seem easy if the critical features that distinguish the targets from the distractors were encoded when the targets were first presented. One such task that most people perform well is face recognition. For example, you have no trouble picking out the face of a friend in a crowded classroom. Is face recognition easy because people do not look very much alike, or because you have so thoroughly learned the critical features of your friend's face? Probably the latter is the correct answer.

One piece of evidence in favor of this interpretation involves people's ability to recognize the faces of individuals of different races. Informal reports suggest, for example, that blacks and whites have difficulty distinguishing among the faces of different Asians. Malpass and Kravatz (1969) found experimental evidence that people can most accurately recognize the faces of the racial types with which they have had the most experience. Both black and white American college students were shown twenty photographs of other college students, half of whom were black and half of whom were white. The students then had to select the twenty photos they had already seen from a new set of eighty. Both blacks and whites recognized the white faces equally well. However, blacks were more accurate than whites at recognizing the black faces.

These results suggest that there are different distinguishing features for recognizing individuals of different races and that these features have to be learned. Many whites in the Unites States see relatively few blacks and therefore do not learn to encode the critical features that distinguish among black faces. But most American blacks see people of both races and therefore learn to recognize faces of both racial types. An important practical implication of the Malpass and Kravatz study is that white eyewitnesses may tend to be less accurate than blacks in identifying black suspects in criminal cases.

## Development of Perceptual Skill

When a person learns to identify a set of complicated inputs, the learning generalizes beyond the instances actually presented, because the partial representations of the instances that are formed during perceptual learning will match perceptual representations of other, similar inputs. Hence the processing of these inputs will be facilitated as well. The degree of generalization depends on the number of features shared among inputs. In the case of faces we have just seen that the highest degree of generalization occurs for those faces of the same racial type. In the case of a set of artificial inputs, characterized by a small number of features, a small set of partial representations composed of those features may be sufficient for identifying all set members. Perceptual learning will therefore generalize to all members of the set. For example, postal workers can sort mail by zip code faster than most of us could even locate the zip code on a letter. Sometimes, the features used to encode set members are quite abstract. One example, which will be discussed in Chapter 12, is the perception of an array of chess pieces by chess experts. When a person has learned to rapidly identify members of a set, they are said to have learned a *perceptual skill.*

Kolers (1979) has studied the acquisition of a novel perceptual skill. He had subjects read 200 pages of text in which the typescript was inverted. At first the readers were extremely slow, as you might expect. The subjects took more than 16 minutes to read their first page of inverted text, as compared with only 1.5 minutes for normal text. But by the time they had finished 200 pages, they were reading inverted text almost as quickly (1.6 minutes per page) as normal text. Kolers also retested his subjects a year later, and he found that their novel perceptual skill was largely preserved. Furthermore, because practice on one body of text improved performance in reading a different inverted text, the subjects learned recurring features or higher-level units, rather than simply particular sequences of inverted letters.

### Incidental-Category Learning

When an input matches a complete, detailed representation, it necessarily also matches the partial representations formed during the learning process. An important consequence of the effects of a match is the storing in memory of prototypes (Chapter 5) for categories whose inputs are complicated enough to require detailed representations and are homogeneous enough so that a set of critical features is shared by all or most instances. For example, consider how someone might learn to recognize instances of the category *bird*. The first time a child sees a bird, a vague representation is stored. On each subsequent occasion that the same bird is seen, the input representation is found to contain features that the memory representation lacks, and a new memory representation is created containing some additional features. Hence the child will have stored in memory a set of successively more detailed representations, all of which match the same input representation. In addition, some of the vaguer representations will match the input representations of other birds. Of course, those representations that match inputs more often have higher levels of activation. If this representation is not a partial representation of any of the noncategory representations, then it will be the category prototype, and its features will be the critical features of the category.

When we discussed category learning in Chapter 5, we described experiments in which subjects presented with exemplars drawn from multiple categories learned representations of the central tendency and variability of each category. Then they used these representations to classify novel instances. In these studies the subjects were told the category to which each of the training instances belonged, and they were explicitly instructed to learn the categories. However, perceptual category learning can take place in a much more incidental fashion. As we will see in Chapter 14, children acquire representations of basic-level natural categories before they learn language. Apparently, mere observation of instances results in learning about the similarities among them.

Reber (1967) has dubbed the incidental acquisition of category representations *implicit learning*. He characterizes implicit learning as a process that occurs naturally when a person attends to the members of a structured set of inputs. Reber and his colleagues have studied implicit learning by using artificial "languages" composed of letter sequences. Such a language is defined by a kind of grammar that determines which letter strings are "grammatical" and which are "ungrammatical." Figure 9.1 illustrates one

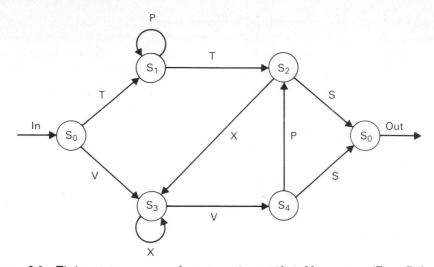

**Figure 9.1 Finite-state grammar for generating artificial language. (From Reber 1967.)**

such grammar, represented as a *finite-state network.* Grammatical sequences are generated by following the arcs from node to node and producing the letter indicated on each arc as it is traversed. An arc that returns to the same node can be traversed any number of times in a row. The sequence always begins at the point labeled "in" and ends at the point labeled "out." For example, for the network in Figure 9.1 the sequence TTS is grammatical, as are TPPPTXVS, VXVPS, and VVS. In contrast, the sequences TVTS and VXXVP do not correspond to complete paths through the network, and hence they are ungrammatical.

As you can see, such finite-state grammars can be quite complex. Subjects who do not have the grammar described to them as a network never spontaneously invent such a representation for it. Nonetheless, Reber has demonstrated that people who observe examples of grammatical strings can learn to make grammaticality judgments about novel strings with reasonable accuracy. More remarkably, Reber (1976) found that subjects were actually more successful in learning a grammar when they simply memorized sample strings than when they actively examined the same set of sample strings and tried to figure out the rule system. This result occurred despite the fact that when they were informed of the existence of a grammar (after having already seen the samples), some subjects in the memorization condition protested that they had learned nothing. When the underlying grammar is relatively complex, implicit learning may be more effective in inducing regularities than are the intentional learning strategies subjects use when they are trying to learn (Reber,

Kassin, Lewis, and Cantor 1980). Reber and Allen (1978) found that even if subjects were not asked to memorize the sample strings but only to observe them carefully, they were later able to make reliable grammaticality judgments.

Reber's results indicate that representations of regularities in perceptual inputs naturally emerge as a product of attending to the inputs. In the case of letter string grammars subjects appear to learn pairs of letters that tend to occur together at particular positions in grammatical strings (e.g., many strings generated by the grammar depicted in Figure 9.1 will end in TS). Such regularities, even though they are imperfect, can be used to make fairly accurate grammaticality judgments (Dulaney, Carlson, and Dewey 1984; Reber and Allen 1978).

More generally, people encode covariations among features that correspond to clusters of similar inputs. Even when examples of multiple categories are intermixed and subjects are not told the category to which any individual item belongs, distinctive categories can still be learned (Evans 1967). Fried and Holyoak (1984) performed experiments on prototype abstraction in which instances of two categories of complex visual patterns were randomly intermixed, without category labels. Even if subjects were not told that they were in a category-learning task until after all the training instances had been presented, they nonetheless proceeded to classify novel instances in a manner indicating they had learned something about the central tendencies and variability of the categories. Thus distinctive natural categories, consisting of discriminable clusters of inputs, are learned as a by-product of perceptual processing.

## CONCEPTUAL ENCODING

When two successive input representations activate the same semantic node, they are perceived as two occurrences of the *same* instance. In contrast, when two inputs activate different semantic nodes, they are perceived as different instances. So an input must activate a new semantic node to be perceived as novel and to be subsequently identified as distinct. We take up here the process by which new nodes are activated.

### Attention and Memory

The formation of a new node in the semantic code is a by-product of conscious attention, but it is not a necessary one. We owe this important finding to the work of Mary Potter (1975, 1976) and Helene Intraub (1980, 1981), who had students perform a task in which they had to detect a target among a sequence of pictures presented for 114 milliseconds apiece, pressing a button when the target appeared. Sometimes, the target was defined quite generally, e.g., a picture that is not house furnishings or decorations. Such a definition required the observer to identify *every* picture in the sequence at the semantic level as either an instance or a noninstance of the specified category (see Chapter 5). Therefore if activation of a semantic node was sufficient to leave a memory trace on trials when the observer accurately detected the distractor in the sequence, implying that all the pictures had been identified, they should have been able to select all or most of the pictures just presented in a subsequent recognition test. However, in the recognition test that immediately followed presentation of the sequence, the observer was able to select few, if any, pictures as a picture that had just been seen. Detection accuracy was almost always much higher than recognition accuracy. Thus, although only a few tens of milliseconds may be needed to construct a representation and find a match in memory, apparently a few hundred milliseconds are needed to establish a new association between that trace and some concept in memory. Merely attending to an input and being briefly aware of it does not automatically lead to a permanent record of that input in memory. Only some portions of the inputs compared with memory will leave some trace of themselves behind.

As we indicated in Chapter 3, the representation of an input can be maintained in active memory by the executive. The longer attention is maintained on an input, the more likely is a representation of it to be stored in long-term memory. In particular, one way that attention influences memory is by allowing the formation of an association between the input's perceptual representation and a new semantic node. The longer the representation is maintained in active memory, the greater is the likelihood that a new node will be formed. Furthermore, as pointed out by Craik and Lockhart (1972), the act of maintaining an input in consciousness is itself a conscious, voluntary process during which a person may focus on different aspects of an input. Recall that many inputs activate multiple representations in multiple codes in memory. A person may bring these various representations into consciousness and hence connect them to the new semantic node. According to Craik and Lockhart, the more aspects of a concept that are attended, the more discriminable will be the memory trace that is formed, and the more associations it will have to other concepts.

Because what is attended determines what is stored, there is a direct relationship between what is attended at the time of encoding and what is later recalled. In a wide-ranging review of memory studies, Hasher and Zacks (1979) showed that many of the differences observed in the learning abilities of people of different ages and among the amount retained in different situations were the result of the differing amounts of attention the people could devote to the inputs. At many points in this chapter and the next, the role of selective attention on the encoding process will be apparent.

## Dynamic Memory Processes

Human memory is a *dynamic* system of representations, i.e., a system constantly undergoing change. To know what part of an input will be encoded on a particular presentation, we must know what came *before* it. To know what part of the input will be recalled at a later time, we must know what occurred during the *retention interval* between encoding and retrieval. The degree to which the processing of other inputs influences the ultimate retrieval of a target depends on their relatedness to the target. Unrelated inputs apparently have little or no effect on its retrieval and so will not be discussed further.

The retrieval of a target is influenced by the processing of those inputs that were either identical, similar, or related to it. First, repetitions of the target during the retention interval will be discussed. As you know, repeating something increases the probability that it will be remembered. Second, the effect of the processing of similar or related inputs will be described. Whether these inputs increase or decrease the likelihood of retrieval depends on their precise relation to the target and the precise nature of the retrieval task. Most often, their processing reduces the likelihood of the target's retrieval. This interference is the major source of forgetting in normal memory.

## Repetition

As we just mentioned, repeating something increases the probability that it will be remembered. A number of recent experiments have shown that repetition can improve memory performance even when people are not deliberately trying to remember the input. One way to demonstrate this result is to show that repetition improves memory even in an incidental-learning situation. For example, Nelson (1977) asked students to read a list of twenty words and indicate as quickly as possible whether each word contained a particular letter sound; e.g., "Does the word contain an r sound?" Half the words contained the letter sound (e.g., *frog*) and half did not (e.g., *knight*). After they had made the classification, half the students were asked to read through the same words (in a new order), again deciding whether they contained a particular letter sound. Shortly after the students finished classifying the words, they were given a surprise test in which the experimenter asked them to recall as many of the words they had just classified as possible. Nelson found that the students who read the words twice recalled more words. (See also Darley and Glass 1975.)

**Massed vs. distributed repetition.**    Recall is better if the repetition of an input is spaced far from the first encounter rather than close to it. In other words, *distributed repetitions* are more effective than *massed repetitions* (Madigan 1969; Melton 1967). For example, if you see an item twice, you will remember it better if the two presentations do not occur one after the other.

Figure 9.2 illustrates a typical spacing effect. In this experiment students were given two presentations: each of forty-eight words. Each presentation involved showing the word for 1.5 seconds. All the points plotted in Figure 9.2 represent the percentage of words recalled after two presentations. The only difference between the points involves the lag between the introduction of the word and its repetition, i.e., the number of items intervening between the two presentations of the same word. For example, with a lag of 0 the two presentations occur one after the other. At the other extreme, a lag of 40 means that the two presentations were separated by the presentation of 40 other items.

As Figure 9.2 indicates, recall is greatly improved by spacing the presentations rather than massing them together. Most of the advantage due to spacing accrues as long as even two items separate the repeated words; but to some extent the advantage continues to increase even up to a lag of 40.

Distributed repetitions produce greater recall because they produce more discriminable memory representations. Spaced repetitions increase discriminability in two ways. As the repetitions of an input become more separated, both the differences in their encoding contexts and the amount of attention paid to each occurrence increase. Let us examine each of these factors.

**Encoding variability.**    Distributed repetitions allow an input such as a word to be encoded in more than one context. When a word is repeated twice in succession, each representation is encoded in the same context. But as the separation between the items increases, the probability of differences in the encoding context increases as well. As we saw in Chapter 7, its encoding context

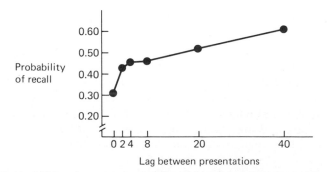

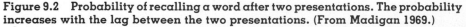

**Figure 9.2    Probability of recalling a word after two presentations. The probability increases with the lag between the two presentations. (From Madigan 1969.)**

provides a useful generation cue for a word (Godden and Baddeley 1975). Distributed presentations produce additional contextual generation cues that massed presentations lack (Glenberg 1979; McFarland, Rhodes, and Frey 1979).

Differences in encoding context contribute to the increase in recall shown in Figure 9.2, from a separation of 2 to a separation of 40. However, this factor cannot account for the initial large increase in recall between a separation of 0 and a separation of 2, because at this small separation the contexts of both presentations are quite similar.

**Attentional hypothesis.** The attentional hypothesis (Hinztman 1974; Johnston and Uhl 1976) assumes that when people receive two presentations of a word, one after another, less attention is devoted to the second presentation. Because the probability of activating a new category node is directly related to the amount of attention devoted to an input, the small amount of attention paid to the repetition of the input only slightly increases its probability of recall.

Why does the repetition of an input receive so little attention? The concept activated by the first presentation of the input is still highly active immediately after its first presentation. At the second presentation even a superficial match with the input causes an identification and terminates its processing. Hence the activation of various representations of the concept by the comparison process is short-circuited, and there is little permanent effect on memory. However, as the interval between the first and second presentation is increased, the activation caused by the first presentation declines. Consequently, a more detailed match is needed to raise the activation of the concept for identification, and more representations of the concept are activated. Thus the ultimate contribution of an additional presentation of an input to the memorability of an input depends on the partial forgetting of its earlier presentation. Cuddy and Jacoby (1982) showed that factors that reduce the likelihood that the second presentation of an input will cue recall of the prior presentation ultimately enhance its recall.

The decrease in attention that occurs with massed repetition was nicely demonstrated by William Johnston and Charles Uhl (1976). They had students do two tasks at the same time. The first task was to listen to several lists of about a hundred words. The words were presented at the rate of one every 5 seconds. The students heard the words in their right ear (by means of headphones). The students were to study and remember each list for a later recall test. Some of the words were repeated four times in the list. If a word was repeated, it could be presented four times in succession (massed) or at four separate times during the list (distributed). As we would expect, the students recalled the words more acccurately after distributed than massed presentations.

The real interest in the experiment, however, involves the second task the students had to perform while studying the words. Their second task was to press a button as quickly as possible whenever they heard a faint tone presented to the left ear. The tones occurred at various times throughout the presentation of the study list.

What in the world, you might ask, does detecting tones have to do with understanding the spacing effect? Johnston and Uhl reasoned as follows: Both encoding words and detecting tones require attention. Consequently, the speed with which tones are detected should provide an index of how much attention was being used to encode words on the other channel. Presumably, the slower the reaction time to the tone, the more attention is being used to process words.

The attentional explanation of the spacing effect makes a clear prediction about how spacing should affect time to detect tones. With massed presentations of a word people should pay relatively little attention to the later repetitions. As a result, people should very quickly detect a tone presented at that time. In contrast, with spaced presentations people should continue to attend to later repetitions of the word. They should therefore take more time to detect a tone at the same time.

The reaction time data from Johnston and Uhl's experiment are presented in Figure 9.3. The points in the graph indicate the average time required to detect the tone when it occurred simultaneously with the first, second, third, or fourth presentation of a word. The results clearly support the attentional hypothesis. When the presentations were massed, the reaction times decreased markedly with each successive presentation of a word. This result suggests that the students paid less attention to each successive repetition. On the

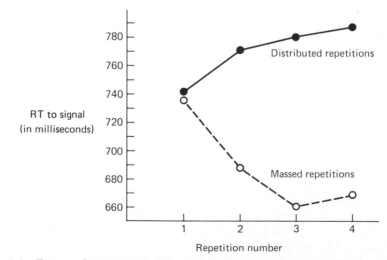

**Figure 9.3   Time to detect a tone. The time decreases over massed presentations of a word but increases over distributed presentations. (From Johnston and Uhl 1976.)**

other hand, with spaced presentations the reaction times actually increased over repetitions. Apparently, when the presentations of a word are separated, people pay more attention to the later repetitions.

Johnston and Uhl's experiment provides a very elegant demonstration of an obvious intuition. As one practices the same thing over and over again, maintaining concentration and keeping one's mind from wandering is almost impossible. So as we will see in the next chapter, repeating something over and over is usually the least effective strategy for learning it.

## Proactive Interference

We saw in Chapter 7 that for a target to be reliably recalled in response to a cue, there must be a unique association between the cue and the target, and the target must have a sufficient level of activation so that the additional activation provided by the cue raises the level past the threshold of awareness. When the results of the distractor task were discussed in Chapter 7, we saw that if a person is prevented from forming a unique association between the cue and target, then the person may be unable to recall even a single consonant trigram after a retention interval of only a few seconds.

The distractor task encapsulates a situation common to daily life. For example, you probably have had the experience of being introduced to several people at a party, one after the other. As you were introduced to the third and fourth person, you felt that sinking feeling as the names began to slip away. Clearly, the cue "people met at party" would not be sufficient to generate all those names you just heard if you were asked to free-recall them.

But what about a cued recall task, where each name is activated by a unique cue? Suppose after hearing all the names, you were asked to point to each individual and say his or her name. In this case each cue (a particular face) is uniquely associated to a different target (its name). Why is it, then, that you do not always learn a person's name in a single trial? The answer is that the representation of the name did not receive sufficient activation during its encoding. So even when re-presented with the face, it does not generate sufficient additional activation to raise the name above threshold to consciousness. As we have discussed, the amount of activation a concept receives is directly related to the attention given to it. When you are introduced to several people at a party, their names do not receive sufficient initial activation to ensure that they can be later recalled.

Let us look a little more closely at what determines the amount of attention, and hence the amount of activation, a representation receives. The first factor is the duration of its initial activation. As we have seen, the longer a representation is maintained in consciousness, the more activation it receives. The second factor is the similarity of the representation to representations that have been processed shortly before it. We have just seen that if an input is repeated after a brief interval, it receives less attention the second time than it received the first. This situation is the limiting case of a more general phenomenon: If we consider the processing of two inputs presented in succession, to the extent that they are similar, the activation of the representation of the first input will be enhanced and the activation of the second input will be diminished. The negative effect of an earlier input on memory for a later one further contributes to *proactive inhibition* (PI).

When similar inputs are perceived in sequence during an interval, the first one or two inputs will be better recalled than subsequent ones (Radtke, Grove, and Talasi 1982). For example, in the party situation you are most likely to recall the names of the first one or two people you meet. This effect is called *primacy*. An important question is, How similar must a set of inputs be for proactive inhibition to produce primacy? As we will see, the answer is quite complex, because it depends on the amount of time a person has to process each input and how the person uses that time (i.e., what encoding strategy they choose), as well as the degree of overlap and similarity among the concepts that the inputs activate.

Generally, if a person is able to activate a representation that is not shared by any concept activated by a prior input, the distinctive representation will not only act as a retrieval cue for the target but will also distinguish it sufficiently from its predecessors so that it will receive as much activation as the first input that was processed. Hence a distinguishing characteristic of an input that will cause release from PI in the distractor paradigm (the effect of category shift discussed in Chapter 7) will also cause the distinctive item to be recalled as well as the first one, if recall of all the inputs is attempted at some time after they all have been presented. This result is known as the *isolation* or *Von Restorff* (1933) *effect*, after its discoverer. In one demonstration Douglas Detterman and Norman Ellis (1972) had students recall serially presented lists of line drawings of common objects (e.g., hat, pill, pencil sharpener). Half the lists contained, in the middle position, one of a set of critical items, which were photographs of groups of male and female nudes with exposed genitalia. Their results are shown in Figure 9.4. A dramatic Von Restorff effect can be seen in the figure.

In a fixed period of time there is only a limited amount of activation possible. The Von Restorff effect increases the activation of one item, and hence the likelihood of its recall, at the expense of others (Newman and Saltz 1958), just as does the primacy effect. Figure 9.4 also clearly indicates that the other pictures in the lists containing the nudes were less well recalled than they were in lists without the nudes. The critical different item is, in effect, a sort of punctuation point that ends one set of items and begins another.

Both the Von Restorff effect and the primacy effect are really manifestations of the same phenomenon: The more distinctive an input is from its predecessors, the more activation it receives. But because the total pool of activation is limited, the encoding of unorganized items is a self-limiting pro-

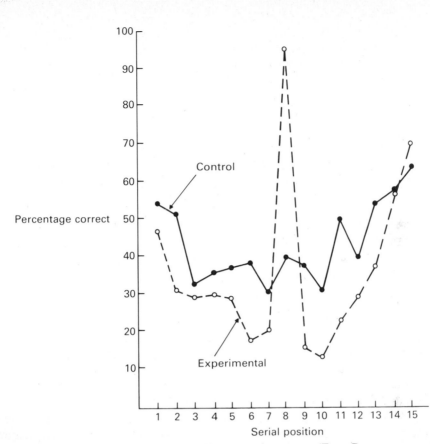

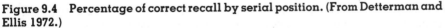

**Figure 9.4    Percentage of correct recall by serial position. (From Detterman and Ellis 1972.)**

cess, just as is their recall (Chapter 7). However, as was the case with recall, there is a way out of the trap. As we will see in the next chapter, it again involves organization.

**Long-term PI.**    Just as encoding the same input in different contexts increases the likelihood of its retrieval because more cues are associated to it, encoding many inputs in the same context reduces their individual likelihoods of being retrieved. In an extensive review Underwood (1957) plotted the results of sixteen studies, all of which involved learning to a criterion of one perfect trial and recall 24 hours later. He plotted the result of each study as a function of the number of prior lists that had been learned by the subject. As shown in Figure 9.5, the more lists a subject had learned, the less was retained (see also Keppel, Postman, and Zavortink 1968). As we will see, the better a list is learned, the less susceptible it is to long-term PI (Warr 1964).

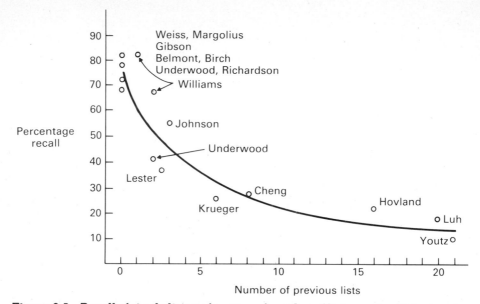

**Figure 9.5**   **Recall of single lists as function of number of lists previously learned. Each point represents an experiment by the investigator named, in which the list was learned 24 hours prior to recall. The more previous lists the subject had learned, the poorer was retention. (From Underwood 1957.)**

**Imageability and discriminability.** A set of inputs that activate concepts with quite different visuospatial representations, which are relatively discriminable, are more easily learned than a set of similar inputs, because discriminable inputs are less susceptible to PI at encoding. Thus words such as *tree* that refer to concrete, easily imaged objects are remembered better than words such as *thought* that are abstract and do not refer directly to anything that can be imaged, whether the test is free recall (Stoke 1929), recognition (Gorman 1961), or paired-associate learning (Paivio 1969). Bevan and Steger (1971) presented both children and adults with a list consisting of a mixture of actual objects, pictures of objects, and names of objects. For both age groups recall (always of the names) was best when the input was an object, next best for pictures, and poorest for words.

Let us consider Allan Paivio's (1969) paired-associate experiment in more detail. He began by having a large group of people rate words according to how easy it was to form a visual image of them (Paivio, Yuille, and Madigan 1968). Paivio then used these norms to create four types of word pairs: concrete-concrete (e.g., *hand-chair*), concrete-abstract (e.g., *hand-age*), abstract-concrete (e.g., *truth-chair*), and abstract-abstract (e.g., *truth-age*). During the study portion of the task all the pairs of words were presented. During the recall portion the first word of each pair was presented and the subject had to recall the second word. Paivio found that people's recall performance for the various types of pairs was ordered (from best to worst) concrete-concrete, concrete-abstract, abstract-concrete, abstract-abstract. Note that not only was performance better overall for pairs with concrete words, but it was better if the first rather than the second word was concrete (i.e., concrete-abstract was superior to abstract-concrete). Apparently, then, the main effect of concreteness in a recall task is to reduce PI during encoding and generation rather than to make targets more discriminable from distractors during the recognition phase of the task.

### Sequence Learning

To this point we have been concerned with the learning of individual instances, and we have seen how it is accomplished through the modification of representations in the perceptual and semantic codes. We now turn to the learning of sequences, that is, a set of items that must be recalled in the same order, such as the alphabet, your phone number, your address, the pledge of allegiance, and the story of Cinderella. The learning of a sequence is the result of encoding either a generative procedure (as we saw in Chapter 8) or even a motor program in which each item in the sequence acts as a stimulus to activate its successor.

Hebb (1961) demonstrated that people do not have to be aware that they are repeating the same sequence to create a generative procedure. The procedure develops automatically as the consequence of the repeated production of the sequence. Futhermore, Tulving (1962) observed that students tend to recall a set of words in about the same order on successive recall attempts, even if the items are represented in different orders on successive study trials. When learning involves successive attempts at recall, the information becomes better organized on each recall trial and hence is easier to recall the next time. What is initially a set of independent items tends to become an organized list of items that can be sequentially generated by accessing the first item on the list.

In general, generative procedures are the result of deliberate learning. To create a generative procedure, one must repeat a sequence over and over in the same order. Very few inputs naturally occur repeatedly in the same sequence in the environment. Only a few short sequences, such as idioms (e.g., "kick the bucket"), seem to be learned as a result of natural repetition. Intentional learning is the topic of the next chapter, so further discussion of the learning of generative procedures will be postponed until then. However, whether a sequence is learned incidentally or intentionally, its fate over a retention interval is the same. Retention is one of the topics of this chapter, so retention of sequences will be discussed now.

The degree of interference to which a sequence is susceptible depends on its degree of learning, which in turn depends on the number of times it has been repeated. Typically, a sequence is learned at the conceptual level, so the production of the conceptual representation of each item activates its successor. Such sequences are susceptible to *retrograde interference* (RI) from the learning of a new sequence that contains the same items in a different order (Briggs 1957; McGeoch 1936; Melton and Irwin 1940). Hence learning a new phone number containing the same digits may interfere with generation of the old number. The generation of an automatized sequence requires that each item have a strong association to its successor only, and the learning of two sequences forms competing associations between an item and its successor in each sequence.

Constant repetition creates an *overlearned* sequence, which is one that has been reduced to a motor program. The alphabet, the integers 1–10, some familiar phrases, and even some familiar songs and nursery rhymes may be learned at this level. Such sequences are not susceptible to interference and are extremely resistant to brain damage. Short of damage to the nervous system that makes the proper movement of muscles producing speech impossible, these sequences may still be produced. Snatches of familiar phrases can be elicited from individuals whose cortex has largely been destroyed and for whom any activity that would be called cognitive has ceased.

## MEMORY AND AGING

Memory is a topic that is of much more concern to the old than to the young. For college students studying cognitive psychology, memory is just one more topic to be studied. Not one student in a hundred worries about his or her own memory. But if a cognitive psychologist says, while in earshot of a group of people past their fifth decade, that he studies memory, inevitably one or more individuals volunteer that their memory is not what it once was and ask if anything can be done. Let us first examine changes in retention and retrieval with time. Then we will examine changes in encoding.

### Retention

The first thing that must be noted about long-term retention and aging is that the topic is extremely difficult to study. If a change in memory performance over a long period of time is observed, it is difficult to determine whether the effect is due to gradual decay of memory traces, interference from later inputs on memory for earlier inputs, or an actual change in memory processes due to aging (Bahrick 1984). In addition, it is difficult for the investigator to know what information was encoded many years ago by subjects and how well it was initially learned.

Despite these inherent difficulties the studies that have been performed so far provide a clear picture of the basic factors influencing long-term reten-

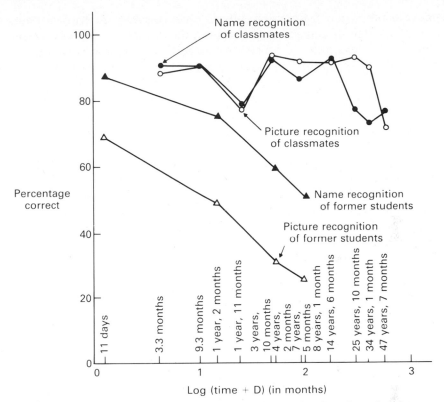

**Figure 9.6    Long-term recognition of pictures of high school students by classmates and teachers. (From Bahrick 1984.)**

tion, and indicate that aging per se, at least through the sixth decade of life, does not lead to the decay of memory traces. The most extensive research on long-term retention has been performed by Harry Bahrick and his colleagues (Bahrick, 1983, 1984; Bahrick, Bahrick, and Wittlinger 1975). They (Bahrick *et al.* 1975) asked groups of alumni to recognize names and pictures from their high school yearbook after intervals ranging up to almost fifty years after their graduation. The results are depicted by the top two lines in Figure 9.6. As the figure shows, ability to recognize classmates' names showed no decline after fourteen years, and ability to recognize classmates' pictures showed no decline after thirty-four years. In contrast, the ability to *recall* the names of classmates, even when cued by their pictures (not plotted in Figure 9.6), remained constant for only three years before beginning a steady decline with time.

The robustness of recognition after so many years leads to many important conclusions. First, perhaps over time, some representations are lost from memory as the result of some basic physiological process, such as the death of brain cells. After all, some of our brain cells die every day, and they are never replaced. This spontaneous process of forgetting over time is called *decay*. The stability of recognition over years demonstrates that decay contributes at most a modest amount to the forgetting of well-learned material. Furthermore, these results support the distinction between familiarity and identification. A face or name may seen familiar because the input achieves at least a partial match with a memory representation. This slight degree of familiarity is still sufficient to discriminate an old input from a new one, even after many years. However, the association of a picture to a name may become inaccessible after prolonged disuse, so the person is unable to make an identification.

Another implication of these results is that the comparison mechanism itself does not deteriorate before a person is in their fifties, because such a change would also cause a change in recognition performance. The ability to retrieve old, well-learned information remains stable, at least until about the seventh decade. As a result, healthy old people are able to retrieve more facts than younger people of equal education, simply because they have lived longer and learned more (Lachman and Lachman 1980).

Later work by Bahrick emphasizes that successful long-term retention depends on the degree of initial encoding. The lower two lines in Figure 9.6 present the recognition performance observed when instructors were asked to recognize the names or faces of their former students at retention intervals of up to eight years. In contrast to the long period without forgetting obtained for classmates, performance by the instructors began to decline soon after exposure, and relatively little information survived eight years. Whereas memory for the names and faces of classmates was based on a four-year period of interaction, instructors' memories of students were based on only ten weeks of much more limited interaction.

Bahrick (1984) investigated the retention of Spanish learned in school at retention intervals ranging up to fifty years. Figure 9.7 plots the subjects' performance on a test of their ability to recall the English translations of Spanish vocabulary items. The data shown are for subjects whose combined Spanish training in high school and college was considered the equivalent of either one, three, or five college courses in Spanish. Overall, recall performance increased with the amount of training the subjects originally received (and, it turns out, with their grades in their Spanish courses). Furthermore, the subjects with a substantial number of courses in Spanish showed a very stable recall level over retention intervals of six to twenty-five years. These results again support the general conclusion that material that is very well learned is not forgotten over long retention intervals.

This generally rosy picture is modified slightly when we consider the results of a free-recall task for a set of relatively unorganized items, such as the names of animals or words beginning with the letter *B*. The number of items

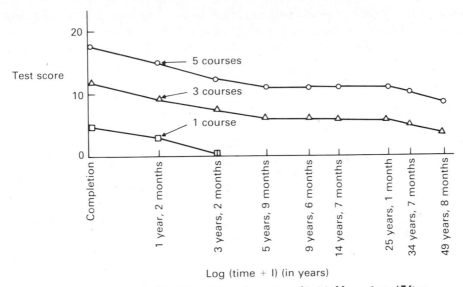

**Figure 9.7   Long-term recall of Spanish as function of initial learning. (After Bahrick 1984.)**

that can be generated within a fixed time period, usually a minute, declines on this task, which is sometimes called a verbal fluency task (Howard 1980; Schaie and Parham 1977; Schaie and Strother 1968). The cause of the decline appears to be quite basic. The executive mechanism simply appears to be less effective at activating representations in memory. This decline in free recall is only one aspect of a larger problem, encoding, to which we now turn.

## Encoding

Though the phenomenon is not well understood, overwhelming evidence now indicates that as people age, there is a general decline in physiological arousal and mental activation, and this decline has a pervasive effect on emotion and cognition. As people age, they become more susceptible to debilitating depression. In the realm of cognition we saw in Chapter 3 that with age an input produces less activation of its perceptual code (Di Lollo, Arnett, and Kruk 1982) and hence people are less successful at dividing attention among multiple inputs (Craik 1977). Furthermore, we have just seen that people are less able to activate targets through self-cuing (e.g., Howard 1980). Though the decline in the ability to bring inputs into awareness and maintain them there can be detected by demanding laboratory tasks, virtually no tasks in daily life place sufficient demands on attention so that the decline in awareness affects task performance. So for the most part, the decline goes unnoticed. The one task in which the decline in activation has a noticeable effect on ordinary levels of performance is the encoding of new information, and many old people are keenly aware of this decline.

Here the effect of the decline in activation is twofold. First, as Deborah Burke and Leah Light (1981) pointed out, an input spontaneously causes less activation. Hence even when young and old subjects use exactly the same mnemonic strategies (e.g., Hulicka and Grossman 1967; Hulicka, Sterns, and Grossman 1967; Hultsch 1971) and when they are given a recognition test, which eliminates any potential retrieval deficit (e.g., Erber 1978; Kausler and Klein 1978), the young subjects remember more. The disadvantage of the older subjects is exacerbated by their less frequent use of mnemonic strategies (Burke and Light 1981; Hasher and Zacks 1979), which will be discussed in the next chapter. Older subjects probably use mnemonic strategies less because they involve the activation of representations, and hence the older subjects find them more effortful and less effective.

In summary, the seriousness of the age-related decline in encoding should be neither minimized nor exaggerated. The decline is real and cannot be wished away. As people age, they must put more time into learning. However, as long as a person is willing to put in the time (see Hulicka and Wheeler 1976; Treat and Reese 1976), the ability to acquire new information remains more than adequate to keep up with changes in the environment and does not impair performance in most human endeavors.

## EPISODIC ENCODING AND RETENTION

What do you remember of the day's events, of yesterday's, and of the day's before that? While you remember many many things, you do not remember everything. Why are some things remembered and not others? To understand what is remembered, we must go back to the moment of encoding and determine what was encoded and what will be effective later for retrieving it. In this section we will use what we have learned about basic encoding processes to examine the course of incidental learning in daily life.

### Factors Influencing Encoding

Many inputs, such as words and sentences, and pictures of objects and scenes, activate complex concepts involving many representations. The particular representations to which a person attends make particularly good retrieval cues. Thus if a comment calls attention to a detail of a scene or picture, the witness is more likely to recognize that detail (Loftus and Kallman 1979), to discriminate it from other pictures lacking the detail (Jorg and Hormann 1978), and to recognize the similarity of other scenes that contain that detail (Bartlett, Till, and Levy 1980). The influence of a label can be quite subtle. Jorg and Horman (1978) found that whether a picture was called a *fish* or a *flounder* influenced the distractors from which it could be discriminated (also see Nagae 1980; Warren and Horn 1982).

Three factors influence which representations activated by the input are attended and hence are stored in memory: the context in which it is perceived, the perceiver's purpose in attending to it, and the characteristics of the input's representations themselves. First, in Chapter 6 we described how the context and a person's expectations influence the memory representation to which the input is matched. These same factors necessarily influence what is attended to and stored in memory. Hence if you see Figure 6.2 in the context of other animals, you will remember a rat. Second, a person's purpose in processing an input influences which representations enter awareness. You will remember different things from this book depending on whether you read it for content or scan it for spelling errors. In general, the more decisions you make about an input such as a word, which is associated with multiple representations, the more representations will be activated and the better remembered the input will be (Johnson-Laird, Gibbs, and deMowbray 1978; Ross 1981). Third, the details to which you attend are influenced by the nature of the inputs themselves. Jacoby, Craik, and Begg (1979) found that more difficult decisions about inputs, which required the retrieval of more details, led to better memory for them. For example, people are better able to recognize and recall the names of animals if they are involved in a difficult mental size comparison (e.g., deciding which is larger, a tiger or a donkey) than an easy comparison (e.g., choosing the larger of a frog and a kangaroo).

Ultimately, automatic activations from the input and from the context and conscious selection based on the demands of the task interact in a predictable but extremely complex way to determine which representations are activated (Hunt, Elliott, and Spence 1979; Nelson and McEvoy 1979; Nelson, Walling, and McEvoy 1979). A basic principle that explains many results is that when a processing task activates some additional representation beyond what the input normally activates, it increases memory for the input. Let us consider the results of two studies that demonstrate this principle. The studies made use of a paradigm developed by Craik and Tulving (1975) in which observers must perform different tasks that orient them toward different aspects of each input, after which incidental memory for the input is tested.

D'Agostino, O'Neill, and Paivio (1977) presented to students, one at a time, either thirty-six abstract words (e.g., *power*), thirty-six concrete words (e.g., *wheel*) or thirty-six pictures of objects named by the concrete words. The students had to perform one of three tasks as each item was presented. One task was to make a judgment about a *superficial* aspect of the visual representation. For words this judgment involved responding whether the word was in uppercase or lowercase; for pictures it involved responding whether the picture presented was large or small. The second task, the *verbal task,* was to respond whether the word, or the name of the object in the picure, rhymed with a word spoken by the experimenter. The third task, the *referential task*, was to respond whether the word, or the name of the object in the picture, fitted in a sentence frame (e.g., ''The _____ rolled down the hill'') spoken by the experimenter. Following presentation of the list, the students were allowed 5 minutes to free-recall all the list items.

The results, shown in Figure 9.8, were that recall was worst for the abstract words, better for the concrete words, and best for the pictures. Presumably, the better-recalled targets automatically activated richer perceptual representations and hence were more discriminable and therefore less prone to interference at both encoding (see above) and recall (Chapter 7). Also, better recall was produced by the verbal and referential tasks, which caused the observer to attend to richer representations, than by the superficial tasks. Finally, the interaction between the type of target (picture or word) and orienting task (verbal or referential) is of great interest. We have seen that pictures automatically activate more detailed visuospatial representations than words do, but words automatically activate lexical representations and pictures do not (McCauley, Parmelee, Sperber, and Carr 1980). For words better recall was produced by the referential task, which presumably activated a variety of representations associated with the semantic node defining the word's referent, than by the verbal task, which only reactivated the automatically activated lexical representation of the word. However, for pictures there was no difference in the recall produced by the verbal and referential tasks. The reason for the lack of difference becomes clear when we consider the results of another experiment, which is described next.

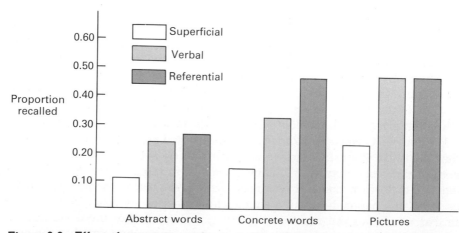

**Figure 9.8   Effect of processing task on recall for different types of inputs. (After D'Agostino, O'Neill, and Paivio 1977.)**

**TABLE 9.1** Description of the Ten Orienting Tasks

| Tasks | Description | Response* |
|---|---|---|
| Verbal | | |
| Naming | What is the name of the item? | Knife |
| Last letter | What is the last letter of the name? | e |
| Imaginal | | |
| Artist time judgment | How long would (did) it take to draw the object? | 3 |
| Explicit imagery | Create an image. How "good" is the image? | 9 |
| Referential | | |
| Size | How large is the real-world object? | 2 |
| Physical complexity | How physically complex? | 1 |
| Animacy | How much movement does the object go through daily? | 2 |
| Function | What is the object used for? You _____ it. | Cut with Blade |
| Relevant features | What must the object have to be that object? | |
| Category member-ship | Is the object artificial (i.e., man-made) or naturally occurring? | Art |

*Source:* From Durso and Johnson (1980).

*All number responses were on a scale from 1 to 10.

Durso and Johnson (1980) obtained consistent results from a more elaborate experiment. They showed students a list consisting of both pictures and concrete words, one at a time, and had them perform one of ten different tasks. The ten tasks are listed in Table 9.1. As shown in the table, they divided their tasks into three kinds: verbal, imaginal, and referential. Afterward, either the students received a surprise recognition task, in which they heard the names of common objects and had to identify the ones for which they had seen corresponding pictures or names, or they were given a surprise recall test. The results of the memory tests are shown in Figure 9.9.

First, notice that, as usual, memory for pictures was somewhat better than memory for words. Second, the imaginal tasks produced better memory for words than the verbal tasks, because the imaginal tasks activated a more detailed visuospatial representation of the word than was automatically activated by the word itself. In contrast, the verbal tasks produced better memory for pictures than the imaginal tasks, because the verbal tasks ac-

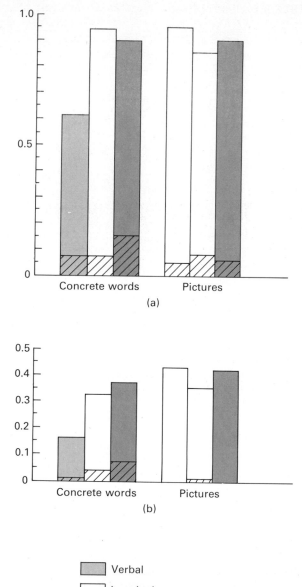

(a)

(b)

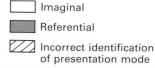

Verbal

Imaginal

Referential

Incorrect identification
of presentation mode

**Figure 9.9  Effect of orienting task on memory for pictures and words: (a) Recognition accuracy; (b) recall accuracy. Shaded regions are the proportion of correct responses that were accompanied by an incorrect identification of presentation mode. (After Durso and Johnson 1980.)**

tivated the lexical representation of the name of the pictured object, which was not automatically activated by the picture itself. Finally, the referential tasks produced about as good memory as the verbal tasks for pictures and the imaginal tasks for words because they activated multiple representations.

Reed Hunt and Gilles Einstein (Einstein and Hunt 1980; Hunt and Einstein 1981) showed that an orienting task could affect recall in other ways. On the one hand, it could direct attention to a perceptual representation of a target, which would increase its discriminability, as we have just seen in the studies described. On the other hand, the orienting task could direct attention to a common semantic node associated with several targets, which could be used as a retrieval cue for those targets.

Hunt and Einstein noted that a well-established hierarchy of retrieval cues already exists for words that name instances of a category, e.g., *animals*, but that the representations of such instances are necessarily similar to each other. So the recall of a list of such words should be greater following an orienting task that directs attention to their perceptual rather than to their semantic representations. The reverse should be true for unrelated words, which activate discriminable perceptual representations but for which no obvious cue hierarchy exists. In fact, Begg (1978a) found that related words were better remembered if the orienting task drew attention to differences among the words, whereas unrelated words were better remembered if similarity relations were processed. Similarly, Einstein and Hunt (1980) found that pleasantness ratings (the perceptual task) produced greater recall for lists of related words than a category-sorting task, but that the reverse was true for lists of unrelated words.

## Understanding and Learning

Notice that activating multiple representations from a single input essentially involves retrieving all you know about it. Hence we are back to another version of the bootstrap model of learning, with which we began this chapter. The more you know about a target, the more varied and detailed a conceptual representation you will access for it, and hence the more discriminable it will be from other targets. As a result, you are more likely to encode additional details about it, the next time it is presented you are likely to recall them as well, and so on. In short, the more you already know about something, the easier it is to learn more. Nowhere is this effect more dramatic than in memory for essays and stories. The better the material is understood, the more of it that is remembered.

As we saw in Chapter 8, people make use of story schemas to encode the events in a story or in their lives. Learning usually does not involve something entirely new but, instead, involves adding more details to a well-developed conceptual network. For example, when you read an account of a baseball game, you do not need to encode every detail about the layout of the field and the rules of the game. All you have to encode is the new information the article provides about the progress of a particular game on a particular day. Conversely, because the writer of the article assumed that you already know how baseball is played, the article will be largely incomprehensible to you if, in fact, you know nothing about baseball.

**Schema instantiation.**    In the encoding of new tokens of familiar types of situations, understanding involves instantiating a schematic structure with details specific to the particular input. In phenomenological terms, people do not feel they understand a description unless they can imagine a concrete example of what is being described. Because understanding requires the elaboration of a schematic structure in memory, much of memory is simply a by-product of understanding. Conversely, failure to understand typically implies that the input has not been associated with existing nodes in the semantic network and therefore will not be retrievable (Dooling and Lachman 1971).

The role of prior knowledge in understanding and learning was demonstrated in the early 1970s in a series of ingenious experiments conducted by John Bransford and his colleagues (Bransford 1979). In a typical experiment students were asked to read the following passage (Bransford and Johnson 1972, p. 722):

> The procedure is actually quite simple. First you arrange things into different groups. Of course, one pile may be sufficient depending on how much there is to do. If you have to go somewhere else due to lack of facilities that is the next step, otherwise you are pretty well set. It is important not to overdo things. That is, it is better to do too few things at once than too many. In the short run, this may not seem important but complications can easily arise. A mistake can be expensive as well. At first the whole procedure will seem complicated. Soon, however, it will become just another facet of life. It is difficult to foresee any end to the necessity for this task in the immediate future, but then one never can tell. After the procedure is completed one arranges the materials into different groups again. Then they can be put into their appropriate places. Eventually they will be used once more and the whole cycle will then have to be repeated. However, that is part of life.

After reading the passage, the students were asked to recall as much of it as they could. Try recalling the passage yourself right now. You will probably find it difficult to remember very much at all, which was also true for the students in the actual experiment. The passage appears to be a set of reasonably intelligible sentences stuck together somewhat arbitrarily. Because the sentences cannot be easily integrated into an existing conceptual structure, the passage is difficult to remember.

Now suppose we tell you that the passage is entitled "Doing the Laundry." Try reading the passage again. You will find that it suddenly all makes sense once you have the cue that makes it possible to retrieve the relevant visuospatial representations and imagine the appropriate sequence of actions described by the sentences. The activation of the schema for washing clothes provides a way of generating cues for the input sentences. In the actual experiment students who were given the title before they read it recalled more of the passage.

**Integrating old and new information.**    Writers of texts, stories, and newspaper articles make use of titles, headings, and opening sentences to activate a schema for encoding the propositions that follow. Kozminsky (1977) demonstrated this fact by having different students read the same story with different titles that biased the reader toward different interpretations of the story. Each interpretation was associated with a different schema, and the structure of each schema implied that different propositions would be the most likely to be recalled. This result is what Kozminsky found: The propositions recalled were consistent with the schema implied by the title given to the study.

Writers also make use of titles, headings, and opening sentences to call up relevant knowledge that can be used to interpret incoming information. The new information is encoded by linking it to the old. This point was cleverly demonstrated by Sulin and Dooling (1974). As we have seen, people usually do not confuse facts learned on two different occasions. You do not mix up what you read in your psychology text with what you read in your history text. However, Sulin and Dooling showed that when people integrate what they are learning with what they already know, they are soon unable to discriminate the new knowledge from the old. They had one group of students read the following passage, entitled "Carol Harris's Need for Professional Help" (Sulin and Dooling 1974, p. 256):

> Carol Harris was a problem child from birth. She was wild, stubborn, and violent. By the time Carol turned eight, she was still unmanageable. Her parents were very concerned about her mental health. There was no good institution for her problem in her state. Her parents finally decided to take some action. They hired a private teacher for Carol.

A second group of students read exactly the same passage, except for one change: the name "Helen Keller" was substituted for "Carol Harris." After reading the passage, all the students were given a recognition test. They were presented with a series of sentences and asked to judge whether or not each had been included in the passage. The most interesting part of the experiment focused on the responses given to one critical test sentence: "She was deaf, dumb, and blind." Since this sentence was not in the passage, everyone should have rejected it. In fact, students who had read the Carol Harris version did exactly that; not one of them claimed that the sentence had been presented.

However, 20 percent of the students who read the Helen Keller version erroneously indicated that they had read the critical sentence. This difference in mistaken recognition was even more dramatic if the recognition test was postponed a week, as we would expect from Reder's (1982) finding that target sentences can no longer be discriminated on the basis of familiarity after a delay (Chapter 8). Only 5 percent of the Carol Harris subjects misrecognized the critical sentence, but a whopping 50 percent of the Helen Keller students indicated that they had read it.

**Retention interval interference.**    Integration and interference are two sides of the same coin. When you take an exam, you want to be able to remember, integrated together, both what you read in this book and what you heard in class. Yet you want to keep it separate from any speculations of your friends about cognition. Spiro (1982) showed that stories that people learn as stories are quite resistant to integration with other information, but stories that people encode incidentally as life events are likely to become integrated with other life events and hence are subject to the kinds of distortions at recall that were described in the previous chapter. He had students read a story and then recall it either two days, three weeks, or six weeks later. Almost all the students who were told that they were in a memory experiment and would have to recall the story did not make *intrusion* errors, where they added or changed a proposition, even six weeks later. In contrast, most students who were told they were in an experiment about how people react to stories involving interpersonal relations, were told the story was true, and were told to think about and react to it made intrusion errors when tested only three weeks later. In particular, the recall of the story was altered to conform to additional information about the characters that was passed to the students 8 minutes after the story was read.

## Retention of Complex Events

Because people rely on generative procedures such as story schemas to encode complex events, the fit between details of the event and the procedure determines what is retained. Some details are more important than others, depending on their place in the hierarchy. Important details will be doubly favored, because their position in the schema being constructed initially causes considerable attention to be given to them during encoding and later gives them a privileged position during retrieval. Conversely, unimportant details may be ignored during encoding and hence may be only poorly learned or not learned at all.

    Arkes and Harkness (1980) performed two experiments that demonstrated the importance of the fit between the schema and the event details.

They pointed out that a diagnosis, whether given by a doctor, a plumber, or a mechanic, is produced by a schema that organizes and interrelates a set of symptoms. In the first experiment they showed sophomore speech and hearing students four symptoms of a problem (Down's syndrome), which they were asked to diagnose. Twelve days later they were again shown these four symptoms, as well as four other symptoms related to the problem and four symptoms unrelated to it, and were asked which symptoms had been presented earlier. Students who had diagnosed the problem from the initial four symptoms were less confident than the students who had not made the diagnosis in rejecting related symptoms they had not seen, but they were more accurate at rejecting unrelated symptoms. However, in the second experiment only four out of five symptoms were consistent with a problem schema. This time the students who were able to diagnose the problem were not more confident in rejecting unrelated symptoms than those who were not.

When a detail is not important within the framework of the encoding procedure and is not itself salient, then it may not be encoded. Later when people attempt to recall the event, they may unwittingly add details learned at other times for those they failed to encode initially, and hence they become confused about what they learned at a particular time. Such effects occur when the person has encoded only a vague representation of the input in memory and so must reconstruct it by referring to the representations of other inputs (e.g., when observers have been given only a limited amount of time to study the inputs, so their representations will contain few details).

The interference between what a person perceived and what they heard about later was extensively studied by Elizabeth Loftus, who, as we mentioned in Chapter 8, is interested in the accuracy of eyewitness testimony. Loftus (1975) demonstrated that in reconstructing an event they have witnessed, people may add some fine details that they actually heard about later rather than actually witnessed. Of course, for all important aspects of the event, people are able to discriminate what they have perceived from what they subsequently heard if there is a conflict. However, the representations of unimportant incidental details that the person was not trying to remember will be low in activation and hence will not appear familiar in a subsequent recognition task.

Loftus (1977) showed that a person may be unable to distinguish such a detail from a distractor which has had its familiarity insidiously raised by a misleading question. She showed 100 undergraduates a series of thirty color slides depicting successive stages of an accident involving a car and a pedestrian. Each slide was shown for 3 seconds. One slide included a green car, not involved in the accident, driving by. Immediately after viewing the slides, the subjects answered a short series of questions. For half the students one question was, "Did the blue car that drove past the accident have a ski rack on the

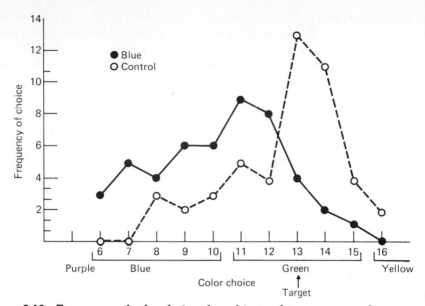

**Figure 9.10   Frequency of color choices for subjects who were exposed to misleading information (blue) and subjects who were not (control). (From Loftus 1977.)**

roof?'' Note that this question implies that there really *was* a blue car (although, in fact, it was green). The other half of the subjects answered the same question except the word *blue* was deleted.

Twenty minutes later, all the students were shown a set of numbered colored strips and asked to select the strip that matched each of ten objects that had appeared in the slides, including the green car. Figure 9.10 plots the frequency with which each strip was selected as the color of the car. Control subjects, who had not answered a misleading question, tended to select colors near the correct choice, but only thirteen of fifty of them got it right, so it was a difficult and uncertain judgment. However, the students who answered the misleading question did even more poorly because they were influenced to shift their judgments toward the blue end of the spectrum.

## ANTEROGRADE AMNESIA

In Chapter 8 we discussed memory disorders, termed retrograde amnesia, that involve the loss of memory for episodes occurring prior to a trauma to the brain. Brain damage can also produce deficits in the ability to learn new information subsequent to the trauma. This disorder, termed *anterograde am-*

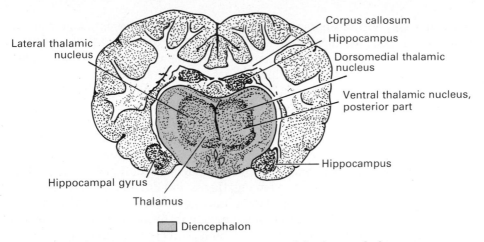

**Figure 9.11    Brain slice. Bilateral lesions in parts of the diencephalon or hippocampus cause anterograde amnesia.**

nesia, can result if certain structures are damaged in the interiors of the temporal lobes.

The temporal lobes are essential to the permanent storage of memory traces. The storage system is quite robust, so damage to the temporal lobe of one hemisphere leaves, at worst, a mild deficit in the retention of either visual inputs (if the right hemisphere was damaged) or auditory inputs (if the left hemisphere was damaged). But if certain structures are damaged bilaterally in the interior of the temporal lobes, either of two kinds of anterograde amnesia can result, corresponding to damage to two different areas, which are shown in Figure 9.11. One type results from bilateral destruction of parts of the diencephalon (exactly which parts is not known). The other type results from bilateral destruction of the hippocampus. The two types of anterograde amnesia seem to reflect impairment of different aspects of the encoding process. Bilateral damage to the diencephalon appears to make it difficult to raise the activation levels of nodes in the semantic network through attention. In contrast, bilateral damage to the hippocampus seems to somehow make memory impermanent, so newly formed traces decay. Let us examine each of these syndromes in turn.

## Diencephalic Amnesia: Korsakoff's Syndrome

**Alcoholism.**    As we mentioned in Chapter 8, the most common cause of Korsakoff's syndrome is alcoholism (though any bilateral injury to the diencephalon will cause the same symptoms). Therefore let us first look at the effect of alcohol on memory. While a person is drunk, the storage of information in memory is impaired (Hartley, Birnbaum, and Parker 1978; Ryan and Butters 1983). The most dramatic aspect of this impairment is the well-known blackout phenomenon. Later when the individual sobers up, he or she is unable to remember what occurred while drunk. This short-term encoding impairment clears up after the alcohol passes through the system, but frequent drinking results in a permanent deficit from the poisonous effects of the drug. The brains of even young alcoholics in their twenties and thirties show cortical atrophy and abnormal electrical activity during target detection (Ryan and Butters 1984). These changes cause a variety of nonverbal cognitive deficits, in particular, deficits involving visuospatial reasoning (Jones and Parsons 1972) and visuospatial attention (Becker, Butters, Hermann, and D'Angelo 1983). Alcohol consumption causes the encoding deficit in particular, because the metabolism of alcohol uses up the supply of thiamine, which is an essential nutrient for neurons that make up parts of the diencephalon. When excessive drinking is combined with a thiamine-poor diet, cells in the diencephalon begin to die. Hence Ryan and Butters (1980) found that detoxified alcoholics performed more poorly than age-matched controls on paired-associate learning tests of unrelated words, and of digits and unfamiliar symbols (see also Ryan and Butters 1983).

Recall that everyone's attentional and encoding abilities decline somewhat with age. This parallelism encouraged researchers to look closely at the effects of alcoholism and aging to determine whether alcohol prematurely aged the brain. While there is considerable overlap in the symptoms of aging and alcoholism, apparently alcohol does not prematurely age the brain (Becker *et al.* 1983; Oscar-Berman, Weinstein, and Wysocki 1983; Ryan and Butters 1984).

**Onset and overview of syndrome.**    The effect of alcohol is insidious. The change in memory from day to day is imperceptible. Furthermore, whatever skills people use in their daily activities remain unimpaired. Frequently, years of gradual mental decline go unnoticed. Hence even a superficially healthy person who is addicted to alcohol—someone who may appear to be functioning as a businessperson, college professor, or student—may suffer from a memory disorder. The memory disorders due to alcohol form a continuum of severity. Alcoholics, patients with borderline Korsakoff's syndrome, and patients with severe Wernicke-Korsakoff's syndrome exhibit increasingly severe deficits when compared with normal individuals. If at some point the person stops drinking, then there is a gradual improvement in some cognitive functions, although the ability to store new information remains permanently impaired (Brandt, Butters, Ryan, and Bayog 1983). Otherwise, the decline continues.

However, not all alcoholics develop Korsakoff's syndrome. The necessary conditions for the development of the syndrome probably include the nutritional factor, lack of thiamine in the diet, mentioned earlier, and possibly a genetic factor. The onset of the syndrome is signaled by a single traumatic event. In a typical case years of chronic alcoholism end in a final binge that leaves the patient severely confused, with difficulties in moving and seeing. This phase is the Wernicke phase of the disorder, named after the German neurologist who first described it. Patients who survive the initial few weeks will recover most of their physical and mental abilities. However, in certain respects the patient during the chronic Korsakoff phase of the syndrome (named after the Russian neurologist who first described it) is a changed person. As discussed in Chapter 8, Korsakoff's syndrome includes a variety of symptoms. Patients with Korsakoff's syndrome have an apathetic personality, exhibit a graded retrograde amnesia, and are deficient in attention as well as memory. But their most salient and debilitating deficit, which is far out of proportion to all others, is an inability to learn new information.

**Encoding deficit.**   To get a feeling for just how devastating this memory loss is, let us consider a specific case. Imagine that you are introduced to a pleasant man in his midfifties. A few minutes of conversation indicate that the man is of normal intelligence. To confirm this impression, you could administer an IQ test, on which the man might score slightly above the normal range. You ask him about himself, and he tells you about his wife, children, and job. There is no apparent memory deficit. At this point you leave him. Five minutes later, you happen to run into the same man again. He shows no sign of knowing you and, in fact, denies ever meeting you before in his life. Now imagine that you continue to meet with this man every day. You rapidly discover that at every meeting you must reintroduce yourself. He never has any memory of the previous meetings. In addition, you may find that his wife had left him years ago and his children are grown up.

How long can this situation go on? Some Korsakoff patients spend many years in the same environment and never learn to recognize the people in attendance on them daily or to find their way from their bedroom to a canteen two floors below. If you ask such a person how long they have been a patient there, they may respond that they have been there only a few days or weeks. If you ask why they are there, you will get a vague response (e.g., "Until they find out what's wrong with me"), a blank response ("I don't know"), or a *confabulation*. A confabulation is a plausible but false story that explains the person's current circumstances (e.g., "I fell down and broke my hip and I'm here to have a pin put in it").

Several characteristics of the encoding deficit are worthy of comment. First, contrary to the initial impression, Korsakoff patients store some kinds of information. Normal perceptual and motor learning takes place. Patients improve on the pursuit-rotor task, in which a stylus must be maintained on a moving target (Cermak, Lewis, Butters, and Goodglass 1973), and in the reading of mirror-imaged writing (Cohen and Squire 1981; Martone, Butters, Payne, Becker, and Sax 1983). However, new nodes corresponding to episodes are usually not formed, which leads to a striking dissociation. The patient may learn a skill normally without having any memory of having ever performed it before. Every day the mirror-tracing apparatus must be shown to the patient as if for the first time, and the patient must be reinstructed in its use. But once he or she takes up the task, the patient shows the same increment in improvement over the previous day's performance as an individual whose memory is unimpaired.

Second, reactivation of many of the old concepts in the memory of a Korsakoff patient also occurs normally, and hence normal priming of a concept can be demonstrated, though the patient is unaware of it. Recall that priming is the automatic activation of a category by the match of an associated representation to an input representation. For example, suppose you ask a Korsakoff patient to remember the names of the cities Albany, Buffalo, and Columbus. If you ask the patient 5 minutes later to recall them, he is unlikely to even remember being asked to remember anything. However, if you cue him by telling him that the cities began with the letters *A, B,* and *C,* he is likely to produce them. Similarly, if you present the names of six cities, he will probably pick out the three that were presented. Finally, if you simply ask him to tell you the names of some cities, Albany, Buffalo, and Columbus are likely to be among the first four or five cities he produces. Hence when the situation is set up properly, Korsakoff patients can be made to select or produce targets in a variety of cued recall and recognition tasks (Kinsbourne and Wood 1975). However, these results constitute something less than successful recall. Even though the *experimenter* recognizes that the patient has produced the target responses, the patient is frequently unaware that he has. To the patient the targets evoke no memory of their having been learned minutes earlier. The process of identification has broken down.

An extended series of investigations by Nelson Butters, Laird Cermak, and their colleagues (Butters and Cermak 1980) has shown that the degree of difference in recall between patients with Korsakoff's syndrome and people with unimpaired memories depends on the kind of material to be learned. If the items to be learned are highly similar to each other, unfamiliar, and/or meaningless, the performance of normal individuals is nearly as poor as the performance of patients with Korsakoff's disease. But if words or pictures are presented, then the normal individual's recall improves dramatically compared with recall of the meaningless material, while the Korsakoff patient's does not, and the patient's severe anterograde amnesia becomes apparent. Even equating attention by having the patients perform the same orienting task as the normal subjects does not substantially improve their recall.

This generally negative view of Korsakoff patients' encoding abilities was modified by Huppert and Piercy's (1977) finding that their short-term recognition of pictures could be improved somewhat by extended viewing times. They serially presented five Korsakoff patients and five age-matched and IQ-matched control subjects with sets of twenty target pictures and then, 20 minutes later, the twenty targets mixed with twenty distractors in a yes-no recognition task. Different sets of pictures were presented for different durations, from 0.5 to 8 seconds. The results are shown in Table 9.2. Notice that at presentation durations of 2 and 4 seconds, the recognition of the Korsakoff patients is as accurate as that of normal individuals who received only one-quarter as much exposure to the target.

Another aspect of the disorder is the superficial attention a Korsakoff patient gives to a task (Talland 1965). Korsakoff patients are unable to spontaneously generate the secondary recall cues necessary for generating the targets in a recall task (McDowall 1979). For example, in the distractor task (Chapter 7) Korsakoff patients do not exhibit release from PI when items from a new category are presented. Recall that the category shift provides a new cue with which to generate the target. Korsakoff patients do not spontaneously use this cue unless special pains are taken to draw their attention to it (Winocur, Kinsbourne, and Moscovitch 1981). Thus the inability to engage in top-down processing and generate cues, combined with their other impairments, interferes with the recall attempts of patients with Korsakoff's syndrome. Their recall is always severely impaired.

Finally, a patient with Korsakoff's syndrome does not spontaneously associate a concept activated by an input either with another concept in memory or with an input presented earlier. Consequently, Korsakoff patients cannot organize their concepts as a sequence of episodes in which each episode acts as a cue for its successor. Patients are therefore unable to update their personal life stories, and they thus lose their time and place in the world. This def-

**TABLE 9.2** Percent Correct in Picture Recognition Task

| Subjects | Duration of study picture presentation (seconds) | | | | |
|---|---|---|---|---|---|
| | 0.5 | 1.0 | 2.0 | 4.0 | 8.0 |
| Korsakoff | 6.05 | 66.5 | 77.5 | 85.5 | 84.5 |
| Control | 79.5 | 89.5 | 96.0 | 96.8 | 98.5 |

Source: From Huppert and Piercy (1977).

icit in the retrieval of episodic memories can make it appear that an amnesic is living in the past. For example, if you ask who is president, on one occasion the amnesic may say "Ford" and on another occasion "Nixon." But if you then ask the patient to name Republican presidents, the response may be "Nixon, Ford, Reagan."

**Thalamic stimulation.**   The severe anterograde amnesia of Korsakoff's disease suggests that the diencephalon plays an important role in encoding. Before we go on to the other main type of anterograde amnesia, let us note in passing that converging evidence for this role comes from electrical stimulation of the thalamus, which is a part of the diencephalon that appears to be a critical way station between it and the cortex. Fedio and Van Buren (1975) stimulated portions of the thalamus during the course of operations to remove a portion of it in order to relieve the symptoms of motor disorders such as Parkinson's disease (see Chapter 3). They found that stimulation of portions of either the right or left thalamus impaired the encoding of visual patterns, but only stimulation of the left thalamus impaired their retention. Ojemann (1977) found a more complex pattern of results in which the stimulation sometimes impaired encoding and sometimes appeared to improve it. However, he replicated the basic finding that the thalamus influences the course of encoding.

## Hippocampal Amnesia

The most famous amnesic in the world is a man known as H. M. H. M. is a man of above-average intelligence who had parts of his hippocampus removed in 1953 to alleviate life-threatening epileptic seizures. He has almost total anterograde amnesia for all events since that time, as has been described in detail by Brenda Milner and her colleagues (Milner, Corkin, and Teuber 1968). A few other people have disorders like H. M. S. S. was an optical engineer who contracted encephalitis, which damaged his hippocampus. R. B. was a computer designer who somehow suffered similar damage during an operation in which an aneurysm in the anterior communicating artery in his brain was clipped (to prevent it from bursting).

The memory disorder from which these patients suffer superficially resembles Korsakoff's syndrome. It combines good perceptual and motor learning (Corkin 1968) with an almost complete absence of episodic learning. However, close examination reveals significant differences. Patients with hippocampal damage do not necessarily show the graded retrograde amnesia characteristic of Korsakoff's syndrome (Chapter 8). They do not have an attention deficit, so their performance on an immediate memory task and further tests for a few hours afterward is superior to that of Korsakoff patients. However, the memory traces they form must be in some way defective, because they retain information less well than either Korsakoff patients or people with normal memories.

This difference in long-term retention was demonstrated by Huppert and Piercy (1979) and by Butters, Miliotis, Albert, and Sax (1983), who both compared patients having hippocampal damage with alcoholic Korsakoff patients and normal controls of the same age. Subjects were first shown 120 photographs of colored pictures, and then they were administered forced-choice recognition tests after 10-minute, 6-hour, and 7-day delays. On each recognition test 40 target-distractor pairs of photographs were shown, and the observer had to indicate which member of each pair had been presented previously. A longer study time (4 to 8 seconds) was used with the patients than with the normal control subjects (1 second) to ensure equivalent initial learning on the 10-minute recognition task.

There were no differences among observers at 10 minutes. The results at 6 hours and 7 days are shown in Figure 9.12. The loss of information during this interval was equivalent for Korsakoff patients and normal controls, but the loss for R. B. and S. S. was much steeper. When Huppert and Piercy (1979) compared H. M. with alcoholic Korsakoff patients on this task, his loss of information was equivalent to that found for R. B. and S. S.

Electric shock causes a temporary anterograde amnesia in addition to a temporary retrograde amnesia (Chapter 8). When Squire (1981) compared patients who received electric shock with alcoholic Korsakoff patients on a yes-

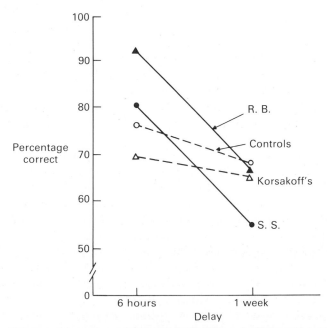

**Figure 9.12   Picture recognition of diencephalic (Korsakoff's) and hippocampal (R. B. and S. S.) amnesics and normal controls at 6 hours and 1 week. (After Butters, Miliotis, Albert, and Sax 1983.)**

no picture recognition task, he found that the patients receiving electric shock showed more forgetting between 2- and 32-hour tests than those with Korsakoff's syndrome.

Milner (1975) found that the severe recall deficit in the few patients with bilateral hippocampal damage was approximated in epileptic patients who had one hippocampus damaged and the other one briefly sedated by an injection of sodium amobarbital (see Chapter 13). During the brief period that the healthy hippocampus was inactive, the patient was shown two pictures and given a sentence to remember. A few minutes later when the drug wore off, patients were first asked to recall and, failing that, to recognize the pictures and sentences. Recall of the pictures was 40 percent accurate and of the sentences 28 percent accurate, but recognition of the pictures was 100 percent accurate and of the sentences 94 percent accurate.

### Emotion and Encoding

Something else besides attention appears to influence encoding, namely, emotion. On the one hand, depression has a general depressing effect on information processing (Hasher and Zacks 1979; Wells 1979). On the other hand, the strongly felt emotions of grief (Brown and Kulik 1977) and joy make an event much more memorable, not only for people with normal memories but also for many amnesics, including those with Korsakoff's syndrome (Zola-Morgan and O'Berg 1980). The effect of emotion on storage is particularly noticeable for those with impairments, because it can create a little island of memory in a sea of amnesia. For example, one of the authors once tested a patient who had been brought in for testing by his family. The man did not know who had brought him to the office (his wife, son, and daughter), what year it was, or who was president. But he volunteered the information that he had been at the same hospital the previous Friday when his brother died. This lone memory was accurate.

Another man was institutionalized for years when he suffered carbon monoxide poisoning. One day his son and daughter-in-law came to visit, placed a baby in his arms, and told him the baby was his granddaughter. Ever after that he always remembered that child and always asked after her by name. However, he always thought of her as a little baby, even after she was a grown woman who gave him her own infant to hold.

No one knows how emotion influences memory, but we have two clues. First, the same brain structures that influence encoding and retrieval influence emotion as well. Second, the excitation of an emotion is associated with the release of hormones, and evidence indicates that hormones somehow influence the process by which representations are permanently stored in memory (McGaugh 1983).

## SUMMARY

Much of what we learn is the incidental by-product of cognitive processing. Perceptual skills and perceptual categories can be acquired in the absence of any direct intention to learn. For complex structured inputs such *implicit learning* is sometimes superior to intentional-learning strategies.

Episodes can also be encoded in an incidental manner. In general, the longer attention is maintained on an input, the more likely it is that a representation of the input will be stored in long-term memory. Repetitions of an input lead to greater recall, especially when the repetitions are *distributed* in time rather than *massed*. Distributed repetitions produce superior encoding because of *encoding variability* and greater attention to individual presentations. When multiple inputs are presented, encoding of later inputs suffers *proactive interference* from earlier inputs. If a later input is highly distinctive, it will suffer less PI (the *Von Restorff* effect). Inputs that are easily imaged, and hence produce more discriminable representations, are also less subject to interference. Learning is intimately related to understanding, since both often depend on the instantiation of a schema with details specific to the particular input.

*Anterograde amnesia* is a deficit in the ability to learn new information as the result of brain damage. In *diencephalic amnesia*, most commonly associated with *Korsakoff's syndrome*, the patient has severe difficulty in encoding events. In contrast, perceptual and motor learning are spared. Korsakoff patients have difficulty maintaining attention on tasks, and they do not encode details and associations that could produce a discriminable memory trace. Patients with *hippocampal amnesia* resemble Korsakoff patients in many respects. However, they do not exhibit an attention deficit. Rather, the memory traces they form are in some way defective, so they retain information less well than either Korsakoff patients or people with normal memories. Even in patients with severe anterograde amnesia, events associated with strong emotion may be encoded and remembered.

## RECOMMENDED READINGS

In addition to the books mentioned at the ends of Chapters 6–8, three books are worthy of mention. Eleanor Gibson's *Principles of Perceptual Learning and Development* (1969) remains the classic in its field. John Bransford's *Human Cognition: Learning, Understanding, and Remembering* (1979) is an excellent introduction to his work on the relationship between understanding and memory. Nelson Butters and Laird Cermak's *Alcoholic Korsakoff's Syndrome* (1980) is a thorough, though already somewhat dated, introduction to this research by two of the leaders in the field.

# CHAPTER **TEN**

# Mnemonics and Memory Skill

## INTRODUCTION

In the previous chapters we examined the mechanisms by which information is encoded into memory and later retrieved. Can we use our understanding of human memory to improve memory performance? Most people certainly are painfully aware that their memories are sometimes fallible. Can we reasonably view memory performance as a skill that can be improved by practice and training?

People have a tendency to view memory as analogous to a "muscle," which can be "strengthened" by sheer exercise. This view once served to justify such educational practices as the rote memorization of long passages of Greek and Latin poetry. However, we now know that sheer practice in and of itself is not an effective means of producing general improvement in memory skill. Rather, memory can be improved by strategic recoding and reorganization of the to-be-remembered material, particularly if the result is to enable one to use more effective retrieval cues later. We do not mean to say that practice is unimportant. However, practice is far more effective when it is directed toward the development and use of appropriate learning strategies, much as people's ability to defend themselves might be improved more by training in judo techniques than by weight lifting.

Strategies for improving memory performance are termed *mnemonics* (pronounced nee-mon'-iks). This term is most often used for various specialized techniques for memorizing particular types of material (e.g., a list of items that must be learned in serial order) so that they can be later recalled. People apparently do not often engage in conscious strategies for recognition because, as we have seen, recognition is so good under most circumstances that there is no need to. We will use the term to refer to all consciously applied strategies that improve memory performance. Some mnemonics, as described in this chapter, are highly general in the range of materials to which they can be applied.

## NATURAL MNEMONIC STRATEGIES

A great deal of information is encoded incidentally as a by-product of what a person attends to. Hence you can probably give a good account of an interesting lecture you heard recently, a show you've seen, or a book you've read. However, sometimes this level of recall is not enough. Sometimes, you are faced with an exam on the details of what you read or heard. The extreme case is one that requires verbatim recall. For a phone number, knowing the approximate order of the digits is not sufficient for placing a call. When people want to recall material to a fine level of detail, they employ a mnemonic.

We have seen that two basic aspects of the encoding process influence whether a target will ultimately be recalled in a particular context. First, sufficient attention has to be directed toward the target so that it is encoded. Second, an association must be formed between the target and some cue that will be present in the recall context and hence available for reactivating the target. The two purposes of all mnemonics are fundamentally the same. First, mnemonics must ensure that sufficient attention is given to each target to encode it. Second, mnemonics must associate the target to a retrieval cue.

Let us begin by looking at the two natural mnemonics that people use to accomplish these goals: rehearsal and imagery. These mnemonics are called natural because instead of their being taught, most people discover these strategies for themselves. The two mnemonics make use of different codes but deal with long lists of targets in the same way: by creating hierarchical organizations for generating them. Hence in the final part of this section we will specifically look at the role of hierarchical organization in encoding.

### Rehearsal

Rehearsal is the most pervasive mnemonic, and it is by far the most intensively studied. We will first look at how rehearsal is used to encode a short sequence, which can be repeated in its entirety after a single hearing. Next, we will look at what happens when someone tries to learn a longer list through rehearsal on the basis of only a single hearing or viewing. Finally, we will see what happens when a person is given free access to a long list and learns it by rehearsing it over and over.

Rehearsal is a perfectly adequate strategy for learning a short sequence, such as a phone number, which can be kept within awareness by cyclicly reactivating perceptual representations of the spoken names of each digit (Drewnowski and Murdock 1980). In this case the act of saying each target reactivates it, so the act of rehearsal maintains the entire sequence in awareness. Conversely, as long as the sequence is in awareness, a person has a model she can reproduce. After a sufficient number of repetitions a generative procedure for the sequence, usually a speech-production program, is encoded (see Chapter 3). At this point the sequence can be allowed to lapse from consciousness because it can be restored at any time by initiating its generative procedure.

Beyond a sequence of about seven items, rehearsal becomes a less effective strategy because the speech-perceptual representation of one or more of the items fades from awareness before the person has a chance to repeat and hence reactivate it. When learning more than seven items, a person's rehearsal strategy changes radically. No longer does the person wait for the entire sequence to be presented and then repeat it from beginning to end. Rather, as each item is first presented, the person attempts one or two rehearsals to boost its activation. Hence the person divides attention between perceiving new items and rehearsing old ones. At least three different codes are involved in the process. When an item is first perceived, its speech-perceptual representation and then the semantic node dominating its conceptual representation are activated. When the item is rehearsed, its speech-production representation is activated, and the act of saying it re-presents the item and reactivates the representations in the first two codes.

The attempt to rehearse a sequence longer than the person's span leads to a characteristic short-term recall function. Suppose subjects are presented with a list of twenty words and asked to immediately recall the words in any order. Then we can examine the probability that a word will be recalled correctly immediately afterward as a function of where it occurred in the study list. The resulting *serial-position curve* for a typical experiment is presented by the solid circles in Figure 10.1. As the figure shows, the curve has a very distinctive bow shape. Recall is highest both at the beginning of the list (the primacy effect) and at the end of the list (the recency effect) and is lowest near the middle of the list.

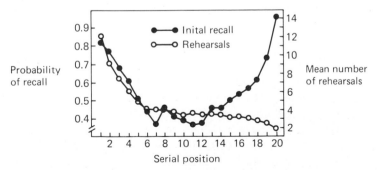

**Figure 10.1   Serial-position curves for immediate free recall and corresponding data on number of rehearsals given items at each position during presentation of list. (From Rundus 1971.)**

**Primacy.**    Rehearsal is a conscious process. It requires attention, and you can only say one word at a time. This requirement is no problem for the early words on the list. But after the subject hears several words, it becomes impossible to rehearse them all. Since later words will have more other items competing for rehearsal at the same time, on average, they will receive less total rehearsal than will earlier words and hence will be less likely to be encoded as a new semantic node. The result will be a primacy effect.

To test this hypothesis, one must show that early words in a list really are rehearsed more than later words. This result was demonstrated in a simple experiment performed by Rundus and Atkinson (1970; Rundus 1971). To obtain a count of the number of rehearsals given each item, Rundus asked students to rehearse the words on a list aloud and tape-recorded their responses. The open circles in Figure 10.1 show how many times the words at each serial position were rehearsed. As shown in the figure, the early words on the list are indeed given the most rehearsals. In fact, the primacy and middle portions of the recall curve have virtually the same shape as the plot of number of rehearsals.

Further experiments conducted by Modigliani (1980) clearly indicated that what is important about the extra rehearsals that the early list items receive is not their number but where they occur. The later rehearsals for the early list items come in the middle and end of the list. Hence a person benefits from distributed practice on the early items (see Chapter 9).

Note that extra rehearsal is not the sole explanation of the primacy effect. Even when the amount of attention paid to each list item is equalized, the first items are sometimes recalled more accurately (e.g., Darley and Glass 1975). As we saw in Chapter 9, the mere fact that an item is presented first makes it more discriminable from nonlist items. Goodwin (1976) found that when a person was presented with several lists in succession, the primacy effect in successive lists was reduced. Presumably, this reduction occurred because the beginnings of later lists seemed less distinctive.

**Recency effect.**    Of course, Figure 10.1 also shows clearly that the high level of recall from the recency portion of the list cannot be explained by extra rehearsal. Even though the later items are not rehearsed very often, they are recalled very accurately. The recency effect has received a great deal of debate, and we can only sketch an explanation here. Briefly, the last words in a list are probably maintained in a speech code of the sort described in Chapter 1 in connection with Conrad's (1964) experiment on memory for letters. A limited number of words can be maintained in a speech code as long as the person attends to them, and for this reason the last items in the list are the ones that subjects usually recall first.

In contrast, the earlier words in a list tend to be encoded in terms of their meaning (Kosslyn, Holyoak, and Huffman 1976; Mazuryk 1974; Smith, Barresi, and Gross 1971). Items represented in a speech code can be recalled very accurately as long as the test is immediate (as in Figure 10.1). But if subjects are given a distractor task, such as counting backward before they recall the list, the recency portion of the recall curve will suffer substantially (Glanzer and Cunitz 1966; Postman and Phillips 1965). The speech code therefore seems to be highly susceptible to interference from other verbal processing. At any rate, the main effect of number of rehearsals is on the early and middle items, which will mainly be encoded in terms of their meaning (since the speech code for those items will suffer interference from the later words).

As is the case for the primacy effect, however, multiple factors apparently can produce recency effects. Some studies have demonstrated *long-term* recency effects—superior recall of the items at the end of a list even after an interpolated task that presumably would have prevented continuous rehearsal in a speech code (e.g., Bjork and Whitten 1974; Rakover 1977; Rundus 1980). Long-term recency effects are typically observed when a distractor task is interpolated between the successive items to be recalled. Such effects are not well understood, but they may result from the higher activation levels of the items at the end of a series relative to items at the beginning and the middle.

**Maintenance rehearsal and delayed recall.**    From what we have said so far, you might think that rehearsal always leads to an improvement in recall performance. However, as Craik and Lockhart (1972) pointed out in a very influential paper, the maintenance of the last few list items in a speech code in order to optimize immediate recall should also lead to a deficit in delayed recall. In fact, such a negative recency effect is indeed obtained when the recall test is delayed (Craik 1970). As we mentioned in Chapter 7, people typically use semantic cues to facilitate long-term retrieval. But if a person has encoded the last few list items only acoustically, few or no semantic cues will be available to aid retrieval. As a result, the last items will be relatively difficult to recall after a delay.

According to this point of view, increasing the amount of maintenance rehearsal (i.e., rehearsal that maintains a speech code) should *not* necessarily increase delayed recall performance. This prediction has been widely investigated, and evidence has accumulated that maintenance rehearsal sometimes does (Dark and Loftus 1976) and sometimes does not (Craik and Watkins 1973) increase delayed recall. We have already discussed experiments in which rehearsals increased recall, so we will consider a typical study in which it failed to improve delayed recall.

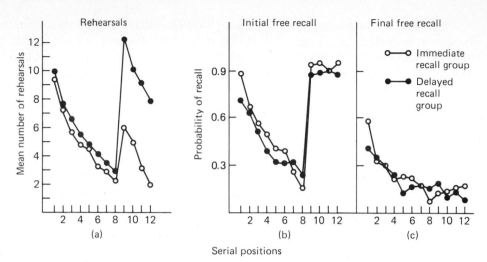

**Figure 10.2   Serial-position functions for immediate and delayed (20-second) recall groups: (a) Number of rehearsals given items; (b) level of initial recall; (c) level of final, end-of-session recall. (From Craik and Watkins 1973.)**

Craik and Watkins (1973) gave subjects lists of twelve words and asked them to rehearse the words aloud, just as Rundus had done. The subjects were told to concentrate especially on the last few words. After each list was presented, the subjects were given an initial recall test. For half the subjects the test was immediate, while for half the subjects the test was delayed for 20 seconds. No distractor task was used, so the subjects were free to rehearse right up to the time of recall. The delayed recall group therefore rehearsed the last few words on the list many more times than did the immediate recall group (see Figure 10.2a). As Figure 10.2(b) indicates, initial recall performance was virtually identical for the two groups, with very high accuracy for the last few words on the list.

After the subjects had gone through twelve lists of words, rehearsing aloud and then recalling each list, they were given an additional surprise recall test. On this final recall test the subjects attempted to recall all the 144 words they had been given during the experiment. As Figure 10.2(c) indicates, delayed free-recall performance was identical for the two groups. Rehearsing the last items on the lists many extra times did not improve recall. Despite all the extra rehearsal the recency part of the serial-position curve for final recall was no higher for the delay than for the no-delay condition.

However, this result doesn't mean that maintenance rehearsal has no effect on the memory representation for an item (Nelson 1977). In fact, even when maintenance rehearsal does not improve free recall, it does improve recognition (Glenberg and Adams 1978; Glenberg, Smith, and Green 1977; Woodward, Bjork, and Jongeward 1973). This result suggests that maintenance rehearsal boosts the familiarity of the items (see Chapter 6). In addition, a number of studies have found that increased time spent on maintenance rehearsal *does* improve recall, unlike the results of Craik and Watkins (e.g., Darley and Glass 1975; Maki and Schuler 1980; Rundus 1980). Why does maintenance rehearsal apparently only sometimes aid free recall? We would expect acoustic maintenance rehearsal to aid free recall if subjects were encouraged to use acoustic cues to generate list items and the list items were acoustically discriminable. On the other hand, if the list items were acoustically similar, or subjects did not adopt an acoustic self-cuing strategy, maintenance rehearsal should have little effect on recall (Moscovitch and Craik 1976).

**Rehearsal and organization.**   When people rehearse over and over a list that exceeds their immediate memory span, they eventually learn the entire list. John Seamon and James Chumbley (1977) showed that this learning is accomplished by creating a hierarchical organization for generating the list members. First, a subject encodes separate generative procedures for subspan segments of the list. For example, a procedure might generate the substring *tree bush fern*. Second, each procedure is associated with a cue that activates it. For example, the procedure for generating *tree bush fern* might be activated by the cue *plant*. Third, another procedure is encoded for generating all the cues. For example, the cues for the substrings *tree bush fern, pony goat lamb, shoe belt vest, bone skin hair* might be *plant, animal, clothes,* and *body parts,* respectively.

Hence the list *tree bush fern pony goat lamb shoe belt vest bone skin hair* may be organized as a two-level hierarchy. The hierarchy, having been created from the bottom up, may be used to generate the list from the top down. First, the higher-level procedure generates the cues, and then the cues are used to activate the generative procedures for the substrings of list members.

Seamon and Chumbley (1977) tested this retrieval model by cuing retrieval of particular list items with their predecessors and/or successors and measuring reaction time to produce targets. According to the model, to retrieve *fern* from *tree bush* _____ requires two steps: first, accessing the cue *plant* from *tree* and/or *bush*, and second, using the cue to activate a generative procedure for the sequence *tree bush fern*. In contrast, to retrieve *fern* from *pony goat* requires six steps. First, the cue *animal* is accessed from *pony* and/or *goat*. Second, the sequence *pony goat lamb* is generated. This sequence does not contain a target before *pony goat,* so the retrieval process must continue. Third, the cue *animal* is reactivated from *pony goat* and/or *lamb.* Fourth, the cue for the cue-generating procedure is activated from *animal.*

Fifth, the higher-level–cue-generating procedure generates the sequence *plant, animal, clothes, body parts.* Sixth, the cue *plant* is used to activate the appropriate procedure and hence generate the sequence *tree bush fern.*

When Seamon and Chumbley correlated the predicted number of steps necessary to generate a target from a cue with the observed reaction time, the correlations in three experiments ranged from 93 to 99 percent, providing powerful support for the hierarchical retrieval model. Though we have used as our example lists in which members of the same substring were also members of the same category in order to clarify the exposition, Seamon and Chumbley showed that the same hierarchical organization is created for lists of unrelated words, though in this case the cues do not correspond to natural categories.

**Development of rehearsal strategies.**    When you come right down to it, rote rehearsal is really a very banal strategy for remembering. But as we have seen, even rehearsal is a more complex process than it might seem at first glance. Still, you might think that rehearsal is such an obvious strategy that any children old enough to perform an intentional memory task would automatically use it. It turns out, however, that they do not. Children up to the age of kindergarten or first grade generally do *not* spontaneously rehearse (Flavell, Beach, and Chinsky 1966; Keeney, Cannizzo, and Flavell 1967).

In a typical study of this sort (Keeney *et al.* 1967), a group of first grade children was shown a set of pictures of common objects. On each trial the experimenter pointed to several of the pictures (the number varied from three to five across trials). The child had to wait 15 seconds (without looking at the pictures) and then had to point to the same pictures in the same order as the experimenter had used. One of the experimenters was a lip-reader and recorded any signs of verbalization during the delay interval. Several striking findings emerged in this study. Children who spontaneously rehearsed remembered the pictures more accurately than did the nonrehearsers. But with a little instruction from the experimenter, the nonrehearsers could also be induced to rehearse; when they did so, their accuracy rose to the same level as that of the spontaneous rehearsers. However, the effect of training was not long lasting. When given the option of either rehearsing or not, more than half of the children who had to be trained abandoned the rehearsal strategy, so their accuracy declined again.

Clearly, then, even a strategy as simple as rehearsal has to be learned. As you would expect, this result is even more true of the more complex memory strategies, we will be discussing throughout the rest of this chapter. An important aspect of development is *metamemory*—the child's understanding of his or her own memory abilities (Flavell and Wellman 1976). Younger children, for example, will wildly overestimate how many pictures pointed out by the experimenter they will later be able to remember. They do not seem to understand how their own memories operate and the limits on how much information they can encode in a short period of time (Flavell 1984).

## Imagery

Rehearsal makes use of the speech-perceptual, semantic, and speech-production codes. To further enhance the discriminability of an item and, hence, its short-term recall, one can activate an item's representation in the visuospatial code as well. As we saw in Chapter 7, the more concrete the input, the more likely it is to be recalled. In addition, instructions to form visual images typically result in improved memory performance. For example, Bower (1972) presented twenty consecutive pairs of nouns to students in a paired-associate task in which subjects had to recall the second word in each pair when given the first word as a cue. When the students were instructed to rehearse the pairs, they recalled only 33 percent correctly; but when they were told to form interacting images for each pair, they recalled 80 percent. Rote rehearsal was greatly surpassed by a more elaborative mnemonic strategy.

Imagery performs both functions of a mnemonic in a paired-associate learning task. First, it creates a discriminable representation that is likely to be encoded. Second, the representation has strong associations to both the cue and the target, so presentation of the cue at recall is likely to activate the target. You may have noted that the imagery instructions we have discussed so far always required subjects to form *interacting* images. For example, Figure 7.14(b) shows an interactive image for the words *girl, chair,* and *flag.* When two or more visuospatial representations are combined into a single compound representation, then each of the component representations becomes a feature of the compound representation. Hence as we saw in Chapter 7, any one of the component representations becomes an effective cue for activating the entire compound representation.

In terms of a paired-associate learning task, if the visuospatial representations of the cue and target are united as features in a compound representation, then when the cue is presented, it will activate the compound representation, thus activating the target. Bower (1972) found that interaction is in large part the key to the effectiveness of imagery when he compared the effects of two types of imagery instructions on paired-associate learning with word pairs. One group of subjects was told to form images of the two objects interacting, while the other group was told to form separate images of the two objects. The compound-image group recalled 71 percent of the words, while the separate-image group recalled only 46 percent.

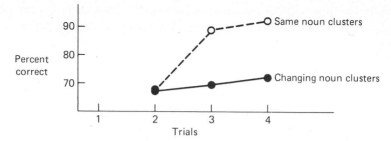

**Figure 10.3   Imagery and recall. Imagery improves recall over trials much more if the same interactive images are repeated. (From Bower, Lesgold, and Tieman 1969.)**

As with rehearsal, the ultimate effect of imagery on long-term recall is to create a hierachical organization for the list so that substrings can be activated by a small set of cues. An experiment performed by Bower, Lesgold, and Tieman (1969) showed that interactive imagery could be used to create compound representations containing clusters of targets analogous to the substrings created by rehearsal. They presented subjects with a list of twenty-four nouns in clusters of four at a time. One group of subjects imaged the same clusters of nouns during four successive presentations of the list, while another group imaged the same words clustered differently on each trial. Figure 10.3 presents the recall results for the two groups on the second, third, and fourth trials. As shown, recall improved much more over trials if the same nouns were clustered together on each trial. So even when imagery instructions are used, a consistent organization is critical for producing accurate long-term recall.

Finally, Bower (1970) demonstrated that the interactive aspect of imagery influences the generation stage of recall (see Chapter 7), as we would expect. He found that when *recognition* of cue words was tested, rather than cued recall, instructions to form interactive images were no more effective than instructions to form separate images (also see Begg 1978b). Recognition does not require generation, so for this task only the effect of imagery on target discriminability is significant.

There appear to be important individual differences in the spontaneous use of imagery. Denis (1982) identified college students who claimed to have relatively vivid or nonvivid imagery, as measured by a standardized questionnaire. He found that subjects with vivid imagery took more time to read a narrative text based on concrete material and subsequently remembered it better. In contrast, no differences were found between vivid and nonvivid images, either in reading time or in memory performance, for a passage based on abstract content (for which no one was likely to form images). These and other findings obtained by Denis indicate that forming images aids memory for concrete meaningful texts, as well as for pairs of unrelated words.

### Instructions to Organize

Another way of demonstrating the importance of organization in mnemonics is to simply instruct the subjects to organize the material and then leave the basis of the organization to them. George Mandler (1967) compared the recall performance of a group of students who were simply told to organize a list with the performance of a group told to recall it. In one experiment students were presented with a sequence of fifty-two words and were asked to write each word as it was presented. Two groups of students were told they would later be required to recall the words, whereas two other groups were not led to expect a later memory test. Each of these two groups was further subdivided either by instructing the students to organize the words into subjective categories or by giving no organizational instructions. Students who were instructed to organize were told to write each word in columns on their paper, with each column representing a group of words that seemed to belong together. The students who were not told to organize simply wrote each word one after the other as they were presented. All of the students were then asked to recall the list.

Table 10.1 presents the outcome of Mandler's experiment for the four groups of subjects. Recall for three of the conditions was virtually identical. Recall performance was high as long as subjects received either recall instructions, organization instructions, or both. Performance was relatively poor only for the group that was not instructed either to organize or to study for recall. Mandler's interpretation of these results is that to study a list essentially means to organize it, because recall fundamentally depends on organization.

**TABLE 10.1** Number of Words Recalled After Recall and Organization Instructions

|                              | Recall instructions | |
| ---------------------------- | ----- | --------- |
|                              | Given | Not given |
| **Organization instructions** |       |           |
| Given                        | 31.4  | 32.9      |
| Not given                    | 32.8  | 23.5      |

*Source:* From Mandler (1967).

Mandler demonstrated in another experiment (Mandler and Pearlstone 1966) that the final organization of a list is more important than how that organization was achieved. In this experiment subjects had to sort fifty-two cards, each with a word on it, into some specified number of categories ranging from two to seven. The cards were then scrambled, and the subject sorted the cards again. This procedure was repeated until the subject sorted the cards the same way twice. Each of these subjects was yoked to a subject in a second group. Subjects in this group had to keep sorting the cards until they achieved the same organization as their partner in the first group. In other words, subjects in the second group were forced to impose another person's subjective organization on the list. As you might expect, subjects in the second group took longer (just over twice as many trials) to achieve the same organization. However, in a subsequent recall test both groups of subjects were able to recall about the same number of words. Thus once the organization was achieved, it aided recall just as much regardless of whether it reflected the subject's own organizing strategy or that of someone else.

Over several experiments Mandler observed that total recall seemed to be determined by the number of categories into which the words were sorted. Subjects generally recalled about five words from each category, so total recall increased with the number of categories. This result suggests that the categories served as secondary recall cues that were used to generate potential target words. Each additional category could apparently serve as a cue for about five additional list words.

Buschke (Buschke 1973, 1976, 1977; Fuld and Buschke 1976) carried this analysis further. Buschke asked people to learn lists of random words and examined the precise order in which they recalled list items. He found that successive recall attempts of the same list revealed the same clusters of words. His results suggested that the process of learning a list involved combining smaller clusters into larger ones. In other words, learning a list involves organizing its members into a hierarchical structure.

## SPECIALIZED MNEMONIC STRATEGIES

We will now examine some specific mnemonic strategies that can facilitate learning. All mnemonic strategies are based on three basic principles. First, the new material to be learned is restructured in order to reduce it to familiar components. To add a few details to an established representation is easier than to create one that is altogether new. Second, the material is organized in such a way as to establish potential retrieval cues for subsequent recall. Third, many mnemonic strategies involve the generation of imagery in order to increase the discriminability of the material. Let us take a detailed look at some specific examples of mnemonic strategies that illustrate these principles.

## Chunking

Chunking is the process by which people organize input items into larger units. In general, chunking occurs whenever several targets are matched against a larger representation in memory. Chunking plays an especially important role in determining how much material can be successfully encoded in one presentation. For example, you could probably repeat a 15-word sentence verbatim, but not 15 random words. Most people can repeat about 7 short words, 7 syllables, or 7 random letters. Yet the 7 words would contain about 35 letters! Clearly, how much is remembered is not equivalent to a simple physical or perceptual characteristic of the input, such as number of letters. Rather, the rate at which information can be encoded into memory depends on the size of the representations that can be formed. A word generally will be encoded as a single unit, or *chunk*, whereas 7 unrelated letters will be encoded as 7 individual chunks. In general, the larger the unit of encoding, the more material can be encoded in a given period of time.

George Miller (1956) performed a demonstration experiment with one subject to show how the rate at which information can be encoded depends on the size of the chunks formed in memory. He first presented the subject with a series of strings of 1s and 0s (e.g, 10011101101), and for each string he asked the subject to repeat the numbers to him in the same order. Not surprisingly, the subject could not remember very long strings of 1s and 0s in perfect order. In fact, a typical person can remember a string of only nine such digits.

However, Miller then went on to teach his subject a trick for remembering strings of 0s and 1s. The basic idea is to give the person a rule for coding the digits into larger chunks. Miller's rule was to code the digits from base 2 (binary) numbers into base 8 (octal) numbers. This technique increases the size of the chunks because one octal number stands for a unique pattern of three 0s and 1s, as follows: 0 = 000, 1 = 001, 2 = 010, 3 = 011, 4 = 100, 5 = 101, 6 = 110, 7 = 111. After learning this simple coding scheme, one can listen to a series of 0s and 1s and quickly translate it into a much shorter string of octal numbers. For example, 010001111011101110010 becomes 2173562, which is no harder to remember than an ordinary telephone number. To recall the original string, one simply has to translate back from the octal code into 0s and 1s. By using this technique, Miller's subject was able to listen to a string of as many as forty 0s and 1s and repeat them back perfectly.

Twenty-five years later, Chase and Ericsson (1982) performed another experiment demonstrating the role of chunking in mnemonics. However, this time they let the subjects invent their own chunking strategies. Chase and Ericsson monitored the course of learning in a digit span task, in which subjects listen to a series of digits read at the rate of one digit per second and then immediately attempt to report the series in order. Two subjects practiced the digit span task for two years, completing well over two hundred sessions. Figure 10.4 plots the growth in their average digit span with practice. One of

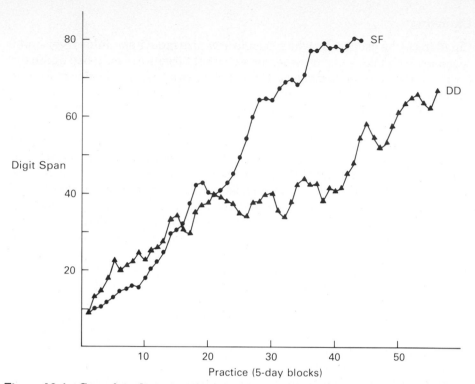

**Figure 10.4    Growth in digit span for two subjects, SF and DD, as function of prac-
tice with recoding strategy. (From Chase and Ericsson 1982.)**

the subjects, Steve Faloon, began like any other naive subject, with an initial
span of seven digits. Ultimately, he attained truly spectacular levels of recall
ability, culminating in a peak performance of eighty-two digits!

What were the mechanisms underlying this tremendous increase in digit
span? The factors identified by Chase and Ericsson are entirely consistent
with what we have learned about mnemonic strategies. First, the subjects
learned to chunk sequences of three or four digits by matching them to
unitized representations already stored in long-term memory. Both subjects
were runners, and their primary coding device was to relate incoming digits to
well-known times of races (e.g., the sequence 351 was coded as the "old world
record for the mile for a long time").

Second, the subjects developed a retrieval structure—a device for index-
ing information in long-term memory, such as the memory locations used in the
method of loci. The two subjects both learned to group their low-level digit

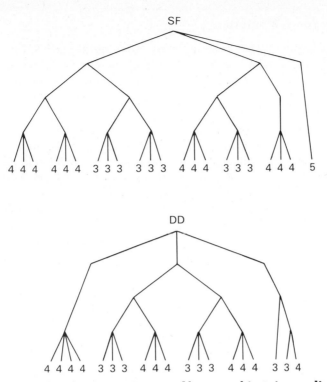

**Figure 10.5   Hierarchical organizations used by two subjects in recoding digit strings. (From Chase and Ericsson 1982.)**

chunks into larger supergroups, hierarchically organized as illustrated in Figure 10.5. By using these retrieval structures, the subjects were able to locate chunks within a long series directly, without necessarily having to repeat the list from the beginning. When the series was being reported, the subjects tended to pause for a longer time between the major boundaries in the retrieval structure. Finally, extensive practice produced an increase in the speed with which the subjects could access the relevant information in long-term memory. These results show how extraordinary memory skill can be produced by learning appropriate strategies and practicing their use.

Other types of material can be encoded in terms of preexisting chunks stored in memory. In the next subsection we will see that meaningless sounds can be recoded as words. Nor are chunks restricted to verbal material and numbers. As we have seen, interactive imagery can be used to combine several targets in a single visuospatial representation, which serves as a chunk. Let us examine different mnemonics that make use of different kinds of chunks.

## Natural-Language Mediation

We saw in Chapter 9 that remembering meaningful material is easier than remembering meaningless material. A useful encoding strategy is therefore to somehow turn a meaningless input into a meaningful one. By associating the input with more meaningful concepts, the person is able to establish a more effective set of retrieval cues.

One such strategy is called *natural-language mediation* (Montague, Adams, and Kiess 1966; Prytulak 1971). This approach is useful for learning unfamiliar technical terms, numbers, and sometimes foreign language vocabulary. Natural-language mediation involves encoding a term by thinking of a real-word association. For example, suppose you had to learn a set of nonsense pairs such as *wis-op, cer-val,* or *klm-ptg*. One way to encode the material is by allowing yourself to free-associate while you are studying in order to come up with a more meaningful representation. In our examples, *wis-op* might remind you of *whistle-stop, cer-val* might translate into *Sir Valiant,* and *klm-ptg* might result in *Dutch airline–paper tiger*.

Experimental evidence suggests that natural-language mediation is an effective encoding strategy. For example, Montague *et al.* (1966) asked subjects to think of natural-language mediators for nonsense syllable pairs like the examples just given. On the recall test the first member of each pair was presented, and the subject had to recall the second nonsense syllable. Montague *et al.* found that subjects were more likely to recall the nonsense syllable if they were also able to recall the mediator they had used to encode the pair.

In addition, experimental studies have demonstrated the effectiveness of a strategy that combines natural-language mediation with imagery to aid in memorizing the meanings of foreign vocabulary items. In the *keyword method* subjects are trained to connect a foreign word to its translation in two steps: First, the foreign word is linked to a similar-sounding word in the native language (the keyword). Then the keyword is linked to the translation by a mental image. For example, the Russian word for "building," *zdanie,* is pronounced somewhat like "zdawn-yeh," with emphasis on the first syllable. One could therefore use *dawn* as the keyword and then form a mental image of the first light of dawn casting its glow over a large building. Students taught to use the keyword method show improved ability in recalling the definitions of foreign vocabulary items (Atkinson and Raugh 1975; Kasper 1983).

## Semantic Elaboration

Recall from Chapter 9 how effective a referential-orienting task was in improving the recall of both words and pictures. The general strategy of creating more meaningful representations can also involve expanding pairs of words into sentences or lists of words into stories. In such cases the strategy is termed *semantic elaboration.*

In one experiment investigating this type of strategy, Bower and Winzenz (1970) presented three groups of subjects with thirty pairs of words, such as *frog-tree*. As in our earlier examples with nonsense syllables, the subjects' task was to learn to produce the second word in each pair given the first word as a cue. The first group of subjects in the Bower and Winzenz experiment was simply told to rehearse the word pairs. The second group was told to form a visual image of the two objects interacting in some way (e.g., visualizing a frog sitting in a tree). The third group was told to think of a sentence that contained both words (e.g., "The frog is sitting in a tree"). The results showed very striking effects of elaboration. The imagery group recalled 87 percent of the words, the sentence group 77 percent, and the rehearsal group only 37 percent.

In another study Bower and Clark (1969) had two groups of subjects learn twelve lists of 10 nouns each, either by rehearsal or by linking all the words together in sentences that formed a story. After the students had been presented with all twelve lists, they were asked to recall all 120 words that had been presented. The difference between the two groups was almost incredible. While the rehearsal group recalled a mere 13 percent of the words, the story group recalled fully 93 percent of them.

### Serial-Order Mnemonics

A common type of memory task is to memorize a set of items in a particular order (e.g., a list of topics to cover in a lecture). Some *serial-order mnemonics* have been taught for centuries as practical aids to memory. We will briefly describe two of them: the *method of loci* and the *pegword method*. Both can be used to remember an arbitrary list of items in an exact order.

**Method of loci.**    The method of loci, or mental-walk technique, is the oldest and probably the best-known mnemonic strategy. It has been described so often and so well that we will not try to describe it again; instead, we will quote from others. We use Gordon Bower's (1970) description of the method. As you will see, Bower in turn quotes Frances Yates, who in turn paraphrases an ancient Roman source (Bower 1970, pp. 496–497).

> The "method of loci" has been known in Western civilization since ancient Greek times. Cicero (in *De Oratore*) claimed that the method originated in an observation by a Greek poet, Simonides, about whom he told the following story: Simonides was commissioned to compose a lyric poem praising a Roman nobleman and to recite this panegyric at a banquet in his honor attended by a multitude of guests. Following his oration before the assembled guests, Simonides was briefly called outside the banqueting hall by a messenger of the gods Castor and Pollux, whom he had also praised in his poem; while he was absent, the roof of the hall collapsed, killing all the celebrants. So mangled were the corpses that relatives were unable to identify them. But Simonides stepped forward and named each of the many

corpses on the basis of where they were located in the huge banquet hall. This feat of total recall is said to have convinced Simonides of a basic prescription for remembering—to use an orderly arrangement of locations into which one could place the images of things or people that are to be remembered.

Cicero relates this story about Simonides in connection with his discussion of memory regarded as one of the phases of rhetoric. In ancient times rhetoric teachers provided memory instruction because, in those days before inexpensive paper and writing implements, public speakers had to memorize an entire speech, or at least the sequence of main topics. For this reason most references to the method of loci come down to us from treatises on rhetoric, such as Cicero's *De Oratore*, the anonymous *Rhetorica ad Herennium*, and Quintilian's *Institutio oratoria*. Frances Yates tells the historical story in fascinating detail in *The Art of Memory* [1966, p. 3] and provides a detailed description of how the method of loci was used in ancient times:

> It is not difficult to get hold of the general principles of the mnemonic. The first step was to imprint on the memory a series of loci or places. The commonest, though not only, type of mnemonic place system used was the architectural type. The clearest description of the process is that given by Quintilian. In order to form a series of places in memory, he says, a building is to be remembered, as spacious and varied a one as possible, the forecourt, the living room, bedrooms, and parlours, not omitting statues and other ornaments with which the rooms are decorated. The images by which the speech is to be remembered . . . are then placed in imagination on the places which have been memorized in the building. This done, as soon as the memory of the facts requires to be revived, all these places are visited in turn and the various deposits demanded of their custodians. We have to think of the ancient orator as moving in imagination through his memory building whilst he is making his speech, drawing from the memorized places the images he has placed on them. The method ensures that the points are remembered in the right order, since the order is fixed by the sequence of places in the building.

To summarize, the prescription for memorizing a series of items is (1) first to memorize a list of "memory snapshots" of locations arranged in a familiar order; (2) to make up a vivid image representing, symbolizing, or suggesting each of the items of information that is to be remembered; and (3) to take the items in the sequence they are to be learned and to associate them one by one with the corresponding imaginary locations in memory. The associations are to be established by "mentally visualizing" the image of the items placed into the imaginary context of the locational snapshots. The same loci are used over and over for memorizing any new set of items. Without this feature—if an entire new set of loci had to be learned for each new list—the use of the method would be uneconomical.

**Pegword method.** Another serial-order mnenonic, the pegword method, works without the spatial imagery involved in the method of loci. This technique involves first learning a series of number-word rhymes. A possible set is as follows: one is a bun, two is a shoe, three is a tree, four is a door, five is a hive, six is sticks, seven is heaven, eight is a gate, nine is a line, and ten is a hen. After this set of rhymes has been thoroughly learned, quickly and accurately learning any new list of ten words is then possible. The technique from this point on is the same as the method of loci. As each new word is presented, you form a vivid image relating the word to one of the pegwords. For example, suppose you wanted to remember the elements in the order of their atomic weights. To memorize the first element, hydrogen, you might image a bun rising out of the mushroom cloud of an exploding hydrogen bomb. For the second element, helium, you might image a shoe suspended from a helium balloon; etc. To later recall the list, you would run through the pegwords in order and retrieve the word associated with each. A nice feature of the pegword method is that because the items are numbered, overlooking an item is impossible. For example, when one comes to *three-tree,* one knows that there is some word that comes with it that must be recalled.

With a little practice both the method of loci and the pegword method produce extremely accurate recall. [For an assessment of both methods, see Roediger (1980).] The methods are limited only by the number of loci or pegwords you have learned. In fact, you can learn several different lists by using the same loci and not confuse them, at least for relatively short retention intervals, just as you would not be likely to confuse events that occurred on two different trips to school (Bower and Reitman 1972; Christen and Bjork 1976). Possibly, these mnemonic devices, which allow items to be learned rapidly, increase the temporal discriminability of multiple lists (Bellezza 1982). Both methods are highly specialized forms of the imagery and organizing tactics we discussed earlier. In each case the new material to be learned is associated with a set of cues that can easily be generated in order. A distinctive retrieval cue for each item is therefore available at the time of recall. Armed with a well-learned set of pegwords or loci (a series of landmarks along a route through campus is often a good choice), you will be ready to astound your friends with your memory ability.

## Detrimental Effects of Mnemonic Strategies

So far all the evidence we have cited consists of striking demonstrations of the effectiveness of mnemonic strategies in improving short-term recall. However, work by Baker and Santa (1977) has demonstrated some important limits on the usefulness of mnemonics. In a particularly interesting experiment they created a situation in which instructions to form interactive images actually *hindered* memory performance.

In this experiment subjects were read a list of twenty-eight concrete nouns, with pauses inserted after every fourth item. Half the subjects were told to form intractive images linking the items within each group of four. The other half of the subjects were not given any special learning instructions. Afterward, the subjects were tested in one of two ways. One test was simply a

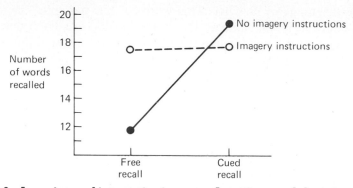

**Figure 10.6    Learning and interactive imagery. Learning words by interactive imagery leads to poorer performance on a cued recall task. (From Baker and Santa 1977.)**

free recall of all the words. The other was a *cued* recall test. This test involved giving the subjects a new list of words, most of which were associates of words from the study list. For example, if the word *cheese* had appeared on the study list, the word *milk* might be presented as a cue. The subjects were told to generate associates of the cue words and to write down any words from the study list that came to mind.

The results of the experiment are shown in Figure 10.6. The free-recall results show the usual large superiority of subjects instructed to form images. However, the picture is quite different for cued recall. With that type of test subjects who did *not* receive imagery instructions actually recalled more words than did those subjects told to use imagery!

What has gone wrong with our trusted mnemonic strategy? As we saw in Chapter 6, an item cannot be entirely separated from its context. You may recall, for example, that Hunt and Ellis (1974) found that if the word pair *file folder* was presented for study, people were less likely to later recognize *folder* if it was presented alone. Similarly, if people are encouraged to encode *cheese* in an interactive image with three other words, then even if they later are able to use the cue *milk* to generate *cheese,* they may not recognize it as a list word because its context will have been changed.

The Baker and Santa study again demonstrates that how we encode something ultimately determines what kind of recall strategy will be successful. Mnemonic devices are effective because they create an integrated context for the memory representations of list items. This context affords a set of potential retrieval cues. However, there is a resulting danger. If the context provided at recall is very different from the context in which the target items were encoded, those potential retrieval cues will not be accessed, and alternative possible retrieval cues will not be as effective as they might otherwise have been.

In general, mnemonics create an especially context-bound memory representation. This conclusion has important educational implications. In order to ensure that material will be retrievable in a wide range of contexts, students should encode the material in a flexible way, perhaps using a variety of different study methods. Otherwise, a rigid encoding may prevent retrieval of the information in a novel context. As we will see in Chapter 12, such memory blocks can inhibit creativity in solving problems.

## Outlining and Hierarchical Organization

A strategy for improving long-term recall that has many practical uses as a technique for studying is *outlining*. A good way to study this chapter, for instance, is to go through it and draw an outline of the main ideas. Your outline should include the major divisions of the chapter: general mnemonic strategies, specialized strategies, and mnemonists. Each of these major parts can be divided into more detailed topics and concepts. By working down through the hierarchy, you will be able to find where we are now—talking about outlining.

Outlining is an abstractive strategy because it is typically used to capture the gist of the material, not the specific wording. In studying this chapter, you don't want to memorize all the sentences but, rather, to grasp the major concepts and the ways in which they relate to one another. In fact, trying to construct an outline can serve as a test of how well you understand the material. Studying the outline will then provide you with an organized memory representation with a large set of potential retrieval cues for recalling important concepts.

Outlining is useful not only for encoding an organized body of information but also for generating one. Drawing up a careful outline is a good way to begin writing an essay, a story, or a chapter in a textbook. Once you have an outline, you can keep the general framework of what you are writing in mind as you work on specific pieces. The process of constructing an abstract representation, such as an outline, starts to take us across the fuzzy boundary between simply recalling what we know and using what we know to generate something new.

The technique of outlining is closely related to the strategy of organizing a list of words into categories, which we discussed earlier. In Chapter 7 we emphasized that a hierarchical memory organization aids recall by providing secondary recall cues. A number of studies support this general conclusion. For example, Bower, Clark, Lesgold, and Winzenz (1969) demonstrated that a list of words will be remembered much better if people are aware that the list can be organized hierarchically. The experimenter showed students four

**TABLE 10.2**  Two Levels of Organization

| Hierarchical condition | | | | |
|---|---|---|---|---|

**Minerals**

| Metals | | | Stones | |
|---|---|---|---|---|

| Rare | Common | Alloys | Precious | Masonry |
|---|---|---|---|---|
| Platinum | Aluminum | Bronze | Sapphire | Limestone |
| Silver | Copper | Steel | Emerald | Granite |
| Gold | Lead | Brass | Diamond | Marble |
|  | Iron |  | Ruby | Slate |

| Random condition | | | | |
|---|---|---|---|---|

**Knee**

| String | | | Ruby | |
|---|---|---|---|---|

| Drum | Arm | Lead | Percussion | Head |
|---|---|---|---|---|
| Flower | Slate | Instrument | Hand | Trumpet |
| Tuba | Foot | Maple | Rose | Marble |
| Neck | Piano | Toe | Birch | Aluminum |
|  | Oak |  | Gold | Violin |

*Source:* Bower, Clark, Lesgold, and Winzenz (1969).

cards, each of which contained approximately 28 words. The students studied each word set for about a minute and then tried to recall as many as possible of the 112 words. The students were then asked to study and recall the word sets three more times, for a total of four study-test trials.

The most interesting aspect of the experiment involved a contrast between two groups of students. One group (the hierarchical condition) saw the words on each card arranged in a sensible hierarchical classification scheme; see Table 10.2. The other group (the random condition) saw each word set randomly scrambled. The recall results for the two conditions over the four trials are shown in Figure 10.7. As the figure shows, subjects in the hierarchical condition consistently recalled many more words than did subjects in the random condition.

How critical is it that subjects actually see the hierarchy when they study the list? Can people make use of the hierarchical organization even if they do

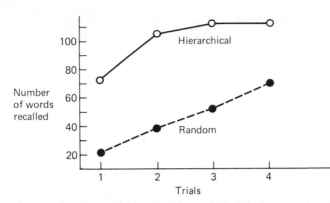

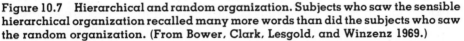

**Figure 10.7    Hierarchical and random organization. Subjects who saw the sensible hierarchical organization recalled many more words than did the subjects who saw the random organization. (From Bower, Clark, Lesgold, and Winzenz 1969.)**

not encounter it until the time of the recall test? These questions were investigated in a study by John Santa and his colleagues (Santa, Ruskin, Snuttjer, and Baker 1975). They had students study lists of the same type as Bower *et al.* had used. One group studied the lists in hierarchical arrangements, whereas two other groups studied randomly arranged lists. After studying the lists, the students tried to recall as many words as possible.

At this point the subjects were given some cues to help them recall more words. The hierarchical group and one of the random groups were given the top three levels of the conceptual hierarchy as cues for further recall. The other random group was given the same cue words, except that the cue words were arranged randomly. Santa *et al.* then counted how many additional words the subjects were able to recall after receiving the cues. The hierarchy cues improved recall most for the students who originally studied the list in hierarchical form (an extra 19 words recalled). The cue words were next most effective for the group that studied the words in a random arrangement but were cued with the hierarchy (10.2 additional words). The cues were least effective when they were arranged randomly (just 4.8 additional words). This experiment demonstrates that organization is most effective when presented for both study and recall; however, it is an aid even when presented only at the time of recall.

## MINDS OF THE MNEMONISTS

The kinds of mnemonic strategies we have been discussing can improve anyone's memory performance. However, there are people who are expert *mnemonists*, masters of mnemonic strategies. Their memory abilities go well beyond anything we have yet considered. Most laboratory tasks are not sufficiently difficult to give expert mnemonists a chance to demonstrate the full range of their abilities. When these abilities are displayed for the first time, they seem almost superhuman. But when we consider what we already know about memory, we can understand them as extensions of our own abilities. We will examine the memory feats of three individuals: a mathematician in Scotland, a history graduate student in Washington State, and a reporter in the Soviet Union.

## Lightning Calculator

For hundreds of years there have been reports of people with exceptional abilities to perform numerical calculations in their heads. Hunter (1962, 1977) presents an interesting case study of one such "lightning calculator," Professor A. C. Aitken of Edinburgh University. Here is one example of his prodigious skill. He was given the task of expressing $\frac{4}{47}$ in decimals. After an initial pause of 4 seconds, he began to produce the answer at the rate of about one digit every $\frac{3}{4}$ second: ".08510638297872340425531914 . . . (a pause of about 1 minute) . . . 191489 . . . (5-second pause) . . . 361702127659574458." At this point he stopped and announced that the decimal pattern repeats itself.

How did Aitken do it? His ability depended on two essential types of knowledge. First, he simply knew an enormous number of facts about numbers. Second, he had many alternative strategies for performing calculations. These strategies in turn relied on the number facts that Aitken knew. He worked a calculation in two steps. First, he examined the problem and decided upon a plan of attack. In doing so, he might translate the problem into a different form that was easier to handle. Second, he actually implemented the method and generated the answer.

Consider a second example, for which Aitken described how he arrived at a solution. The problem was to express $\frac{1}{851}$ in decimals. The first thing he did was recall that 851 equals 23 × 37 (a number fact). Then he also recalled that $\frac{1}{37}$ equals 0.027027027 . . ., repeating. As a result, his chosen plan of attack was to divide $\frac{1}{37}$ by 23. At this point Aitken began to produce the answer in the following way:

$$23 \text{ into } 0.027 = 0.001 \text{ with remainder 4;}$$
$$23 \text{ into } 4027 = 175 \text{ with remainder 2;}$$
$$23 \text{ into } 2027 = 88 \text{ with remainder 3;}$$
$$23 \text{ into } 3027 = 131 \text{ with remainder 14;}$$
$$23 \text{ into } 14{,}027 = 609 \text{ with remainder 20; etc.}$$

In addition, Aitken could easily calculate how far the solution would go before repeating. He knew that $\frac{1}{37}$ repeats after 3 places and that $\frac{1}{23}$ repeats after 22 places. As a result, $\frac{1}{851}$ must start to repeat after 3 × 22 = 66 places.

The basic principle motivating Aitken's choice of a plan of attack was always to minimize the amount of conscious processing he had to do at one time. Most of us have great difficulty with such mental calculations because we have to compute and remember so many partial results as we go along. Aitken minimized this problem of limited capacity by using his enormous repertoire of number facts that were already stored in memory and could be retrieved without computation. We all know, for example, that $8 \div 4 = 2$. But Aitken also knew all the prime numbers up to 1000 and the factors of all the nonprimes (e.g., $851 = 23 \times 37$). When the year 1961 was mentioned, for example, he commented that 1961 was $37 \times 53$, also 44 squared + 5 squared, as well as 40 squared + 19 squared.

Unlike most of us, Aitken thought of large numbers as single chunks rather than as combinations of digits. He said that all numbers up to 1000 seemed like "one idea," while numbers from 1000 to 1 million seemed (regrettably) like "two ideas." As a result of having such compact chunks for numbers, Aitken had no trouble repeating fifteen digits either forward or backward when they were read out to him at the rate of five per second (Baddeley 1976, p. 367). As we will see in Chapter 12, the use of extensive stored knowledge and plans also typifies expert players of complex board games such as chess.

Before the age of electronic calculators and computers, lightning calculation was a very valuable skill for a mathematician. Today it may be a dying art. One of the saddest days in Professor Aitken's life was in 1923 when he first used a mechanical calculator. After that first encounter he lost interest in extending his abilities any further, and he believed that his skills deteriorated. Of course, as we saw in Chapter 4, mental calculation based on a specialized mnemonic strategy (mental abacus) is still taught and used extensively in Asia.

## Mnemonist V. P.

While Professor Aitken used his memory skills primarily for mental calculation, two other mnemonists we will talk about were more general. The first of these, known to science as V. P., was born in Latvia but has lived for many years in the United States. He is a very intelligent man (with an IQ of 136). When V. P. was tested systematically (Hunt and Love 1972), he was able to repeat seventeen digits in order. He also recalled Bartlett's story *War of the Ghosts* almost verbatim six weeks after being presented with it. V. P. apparently relied mainly on linguistic and semantic associations to elaborate what he was trying to remember. In doing so, he was aided by an extremely wide knowledge of languages (he could read almost all modern European languages). Since virtually all consonant sequences approximate a word in one language or another, he found it very easy to generate natural-language mediators for any nonsense syllable.

V. P. had his own views about how his skills developed. He regarded his memory abilities as the result of Jewish culture, which valued and encouraged rote memory. He viewed good memorizers such as himself as basically passive individuals who are prepared to devote their energies to encoding the presented material, without being particularly concerned with the purpose of remembering it.

### Mnemonist S.

The most extensively studied of all mnemonists, known to us as S., was born a few miles from V. P.'s birthplace, shortly before the turn of the past century. In the 1920s he was a newspaper reporter in Russia. When the editor gave out assignments for the day, S. never took notes. One day the editor started to reproach him for being inattentive, but S. repeated the assignment word for word. The editor then sent him to a psychology laboratory. There he met the great Russian psychologist A. R. Luria. Luria studied S.'s memory abilities for almost thirty years, and he published his findings in a fascinating book called *The Mind of a Mnemonist* (1968).

**Memory abilities.**    S.'s abilities were truly astounding. He could repeat seventy or more items in order without error, whether they were words, letters, nonsense syllables, or sounds. He could repeat the series either forward or backward. Furthermore, his recall of such lists was still perfect when tested after fifteen years, despite the fact that by that time S. had become a professional mnemonist, who had learned thousands of similar lists. To recall a particular list, he would carefully reconstruct the situation, as the following example demonstrates (Luria 1968, p. 12):

> "Yes, yes. . . . This was a series you gave me once when we were in your apartment. . . . You were sitting at the table and I in the rocking chair. . . . You were wearing a gray suit and you looked at me like this. . . . Now, then, I can see you saying. . . ." And then he would quickly recall the entire list.

**Encoding process.**    How did S. encode the material? In large part he relied on extraordinarily vivid visual imagery. For example, when S. was presented with a list of 50 digits shown in Table 10.3, he reported that he could still "see" the numbers even after they were removed. As a result, he was able to rapidly read off the numbers by rows, columns, or diagonals of four. After four months he needed more time to "recapture the situation" before beginning to recall, but then he performed as quickly and accurately as ever.

Part of S.'s encoding ability depended on an extreme form of *synesthesia*. Synesthesia occurs when an input evokes an image in a different sense modality. Many people experience synesthesia occasionally, as when a piece

**TABLE 10.3**  Fifth Digits Used to Test S.'s Memory

| |
|---|
| 6680 |
| 5432 |
| 1684 |
| 7935 |
| 4237 |
| 3891 |
| 1002 |
| 3451 |
| 2768 |
| 1926 |
| 2967 |
| 5520 |
| 01 |

of music arouses visual images. But S. experienced synesthesia in response to virtually any input. For example, Luria (1968) reports S.'s reaction to a particular tone (p. 23): "S. saw a brown strip against a dark background that had red, tongue-like edges. The sense of taste he experienced was like that of sweet and sour borscht, a sensation that gripped his entire tongue." His synesthesia allowed S. to easily form visual images of essentially anything—words, numbers, or nonsense material. Here, for example, is how S. imaged digits (Luria 1968, p. 31): "Take the number 1. This is a proud, well-built man; 2 is a high-spirited woman; 3 is a gloomy person (why, I don't know); 6 is a man with swollen feet; 7 a man with a mustache; 8 a very stout woman."

**Nature of his errors.**    Did S. ever forget? He did occasionally make errors, but these seemed to be not so much defects of memory as defects of *perception*. For example, a noise during the reading of a list might be imaged as "puffs of steam" or "splashes," which would make it difficult for S. to encode the table. During recall he might do something like "misread" the digit 8 as a 3. He often used the method of loci, which he appeared to have rediscovered for himself. Sometimes, he would omit words during recall because he couldn't "see" them clearly in his image. For example, on one occasion he missed the words *pencil* and *egg* in recalling a list by the mental-walk technique. Here is his explanation for the errors (Luria 1968, p.36):

> I put the image of the pencil near a fence . . . the one down the street, you know. But what happened was that the image fused with that of the fence and I walked right on past without noticing it. The same thing happened with the word *egg*. I

had put it up against a white wall and it blended in with the background. How could I possibly spot a white egg up against a white wall?

While S.'s amazing abilities were in some ways an extraordinary benefit, they were also an extraordinary burden. Because *everything* aroused a distinctive image, he had trouble with any task requiring the ability to think more abstractly. For example, he sometimes had difficulty recognizing faces or voices. For him, a different expression or tone would seem to change the face or voice entirely. His vivid imagery also interfered with his ability to understand metaphorical or abstract language. Each word would conjure up a specific image, and he would have difficulty in ignoring these images to get to the meaning of the entire sentence. For example, consider how much trouble he had with the apparently simple sentence "The work got under way normally" (Luria 1968, p.128):

> I read that "the work got under way normally." As for *work*, I see that work is going on . . . there's a factory. . . . But there's that word *normally*. What I see is a big, ruddy-cheeked woman, a *normal* woman. . . . Then the expression *got under way*. Who? What is all this? You have industry . . . that is, a factory, and this normal woman—but how does all this fit together? How much I have to get rid of just to get the simple idea of the thing!

The power of S.'s imagination was extraordinary. He was able, for example, to make the temperature of his left hand go up while making the temperature of his right hand go down. He did so by imagining his left hand on a hot stove and his right hand holding ice. But his mental powers also created problems. To a large extent he lived in his imagination. He changed jobs dozens of times, working as a reporter, vaudeville actor, efficiency expert, and professional mnemonist. Although his life was rather unstable, he always believed he would somehow achieve greatness. Although he did not really succeed, through Luria he has given us a fascinating look at a phenomenal memory.

## Normal and Expert Memory

There are clearly both similarities and differences among the three mnemonists we have described. One commonality is their use of special encoding strategies. In Chapter 9 we saw that defective encoding was in part responsible for the recall difficulties of chronic amnesics. Conversely, we find that the skilled use of encoding strategies by the master mnemonists serves to improve their recall ability. The mnemonists illustrate the general point that encoding and retrieval depend on each other. For example, because Professor Aitken knew so much about numbers, he was able to rapidly encode new numerical information.

Also interesting is that all three mnemonists used strategies that improve recall for average individuals as well. But the mnemonists are much more proficient in their use of these strategies. This point raises an interesting question: Could anyone develop his or her memory to a similar level of proficiency with sufficient practice?

The answer to this question suggests how the mnemonists differ from one another. The abilities of Aitken and V. P. seem to rest on two major factors. First, each has stored in memory a vast body of knowledge about a specialized area (numbers for Aitken, languages for V. P.). Second, both are highly practiced in using the knowledge to facilitate encoding. Such knowledge and skills seem to be the kind of thing that could be learned with extensive practice.

Of course, most of us would probably never achieve their level of performance within a reasonable length of time. For one thing, most people simply would not be willing to devote years of concentrated effort to the task, any more than they would be willing to devote years of practice to becoming a championship bowler. Still, the abilities of Aitken and V. P. do not seem all that mysterious in view of what we know about normal human memory.

However, S. is a different case. His extraordinary synesthesia is not the kind of thing we would expect to develop through practice. Although he used some standard mnemonic devices like the method of loci, his encoding processes were generally highly unusual. Instead of abstracting only certain critical features of a sensory input in order to construct a representation of it, as people normally seem to do, he apparently retained a virtually exact representation of the entire experience. As we have seen, this detailed type of encoding affected not only his memory but other aspects of his thought processes as well.

## SUMMARY

Memory skill depends on the use of *mnemonic strategies* for encoding and retrieving information. The most basic types of strategies are *rehearsal, imagery,* and *organization*. Rehearsal—the self-generation of repetitions of an item—is the main source of the *primacy effect* in free recall, because early items in a list tend to receive more rehearsal than later items and hence are better recalled. The last items in a list are also recalled well on an immediate test (the *recency effect*) because they can be maintained in a speech code. However, simply maintaining items in a speech code (*maintenance rehearsal*) does not always improve later recall of the items. Even a strategy as apparently simple as rehearsal is a technique children have to learn. The more complex strategies based on imagery and organization require further training and practice.

Effective mnemonic strategies involve the reduction of the new material to familiar components, organization, and imagery. Examples of mnemonic strategies include *chunking, natural-language mediation, semantic elaboration*, various serial-order mnemonics (including the *method of loci* and the *pegword method*), and *outlining*. While such mnemonic strategies usually aid recall a great deal, some of them tend to tie the information to a relatively specific context. If the recall context is very different, retrieval can sometimes fail.

*Mnemonists* are people who use extremely sophisticated strategies to perform memory feats, such as lightning calculation and verbatim recall of long, meaningless lists. Such expert memorizers generally have large bodies of specialized knowledge stored in memory, along with well-practiced encoding strategies. In one well-documented case (Luria's S.) the mnemonist encoded virtually all material as vivid images. With practice and the development of specialized mnemonic strategies, normal individuals can achieve spectacular levels of performance in tasks such as digit span tests.

## RECOMMENDED READINGS

Four interesting books on mnemonists and mnemonics are Luria's *Mind of a Mnemonist* (1968), Smith's *Great Mental Calculators: The Psychology, Methods, and Lives of Calculating Prodigies, Past and Present* (1983), Lorayne's *Remembering People* (1975), and Lorayne and Lucas's *Memory Book* (1974).

# CHAPTER ELEVEN

# Reasoning and Decision Making

## INTRODUCTION

The processes of reasoning, decision making, and problem solving are mental activities that form the core of what most people regard as thinking. Thinking involves the active *transformation* of existing knowledge to create new knowledge that can be used to achieve a goal. The goal may be relatively simple, such as answering a novel question, or extremely complex, such as designing a reusable spacecraft. Human thought has clearly yielded stupendous intellectual achievements, and psychologists have only begun to understand how our thought processes operate.

Reasoning, decision making, and problem solving are highly interrelated cognitive processes; indeed, drawing sharp distinctions among them is difficult and probably unnecessary. Situations that naturally seem to require thinking typically involve some initial doubt or difficulty in deciding what to do or believe. *Reasoning* involves drawing further inferences from current knowledge and beliefs; *decision making* involves the evaluation of alternative outcomes or making choices among them. *Problem solving*, the topic of Chapter 12, involves attempts to achieve any of a wide variety of types of goals. Reasoning is clearly involved in decision making, and both reasoning and decision making are required to solve problems. In addition, drawing inferences and making decisions can readily be viewed as types of problem solving.

### Descriptive vs. Normative Models

Somewhat paradoxically, given the obvious power of human intellect, experimental investigations of thinking have revealed a wide range of apparent shortcomings in human reasoning and decision making. These shortcomings are not simply errors; many of our judgments are necessarily based on imperfect information, making mistakes inevitable. Rather, the shortcomings psychologists have identified involve the *way* in which information is used to make decisions. Relevant information is sometimes ignored; irrelevant information sometimes has an unwarranted impact; and multiple pieces of information are often not integrated as they should be.

The identification of reasoning errors depends on an important conceptual distinction between *descriptive* and *normative models* of reasoning. A descriptive model is intended to describe *how* people perform cognitive tasks. The construction of descriptive models is the central task of cognitive psychology, and all the models we have encountered in this book (of attention, memory, etc.) have been of the descriptive variety. A normative model is quite different. A normative model describes not how people actually perform a task but how it *ought* to be performed to meet some criterion of optimality. Normative models are especially prominent in the areas of reasoning and decision making because such disciplines as logic and statistics have produced normative models that can be applied to reasoning tasks that people perform. When an accurate descriptive model violates principles embodied in a corresponding normative model, a shortcoming of human reasoning is pinpointed.

As an example of such a shortcoming, let us consider the *conjunction fallacy* identified by the two foremost contributors to the psychology of human judgment, Amos Tversky and Daniel Kahneman (1983). The relevant normative model in this case comes from probability theory. One of the basic laws of probability is that increasing the specificity of an event or outcome can only decrease its probability. For example, the probability that a person is both a lawyer and a tennis player must be less than the probability that the person is a lawyer. More generally, the probability that both condition $A$ and condition $B$ are met can only be less than the probability of meeting condition $A$ alone; i.e., $P(A\&B) \leq P(A)$.

Even though this normative principle is one that most people find intuitive when it is directly stated, Tversky and Kahneman were able to demonstrate that college students—including statistically sophisticated graduate students in the Stanford Business School—systematically violate it when asked to make probability estimates. One of Tversky and Kahneman's demonstrations involved having subjects read the following brief personality sketch (1983, p. 297):

> Linda is 31 years old, single, outspoken, and very bright. She majored in philosophy. As a student, she was deeply concerned with issues of discrimination and social justice, and also participated in anti-nuclear demonstrations.

After they had read the description, the subjects were asked to rank-order the probabilities that various statements about Linda were true. Among these statements were the following two:

1.   Linda is a bank teller.
2.   Linda is a bank teller and active in the feminist movement.

If you understood the law of probability described above, you realize that the second of these statements, which is a conjunction that includes the first statement, can only be less probable. That is, if we call "is a bank teller" condition $A$, and "is active in the feminist movement" condition $B$, then $P(A\&B)$ must be less than $P(A)$. However, over 80 percent of the subjects Tversky and Kahneman tested said that the conjunctive statement was *more* probable—a clear violation of the normative model of probability. Furthermore, subjects with statistical training were just as prone to this conjunction fallacy as were subjects who lacked such training.

What kind of descriptive model might account for this deviation from the normative standard? The first thing to note is that the description of Linda seems to "fit" very well with her being a feminist but not particularly well with her being a bank teller. To use Kahneman and Tversky's (1973) term, Linda seems more "representative" of the category "feminist" than of the category "bank teller." That is, Linda is more similar to a typical feminist than to a typical bank teller. As a result, even though Linda is not a typical bank teller, she seems somewhat more similar to a *feminist* bank teller. In fact, when Kahneman and Tversky (1982) asked subjects to evaluate "the degree to which Linda resembles the typical member of that class," they rated her as more similar to the compound "feminist bank teller" than to "bank teller." Apparently, then, the subjects who made probability judgments based their assessments on implicit *similarity* judgments; i.e., since Linda was viewed as more similar to a feminist bank teller than to a bank teller, subjects judged the conjunction to be more probable. Under this interpretation the conjunction fallacy reveals that people tend to judge *probability* on the basis of *similarity*, even though the two concepts are by no means equivalent.

## Deduction vs. Induction

There are two basic forms of logic: deduction and induction. A deduction is a judgment that something *must* be true if other things are true. For example, the conclusion "The earth circles a star" based on the premises "The earth circles the sun" and "The sun is a star" is a deduction. An induction is a judgment that something is *probably* true on the basis of experience. The conclusion that night will follow day because it always has in the past is an induction. As these examples suggest, both deduction and induction play an important role in human reason, and normative models have been developed to improve reasoning in both areas. In the first half of this chapter we will compare untutored human reason with normative models of deduction. In the second half of the chapter human reason will be compared with normative models of induction.

## DEDUCTIVE REASONING

Deductive reasoning requires that the reasoner integrate two or more separate assertions in order to deduce a new assertion as a necessary consequence. Deductions typically center on so-called logical words, such as quantifiers (e.g., *all, some, none*), connectives (e.g., *and, or, if-then*), and comparatives (e.g., *more, less*). The standard normative models of deductive reasoning are based on various types of formal logic. The most venerable of these types is *syllogistic logic*—the logic of quantifiers—which was constructed by Aristotle and provided a framework for a number of the earliest psychological investigations of deductive reasoning (Wilkins 1928; Woodworth and Sells 1935). Here is an example of syllogistic argument:

> Some taxpayers are foreigners.
> No foreigners are citizens.
> ———————————————————
> Therefore some taxpayers are not citizens.

In this and other deductive arguments, the statements above the line are called *premises.* The reasoner is to take the premises as "given" (i.e., assume they are true). The statement below the line is the putative *conclusion.* The argument is *valid* if and only if the truth of the premises guarantees the truth of the conclusion. Note that validity is *not* the same thing as truth. An argument is valid if and only if the truth of the conclusion depends on the truth of the premises and the form of the argument.

How can we tell whether or not an argument is valid? In the case of syllogisms one procedure is to use *Venn diagrams,* as depicted in Figure 11.1. In these diagrams A and B represent two categories, and the regions of overlap represent instances that belong to both categories. There are exactly five possible *set relations* between two categories. In situation 1, A and B are *identical;* i.e., all instances of A are also instances of B, and vice versa. In situation 2, A is a *subset* of B. In situation 3, B is a subset of A. In situation 4, A and B *overlap.* And in situation 5, A and B are *mutually exclusive,* with no common instances.

The various statements with quantifiers correspond to possible set relations, as follows:

| Statement | Possible situations |
|---|---|
| All A are B. | 1, 2 |
| Some A are B. | 1, 2, 3, 4 |
| No A are B. | 5 |
| Some A are not B. | 3, 4, 5 |

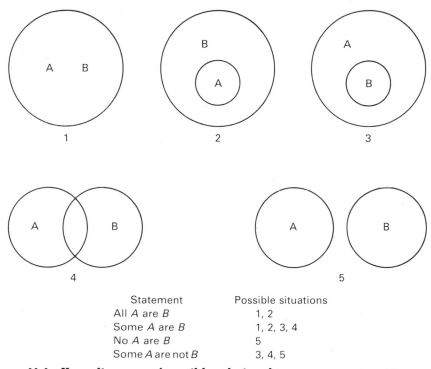

|  Statement | Possible situations |
| --- | --- |
| All *A* are *B* | 1, 2 |
| Some *A* are *B* | 1, 2, 3, 4 |
| No *A* are *B* | 5 |
| Some *A* are not *B* | 3, 4, 5 |

**Figure 11.1   Venn diagrams of possible relations between two sets.**

We can use these correspondences to decide whether any syllogism is valid or fallacious. The procedure is as follows: Determine whether there is any situation in which both premises could be true but the conclusion false. If such a situation exists, the argument is fallacious; otherwise, it is valid. "Some taxpayers and foreigners" could correspond to any of situations 1–4, in which at least some instances of the set "taxpayers" are included in the set "foreigners." For each of these possible cases we can now add a third set, "citizens," which is mutually exclusive with "foreigners," as asserted by the second premise, "No foreigners are citizens." If you carry out this exercise, you will discover that you will always be forced to make the set relation between "taxpayers" and "citizens" correspond to one of situations 3–5, i.e., just those situations in which "Some taxpayers are not citizens" is true. Accordingly, the argument is valid.

## Validity vs. Truth

If you attempted the exercise just described, you probably also discovered that manipulating Venn diagrams to evaluate a syllogistic argument is no easy task. Furthermore, people who haven't received training in the use of Venn diagrams are unlikely to use them at all. In general, we have no reason to believe that descriptive models of deductive reasoning bear any close resemblance to normative models. In fact, a great deal of evidence indicates that everyday reasoning differs greatly from the logical systems devised by logicians.

The distinction between *validity* and *truth,* for example, is basic to deductive logic. However, many people find the distinction difficult to grasp. A conclusion is valid if it can be deduced from the premises; but validity neither requires nor ensures that the conclusion is true of the real world. For example, consider the following deductive argument:

> If grass is pink or elephants fly, then the moon is square.
> Grass is pink.
> _____
> Therefore the moon is square.

In this example both the premises and the conclusion are in fact false; nonetheless, the conclusion follows as a valid deduction. That is, if we *assume* that the premises are true (as the logical task requires), then the conclusion is also necessarily true. Validity depends only on the *form* of the argument, not on its content.

More abstractly, the above argument has the following form:

> If *p* or *q,* then *r.*
> *p.*  _____
> Therefore *r.*

This argument form is valid regardless of the actual truth of the statements we might substitute for *p, q,* and *r.*

Sometimes, however, people have difficulty separating the form of an argument (which determines its validity) from its content (the truth of the premises and conclusion). Consider the following syllogistic argument:

> All dogs are animals.
> Some animals are pets.
> _____
> Therefore some dogs are pets.

This syllogism is invalid; however, people are likely to have difficulty detecting its invalidity because the conclusion is something they know to be true. In contrast, the fallacy is obvious if the conclusion is known to be false, as in the following version, which has the same form but different content:

All sharks are animals.
Some animals are pets.
Therefore some sharks are pets.

People thus exhibit *belief-bias effects.* They are biased to accept arguments that attempt to deduce a conclusion they believe to be true, and to reject arguments that attempt to deduce a conclusion they believe to be false (Evans, Barston, and Pollard 1983). In some sense belief-bias effects are quite understandable; after all, in real life knowing what is true is usually far more important than knowing what is valid. However, in many situations biases based on prior beliefs lead to consequences that are clearly undesirable. In particular, such biases may tend to make people's beliefs impervious to rational arguments.

Belief bias occurs when the deduction relation between the premises and the conclusion is not obvious. As we will see, the relation is not obvious when a person cannot transform a representation based on the premises into one corresponding to the conclusion by a single mental operation, i.e., in a single step. In such cases the procedure necessary for determining the validity of a syllogism is apparently an artificial one that must be learned. In contrast, the premises and conclusions automatically activate representations in memory, so their truth or falsity is apparent.

We can learn about human reason by determining which normative deductions are obvious and which are not. The obvious deductions may reveal basic mental operations. In contrast, the nonobvious deductions seem to require a learned sequence of operations.

### Transitive Inferences Based on Linear Orderings

One important type of deductive inference is based on the transitivity of comparative relations. A basic transitive inference is the following:

A is greater than B.
B is greater than C.
Therefore A is greater than C.

A number of psychologists have investigated the way in which people solve such "three-term series problems" (Clark 1969; DeSoto, London, and Handel 1965; Huttenlocher 1968). In general, people make such transitive inferences quickly and accurately.

More recent work has examined inferences based on longer transitive chains. Suppose someone is given the following information as a set of premises: "Bill is taller than Sam," "Sam is taller than Dave," "Dave is taller than Bob," "Bob is taller than Pete." Now the person is asked to decide as quickly as possible whether the conclusion "Bill is taller than Pete" is valid. One way to formulate the process of reaching a decision as a series of inference steps is as follows:

1.   Bill is taller than Sam.
     Sam is taller than Dave.
     Therefore Bill is taller than Dave.

2.   Dave is taller than Bob.
     Bob is taller than Pete.
     Therefore Dave is taller than Pete.

3.   Bill is taller than Dave.
     Dave is taller than Pete.
     Therefore Bill is taller than Pete.

This procedure produces the correct solution, but it requires three inference steps. In general, the further apart in the ordering two terms are, the more inferences will be required to evaluate the relation between them. Thus if people used this inference-chaining procedure to derive conclusions, their decision time would be expected to increase with the "distance" between the terms in the conclusion to be evaluated.

**Mental arrays.** George Potts (1972, 1974) performed the first studies that used longer series. In a typical experiment he first taught subjects an arbitrary ordering by presenting them with sentences describing the relation between pairs of adjacent items, as illustrated in the sequence just given. The entire ordering contained six terms. After subjects had learned the ordering, they made true or false judgments about sentences describing all possible pairs of items. The results were dramatically different from those inference chaining would predict. Reaction time actually *decreased* with the distance between the items. Sentences based on a pair of remote items (e.g., "Bill is taller than Pete") were evaluated more quickly than the sentences based on adjacent items (e.g., "Dave is taller than Bob"), even though only the latter sentences had actually been presented during learning.

How do people manage to make transitive inferences more quickly than they can evaluate the original premises? A possibility that has acquired considerable support is that subjects learn an ordered list by coding the items onto a linear mental array in the visuospatial code (see Chapter 4). As a result, the time to make comparisons depends not on the specific sentences used to learn the ordering but on the ease with which the items can be accessed in a linear array. In general, the terms at the two ends of the array (often called "end anchors") are accessed very quickly, whereas terms near the center of the array are accessed much more slowly. Since remote pairs tend to be nearer the ends of the list, more remote inferences can be made relatively quickly. This basic pattern has been obtained for linear orderings containing as many as sixteen items (Woocher, Glass, and Holyoak 1978).

A similar reaction time pattern is found when people judge the relative position of items in a perceptual array [e.g., a series of lines ordered from left to right (Holyoak and Patterson 1981)]. The processes used to make transitive inferences may therefore have some important similarities to basic perceptual processes. Perhaps for this reason even children as young as five or six years old seem to be able to use mental arrays to represent the relations between ordered items and hence make transitive inferences (Trabasso, Riley, and Wilson 1975).

**Symbolic-distance effect.**    Similar processes appear to be used to make comparative judgments about well-learned concepts that form a unidimensional ordering. Across many different types of concepts, reaction time measures show a *symbolic-distance effect:* The further apart the items are on the relevant dimension, the faster a comparative judgment can be made. For example, people are faster to choose the larger animal of the pair *horse* and *cat* than of the pair *horse* and *goat* (Moyer 1973); they are faster to choose the larger digit of the pair 2 and 8 than of the pair 2 and 3 (Moyer and Landauer 1967). Symbolic-distance effects have also been found in judgments of animal intelligence (Banks and Flora 1977); e.g., people can decide that horses are smarter than sheep.

Even with abstract dimensions, memory for subjective magnitude can be quite detailed. Holyoak and Walker (1976) had subjects perform mental comparisons with pairs of words from semantic orderings, such as quality terms (e.g., *poor, fair*) and temperature terms (e.g., *cool, hot*). One group of subjects was asked to rate the psychological distance between the terms in each ordering. These ratings were used to derive a scale for each set of terms. Figure 11.2 shows how the quality and temperature terms were placed. As the figure shows, the terms are not spaced evenly. For example, the two central terms in the quality scale, *fair* and *average,* are very close. In contrast, the central terms in the temperature scale, *cool* and *warm,* are very far apart (i.e., people feel that the temperature difference between *cool* and *warm* is greater than that between, say, *cold* and *cool*).

A different group of subjects then performed a reaction time task in which they chose the "better" of each possible pair of quality terms and the "warmer" of each possible pair of temperature terms. A symbolic-distance effect was found for each scale: The greater the distance between the terms, the

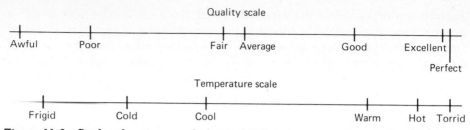

**Figure 11.2    Scales showing psychological differences among terms for quality and for temperature. (From Holyoak and Walker 1976.)**

faster the comparison was made. The exact spacing of the terms affected decision time. For example, the "close" pair *fair-average* was compared very slowly, whereas the more "distant" pair *cool-warm* was compared rapidly. These results indicate that not only does the order of the terms matter but also the psychological distance between them on the scale.

Symbolic-distance effects have posed a puzzle for psychologists of human reason. *Number, intelligence,* and *goodness* are all abstract dimensions, so it is unlikely that the symbolic-distance effect requires visuospatial representation. How, then, are these judgments made, and why does the symbolic-distance effect occur? A firm conclusion has yet to emerge.

### Evaluating Conditional Rules

**Modus ponens and modus tollens.**    An interesting comparison involves two inference rules based on conditional statements of the form "If *p,* then *q.*" A conditional statement can be falsified by one situation: the occurrence of *p* in the absence of *q.* In standard logic two rules follow from this fact, which are traditionally called by the Latin names *modus ponens* and *modus tollens.* Modus ponens has the following form:

> If *p,* then *q.*
> *p.*
> ———————
> Therefore *q.*

Modus tollens is as follows:

> If *p,* then *q.*
> Not *q.*
> ———————
> Therefore not *p.*

Both of these rules are clearly valid. For example, suppose our initial premise is "If it is Friday, then Bill is wearing a blue shirt." Modus ponens then gives the following:

If it is Friday, then Bill is wearing a blue shirt.

It is Friday.

Therefore Bill is wearing a blue shirt.

Modus tollens gives the following:

If it is Friday, then Bill is wearing a blue shirt.

Bill is not wearing a blue shirt.

Therefore it is not Friday.

But while both rules are valid, you have probably already noticed that they do not seem of equal difficulty. Modus ponens is immediately obvious, whereas modus tollens seems to require careful thought. And, in fact, studies have shown that whereas virtually all college students endorse modus ponens as valid, a substantial proportion fail to endorse modus tollens (Taplin 1971; Taplin and Staudenmayer 1973). Seemingly modus ponens is an intuitive rule of logic, whereas modus tollens is not.

Modus ponens can be verified through a straightforward matching strategy. If the second premise matches the first term of the first premise, then the conclusion is true. However, modus tollens involves negation, which inevitably increases processing difficulty (Clark and Chase 1972). Probably the clearest justification of modus tollens is to reason as follows (using our earlier example):

I know that if it is Friday, Bill is wearing a blue shirt. I also know that Bill is *not* wearing a blue shirt. Now suppose it were Friday. Then (by modus ponens) Bill would be wearing a blue shirt. But that contradicts the fact that Bill isn't wearing a blue shirt. So my supposition must be false: It is not Friday.

Although most people find this justification of modus tollens compelling, it clearly involves several inference steps. In contrast, the simple matching operation for modus ponens is easily applied so that the deduction is immediately recognized as valid. This discussion suggests that modus ponens is part of our cognitive repertoire of rules for everyday reasoning, whereas modus tollens is not.

**Wason's selection task.**   The kinds of knowledge people have available for reasoning about conditional statements has been extensively investigated by using a paradigm called *Wason's selection task*, after its originator, Peter Wason (1966,1968). In its original version the task is deceptively simple. Wason presented his subjects with four cards, which were placed in front of them, showing symbols such as the following:

A     M     6     3

They were told that each card has a letter on one side and a number on the other. Then they were given a rule: "If a card has a vowel on one side, then it has an even number on the other side." The subjects' task was to name those cards, and those cards only, that needed to be turned over in order to determine whether the rule was true or false.

What do you think is the correct answer? Almost all the subjects in Wason's experiment said either "A and 6" or "only A." But the correct answer is "A and 3." If you think about the problem carefully, you will see why this answer is correct. Card "6" is incorrect because even if there isn't a vowel on the other side, it would not falsify the rule. The rule says only that if a card has a vowel, then it will also have an even number. But the "3" is a critical card. For if a card with an odd number turns out to have a vowel on the other side, the rule will have been falsified.

The solution to Wason's selection task is closely related to the two inference rules for conditional statements we discussed above. The rule to be tested has the conditional form "If $p$, then $q$." As we saw earlier, conditionals are falsified just in case $p$ occurs without $q$. Modus ponens implies that if we have established $p$, we need to check that $q$ holds. So in the selection task we have to check the "A" card. Modus tollens implies that if $q$ does *not* hold, $p$ must not hold either. Accordingly, we need to check the "3" card (i.e., the noneven number) to ensure there is not a vowel on its back. Subjects' failure to select the "3" card (or, more generally, the not $q$ case) thus confirms that modus tollens is not a readily available inference rule.

Since the selection task basically involves the evaluation of a conditional statement, clearly one can construct a host of logically equivalent problems. As it turns out, performance on the task can be radically altered by varying

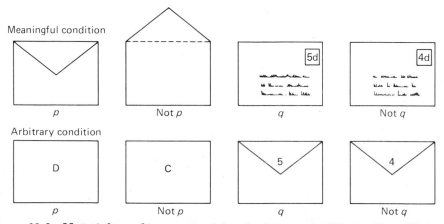

**Figure 11.3   Materials used in meaningful and arbitrary conditions. (From Wason and Johnson-Laird 1972.)**

the content of the rule. Figure 11.3 illustrates two versions of selection problems studied by Johnson-Laird, Legrenzi, and Legrenzi (1972). One condition used a meaningful rule, and another used an arbitrary rule.

In the meaningful condition the subjects were told to imagine they were postal workers engaged in sorting letters. They were to decide if the following rule was being followed: "If a letter is sealed, then it has a 5d stamp on it." (The experiment was conducted in England, and d is the symbol for "pence.") The choices were the four envelopes shown at the top of Figure 11.3: a closed envelope (p), an open envelope (not p), a 5d stamp (q), and a 4d stamp (not q).

In the arbitrary condition the rule was stated as follows: "If a letter has a D on one side, then it has a 5 on the other." The choices shown at the bottom of Figure 11.3 corresponded to the four alternatives in the arbitrary version.

The logic of the rule was exactly the same in both the meaningful and the arbitrary conditions. The two relevant cases to check were always p and not q, i.e., the closed envelope and the 4d stamp in the former version, and the D and the 4 in the latter version. However, performance on the two versions was strikingly different. In the meaningful condition twenty-one of the twenty-four subjects were correct, whereas in the arbitrary condition only two of the same twenty-four subjects were correct. Moreover, no transfer occurred between the two conditions: Getting the correct solution to the meaningful version did not improve performance on the arbitrary version.

The results of Johnson-Laird *et al.* thus indicated that people are much more successful at reasoning about a meaningful rule than a logically equivalent arbitrary rule. Why they are, however, has not been entirely clear. The reason is not simply that meaningful rules involve more concrete objects, since not all concrete versions produce facilitation (Griggs and Cox 1982; Manktelow and Evans 1979; for reviews see Evans 1982; Griggs 1983; Wason 1983). Indeed, Johnson-Laird and colleague's postal rule version does not always produce the good performance it did in the original experiment. Griggs and Cox (1982) failed to find facilitation for American subjects.

At the time of the original Johnson-Laird *et al.* study, there was, in fact, an actual British postal rule of this sort: A sealed envelope signified first-class mail, which required more postage. The postal rule version of the selection task was thus very similar to a rule with which the subjects were familiar. Since no such rule existed in the United States at the time of the Griggs and Cox study, their results suggested that direct prior experience might be essential to produce facilitation. A study by Golding (1981) provided further support for this possibility. Golding found that the postal rule version produced facilitation for older British subjects who were familiar with the rule, which was by then defunct, but not for younger British subjects who were not familiar with it.

Such evidence suggested that everyday reasoning is highly dependent on memories of specific experiences. However, other research indicates that people are more flexible than these results suggest. Cheng and Holyoak (1985) gave the postal rule problem both to students in the United States, who were unfamiliar with it, and to students in Hong Kong, where the post office still enforced such a rule. As would be expected given earlier results, the Hong Kong subjects selected the correct alternatives more often than did the American subjects. However, Cheng and Holyoak also tested conditions in which a rationale was provided along with the rule. Subjects in the rationale condition were simply told that the post office defined sealed mail as first-class. When the rationale was provided, students in the United States performed just as well as Hong Kong students with prior familiarity with the rule.

How might provision of a rationale facilitate performance? One possibility is that a rationale, like direct experience with a similar rule, encourages people to bring their relevant knowledge about regulations to bear on the problem. One thing we learn about regulations is how to check that they are followed. Many regulations, like the postal rule, have the form "If a certain action (such as sealing an envelope) is to be taken, then a certain condition (such as providing adequate postage) must be met." If the action is taken, we need to check that the condition was met; and if the condition wasn't met, we need to check that the action wasn't taken. This kind of regulation schema thus permits inferences equivalent to both modus ponens and modus tollens, in effect providing a shortcut procedure for deriving the latter inference, which is otherwise very difficult.

The work on Wason's selection task thus illustrates how both specific and more schematic knowledge can augment the inference rules available for everyday deductive reasoning. In fact, as we will discuss later, the reliance on strategies for applying prior knowledge to new situations leads to many of the unique strengths and weaknesses of human reason.

## HEURISTICS OF HUMAN JUDGMENT

Everyday reasoning and decision making involve much more than drawing certain deductions from premises known to be true. We often have to make decisions in the face of uncertainty, with sketchy information about the situation, on the basis of suggestive but inconclusive evidence. Cognitive psychologists, inspired by the seminal work of Kahneman and Tversky (1972, 1973; Tversky and Kahneman 1973) have begun to identify the reasoning processes that people use to cope with such uncertainty. People use a variety of *judgment heuristics*—strategies that can be applied easily in a wide variety of situations and that often lead to reasonable decisions.

However, judgment heuristics are very different from valid deductive arguments. Such heuristics can generate plausible conjectures but not irrefutable conclusions. Indeed, in some situations, which researchers have begun to identify, judgment heuristics lead to violations of normative models. The conjunction fallacy ("Linda, the feminist bank teller") that we discussed at the beginning of this chapter is, as we will see shortly, an example of the suboptimal decisions that can result from use of judgment heuristics. These heuristics can yield both quick, intuitive insights and dramatic lapses of logic. Furthermore, judgment heuristics are used not only by laypersons in everyday life but also by professional decision makers—doctors, government leaders, military strategists—whose judgments may have life-and-death consequences. Therefore understanding how the heuristics operate is critically important.

## Similarity Judgments

One of the most basic concepts involved in understanding judgment heuristics is similarity. As we saw in Chapter 5, categorization decisions often seem to involve assessment of the similarity of an instance to the prototype of a category. What is similarity, and how is it judged? The assessment of similarity depends on a familiar concept—the decomposition of inputs into features (see Chapter 1). If we take two concepts, each defined by a number of features, then the similarity of concepts increases with the number of shared features—features that are true of both concepts. So the concepts "robin" and "sparrow" are similar because they share many features (e.g., "flies," "small size"); in contrast, "robin" and "penguin" are relatively dissimilar because they share fewer features.

Note that "number of shared features" is always independent of the order of the two concepts. By definition, "robin" shares as many features with "sparrow" as "sparrow" does with "robin." If similarity depended only on shared features, it would therefore always be the case that concept A is as similar to concept B as concept B is to concept A. In other words, similarity would be a symmetrical relation. In fact, however, similarity is not always symmetrical. Note that in the expression *A is similar to B*, the concepts A and B serve different semantic roles. A has the role of *subject*, while B is the *referent*; i.e., A is being compared to B, not vice versa. The difference between the roles of the subject and the referent is a source of potential asymmetry in the similarity relation. This is particularly striking in figurative uses of language, such as metaphor or simile. For example, the simile *A rattlesnake is like lightning* suggests that rattlesnakes share some of the salient properties of lightning (rapid motion, sudden extension). But the reversed simile, *Lightning is like a rattlesnake*, suggests that lightning shares some of the salient properties of rattlesnakes (potentially deadly, unpredictable, striking suddenly). In each case the simile asserts that some salient properties of the referent are also true of the subject; as a result, the interpretation differs depending on which term fills which role.

Concept *A*          Concept *B*

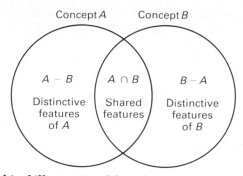

**Figure 11.4    A graphical illustration of the relations between the features of two concepts. (After Tversky 1977.)**

Asymmetries in similarity judgments suggest that our ideas about how people judge similarity need to be modified. Tversky (1977) has developed a detailed theory of how people use features to judge the similarity between two concepts. Figure 11.4 depicts the relation between the features of two concepts, *A* and *B*, using Venn diagrams. The features of each concept are represented by a circle. The features can be partitioned into three sets. The area where the circles overlap represents the shared features of the concepts. This set is referred to as "*A* ∩ *B*" (read "*A* and *B*"); i.e., these are features that are true of both *A* and *B*. The other two sets represent distinctive features. "*A* − *B*" is the set of distinctive features of concept A (i.e., those true of *A* but not of *B*); similarly, "*B* − *A*" is the set of distinctive features of concept *B*.

Our simple model of similarity assumed that similarity depended only on the shared features, *A* ∩ *B*. But Tversky points out that the distinctive features, *A* − *B* and *B* − *A*, are probably also important. In general, the three types of features will affect similarity judgments in the following way:

**1.** Increasing *A* ∩ *B* increases similarity.

**2.** Increasing *A* − *B* decreases similarity.

**3.** Increasing *B* − *A* decreases similarity.

In other words, increasing the shared features of two concepts will increase their similarity, whereas increasing their distinctive features will decrease their similarity. How can asymmetries in similarity arise? This is quite simple: the distinctive features of the subject are usually given more weight than the distinctive features of the referent. That is, similarity is reduced more by the unique features of the subject than by the unique features of the referent. In addition, if one item is more salient than another (because it is more focal, more familiar, more intense, more informative, or whatever), the distinctive features of the more salient item will receive greater weight. As a result, the similarity of two items will be reduced if the more salient stimulus is placed in the subject position, in which its distinctive features will be weighted heavily. It follows that a focal item will seem less similar to a variant (Rosch 1975).

Asymmetries arise whenever one item is more salient than another. For example, Tversky and Gati (1978) selected pairs of countries in which one was more prominent than the other (e.g., *China–North Vietnam, Belgium–Luxembourg, Russia–Poland*). They asked two groups of college students to rate how similar each pair of countries was. For each pair, one group was asked to compare the more prominent country with the less prominent one (e.g., "How similar is Russia to Poland?"), whereas the other group was asked to compare the less prominent country with more prominent one (e.g., "How similar is Poland to Russia?") As predicted, the less prominent country was usually judged to be more similar to the prominent country than vice versa.

Not only can similarity judgments be asymmetrical, but the judged degree of *difference* between items is not necessarily the same as "similarity in reverse." Tversky argued that whereas similarity judgments primarily stress shared features, difference judgments stress distinctive features. This change in focus can have striking effects on people's judgments. For example, do you think it is possible for one pair of items to be both more similar and more different than another pair? Figure 11.5 illustrates the way this possibility might arise. China and Japan are two prominent countries that most people

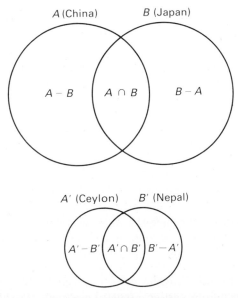

**Figure 11.5   Similarity vs. differences. China and Japan are perceived as both more similar to and more different from each other than Ceylon and Nepal are similar to or different from each other. (After Tversky and Gati 1978.)**

know a lot about. As a result, each country has many features. On the other hand, Ceylon and Nepal are two countries that most people know relatively little about. As a result, the two prominent countries have more shared features than do the less prominent ones (i.e., $A \cap B$ is larger than $A' \cap B'$). But in addition, the more prominent countries also have more distinctive features (i.e., $A - B$ plus $B - A$ is larger than $A' - B'$ plus $B' - A'$). In other words, people can think of many similarities between Japan and China, and also many differences. But since people do not know very much about Ceylon and Nepal, those countries do not seem either so similar and more different than pairs of less prominent countries.

Tversky's careful analysis of the way people think about features when they judge degree of similarity of difference has many important implications. For example, the studies we have described illustrate the subtle ways in which the exact way a question is worded can influence people's judgments.

## Representativeness

Judgments of similarity underlie one of the most basic judgment heuristics, which Kahneman and Tversky (1972, 1973) term *representativeness*. In one experiment (Kahneman and Tversky 1973) a group of sixty-five college students were presented with the following personality sketch (p.238):

> Tom W. is of high intelligence, although lacking in true creativity. He has a need for order and clarity, and for neat and tidy systems in which every detail finds its appropriate place. His writing is rather dull and mechanical, occasionally enlivened by somewhat corny puns and by flashes of imagination of the sci-fi type. He has a strong drive for competence. He seems to have little feel and little sympathy for other people and does not enjoy interacting with others. Self-centered, he nonetheless has a deep moral sense.

The subjects were asked to rate how similar Tom W. seemed to the typical graduate student in either computer science or the humanities. Overwhelmingly, they thought that Tom W. was more similar to a typical computer science student.

The same sketch was then given to a different group of 114 psychology students, along with the following additional information:

> The preceding personality sketch of Tom W. was written during Tom's senior year in high school by a psychologist, on the basis of projective tests. Tom W. is currently a graduate student.

Subjects were then asked to predict whether Tom W. was more likely to be in computer science or in humanities. Overwhelmingly, they decided on computer science.

Well, you might ask, what's surprising about that? After all, people think the sketch of Tom W. fits a computer science student. Three things make the result remarkable. First, yet another group of subjects simply estimated the relative frequencies of the two types of graduate students. Humanities students were judged to be about three times more numerous. So the *prior odds*—the odds based simply on this background information—were rather heavily against Tom W. being in computer science. Second, the same subjects who made the predictions were also asked how reliable they thought projective tests (e.g., inkblot tests) were. They thought projective tests—the source of Tom W.'s personality sketch—were very unreliable. Third, even if the description was valid when Tom W. was in high school, everyone would agree he may well be very different by the time he is in graduate school. So seemingly, in making their predictions, subjects ignored the prior odds and based their decisions entirely on information they would readily admit was very likely wrong. The sketch was considered highly "representative" of the personality of a computer science student, and this high degree of representativeness appeared to overwhelm all other considerations.

Most people probably use the representativeness strategy in making intuitive predictions. Sometimes, it is a rather accurate way to make quick decisions, as when instances are categorized on the basis of similarity to a category prototype. But when applied to prediction, the strategy can be quite misleading. For example, we may decide a child is likely to be a scientist if he or she fits our idea of what a scientist is like (inquisitive, bookish, or whatever). In such examples representativeness is evaluated with respect to social stereotypes that may be inaccurate measures of future performance. And as you should now see clearly, the conjunction fallacy, which violates a basic law of probability, is due to use of the representativeness heuristic.

**Dominance of representativeness.**   You may not have believed that the use of representativeness was such a poor choice of decision strategy in the Tom W. example. After all, the information that argued that Tom was probably not a computer science student (very few people are) and the poor quality of the information about Tom (from a projective test given years earlier) were not made very salient to the subjects in the experiment. In contrast, the similarity of the description of Tom to the stereotype of a computer science student was very salient. Hence when the subjects made their decision, they may have remembered only the similarity of the description to that of a computer science student and may not have recalled that the information in it was of poor quality or that relatively few people ever become computer science students.

In further experiments, therefore, Kahneman and Tversky attempted to make the prior odds as salient as possible. In one experiment they presented subjects with a series of five personality descriptions. The subjects were told that the descriptions were drawn from a set of 100 descriptions of engineers and lawyers. For each description the subjects had to decide whether the person was more likely to be a lawyer or an engineer. So that the prior odds were salient, half the subjects were told that the set of descriptions consisted of 70 lawyers and 30 engineers, while half were told it consisted of 30 lawyers and 70 engineers.

Kahneman and Tversky found, however, that the prior odds had almost no effect on people's judgments. That is, a particular description was just as likely to be judged an engineer regardless of whether the engineers were the majority or the minority. The only factor subjects seemed to consider was how representative the description was of the alternative occupations. This result doesn't mean that subjects were entirely unaware of the prior odds. For example, suppose a subject was told that 70 descriptions were lawyers and 30 were engineers, and then the subject had to make a prediction for one individual without any description at all. In that case the subject would estimate that the chances were 70 percent that the individual was a lawyer.

But now suppose, instead, that the subject was given the following description:

> Dick is a 30-year-old man. He is married with no children. A man of high ability and high motivation, he promises to be quite successful in his field. He is well-liked by his colleagues.

Most people agree that this description is equally likely to be true of a lawyer or an engineer. It simply provides no information about Dick's occupation. Since this description is no more useful than no description at all, you might think that subjects would use the prior odds and assign Dick a 70 percent chance of being a lawyer. But they gave him a 50 percent chance. Apparently, as soon as subjects are given any kind of information about an individual case, even if it is vacuous, they base their judgments solely on that information and ignore the prior odds. People's predictions appear to be dominated by the representativeness strategy.

What makes representativeness such a compelling prediction strategy, in spite of the fact that it often leads to errors? Kahneman and Tversky suggest that we fail to distinguish between evaluation and prediction. For example, suppose your roommate introduces you to another student. After talking to the person for awhile, you decide, without being told, that the student is a computer science major. This decision is a case of evaluation on the basis of representativeness: The student appears similar to your stereotype of a computer science major. Now suppose you are asked what the student will be doing five or ten years from now. Of course, many things may change in that time, such as the student's interests or the job market. You should therefore be less certain about what the person will be doing at some time in the future than you are about what the person is doing today. However, the representativeness strategy operates in the same way regardless of whether it is used for evaluation or for prediction. As a result, the predictions people make about the future are often the same as their evaluations of the present.

Furthermore, people are just as confident about predictions as evaluations. For example, Tversky and Kahneman (1974) presented subjects with several paragraphs, each describing the performance of a student teacher during a particular practice lesson. Some subjects were asked to evaluate the quality of the lesson. Other subjects were asked to predict the standing of each student teacher five years after the practice lesson. The judgments made under the two conditions were identical.

**Representativeness vs. Bayes's theorem.**   You might think that people (often mistakenly) rely on the representativeness strategy only in situations where they have little information to guide them. But even when people have sufficient information to calculate the statistically optimal prediction, representativeness still guides their intuitions. To demonstrate this situation, let us turn from real-world decision making to an artificial example and examine a situation where we can work out the optimal prediction exactly.

Consider the following simple game: Let's say I have two bags, each containing a mixture of red and blue poker chips. Specifically, their contents are as follows:

Bag A: 10 blue, 20 red;
Bag B: 20 blue, 10 red.

On each trial I select one bag, and your problem is to guess whether it is bag A or bag B. However, you get some information to help you decide. First, you know the number of blue and red chips in each bag. Second, you know that I will select bag A 80 percent of the time and bag B 20 percent of the time. Third, you get to draw three chips from the bag and see what color they are. Each time you draw a chip, it goes back in the bag after you've seen it.

Let's say that on one particular trial you draw three chips, and they are two blues followed by one red. Which bag do you think I selected? How confident are you in your decision? If you are like most people (at least most people who haven't just read about representativeness!), you have probably decided that it was fairly likely to be bag B. After all, two-thirds of the chips you drew were blue, which is exactly the proportion of the blue chips in bag B. At any rate, you may be surprised to know that the true odds are 2 to 1 that it was actually bag A rather than bag B.

How do we know the true odds? Calculating the exact odds for this game can be done by using *Bayes's theorem*. Bayes's theorem uses two pieces of information. The first is the odds *before you draw the sample* that the chosen bag is A rather than B. These *prior odds* are 4 to 1, since you knew I select bag

A 80 percent of the time and bag B only 20 percent of the time. The second piece of information is the odds that the sample (two blues and one red) comes from bag A vs. bag B. These odds are called the *likelihood ratio* (the ratio of the probability that the sample comes from A to the probability that it comes from B).

The likelihood ratio is calculated as follows: Probability theory tells us that if $p$, $q$, and $r$ are the probabilities of three independent events, the probability of all three occurring is $p \times q \times r$. In this case $p$, $q$, and $r$ are the results of each draw of a chip, i.e., blue, blue, and red. Suppose the bag selected is actually A. Then the probability of drawing a blue ($p$ and $q$) is $\frac{10}{30}$, or $\frac{1}{3}$; the probability of drawing a red ($r$) is $\frac{20}{30}$, or $\frac{2}{3}$. So the probability of the obtained sample is $\frac{1}{3} \times \frac{1}{3} \times \frac{2}{3} = \frac{2}{27}$. Now suppose the bag is actually B. In that case the probability of drawing a blue is $\frac{2}{3}$, and the probability of drawing a red is $\frac{1}{3}$. So the probability of the sample is $\frac{2}{3} \times \frac{2}{3} \times \frac{1}{3} = \frac{4}{27}$. The likelihood ratio, then, is simply $\frac{2}{27}$ (the probability that the sample came from A) divided by $\frac{4}{27}$ (the probability that the sample came from B), which gives us odds of 1 to 2 that the sample is from bag A rather than from bag B. In other words, the obtained sample is half as likely to have come from A as from B.

Finally, what we want to calculate are the odds that the bag is A vs. B given all that we know *after* taking the sample. These odds are the *posterior odds*. Bayes's theorem gives this calculation:

$$\text{posterior odds} = \text{prior odds} \times \text{likelihood ratio}.$$

Since the prior odds are 4 to 1, and the likelihood ratio odds are 1 to 2, we find:

$$\text{posterior odds} = \frac{4}{1} \times \frac{1}{2} = \frac{2}{1} \text{ (in favor of bag A).}$$

That is, the final odds are 2 to 1 that the bag is A rather than B.

Why do people usually find this result surprising? The answer is clear —they tend to ignore the prior odds. True, if we consider just the obtained sample, it is indeed more likely to have come from bag B. But while the sample is twice as likely to have come from bag B, this result isn't enough to compensate for the fact that bag A is four times more likely to be selected in the first place.

So people concentrate on the proportion of blue and red chips in the sample and neglect the prior odds. Why do they do so? Kahneman and Tversky argue that people do not make intuitive judgments of this sort by applying anything like a statistical formula such as Bayes's theorem. Rather, they use the representativeness heuristic. This strategy involves a judgment of the degree to which a sample is similar in essential characteristics to the class from which it may have been drawn. In our poker chip example the proportion of blues is two-thirds in both the sample and bag B. Accordingly, the sample is very representative of B. In fact, you might think of two blues and one red as a prototypical sample for bag B. Prior odds just don't fit into the representativeness heuristic. As a result, people seem to ignore prior odds and select bag B because its composition seems so similar to that of the sample.

**Causal interpretation of prior odds.**    You should not think, however, that people never integrate prior odds in making decisions. Prior odds are considered in situations in which they seem to plausibly *cause* variations in the outcome (Ajzen 1977; Tversky and Kahneman 1978). For example, Tversky and Kahneman told subjects that a particular town had two cab companies, the Blue Company and the Green Company. An accident had taken place, and a witness made an uncertain judgment about whether the cab involved was blue or green (visibility had been poor). One group of subjects was told that 85 percent of the cabs in town were blue and 15 percent were green. These subjects, like those in the studies discussed above, largely ignored the base rates and based their decision about which company was involved in the accident primarily on the apparent reliability of the witness. A second group received base rate information in a different way. They were told that although the blue and green cabs were equal in number, 85 percent of all accidents involving cabs were due to blue cabs and only 15 percent were due to green cabs. In this case the prior odds had a clear causal interpretation: The drivers of the blue cabs were more careless. This second group of subjects were heavily influenced by the base rate information. When prior odds are given a causal interpretation, and hence influence decisions, the representativeness heuristic is apparently supplemented by the more sophisticated simulation heuristic, which we will describe shortly.

## Availability

The representative heuristic depends on a very basic cognitive process, the assessment of similarity. A second judgment heuristic identified by Tversky and Kahneman (1973) depends on another basic process, memory retrieval. This heuristic can be illustrated by a task that requires prediction of memory ability. Suppose you are presented with the name of a category, e.g., flowers or Russian novelists, and given just 7 seconds to estimate how many instances you will be able to recall in 2 minutes. Do you think you can make accurate estimates? Tversky and Kahneman performed exactly this experiment and found that people were relatively accurate in predicting how many instances they would eventually be able to recall.

How is it possible to estimate your total recall after just 7 seconds? Tversky and Kahneman suggested that people accomplish this feat by using the *availability heuristic*. The availability heuristic involves basing judgments on the ease with which relevant instances can be retrieved from memory. In the instance generation task subjects seem to note how easy or difficult it is to think of instances in the first 7 seconds, and then they use this initial information to estimate what their total recall will be.

The availability heuristic is based on one of the oldest laws of memory—associations are strengthened by repetition. The heuristic turns this law around; it is based on the assumption that if memory associations are strong, then the events or instances in question must be frequent. Since availability does increase with frequency, the heuristic is often quite accurate. But availability is also affected by other factors as well, which can lead to systematic biases.

For example, consider this question: Of words three or more letters long, is the letter r more likely to appear in the first position or in third position? Tversky and Kahneman found that most people think r is more frequent in first position (e.g., raft). But, in fact, there are more words with r as the third letter (e.g., strike). However, to retrieve words according to their first letter is much easier than to retrieve them according to their third letter, so the availability heuristic leads to an incorrect decision.

Availability can also lead to biases in direct perceptual judgments. Consider Figure 11.6. A path in either structure (a) or structure (b) is a line that connects an element in the top row to an element in the bottom row and passes through one and only one element in each row. Which structure has more paths? How many paths do you think are in each structure?

When Tversky and Kahneman asked fifty-four subjects these questions, the median responses were that structure (a) had 40 paths and (b) had only 18. In fact, there are an equal number of paths through the two structures (512). Why do people see more paths in structure (a)? There are at least three reasons. First, the columns are the most obvious paths, and there are more columns in (a). Second, the paths in (a) cross each other and are therefore more distinctive. Third, the paths in (a) are shorter and hence easier to visualize. All these factors operate to make the paths in (a) more perceptually available than those in (b).

Probably the most striking demonstrations of availability involve the real-life impact of salient events. Your subjective estimate of the probability of a

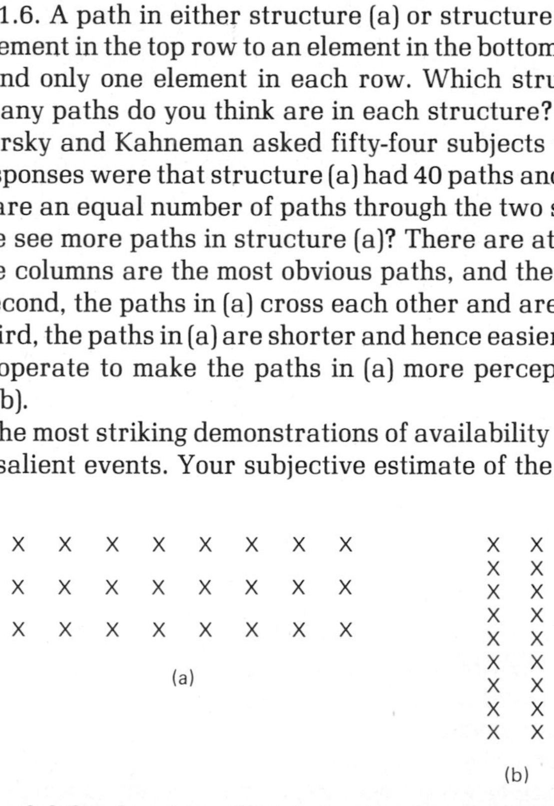

```
        X  X  X  X  X  X  X  X        X   X
                                      X   X
        X  X  X  X  X  X  X  X        X   X
                                      X   X
        X  X  X  X  X  X  X  X        X   X
                                      X   X
                 (a)                  X   X
                                      X   X
                                      X   X
                                      X   X

                                        (b)
```

**Figure 11.6   Availability heuristic. Which structure has more paths, (a) or (b)?**

car accident is likely to shoot up after seeing an overturned car beside the road. For many people, stepping onto an airplane calls to mind memories of airplane crashes, leading to overestimation of the danger. One consequence of the availability heuristic, observed by Lichtenstein, Slovic, Fischhoff, Layman, and Combs (1978), is that people overestimate the frequency of well-publicized causes of death while underestimating the frequency of less notorious causes. For example, Lichtenstein *et al.* found that homicides are judged to be about as frequent as death by stroke in the United States population, whereas in fact stroke is over ten times more common than homicide as a cause of death.

The availability heuristic has important implications for clinical judgment. For example, suppose a clinician encounters a depressed man and wishes to estimate how likely it is that the patient will attempt suicide. What are the relevant instances? Clearly, the clinician should recall previous instances of depressed patients and determine how many attempted suicide. However, the clinician may well find it easier to recall previous instances of suicidal patients, since suicide is a much more striking occurrence than simple depression. Very probably, all previous suicidal patients were depressed, even though in fact few of the previous depressed patients attempted suicide. In this case availability may lead to a logical error and consequent overestimation of the probability that a particular depressed patient will attempt suicide. The logical error is to assume that if $A$ implies $B$, then $B$ implies $A$ (i.e., confusing a conditional statement with a biconditional). In other words, just because all suicidal patients were depressed ($A$ implies $B$), one can't conclude that all depression leads to suicide ($B$ implies $A$). By the same erroneous logic, if all suicidal patients ate mashed potatoes, then mashed potatoes lead to suicide.

Finally, availability produces a *hindsight bias,* the bane of every football coach who had his team go for it in a fourth-down-and-one-yard situation only to have the effort fail. In retrospect, the risky decision tends to seem just plain stupid, since the negative actual outcome is now by far the most available. People tend to neglect the fact that the outcome *could* have been quite different and that the calculated risk was perhaps justified (Fischoff 1975).

## Analogical Reasoning

Another judgment heuristic, which incorporates elements of both representativeness and availability, is the use of *analogical reasoning* to make decisions. When faced with a novel situation, the decision maker may recall a more familiar situation that seems related, evaluate its similarity to the new case, and use the known case to make predictions about the novel one. Analogical reasoning has been studied by psychologists who have recorded and analyzed naturally occurring reasoning patterns (Collins, Warnock, Aiello, and Miller

1975). For example, consider this hypothetical dialog between a teacher and a student on the topic of geography:

> Teacher: Is the Chaco [a region in Argentina] cattle country?
>
> Student: Well, I'm not sure. I guess the climate is a lot like western Texas, and they raise cattle there. So, yes—I suppose the Chaco probably is cattle country.

In this example the student is reasoning by analogy, noting that the Chaco is similar to western Texas in that the two regions share certain attributes. Furthermore, we can be sure the student was thinking of attributes known to be relevant to cattle raising (e.g., temperature, rainfall, and vegetation). The student picks out those attributes that are the functional determinants of cattle raising and, on that basis, compares the region under question (the Chaco) with the region known for cattle raising (Texas). The same reasoning process would have produced a negative decision if the question had been whether the Chaco produces rubber. By comparing the Chaco with a rubber-producing region, such as the Amazon jungle, with respect to the functional attributes for rubber production, multiple mismatches on the relevant attributes would lead to a "no" response.

Like representativeness, analogical reasoning requires an assessment of similarity. But as the example illustrates, the kind of similarity assessment required is of a particularly sophisticated kind. The reasoner needs to base the decision on those attributes of the known case that are *functionally relevant* to the required decision. Thus western Texas provides a better analogy with the Chaco than does the Amazon because western Texas is more similar in terms of functionally relevant attributes. The fact that the Chaco is more similar to the Amazon on other attributes, such as geographical proximity, is irrelevant to the required decision.

Sometimes, however, functionally irrelevant attributes can influence the choice of the known situation to use as an analogy. That is, certain attributes of a novel situation may serve to remind the person of a superficially similar prior situation, which will in turn influence the decision. A study by Gilovich (1981) provides an interesting demonstration of this possibility. Gilovich pointed out that modern American foreign policy has been heavily influenced by two salient historical analogies: the Munich analogy, in which misguided attempts were made to appease Hitler prior to World War II, and the Vietnam analogy, in which American interference in a foreign country led to disaster. Gilovich reasoned that if a new crisis situation contained cues associated with Munich, people would tend to advocate intervention; whereas if the crisis cued Vietnam, people would tend to favor a hands-off policy.

To test this hypothesis, he gave students in a political science course (dealing with conflict from World War I to the present) a description of a hypothetical crisis. The crisis involved a threatened attack by a large totalitarian country, country A (see Figure 11.7), against a small democratic country,

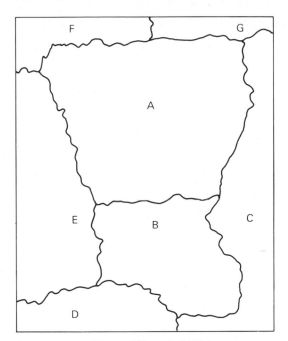

**Figure 11.7    Map of crisis area. (From Gilovich 1981.)**

country B. The subjects were asked to select an option for the United States to follow, ranging from extreme appeasement of country A to direct military intervention.

Two versions of the crisis were constructed, which were intended to cue either the Munich or the Vietnam analogy. For example, the Munich version referred to the impending invasion as a "blitzkrieg," whereas the Vietnam version referred to it as a "quickstrike." The Munich version described how minority refugees were fleeing from country A, in boxcars on freight trains, to country G. In contrast, the Vietnam version indicated that minority refugees were fleeing from country A in small boats that sailed up the "Gulf of C" to country G. These alternative descriptions thus made the crisis seem superficially similar to either the situation in World War II or Vietnam.

However, most people would agree that these cues have no functional relevance to a decision about how the United States should respond to the hypothetical crisis. After all, why should it matter whether refugees are fleeing in boxcars or small boats? Nevertheless, Gilovich's subjects tended to make decisions of a more interventionist nature when they read the Munich version rather than the Vietnam version. This result indicates that functionally irrelevant similarities can guide the selection of an analogy, resulting in a normatively unjustified influence on decisions. We will have more to say about analogical reasoning when we discuss problem solving in the next chapter.

## Simulation Heuristic

The availability heuristic is based on the retrieval of examples from memory. However, one can also base decisions on examples or scenarios that are *constructed* by the reasoner. This basis is especially evident in reasoning about *counterfactual* statements—claims made about what *would* have been true had conditions been otherwise. Compare the following two counterfactual statements:

1. If Hitler had had the atomic bomb in 1943, Germany would have won World War II.
2. If Hitler had had one more airplane in 1943, Germany would have won World War II.

Both of these statements make claims based on an overtly false premise —Hitler had neither the atomic bomb nor an extra airplane in 1943. Nevertheless, we feel confident that statement 1 is highly plausible whereas statement 2 is almost certainly false.

How do we make such judgments? One general hypothesis involves what Kahneman and Tversky (1982) call the *simulation heuristic.* We can form a general mental model of the situation at the height of World War II, and then we imagine the different outcomes that various changes in the situation would produce. We know that possession of the atomic bomb would yield an enormous shift in the balance of military strength, whereas one more airplane would yield only a tiny change. Our mental simulation thus indicates that statement 1 is a much more believable claim than 2, even though both are counterfactual.

Kahneman and Tversky (1982) provide an illuminating illustration of the emotional consequences of the simulation heuristic. Consider the following scenario:

> Mr. Crane and Mr. Tees are scheduled to leave the airport on different flights at the same time. They travel from town in the same limousine, are caught in a traffic jam, and arrive at the airport 30 minutes after the scheduled departure time of their flights.
>
> Mr. Crane is told that his flight left on time. Mr. Tees is told that his flight was delayed, but it left 5 minutes ago.
>
> Who will be more upset?

Virtually everyone agrees that Mr. Tees will be more upset. But notice that objectively the two unfortunate travelers suffered exactly the same fate. Both presumably expected to miss their planes because of the slow limousine trip, and both did so. Why should Mr. Tees be more disappointed than Mr.

Crane? The difference is that he will find it easier to imagine how the mishap could have been avoided. *If only* the limousine had been a little faster, or the plane had been delayed just a bit more, he would have caught his flight. Because the simulation heuristic indicates that small changes in reality would have produced a dramatically better outcome, Mr. Tees suffers greater disappointment. In general, defeats *almost* avoided and victories *almost* gained are the source of life's most trying moments.

The simulation heuristic can be used to evaluate the probability of an event by the ease with which you can construct a plausible scenario leading to that outcome. For example, one way a clinician might estimate the likelihood of a suicide attempt is by trying to imagine a chain of events that might occur in the patient's life to worsen the depression. If such a causal scenario is easy to imagine (e.g., the patient's wife is ready to leave him, or he is in danger of losing his job), the clinician may conclude that a suicide attempt is relatively likely. The simulation heuristic plays a role in many kinds of situations in which people are trying to understand events happening around them.

### Heuristics vs. Statistics

A great deal of evidence indicates that the judgment heuristics we have described, and other variants of them, are extremely pervasive (see Kahneman, Slovic, and Tversky 1982; Nisbett and Ross 1980). They are pervasive because the heuristics rely on very basic cognitive processes—most notably, memory retrieval and similarity assessment—that are central to human information processing. In many situations the heuristics may generate reasonable judgments without undue delay or excessive cognitive effort. When the cost of error is not high, applying more effortful, albeit more normative, judgment procedures may not be worthwhile. In other situations, such as deciding whether to permit a new drug to be used, formal statistical procedures are extremely useful, even if the procedures are difficult to use. The challenge for the future is to devise means of minimizing the potential errors that can result from heuristic judgments while, at the same time, maintaining their beneficial aspects. Recent research suggests that it is possible to foster appropriate use of statistical reasoning in everyday decision making (Nisbett, Krantz, Jepson, and Kunda 1983).

## SUMMARY

The study of human reasoning and decision making focuses on discrepancies between *descriptive models* of how people actually reason and *normative models* of how they ought to reason. Many important differences have been identified. In the case of *deductive reasoning*, which requires evaluating whether a conclusion necessarily follows from given premises, everyday reasoning differs from formal logic in several respects. People have difficulty evaluating the *validity* of an argument independently of their belief in the truth of the conclusion. Many logic terms, such as *if-then*, are interpreted differently in natural language and in standard logic. Furthermore, people base some kinds of inferences on special types of representations, such as the use of mental arrays to make transitive inferences about linear orderings. The way people reason about *conditional statements*, particularly in *Wason's selection task*, illuminates various distinctions between human deductive reasoning and logic.

Many inferences are not valid deductions but simply plausible (but error-prone) conjectures. The inferences upon which many everyday decisions are based are the result of various *judgment heuristics*. The *representativeness heuristic* involves assessing the *similarity* of an instance to a prototype, and the *availability heuristic* depends on the retrieval of particularly salient instances. *Analogical reasoning* requires retrieving a related situation from memory and comparing it with the situation at hand. The *simulation heuristic* involves forming a mental model of a situation and imagining the outcomes that would result from various possible changes in the situation. Although all the judgment heuristics sometimes produce suboptimal decisions, they often produce reasonable judgments quickly and without a great deal of cognitive effort.

## RECOMMENDED READINGS

A survey of the various paradigms that have been used to study deductive reasoning is available in *The Psychology of Deductive Reasoning* (1982) by Evans. Evans has also edited a collection of papers on reasoning entitled *Thinking and Reasoning: Psychological Approaches* (1983). A good collection of readings in the broad domain of reasoning is contained in *Thinking* (1977), edited by Johnson-Laird and Wason. *Judgment Under Uncertainty: Heuristics and Biases* (1982), edited by Kahneman, Slovic, and Tversky, provides an outstanding collection of major papers dealing with judgment heuristics. *Human Inference: Strategies and Shortcomings of Social Judgment* (1980), by Nisbett and Ross, gives a thorough treatment of judgment heuristics from the perspective of social psychology. *On Scientific Thinking* (1981), edited by Tweney, contains papers on reasoning as it relates to hypothesis testing and other aspects of scientific thinking.

A major area of decision making, often called *behavioral decision theory*, was not described in this chapter. Work in this area has been heavily influenced by economic models and often involves mathematical analyses of choice behavior. Although this work is relevant to cognitive psychology, it is difficult to integrate with the rest of the field. This difficulty is reflected in the fact that there are no books that provide cognitive approaches to behavioral decision theory. If you are interested in exploring this area, overviews of theoretical concepts can be found in *Mathematical Psychology* (1970) by Coombs, Dawes, and Tversky and *Decision Theory and Human Behavior* (1971) by Lee. A good collection of papers in the area is contained in *Cognitive Processes in Choice and Decision Behavior* (1980), edited by Wallsten.

# CHAPTER **TWELVE**

# Problem Solving and Creativity

## INTRODUCTION

### Problem Solving: Basic Definitions

In many ways this chapter is the culmination of those that have come before it. All the basic cognitive processes we have explored in earlier chapters—perceiving, categorizing, remembering, and reasoning—are used in dealing with problems. Problem-solving skills hinge on the way information can be represented in memory and later retrieved and applied in novel situations. The ability to formulate creative solutions to problems is what most people consider the most central aspect of thinking.

At an intuitive level everyone knows what a problem is; we all have them from time to time. Consider a few examples:

| | |
|---|---|
| Deciding how to lose weight | Designing a house |
| Solving a crossword puzzle | Building a spaceship |
| Selecting a good chess move | Writing a play |

Basically, a person has a problem when he or she wants something that is not immediately attainable. The goal of the problem may be quite specific (solve today's crossword puzzle) or more general (write a story good enough to win an award). The actions involved in obtaining the goal may range from physical activities (e.g., walking) to acts of the imagination (e.g., visualizing the problem). While problems can be extremely diverse, all have four basic components:

1. A *goal,* or a description of what would constitute a solution to the problem.

2. A description of *objects* relevant to achieving a solution, such as resources that can be used, the problem solver, and any allies or opponents that may be involved.

3. A set of *operations,* or actions that can be taken to help achieve a solution.

4. A set of *constraints* that must not be violated in the course of solving the problem.

For example, consider the problem of solving a crossword puzzle. The object description would include the pattern of blank spaces on the puzzle, a specification of where each word has to fit in, and a set of clues for what each word means. The operations that a person might employ include searching semantic memory, counting the number of letters in a word, and assigning possible words to spaces. The goal state is a complete set of assignments of words to spaces, with all words correctly spelled and appropriate in meaning. Constraints might include strictures against cheating in getting the solution (e.g., getting a friend who is an expert at crossword puzzles to do it for you).

The term *problem* is typically reserved for situations in which the goal is not achieved by an automatic process of perception or recognition. Rather, problems are cases in which some obstacle initially blocks achievement of the goal. In a complex problem there may be many false starts, dead ends, and intervening steps before a solution is achieved. Problems such as the examples listed earlier will usually require a substantial amount of time to reach the goal—at least several seconds, often minutes or hours, sometimes years.

## Problem-Solving Process: Overview

Just as a problem has basic components, the process of solving one can be described in terms of several major steps. While the schemas for solving different kinds of problems are somewhat different, they all have some general steps in common. A general problem-solving schema is diagramed as a flowchart in Figure 12.1. The four major steps in the process are (1) forming an initial representation of the problem (in terms of goal, objects, operations, and constraints); (2) using problem-solving methods to plan a potential solution; (3) if necessary, reformulating the problem; and (4) executing a procedure to carry out a plan and checking the results.

To take a relatively simple example, consider the problem of proving a geometry theorem of the sort you probably encountered in high school. Step 1 in the solution process might involve listing the information given and drawing a diagram. Step 2 would involve applying operations (e.g., relevant theorems) to construct a sequence of steps that actually yield a proof. If step 2 cannot be done on the first attempt, you might have to try to reformulate the problem in

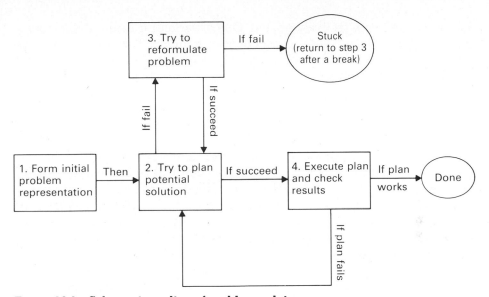

**Figure 12.1   Schematic outline of problem-solving process.**

some way (step 3). For example, you might try reducing a problem given in three dimensions to a similar one that you know how to solve in two dimensions; then you use the result to help develop a plan for the more complex problem. If attempts to reformulate a problem initially fail and you are stuck, taking a break and returning to the problem later may be helpful. (We will consider the possible benefits of such *incubation* later when we discuss creative thinking.)

Once a potential plan has been generated, step 4 would involve actually giving an explicit step-by-step statement of the proof. In addition, you might then check the results by using a different method, or by trying the same method on a similar problem, to make sure that the solution is correct.

We will discuss the process of solving problems in more detail later, but a few points deserve emphasis at the outset. A major point concerns the concept of a *plan*. A plan is a procedure for a sequence of actions that implicitly makes a prediction: "If I take the following actions, then I will achieve a solution." One of the most basic aspects of problem solving is that a plan is often created and then mentally tested *before* overt actions are taken. This step is extremely important, because many problems are unforgiving of errors. For example, suppose the police are trying to rescue hostages being held by a gunman. If the police attempt to solve this problem by a sudden raid on the building and something goes wrong, the hostages may be killed. In such a situation the police must plan with great care in advance, since there will probably be no second chance. In terms of the flowchart in Figure 12.1, the arrow returning from step 4 to step 2 is effectively erased. One criterion for evaluating plans, in fact, involves anticipating the consequences of failure. For example, negotiation is often preferable to attack in a hostage situation, because the police can explore different approaches to negotiation, whereas they can usually expect to attack only once.

## Well-Defined vs. Ill-Defined Problems

A major dimension along which problems vary is the extent to which they are *well defined* (Newell 1969; Reitman 1964; Simon 1973). In a well-defined problem the components are all completely specified. A good example is an algebra problem (e.g., solve the equation $ax - b = x$ for $x$). The objects involved (the algebraic symbols) are clear to any algebra student; the operations are the rules of algebra (e.g., add a constant to both sides of the equation); the goal state is to have only $x$ on the left side of the equal sign and everything else on the right; and the main constraint is to use legal algebraic manipulations.

Ill-defined problems, on the other hand, are those for which the problem solver has more uncertainty concerning the given information and starting materials, the operations that can be used, and the final product that must be achieved. Unfortunately, the term *ill-defined problem* has a slightly negative ring to it. In fact, however, many ill-defined problems are very creative tasks. When people decide to paint pictures, write books, or perform experiments, they are all undertaking ill-defined but creative tasks.

Virtually all real-life problems are actually ill defined in one way or another. Take an apparently simple problem like cooking dinner. The available objects may not be precisely determined (Shall I use whatever is in the house or go shopping in a gourmet food store?), nor the possible operations (Shall I fry hamburgers or use a recipe in my Tibetan cookbook?), nor the goal state (Do I really need dessert?). Most problems are even less well defined than this one. For example, consider the problem of writing a novel. How would we define the initial-knowledge state of the author? Not only do writers use a vast store of information based on knowledge of other novels, but they also often base the content of the book on some real-life experiences. So at first glance the initial-knowledge state seems virtually unlimited. Similarly, the rules of composition, which are the operations used in writing a novel, are not clearly specified.

The goal state is particularly critical in ill-defined problems, because to specify what will count as a successful problem solution is difficult. Many problems like this one are so open-ended that finding a "perfect" solution, or even recognizing one should you stumble upon it, is virtually impossible. In the case of the novelist, how would he or she decide that the story is finished? Usually, one must stop after achieving a solution that is good enough by some criterion. For example, a student may adopt a certain satisfaction criterion in writing a term paper and may decide to turn in a paper that he or she expects will receive a B grade, because to produce an A paper would require more time than the student is willing to put into it. In general, a problem solver needs to be able to evaluate progress toward a solution and also to be able to decide when an acceptable solution has been reached.

Because of the uncertainties involved in ill-defined problems, the problem solver must often devote a great deal of time to both the step of forming an initial representation of the problem and the step of reformulating it. Often a more specific reformulation will go a long way toward solving the problem; e.g., in the dinner problem, deciding on the meal one wants to cook constrains the choice of grocery stores. In some ill-defined problems the plan that is first generated does not remain fixed. For example, writers often get an idea and then let the plot and characters unfold as the story progresses, without having a clear conception of how the story will end. In other words, the planned solution may actually evolve during the course of writing. This idea is expressed very clearly by the novelist John Fowles (1969, pp. 81–82):

> You may think novelists always have fixed plans to which they work, so that the future predicted by Chapter One is always inexorably the actuality of Chapter Thirteen. But novelists write for countless different reasons. . . . Only one same reason is shared by all of us: *we wish to create worlds as real as, but other than the world that is.* Or was. That is why we cannot plan. We know a world is an organism, not a machine. We also know that a genuinely created world must be independent of its creator; a planned world (a world that fully reveals its planning) is a dead world. It is only that when our characters and events begin to disobey us that they begin to live.

For ill-defined problems the first step in problem solving, forming an initial representation, deserves special emphasis. This step actually includes the process of *finding* a problem in the first place. The ability to create problems appears to be a peculiarly human ability. People not only bring images of things they have seen into consciousness but also manipulate them and so imagine a green horse or a mouse flying through the air. We call this ability to create new representations *imagination,* and at its core is the ability to manipulate perceptual representations through imagery. But humans can also manipulate conceptual representations and hence imagine machines that turn lead into gold and sunlight into power. A great deal of what we call creative thinking occurs in finding a problem that is *worth solving.* A writer must find a story worth telling, a painter an idea worth capturing on canvas, a scientist a question about nature that needs to be answered.

Finding a problem to solve is as important, and often as difficult, as solving it. Many students working on a Ph.D. dissertation find that getting a good idea is harder than doing the actual research. For any creative problem solver, such as an artist, writer, or scientist, few experiences are more painful than a dry period without a project worth pursuing.

### Problem Representations in Chimpanzees and Humans

Problem-solving behavior requires such extensive conscious manipulation of representations that we would not expect to find much evidence of it in nonhuman species. In fact, only a few animals engage in anything that closely resembles human problem-solving behavior. In particular, the classic studies of the Gestalt psychologist Wolfgang Kohler (1925) demonstrated that chimpanzees can sometimes overcome functional fixedness. In one sequence the chimp Sultan was in a cage and noticed a banana lying outside out of reach. In the cage was a bushy tree. Sultan suddenly went to the tree, broke off a branch, ran back to the bars and used the branch to bring the banana into reach. What was at first not even a separate object was suddenly recognized as a potential tool.

More recently, David Premack and his colleagues have conducted an extensive investigation of problem solving by chimpanzees (Premack and Woodruff 1978). Rather than have chimps actually execute problem solutions, they tested the chimps on their ability to *comprehend* solutions. In a typical experiment a chimpanzee was shown a videotape of a human actor struggling to obtain bananas that were attached to the ceiling out of reach. Then the animal was shown a pair of still photographs, one illustrating a solution to the problem and the other a nonsolution. For example, the solution scene might show the actor stepping onto a box, while the nonsolution scene might show him moving a box aside. The two alternatives were placed in a cardboard box, and the experimenter then left the room. The chimp had to pick up the correct picture, place it in a designated location, and ring a bell to recall the experimenter. The experimenter would then say either "Good, that's right" or "No, that's wrong."

Such problems were presented to Sarah, a chimp who became famous for her performance in studies of "language" training (see Chapter 14). When tested at the age of fourteen years (about eight years after the studies of language training had ended), Sarah was able to reliably choose the correct alternative in tasks such as that just described (Premack and Woodruff 1978). Moreover, Sarah's choices were influenced by some very humanlike motives. In one experiment the actor in the videotape of the problem situation was varied. When the actor was Sarah's favorite trainer, she invariably selected the correct-solution photograph. But when the actor was a man who Sarah was known to dislike, Sarah was likely to pick out a photograph of a bad outcome, such as the actor stepping right through the box. Seemingly, Sarah not only knew how to solve problems but also knew when she would just as soon see the problem solver fail.

An intriguing observation that Premack has made is that chimps like Sarah, who have received language training, seem to be especially adept at complex problem-solving tasks. Although it remains a speculative possibility, such training may serve to develop internal representations that facilitate problem solving. In any case, humans clearly have a unique ability to manipulate representations and to transfer information between various codes, and this ability allows them to solve a wide variety of problems. Foremost among those codes used to solve problems are the visuospatial representation and those codes involved in language, which will be collectively referred to as the verbal representation.


## PROCESS OF PROBLEM SOLVING

We will now examine each of the four basic steps of problem solving in more detail.


### Forming an Initial Representation

**Problem representation.**  A key to understanding the first step of problem solving is to gain some insight into how the problem solver arrives at an initial problem representation. For example, consider the following problem:

> The price of a notebook is four times that of a pencil. The pencil costs 30¢ less than the notebook. What is the price of each?

This problem is presented in a purely verbal form. However, this form is not a very good representation for solving it. If you are like most people who have learned algebra, you will probably translate the problem into a different representation, perhaps as follows:

Let $n$ = notebook and let $p$ = pencil.

Initial state: $n = 4p$, and $p = n - 30$.

Substitute for $n$: $p = 4p - 30$.

Subtract $4p$ from both sides: $-3p = -30$.

Therefore $p = 10$ and $n = 40$.

An algebraic representation makes use of both the verbal and the visuospatial representations to bring into play a set of operations for manipulating equations, making the problem quite simple to solve. Algebra makes use of the name relation in the semantic code (Chapter 5) to identify variables, but it also makes use of the visuospatial code in substituting variables and moving them from one side of the equation to the other.

However, one can also translate the verbal representation directly into the visuospatial code. When this problem was given to S., the remarkable mnemonist studied by Luria (see Chapter 10), S. reported imagining a series of visual equations, as illustrated in Figure 12.2. In Figure 12.2(a) he imagined a notebook beside four pencils. Then in Figure 12.2(b) he mentally pushed three pencils aside and replaced them with 30¢, since one pencil plus 30¢ equals the value of the notebook. Since 30¢ therefore is equivalent to three pencils, S. immediately realized (presumably by simple arithmetic) that one pencil was worth 10¢ and the notebook was worth 40¢. Some of S.'s major problem-solving operations were thus manipulations of visual images.

**Importance of task analysis.**    The example of the algebra problem illustrates the fact that a problem can have more than one representation, because the person often defines the problem in his or her own way. The question is, What is the best way to think of a problem in order to solve it more easily? Here we find some individual differences; e.g., some people claim they usually think visually. However, some problems can be solved much more easily with one form of representation than another.

One common example of a dramatic shift in representation is the game of number scrabble (Newell and Simon 1972), which can be described as follows:

> Each of the digits 1 through 9 is written on a separate piece of paper. Two players draw digits alternately. As soon as either player gets any three digits that sum to 15, that player wins. If all nine digits are drawn without a win, then the game is a draw.

Most people who play this verbally encoded game a few times are still surprised when told that it is actually equivalent to the visuospatially encoded

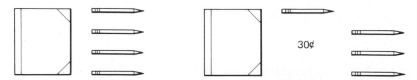

**Figure 12.2    Visual equations that S. used to solve pencil-and-notebook-problem: (a) Orignal equation; (b) substituting 30¢ for three pencils. (From Luria 1968.)**

game tic-tac-toe. Figure 12.3 illustrates why they are equivalent. The nine digits can be placed on the squares in such a way that each horizontal, vertical,
or diagonal row sums to 15. As a result, the rule for winning number scrabble
(select three digits that add to 15) is equivalent to the rule for winning tic-tac-
toe (occupy three squares in a row).

Even though the two games are equivalent, so that we can represent one in
terms of the other, most people find tic-tac-toe easier. For one thing, the digits
disappear; we no longer have to compute sums of numbers, as in number
scrabble. Also, in tic-tac-toe scanning all possible solutions is easier. If players actually discover that number scrabble can be represented as tic-tac-toe,
this insight may substantially alter the way they play the game. For example,
many people know that a good strategy in tic-tac-toe is to occupy the corner
squares. The equivalent strategy in number scrabble is to select even digits.
This strategy might not occur to you unless you thought about it in terms of tic-
tac-toe. This point is a general point about problem-solving strategies: the kind
of representation will affect the strategies chosen.

Another example of how problem representation can affect the ease of solution is the Buddhist monk problem. This problem, like many of those commonly dicussed by psychologists, originated with the Gestalt psychologists
of the early twentieth century (in this case, Karl Duncker). The problem is as
follows:

> One morning, exactly at sunrise, a Buddhist monk began to climb a tall mountain.
> A narrow path, no more than a foot or two wide, spiraled around the mountain to a
> glittering temple at the summit. The monk ascended at varying rates of speed,
> stopping many times along the way to rest and eat dried fruit he carried with him.
> He reached the temple shortly before sunset. After several days of fasting and
> meditation he began his journey back along the same path, starting at sunrise and
> again walking at variable speeds, with many pauses along the way. His average
> speed descending was, of course, greater than his average climbing speed. Show
> that there is a spot along the path that the monk will occupy on both trips at pre-
> cisely the same time of day.

People who think about this problem verbally or algebraically are unlikely
to solve it. They may conclude that it would be an improbable coincidence for

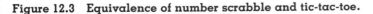

|  8  |  1  |  6  |
| --- | --- | --- |
|  3  |  5  |  7  |
|  4  |  9  |  2  |

**Figure 12.3   Equivalence of number scrabble and tic-tac-toe.**

the monk to find himself at the same spot at the same time on two different days. But one can actually visualize the solution, as the following report by a young woman suggests (Koestler 1964, p. 184):

> I tried this and that, until I got fed up with the whole thing, but the image of the monk in his saffron robe walking up the hill kept persisting in my mind. Then a moment came when, superimposed on this image, I saw another, more transparent one, of the monk walking down the hill, and I realized in a flash that the two figures must meet at some point in time—regardless of what speed they walk and how often each of them stops. Then I reasoned out what I already knew: whether the monk descends two days or three days later comes to the same; so I was quite justified in letting him descend on the same day, in duplicate so to speak.

Figure 12.4 provides a somewhat more abstract, visual solution to the problem. This graph plots the altitude of the monk on the mountain as a function of time of day, for both his ascent and his descent. We see that the two paths must cross, regardless of the monk's variable rates of progress. The point of intersection is the point on the path that the monk will occupy at the same time of day on both trips.

In the report quoted above the problem solver experiences a flash of *insight* when she visualizes the solution. Insight, a concept stressed by Gestalt psychologists who investigated problem solving, seems to involve a rapid reorganization of a problem representation that proceeds finding a solution. We will encounter other illustrations of insight as our discussion proceeds.

The successful visual solution to the Buddhist monk problem can be contrasted with the solution to the following mental paper-folding problem (from Adams 1974, p. 63):

> Picture a large piece of paper, 1/100 of an inch thick. In your imagination, fold it once (now having two layers), fold it once more (now having four layers), and continue folding it over on itself 50 times. It is true that it is impossible to fold any actual piece of paper 50 times. But for the sake of the problem, imagine that you can. About how thick would the 50-times-folded paper be?

At first glance this problem might seem like another problem requiring a visual solution. But in fact a visual solution is impossible. Note that the first fold will result in 2 times the original thickness, while the second fold will result in $2 \times 2 = 4$ times the original thickness. In fact, each fold increases the thickness by a factor of 2. So 50 folds will increase the paper's thickness by a factor of 2 multiplied by 2 exactly 50 times, or $2^{50}$. This number works out to about 1,100,000,000,000,000, a number so large that the resulting thickness of the folded paper would approximate the distance from the earth to the sun.

Obviously, visual imagery cannot produce this result. People who try to visualize a few folds and then extrapolate to estimate the thickness resulting

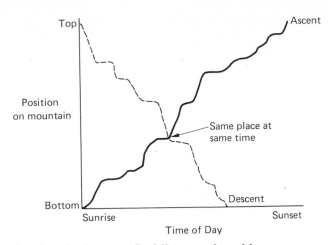

**Figure 12.4   Graphical solution to Buddhist monk problem.**

from fifty folds (a kind of visual application of the availability heuristic) invariably wildly underestimate the correct answer. In this case only a mathematical representation can easily produce an accurate solution.

The contrast between the Buddhist monk problem and the mental paper-folding problem highlights the importance of *task analysis*. Understanding the nature of the task and defining what is necessary for a solution is usually a major step toward finding a representation that can be used effectively to solve the problem. This principle is a useful one to remember when you are studying problem solving. Often by thinking about how a problem *could* be solved, one can get a good idea of how an intelligent problem solver actually *would* solve the problem.

We see, then, that a major part of forming an initial problem representation is selecting the best code to represent it in. This selection process requires making implicit information explicit, weeding out irrelevant information, and noting what is forbidden and what is permitted by the problem. We will see shortly that if the initial problem representation proves inadequate, these same considerations arise again in the step of reformulation.

**Planning a Potential Solution**

As the flowchart in Figure 12.1 indicates, the three final steps of the problem-solving process do not follow each other in a fixed order. Rather, the problem solver is basically trying to plan a potential solution (step 2). However, if no plan can be constructed (perhaps because the representation is ill defined in some way), an attempt will be made to reformulate the problem (step 3), after which step 2 will be repeated. Once a plan is actually constructed, it can be tested (step 4); if the plan fails, the process cycles back to step 2 to generate a new plan. In this section we will consider how a solution plan can be generated (step 2) if the problem representation is adequate. However, you should keep in mind that in actual problem solving steps 3 and 4 may intervene many times before an adequate representation is achieved.

In order to create a plan, one must use problem-solving methods. Let us examine some of the most important such methods.

**General methods for problem solving.**    The process of generating a problem solution can be viewed as a *search* through a space of *possible* solutions (Newell and Simon 1972). In many problems a major difficulty is that the space to be searched is potentially enormous. A good example is the problem of winning a game of chess.

The course of a chess game can be represented as a tree similar to the one shown in Figure 12.5. The top node in the tree represents the initial position on the chessboard. Each of the possible alternative moves will lead to a different new position. At an average choice point a chess player may have twenty or thirty possible alternatives; for simplicity only three alternatives are shown at each choice point in the figure. At the second level in the tree the opponent will select a move, again changing the board position. The first player then chooses one of the next set of possible moves, etc. As Figure 12.5 illustrates, the final positions at the bottom of the tree determine how the game ends—whether the first player wins, ties, or loses. The dark line in the figure shows a path through the tree (i.e., a sequence of moves) that leads to a win. Only a few of the possible paths are shown in Figure 12.5, and all the paths are just four moves long. An actual chess game will often be fifty or more moves long.

There is a clear way to win a game that can be represented as a decision tree, as in Figure 12.5. This method is to explore every possible path in the tree

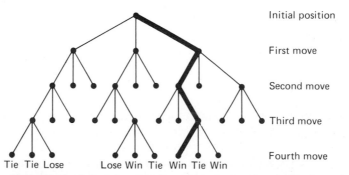

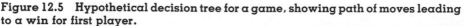

**Figure 12.5    Hypothetical decision tree for a game, showing path of moves leading to a win for first player.**

to determine its final outcome and then to always select a move that sends the game along a path that cannot end in a win for the opponent. The problem with this approach is that the number of paths that would have to be considered at each choice point may be astronomical. An astronomical number will certainly arise in a complex game like chess, in which the tree of possible moves is both very wide (many alternatives at each choice point) and very deep (many moves to complete a game). As a result, the only effective way to play a good chess game—even for a computer—is to use intelligent problem-solving methods that sharply restrict the search space.

As Newell (1969) pointed out, problem-solving methods range from those that are very general (applicable to almost any problem) to those that are very specialized (applicable to only a small class of problems). An example of a specialized method is a procedure for solving quadratic equations; it works very well on quadratic equations, but it is no use at all for playing chess. If a suitable specialized method is available, it will make it far easier to solve the kind of problem for which the method is tailored. As we will see shortly, expertise in a problem domain is based in part on knowledge of specialized methods.

The number of specialized methods is, of course, extremely large, since many vastly different types of problems present themselves. In contrast, there seem to be only a handful of truly general methods. Here we will discuss two representative examples.

**Generate-test method.**     The most basic general method is the *generate-test method* (Newell and Simon 1972). This method is extremely similar to the generate-recognize process of recall that was described in Chapter 7. In fact, we can illustrate the generate-test method with a simple memory search problem: Produce the name of a fruit that has a vowel as its fourth letter.

As its name implies, the generate-test method has two steps:

1.  Generate a candidate for a solution.
2.  Test to see whether it is actually a solution.

If the candidate fails the test, another candidate is generated, and the cycle repeats until a solution is found. For the fruit-letter task a person might generate a series of fruits and test each one to see whether it has a vowel as its fourth letter, e.g., apple (no), orange (no), peach (no), banana (yes!).

Newell and Simon (1972) discuss four potential sources of difficulty for the generate-test method:

1.  Generating each candidate may be hard. For the fruit-letter problem, generating the first few candidates is usually easy, but then thinking of new possibilities may become quite difficult.

2.  Testing whether the candidate is actually the solution may be hard. The test is simple for the fruit-letter problem (check the fourth letter), but in many problems testing is the hardest part. For example, generating a possible chess move is easy, but testing whether it is the best move possible is very difficult.

3.  The size of the search space may be very large. This feature is the principle behind the use of combination locks. If a lock on a bank vault has ten dials, each of which can be set at any number from 00 to 99, then there are $100^{10}$, or 100 billion billion, combinations. Since only one randomly chosen combination will open the lock, the sheer size of the search space will protect the bank vault from a thief who tries to use the generate-test method to discover the correct combination.

4.  The correct solution may be low in the sequence of candidates that will be generated. This feature also provides the effectiveness of the combination lock; the correct solution will, on average, be found after one tests half the possibilities (i.e., after 50 billion billion tries). Compare this difficulty with the problem of naming a fruit that begins with an *a*. Even though you know many fruits, and almost none of them start with *a*, it is quite likely that *apple* will be the first possibility that you generate, since it is a highly typical fruit. No matter how big the search space is, the problem will be easy if the correct solution is generated early in the sequence.

The generate-test method thus has two major drawbacks as an approach to problems. First, it does not provide a mechanism for selecting good candidate solutions to be tested. If the search space is large, preselecting candidate solutions becomes critical so that one does not waste time testing candidates that are obviously wrong. A good problem solver will tend to select candidate solutions that are increasingly close to the desired goal. The name "heuristic search" is usually reserved for "intelligent" methods of selecting possible solutions to a problem. (The term *heuristic*, as we saw in Chapter 11, refers to a procedure that tends to produce successful solutions, even though success is not guaranteed.)

Second, the simple generate-test method involves generating a complete possible solution before testing it to see whether it is correct. For many problems this procedure is clearly very inefficient. For example, you would not try to solve a crossword puzzle by filling in all the spaces and only then checking to see whether you had a correct solution. Rather, you would work on the problem one word at a time. Finding even one correct word is clearly a partial solution that brings you closer to a full solution to the problem. This example illustrates the general usefulness of breaking down a problem into parts, sometimes called the *problem reduction approach* (Nilsson 1971). In this approach the original problem is broken down into subproblems, or subgoals, so that a solution to all the subproblems implies a solution to the overall problem. In the example of the crossword puzzle, if we set up subgoals of solving each word, the crossword puzzle will be solved once all the words have been found. A set of subgoals constitutes a plan for finding a problem solution.

One way the generate-test method could be elaborated to solve a crossword problem is to generate words of the specific lengths given in the puzzle and then to test whether the words match at intersections (Newell and Simon 1972). Note that the problem reduction approach does not eliminate search from the problem-solving process. The person now has to search for good subproblems to solve.

**Means-ends analysis.**   A heuristic strategy for finding subgoals is *means-ends analysis*. This procedure requires problem solvers to determine the ends they are trying to achieve and the means that will serve to reach these ends. In doing so, problem solvers set up subgoals. Means-ends analysis is used frequently in everyday life. Consider the problem of cooking a Chinese dinner. You might work through this problem by using means-ends analysis and by thinking approximately as follows: "What's the difference between what I have now (my initial state) and dinner (the goal state)? A cooked meal. What is needed to cook a meal? Food, an oven. I have an oven. I also have some food, but not Chinese food. What do I do to get Chinese food? Go to the grocery store. The grocery store is down the street, but I haven't any money. What can I do to get some money? Go to the bank, which is beside the grocery store. How can I get there? Walk." And so on.

As you can see from this example, a major component of means-ends analysis consists of two steps applied repeatedly: (1) identifying the differences between the current state and the desired goal, and (2) applying an operation to reduce one of these differences. This two-step procedure is often called *difference reduction*. The method can be illustrated by using the simple algebra problem mentioned earlier: Solve the equation $ax - b = x$ for $x$. The steps to a solution are outlined in Table 12.1. The goal state for this problem can be described as "term $x$ on the left-hand side of the equation; all other terms on the right." At each step the current known version of the equation is compared with the goal state and differences are noted. Then an algebraic operation (e.g., "add a term to both sides of the equation"), which will eliminate one of the differences, is selected and applied. The process is then repeated until no differences remain.

Note that a major difference between the algebra problem and the dinner problem is that the algebra problem does not require subgoals. Everything needed to solve the algebra problem is available from the start, which was not the case in the example of cooking dinner. Since the required food was not im-

**TABLE 12.1** Method of Difference Reduction Applied to Simple Algebra Problem

Problem: Solve the equation $ax - b = x$ for $x$.

Goal state: Term $x$ on the left-hand side of the equation; all other terms on the right.

Steps

1.  Current state: $ax - b = x$.
    Differences: $a$ on left, $b$ on left, $x$ on right.
    Apply operation: Add $b$ to both sides.

2.  Current state: $ax = x + b$.
    Differences: $a$ on left, $x$ on right.
    Apply operation: Subtract $x$ from both sides.

3.  Current state: $ax - x = b$.
    Differences: $a$ on left, $x$ on left twice.
    Apply operation: Factor $x$ on left.

4.  Current state: $x(a - 1) = b$.
    Differences: $(a - 1)$ on left.
    Apply operation: Divide both sides by $(a - 1)$.

5.  Current state: $x = b/(a - 1)$.
    Differences: None.
    Problem solved.

mediately available, we had to set up a subgoal of getting food, and then a subgoal of getting money, etc. Problems that require subgoals are often difficult because they require extra information to be stored in memory. The person has to remember what the subgoals are and the reasons for achieving them. If we didn't remember why the subgoals were established in the first place, we might find ourselves in the position of going to the bank and then forgetting why we went there.

A more complex problem that illustrates the importance of planning and setting up subgoals in the strategy of means-ends analysis is the well-known, Tower of Hanoi puzzle depicted in Figure 12.6. A number of disks (three in Figure 12.6) must be moved from peg A to peg C. Only one disk (the top disk on a peg) can be moved at a time, and no disk can ever be placed on top of a disk smaller than itself. This puzzle derives its name from a legend that a group of monks near Hanoi are working on a version of the puzzle that uses sixty-four disks. The legend says that the world will end when they finish the puzzle, which at the rate of one perfect move every second, will take them about a trillion years (Raphael 1976).

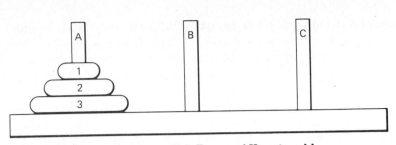

**Figure 12.6    Initial state for three-disk Tower of Hanoi problem.**

The three-disk version of the puzzle is considerably more tractable, but it still requires a degree of planning in selecting moves and generating subgoals that will bring the problem closer to a solution. For example, clearly the solution to the puzzle in Figure 12.6 requires that the largest disk (disk 3) be placed on peg C first. (This approach is an illustration of working backward from the goal to solve a problem.) Therefore we begin by setting up a subgoal of getting disk 3 to peg C. Also clear is that disks 1 and 2 have to be moved from disk 3 before the latter can be moved. This step results in a further subgoal of moving disks 1 and 2, which in turn sets up a subgoal of first moving disk 1.

But should disk 1 go to peg B or peg C? Here looking ahead a few moves will help. For if we move disk 1 to peg B, then disk 2 will have to go on peg C. But then disk 3 won't be able to go on peg C. On the other hand, if we begin by moving disk 1 to peg C, the following sequence will accomplish the subgoal of moving disk 3 to peg C:

Disk 1 to peg C;

Disk 2 to peg B;

Disk 1 to peg B;

Disk 3 to peg C.

Having completed the initial subgoal, we can set up the next subgoal, getting disk 2 onto peg C. This step is easily accomplished:

Disk 1 to peg A;

Disk 2 to peg C.

Then a final move (disk 1 to peg C) completes the puzzle.

Note that this approach to the Tower of Hanoi puzzle involves formulating a hierarchy of subgoals (e.g., the subgoal "move disk 3 to peg C" generates the subgoal "move disk 2 off disk 3," which in turn generates the subgoal "move disk 1 off disk 2"). This puzzle becomes increasingly difficult when more disks are used, because the subgoal hierarchies get deeper. Thinking far enough ahead in planning moves and remembering how all the subgoals that are generated relate to each other becomes difficult. Egan and Greeno (1974) observed subjects as they worked on a six-disk, Tower of Hanoi problem, and they found that the probability of a subject's making an error on a move increased with the number of subgoals that had to be set up between the preceding move and the current one.

Note that means-ends analysis solves the first problem for the generate-test method that we noted earlier. Each new knowledge state is closer to the desired goal than was the previous one. Whereas each test in the generate-test method gave very little information—just "yes, it's a solution" or "no, it's not"—each test in means-end analysis provides information about how the current state differs from the goal state and how this difference can be reduced.

## Reformulating Problem Representations

As noted earlier, the initial problem representation may not be adequate for the task of planning a solution. In such cases the representation must be somehow reformulated (step 3 in the overall problem-solving process depicted in Figure 12.1). In many ways the reformulation process resembles the process of forming an initial representation; in fact, in extreme cases the problem solver may essentially discard the initial representation and construct a new one.

**Removing unnecessary constraints.**    In other cases, however, the initial representation may undergo much more subtle changes. An example is provided by the well-known nine-dot problem. The problem is to draw four straight lines through all the nine dots depicted in Figure 12.7(a) without lifting the pencil from the paper. The Gestalt psychologists noticed that people see a square boundary around the nine dots, owing to the perceptual principle of closure (see Chapter 4). As a result, when most people are given this problem, they tend to assume that the four lines can't go outside the imaginary boundary. But, in fact, the problem can be solved only by extending some of the lines beyond the boundary, as in Figure 12.7(b).

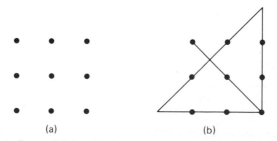

(a)                              (b)

**Figure 12.7    Nine-dot problem: (a) Configuration of nine dots; (b) possible solution.**

Adams (1974) calls this difficulty a "conceptual block"; problem solvers impose an unnecessary constraint on the problem that actually blocks its solution. If problem solvers can modify their internal representation of the problem by eliminating this constraint, they may be able to develop a solution. Weisberg and Alba (1981) tested this possibility by instructing some subjects, after they had made several unsuccessful attempts, that it was necessary to draw lines outside the boundary to solve the problem. Although the problem still proved far from easy, about 25 percent of these subjects eventually solved the problem, whereas subjects in a control condition that did not receive such a hint invariably failed.

**Noticing and applying analogies.**   Often a problem must be reformulated in order to define it more clearly. This type of reformulation seems to be especially important in relatively creative types of problem solving. One method that can be used to reformulate a problem is to model its representation after that of some structurally similar or *analogous* problem. An analogy can result in the reformulation of a problem such that the solution to a known problem can be used to plan a solution to the new one. Analogies are important in developing new scientific theories. For example, the wave theory of light was based on an analogy with sound waves (Oppenheimer 1956).

As this example suggests, useful analogies can sometimes be found between concepts that are superficially very different. Gick and Holyoak (1980, 1983) have investigated the use of such analogies in solving relatively ill-defined problems. Their results indicate that analogies are indeed useful in reformulating problems, at least once their relevance is noticed by the problem solver. The problem they studied most extensively was the radiation problem made famous by the Gestalt psychologist Karl Duncker (1945). The problem runs as follows:

> Suppose you are a doctor faced with a patient who has a malignant tumor in his stomach. To operate on the patient is impossible, but unless the tumor is destroyed, the patient will die. A kind of ray, at a sufficiently high intensity, can destroy the tumor. Unfortunately, at this intensity the healthy tissue that the rays pass through on the way to the tumor will also be destroyed. At lower intensities the rays are harmless to healthy tissue but will not affect the tumor, either. How can the rays be used to destroy the tumor without injuring the healthy tissue?

This problem is reasonably realistic, since it describes a situation similar to what actually arises in radiation therapy. Most of the problem components are reasonably well specified; however, the operations are extremely vague. The problem solver might imagine the possibilities of altering the effects of the rays or of avoiding contact between the rays and the healthy tissue. However, none of these operations immediately specify realizable actions; they remain at the level of wishful thinking.

Gick and Holyoak (1980) wanted to find out whether college students could use a remote analogy to develop a clearer problem representation and hence solve the problem. To provide the students with a potential analogy, the experimenters first had them read a story about the predicament of a general who wished to capture a fortress located in the center of a country. Many roads radiated outward from the fortress, but these roads were mined so that although small groups could pass over them safely, any large group would detonate the mines. Yet the general needed to get his entire large army to the fortress in order to launch a successful attack. Thus the general's situation was analogous to that of the doctor in the radiation problem.

Different versions of the story described different solutions to the military problem. For example, in one version the general divided his men into small groups and dispatched them simultaneously down multiple roads to converge on the fortress. All subjects were then asked to suggest solutions to the radiation problem, using the military story to help them. Subjects who received the multiple-road version were especially likely to suggest a convergence solution—directing multiple weak rays at the tumor from different directions. This solution is in fact similar to actual medical procedures for radiation therapy. About 75 percent of the subjects who received the relevant story generated this solution, compared with fewer than 10 percent of control subjects who did not receive an analogy.

The correspondences between the convergence version of the military story and the radiation problem are shown in Table 12.2. Even though the particular objects involved (e.g., army and rays, fortress and tumor) are very different, the basic relations that make the convergence solution possible are present in both. The goal, resources (and other objects), operations, and contraints are structurally similar, and they can be matched, or "mapped," from one problem to the other. Because the military story provides clear operations (e.g., "divide the army"), subjects are able to use the mapping to construct corresponding operators (e.g., "reduce ray intensity") that can be used to solve the ray problem. The abstract structure common to the two problems can be viewed as a schema for convergence problems. The schema is described at the bottom of Table 12.2.

Other experiments by Gick and Holyoak (1980, 1983) revealed that subjects often fail to make use of a potentially helpful analogy unless its relevance is pointed out to them. The difficulty of noticing distant analogies is perhaps not surprising, since the underlying schema is quite abstract, whereas the many superficial differences between the two cases are very obvious.

Sometimes, people are explicitly taught to think about one domain in terms of a very different one so that the problem of noticing the analogy is

**TABLE 12.2**    Correspondences Between Two Convergence Problems and Their Schema

**Military problem**

Representation
  Goal: Use army to capture fortress.
  Resources: Sufficiently large army.
  Operators: Divide army, move army, attack with army.
  Constraint: Unable to send entire army along one road safely.
Solution plan: Send small groups along multiple roads simultaneously.
Outcome: Fortress captured by army.

**Radiation problem**

Representation
  Goal: Use rays to destroy tumor.
  Resources: Sufficiently powerful rays.
  Operators: Reduce ray intensity, move ray source, administer rays.
  Constraint: Unable to administer high-intensity rays from one direction
        safely.
Solution plan: Administer low-intensity rays from multiple directions
        simultaneously.
Outcome: Tumor destroyed by rays.

**Convergence schema**

Representation
  Goal: Use force to overcome a central target.
  Resources: Sufficiently great force.
  Operators: Reduce force intensity, move source of force, apply force.
  Contraint: Unable to apply full force along one path safely.
Solution plan: Apply weak forces along multiple paths simultaneously.
Outcome: Central target overcome by force.

*Source:* From Gick and Holyoak (1983).

avoided. For example, students are often told that electricity behaves like a hydraulic system. As depicted in Figure 12.8, electricity is analogous to water flowing through a pipe; batteries act like reservoirs, and resistors act like constrictions in the pipe. Gentner and Gentner (1983) have demonstrated that the ease with which high school and college students solve particular types of electricity problems depends on the degree to which the analogy they have been taught generates correct inferences about the relevant electrical concepts.

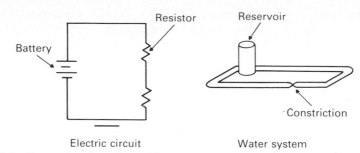

**Figure 12.8   Example of analogy: Electric current and water system.**

Another way in which the difficulty of noticing distant analogies can be overcome is by encouraging abstraction of the underlying schema. Notice that the schema captures the commonalities among different examples of a type of problem while deleting the differences among them. As a result, a novel example will be more similar to the schema than to another example (Tversky 1977). If retrieval depends on similarity, then a novel problem is more likely to cue recall of a schema than of a stored problem.

Gick and Holyoak (1983) tested this hypothesis by having subjects first read *two* convergence stories, such as the military story and a story about fire fighting (e.g., a story in which the hero extinguished an oil well fire by using multiple small hoses). The subjects were asked to describe ways in which the stories were similar, thus encouraging them to map the two stories with each other and hence to potentially abstract the shared convergence schema. When such subjects subsequently attempted to solve the radiation problem, they were much more likely to generate the parallel solution (either with or without a hint to use the stories) than were subjects who received just one prior story.

These results suggest that analogical mapping is used not only to reformulate novel problems but also to learn more abstract problem schemas that can be stored in memory and later retrieved and applied. As we will see shortly, the acquisition of problem schemas seems to be a key factor in the development of expertise in problem solving.

**Executing a Solution Plan**

Once a solution plan has been developed, the problem solver can actually execute and test it. This final step in problem solving often lacks the excitement that can be generated by a creative reformulation of the problem, but it is nonetheless essential. Often enough, the initial plan will prove inadequate when it is actually tried. Information about *why* the plan fell short may be used in cycling back to generate a modified plan. For example, if an analogy was used to construct the initial plan, the shortcomings of the plan may lead to a critical evaluation of the analogy. The plan may then be altered slightly or abandoned in favor of an entirely different approach.

# EXPERTISE IN PROBLEM SOLVING

One of the most intriguing issues involving problem solving concerns the differences between novices and experts. Obviously, training and practice are important, but what is it that experts learn that makes it relatively easy for them to solve new problems in their knowledge domain? We will look at two domains in which a great deal of research has addressed this question: playing complex board games, such as chess, and solving problems in physics.

## Expertise in Chess

**Memory and perception.**    The pioneering work on chess skills was done by De Groot (1965). His basic question was simple: What makes a master chess player better than a weaker player? To investigate this question, he collected protocols from some of the best chess players in the world as they selected chess moves.

De Groot's findings were quite different from what most people might expect. The master chess players did not seem to reason in any unusual ways. Nor did the masters search through more possible moves before selecting one. In fact, if anything, the masters considered fewer alternatives than did ordinary players. The difference was that the masters explored particularly good moves, whereas weaker players spent more time considering bad moves. Somehow, the good moves seemed to be immediately apparent to the master players.

The most striking difference between masters and weaker players emerged in a test of perceptual and memory abilities. In this test a chess position, such as the middle game (board position in the middle of an actual game) shown in Figure 12.9(a), was displayed for 5 seconds and then removed. The player then had to reconstruct the board position from memory. Chase and Simon (1973) performed this experiment with a master player (an expert), a class A player (a very good player), and a beginning (B) player. Figure 12.10(a) plots the number of pieces correctly recalled by each player over seven trials. As shown, memory performance is ordered in the same way as the level of chess skill: the master recalled the most pieces, followed by the class A player and the beginner.

This result might suggest that master players simply have the best memories. But this conclusion is not quite right. Chase and Simon also performed the memory test with positions in which the pieces were arranged

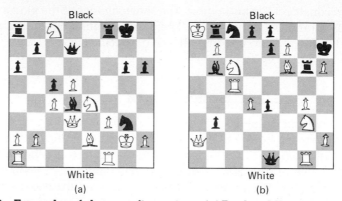

**Figure 12.9   Examples of chess configurations: (a) Real middle game; (b) random counterpart. (From Chase and Simon 1973.)**

randomly, as in Figure 12.9(b). With these random games the superiority of the master player completely disappeared. In fact, as Figure 12.10(b) indicates, the master actually tended to recall fewer correct pieces than the weaker players.

Apparently, then, the master players are especially good at a very specialized task—encoding actual chess positions. If you recall our discussion

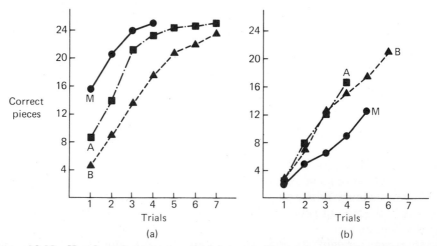

**Figure 12.10   Number of pieces recalled correctly by master (M), class A player (A), and beginner (B) over trials: (a) For actual board positions; (b) for random board positions. (From Chase and Simon 1973.)**

of perceptual learning in Chapter 9, you might wonder whether the master players perform so well because they can recognize large meaningful chunks in board positions. Chase and Simon (1973) found evidence that this recognition is indeed the case. They timed how long the subjects paused between each placement of a piece as they recalled the positions on the first trial. If the pause was less than 2 seconds long, the two successive pieces were defined as belonging to the same chunk. If the pause was longer than 2 seconds, the two pieces were defined as belonging to different chunks. Chase and Simon found that pieces belonging to the same chunk tended to be recalled together on both the first and second trials, even though the order of recall within a cluster varied. This result suggests that each chunk is stored in memory as a single compound representation.

If the unitization hypothesis is correct, the master should have recalled larger chunks than the weaker players. And as Table 12.3 indicates, the master did. In addition to recalling larger chunks, the master also recalled more chunks. This result suggests that the master is able to establish more associations in memory between chunks, so that one chunk can serve as a retrieval cue for another.

Recall that only a limited number of representations can be maintained in awareness. Britton and Tesser (1982) hypothesized that if experts activated more knowledge when performing a problem-solving task, they would be slower to detect a target that was part of a secondary task. Both expert and novice chess players were given chess problems to solve, but they were also told to press a telegraph key when they heard a click. The expert took longer than the novices to respond to the clicks.

Related evidence has been found with another complex board game, the oriental game of go. The game involves placing black and white stones on a grid and fighting for territory on the board. A player can capture an enemy stone by surrounding it with his or her own pieces. Judith Reitman (1976) studied a go master and a beginner, using the kinds of memory tests used earlier with chess players. As in chess, the go master player showed superior memory for real go positions but not for random positions.

**TABLE 12.3** Number and Average Size of Units Recalled on First Trial

|  | Number of units | Size (number of pieces) |
|---|---|---|
| Master | 7.7 | 3.8 |
| Class A player | 5.7 | 2.6 |
| Beginner | 5.3 | 2.4 |

*Source:* From Chase and Simon (1973).

The go master also tended to recall pieces in clusters. Figure 12.11 shows several examples of board positions (labeled A through D) that were presented to the master. The circles show how the master himself partitioned the pieces into chunks. Note that the go master saw the chunks as overlapping in many different ways. That is, the same piece was often included in several different clusters. The numbers on the pieces in Figure 12.11 give the order in which the pieces were recalled on that trial (if there is no number, the piece was not recalled). As shown, pieces that were part of the same pattern had a very strong tendency to be recalled together.

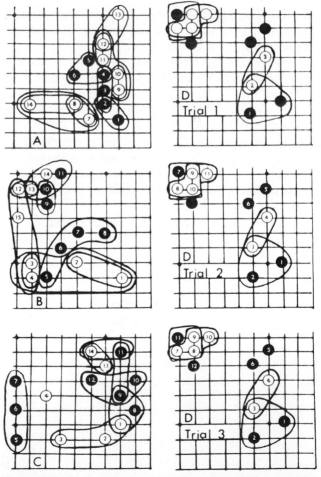

**Figure 12.11    Examples of go master's penciled partitioning of meaningful patterns and orders in which he recalled elements. (From Reitman 1976.)**

What is the basis for the perception of a chunk? One might expect that two pieces would be united together if they were related in some way that was important to the game. Chase and Simon (1973) examined five relations between two pieces that are important in chess:

1. One piece can attack another.
2. One piece can defend another.
3. Two pieces can be on adjacent squares.
4. Two pieces can have the same color.
5. Two pieces can be of the same type (e.g., both pawns).

Figure 12.12 plots the length of the pause between the recall of one piece and the next as a function of the number of relations between them. As the figure shows, the more relations there were between the two pieces, the shorter was the pause. This result suggests that the more ways two pieces are related, the more likely they are to be coded into a single chunk. Similarly, in go, chunks seem to be defined by attack-defense relationships, groups of stones of the same color, and other meaningful configurations. Chunks therefore contain information about important relations between pieces that will make this information readily available to help plan the next move.

Simon and Gilmartin (1973) developed a computer program that simulates the way chess players store board positions in memory. The program contains information about many familiar patterns of pieces. Simon and Gilmartin used the performance of their program to estimate how many patterns a master chess player has stored in memory. Their estimate was 30,000. This estimate

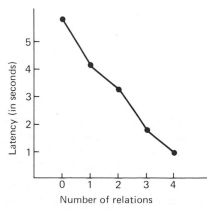

Figure 12.12    **Average latency between two pieces as function of number of relations between them. (From Chase and Simon 1973.)**

may seem like a very large number of patterns, but it is no larger than the number of words (another type of meaningful pattern) that a good reader can recognize. And a master chess player will have spent as much time studying chess positions as a good reader will have spent reading. In fact, the most basic requirement for becoming a master player appears to be an incredible amount of practice: as many as 50,000 hours spent working with chess positions. As a result of this practice, the master is able to recognize complex chess patterns as chunks, just as a skilled reader recognizes words as chunks.

**Perception and thought.**    The fact that skilled chess and go players seem to have their knowledge of board positions organized into large perceptual chunks has important consequences for how they select moves. Good players often seem to know immediately after looking at a board what the best move is. Simon (1973) suggests that the selection of chess moves is partly based on a set of rules, built up through years of experience. These rules can be stated in an if-then form (see Chapter 3): "If a particular board configuration is present, then a particular move should be taken." In other words, perception of a familiar perceptual chunk leads directly to an appropriate action.

This human style of play is very different from that of computer programs, such as the many programs that have been developed to play chess, which operate by searching through game trees of the sort depicted in Figure 12.5. Most chess programs do have heuristics to restrict the number of possible moves they consider, but these heuristics don't involve incorporating chunks into the knowledge available to the program. Part of the reason that existing chess programs can be beaten by good human players may be that current programs do not use chunks. Some chess enthusiasts such as Hearst (1977) have advised programmers to model their programs more closely on human characteristics, such as the use of perceptual chunks.

### Expertise in Other Domains

**Problem schemas in physics.**    Recent work on differences between novices and experts in domains such as physics problem solving has largely confirmed the major conclusions derived from work on board games (Larkin, McDermott, Simon, and Simon 1980). In domains such as physics, in which knowledge is highly systematized, the role of specialized problem schemas is especially apparent. A major factor differentiating experts from novices is that experts have both more and better problem schemas, which allow them to rapidly classify problems and retrieve relevant solution procedures.

A study of experts and novices in the domain of physics problems by Chi, Feltovich, and Glaser (1981) is especially illuminating. When subjects were asked to sort problems into clusters on the basis of similarity, novices tended to form categories based on relatively surface features of the problem state-

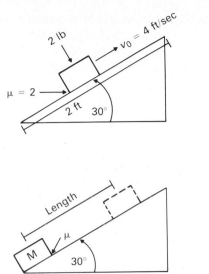

Novice 1: "These deal
   with blocks on an
   incline plane."
Novice 2: "Inclined plane
   problems, coefficient
   of friction."
Novice 3: "Blocks on
   inclined planes with
   angles."

**Figure 12.13    Diagrams of two problems categorized together by novices, and samples of explanations given. (From Chi, Feltovich, and Glaser 1981.)**

ments (e.g., inclined-plane problems). In contrast, experts sorted the problems with respect to applicable physical laws (e.g., problems solvable by the principle of conservation of energy). If you compare the problem pairs depicted in Figure 12.13, which were grouped together by novices, with those depicted in Figure 12.14, which were grouped by experts, you will get a sense of the

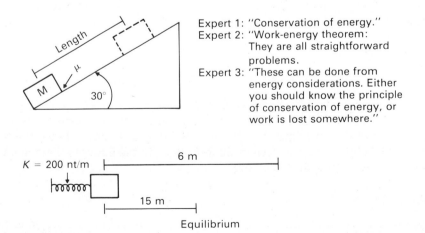

Expert 1: "Conservation of energy."
Expert 2: "Work-energy theorem:
   They are all straightforward
   problems.
Expert 3: "These can be done from
   energy considerations. Either
   you should know the principle
   of conservation of energy, or
   work is lost somewhere."

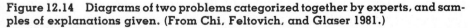

**Figure 12.14    Diagrams of two problems categorized together by experts, and samples of explanations given. (From Chi, Feltovich, and Glaser 1981.)**

greater degree of abstraction involved in the experts' problem categories. Further differences were apparent in protocols in which subjects described their problem categories. The experts were able to articulate the equivalent of rules for realizable actions—i.e., explicit solution procedures for problems of a given type. The novices' protocols, on the other hand, even when they mentioned abstract problem features, usually did not reveal such rules for action. Rather, their rules seemed to set further abstract subgoals that lacked specific solution procedures.

**Expertise and problem definition.**    The richer problem schemas of the expert can account for the observation that the degree to which a problem is ill defined depends on the knowledge of the problem solver. To use an example discussed by Simon (1973), most of us would find the problem of designing a house quite ill defined. The list of alternative styles (ranch, colonial, neo-Gothic) and materials (wood, brick, Plexiglas, camel's hide) could go on indefinitely. An architect, however, can quickly call up a hierarchy of relevant schemas that effectively decompose the problem, providing clear solution procedures.

The first step is to determine some general constraints: What basic design is desired? How much money is available? The architect knows that a home consists of a general floor plan plus structure; a structure consists of roofing plus siding plus utilities; utilities consist of plumbing plus heating system plus electrical system; etc. Once the problem is broken down in this hierarchical way, the number of reasonable alternatives at each choice point will usually be fairly limited. The heating system, for instance, may reduce to a choice between a gas or an electric furnace. For the expert with specialized problem schemas, this ill-defined problem eventually becomes a series of well-structured problems. If this process of problem reformulation proceeds rapidly enough, the expert may scarcely notice that the original problem statement was vague.

## BLOCKS THAT HINDER PROBLEM SOLVING

So far we have been discussing ways in which prior knowledge stored in memory is helpful in solving problems. But in some cases the problem solver's knowledge actually hinders the ability to achieve a solution. Let's examine some of these blocks to effective problem solving in the light of what we know about memory and problem solving.

### Problem-Solving Set

As we saw in earlier chapters, a very general principle of behavior is that activities, both physical and mental, tend to be strengthened by repetition. In the case of problem solving people often exhibit a *problem-solving set*—a tendency to repeat a solution process that has been previously successful.

The classic demonstration of a problem-solving set (*einstellung* in German) was a series of experiments by Luchins (1942; Luchins and Luchins 1950). Luchins tested over nine thousand subjects, ranging in age from elementary school children to adults, on water jar problems. A typical series of problems is shown in Table 12.4. The subject is asked to imagine three jars of various specified capacities and told to find a way to get a required amount of water. For the first problem in Table 12.4 the solution is to fill jar $B$, then to take out the volume of jar $A$, and then to take out the volume of jar $C$ twice. The series of problems is set up so that this same general solution ($B - A - 2C$) works for the first five problems. This series is designed to establish a problem-solving set.

On trials 6 and 7 there are two possible solutions: the previously successful formula and also a simpler one. One measure of the effect of a set is how often people discover the simpler solution. Finally, trial 8 is a problem for which the earlier formula won't work but a simpler one ($A - C$) will. Luchins found that subjects very often failed to notice the simpler solutions to problems 6 and 7 and sometimes failed to solve problem 8 at all. Seemingly, an initially successful solution procedure tends to be repeated, blocking discovery of alternative solutions.

The set effect is hardly surprising given what we know about learning and memory. Attempting to apply previously successful solution procedures to similar new problems is only reasonable. Educators can minimize the negative

**TABLE 12.4** Typical Series of Water Jar Problems

| Problem | Capacity of given jars (in quarts) | | | |
| | $A$ | $B$ | $C$ | Amount of quarts to get |
|---|---|---|---|---|
| 1 | 21 | 127 | 3 | 100 |
| 2 | 14 | 163 | 25 | 99 |
| 3 | 18 | 43 | 10 | 5 |
| 4 | 9 | 42 | 6 | 21 |
| 5 | 20 | 59 | 4 | 31 |

($B - A - 2C$ is the solution to the first five problems.)

| | | | | |
|---|---|---|---|---|
| 6 | 23 | 49 | 3 | 20 |

($A - C$ also works.)

| | | | | |
|---|---|---|---|---|
| 7 | 15 | 39 | 3 | 18 |

($A + C$ also works.)

| | | | | |
|---|---|---|---|---|
| 8 | 28 | 76 | 3 | 25 |

($A - C$ works, but $B - A - 2C$ doesn't.)

*Source:* Based on Luchins (1942).

aspects of set by carefully selecting the examples used to teach skills in solving a particular type of problem. To begin by exposing the students to only a narrow range of examples is unwise. Although the students may learn how to solve the initial examples, the limited problem-solving rules that they acquire may actually interfere with their ability to solve a wider range of problems.

### Functional Fixedness

Another kind of negative influence of memory on problem solving is illustrated by the following experiment. Duncker (1945) presented subjects with several objects lying on a table and asked them to find a way to use them to support a board. The available objects included two iron joints and a pair of pliers. The solution to the problem was to use the iron joints to support one end of the board and the pliers to support the other. In one condition the subject first had to use the pliers to free the board.

Duncker found that subjects who began the experiment by using the pliers to free the board were less likely to find the solution of using the pliers as a support. He called this phenomenon *functional fixedness*: If an object has one established use in a situation, subjects have difficulty in using the object in another way.

Functional fixedness, like set, is a block to effective problem solving resulting from prior experience. But whereas set is a tendency to repeat previously successful problem-solving operations, functional fixedness is a tendency to think of past uses of an object to the exclusion of novel potential uses. Functional fixedness can also be understood in terms of memory processes. The most familiar functions of objects are likely to be directly stored with the concept in the semantic network (e.g., the concept *pliers* might be associated with the function "used for grasping objects"). These familiar uses will be the most available ones, especially if they have already been activated in the current context (as occurred when the pliers were used to free the board). But the perceptual attributes of an object (e.g., its shape, size, or weight) may be compatible with other potential uses, sometimes called *affordances* (J. J. Gibson 1966). A pair of pliers can therefore be used as a support. However, these potential uses are usually harder to think of than functions that have already been stored in memory.

As is the case for the set effect, functional fixedness can be viewed as a negative side effect of a generally useful property of memory organization, which is also reflected in the availability heuristic (Chapter 11). Whatever functions of objects are activated in a given context will be most readily available for generation of a solution to a problem. Indeed, Per Saugstad showed that success in generating a problem solution can be predicted by measures of the availability to the problem solver of the functions required for a solution.

Saugstad (1955) showed 57 college students objects to be used later in a problem in which some hollow tubes and putty had to be used to blow out a candle 6 feet away. Nothing was mentioned of the problem itself. Subjects were simply instructed to list all the possible functions that the objects might serve. All 13 subjects who listed functions for the objects that were later necessary to solve the problem did, in fact, solve the problem. In contrast, only 58% of the remaining subjects solved the problem. In another experiment, Saugstad and Raaheim (1960) demonstrated the functions of some objects, which turned out to be critical to the solution of a problem, to 20 male high school students. Nineteen of the boys later solved the problem. In contrast, only 10 of 45 boys who had not seen the demonstration were able to solve the problem.

Another task that illustrates functional fixedness is the so-called candle problem (Duncker 1945). In this problem subjects are given the task of affixing a candle to a wall and lighting it. The objects available for use are some matches, a candle, and a matchbox filled with thumbtacks. The optimal solution, as defined by Duncker, is to use the tacks to fix the matchbox to the wall, put the candle on the box, and then light it with the matches. Duncker found that more subjects used the box as a candle holder when it was presented empty than when it was full of tacks. He considered functional fixedness to be a perceptual problem. Seeing the box as a container for tacks makes it difficult for subjects to see it also as a platform. Presenting it empty makes it easier for them to perceive the box as a candle holder.

Samuel Glucksberg, Robert Weisberg, and their colleagues (Glucksberg and Danks 1968; Glucksberg and Weisberg 1966; Weisberg and Suls 1973) performed several experiments that illustrate how subtle changes in the experimental situation can affect how the candle problem is solved. For example, sometimes the experimenter would name the box while giving instructions to the subject, while sometimes he only named the tacks. More subjects solved the problem by using the box as a platform (the box solution) when the box itself was labeled. One way to interpret this result is to suppose that when only the tacks are labeled, the box that holds them is not really "seen" as a separate object. But once the name box is heard, the subjects become aware not only of the box as an object but also of the various familiar uses of boxes that are stored in the conceptual network. Since these familiar uses are likely to include the use of boxes to support other objects, hearing the name box makes it easier to find the solution.

Glucksberg and Danks (1968) also found cases where hearing the name of an object actually hindered problem solving. In this experiment the subject's task was to complete an electric circuit. The objects provided were batteries, a bulb, a switch, and a wrench. The solution was to use the wrench to complete the circuit. In this case subjects were more likely to find the solution when they were required to refer to the wrench by a nonsense name such as *vorpin* rather than by the familiar name *wrench*.

Why did the name *wrench* interfere with solving this problem, whereas the name *box* facilitated the process in our previous example? The critical difference is that the box had to be used in a relatively familiar way (as a support), whereas the wrench had to be used in a more novel way (to conduct electricity). The name *wrench* therefore activated known uses stored in memory that actually conflicted with the critical potential use, which could be discovered by exploring the perceptual properties of the object.

However, Weisberg and Suls (1973) offer a different interpretation of the functional fixedness observed in the candle problem. They point out that the experimenter decides in advance that the box solution is the "best." Perhaps if subjects do not realize that there is a best solution, they may simply attempt to produce a solution in the most obvious way, which is probably to try to tack the candle directly to the wall. However, if the experimenter gives a clue about what solution is desired (by leaving the box empty or by labeling it), the subject may catch on that the experimenter wants him or her to use the box. According to this interpretation, then, subjects may not be inhibited from using objects in a novel way. That is, unless the experimenter somehow indicates that he or she is looking for a novel solution, subjects will solve the problem in the most straightforward way.

But while the experimenter's expectations may play a role in producing the functional fixedness phenomenon, those expectations are probably not the whole story. Sometimes, there is simply no way to solve a problem without putting some object to a novel use. For example, if you forget your frying pan on a camping trip, you might end up cooking pancakes on a flattened tin can.

### Productive Thinking

What is learned from experience with examples of a type of problem can differ with respect to later transfer to novel cases. One can learn a procedure by rote, which Max Wertheimer (1959) termed *reproductive thinking,* or one can learn it in a way that makes it easy to generalize to new situations. Wertheimer termed this second, more flexible type of problem-solving procedure *productive thinking.* An example that illustrates the contrast between reproductive and productive thinking is Wertheimer's parallelogram problem, illustrated in Figure 12.15(a).

Consider the problem of finding the area of this parallelogram. One method taught in a class observed by Wertheimer was to draw two perpendicular lines, one from each upper corner, as shown by the dotted lines in Figure 12.15(a). Students are then told to prove that the area of the parallelogram is the product of the length of the base times the altitude by using the fact that the two triangles formed by the perpendicular are equivalent. However, as shown in Figure 12.15(b), some of the students blindly drew perpendiculars from the upper corners and then became confused, since the resulting figure didn't resemble the parallelogram they had been trained on. That is, the stu-

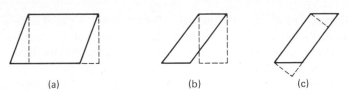

(a)          (b)          (c)

**Figure 12.15   Wertheimer's parallelogram problem: (a) Solution initially taught; (b) erroneous reproductive solution; (c) correct productive solution.**

dents were unable to form two triangles, one inside and one outside the parallelogram. These students had been thinking reproductively.

Another group of students, however, drew the dotted lines as in Figure 12.15(c). These students were thinking productively. They had grasped the critical relations between the parts of the figure (the triangles) and the whole (the parallelogram). These students realized that the essential principle underlying the method is that the parallelogram is really like a rectangle. That is, removing the inner triangle from the parallelogram and adding on the outer triangle produces a rectangle. Since the triangle removed and the triangle added have the same area, the original parallelogram must have the same area as the resulting rectangle. However, merely drawing perpendiculars from the upper corners of all parallelograms will not form the necessary triangles. The student who understands the underlying principle can search for alternate ways to draw the perpendiculars such that the necessary triangles will be formed. The ability to think productively seems to depend on learning the kinds of abstract problem categories that, as we saw earlier, distinguish expert from novice problem solvers.

## ANALYZING PROBLEM-SOLVING BEHAVIOR

One of the most important aspects of the study of problem solving is the methods that are used. How can we tell what representations and strategies are being used in particular problem-solving tasks? We have already mentioned a few possible methods, such as observing the frequencies of certain specific types of solutions or errors. In the case of problems that require explicit moves, one can also time how long it takes a person to make each move. However, most problems do not have such a rigid format. Clearly, the most interesting aspects of problem solving take place in the person's head. Given that we can't read minds, is there any way to observe this internal problem-solving behavior?

### Protocol Analysis

One important technique, used extensively by Newell and Simon (1972), is *protocol analysis*. This technique involves asking a subject to think out loud while solving a problem, with the experimenter recording the resulting protocol (a verbatim transcript of the session) for later analysis. Newell and Simon used this technique to study the ways in which people solve "cryptarithmetic" problems. In these puzzles the problem solver must substitute digits for letters to represent an arithmetic problem. Each letter represents a distinct digit, and each assignment is unique. The following is a simple example and its solution:

$$
\begin{array}{cc}
AA & 22 \\
+BB & +99 \\
\hline
CAC & 121
\end{array}
$$

Some more complex puzzles include the following:

$$
\begin{array}{lll}
\text{SEND} & \text{DONALD} \quad (\textit{Hint:}\ \text{D} = 5) & \text{CROSS} \\
+\text{MORE} & +\text{GERALD} & +\text{ROADS} \\
\hline
\text{MONEY} & \text{ROBERT} & \text{DANGER}
\end{array}
$$

You might like to try solving one or more of these brainteasers to get a feeling for what cryptarithmetic puzzles are like. The answers are given at the end of this chapter.

Tables 12.5–12.7 present three examples of fragments of protocols taken from subjects solving cryptarithmetic problems. In one technique for doing a protocol analysis, the first step is to break up the transcript into fragments that correspond to different states of the subject's knowledge or mental activity. This division is done intuitively by the experimenter. The result is a series of labeled statements, as illustrated in Tables 12.5–12.7.

**TABLE 12.5**  Beginning of Protocol for Subject on
CROSS + ROADS = DANGER Problem

---

1. Experimenter: R is 6.

$$
\begin{array}{c}
\text{C6OSS} \\
+\text{6OADS} \\
\hline
\text{DANGE6}
\end{array}
$$

2. Since R is 6 and the two S's are equal...
3. S must be equal to 3, or 8.
4. And D must be equal to 1...
5. Because C plus R can't be greater than 19...
6. Or greater than 16 in this case.
7. So D must be a 1.
8. Would you make D a 1?
9. Experimenter: D is 1.
10. And seeing that two S's are equal...

(continued)

**TABLE 12.5** (continued)

11. They must be either 3 or 8.
12. If they are 8...
13. Then E would be 0.
14. If they are 3...
15. Then E would be 4.
16. So let's try the S's as 8.
17. Could you make the S an 8?
18. Experimenter: S is 8.
19. That would make E a 0.
20. Would you make E a 0?
21. Experimenter: E is a 0.

*Source:* From Newell and Simon (1972).

The next step is to identify the general approach to the task that the subject is using. The protocol from the subject in Table 12.5 reveals that he is working on the problem in a way typical of most college students. He realizes that the task involves a relationship between numbers and letters and that his task is to discover that relationship. In working on the problem, he assigns numbers to letters and makes inferences by using his knowledge of arithmetic to check that each number assignment is consistent with the rest of the letters (for example, line 5 in Table 12.5).

**TABLE 12.6** Fragment of Protocol for Subject on
DONALD + GERALD = ROBERT Problem

1. Make the N 7.
2. Experimenter: N is 7.
3. Make the R 8.
4. Experimenter: R is 8.
5. Er...change the R to 6.
6. Oh...G is 6...
7. Er...6, 7.
8. Experimenter: Please speak.
9. Change the R to 7.
10. Experimenter: R is 7.
11. Make the E 4.
12. Er...change the 0 to 1.
13. Make the E 4.
14. Experimenter: 0 is 1, E is 4.
15. Right. Er...something's wrong here. We have both N and R as 7s.

*Source:* From Newell and Simon (1972).

In contrast, the subject in Table 12.6 is less systematic in his approach. Although he realizes the task involves a relationship between numbers and letters, he merely tries different assignments of numbers to letters, tests them, and changes them if something goes wrong (e.g., by line 6 he has assigned the value 6 to both G and R). He doesn't notice systematic restrictions on the possible values for a letter (e.g., if it has to be even or less than 2).

The subject in Table 12.7 is even less efficient. He cannot seem to get a grasp of the problem, and he changes his approach repeatedly, trying out new hypotheses. For example, in lines 1 to 3 he considers the possibility that the problem involves some relationship between the appearance of numbers and letters. He also considers the hypothesis that the problem is algebraic (lines 4 to 7) or involves some relation between the words as a whole and numbers as a whole (lines 8 to 10). This subject is really having trouble with the first step of the problem-solving process: understanding the problem and forming an initial representation of it.

Once the subject's general approach has been identified, the experimenter may attempt to identify the specific operations that the subject is using to move from one knowledge state to the next. For example, in the protocol of the subject in Table 12.5 we see in line 2 that the subject is processing the

**TABLE 12.7**  Fragment of Protocol for Subject on
LETS + WAVE = LATER Problem

---

1. I guess it's also possible that certain number . . . letters look like numbers.
2. For example, an E looks a lot like a 3.
3. But er . . . I'm afraid I'm not going to get very far with this idea because er . . . I can't see any other letters that look much like numbers.
   [Later.]
4. So I keep coming back to the idea of er . . . I keep coming back to the idea of . . . of trying some sort of algebraic equations.
5. But the more you think about this, the more ridiculous it gets . . .
6. I can't be attacking trying to set up any equations . . .
7. I'm really stymied at this point.
   [Later.]
8. I don't imagine it's possible that the words have any significance . . . LETS, WAVE, LATER.
9. This doesn't seem likely that the words LETS, WAVE, and LATER would give me any clues to any four-digit or five-digit numbers.
10. Er . . . they certainly don't.

---

*Source:* From Newell and Simon (1972).

rightmost column. The experimenter's clue has identified R as 6, and now the subject is processing it to try and discover what S is. Another operation is illustrated by line 7, where the subject assigns a value of 1 to D.

**Problem behavior graphs.** The results of the protocol analysis with the operations that have been identified can be summarized in a *problem behavior graph,* such as the one shown in Figure 12.16. This graph corresponds to the protocol for the subject in Table 12.5. Each box represents a new knowledge state, and the arrows represent operators that change one knowledge state into another. The numbers in the upper left corner of each box refer to the first line in the protocol that appears to correspond to that knowledge state. For example, at line 4 the subject states that D is 1, and the next few lines simply expand on why he has reached that conclusion. The vertical lines on the graph mark places at which the subject returns to an earlier knowledge state. For example, at line 10 the subject once again notes that the two S's must be equal, and he starts to process that piece of information for a second time. Note that to read the graph in the order in which the subject's knowledge states occurred in time, you read across the top row to the far right, then go down to the next row, across to the right again, etc.

The problem behavior graph makes a notable feature of problem-solving behavior very explicit. The subject's line of thought does not move in a direct line to the solution. Rather, he explores one line of thought as far as he can, and then he returns to an earlier state and starts out again. Sometimes, he finds an important piece of information before reaching a dead end (e.g., his first attack leads to the conclusion that D is 1). But other times, an approach will end up with an error, and everything will have to be undone back to an earlier point. This feature is shown at line 16, where the subject decides to tentatively assume that S is 8. As it turns out, this assumption is wrong (S is really 3). About fifty lines later in the protocol the subject finds himself trapped in a contradiction and has to return to the same knowledge state as line 14.

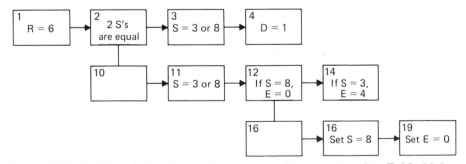

**Figure 12.16 Problem behavior graph corresponding to protocol in Table 12.5.**

**Limitations of protocol analysis.**   Protocol analysis is often a useful technique for analyzing problem-solving behavior, especially when it can be complemented by nonverbal measures, such as recordings of eye movements (Ericsson and Simon 1980). However, the technique has its limitations. Often a protocol will seem to have gaps in which the subject forgets to speak (e.g., the subject in Table 12.6, line 8) or takes a "mental leap," reaching some conclusion without mentioning any intermediate steps. Sometimes, the protocol will be ambiguous or difficult to interpret. Protocol analysis is always a cumbersome method, requiring painstaking and tedious work.

There are also other, more serious limitations. These limitations relate to the fact that protocols are obviously verbal. It is virtually impossible to get a useful protocol from a young child, and it is difficult with many subjects other than highly verbal college students. There are probably restrictions on the problems that can be studied as well as on the subjects. It may be difficult to provide a detailed verbal description of what you are thinking if you are using visual imagery or some other nonverbal representation. Also, if there are important unconscious components to problem solving, they will, of course, not be reported in a protocol. Furthermore, since subjects are being watched, they may use a more systematic method than usual, because they are aware that the protocol is being carefully recorded. As a result, the strategies inferred from the protocol may not tell you what subjects normally do in private. But despite these limitations, protocol analysis is currently an important technique for studying problem-solving behavior.

### Computer Simulation of Problem Solving

**GPS.**   One of the most important tools for developing theories of problem solving is simulation by computer programs. An early example of this approach, which has greatly influenced more recent computer models, is the *General Problem Solver,* or *GPS* (Ernst and Newell 1969). The GPS is a kind of theory of how humans might do various tasks, against which human performance can be compared.

The general strategy that GPS uses is means-ends analysis. The program operates by breaking a problem into subgoals and then attacking each subgoal in turn by using a difference reduction strategy. The GPS requires a variety of information in order to tackle a new problem. The most important information includes the following:

> (1) A description of the initial state, goal state, and operations. (2) A description of the possible differences among states. (3) A specification of which operations can be used to reduce each possible difference.

How does the performance of GPS compare with that of human problem solvers? In many cases, such as the Tower of Hanoi puzzle and logic problems, the performance of GPS bears a close resemblance to human performance. For example, in the Tower of Hanoi problem people take the most time and make the most errors on moves on which GPS would have to set up a series of subgoals (Egan and Greeno 1974). Such similarities are not surprising, given that people, like GPS, tend to use the strategy of means-ends analysis.

There are some problems, however, that people tend to solve somewhat differently from GPS. One example that has been studied extensively is the missionaries and cannibals problem (sometimes known as the hobbits and orcs problem), which can be stated as follows:

> Three missionaries and three cannibals are on one side of a river, and all of them must get to the other side. They can row themselves across with a rowboat that can hold two people. There is one important thing to remember: The cannibals must never outnumber the missionaries on either side of the river. Find a sequence of river crossings that will get all six people safely to the other side. Remember that someone will have to row the boat back after each trip across.

Try your hand at solving the missionaries and cannibals problem for a few minutes, and then work through the solution path shown in Figure 12.17. Each box shows where the missionaries, cannibals, and boat are located at each state on the way to the solution. The arrows show which people cross the river on a particular trip. Note that the trips following even-numbered states are always to return the boat.

The interesting thing about this problem is that the correct sequence is almost completely determined by the rules. Only the trips following the first and tenth states involve a choice (more than one path leading from a given state). In all other cases there is only one legal move (this solution ignores such dead ends as taking the same people back and forth repeatedly).

Nevertheless, many people find this problem quite difficult. Much of the difficulty for people occurs at the sixth state, which is usually the key to the solution (shown as boldface type in Figure 12.17). This *return* trip must send across a missionary *and* a cannibal. There is no other way to avoid having the cannibals outnumber the missionaries on one side or the other. People usually pause for a long time before making this move and are especially likely to make an error at this point (Thomas 1974).

Since there is no other legal move available, why do people find this step in the problem so difficult? The reason is that it appears to lead away from the final goal state. People naturally try to maximize the number of people on the other side of the river after each trip. Thus they prefer to send two people across and just one back. The critical sixth trip is a kind of detour—the

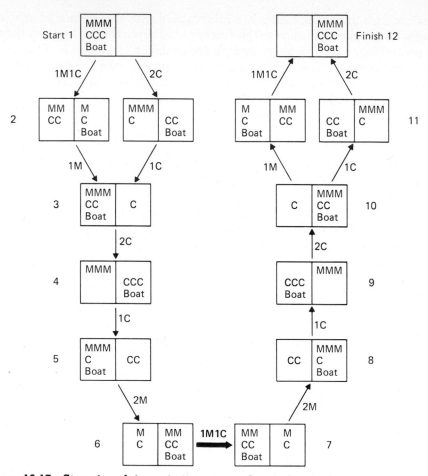

**Figure 12.17    Steps in solving missionaries and cannibals problem.**

difference between the current state and the goal state has to be temporarily increased in order to solve the problem.

The missionaries and cannibals problem is one in which people usually consider just one move at a time. There is little or no choice at each decision point once the illegal moves have been eliminated. As a result, people appear to use a difference reduction strategy, but without setting up subgoals (Jeffries, Polson, Razran, and Atwood 1977; Simon and Reed 1976). The performance of GPS on the problem differs in some ways from that of human problem solvers (Greeno 1974). For example, people run into trouble at state 6 because they are always comparing the current state directly with the final goal state. Since GPS solves the problem by generating subgoals and executing each in turn, it avoids this difficulty. However, the human strategy affords an advantage at state 11, where people immediately bring back both the rower and the cannibal to achieve the final goal. In contrast, GPS at this point is working on the subgoal of bringing back the one cannibal that was on the left side at state 10. As a result, at state 11 the program first considers sending only the one cannibal back to the other side. In this instance GPS has a tendency to be trapped by its rigid adherence to subgoals.

There are other, more fundamental limitations to GPS and similar programs as models of human problem solving. One is that GPS can only operate on well-defined problems. Without a clear description of the goal state, for example, the program cannot compute the difference between the goal state and the current state; as a result, GPS cannot apply means-ends analysis. More generally, GPS is unable to reformulate a problem representation in any way. A second severe limitation is that GPS learns nothing at all from its problem-solving experiences. Solving a problem does not help in solving the same problem again, far less in solving a different one. No matter how many problems it is given, GPS will remain a novice.

**Expert systems.**  As the name *General Problem Solver* implies, GPS uses general methods to solve problems. But as we saw in our discussion of expertise, experts appear to use solution methods that are specialized for particular categories of problems. Many problem-solving programs developed by researchers in artificial intelligence have, in fact, taken what is called an "expert systems" approach (Davis, Buchanan, and Shortliffe 1977; Feigenbaum, Buchanan, and Lederberg 1971). The programmer builds in a tremendous amount of specialized knowledge that the program can  use, consulting extensively with human experts in the process. Such programs can contribute to complex problem-solving tasks such as medical diagnosis and chemical analyses. Nonetheless, current expert systems are also severely limited in their ability to learn from experience, and for this reason they fall far short of human flexibility (for a review, see Duda and Shortliffe 1983).

**Machine learning.**  Some progress is now being made in developing computer programs that can learn from experience in problem-solving tasks. For example, Lenat (1979) incorporated a variety of heuristic strategies in a computer program called AM that searches for interesting concepts in elementary mathematics. He has a list of 250 heuristics for searching for interesting new concepts. Some of the heuristics are used to select problems that are likely to yield interesting concepts. For example, one heuristic is to explore more general concepts, like *number,* before more specific ones, like *even number.* Other heuristics are used to decide what to do once a concept has been selected for study, such as to examine extreme examples. A person might investigate the concept *set* and find that some sets have no members. Since such extreme examples of a concept are likely to be interesting, the person might create the new concept *empty set.*

Another heuristic is to find examples of a concept for which no examples are yet known. For instance, suppose you start with the concept *divisor of a number* but have no examples of the concept. You might begin by simply producing examples; e.g., the divisors of 6 are 1, 2, 3, and 6. Then you might decide to look at extreme examples, like numbers with small sets of divisors. This step might cause you to find examples of numbers with only two divisors, e.g., 2 (1, 2), 3 (1, 3), 5 (1, 5), 7 (1, 7), 11 (1, 11). You might then notice that for all such numbers one divisor is 1 and the other is the number itself. Since this result is an unexpected and therefore interesting regularity, you would store in memory a new concept that we call *prime number.* Some of these heuristics are similar to those discussed by Polya (1973).

A major limitation of the AM program is that it does not learn any *new* heuristics for investigating mathematics. In more recent work Lenat (1983) is developing a program called Eurisko that uses heuristics to modify its own set of heuristics. Eurisko has been used to generate the design for a novel and potentially useful type of computer chip. Nonetheless, the development of automated learning systems is still in its infancy. Human beings, despite their propensities to be trapped by set effects and functional fixedness, remain the most flexible and adaptive of all known intelligent systems.

## CREATIVE THINKING

A work of art, whether a painting or piece of music, appears creative if it is both good (i.e., emotionally moving or intellectually stimulating) and looks or sounds like nothing the observer or listener has ever seen before. Similarly, a scientific theory is viewed as creative if it makes use of some new assumption about the world to generate interesting predictions and explanations.

Where do good new ideas come from? Is it a matter of luck? Studies of creative individuals and acts of creation indicate that there is more to creativity than just chance. Some individuals appear more likely to come up with creative solutions than others.

### Talent

Talent must stand as the most obvious, least understood, and least studied factor in creativity. Clearly, some people are born with extraordinary abilities to draw lifelike pictures, remember musical compositions, solve mathematical problems, etc. Many outstanding figures in these areas were child prodigies who exhibited their talent at an early age before they had received much formal training. Furthermore, talent in one area does not guarantee ability in other areas. On the one hand, Leonardo Da Vinci coupled an extraordinary drawing ability with a variety of superior skills. But in stark contrast, some children are *idiot savants* who combine an extraordinary drawing, musical, or mnemonic ability with a profound retardation in language and reasoning. Unfortunately, there have been few detailed studies of idiot savants published, which is why Selfe's (1977) study of Nadia, an autistic child with extraordinary drawing ability, is so important.

Nadia was born in Nottingham, England, in 1967. From the first her development was slow. As an infant she was unresponsive and would not turn at her mother's approach. Her first words appeared at nine months; but at eighteen months, two-word utterances, which normally appear, did not develop, and she used the single-word utterances she had acquired less and less frequently. During this time she became increasingly isolated emotionally, and her family began to worry that her development was not proceeding normally.

Nadia entered a special school for severely subnormal children in 1972. She was physically large for her age, but she was slow and lethargic in her movements. Her typical behavior exhibited passivity and excessive slowness, and she was mute and inactive. She had an effective vocabulary of less than ten words. She could not dress herself without assistance.

When she was $3\frac{1}{2}$ years old, Nadia suddenly displayed an extraordinary drawing ability. Over the next three years she created many striking drawings. From the beginning her drawings were three-dimensional, lifelike, and quite beautiful. Nadia drew pictures of horses, with and without riders, of birds, of other animals, of trains, and of people. Her drawings were based on both pictures she had seen and solid objects, but her drawings were not copies. Rather, elements of what she had seen appeared in drawings done weeks later in new and original perspectives. Her drawings were not wooden portraits but contained scenes of vigorous action, sometimes containing strange, new creatures. For example, one of her animals looks part giraffe and part donkey. A comparison of Nadia's drawings with 24,000 "pictures of mommy" from a local newspaper contest made it clear how unique Nadia was. A further search of the psychological literature revealed no documented case of such exquisite drawing ability emerging at such an early age.

Nadia was left-handed and drew with a ballpoint pen, which she held firmly and comfortably. She rapidly executed strokes with the kind of command that suggests years of training. She could stop a line exactly where it met another even while drawing quite rapidly. She could change the direction of a line and draw lines at any angle toward or away from the body. She could draw a small but perfect circle in one movement and place a dot in the center.

Nadia drew intensively for varying intervals of time up to a minute and then usually sat back to survey the effect, moving her head perhaps to vary the viewing angle. This study usually gave her great pleasure, and after surveying intently what she had drawn, she often smiled, babbled, and shook her head and knees in glee. During her most productive period she drew four or five times a week.

Nadia entered a school for autistic children when she was seven, and in the next two years her sociability and language improved greatly. However, she virtually stopped drawing spontaneously, though she would produce a recognizable sketch of a classmate upon request.

Nadia's remarkable talent emphasizes that we still know very little about the sources of individual differences in creative potential. Let us now examine the general nature of the creative process in more detail.

### Creative Process

In an early analysis Wallas (1926) proposed that the creative process has four steps:

1. *Preparation*: Formulating the problem and making preliminary attempts to solve it.
2. *Incubation*: Leaving the problem to work on other things.
3. *Illumination*: Achieving insight into the solution.
4. *Verification*: Making sure that the solution really works.

Certainly, not every example of creative problem solving shows all these separate phases, and Wallas's framework has been criticized for this reason and others (Perkins 1981). However, one famous example that apparently illustrates the four phases is an introspective report by the French mathematician Henri Poincaré (1913). He was attempting to develop a theory of Fuchsian functions (what these are is not important to understanding how Poincaré discovered them). He reports that he began by working on the problem almost constantly for fifteen days, until one sleepless night when "ideas rose in crowds; I felt them collide until pairs interlocked, so to speak, making a stable combination." Poincaré continues (1913, pp. 387–388):

> I wanted to represent these functions by the quotient of two series; this idea was perfectly conscious and deliberate; the analogy with elliptic functions guided me. I asked myself what properties these series must have if they existed, and succeeded without difficulty in forming the series I have called theta-Fuchsian.

> Just at this time I left Caen, where I was living, to go on a geologic excursion under the auspices of the school of mines. The changes of travel made me forget my mathematical work. Having reached Coutances, we entered an omnibus to go

some place or other. At the moment when I put my foot on the step the idea came to me, without anything in my former thoughts seeming to have paved the way for it, that the transformations I had used to define the Fuchsian functions were identical to those of non-Euclidean geometry. I did not verify the idea; I should not have had time, as, upon taking my seat in the omnibus, I went on with a conversation already commenced, but I felt a perfect certainty. On my return to Caen, for conscience's sake, I verified the result at my leisure.

Here we see that the preparatory period for Poincaré consisted of fifteen days of intense work, culminating in some new ideas that arose one restless night and formed a "stable combination." Poincaré then wished to define the class of functions he had discovered more clearly. In doing so, he developed an analogy with another class of functions. Then followed a period of incubation during his travel, leading to his experience of illumination. Later he verified his results.

**Preparation.**     Where did Poincaré's "stable combinations" come from? What kind of mental activity was occurring during those fifteen days of intensive preparation? This period seemed to involve the generation of many combinations of ideas and then the discarding of some and the selection of some to pursue further. Actually, to say that the preparation period for Poincaré lasted fifteen days is a bit misleading. Although this intensive two-week period was important, Poincaré's preparation really consisted of his entire mathematical education up to that point. Without his vast stock of acquired mathematical knowledge, he could not have made his discovery. For example, this knowledge was necessary to develop the analogy with elliptic functions, which played an important role in the development of Poincaré's ideas about Fuchsian functions. In general, without thorough training and an intense initial period of work on a problem, it is unlikely that an incubation period will be fruitful. Successful incubation requires an intense dedication to finding a solution, a motivation to acquire as much relevant knowledge as possible, and a willingness to return to the problem over periods of perhaps years.

In fact, if we look at other areas of discovery, we find that the period of preparation plays an even more fundamental role: It influences the selection of the problem in the first place. There is a saying in science, "Chance favors the prepared mind." What this saying means is that no discoveries are made simply by accident. For example, a well-known story of an "accidental" discovery is Alexander Fleming's discovery of penicillin, when he noticed that a culture of staphlylococcus did not grow near a contaminant that had literally dropped out of the air onto the culture dish. However, such contamination was routine in every laboratory in the world. Only Fleming realized its significance and did not simply wash the contaminant away. The large body of knowledge provided by an intense period of preparation makes it more likely that creative individuals will recognize an important problem when they see it.

The importance of preparation to problem selection becomes even more significant when we turn from science to art and music. The composer Arnold Schönberg turned away students who had come to learn his twelve-tone system, saying that they could not learn the new music until they had mastered the old. Schönberg's point was that first people must thoroughly master the art of their times, so creating a work in the contemporary style is no longer a novel and creative act for them personally. Only then are they in a position to take the next step forward and create something that no one else has done before.

**Incubation.**    Perhaps the most fascinating aspect of the creative process is the incubation phenomenon. Why should an interruption of problem solving help one to reach a solution? There are several possible explanations (Posner 1973):

1. Interruption permits one to *recover from fatigue*. Problem solvers may simply tire of working on the problem and will work harder again after a rest. The few experimental demonstrations of improved performance on a problem-solving task after a break (Fulgosi and Guilford 1968; Murray and Denny 1969; Silveira 1971) can largely be explained on this basis alone.

2. Interruption allows one to *forget inappropriate approaches*. Over time, problem solvers may forget what they were doing when they last worked on the problem. If what they were doing was exploring a dead end, an interruption may make it more likely that they will take a more fruitful approach when they tackle the problem again. This explanation is supported by evidence that the effect of functional fixedness can be diminished by increasing the delay between the initial use of an object and presentation of the new problem (Adamson and Taylor 1954).

3. Interruption may promote *conscious problem solving*. Problem solvers may actually work on the problem from time to time during the break. Many people commonly find themselves thinking about an important problem in the middle of doing something else. Problem solvers may often forget about having returned to the problem, so later they are unaware of having worked on the problem during the interlude.

4. Interruption permits one to *reorganize*. We saw in Chapters 8 and 9 that after a retention interval when a person attempts to recall, various facts that were learned at different times about a common topic are recalled together. This grouping leads to a novel organization in memory. Such novel organizations may make fresh approaches to a problem possible.

**Illumination.**  The essence of creative thought is the synthesis of new concepts. In the moment of illumination there is a *juxtaposition of ideas,* ideas that until then were only thought of separately are brought together. Creative thought is therefore closely tied to reasoning by analogy.

As we saw, Poincaré felt he was aware of his own unconscious processes at work during the sleepless night that led to his initial progress. In another famous incident the chemist Kekulé describes the origin of his idea of the benzene ring (from Koestler 1964, p. 118):

> I turned my chair to the fire and dozed . . . Again the atoms were gamboling before my eyes . . . My mental eye . . . could now distinguish larger structures, of manifold conformation; long rows, sometimes more closely fitted together; all twinning and twisting in snakelike motion. But look! . . . One of the snakes had seized hold of its own tail, and the form whirled mockingly before my eyes. As if by a flash of lightning I awoke.

Kekulé realized that the structure of certain organic compounds is like that of the snake biting its own tail—a closed chain or ring. This case provides a striking example of a visual analogy. Other statements by creative individuals also indicate that the period preceding illumination is often occupied by sleep or dreaming.

Conceptual synthesis is apparent in the development of other scientific theories, as reconstructed in historical case studies. Gruber's (1974) analysis of the origin of Charles Darwin's theory of natural selection illustrates how multiple analogies can contribute to a new conceptual structure. Darwin was aware of *artificial* selection—the procedures by which breeders mold varieties of animals and plants by selecting specimens with desirable traits for reproductive use. He therefore considered the hypothesis that species are molded by some type of *natural* selection analogous to artificial selection. However, this analogy was clearly imperfect. For one thing, the criterion for selection had to be different: Forms were not adapted to serve human purposes but to fit natural environments. For another, and most critically, it was not clear what constituted the *agent* of natural selection, since it obviously was not human breeders.

Darwin used a very different analogy to solve this central problem. He learned of Malthus's theory of population, according to which human populations will inevitably outstrip their food supply, because human reproduction will outstrip agricultural production. Darwin generalized this idea beyond just human populations to an incessant "struggle for existence" everywhere in nature. As a result of this struggle, only the fittest would survive and reproduce. In this way Darwin arrived at a causal mechanism that could drive natural selection. Thus the overall theory was a conceptual synthesis based on two previously unrelated analogies.

Imagination—i.e., the ability to take things from different domains and put them together—is a fundamental human ability. As a simple example, Figure 12.18 presents a child's solution to the problem of improving the design of the human body. The child who drew this picture thought that an aerial could be added to detect attackers and that springs would make useful legs (at least for a person who wants to be a good goalie in soccer). The recommendations of three noses to improve smell and three eyes to see with seem to be based on a time-honored heuristic: "More is better." The resulting design is an amalgam of various ideas intended to upgrade certain functions of the human body.

Real inventions sometimes have a similar origin. For example, at one time television aerials came in pieces and had to be assembled on the rooftop—not an easy job, especially in bad weather. More recently, the design was improved by constructing aerials that fold up like umbrellas, so they can simply be opened up on the roof, with minimal assembly. Just as in the child's drawing, the improved design depended on the import of an idea from a different problem domain.

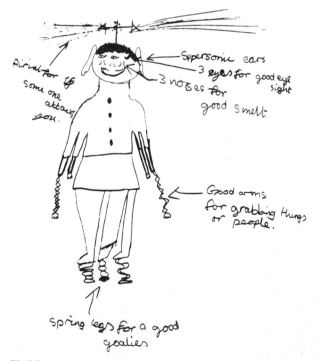

**Figure 12.18   Child's solution to problem of designing some improvements for human body. (From de Bono 1972.)**

Analogies may be verbal as well as visual. Metaphors, for example, have the creative element of pointing out a hidden analogy. Geoffrey Leech (1974, p. 44) gives the example of the Anglo-Saxon expression *mere-hengest* ("sea-steed"), which is used in a poem as a metaphor for *ship*. The meanings of *ship* and *steed* are connected by their shared properties. Both ships and horses carry men from one place to another, with an up-and-down movement. In the context of the heroic poem both are associated with journeys for adventure and warfare. When the meanings of the two words are combined in a metaphor, the similarities are emphasized, while the obvious dissimilarities (horses are animate, ships are not; horses move on land, ships on the sea) are pushed into the background. The result is a new concept that focuses on the analogy between ships and horses.

Thus Koestler (1964) argues that the diverse forms of creativity that can be found in literature, art, and science are basically similar. All have the fundamental property of synthesizing novel combinations of ideas. According to Koestler, even a good joke has this property of juxtaposing ideas, as well as the critical element of surprise. Here is a "Freudian joke" paraphrased from Koestler (1964, pp. 32–33):

Two women meet while shopping at a supermarket in the Bronx.
One looks cheerful, the other depressed. The cheerful one inquires:
"What's eating you?"
"Nothing's eating me."
"Death in the family?"
"No, God forbid!"
"Worried about money?"
"No...nothing like that."
"Trouble with the kids?"
"Well, if you must know, it's my little Jimmy."
"What's wrong with him then?"
"Nothing is wrong. His teacher said he must see a psychiatrist."
Pause. "Well, well, what's wrong with seeing a psychiatrist?"
"Nothing's wrong. The psychiatrist said he's got an Oedipus complex."
Pause. "Oedipus-Schmoedipus! I wouldn't worry so long as he's a good boy and loves his mama."

If you missed the punch line, your Freudian psychology is rusty—an Oedipus complex is the sexual desire of a boy for his mother. The humor is generated by the conflict between two notions of what "loves his mama" means: the duty of a child to treat his mother with affection, and the Freudian view that the son-mother relationship can involve frustrated sexual attraction. One is good, the other is bad; and the humor is increased by the fact that the speaker is obviously unaware of the contradiction in what she is saying.

**Verification.**   One can become so bedazzled by the drama of the moment of illumination that the importance of verification to the creative process may be overlooked. Verification is important because there may be false moments of illumination whose flaws appear only when a systematic attempt at verification is made. In addition, often the only way a person who has attained a moment of illumination can share it with others is by taking them through the process of verification.

In the history of science we find, paradoxically, that some of the most original scientific discoveries occur as ideas to several different people at different places and times. But only when one of those individuals has the ability, persistence, and courage to verify the idea does it become accepted by the entire scientific community. For example, the theory of evolution was worked out independently by Charles Darwin and Alfred Wallace, but Darwin spent twenty years gathering data that supported the theory before he published it. As another example, you might think that the importance of such a useful substance as penicillin would be obvious. However, years before Fleming's fateful ruined culture, penicillin had been discovered, presented in a scientific paper, given no interest, and completely forgotten. Fleming's own original report was also ignored, but Fleming had the confidence in his own insight to continue to work with penicillin until its importance was verified.

Painters, musicians, and other artists have even more difficulty than scientists in sharing their insights with others. They must validate their visions by creating original works that will have sufficient dramatic appeal to attract attention.

### Problem Solving and the Creative Process

The steps involved in the creative process can be related to the general problem-solving steps we discussed earlier (see Figure 12.1). The preparation step in creative thinking is simply an extended case of forming an initial problem representation. Incubation, as we saw, is poorly understood; however, it can be viewed as a means of overcoming difficulties in reformulating a problem (i.e., getting stuck in the flowchart of Figure 12.1). For example, if incubation serves to allow inappropriate approaches to be forgotten, thus reducing initial difficulties due to set and functional fixedness, the problem solver may then achieve a new reformulation. Illumination may simply correspond to the result of achieving such a reformulation. Finally, verification appears to correspond to the problem-solving steps of planning a concrete solution and then executing and testing it. An act is recognized as creative when it is a new solution to an old problem and when it is a solution to a problem that has never been solved before.

## SUMMARY

Our discussion in this chapter has dealt with human performance in complex problem-solving tasks, ranging from *well-defined* puzzle problems (e.g., the Tower of Hanoi) to such *ill-defined,* creative problems as invention and scientific discovery. Although these tasks seem very different, certain global similarities in the problem-solving process can be identified. Problem solving involves the steps of forming an initial *problem representation,* trying to *plan* a potential solution, *reformulating* the problem if necessary, and *executing* and testing the solution plan. The planning step usually requires heuristics such as means-ends analysis. Problem reformulation, which is often critical in solving ill-defined, creative problems, often involves noticing and applying an analogy. The skill of experts on many types of problems, including complex board games and physics, can be largely attributed to knowledge and perceptual abilities specifically related to the expert's task domain. In some cases, however, problem-solving experience can have deleterious effects, as evidenced by the phenomena of *functional fixedness* and *set.*

Some useful tools for studying problem solving and creative thinking are *protocol analysis* (theorizing from verbal reports) and computer simulation. The *GPS* is a simulation model based on means-ends analysis. Recent work in artificial intelligence has been directed toward the development of *expert systems* based on specialized, prestored knowledge. Some work is being done on the development of computer programs that can learn in a problem-solving environment. Experimental techniques have also been developed for studying complex problem solving by nonhuman primates, especially chimpanzees.

Creative thinking can be viewed as a type of problem solving in which reformulation based on conceptual synthesis is often critical. A period of *incubation* in which the problem is set aside is often important in achieving a successful reformulation. Conceptual synthesis is exhibited in such diverse phenomena as humor, literature, invention, and generation of scientific theories.

## RECOMMENDED READINGS

There are many good sources for further reading about problem solving. Three important works in the Gestalt tradition are Kohler's *Mentality of Apes* (1925), Wertheimer's *Productive Thinking* (1945), and Duncker's monograph *On Problem-Solving* (1945). An important book in the information-processing tradition is *Human Problem Solving* (1972) by Newell and Simon. This book remains influential, but it is also extremely long (over nine hundred pages) and difficult to read. *Cognitive Skills and Their Acquisition* (1981), edited by Anderson, contains a number of papers on learning and problem solving. A good introduction to artificial-intelligence models of problem solving is provided in textbooks by Winston (1984) and Rich (1983). The collection of papers in *Machine Learning* (1983), edited by Michalski, Carbonell, and Mitchell, gives a state-of-the-art treatment of computer programs that learn.

There are a number of good how-to books on problem solving. Two of the best are Polya's *How to Solve It* (1957) and Wickelgren's *How to Solve Problems* (1974). *Conceptual Blockbusting* (1974) by Adams is easy and fun. Koestler provides an interesting discussion of creativity in *The Act of Creation* (1964). This book is very long, and the first part (Book One) is the best. *The Mind's Best Work* (1981) by Perkins is an engaging discussion of the creative process.

### Solutions to Cryptarithmetic Problems

| S END | 9,567 | DONALD | 526,485 | CROSS | 96,233 |
|---|---|---|---|---|---|
| +MORE | +1,085 | +GERALD | +197,485 | +ROADS | +62,513 |
| MONEY | 10,652 | ROBERT | 723,970 | DANGER | 158,746 |

# CHAPTER **THIRTEEN**

# Language and Hemispheric Specialization

## INTRODUCTION

In the previous chapter we discussed human creativity. In the remaining chapters we will examine a major vehicle for human creativity—language. Humans are unique in their ability to learn and understand language, because human brains alone have evolved to make it possible. In this chapter we will examine the neurological underpinnings of language in some detail.

The human cerebral cortex, as was described in Chapter 2, is divided into a left and a right hemisphere. If research on the functioning of the cerebral hemispheres were restricted solely to primates and other animals related to human beings, the conclusion would be that the two hemispheres duplicate each other in both structure and function, in the way that our two eyes, two lungs, and two kidneys do. If only one hemisphere in a cat or monkey is damaged, the effect of the damage on the animal's overall cognitive ability is analogous to the effect that the loss of a single eye would have on its perceptual ability. For example, if a cat lost its right eye, its ability to see something on the right of it would, of course, be restricted; conversely, if it lost its left eye, its ability to see something on the left would be restricted. Tasks such as depth perception, which depend on two eyes, would be equally affected by the loss of either eye.

Similarly, if only one hemisphere of the brain of a nonhuman primate is damaged, the ability to discriminate two shapes, to run a maze, or to avoid shock is influenced in the same way as by an equal amount of damage in the same location in the opposite hemisphere. Neither previously learned abilities nor the acquisition of new abilities is selectively impaired by damage to a single hemisphere (Doty and Overman 1977; Hamilton 1977).

When we turn our attention to human beings, a radically different picture emerges. The left hemisphere has developed special mechanisms for producing and comprehending language. So language and hemispheric specialization are closely linked. In order for language to develop to the point that it has, the left hemisphere had to develop specialized functions. But why was the specialization of the hemisphere necessary? No one knows for sure. But as more is learned about the nature of the specialization, some hypotheses have emerged. We will discuss one here.

## Origin of Lateralization

A common proposal (Bever 1975; Gazzaniga 1977; Lenneberg 1967; Levy 1977; Pribram 1977) is that the factor that led to the specialization of the hemispheres was the development of spoken language. To a large extent, the act of speaking is the limiting factor, or bottleneck, in the language communication process. In particular, people can understand speech faster than they can speak it. Consequently, how fast people can speak determines the rate at which information is transmitted in a conversation. In turn, the rate at which people can speak depends on the number of different sounds they can make and the rate at which they can make them. The timing required for producing the sounds used in speech pushes the nervous system to its limit. Recall that a neuron takes about a millisecond to transmit an impulse. Speech requires successive motor acts that are only a few milliseconds apart. If the control of speech were spread across two hemispheres, so that signals had to travel between them to coordinate their commands, the rate at which a person could speak would be significantly slowed. (In fact, such slowed commands may be the cause of congenital stuttering, as "echo" commands from the right hemisphere produce the stutter.)

Interestingly, certain songbirds, including canaries, also have specialized hemispheres. The songs of these birds are under the control of the left hemisphere (Nottebohm 1977), just as speech is in human beings. Of course, birds are very different from people. However, these findings for birds make more salient the advantage to having the production of a complex vocal response lateralized. Hence the original cause of left-hemisphere specialization may have been pressure to increase the rate of speech. In that case the oldest area with a lateralized function would be Broca's area.

So that spoken language would be possible, a special procedure for perceiving speech also developed. Because this procedure required detailed information about how speech was produced in order to perceive it (as we will see later), it became installed in another lateralized area of the brain near the speech-production center. As the left hemisphere came to control language functions, it left the right hemisphere free to control nonlinguistic functions. Hence the right hemisphere came to control responses to visual inputs, even though the left hemisphere retains the capacity to process visuospatial information. (Recall the asymmetry of the neglect syndrome discussed in Chapter 2.)

### Overview of Language Processing

Figure 13.1 is a flowchart of the process by which language is produced and comprehended. Speech production and perception involve special mechanisms that have evolved to make speech possible. An utterance to be produced begins as a proposition constructed from concepts in memory (see Chapters 5 and 8). The syntactic translation procedure translates that proposition into a *syntactic representation,* which specifies a temporal sequence of semantic categories and relations. This string is compared with memory by the comparison mechanism, which activates the words associated with the categories and relations, thus producing a word string recognizable as a *sentence.* The sentence, in turn, is translated into a sequence of motor commands that produce it as speech.

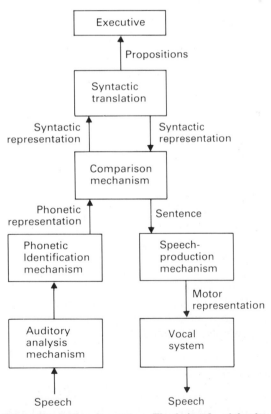

**Figure 13.1    Outline of speech processing. The left side of the figure represents processes of speech perception, and the right side represents processes of speech production.**

The speech-perception mechanism of a listener detects speech sounds in the auditory input. Strings of these sounds are compared with memory and recognized as words. As each word is recognized, its semantic category or relation is automatically activated (as described in Chapters 1 and 2). Notice from Figure 13.1 that the speech-perception process is a top-down process under control of the executive. Finally, the syntactic translation procedure attempts to translate the syntactic representation into a proposition.

As shown in Figure 13.1, the syntactic translation procedure is directly controlled by the executive. In fact, the syntactic translation procedure may be considered a part of the executive, and as with other executive procedures, the representation it operates on is in awareness. The syntactic procedure is also closely integrated with the speech-production and speech-perception mechanisms. In most individuals these three procedures are lateralized in specific portions of the left hemisphere. Their general locations are shown later in Chapter 15 (Figure 15.5).

## PERCEPTION OF SPEECH

The very first step in understanding spoken language is to identify the words being spoken. You probably learned as far back as elementary school that a word is made up of *syllables* and that syllables are made up of *consonants* and *vowels*. For example, the word *lady* contains the syllables /la/ and /dy/, which in turn contain the consonants /l/ and /d/ and the vowels /a/ and /e/. These vowels and consonants of English (or any other language) are called *phonemes*. (Slightly more technically, a phoneme is the smallest part of the speech input that makes a difference in a word's meaning.)

There is an obvious, possible bottom-up model of speech perception. First, features corresponding to phonemes would be detected in the speech signal. These phonemes would then be combined into syllables, the syllables into words, etc. Finally, the word meanings would be retrieved from memory. As it turns out, this simple model of speech perception is about as wrong as it could be. We will review some of the relevant evidence here, which includes some of the most astonishing perceptual phenomena that have ever been discovered. A good deal of this evidence, as you will see, suggests that top-down processes play important roles in speech perception.

### A Look at the Speech Input

We think you will agree with us that when you listen to someone speak, most of the words sound distinct. That is, each word is perceived as having a definite beginning and ending. The words do not blend into one another. However, when the sound input is examined, it often does not contain discrete patterns corresponding to the individual words of a sentence. For instance, Figure 13.2 is a speech spectrogram of the sentence *The steward dismissed the girl.* The vertical axis represents frequency (roughly, the pitch of the sound pattern), and the horizontal axis represents time. The darkness of a point on the spectrogram represents the amplitude of that frequency at that point in time (roughly, its loudness).

The easiest way to read a spectrogram is as a series of columns. By examining which parts of a column are dark and which are light, we can determine which frequencies were heard and which frequencies were not at a given moment in time.

As you can see from the spectrogram, there are some relatively white areas. The white areas represent moments of relative silence, and you therefore might imagine that they correspond to breaks between words. However, if you examine the bracketing at the bottom of the figure, you will see that they do not. This bracketing shows approximately where one word ends and another begins. Notice that the word *the* blends into the word *steward* in the higher-frequency ranges. There is no break between the words at all. The first blank area occurs within the word *steward.* Similarly, *steward* blends into *dismissed,* which itself contains two white areas, and the second *the* blends into *girl* in the low-frequency ranges. Hence moments of relative silence are as likely to occur within words as between them. The breaks and pauses we hear

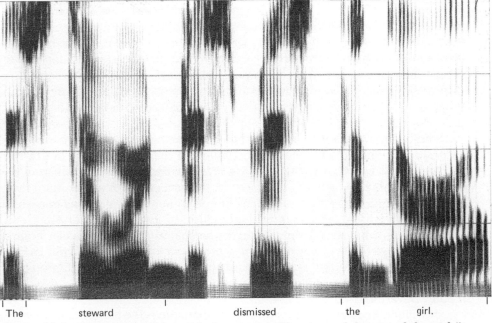

The          steward                    dismissed          the          girl.

**Figure 13.2  Spectrogram of sound of sentence "The steward dismissed the girl."**

when we listen to speech do not directly correspond to changes in the physical signal at all. In less than a tenth of a second of processing, that continuous input is transformed into the discrete intelligible words that are perceived.

## Consonant and Syllable Perception: Segmentation of the Speech Signal

Even though the speech input is essentially continuous, as shown in Figure 13.2, it is split up into discrete components, occurring in successive epochs of time. Each of these components is perceived as a syllable. Many syllables begin with a consonant and end with a vowel sound (e.g., /be/, /ta/, /du/). You might therefore expect that if we examined a pattern of sound waves that we perceive as an entire syllable, we would find that the beginning of the speech input contained the sound of the consonant, while the end contained the vowel.

In Haskins Laboratory, Al Liberman and his colleagues have been able to test this obvious hypothesis by generating brief segments of synthetic speech. Without going into details of how synthetic speech is generated, let us simply say that it allows us to produce and listen to just the very beginning of a syllable. However, the result does not sound like a speech sound at all but like a whistle (Liberman, Cooper, Shankweiler, and Studdert-Kennedy 1967). Furthermore, when the beginnings of different syllables containing the *same* consonant are played, they sound different from each other. For example, the beginning of the tape for /di/ sounds like a rising whistle, while the beginning of the tape for /du/ sounds like a falling whistle (Lieberman *et al.* 1967). Thus two different sound patterns may be perceived as the same consonant, depending on the following vowel. Also, the same sound pattern may be perceived as different consonants when the vowel context is changed. For example, the identical initial sound will produce /pi/ when paired with /i/ and /ka/ when paired with /a/ (Schatz 1954).

These findings clearly demonstrate that our perception of a consonant sound is not determined by just the beginning of the syllable input but by the entire input, from its beginning to its end. When we widen our level of analysis from the syllable to the word, we find that the perception of a consonant may be entirely determined by what comes before it. For example, consider word pairs like *writer* and *rider* or *latter* and *ladder*. In some dialects of American English the only physical difference in the sound patterns of these word pairs is the length of the first vowel. The vowel will be longer in *rider* and *ladder* than in *writer* and *latter*. In these cases the same sound pattern can be perceived as either a /d/ or a /t/, depending on the length of the preceding vowel (Fodor, Bever, and Garrett 1974, p. 292).

Still more striking is the fact that silence produces the perception of a consonant in the proper context. Thus one can convert a recording of the word *slit* into *split* by inserting a pause of 75 milliseconds between the /s/ and /l/ (Liberman, Harris, Eimas, Lisker, and Bastian 1961). The analogous operation converts *sore* to *store* (Bastian, Eimas, and Liberman 1961) and *say* to either *stay* or *spay*, depending on the precise form of the vocalic portion of the input (Dorman, Raphael, and Liberman 1979; Liberman 1982). In these contexts the consonant is heard in the segment immediately following the silence.

A patch of silence can also produce the perception of a consonant in the segment that comes immediately before it. Figure 13.3 shows the spectrogram of the phrase *gray ship*. The perception of this segment depends on both the length of the silent segment and the length of the segment labeled "fricative noise." It is heard as *gray ship* as long as the silence is less than 10 milliseconds long. If the silence is expanded to 40 milliseconds and the fricative noise section is 62 milliseconds long, then *gray chip* is heard. Hence as in the previous examples, the perception of the sound segment immediately following the silence is altered. But if the silence is 40 milliseconds when the fricative noise segment is 142 milliseconds long, then *great ship* is heard. Thus the perception of the sound segment immediately before the silence can also be altered (Repp, Liberman, Eccardt, and Pesetsky 1978).

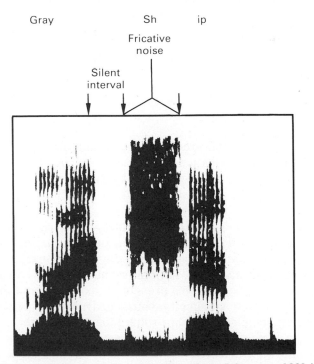

**Figure 13.3   Spectrogram of words *gray ship*. (From Liberman 1981.)**

The reason for this peculiar situation, in which speech doesn't sound at all like the sounds that make it up, involves the sluggishness of our articulatory mechanism (i.e., our vocal tract and mouth). When you attempt to make a single speech sound, you must adjust your lips, teeth, tongue, vocal cords, and lungs in unison. When you try to speak, the signals for all the successive, distinct sounds that must be made if you are to speak at a reasonable rate come too fast for the vocal apparatus to react separately to each one. Instead, the movements for the various sounds become jumbled up and compromised. As a result, the actual speech produced sounds different from the way it would if each speech sound were separately articulated.

To understand spoken language, we need a special mechanism that interprets segments of speech and yields a representation of the sequence of speech sounds that the speaker was trying to produce. For example, when you produce a /p/ or /t/, you momentarily close your vocal tract and stop the flow of air from your lungs. (For this reason /p/ and /t/ are called *stop consonants*.) This stoppage produces a moment of silence in the speech signal. Hence a moment of silence produces the perception of a /p/, /t/, or some other stop consonant when it is part of a speech segment (Liberman 1982). It is the representation produced by the phonetic identification mechanism that is heard.

The phonetic identification mechanism must also deal with variations between speakers. For example, the faster you speak, the briefer is the silence signaling a stop consonant. Accordingly, the phoneme identification mechanism must calculate the speaking rate to determine whether a stop consonant has been produced (Miller 1981; Miller and Grosjean 1981).

### Speech Perception and the Brain

Phonetic identification is the product of evolution. Special cortical mechanisms make phonetic identification possible. One can demonstrate the special processing speech inputs receive through the dichotic presentation of artificial sounds that can be interpreted as either speech or nonspeech (Best, Morrongiello, and Robson 1981).

For example, Rand (1974) split the syllable /ga/ into two components. One piece, the *base*, consisted of most of the segment, including its vowel. The other part was the portion of the very beginning that determines whether the entire segment is heard as /ga/ or /da/. This segment sounds like a chirp in isolation. When the base segment was presented to one ear and the initial segment to the other, the listener simultaneously heard /ga/ in the base ear and a chirp in the other (see also Liberman 1982; Liberman, Isenberg, and Rakerd 1981). Hence the same sound input was processed by one portion of the brain as a natural sound and combined with the base by another portion of the brain and processed as a speech sound. (See Figure 13.1.)

**Kimura effect.**    Additional evidence that speech is processed by a lateralized mechanism in the brain comes from other dichotic-listening tasks, which partially isolate each hemisphere's processing of natural-speech sounds. Recall that in a dichotic-listening task a person wears headphones and different sounds are presented simultaneously to each ear. This task is very different from normal listening, since in normal listening the same sound is heard with both ears and reaches both hemispheres of the brain at almost the same time. The dichotic-listening experiment sets up an unnatural situation in which there is competition between the two sounds that are heard with different ears. To understand how this competition arises, we must consider the anatomy of the auditory system.

Each ear is connected to both hemispheres by a direct neural pathway. Although the connection to the contralateral (opposite-side) hemisphere is stronger, the connection to the ipsilateral (same-side) hemisphere is strong enough so that if a sound is simply directed to a single ear, the input will reach both hemispheres. As a result, monaural presentation (one input to one ear) generally fails to produce any significant differences between ears, presumably because both hemispheres receive roughly the same information (Kimura 1961, 1967; but also see Bakker 1970).

When two sounds are presented dichotically, researchers believe that stimulation of both contralateral pathways inhibits the ipsilateral information reaching the hemispheres. In other words, if the left hemisphere receives different inputs from the left ear (along the ipsilateral pathway) and from the right ear (along the contralateral pathway), the left hemisphere processes only the input from the right ear. The information from the left ear will reach the left hemisphere more slowly, after first reaching the right hemisphere by the contralateral pathway and then crossing the corpus callosum.

In a typical experiment one ear will be presented with a syllable (e.g., /da/) while simultaneously the other ear will be presented with a different syllable (e.g., /ba/). The subject is then asked to report what he or she heard. Sometimes, instead of being followed by a simple report procedure, the dichotic presentation is followed by four different test syllables that were presented in succession. The test set contains both syllables that were presented dichotically. The person participating must state which of the syllables had been presented dichotically. Whichever procedure is used, the syllable presented to the right ear is more likely to be recognized or reported than is the syllable presented to the left ear. In other words, the syllable presented to the left ear appears to have been suppressed.

The suppression of the left-ear (right-hemisphere) syllable has been called the *Kimura effect* after its discoverer, Doreen Kimura (Kimura 1961). This effect is consistent with other results showing a right-ear advantage for language (Bohannon and Baker-Ward 1981). However, as Berlin (1977) points out, the right-ear advantage is small, and it can vary considerably across individuals or even within an individual from one test session to the next. So keep in mind that these studies reveal subtle differences, not drastic ones, and that in a healthy brain every input reaches both hemispheres rapidly.

Interestingly, when Kimura (1974) presented listeners with brief excerpts of classical melodies dichotically, the results were reversed. The listeners recognized the left-ear (right-hemisphere) melody more frequently. Evidence obtained using dichotic-listening studies is in close accord with studies of brain-damaged patients. Aphasic patients are likely to retain any prior musical abilities; while Amytal injections (as discussed later) in the right hemisphere reliably suppress melodic production (Gardner 1976, p. 344). The collective impact of these different kinds of studies is to reinforce the conclusion that the left hemisphere is the language hemisphere, whereas the right hemisphere space is more important for other kinds of perceptual processing (in this case, music).

Actually, the results of studies on the perception of music are quite complex. The advantage of one ear over the other depends on the precise nature of the task (Efron, Bogen, and Yund 1977; Gordon 1970, 1974; Robinson and Solomon 1974) and on the musical experience of the listener (Bever and Chiarello 1974; Gordon 1980). The kind of judgment required determines which hemisphere controls the input's processing.

**Aphasia.**    The oldest and clearest evidence of the specialization of the left hemisphere is the distribution of the locations of injuries that cause a deficit in the production and comprehension of language, i.e., *aphasia*. Over 98 percent of all aphasias suffered by right-handed human beings result from injuries to the left hemisphere (Bogen and Bogen 1976; Russell and Espir 1961); for ambidextrous and left-handed individuals the percentage is somewhat less (Gloning 1977; Russell and Espir 1961).

Lesions in different areas of the cortex damage different mechanisms, thus causing different deficits. For example, once in a while a highly localized lesion destroys the path of the auditory input to Broca's area. In cases of pure *word deafness* the person can still hear sound but apparently can no longer construct phonetic representations. As a result, such people can't identify words or understand what is being said. They can still speak and read and write, and they are functionally similar to the deaf, except for the fact that they can still hear (Geschwind 1965).

### Top-down Processing of Speech

After the speech input is segmented into the units that will eventually be heard as syllables, these *protosyllables* must be combined into words. Matching a string of protosyllables to a set of syllabic representations of words is more like reading handwriting than typescript, because the same protosyllable can be perceived as several different syllables, depending on the context it appears in. To see how this perception occurs with writing, examine Figure 13.4(a). What letter is shown, if any? As you can see from Figures 13.4(b)–13.4(e), it may be an *e, i, l,* or part of a meaningless pattern, depending on its context.

Several clever experiments have demonstrated the effect of context on the perception of syllables. Some studies have been based on the observation that when people listen to continuous meaningful speech, they generally do not notice minor mispronunciations (Cole 1973). When people are asked to shadow (i.e., repeat back) speech, they typically correct mispronunciations. For example, if the input sentence is *We had a lot of compsiny over the weekend,* the subject will usually repeat the sound *compsiny* as *company* (Marslen Wilson 1975). This correction occurs only when the mispronounced word fits into the sentence context in a meaningful way. You may think that subjects who are shadowing passages might correct mispronounced words by deliberate choice. However, people actually produce the corrected word just as quickly as they are able to repeat words that are not mispronounced (Marslen-Wilson and Welsh 1978). This result suggests that people often do not even perceive the mispronunciation.

Similarly, Ganong (1980) found that the same sound was heard as /d/ when part of /dash/ but as /t/ when part of /task/. The syllables /tash/ and /dask/ are possible words that don't happen to exist in English. This result thus shows that the production of /t/ and /d/ is not solely the result of their physical context but depends on the lexical representation they match in memory.

**Phonemic restoration effect.**    Another demonstration of how context influences perception of less-than-perfect speech is the *phonemic restoration effect.* This effect was first demonstrated by Richard Warren in 1970 and has since been investigated in detail by him and his colleagues (Obusek and Warren 1973; Warren and Obusek 1971; Warren and Warren 1970).

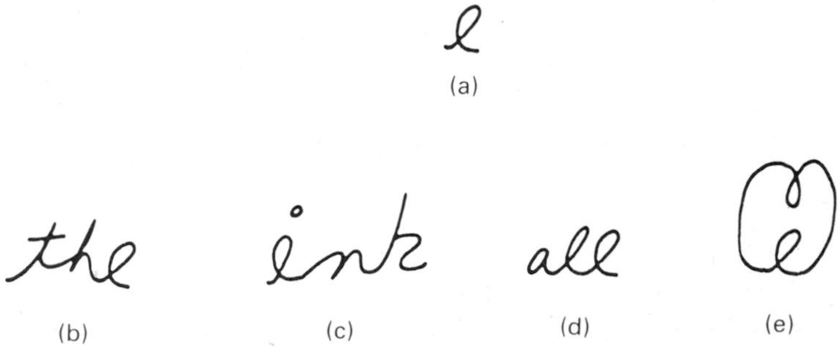

(a)

(b)                    (c)                    (d)                    (e)

Figure 13.4    Alternative interpretations of a line segment: (a) An *l* in isolation; (b) an *e* in *the;* (c) an *i* in *ink;* (d) an *l* in *all;* (e) part of a meaningless pattern.

In one experiment Warren presented twenty people with a recording of the sentence *The state governors met with their respective legi*latures convening in the capital city.* The asterisk indicates a 0.12-second portion of the recorded speech that had been carefully removed and replaced with the sound of a cough. The subjects were asked if there were any sounds missing from the recording. Nineteen of the twenty subjects said there was no missing sound, and the other subject identified the wrong sound as missing. In fact, Warren himself heard the missing sound. When a larger portion of the word was obliterated and replaced by a tone or a buzz rather than a cough, the word was still perceived as intact. However, the missing portion was noticed if it was replaced simply with silence. So though silence can sometimes be perceived as a speech sound, as discussed earlier, that effect occurs only in a very limited set of contexts.

However, there appears to be a great deal of variety in the consonants the same sound pattern may be perceived as, given sufficient context. Warren and Warren (1970) demonstrated this result by presenting different people with one of the following four sentences:

It was found that the *eel was on the *axle.*

It was found that the *eel was on the *shoe.*

It was found that the *eel was on the *table.*

It was found that the *eel was on the *orange.*

The only difference among these sentences was the final word spliced onto the end of the tape—*axle, shoe, orange,* or *table.* But depending on the version people listened to, *eel was perceived as *wheel, heel, meal,* and *peel,* respectively. We do not mean to say that the physical characteristics of the auditory input play no role in perception. Samuel (1981) found that the inserted non-speech sound is more likely to be perceived as a speech sound that it vaguely resembles than as a totally dissimilar sound.

The phonemic restoration effect clearly demonstrates that the phoneme identification procedure is supplemented by additional comparison procedures that use meaning to select the appropriate representation of the speech input (see Figure 13.1). In Warren and Warren's (1970) experiment the same sound pattern was perceived as either /wh/, /h/, /m/, or /p/, depending on the meaning of a word that followed it in the sentence. Clearly, the perceptual representation could not have been constructed by using only information from the physical input. Higher-level information in memory—the meanings of the words—was also used in constructing the representation.

**Contextual constraints.**    The effect of context on syllable perception demonstrates that speech perception involves a substantial amount of top-down processing. When you listen to a sentence, you have a certain amount of knowledge about what you are going to hear. You use this information to guide the construction of the representation of the speech input.

Your main source of information for constructing a representation of the speech input is your knowledge of the language that is being spoken. Each language consists of a finite number of words, some of which are used over and over again, and these words can be combined only into certain recurring patterns to form meaningful sentences. The structure of the language restricts the sounds we are likely to hear. First, there are grammatical restrictions on what words may form a sentence and the order they must be in. For example, *I ate an I scream cone* and *John Sam an* are not sentences, but *I ate an ice cream cone* and *John's a man* are. Second, the fact that sentences usually have meaning further restricts the word sequences that are likely to occur. For example, *John is a man I know* is a meaningful sentence, whereas *John is a moon I know* is not.

Apparently, then, a listener can use knowledge of grammar and meaning to fill in details in the perceptual representation. This top-down model of the speech-perception process suggests that the listener does not construct a perceptual representation for individual words but for a group of words at a time. For example, the same sound pattern might be potentially heard as either *can* or *cone*. But when this pattern is part of a longer input that could be heard as *Can I eat?*, the ambiguous sound will be heard as *can*, since *Cone I eat?* would be highly improbable.

**Perceptual learning.**   One implication of the top-down processing of speech deserves special mention. As we saw in Chapter 5, a red apple would look the same to you whether you were raised in America, Norway, or New Guinea, because innate, bottom-up form and color-processing procedures, uninfluenced by learning, determine your perception. However, a speech sound of English would not sound the same if you had learned some other language instead. For example, imagine how someone who did not know English would hear the cough in Warren and Warren's (1970) experiment. What a speaker of English hears as four different sounds, a nonspeaker would hear as the same sound. Similarly, native speakers of Japanese, a language that does not distinguish between the English phonemes /r/ and /l/, have great difficulty even hearing this distinction when they try to learn English. The perception of speech is thus highly dependent on perceptual learning.

## Speech Perception by Computer

Top-down processes also appear to play a critical role when the listener is a computer. One of the most advanced current systems is called Hearsay II, which was developed at Carnegie-Mellon University (Erman, Hayes-Roth, Lesser, and Reddy 1980). Hearsay is designed to perform such tasks as allowing a user to speak to the computer in English and ask it to retrieve wire service news stories. When the computer is given a speech input, it extracts an acoustic representation of the utterance, which includes the kind of information present in a spectrogram such as Figure 13.2. In addition, the system has knowledge of how simple English sentences are structured. It also knows something about the topics of the current news items. The system uses all this information—acoustic analysis of the input, grammatical constraints, and potential topics—to arrive at a decision about what the speech input actually says.

Like visual perception, speech perception by computer is still in its infancy. The Hearsay system has been tested only by having people read prepared scripts containing words and phrases the computer is programmed to recognize. Still, the system is interesting because it resembles a human being in its use of top-down processes in speech analysis. Because the system uses knowledge about grammar and meaning, it clearly involves top-down processing. Just as is the case for people, top-down processes are critical for Hearsay. An earlier version, Hearsay I, was tested on its ability to recognize speech read from a script by five different speakers. In this test the system identified 93 percent of the words, using all its sources of knowledge. Without knowledge of meaning, performance dropped to 70 percent, and without grammatical knowledge, it fell to 39 percent.

## LATERALIZATION, ATTENTION, AND ACTION

The model of attention and performance presented in Chapters 2 and 3 must now be reexamined in the light of the role that lateralized mechanisms play in the processing of inputs and the initiation of actions.

### Split-Brain Patients

The discovery that the left hemisphere was specialized for language production and comprehension has raised many questions about each hemisphere's contribution to cognition. What is needed to help settle the question of how each hemisphere functions is the careful examination of a single, relatively intact hemisphere of the brain, to catalog exactly what it can accomplish on its own. Such experiments sound like a piece of science fiction, but first approximations to them are going on today. In these experiments single hemispheres are being studied, although they are damaged rather than intact. This work was begun by R. W. Sperry and was continued by Sperry and his collaborators Michael Gazzaniga, Jerre Levy, and Eran Zaidel. Their studies are the byproduct of a surgical procedure for saving lives threatened by epileptic seizures.

Most cases of epilepsy can be controlled by medication. However, in some cases the seizures become so violent that they cannot be controlled by medication and eventually threaten the life of the sufferer. Recall that information is transmitted between the hemispheres across the corpus callosum. One surgical procedure occasionally used, depending on the location and extent of the damage, is to sever the corpus callosum (the bundle of nerve fibers connecting the two hemispheres) in order to prevent the seizure from spreading. This operation greatly reduces the size of the seizures, and it leaves the patients with their intellects and personalities relatively intact. In fact, it was only upon careful testing that the cognitive effects of the operation were discovered.

This testing involved presenting an input to only a single side of the body. For example, an object would be placed in either the right hand or the left; or a sound would be played in either the right ear or the left while a masking sound was played in the other ear; or while the patient kept his or her eyes on a fixation point, a word or picture would be presented in the right or left visual field. When such an input is presented to a person with an intact brain, the information reaches both hemispheres, because it can cross the corpus callosum from one hemisphere to the other. Even a person with a split brain can still get information to both hemispheres in a normal situation. For example, as a person's eyes scan over an object, it will appear in both visual fields and hence provide direct information for both hemispheres. However, we can thwart these strategies in an experimental situation by blindfolding the person when an object is placed in one hand or by presenting a visual input very rapidly in one visual field so the person doesn't have time to scan it. When these precautions are taken, the stimulus is effectively presented only to one hemisphere of the split-brain patient.

When most inputs are presented only to a single hemisphere of a split-brain patient, either hemisphere can respond by making a motor response. The left hemisphere has good control of the right hand and poor control of the left hand, whereas the right hemisphere has good control of the left hand and poor control of the right. However, if forced to, either hemisphere can make gross movements with either hand.

This equality of control is not extended to language. When the patient has an intact left hemisphere, uninjured by epilepsy, its performance on linguistic tasks is essentially normal. That is, it can understand sentences and produce speech. However, the linguistic skills of the right hemisphere are much less certain and very controversial (Gazzaniga 1983 vs. Myers 1984). At a minimum the linguistic performance of the right hemisphere differs markedly from patient to patient.

The linguistic capacities of the right hemisphere have been studied in only a handful of split-brain patients (Myers 1984). In the earliest studies the linguistic ability of the right hemisphere was nil. Only the left hemisphere could produce a verbal response. If an object was placed in the right hand of the patient, he or she could name it. The patient could also read words and identify pictures presented in the right visual field. But if the object was placed in the left hand, the patient claimed not to know what it was. If a word or picture was presented in the left visual field, the patient claimed to have seen nothing.

This result did not mean that nothing was actually seen. If the person was presented with a selection of pictures, words, or objects and asked to point out which one was the same as the one that had just been presented in the left visual field, the person pointed out the correct one. Hence when carefully tested, a split-brain patient performed paradoxically when something was presented in the left visual field. At the same time that the person was denying seeing anything, he or she might be pointing out exactly what was seen. Similarly, at the same time that the person denied knowing what was placed in the left hand, the person might be selecting a picture of the object with the left hand (Gazzaniga 1970, Chapters 3 and 6).

The right hemisphere thus appeared to have no control over the production of speech. Verbal responses were made only to inputs to the left hemisphere, whether it was an object placed in the right hand, a sound in the right ear, or a pattern in the right visual field. When the comprehension of language was examined, the pattern of results was the same. When a linguistic input, be it word or sentence, was presented in the right visual field (to the left hemisphere), the split-brain patient generally performed the task as well as he or she could prior to surgery. For example, if presented with a word, the patient could read it or select a word that rhymed with it, was associated with it, or meant the same thing. However, when the same words and sentences were presented in the left visual field (to the right hemisphere), patients were unable to indicate that they understood it in any way.

Finally, when tested on Kimura's (1961, 1967) dichotic-listening task for speech sounds, performance for those speech sounds presented in the right ear was normal. In contrast, recognition of left-ear-presented speech sounds was near zero (Milner, Taylor, and Sperry 1968; Sparks and Geschwind 1968).

Subsequent examinations of other patients revealed considerably more right-hemisphere linguistic abilities. In particular, three intensively studied split-brain patients showed considerable right-hemisphere, visual, word identification skills (Gazzaniga 1983; Zaidel 1976, 1978a, 1978b), but these patients have either little (Zaidel 1983) or no (Gazzaniga and Hillyard 1971) right-hemisphere syntactic comprehension and no right-hemisphere, speech-production ability (Gazzaniga 1983). Two other patients have essentially equal command of production (including speech) and comprehension in the left and right hemispheres (Gazzaniga 1983). However, one of the patients with right-hemisphere speech production is known and the other is presumed to have suffered left-hemisphere damage early in life (Myers 1984). As we will see, early brain damage radically alters the brain's functional organization, so we cannot draw conclusions about normal organization from these patients.

To summarize, the study of split-brain patients confirms the conclusion that has been reached with aphasics with regard to language production and comprehension. For most individuals the left hemisphere contains procedures essential for both production and comprehension.

### Hemispheric Control in Split-Brain Patients

Because the connections between them are severed, we can present different visual inputs simultaneously to each hemisphere of a split-brain patient. This task has provided considerable insight into the relationship of the hemispheres to each other. In a typical experiment, while the patient centers his or her gaze on a fixation point, a word is briefly presented so that half the letters fall to one side of the point and half the letters fall to the other side. For example, as Figure 13.5 illustrates, if the word *target* were briefly presented, the letters *tar* would fall in the left visual field and be processed by the right hemisphere, while the letters *get* would fall in the right visual field and be processed by the left hemisphere. After such an input is presented, the patient is given a choice of four alternatives and asked to point to the one that was presented. For example, the alternatives might be *tar, get, cow,* and *pea.*

You might think that since each hemisphere has processed a separate three letters, the person would choose two alternatives and point to *tar* with the left hand and *get* with the right. However, this result did not occur when words were presented to most patients. Instead, the person pointed to the right-visual-field input (e.g., *get*), whether asked to respond with the right or the left hand (Gazzaniga 1977). Only two patients with bilateral linguistic representations selected both words (Gazzaniga 1983). Thus the left hemisphere typically controls the response to conflicting linguistic inputs.

When conflicting *nonlinguistic* inputs are presented to the hemispheres, by contrast, it is the right hemisphere that controls the response. Levy, Trevarthan, and Sperry (1972) obtained evidence that the right hemisphere deter-

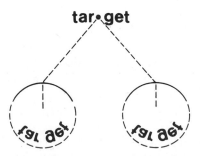

Figure 13.5    **Hemispheric control. If the subject's gaze is fixed on the center of *target, tar* falls in the left visual field and *get* in the right.**

**Figure 13.6   Chimeric face. (From Levy, Trevarthan, and Sperry 1972.)**

mines the response to visual patterns such as the one shown in Figure 13.6. They called inputs like this one "chimeric" stimuli because they look like pictures of impossible creatures.

Such pictures, made up by putting the right and left halves of two different faces together, were flashed at each of four split-brain patients for 150 milliseconds. They were then asked to select which of three intact faces they had seen. None of these faces was the chimeric one actually presented. However, Levy *et al.* (1972) reported that patients failed to notice this fact. Instead, when the patients were asked to choose which face had been presented, the half shown in the *left* visual field (to the right hemisphere) was usually chosen. Patients made approximately the same responses whether asked to respond with the left or right hand, indicating that for this task the right hemisphere had taken control of the motor response mechanism. Similar results were obtained with nonsense shapes and pictures of common objects (Levy and Trevarthan 1976, 1977).

This balance between the right and left hemispheres can be tipped one way or the other by the precise question asked. When the four split-brain patients were taught names for the three faces used in making up the chimeric stimuli and then asked to respond with the name of the face that had been presented, they most often responded with the name of the face corresponding to the *right* half of the picture (perceived by the left hemisphere).

Similarly, when separate pictures were presented in the right and left visual fields, split-brain patients usually pointed to something visually similar to the left-visual-field input when asked to select what they had seen. However, when they were asked to point to a picture of something with a name that rhymed with that of something they had seen, they pointed to a picture with a name that rhymed with that of the picture presented on the right. Hence the kind of judgment that must be made about the input determines the hemisphere that controls the response.

## Hemispheric Control in People with Normal Brains

The work with split-brain patients stimulated the investigation of hemispheric control in normal human brains. This task has been difficult, because in the normal brain information presented to one hemisphere is rapidly transmitted across the corpus callosum to the other. As a result, researchers are never certain what each hemisphere is contributing to performance on a given task. Nevertheless, persistent efforts eventually led to a consistent pattern of results from which inferences about hemispheric specialization could be drawn.

We have already seen that dichotic presentation of auditory inputs reveals the lateralized phonetic identification mechanism (Kimura 1961; Rand 1974). Another technique for isolating the processing of each hemisphere is to present a visual input to the left or right visual field. The observer's task is to make a judgment and response as rapidly as possible to a briefly presented visual input. Observers fix their eyes on a central *fixation point,* and the visual input is presented a few degrees to the right or left of the fixation point.

Recall that inputs in the left visual field go first to the right hemisphere, and vice versa for inputs to the right visual field (see Chapter 2). We assume that if the input arrives first at the hemisphere that controls the processing for the judgment, then reaction time will be faster than if it arrives first at the opposite hemisphere. Accordingly, faster reaction time to left-visual-field inputs is used as an indication of right-hemisphere processing and vice versa. Whether reaction time was faster for left- or right-visual-field presentation depended on the precise nature of the task (Bryden and Allard 1976; Hellige, Cox, and Litvac 1979; Zaidel 1978b). In general, linguistic tasks elicited faster responses with right-visual-field presentations, and visual-pattern analysis tasks elicited faster responses with left-visual-field presentations. (See also Helige 1980.)

These small differences in reaction time are important because they are evidence that some mechanisms are lateralized in the normal brain. However, you should not forget that they are only a few milliseconds long and were obtained under conditions that do not exist in the natural environment. So these results also confirm that inputs from both the left and right are transmitted by the normal brain so efficiently to lateralized mechanisms that there are essentially no biases in attention or perception as a result of lateralization.

## Language and Handedness

Most human beings are strongly right-handed. In this respect humans are unique, for we are the only animals who show any consistent hand preference as a population (Warren 1977). You might expect a link between handedness and other lateralized abilities, which seems to be the case. Kinsbourne and Cooke (1971) had people balance a dowel on either the right hand or the left hand. Then they asked them to spell *Mississippi* while balancing the dowel. Kinsbourne and Cooke hypothesized that since the right hand is primarily controlled by the left hemisphere, and since language is controlled by the left hemisphere, spelling and balancing the dowel with the right hand would give the left hemisphere two things to do at the same time. Sure enough, people balanced the dowel with the right hand for a shorter amount of time when they had to spell than when they did not. In contrast, spelling did not interfere with left-handed dowel balancing.

Evidence also shows that the degree of linguistic lateralization is related to the degree of right-handedness. Left-handers do not show the normal pattern of faster, more accurate linguistic judgments for left-visual-field inputs and faster, more accurate visuospatial judgments for right-visual-field inputs (Jones 1980). Further evidence of the relationship between lateralization and handedness comes from surveys of people with aphasia and epilepsy.

**Handedness and aphasia.**   As we have mentioned, the relationship between head injury location and aphasia is different for right-handers and non-right-handers. Virtually no aphasias in right-handers result from right-hemisphere injury. In contrast, a significant, though small, percentage of aphasias in non-right-handers result from right-hemisphere injury (Gloning 1977; Russell and Espir 1961). Non-right-handers also tend to make better recoveries from unilateral lesions in either hemisphere. Thus non-right-handers appear to be less likely to be completely lateralized for language.

**Sodium amobarbital injection.**   The second source of evidence for the relationship between language and handedness is based on a study of epileptics. Epilepsy can lead to a reorganization of the locations of various specialized hemispheric areas, so these results must be evaluated with caution.

In 1949 a neurologist (Wada 1949) introduced a new technique for studying a single hemisphere's function (Rasmussen and Milner 1977). The carotid artery in the neck is the main source of the blood supply for the cerebral cortex. By injecting sodium amobarbital, a barbiturate, in the appropriate branch of the artery, Wada was able to selectively anesthetize either the left or the right hemisphere. He could then effectively test the cognitive functioning of the hemisphere that was still awake.

The amobarbital solution is injected in the internal carotid artery while the patient is counting, lying down with both knees drawn up, both hands raised, and the fingers moving. The contralateral arm and leg fall to the bed with a flaccid paralysis a few seconds after the injection is completed. In other words, if the left hemisphere is anesthetized, it is the right arm that falls. If the injected hemisphere is nondominant for speech, the patient continues to count and can perform verbal tasks, including naming and repetition tasks. Some patients stop counting temporarily for a period of up to 20 or 30 seconds but resume normal speech with urging. When the injected hemisphere is dominant for speech, the patient typically stops talking near the end of the injection and remains completely aphasic for a few minutes. Speech doesn't begin to return until control of the arm begins to return as well. Notice that this procedure tests only for language production, not comprehension.

If a patient suffers from intractable epilepsy due to damage to the cerebral cortex, a surgeon may cut away the damaged portion in order to relieve the epilepsy. By first injecting the patient with amobarbital, the surgeon can determine whether the damaged hemisphere is dominant for language. This procedure can therefore help determine the likelihood that the surgery will replace epilepsy with aphasia. At the Montreal Neurological Institute the test is accordingly carried out routinely on all left-handed or ambidextrous patients with intractable epilepsy who are candidates for surgery. The test is also carried out on right-handed surgical candidates whenever there is some hint that the speech functions might not be represented in the left hemisphere.

Theodore Rasmussen and Brenda Milner (1977) reported on their results with 296 patients who received amobarbital injections. Their results are summarized in Table 13.1. As shown in the table, 96 percent of the right-handed patients and 70 percent of the non-right-handed patients showed left-hemisphere dominance for language. These percentages agree well with the percentages derived from studies of aphasia and handedness.

**TABLE 13.1** Speech Lateralization as Related to Handedness; Based on 262 Patients

| Handedness | Number of cases | Speech representation | | |
| --- | --- | --- | --- | --- |
| | | Left | Right | Bilateral |
| Right | 140 | 96% | 4% | 0.0% |
| Left or mixed | 122 | 70% | 15% | 15 % |

Source: From Rasmussen and Milner (1977).

Notice also that there were some patients for which neither hemisphere was language-dominant. They continued to count when either hemisphere was injected, but their speech contained some errors, such as mispronunciations and pauses. Furthermore, there was a pattern to the errors. Anesthetization of one hemisphere produced naming errors but little or no disturbance in serial-repetition tasks, such as counting and saying the days of the week. Anesthetization of the other hemisphere produced the opposite pattern. The reason for this intriguing result is not known.

**Conclusion.**   These results indicate that in the human population as a whole there is a dependent relationship between language lateralization and handedness, and that there are fewer left hemispheres specialized for handedness than there are for language. This distribution suggests that lateralization for handedness is an effect of lateralization for language.

Why should left-hemisphere speech control lead to right-handedness? Again, at our present state of knowledge we can only speculate at a very general level. Perhaps all the procedures involved in directing the fine-motor movements for speech can also be recruited for other skills and hence give the left hemisphere an advantage. Or perhaps the connection between language and the first stage of motor skill learning, described in Chapter 4, leads to the final skill also being controlled from the left hemisphere.

Annett (1975) has proposed a theory in which the handedness of an individual is the result of an interaction between heredity and environment. According to the hypothesis, the lateralization of some procedures in the left hemisphere is an inherited trait. People born with it are right-handed. People born without it become left-handed, right-handed, or ambidextrous on the basis of either gestational factors or postnatal experience. According to the hypothesis, the presence of left-handedness in the immediate family of an individual should be a better predictor of a person's lateralization than a person's own handedness, because a family that produces left-handers does not carry the genetic trait for lateralization. Annett found evidence in support of this hypothesis.

## HEMISPHERIC DEVELOPMENT AFTER BIRTH

Further evidence that the left hemisphere is genetically programmed for speech processing comes from the study of neonates. When newborn infants are laid down to rest, most of them turn their heads to the right (Turkewitz and Birch 1971). Furthermore, newborn infants process inputs differently with the two hemispheres, even before language is learned. This issue has been difficult to investigate because newborn infants are not easy subjects to work with. There is not much that they will do to let you in on what is going on in their minds. However, new research techniques are overcoming this problem.

The electrical activity of different parts of the brain can be measured by taping recording electrodes to the scalp. With this technique researchers typically find that when a single input is presented to both hemispheres, the electrical activity in the two differs. The advantage of this technique is that it requires no overt response on the part of the subject. The subject is simply presented with either a long succession of clicks or light flashes, and the potentials evoked by all presentations are averaged. When this average is calculated, the hemispheres of infants show the same between-hemisphere differences in average evoked potentials to auditory and visual inputs that are found in adults (Molfese, Nunez, Seibert, and Rammanaiah 1976; Wada 1977).

Also worth mentioning is the fact that there are anatomical differences between the left and right hemispheres of both adult and infant brains (Geschwind and Levitsky 1968; Witelson 1977), although the meaning of this differentiation is far from clear (Whitaker and Ojemann 1977). In fact, when measured carefully, human beings generally turn out to be slightly asymmetrical (e.g., one foot is usually larger). Also, similar anatomical differences occur in the brains of primates, including chimpanzees, gorillas, monkeys and orangutans (Witelson 1977), which, despite major investigative efforts, have provided virtually no evidence of functional lateralization (the exception is Beecher, Peterson, Zoloth, Moody, and Stebbins 1979). Thus anatomical asymmetry does not necessarily have functional significance.

Although relatively few studies with infants have been done, all their results are consistent. The hemispheres are specialized at birth to some degree. However, these results leave open the possibility that further specialization takes place as the child grows older, either through maturation or under the influence of the environment (Krashen 1975).

## Hemispheric Specialization and Language Acquisition

The ratio of aphasias caused by left-hemisphere vs. right-hemisphere lesions is almost as large for children as it is for adults (Woods and Teuber 1978). So from the beginning the specialized language mechanisms develop within a single hemisphere. However, children make much fuller recoveries from aphasia than adults usually do. This result is consistent with the finding that, in general, children make much better recoveries from brain damage than adults. When the brain is still young, another section can apparently take over the function of a part that has been lost.

Dennis and her colleagues examined the limits of cortical plasticity by comparing the effects of left and right hemidecortication on children (Dennis 1980; Dennis and Kohn 1975; Dennis and Whitaker 1976). In this operation most of the cortex of either the right or left hemisphere is removed. They found that after the removal of either cortex, the children's acquisition of language still approached normal limits. However, the children with intact left hemispheres were superior to the children with intact right hemispheres in the comprehension of syntactically complex sentences. Therefore the right hemisphere does have the capacity to acquire language, if necessary, though whether it can acquire it quite as well as the left hemisphere remains an open question.

These speculations about how the hemispheres develop bear on the *critical period hypothesis* for language learning. According to this hypothesis, before puberty human beings can learn one or more languages easily, perhaps because their hemispheres are not yet completely specialized. But once a person is past puberty and the hemispheres have completely matured, he or she can no longer learn a new language as well. That is, there should always be an obvious decrement in performance indicating that the language was learned (only imperfectly) after the hemispheres had matured and the period for natural-language learning had ended.

What is needed to test the critical period hypothesis is a person past puberty who has never learned a language before. Unfortunately, owing to horrifying instances of long-term child neglect, such cases occasionally arise. Some time ago, a girl was discovered in an attic; she had been tied to a bassinet since birth and never taught to talk. The child, known as Genie, was twelve years old when she was found. Since then, the child has been extensively examined and given special education in the hope of making her a whole human being. In addition, her plight provides some clues about whether a critical age for language development exists.

In the first few years of her education Genie learned a great deal of language. On the other hand, careful testing revealed that although she acquired vocabulary at an excellent rate, her syntax developed much more slowly than it does in normal two- or three-year-olds. Also, although she is right-handed, a dichotic-listening test revealed that all auditory inputs, both linguistic and nonlinguistic, were processed in the right hemisphere. This extreme left-ear advantage is totally unknown in normal right-handers. It suggests atypical language development (Curtiss, Fromkin, Krashen, Rigler, and Rigler 1974; Curtiss 1977) and provides support for the critical period hypothesis. Of course, a case study of a single atypical child is not very strong evidence on which to base an entire theory. However, such a case makes clear how little is known about how the hemispheres develop.

## Consequences of Atypical Organization

Taken as a whole, studies of brain-damaged and normal individuals reveal a consistent pattern. For most people the left hemisphere has unique procedures for language and hand movements, while the right hemisphere is active in the processing of visuospatial information. However, when we turn our attention from the group to the individual, we discover considerable diversity in the ways in which the hemispheres may be organized. A person may be right-handed, left-handed, or ambidextrous. A person may have language controlled by the left hemisphere, the right hemisphere, or both. Although in most individuals the same hemisphere controls both hand and word, in some individuals they are controlled by opposite hemispheres.

What are the consequences for you if you have atypical lateralization? With the exception of handedness—how you hold a pencil when you write (Levy 1976)—and perhaps a few even more subtle undiscovered differences, there appear to be no consequences. As long as certain functions are controlled by a single hemisphere, it does not matter which hemisphere it is. Remember that in a normal, healthy brain information is transmitted in parallel, very rapidly, to all of its parts. As a result, the physical location of the neural basis for a cognitive procedure appears to be remarkably unimportant.

## SUMMARY

In the majority of the population language is primarily controlled by the left hemisphere of the cerebral cortex. A variety of sources of evidence, the most dramatic of which are studies of *asphasic* and *split-brain* patients, support this general conclusion. One hypothesis regarding the evolutionary origin of hemispheric specialization is that it arose as a response to the need to increase the rate of speech. As the left hemisphere came to control language functions, it left the right hemisphere free to control various nonlinguistic functions.

One complex aspect of language use is speech perception. The continuous speech stream must be segregated into discrete *phonemes* and *syllables*. The perception of these elements depends on the acoustic context as well as the syntax and meaning of the utterance. Computer systems for speech recognition, such as *Hearsay*, also make use of contextual cues. A variety of evidence, such as the *Kimura effect* and the distribution of injuries resulting in *aphasia*, indicates that speech perception depends on localized areas of the left hemisphere.

When conflicting linguistic inputs are presented to the two hemispheres, the left hemisphere typically controls the response. Conversely, the right hemisphere controls the response to conflicting nonlinguistic inputs. Hemispheric specialization is linked to handedness. Left-handed people are typically less clearly lateralized for language than are right-handed people. The hemispheres are already differentiated to some degree at birth, but specialization probably continues to develop through childhood. The *critical period hypothesis* suggests that language acquisition is substantially more difficult after specialization is complete.

## RECOMMENDED READINGS

Again, Gardner's *Shattered Mind* (1976) is a good introduction to the topic of this chapter. Two relevant journals are *Behavioral and Brain Sciences* and *Brain and Language.*

# CHAPTER **FOURTEEN**

# Language and Its Acquisition

## INTRODUCTION

The use of language is perhaps our most remarkable cognitive ability, and yet we usually take it very much for granted. We learn to speak at such an early age that we have no recollection of expending any effort doing so. In fact, this ease of learning is part of what is so fascinating about language. Schoolchildren differ in their abilities to learn arithmetic, for example; yet at an even earlier age almost all children learn to speak, even though language appears to be a vastly more complicated system than arithmetic. Computers routinely perform arithmetic, but despite years of trying no one has been able to program a computer to use language as well as a four-year-old can.

Language appears to be universal across all human societies. In the 1970s a Stone Age tribe, the Tasaday, was found in a remote part of the Philippines. The tribe had not had any contact with the rest of the world. Yet no one was surprised that they spoke their own language, nor was anyone surprised that an American could learn their language, just as a Tasaday could learn English. Despite the apparent diversity of human languages, all societies use language in similar ways, and any language can be learned by anybody. Accordingly, languages must have some underlying similarities.

## NATURE OF HUMAN LANGUAGE

### Language Functions

Consider the functions of language. How do we use language? It is part of virtually every social interaction. Language is used to teach students, to command armies, to convey our feelings to friends and enemies. Usually, when we speak, we are *doing* something in the process. Someone who says "I bet you ten bucks the Michigan Wolverines will win the Rose Bowl next year" is making a bet. To say "I'll give you your book back on Monday" is to make a promise. These kinds of language activities are called *speech acts* (Austin 1962; Searle 1969).

Three of the most pervasive speech acts correspond to different types of sentences. A *declarative sentence* conveys information (e.g., *Albany is the capital of New York*). A *question* asks the listener to provide information (e.g., *Is it snowing outside?*). An *imperative* conveys a command (e.g., *Shut the door*). Sometimes the boundaries between these different types of sentences begin to blur. For example, the sentence *Can you shut the door?* looks like a question, but in most contexts it would be strange for someone to answer "yes" and do nothing else. The sentence really conveys a request, but in a more polite way than by a direct command.

Whatever the purpose of the speech act, it almost always requires that information be conveyed to a listener. Even when you make a request or command, someone must understand what needs to be done. So the basic requirement of language is that it be able to convey information. Furthermore, it must be extremely flexible in the kind of information it can convey. When we begin to investigate language, we cross an indefinite boundary between recognition of the old and comprehension of the new. To learn a language is *not* to learn to recognize a particular set of sentences. Rather, it is to learn a set of rules for constructing and understanding novel sentences. As a result, when you read this book and other textbooks, you understand sentences you never saw before and thereby gain knowledge. If you read a fantasy, like Lewis Carroll's *Alice in Wonderland,* you gain knowledge of a world that never did and never will exist.

Now that we've outlined some of the distinctive aspects of human language, we can consider the question of whether animals have language too. Could we, like Dr. Doolittle, learn to understand them? Because this question sheds light on the nature of human language, we will briefly consider it.

## Natural Animal Communication Systems

The first thing to remember is that language is not the same thing as communication. Human beings have many ways of communicating besides language, such as by using gestures, body movements, and nonspeech sounds. It is certainly true that most animal species have communication systems and many of these systems are very elaborate. Wolves convey emotions by the position of ears, lips, and tail. Primates and cats use facial expressions to signal fear or aggressiveness. Birds have songs that indicate sexual readiness and possession of territory. One of the most intricate communication systems has been found in varieties of the lowly honeybee (Von Frisch 1967). A bee that has found a food source returns to the hive and performs a kind of dance, which conveys information about the direction, distance, and quality of the food. This dance allows the rest of the hive to find the location of the food.

Are such animal communication systems really languages? This question is probably the wrong one to ask, since the answer depends completely on how we define *language*. A more useful question to ask is, What important features of human languages are shared by animal communication systems (Hockett 1960)? Let's look at a few such features.

**Use of speech.**   Many animal communication systems involve vocalizations (e.g., the calls of monkeys), but none involves humanlike speech sounds. However, human language doesn't always involve speech either. Language can also be written on paper or expressed in Braille or Morse code. The deaf often use languages based on gestures, such as American Sign Language. So the use of speech doesn't seem to be a critical feature of human language.

**Arbitrary associations.**   Human language involves essentially arbitrary relations between words and what the words refer to. However, some animal systems involve similar arbitrariness. For example, the particular song that a bird uses to signal readiness to mate seems quite arbitrary.

**Naming.**   Human languages introduce different words to name different objects in the environment. Does any animal system involve naming? A possible candidate is the warning calls of some monkeys (Marler 1967). A monkey will produce a different call for different types of predators, and the other monkeys will then respond appropriately. If the monkey sees a snake, it will give a "chutter" sound. The others will then approach the snake and look at it from a safe distance. If the monkey sees a leopard, it will give a "chirp," causing the others to run to trees and climb to the top. Quite the opposite happens if one monkey spots an eagle. The monkey gives a "rraup," and the others climb down from the trees and run from open areas into thickets. Interestingly, the monkeys will respond in the same way when they see a predator and when they hear the appropriate warning call.

While this signaling system certainly resembles naming, the range of what can be named and the range of responses to those names are clearly quite limited. The degree of cognitive competence reflected in such signaling systems is a matter of debate (Dennett 1983).

**Generativeness.**   Generativeness is the strongest candidate for a property that distinguishes human languages from animal systems. There are no convincing examples of animal systems in which new messages are regularly or frequently constructed by rearranging a finite set of basic units. There are some bird songs in which certain basic motifs are rearranged in different ways to create new variations, but these variations don't seem to convey different information. There are no examples of abstract syntactic structure of the sort that characterizes human language.

**Expressive power.**    Similarly, no animal system can convey anything remotely approximating the range of thoughts expressible in human languages. Take the example of monkey calls. When a monkey gives a "rraup," that means something like "I see an eagle." But the monkey has no way of saying "I don't see an eagle," or "Thank heavens that wasn't an eagle," or "Are you afraid of eagles?" or "That was some huge eagle I saw yesterday." As we pointed out earlier, the range of expressible ideas depends on the generative nature of language. That is why we think generativeness is the most fundamental property of human language, one that sets it apart from other communication systems.

## Conversations with Chimpanzees

If we agree that human language has unique properties, we can raise another question: Can only human beings learn a human language? To find out, some psychologists have made monumental efforts to teach language to animals. The favorite subjects have been fellow primates, including several chimpanzees and at least one gorilla. In the 1940s Keith and Cathy Hayes (Hayes 1951) attempted to train a chimp named Vicki to pronounce English words. Vicki was taught to say "mama" by having someone manipulate her lips as she said "ah." She received food rewards for producing approximately the right sound. Eventually she could say "mama" herself, often by holding her own lips. Vicki's achievements as a speaker of English were stupendously unimpressive. After six years of dedicated training, she was able to say just three words—mama, papa, and cup—and even these words were sometimes confused and used incorrectly.

One could draw either of two conclusions from Vicki's lack of fluency. Either chimps can't learn language, or chimps can't make human vocal sounds. We now know that the second conclusion is the correct one. Chimpanzees simply don't have the kind of vocal tract or cortical mechanisms necessary to produce speech sounds. Can chimpanzees learn a language that does not require speech?

In the 1960s two major attempts to train chimps to use language got underway. David Premack (Premack 1971; Premack and Premack 1972) developed an artificial language in which the "words" were colored plastic shapes that could be attached to a magnetic board. A chimp named Sarah was rewarded for placing these symbols on the board in fixed orders that formed "sentences." For example, there were symbols for *question, red, apple,* and the relation "color of." Sarah would be shown a sequence of shapes corresponding to ?—*red*—color of—*apple* (in English, "Is an apple red?"). She would have to replace the"?" symbol with the correct answer, the symbol for "yes," in order to be rewarded. She succeeded in learning to manipulate symbols corresponding to complex concepts such as *same, different,* and negation (*not*). However, Sarah used the symbols only when she was being rewarded by tidbits of food and drink. She never initiated spontaneous "conversations." While her symbol system was structured like language, it had none of the characteristic social functions of human languages. Some other chimps have since been trained with similar systems (Rumbaugh, Gill, and Von Glaserfeld 1973).

Beatrice and Allen Gardner (1969,1975) of the University of Nevada pioneered an entirely different approach to teaching language to chimpanzees. Since chimps spontaneously use gestures, they decided to try to teach a chimp named Washoe to use American Sign Language (ASL). As we noted earlier, ASL is a language in which gestures are used to represent words, and sequences of gestures represent sentences. At first the results were encouraging. In about four years Washoe learned 130 signs, and she began to form sequences of two or more signs. Another chimp, Nim, educated at Columbia University, learned equally quickly (Terrace 1979).

A human child rapidly progresses beyond two-word utterances and produces utterances of increasing complexity and informativeness. However, the intellectual differences between chimps and people make two-word utterances the upper bound on chimpanzee linguistic achievement (Limber 1977). When chimpanzee sequences were compared with those of children at a similar age, researchers found that the average length and the complexity of the children's utterances were rapidly increasing along with their vocabulary, but the chimpanzees' average length of utterance hardly increased at all.

So while the chimpanzees were certainly learning an impressive communication system, close scrutiny of it provided little evidence that it consisted of anything like "sentences" of human language. In addition, chimpanzees do not use their signs in combination with gestures, as children do in communicative contexts (Savage-Rumbaugh, Pate, Lawsen, Smith, and Rosenbaum 1983; Sugarman 1983). Human language is unique in its complexity and the range of expression it provides. As Bertrand Russell so memorably put it, "No matter how eloquently a dog may bark, he will never tell you that his parents were poor but honest."

## Language Structure

Look again at Figure 13.1. The production and comprehension of language involves four different levels of representation and four different procedures that recode representations from one level to the next. At the lowest level a spoken language is either a motor representation produced by the speech-production mechanism or an auditory representation that is detected by the phonetic identification mechanism. At the second level the representations correspond to strings of words. On the production side each word is represented as an individual entity. In contrast, on the comprehension side we have seen that the words are only implicit within the phonetic representation and must be identified through comparison with memory.

At the third level each word in the string has been replaced with its semantic category and some of the relations associated with it in the semantic code, which form the syntactic representation. Finally, the syntactic translation procedure recodes the syntactic representation to a propositional one. This procedure involves selecting among relations activated by different words and combining them in a new representation. The way the relations are combined is in part specified by their order in the sentence.

The key to the generative power of language is the syntactic translation procedure. This procedure recodes sequences of semantic categories and relations as propositions and vice versa. As long as the category-relation sequence is one of a set of repetitive patterns, the translation procedure can recode it into a proposition. In principle, there is no limit on either the number or the length of possible sentences. For example, look at how a familiar old nursery rhyme is built up:

This is the house.

This is the house that Jack built.

This is the cheese that lay in the house that Jack built.

This is the dog that chased the cat that chased the mouse that ate the cheese that lay in the house that Jack built.

We could keep adding to this sentence to make it even longer. Eventually it would get so long that no one could say it or understand it. But as long as the procedures for building sentences were applied correctly, the resulting sentence would be English.

The generativeness of language is clearly tied to its function as a tool for conveying novel information. For example, consider this sentence:

Napoleon Bonaparte invaded the United States in 1990, leading his army across the Rockies on pink elephants that trampled the corn fields of Iowa before they perished in a blizzard on the outskirts of Cleveland.

This sentence is undoubtedly one you've never seen or heard before. It probably strikes you as utterly ridiculous, but nevertheless you can clearly understand what it means. Since there is no known limit on possible human ideas, the procedures for constructing propositions, which are the meanings of utterances, must also be generative.

In Chapters 9 and 10 we saw that the most difficult learning task is the acquisition of a generative procedure. Yet all children acquire the complex syntactic translation procedure for language in only a few years. In this chapter we examine how they do so.

## LANGUAGE ACQUISITION

In assessing the results of attempts to teach language to chimpanzees, we noted that their acquisition falls far short of that exhibited by human children. How do children learn language so readily? A few decades ago surprisingly little was known about how we learn to speak so quickly and so well. The rapidity and the early age of language acquisition conspire to leave us with few adult memories of the learning process. Furthermore, the direct observation of children learning a language can be a highly frustrating and not very enlightening experience. Little children cannot be easily cajoled into attempting experimental tasks, and what children may happen to say or do does not provide all that much information about their total linguistic knowledge. Witness this classic exchange between an investigator and a two-year-old (Brown and Bellugi 1964):

> Interviewer: Adam, which is right, two shoes or two shoe?
>
> Adam: Pop goes the weasel.

Despite such difficulties recent years have brought both new hypotheses and new investigative techniques for assessing a child's linguistic knowledge. A great deal has been learned, but a clear account of the entire process of language acquisition has yet to emerge. Here we can give only a progress report on some of what has been learned so far.

### First Speech Sounds

One of the most important facts about language acquisition is that children around the world learn their varied languages in strikingly similar ways (Slobin 1973). Some of the most impressive regularities involve the acquisition of speech sounds (Jakobson 1968). Babies universally begin to babble at about the age of six months. At about the age of one year their sounds become more speechlike.

First the child produces vowel sounds, like /ah/, and then consonant-vowel combinations. The first consonant sounds are also highly regular. They are typically sounds like /m/, /b/, and /p/, which are produced by modulating the air at the lips. In fact, in many unrelated languages the first words used as names for the parents sound something like the English *mama* and *papa*, which are easily pronounced by children. Both of these English words illustrate another universal tendency of children—to produce *reduplications* of consonant-vowel combinations. It is probably no accident that the words parents are so anxious to hear are designed to be exactly what the infant is naturally most likely to produce.

## Making Sense of Adult Speech

For someone who knows only English, listening to people speaking in a foreign language can be a very disconcerting experience. Imagine sitting in a Paris bistro, eavesdropping on a conversation at a nearby table. If you don't know French, you will probably have a great deal of trouble even in segmenting the sound stream into words. Everybody will seem to be speaking incredibly fast, so you will not remember more than a handful of sounds. Such an experience may make it difficult for you to understand how anyone, least of all an infant, could figure out the basic structure of a language just by listening to it being spoken.

Trying to learn a language by listening in on the conversations of fluent speakers is a difficult and perhaps impossible enterprise. However, it is not the one an infant has to engage in. First of all, children primarily learn to speak by being spoken to. Rather than just listening in on the conversations of others, children are typically actively involved in conversations. In fact, in many cultures, babies that are still too young to talk are often treated as if they could carry on a conversation. A parent may carry on a "dialog" with an infant in which the adult does all the talking, while treating the baby's burps, yawns, and smiles as "turns" in the conversation (Snow 1977). By the time the child is a year old, he or she will actually be using one-word utterances in conversational context.

In addition, speakers addressing young children go to great lengths to get the child to attend to what is being said. They use the child's name frequently, particularly at the beginning of an utterance (Shatz and Gelman 1973). Adults also tend to speak to a young child in particularly high-pitched voices, and they frequently touch the child as they start to talk. These attention-grabbing devices are clearly important, since the child is unlikely to learn the language unless actively processing the speech that is heard.

People also simplify their speech when addressing children (Broen 1972; Phillips 1973; Sachs, Brown, and Salerno 1976). They speak more slowly and distinctly, with extra pauses. They use short sentences, with few complex syntactic constructions. Function words and inflections are sometimes omitted. Simple sentence frames like "Look at _____," "That's a _____," and "Here comes _____," are repeated over and over. In addition, adults tend to repeat themselves when giving instructions to children, as in the following example (Snow 1972, p. 563):

Pick up the red one. Find the red one. Not the green one. I want the red one. Can you find the red one?

Finally, adults talking to children frequently punctuate and supplement their utterances with gestures that help clarify what they are saying. A mother may shake a stuffed animal in front of the child while naming it, or she may shove food in the child's mouth while commanding the child to eat it.

Incidentally, it is not only adults who modify their speech to young children. Shatz and Gelman (1973) found that four-year-olds simplify their speech when they are talking to two-year-olds.

The content of what adults say to children is also relatively simple and straightforward. (You would hardly expect parents to be discussing philosophy with two-year-olds.) Parents typically talk about things in the child's immediate environment, like food or the household pet. Very often they are trying to get the child to *do* something. You shouldn't get the idea that adults modify their speech as an exercise in language training. It's simply that they want the child to understand them and to follow commands. All of the adults' speech modifications are very natural ones, given that they are trying to make themselves understood by someone who knows little either of their language or of what the world is like.

The net effect of these various modifications is to greatly increase the comprehensibility of speech. A psychologist who knew French only imperfectly described this effect from experience (Taylor 1976, p. 231):

> I observed a French woman talking to a 10-month-old baby. She would say slowly and clearly, "red," "yellow," "orange," or "look, this one has a hole," holding appropriately colored and shaped toy objects. Furthermore, she repeated the whole sequence two or three times. I could understand everything she said in French to the baby, but could catch only odd words or messages when she was talking to the baby's mother in rapid, normal French.

## Role of the Child in Language Acquisition

You should not suppose, however, that the fact that people speak in a relatively simple manner to children constitutes an explanation of language acquisition. The analytic abilities of the young child are certainly critical. Indeed, speech simplifications by adults are probably not a necessary condition for language acquisition (Hoff-Ginsberg and Shatz 1982).

Research indicates that variations in adult speech to children have only modest and quite subtle effects on the rate at which children acquire language. For example, Newport, Gleitman, and Gleitman (1977) found that although the rate of growth in the use of auxiliary verbs (e.g., *can, must*) was unrelated to the absolute frequency of auxiliaries in maternal speech, it was positively correlated with the frequency of yes-no questions. Yes-no questions frequently prepose an auxiliary (e.g., *Can you run?*). This position may make the auxiliary perceptually more salient, because children pay greater attention to the beginnings of utterances. Also, children may need examples of auxiliaries both in questions and in declarative sentences (e.g., *You can run*) in order to induce the special role of auxiliary placement in generating yes-no questions. In general, comparisons across multiple examples of sentences may play a significant role in syntax acquisition (Maratsos and Chalkley 1980).

Another finding of Newport *et al.* (1977) was that growth in the child's use of noun inflections (e.g., the plural marker s) was positively related to the frequency of *deictic utterances* in maternal speech. A deictic utterance is a construction that linguistically "points" to an object in the world, as in sentences with pronouns *this* or *that* (e.g., *That's a truck*). One possible explanation of the positive impact of deictic utterances is that they make it especially likely that the child will comprehend the referent of the noun (e.g., they will understand that *truck* refers to a certain object that is being mentioned). Children may only tend to learn syntactic markers such as inflections when they grasp the referent of the word being inflected.

Clearly, the analytical skills that children use to learn language are closely tied to the context of communication (Shatz, 1983). Some evidence indicates that simply listening to speech is not sufficient for language learning. For example, when deaf parents have a child who hears normally, they may leave their radio or TV on constantly so that the child will be exposed to speech. However, such children typically know much less language than other children at the time they enter school, although they will quickly catch up (Sachs and Johnson 1976). Similarly, a study of Dutch children who watched German television every day found that they knew virtually no German (Snow, Arlman-Rupp, Hassing, Jobse, Joosten, and Vorster 1976).

Why do children seem to learn so little language from radio or TV? There are two main differences between this kind of exposure to language and normal adult-child conversations. First, the speech on TV or radio is not simplified, as adult speech to children is. Second, even with TV the child will probably have great difficulty understanding what is being said given only the accompanying picture as context. Watching TV is not like carrying on a conversation about the child's world.

In striking contrast to the failure of children to learn language from linguistic inputs that lack a communicative context is evidence that children will sometimes invent a language of their own in the absence of linguistic inputs. Deaf twins have been observed to create their own rule-governed, languagelike gesture systems (Feldman, Goldin-Meadow, and Gleitman 1979). Such cases emphasize the extent to which language is not simply imposed on the child by adults but, rather, constructed by the child's own analytical skills.

## First Words

What exactly are children learning as they listen to language? Often, as it turns out, something different from what they might at first glance appear to be learning. For example, suppose a father points to Rufus, the family dog, and says to his eighteen-month-old daughter, "That's a dog." How does the child know whether *dog* refers to that one animal, to all dogs, to all furry four-legged animals, to all four-legged animals, or to all animals?

**Overextensions.**   In fact, the child may apply the word *dog* not only to dogs but also to horses, cows, sheep, and various other creatures. This phenomenon is termed *overextension*. It is commonly observed in the speech of children between the ages of one and two-and-a-half years. Another example (Clark 1975) is a child's use of the word *ticktock*. One child first used this term to refer to a watch but later extended it to clocks, a gas meter, a fire hose wound on a spool, and a bathroom scale with a round dial.

As these examples suggest, most overextensions seem to be made on the basis of shape, although other properties are often involved as well. What may be happening is that the first nouns the child learns are associated with basic-level visuospatial representations. Hence the more similar the shape of an input to that of the first creature called *dog*, the more likely it is that it will be given the same name. As the child learns more words and learns more about the words' referents (e.g., dogs have fur, bark, and come in a particular range of shapes and sizes), the representation associated with the word becomes more detailed, and the child's usage converges with that of adults.

As we mentioned in Chapter 5, words referring to basic-level categories tend to be the earliest acquired by children (Rosch, Mervis, Gray, Johnson, and Boyes-Braem 1976). The commonest type of overextension is for children to use basic-level terms to refer to other objects in the same superordinate category (Rescorla 1980). For example, children are very likely to extend *car* to include other vehicles. Thus children's initial categories may actually be somewhat broader than the adult's basic level because the young child's definition has little additional information besides a visuospatial representation.

Rosch et al. (1976) argued that expertise in an area produces more specific basic-level categories; e.g., an airplane mechanic will have a different basic level than most people for the domain of airplanes. Young children are not expert in any domain, so their basic levels are more general than those of adults. If young children are relying on visuospatial representations to define categories, then even though they make overextensions, they should view some referents as better than others (Thompson and Chapman 1977), just as adults do. For example, what would happen if one showed a little girl pictures of both a dog and a horse and requested, "Show me a dog" (Huttenlocher 1974)? Quite likely, she would usually pick out the dog picture.

Children may also sometimes overextend words simply because they don't know what else to call something. In a similar way, someone struggling with a foreign language may not know the word for "desk" and therefore call a desk a table. The person may know very well that table is the wrong word but use it anyway in the hope of being understood. At any rate, the girl described above will probably narrow her usage for *doggie* as soon as she learns the words *horse* and *sheep*.

**Conceptual development.**     Sometime between the ages of three and five a child develops sufficient communicative ability to provide detailed information about what words mean.   Keil (1979) asked preschoolers as young as three years old, as well as children in kindergarten and second, fourth, and sixth grades, to say whether sentences such as "The rabbit is sorry" and "The chair is awake" were "okay" or "silly." He used predicates that could be combined with different kinds of category concepts to examine the child's understanding of the meaning of each word. For example, if a child agreed that *either* "A chair is heavy" or "A chair is light" were "okay," then Keil concluded that the child thought a chair was a physical object. Conversely, if the child thought that "A chair is alive" and "A chair is dead" were both silly, Keil concluded that the child realized that a chair was not a living thing.

Keil tested each child with a variety of nouns and predicates. The youngest children with the most primitive semantic development responded as if all concepts represented physical objects. For example, even if they used the word *idea*, they thought that an idea could be tall and heavy. The children distinguished between only two types of concepts: living (e.g., *girl, rabbit*) and nonliving (e.g., *chair, water, recess, fight, ideas*). A comparison of the responses of younger and older children revealed the following sequences of steps in conceptual development:

1. Living and nonliving.
2. Artifacts (*chair*) and other nonliving physical objects (*water, thunderstorm, fight, love*).
3. Events (*thunderstorm, fight, love*) and physical objects (*water*).
4. Intentional events (*fight, love*) and other events (*thunderstorm*).
5. Abstract concepts (*love*) and events (*fight*).

Keil's results indicate that children initially rely on visuospatial representations generated by bottom-up perceptual processes to define concepts, and only later do they augment these definitions with functional and relational information.

**First Sentences**

A child's earliest use of language involves a variety of desires, concerns, and comments. Table 14.1 contains some two-word utterances of children a few months older than one year. From the very beginning the child is not naming for the sake of naming—or learning the language for its own sake—but is trying to communicate. The first one- and two-word utterances resemble adult communications in the kinds of relations they express about things in the world: Location, possession, description, negation, etc., are the kinds of relations adults make use of in talking about the world.

However, the child's utterances are much more limited than those of adults in what a single utterance can express. A one- or two-word utterance can express only a single relationship to a single object, whereas an adult sentence can express several relationships between as many objects. A one- or two-word utterance can have many interpretations, so the speaker must rely on the context in which it is uttered, and perhaps on accompanying gestures and inflections, to fill in its meaning and disambiguate it. In contrast, an

**TABLE 14.1** Functions of Two-Word Utterances in Child Speech

| Function | Examples |
|---|---|
| Locate, name | There book <br> That car <br> See doggie |
| Demand, desire | More milk <br> Give candy <br> Want gum |
| Negate | No wet <br> No wash <br> Not hungry |
| Describe | Bambi go <br> Mail come <br> Hit ball |
| Possession | My shoe <br> Mama dress |
| Modify | Pretty dress <br> Big boat |
| Question | Where ball |

*Source:* From Slobin (1979).

adult sentence can be explicit enough to be understood when printed on a piece of paper and read in contexts far removed from where it was written and by individuals with no knowledge of who wrote it. The one- and two-word utterance stage is still relatively close to the gesture communication systems that have been taught to other primates.

## Invention of Syntax

**Word classes and syntax.** There are two different ways that a toddler uses language to designate a desired object. A pronoun such as *this* or *that* substitutes for or complements the physical act of pointing. Such pronouns refer to an object in the environment by virtue of the object's location rather than physical features such as its form or color. In order to do so, the pronoun must activate some procedure within the spatial component of the visuospatial code, which selects its referent. In contrast, a noun, such as *doll,* refers to an object by accessing a concept that contains a visuospatial representation of its form. The ability to communicate by using names is limited only by the development of categorization skills.

Around two years of age the child "invents"syntax. The invention of syntax occurs when the child realizes that she can use words in relation to other words as well as to objects in the world. With this insight a sharp division develops in the kinds of words the child uses. Words that refer to the properties of things, called *content words* (e.g., *dog, chase, red,* and *awkwardly*), form a very large open-ended class of words containing many thousands of entries. This class is open-ended because a new class member can be added by simply inventing a new name for something. Words that express relations between other words, called *function words* (e.g., *who, of, in,* and *and*), number less than a hundred and form a closed class. New words are rarely invented and added to this class.

A string of words in which some words relate to other words is either a phrase, a clause, or a sentence. The relationship between the words is the *syntax* of the word string. One word can refer to another in any of three ways. First, the order of the words can determine the relationship between them. Consider the phrase *Fred's radio,* which expresses the relationship of possession between *Fred* and *radio. Fred* refers to the possessor in part because it is the first word in the phrase. *Radio Fred's* means something entirely different.

Second, an *inflection* in a word can mark the relationship between it and another word. An inflection can be any of a variety of changes in a word, such as the change from *strike* to *strikes* and from *strike* to *struck.* In the phrase *Fred's radio* the possessive relation is indicated by the inflection -*s* on *Fred.*

Third, a function word frequently marks the relationship between two or more content words. In the phrase *the radio of Fred,* the function word *of* marks the possessive relationship between *the radio* and *Fred.*

All languages use some mixture of word order, inflections, and function words for marking the relationships between words. Notice that in all the examples of the possessive, word order played some role in defining the relationship between the content words. English relies most heavily on word order and function words and least on inflections. Other languages rely much more heavily on inflections and much less on word order. In such a language, in which the relationship between two adjacent words is completely determined by their inflections, expressions corresponding to *Fred's radio* and *radio Fred's* would mean the same thing.

**Stages in syntax acquisition.**     The learning of syntax appears to pass through three phases. In the first phase the meanings of individual words are learned, and the words are combined in short utterances to express the variety of semantic relations shown in Table 14.1. During this phase children may use correctly whole words and even whole phrases that they hear frequently, including such high-frequency irregular verbs as *came, broke,* and *did.* One type of utterance that emerges during this period, which is critical for further syntactic development, is the type that describes one thing (the *agent*) performing some *action* that affects some other thing (the *object*). Some examples of agent-action-object utterances are *The sun melts the ice* and *Laurie broke the doll.* Agent-action-object utterances provide the model for the basic syntactic structure for the entire language.

In the second phase the child seems to be looking for *rules* that can be applied to a whole class of words to define the relations between them when they appear in an utterance. At this point the word order of agent-action-object utterances becomes the model for utterances in general. In some languages word order is more variable than in others, but every language has at least a preferred order for the two nouns and a verb in the basic agent-action-object relationship. The orderings known to exist in different human languages are agent-object-action, agent-action-object, and action-agent-object (Greenberg 1963; Pullum 1977).

During the second phase of language acquisition the child also becomes aware that some words are produced by combining root forms with inflections and begins to apply rules of inflection. One fascinating consequence of this awareness is the phenomenon of *overregularization:* a rule or strategy is first applied more widely than it should be. For example, after the child learns the general rule for forming the past for regular verbs—add -*ed,* as in *walked* or *kicked*—she is likely to also regularize the irregular verbs. So *came* becomes *comed, did* becomes *doed, broke* becomes *breaked,* etc., for the next several months (Ervin 1964). Overapplying the new rule actually causes the child to make errors with verbs that had previously been used correctly.

Similar instances of overregularization can be found with complex sentence constructions. For example, in the sentence *John told Bill to leave,* Bill is the one who will be leaving. Usually, the subject of the verb in such a complement sentence is the noun phrase immediately preceding it. However, there are some exceptions. One exception is *promise:* in *John promised Bill to leave,* it is John rather than Bill who is going to leave. Carol Chomsky (1969) found that even six-year-olds often misinterpreted sentences with *promise.* They had not yet learned the exceptions to the rule.

During the second phase of acquisition the child also learns the uses of the function words of the language. Function words mark the boundaries between phrases (e.g., *a, the*) and express relations between phrases (e.g., *in, of*). When a sequence of function words and phrases are combined, the function words express relations between entities in the world. Thus in the sentence *Marcie borrowed the book from Lynne, from* marks a relationship between *borrowed, the book,* and *Lynne.* Function words also mark relations between sentences. For example, two (or more) sentences can be concatenated into longer sentences, such as *Marcie borrowed the book from Lynne and she lent it to Barbara.* Sentences that are parts of longer sentences are called *clauses.* Since any number of phrases and clauses can be combined, there is no fixed limit to the length of a sentence.

The final phase of syntax learning begins around the age of six or seven and continues throughout the primary school years. During this period the child's processing of sentences gradually becomes more automatic and hence requires less conscious effort (see Chapter 3). There are two consequences of this automatization. First, the child is able to understand sentences of greater syntactic complexity. Second, the syntactic processing of a sentence is no longer influenced as heavily by the referents of its words.

For the younger child language comprehension requires conscious effort, the kind of effort you would require to understand a sentence of a foreign language you were learning. At this point the child relies heavily on the referential meaning of individual words to construct an interpretation of the entire utterance. For example, *Joy pushed the bicycle* and *The bicycle was pushed by Donna* may be understood correctly, but *The bicycle pushed Joy* and *Donna was pushed by the bicycle* may not be. In contrast, after the sentence construction procedure is automatized, the relationships among the words' referents are computed rapidly and unconsciously from the positions of the words in the sentence. As a result, even absurd statements about bicycles pushing people can be understood (Slobin 1966). At the point at which the words of a sentence are assigned agent-action-object relations solely on the basis of their positions in the string and/or the inflections they carry, the child's agent-action-object representation of an utterance has given way to the adult's subject-verb-object representation of a sentence.

## Complexity of Adult Syntax

Our overview of the acquisition of syntax has given only a very broad outline of the myriad ways of expressing relationships that a single language encompasses. A man can *sing while shaving* or he can *sing during his shave*. A man can *be strong* or he can *have strength*. We have so many ways of expressing essentially the same thoughts that every attempt to exhaustively list all the possibilities has so far been defeated. Just to take one example, consider all the parts of the language that can actually be used as the subject of a sentence. These include the gerunds of verbs (e.g., *Flying is dangerous*), the infinitive forms of verbs (e.g., *To dance is divine*), and adverbs (e.g., *More is not enough*). This sort of syntactic flexibility tends to turn every attempt to list all the rules of a language into a list of the exceptions to those rules.

At this point you may be wondering exactly why the grammatical structure of a language is as complicated as it is. Is it really necessary to have so many different kinds of verbs and function words, each with its own rules of usage? Could not the same flexibility have been achieved with greater economy of structure?

The complexity of language arises because it is not a fixed entity that is passed down through the generations like an heirloom but is an ever-changing set of conventions. These conventions, like the tax code, are subject to conflicting forces. The resulting process of give and take renders the final compromise extremely complicated.

Four major forces that influence language structure are expressive needs, economy, clarity, and learnability. As our society changes, new knowledge is added and new things become important, and the language must be stretched to express them. New words are added and new grammatical functions are created for old words. In addition to expressive needs, there is a need for language to be economical. As a result, speech is elliptical. Unnecessary words are omitted. *The girl who the dog bit cried* becomes *The girl the dog bit cried*. *Houses for dogs* becomes *doghouses*, and *houses in trees* becomes *tree houses*.

However, economy cannot be pushed too far before it must give way to the demand for clarity. If we call men who fight fires *firemen*, then men who start fires must be called something else, like *firebugs*. When syntactic cues become too abbreviated, grammatically ambiguous sentences are generated. Although the phrases *growing a plant* and *a growing plant* each have one meaning, the sentence *Growing plants can be interesting* has two. The sentence *John fired the employee because he was ill-tempered* does not make it clear whether John or the employee was ill-tempered. However, phrases like *John, who was ill-tempered* and the *ill-tempered employee* tell us exactly where the fault lies.

Finally, a language that is a result of all these pressures must have a learnable structure if it is to be passed on to the next generation. Thus it must have as few basic sentence types as possible, each with the widest possible application. For example, one would not want to add a new type of constituent to the basic subject-verb-object sentence structure if one could avoid it. Preferably, one accommodates linguistic change by adding new words or constructions that obey as many of the old rules as possible. For example, what are the subjects of sentences like *It is raining* and *There is nobody here?* Do *it* and *there* really mean anything in these sentences, or are they there just to preserve the generalization that every declarative sentence has a subject, so that the basic structure of a sentence need not be altered?

This kind of compromise between new demands and old structures is what complicates syntax. Part of the syntactic structure of any language no longer serves any real function but remains as a vestige of the linguistic past.

## SUMMARY

Language is perhaps the most distinctly human of all cognitive skills. The basic properties of human language are *generativeness* and *abstract structure.* For example, the rules of syntax can be used to construct an indefinitely large number of possible English sentences. Although natural animal communication systems share various properties with human language, no animal systems offer convincing examples of generativeness. Recent attempts to teach sign language to primates also indicate that although animals can learn to use signs to refer to objects and actions in their environment, their ability to learn abstract syntax is severely limited.

One of the most fascinating aspects of language is the ease with which children learn such a complex system. The earliest speech sounds emitted by children tend to be universal across different languages. Children learn to speak primarily by engaging in conversations in which adults speak to them in a simplified way. Children strive to learn tacit rules for using words and constructing sentences. Often their early hypotheses about word meanings are not entirely correct, so they do not use words in accordance with adult meanings.

A common observation is that children *overgeneralize* word meanings, using words to refer to a broader range of instances than is correct. As they acquire syntax, they often at some point will learn general rules that lead to *overregularization,* which involves applying a general rule even to cases that are in fact exceptions. Children often use simple strategies for comprehending sentences, which generally lead to correct interpretations but sometimes do not. The complexity of adult syntax is the result of various conflicting pressures, of which the learnability of the language is an important one.

## RECOMMENDED READINGS

The relationship between language and human intelligence is discussed by Noam Chomsky, the most influential linguist of this century, in his *Language and Mind* (1972). Chomsky's stress on the innateness of much linguistic knowledge is highly controversial but is important to understand because of the impact of his position on the development of psycholinguistics. A good introduction to the study of linguistics is provided by Fromkin and Rodman's *Introduction to Language* (1978). Two good recent collections of papers on language acquisition are *Language Acquisition* (1982), edited by Wanner and Gleitman, and *The Child's Construction of Language* (1981), edited by Deutsch. *Child's Talk* (1983), by Jerome Bruner, is an enjoyable discussion of language acquisition.

# CHAPTER **FIFTEEN**

# Language Processing

## INTRODUCTION

When you hear an utterance, you usually have the illusion that you comprehend it immediately. Actually, your awareness of the meaning of an utterance
is the result of a complex series of processing steps. You must briefly maintain
several words in consciousness, combine categorical and relational information associated with the words into a single proposition, and supplement the
propositional representation with visuospatial information (see Figure 15.1).
Any of these steps can be impaired by an injury to the brain. In this chapter we
will examine this complex process and how it may be impaired.

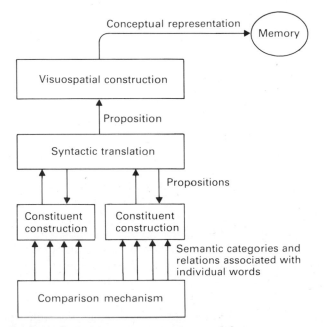

**Figure 15.1   Outline of constituent-processing model.**

## LANGUAGE COMPREHENSION

Language comprehension is under conscious control, which has both advantages and disadvantages. On the one hand, conscious processing allows one to select different interpretations of words and sentences in different contexts, which contributes to the generativeness of language. On the other hand, the propositional representation of a sentence must be constructed in piecemeal fashion, only a few words at a time, because of the severe limitation on the size of a representation that may be maintained in consciousness (see Chapter 3).

In normal conversation we usually understand the meanings of the utterances we hear without conscious effort. We are not aware of piecing together the syntactic and semantic structure of the sentence in order to understand it. Yet this piecing is what we must do. The fact that language comprehension proceeds with such little difficulty is a tribute to the sophistication and efficiency of the processing system responsible for it.

### Steps in the Comprehension Process

A great many cognitive processes are involved in the comprehension process, including the retrieval of word meanings from the semantic code, the application of syntactic-recoding operations, the generation of propositional representations for sentences, and the integration of the current linguistic input with prior knowledge. These processes, shown in Figure 15.1, operate partially in parallel and interact in complex ways. The following steps appear to be major components of the comprehension process:

1.  The meanings of individual words are accessed in memory by the comparison mechanism. This bottom-up process generally occurs as soon as each word is heard or read and is largely automatic.

2.  The lexical information, i.e., the semantic categories and relations accessed by the words, is used by the syntactic translation procedure to construct propositions. This step is a partly top-down procedure, which constructs the proposition in several steps. First, groups of syntactic categories that form *constituents* such as phrases and clauses are combined into larger propositional representations for the entire sentence, as indicated by the upward arrows in Figure 15.1. If at any time an inconsistency is detected (e.g., the meaning selected for an ambiguous word proves incompatible with the context), an attempt is made to find an alternative interpretation. At the ends of constituents and sentences various wrap-up procedures serve to complete the construction of integrated interpretations, as shown by the downward arrows in Figure 15.1.

3.  From the propositional representations a visuospatial representation may also be constructed. This representation is integrated with other representations stored in long-term memory.

Let us examine some of the evidence supporting this general conception of the comprehension process.

## Lexical Access

Normally, when you hear an ambiguous word in a sentence, you do not recognize that it is ambiguous; you are only aware of the meaning that fits the sentence. For example, for the sentence *They need a new sink*, you only perceive the noun meaning of *sink* and not the verb meaning. In fact, however, Tanenhaus, Leiman, and Seidenberg (1979) showed that *both* meanings of an ambiguous word are initially retrieved, and then the appropriate one is selected and integrated into the sentential representation at a subsequent step of the comprehension process. These investigators made use of the fact that if two words that are related in meaning are read in succession, the first word primes the second word so that the time needed to read it is decreased (see Chapter 2). For example, if *sink* is read, followed by *swim*, *swim* is read unusually quickly.

It is not especially surprising that priming facilitates reading of a word when its meaning is related. However, Tanenhaus *et al.* also found that if *swim* immediately follows *They need a new sink*, its reading time is still primed. This result indicates that the verb meaning of *sink* is automatically activated when the word is first processed, even if the sentence context requires a noun. However, if *swim* follows *They need a new sink* by 200 milliseconds, it is no longer read any faster than when preceded by an unrelated sentence. Already, one meaning has been selected (see also Seidenberg, Tanenhaus, Leiman, and Bienkowski 1982; Swinney 1979).

These results suggest that initial lexical access is both immediate and largely independent of context. So multiple interpretations are accessed for ambiguous words, and context is subsequently used to immediately select an appropriate meaning and, perhaps, to actively suppress inappropriate ones, as shown in Chapter 2 (Neely 1977).

## Constituent Processing

**Detection of inconsistencies.**   When a word activates more than one meaning, one has to be selected on the basis of the context. When the wrong meaning is at first selected, the inconsistency is noticed immediately. In one study of the detection and resolution of inconsistencies, Carpenter and Daneman (1981) had subjects read "garden path" passages such as the following:

> The young man turned his back on the rock concert stage and looked across the resort lake. Tomorrow was the annual, one-day fishing contest and fishermen would invade the place. Some of the best bass guitarists in the country would come to

this spot. The usual routine of the fishing resort would be disrupted by the festivities.

When they read this passage aloud, most people initially pronounced the ambiguous word *bass* in accord with its "fish" meaning, which had been primed by the preceding references to fishing. However, the "fish" interpretation is inconsistent with the immediately following word *guitarists*, which forces the interpretation related to low musical notes. Carpenter and Daneman measured subjects' eye fixations as they read the passage, and they found that people kept their gaze on *guitarists* a relatively long time as the inconsistency was detected, and then they regressed to reread the word *bass*. People thus use the context both to select meanings and to detect inconsistencies as early as possible.

**Intrasentence integration.**  Although people continually attempt to develop consistent interpretations of utterances, additional wrap-up processing (Carpenter and Just 1983) is especially likely to occur at the ends of major constituents, such as clauses and sentences. Constituents form natural meaning units, and it is at such points that the information required for higher-order integration often first becomes available. The function and content words in a constituent, when taken together, specify the meaning of the entire constituent. Word order and function words can then serve to indicate how the constituent meaning should be integrated into the meaning of the full sentence. A simple example will make this integration process clear.

Consider the meaning of *to* in the following three sentences:

Laurie went to the store.

Arthur went to get a pencil.

Lillie went to sleep.

In all three sentences *to* connects its constituent to the verb *went*, but in each case it marks a different semantic relationship between the verb and the following constituent. The entire constituent is required to specify the relationship. In the first sentence *to* marks the final location of something after a change in position in space. In the second sentence it marks the purpose of the movement. And in the third sentence it marks a change in psychological state. In all three sentences the entire constituent is needed to understand the nature of what is being referred to (i.e., a location, a purpose, or a state).

The word *to* is by no means a special case. Almost any function word you can think of is vague enough to refer to more than one relationship in isolation. But it is usually restricted to a single relationship when bound to a constituent. For example, consider the words *by* and *of*:

Lee was seated by the waiter.
Susan was seated by the fire.

Vince made a bowl of wood.
Pat made a bowl of soup.

Because we can assign meanings to constituents and combine these constituent meanings to form the meaning of the entire sentence, we feel that we grasp the sentence meaning directly. Syntactic information specifies how the constituent meanings are related, while the constituents, in turn, specify details of the function word's relation.

How are constituent meanings actually combined? There seems to be no single automatic procedure. In fact, sometimes there is more than one way to put constituents together, and one must decide which possibility best fits with the rest of the sentence or the overall context. For example, in the sentence *Lee was seated by the waiter*, Lee may be seated beside the waiter rather than with the waiter's assistance. To decide which meaning is intended, the listener must consider the overall context and what is known about waiters.

**Intersentence integration.** Sentences are not understood in isolation but as segments of conversations, essays, or stories. Hence some wrap-up processes involve integrating a sentential proposition with those that came before it by associating it to a node generated by a story schema (see Chapters 8 and 9). Karl Haberlandt and his students (Haberlandt, Berian, and Sandson 1980) studied this process by measuring the times needed to read individual sentences of stories that could be generated by a simple schema. Each story consisted of a setting (S) and two episodes, where each episode consisted of a beginning (B), reaction (R), goal (G), attempt (A), outcome (O), and ending (E). An example is shown in Table 15.1. Readers were instructed to read a story for the purpose of recalling it as closely to verbatim as possible.

When they controlled for factors that influenced the reading times of the individual sentences, the researchers found that reading times were longest at the beginnings and ends of the episode and declined for sentences in the middle. Haberlandt suggested that at the beginning or the reaction the story schema activates a new semantic node in the story hierarchy for the episode. At the end of the episode the individual sentence propositions are combined into a single proposition for the entire episode, which involves such operations as deleting redundant elements. These extra operations increase reading times at the beginnings and ends of episodes. A similar effect on sentence time was found by Cirilo and Foss (1980) for somewhat longer and more interesting stories.

**Decay of verbatim memory.** We have seen that until the proposition corresponding to a constituent is integrated with the propositional representation of the entire sentence, it is subject to reinterpretation. Hence maintaining a detailed representation of the constituent in consciousness is necessary. If

**TABLE 15.1** Sample Story Consisting of a Setting and Two Episodes

| | |
|---|---|
| S | Once upon a time there was a king. |
| | The king had three lovely daughters. |
| | The king's daughters went for a walk in the woods every day. |
| B | One afternoon a dragon came into the woods and kidnapped the daughters. |
| R | They were frightened by the dragon. |
| G | So they planned to escape from the dragon. |
| A | The daughters tried to distract the dragon by singing songs. |
| O | But they remained the dragon's prisoners. |
| E | The daughters cried desperately. |
| B | Three knights heard the cries. |
| R | They took pity on the daughters. |
| G | They wanted to free the daughters. |
| A | The knights attacked and fought the dragon. |
| O | Finally they killed the fierce monster. |
| E | The knights had saved the king's daughters. |

*Source:* From Haberlandt, Berian, and Sandson (1980).

such a detailed representation is maintained (perhaps at the phonetic or lexical level), then if we interrupt a discourse in the middle or just at the end of a constituent, the listener is likely to remember all of the constituent's words verbatim. Conversely, the words of earlier constituents should not be recalled verbatim, since people do not typically memorize the words they hear but merely retrieve their meanings.

Jarvella (1970, 1971) tested this prediction directly. He had people listen to long passages. The subjects were instructed that when the passage stopped, they were to write as much of the end of it as they could remember exactly. In one study Jarvella found that people remembered the last clause verbatim 86 percent of the time, the second-to-last clause 54 percent of the time, and the third-to-last clause only 12 percent of the time. These results were obtained when the last two clauses were part of the same sentence. When the second-to-last clause was not in the same sentence as the final clause, people recalled it verbatim only 20 percent of the time. Furthermore, even though Jarvella found decay in verbatim recall between clauses, he did not find it within a clause. That is, people who did not remember the whole clause were not especially likely to get just its end correct. This pattern would be expected if people were retaining all the words in a clause until its end was reached then letting them go all at once.

A study by Caplan (1972) also provides evidence linking constituent boundaries with the availability of verbatim representations. In this study the subject heard a sentence, and at the completion of the sentence a probe word was presented. The subject had to respond as rapidly as possible about whether the probe word appeared in the sentence. We are interested in probe words that had actually occurred in the sentence. For some sentences the probe word (which in this example is *oil*) appeared in the last clause:

Now that artists are working fewer hours oil prints are rare.

For other sentences it appeared in the next-to-last clause:

Now that artists are working in oil prints are rare.

As you can see from the examples, the sentences were cleverly constructed so that regardless of whether the probe word was in the last or the next-to-last clause, it was the same number of words from the end of the sentence. If the words of the last clause are maintained in active memory, then a probe word from the last clause should be matched rapidly. If the words of the next-to-last clause are not being maintained in active memory, then the probe word should be matched more slowly on the basis of its meaning. As predicted, the probe word was identified faster when it had occurred in the last clause.

An obvious consequence of the purging of verbatim representations at the ends of constituents is that inconsistencies in the interpretation of an utterance that are only detected after a constituent has been closed are exceptionally disruptive to comprehension. This disruption is particularly true for poor readers, for whom reading is sufficiently difficult to continually tax the capacity of active memory (Daneman and Carpenter 1983). For example, poor readers have a great deal of difficulty recovering from the garden path sequence:

There is also one sewer near our home. He makes terrific suits.

They have less difficulty when the inconsistency manifests itself before a sentence boundary has been crossed, as in the following sentence:

There is also a sewer near our home who makes terrific suits.

## Comprehension Difficulty

Individual phrases and clauses differ greatly in the ease with which they can be understood. In particular, the activation limit on human information processing (see Chapter 2) constrains the number of units that can be held in consciousness during the construction of constituents, and it ultimately influences the ease of comprehending sentences.

**Constituent size.**    One obvious factor that affects comprehension is the number of words each constituent contains. For example, in the sentence *The boy bought a comic book,* maintaining the phrase *the boy* in active memory does not require much effort. Since the entire sentence consists of a single clause with a basic subject-verb-object (SVO) structure, the entire sentence can be assigned a meaning after the word *book.*

In contrast, the sentence *The very thin, grubby-looking, tattered, little boy bought a comic book* also consists of a single, basic SVO clause. However, the subject noun phrase in this sentence contains many more words than the corresponding phrase in the first sentence. Maintaining all those words while trying to process the rest of the sentence would clearly overburden attentional capacity. Accordingly, a meaning must be assigned to the subject phrase in the second sentence so that its words no longer have to be maintained in active memory by rehearsal.

In other words, if a clause is relatively short, it may be processed as a single constituent. But if attentional capacity is heavily burdened, constituent meanings may be constructed at every phrase boundary in order to reduce the processing load as much as possible.

**Lexical complexity.**    Comprehension difficulty is also increased by the use of relatively complex words, such as *unhappiness.* Recall that the flexibility of language structure often affords many ways of expressing the same meaning. For example, we can say that someone is *not happy, unhappy,* or *sad.* Similarly, we can report that someone is *not present* or *absent.* We can construct a meaning out of two words, as with *not happy;* out of a word plus an inflection, as with *un-* and *happy;* or we can simply retrieve the meaning as a single unit, as with *sad.* In general, the more units that are involved, the more conscious processing is required. In addition, a separate word like *not* increases the processing load more than an inflection like *un-* (Clark 1974). Accordingly, *not happy* will take longer to process than *unhappy,* which in turn will take longer than *sad.* Similarly, *not present* will require more time than *absent.*

As a general principle, we can say that processing time tends to increase with the number of units that have to be integrated. Unfortunately, determining how many units are actually involved is usually very difficult. For example, the noun *strength* is actually derived from the adjective *strong* (just as *length* is derived from *long*). But most likely, the meaning of a noun like *strength* is stored in memory as a single unit. But now consider nouns like *happiness, friendliness, prettiness,* etc. Possibly, we recognize a word like *happiness* as the word *happy* with the inflection *-ness* stuck on the end. The meaning of *happiness* may actually be constructed according to a rule that says any adjective with *-ness* on the end is to be interpreted as a noun.

This example is a case in which one rule may literally be worth a thousand memory units. We can understand many similar nouns, such as *sexiness, hardness, wretchedness,* and *redness.* Furthermore, if tomorrow we learned a new adjective like *bloogie,* we could use the rule to help understand an expression like *the blooginess of the floogle.* However, the word creation rules have many exceptions. Just because *rewrite* means *to write again* and *revisit* means *to visit again,* we do not think that *retire* means *to tire again.*

Not only may some units be smaller than words, but some are undoubtedly larger. The best examples of such larger units are *idioms,* such as *kicked the bucket.* The fixed meaning of this expression (i.e., *died*) must simply be retrieved; it certainly cannot be constructed out of the individual words. In addition, stock phrases like *How's it going?* may also be stored as units.

The units stored in memory may therefore be of various sizes. And to know exactly what the units are is often difficult. For example, a word like *helper* may be processed as two units, *help* and *-er,* which are combined to form the meaning *one who helps.* In contrast, the word *teacher* may be stored in memory as a single unit, since it is a high-frequency word that is learned early in life. Also, some rules for forming words, like the *-ed* that produces past-tense verbs, are applied so often that little effort is probably required. Probably the words recognized most quickly will include both those that have common inflections, like *sliced* in *Jerry sliced the steak,* and those sufficiently frequent to be stored as single units, like *ate* in *Virginia ate the apple.*

### Comprehension and Prior Knowledge

Obviously, people usually understand sentences in a larger context. Often one sentence will refer to an entity or topic that has already been mentioned in the conversation. One of the aspects of language that makes it so efficient is the fact that we do not have to repeat information. Instead, we keep referring to the old information as new information is added. Pronouns especially illustrate this feature of language:

Did Dave like the movie?

No, he didn't.

The distinction between prior or "given" information and new information (Clark and Haviland 1977) plays a major role in determining how we store information in memory. If some topic is being discussed and you are told something new about it, you will want to store the new information in memory along with other information about the same topic. Thus in the previous example the pronoun *he* in the second sentence is a cue to search for an earlier referent about whom a new fact is being provided.

Language has many devices for distinguishing between given and new information. One of the most important devices is extra stress. Compare the following sentences:

**1.** Arnold loves *Lynne.*

**2.** *Arnold* loves Lynne.

**3.** Arnold *loves* Lynne.

All these sentences convey essentially the same information. But they differ in what information the listener is assumed to already know. In each case the stressed item conveys new information. So sentence 1 assumes it was known that Arnold loves someone and adds the new information that the person was Lynne. Conversely, sentence 2 assumes it was known that someone loves Lynne and adds that the person was Arnold. Finally, sentence 3 assumes it was known that there was some relation between Arnold and Lynne and adds that the relation was love.

New information can also be marked by special syntactic devices. So sentences 1′ and 2′ divide the information into given and new in the same way sentences 1 and 2 did:

**1′.** It was Lynne whom Arnold loved.

**2′.** It was Arnold who loved Lynne.

As we pointed out in earlier chapters, the encoding of new information almost always involves the retrieval of old information. To understand a sentence, a person often has to fill in details that aren't specified by the words of the sentence. People are so practiced at integrating new information with old information in memory that they usually don't realize how meaningless individual sentences could be if connections could not be made.

Consider these two sentences (Bransford and Johnson 1973):

**1.** The notes were sour because the seam was split.

**2.** The haystack was important because the cloth ripped.

Both sentences are perfectly grammatical sentences. But understanding or remembering them is difficult because we are unable to connect the sentences to anything we already know. When we hear sentence 1, many unanswered questions arise: What notes? What seam? How can splitting a seam produce sour notes? But a single word can provide a referent that makes each sentence perfectly comprehensible and memorable. The words are *bagpipes* and *parachute,* respectively.

These sentences do not become fully meaningful until the propositional representation is supplemented with visuospatial information that designates specific referents for the nouns. Thus nonlinguistic information is also used in the comprehension of a sentence. Producing a sentence like sentence 1 in the presence of an out-of-tune bagpipe is just as good a clue to its meaning as stating the referent verbally. The nonlinguistic context can be just as important as the linguistic context in influencing comprehension.

## READING

In literate societies such as ours language comprehension is not restricted to the processing of speech. Rather, we can also understand the written word. Reading, as we saw in Chapter 1, illustrates many basic principles of cognitive processing. Most of what we said about comprehension in the preceding section holds for reading as well as for processing spoken language. Here we will discuss reading more fully as a mode of language comprehension.

### Overview of the Reading Process

When you read a page of text, your eyes skip from word to word, briefly fixating on almost every word before going on to the next. During a fixation you can see about ten letters to the right of the fixation point clearly, and these are the letters you read. (You don't pay any attention to letters to the left of the fixation point.) In addition, you can pick up word length information about fifteen letters to the right (McConkie and Rayner 1975). This information is used to determine the next fixation point, which, depending on the length and difficulty of the words, is usually about eight letters to the right. No letters can be seen during the actual saccade (eye movement).

On the average, you fixate on each word for about a quarter of a second, though this average is misleading because there is great variability in the length of each fixation. Figure 15.2 shows the record of the eyes of a person moving across a line of text. As the figure shows, a fixation can last from less

| 1 | 2 | 3 | 4 | 5 | 6 | 7 | 8 | 9 | 1 |
|---|---|---|---|---|---|---|---|---|---|
| 1566 | 267 | 400 | 83 | 267 | 617 | 767 | 450 | 450 | 400 |

Flywheels are one of the oldest mechanical devices known to man. Every

| 2 | 3 | | 5 | 4 | 6 | 7 | 8 | | 9 | 10 |
|---|---|---|---|---|---|---|---|---|---|---|
| 616 | 517 | | 684 | 250 | 317 | 617 | 1116 | | 367 | 467 |

internal combustion engine contains a small  flywheel that converts the jerky

| 11 | 12 | | 13 | 14 | 15 | 16 | 17 | | 18 | 19 | 20 | 21 |
|---|---|---|---|---|---|---|---|---|---|---|---|---|
| 483 | 450 | | 383 | 284 | 383 | 317 | 283 | | 533 | 50 | 366 | 566 |

motion of the pistons into the smooth flow of energy that powers the drive shaft.

**Figure 15.2   Eye fixations of college student reading scientific passage. Gazes within each sentence are sequentially numbered above the fixated words, with the durations (in milliseconds) indicated below the sequence number. (After Just and Carpenter 1980.)**

than 100 milliseconds to more than a second (Just and Carpenter 1980). On the average, the more predictable a word is from the preceding passage, the less time is spent fixating on it (Ehrlich and Raynor 1981). During reading, a small number of *regressions* also occur. That is, the eyes move to the left and fixate on a word for a second time. A college student makes about 75 forward fixations and 15 regressions to read 100 words of text. From these numbers a gain of 1.33 words per forward fixation can be calculated (Crowder 1982, p. 9).

The first step in reading is the identification of the visual pattern a written word forms on a page. We saw in Chapter 1 that for most words the pattern information that is recognized is quite detailed, including information about all the individual letters. However, for very common words (e.g., *the*) it is less detailed, mainly involving only the outer configuration of the pattern (e.g., Healy 1981). In either case it is the pattern the letters make lined up next to each other that is recognized during normal reading. If words are presented a letter at a time, so that they must be mentally spelled out, reading is slowed enormously (Mewhort and Cambell 1980).

One important issue in reading has been the route from the visual identification of a word to its meaning. Figure 15.3 shows the two routes available. In route A the visual representation of the word leads to the activation of the auditory representation of the word, which in turn leads to the activation of the word's meaning. In route B the visual representation of the word directly activates its meaning.

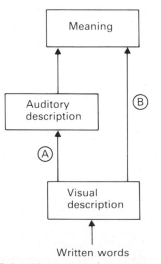

**Figure 15.3 Alternative models of how written words are read.**

The results of most experiments (e.g., Kleiman 1975; Levy 1978) suggest that most of the time the visual representations of words access their meanings directly (route B). Or at a minimum, the activation of the word meaning is sufficiently automatized that any intermediate auditory representation has not been detected. For example, Taft (1979) found that breaking a written word up according to phonological rules disrupts its encoding more than dividing it according to orthographic rules. Even children in the first grade, just learning to read, do not appear to rely on auditory recoding of print to determine meaning (Barron and Baron 1977). Only when material is difficult is evidence of auditory recoding obtained (Hardyck and Petrinovich 1970).

## Dyslexia

In school most children learn to read at least well enough to read a newspaper without special tutoring. But a few children have enormous difficulty learning to read. Extreme difficulty in learning to read is called *dyslexia*. Its cause has remained elusive.

At first researchers thought that dyslexics had trouble seeing the letters on the page. They claimed that somehow dyslexics saw letters upside down or mirror-imaged, because a dyslexic sometimes misread a *b* as a *p* or a *d*. We now know that dyslexics see letters exactly the same way as everyone else sees them and that nondyslexic children who are learning to read make the same errors as dyslexics (Benton 1975; Ellis and Miles 1978; Rourke 1978; Vellutino 1979).

Most dyslexics appear to have a general language comprehension problem (Benton 1975; Mattis, French, and Rapin 1975; Rourke 1978; Rutter 1978; Vellutino 1979). That is, they perform more poorly than normal children on tests involving spoken comprehension as well. The deficit is only noticeable for written material because only comprehension of written material is typically tested. Schoolchildren are never asked to listen to a story and then take individual oral exams. Instead, they are always asked to read a story and then take a written exam. Dyslexic children understand language well enough to understand normal conversation. However, when the material is difficult, as in a textbook, where the whole point is to teach something new, the dyslexic ends up understanding much less than other children.

No one yet knows why dyslexics understand less. What is known is that dyslexia is familial (Owen 1978). Dyslexics are more likely to beget dyslexics than are nondyslexics. Also, dyslexia is lifelong. Although most dyslexics eventually learn to read, they always have more difficulty reading than other people (Scarborough, 1984). These findings imply that dyslexia may be something a person is born with.

The outlook for dyslexics is not all gloomy. Dyslexics, as a group, are as intelligent as the population as a whole. Few occupations require constant reading. With assistance dyslexics can go to college and become doctors, engineers, etc. Though dealing with dyslexia requires hard work, it can be overcome when recognized. The real tragedy occurs when the deficit is not recognized and the student, parents, or teachers conclude that the student is stupid or unwilling to learn.

Unfortunately, even when dyslexia is recognized, proper training does not necessarily follow. Most dyslexics are still told that they see letters reversed. Much money is spent on quack treatments, including drugs. The only proven remediation method is both tedious and expensive—patient and supportive tutoring in reading.

## APHASIA

Aphasics always have difficulty identifying the referents of familiar words. For example, when asked to touch an ankle, they may not know what to do or may touch their leg instead (Goodglass and Geschwind 1976). When asked the name of a familiar object, such as a spoon, they may be unable to respond or they may call it a knife. Even if aphasics produce the correct answer, they may take much more time than a normal subject would and might be unsure that they were right.

Figure 15.4 illustrates schematically the central deficit of aphasia. The naming function, which sets the human brain apart from other brains, is impaired so that many names are lost and the person is unable to relearn them. We will discuss the nature of aphasia in more detail in succeeding sections.

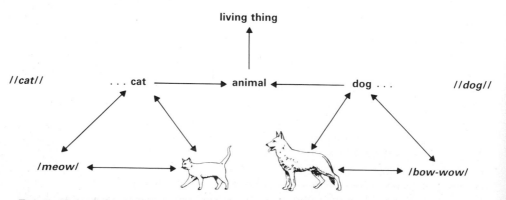

**Figure 15.4    Schematic description of aphasic memory. The dotted lines represent broken connections between names and concepts. Compare this figure with Figure 5.1.**

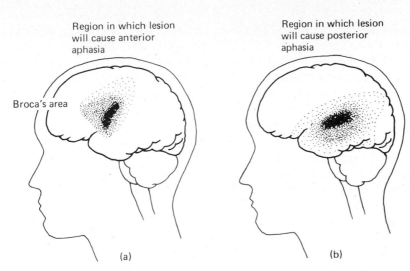

**Figure 15.5    Regions of left hemisphere associated with aphasia: (a) Anterior aphasia; (b) posterior aphasia. Injury to the dark, intermediate, and lighter areas is, respectively, 90, 50, and 10 percent likely to result in aphasia.**

## Types of Aphasia

In addition to their basic difficulty in word finding, different types of aphasics have other symptoms that result from different steps of the language comprehension process (Goodglass and Kaplan 1972). The different deficits result from damage to different areas of the brain. Figure 15.5 shows the regions on the cortex of the left hemisphere associated with the two main types of aphasia (Benson 1967). One type results from a *lesion* (i.e., a destruction of tissue) in a specific area of the frontal cortex (the anterior region), whereas the other results from lesions to the temporal and parietal cortex (the posterior region).

Causes of anterior aphasia are represented in Figure 15.5(a), and causes of posterior aphasia are represented in Figure 15.5(b). The density of dots represents the probability of developing aphasia from a lesion in that area. As the figure suggests, the likelihood of aphasia from certain injuries to two specific locations (one anterior and one posterior) exceeds 90 percent. As one moves from these loci, the likelihood of aphasia drops rapidly.

The two types of aphasia have received many different names. The first type includes the following:

1. *Anterior aphasia,* after the location of the lesion that causes it.
2. *Broca's aphasia,* after the French physician Paul Broca, who first described its symptoms and localized the lesion area primarily associated with it.

3.  *Expressive* or *nonfluent aphasia,* after its most obvious symptom, halting and labored speech.

Broca's aphasia results from damage to the lower levels of the language production and comprehension processes, in which the meanings of the words are retrieved and the syntactic representation of the sentence is constructed. The Broca's aphasic has difficulty retrieving the meanings of words, holding them in consciousness, and combining them to build constituents. This difficulty greatly reduces the syntactic complexity of the speech that a Broca's aphasic can understand. The area associated with Broca's aphasia is adjacent to the part of the cortex called the *motor strip,* which controls voluntary movements. Hence apparently, Broca's area (as it is called) is the place where sentences are turned into the motor commands that produce speech and where phonetic representations are recoded as syntactic representations during comprehension.

The second type of aphasia has been given the following names:

1.  *Posterior aphasia,* after the location of the lesion that causes it.
2.  *Wernicke's aphasia,* after the German physician Carl Wernicke, who first described and localized it.
3.  *Receptive* or *fluent aphasia,* after its two most obvious symptoms, a lack of comprehension and fluent production of meaningless sentences.

Wernicke's aphasia appears to be the result of impairment of the second and third steps of the language comprehension process, in which the categorical and visuospatial representations are combined to form the meaning of the sentence. Wernicke's aphasia results from severe disruption of the connections between the semantic and visuospatial representations. The temporal lobe area associated with Wernicke's aphasia is in the posterior portion of the brain, close to the temporoparietal and occipital areas in which visuospatial processing takes place. Wernicke's aphasia is not restricted to poor comprehension of language; rather, it affects visual categorization as well (see Chapter 5). Thus Wernicke's aphasia involves a general inability to understand natural categories, and the left temporal and parietal cortex seems to be the location of the categorical representation.

Let us now examine each of the two basic types of aphasia more carefully.

## Anterior Aphasia

If Broca's area is injured, a person may have extreme difficulty in producing speech sounds. The person's speech is filled with pauses and stutters. Harold Goodglass (1968, 1976) and his co-workers (Goodglass and Berko 1960;

Goodglass, Fodor, and Schulhoff 1967; Goodglass, Quadfaseal, and Timberlake 1964) have demonstrated that some sounds are hard for aphasics to produce. Goodglass suggests that aphasics leave out the sounds that are hardest for them to produce.

**Syntactic deficits.**    However, the aphasic's difficulty involves more than articulation problems. It also involves syntax. A person suffering from anterior aphasia generally has more difficulty pronouncing function words and inflections than pronouncing content words (Gardner 1976, p. 63; Geschwind 1970). Futhermore, Goodglass has shown (Goodglass and Hunt 1958; Myerson and Goodglass 1972) that one inflection may be harder to produce than another, even when both consist of the same sound. For example, he studied patients who inflected nouns but not verbs. As a result, a person might produce "The boy eats beets" as "The boy eat beets." The final s would be dropped from the verb (eat) but not the noun (beets). This pattern suggests a specific grammatical deficit. In addition, the same types of errors usually appear when the patient tries to write (Gardner 1976, p. 65).

A deficit in the ability to produce and comprehend grammatical sentences is called *agrammatism*. A person suffering from this disorder will tend to leave out function words and inflections. For example, someone trying to say "Hattie bought a dress" might say "Hattie buy dress" or even "Hattie dress."

However, the full extent of the patients' disorder is frequently not obvious from the sentences they produce. It is not obvious because people of normal intelligence can apply special strategies to use the language remaining to them to speak normally. For example, people may use only simple SVO constructions and many overlearned stock phrases like "That's a" and "There is a." In extreme cases people may restrict their speech to very short (but correct) phrases such as "That's right," "Over there," etc. However, the deficit becomes obvious if they are asked to repeat a grammatical sentence that is not in their repertoire. For example, suppose they are asked to repeat the sentence "Keith bought the dress for Hattie." The repetition may contain errors (e.g., "Keith, uh, uh, Hattie, uh, uh, dress"). It may be simplified (e.g., "Keith buy dress Hattie"). The patients may stutter over inflections or may not be able to repeat the sentence at all.

Aphasics may also appear to comprehend more syntax than they are really able to. In many cases if they are aware of some word meanings and the context in which the words are uttered, they can make sense of what is said even if they understand none of the syntax. For example, if a waiter holding a cup of coffee asks, "Do you take cream or sugar in your coffee?" patients will probably be able to respond appropriately even if they understand only the words *cream* and *sugar*.

Alfonso Caramazza and Edgar Zurif (1976) performed an experiment that demonstrated just how dependent aphasics are on word meanings when interpreting complex sentences. They would read a patient a sentence and ask the person to choose which of two pictures the sentence described. Some sentences could only have one reasonable interpretation on the basis of their lexical items. For example, even if one understands only the four main content words in *The bicycle that the boy is holding is broken,* about the only thing the sentence can mean is that the boy is holding the broken bicycle. In comparison, the sentence *The lion that the tiger is chasing is fat* might be interpreted at least four ways if only the content words were understood: the tiger might be chasing the fat lion, the lion might be chasing the fat tiger, the fat tiger might be chasing the lion, or the fat lion might be chasing the tiger. With this type of sentence the aphasics were unable to select the correct picture any more often than would be expected by chance. Apparently, then, anterior aphasia results in a general loss of syntax, both in production and in comprehension (Bradley, Garrett, and Zurif 1980).

**Anterior aphasic vocabulary.** Individual aphasic people vary widely in the degree of their naming difficulties. To casual observation, aphasia presents a crazy-quilt pattern of vocabulary loss, with each aphasic person apparently able to remember a different set of words. However, when groups of aphasic people are tested systematically, a degree of order emerges in the pattern of destruction. Furthermore, more parallels with normal language use become apparent.

If an aphasic patient makes an erroneous response in a naming task, it is likely to be a high associate of the correct response (e.g., substitution of *comb* for *brush*). In fact, when aphasic people are simply asked to produce associations to words, their typical responses are essentially the same as those of normal speakers, although they produce fewer associations and produce them more slowly (Howes 1967). In addition, in a picture-naming task aphasic individuals are most likely to produce nouns that they have learned early in life (Rochford and Williams 1962, 1963) or have used most frequently (Newcomb, Oldfield, and Wingfield 1965). Interestingly, these same factors have been shown to influence how quickly and accurately normal speakers can produce responses in a picture-naming task (Carroll and White 1973; Lachman, Shaffer, and Henrikus 1974; Oldfield and Wingfield 1964, 1965).

Also, anterior aphasic patients are able to produce and comprehend concrete nouns much better than any other kind of word (Caramazza and Berndt 1978). As we saw earlier, concrete nouns seem to play a special role in the vocabulary of normal speakers as well. But in aphasia the difference between facility with concrete nouns and the rest of the vocabulary is enormously exaggerated.

Finally, when aphasic people are asked to rate how similar pairs of words are in meaning, their responses are similar to those of normal speakers (Zurif, Caramazza, Myerson, and Galvin 1974). However, subtle differences do emerge. In this study both normal people and aphasic patients were presented with triads of words and were asked to decide which two were most similar in meaning. This test was done for all possible combinations of twelve words, which included terms for human beings and animals. Zurif *et al.* then used a statistical technique called *clustering analysis* to form a picture of how the subjects viewed the similarity of all twelve words to one another. They found that normal speakers separated the words into human vs. animal terms. The animal terms were then subdivided into three groups consisting, respectively, of fish, reptiles, and mammals: shark and trout, crocodile and turtle, and tiger and dog.

The anterior aphasic patients also divided the words into human and animal terms. However, they subdivided the animal terms in a different way than the normal subjects. The aphasic patients generated two main clusters, one consisting of dangerous animals (shark, crocodile, and tiger), and the other consisting of harmless water animals (trout and turtle). The aphasic patients' clustering scheme may have emerged because the categories *fish, reptile,* and *mammal* were no longer readily available for these subjects.

**Recovery from anterior aphasia.**    Further knowledge of anterior aphasia comes from a survey by J. P. Mohr (1976). First, Mohr's study confirmed Broca's classic observation that difficulties in articulation result from anterior injuries. Second, he found that if the damage to the brain is relatively slight and confined to the front portion, the symptoms of aphasia are likely to clear up after a few weeks or months. On the other hand, the patient who has suffered extensive damage that includes other parts of the hemisphere may initially lose all language use, gradually improving to the level of severe and permanent aphasia. In general, the more severe the initial disorder is, the more severe the long-term disorder is likely to be.

Let us consider what happpens to patients who suffer from a moderately severe initial disorder that shows substantial improvement. As we have seen, at first the patients appear to be suffering from a severe speech disorder. Although they have difficulty talking, they usually appear to be able to understand the conversations going on around them. After a few weeks or months the speech disorder will largely disappear, and to the casual observer the patients may seem fully recovered. However, careful testing often reveals that they have not fully recovered. The patients' ability to produce and comprehend grammatical sentences remains limited.

The degree of aphasic impairment varies over the widest range possible, from those individuals whose ability to speak and comprehend is so slightly impaired that it can be detected only by special testing, to those who are mute and understand nothing. At the mild end of the scale aphasia may manifest itself as a limit on the amount the person can comprehend at one time. For example, an aphasic person who will perform each of three simple commands perfectly (e.g., "Put the key in the cup," "Open the door," and "Touch your head with your hand") when given separately, may be unable to perform any when they are given in combination. Similarly, an aphasic person may be able to take dictation two words at a time yet be totally unable to take it four words at a time (Schuell 1974, p. 111).

Sometimes, aphasia is only a transient rather than a permanent condition. The smaller the size of the lesion and the younger the person is when injured, the more likely it is that a full recovery will be made (Lebrun and Hoops 1976; Sarno 1976). When these temporary aphasic patients recover, they sometimes give an account of what it was like to be aphasic (Moss 1972). As we noted earlier, one difficulty frequently reported is that other people seemed to speak to them too fast during the period of aphasia. Another common report is that the speech of other people was not quite comprehensible. Imagine that you are listening to a stream of speech that sounds awfully familiar but that you cannot quite understand. That is what it feels like to be aphasic.

Unfortunately for aphasic patients, the people around them frequently do not understand their problem, so the aphasic patients do not get the support they need. For example, Helmick, Watamori, and Palmer (1976) found that the spouses of aphasic patients generally did not understand the communication difficulties of their mates, viewed their language as less impaired than it actually was, and did not modify their speech when talking to them (see also Artes and Hoops 1976). This lack of understanding is very unfortunate; our use of language is such an essential part of our daily thoughts and lives that even a slight impairment causes great suffering. For example, Hildred Schuell, a noted aphasia researcher, related the following sad story (Schuell 1974, p. 125):

> I once saw a patient who entered the hospital for seizure control two years after a head injury incurred in the war. He showed no obvious aphasia, but an alert resident referred him for examination because there was a history of transient aphasia on his military record. I found a mild word-finding difficulty and a mild reduction of verbal retention span running through all language modalities. I told the patient what I found and said that it was the result of his head injuries. I told him that it was very mild and that I would not have detected it if I had not tested him. I also told him that there were things that he could do at home to improve it if he were interested. Then he began to talk.
>
> He said it would have made all the difference in the world to him if someone had told him this two years before. He said that he had never heard of aphasia before. He did not know he'd been aphasic after his injury. He said that he went back to his hometown, saw people he had known all his life, and could not remember their names. He could not remember addresses or telephone numbers that he had known most of his life. One night he played cards and found that he could not keep score. He tried to balance his checkbook and found he was not able to do this. He read the paper and did not know what he had read. He listened to news on the

radio and did not know what he had heard. He thought he was losing his mind and he lived in the terror that if someone discovered this he would most certainly be committed to an institution. He began to avoid people. He did not dare to get a job. He said that he had sat home and watched television for two years.

**Language and thought.**    In a case of anterior aphasia a normal, intelligent man may wake up one day (usually the victim of a blood clot in the brain) and discover that he can no longer understand what people around him are saying nor find the words to make himself understood. One striking aspect of this situation is the dissociation between language and thought.

We have good reason to believe that some aphasic people retain many other cognitive abilities while they are aphasic. This belief argues that language is not necessary for intelligent thought. But aphasia also demonstrates that intelligent thought is not by itself sufficient to learn language. So some aphasic individuals retain sufficient cognitive skills to again lead productive lives, yet they never entirely regain their preinjury language competence even after years. [See Gardner (1976, Chapters 8 and 10) for case histories.] When the part of the brain that interprets language is destroyed, one may not always be able to relearn what has been lost.

## Posterior Aphasia

When we turn from anterior aphasia to posterior or Wernicke's aphasia, we find additional evidence for the dissociation of language and thought. As might be inferred from the various descriptive names for the two aphasias mentioned earlier, the two types are about as different as they could be. We have seen that although anterior aphasic patients' words are labored, their thoughts are clear. In contrast, although posterior aphasic patients' speech is fluent, their thinking appears to be very disturbed.

**Symptoms of posterior aphasia.**    If you casually heard a posterior aphasic speak, you would have the impression that you were listening to someone articulate, amiable, and loquacious. His or her speech would seem to come out rapidly and effortlessly, with normal rhythm and intonation. However, if you listened more closely, your impression would quickly change.

The first thing you would note is that the patient's speech was utterly devoid of content. At best, such speech is filled with pronouns that do not refer to anything (e.g., "He went over there, and did that, and came over here and did this," etc.). The patient has difficulty finding words, but this difficulty is exactly the opposite of the anterior aphasic patient's word-finding problems. Whereas the anterior aphasic patient retains concrete nouns the best, the posterior aphasic retains them the worst (Caramazza and Berndt 1978). In the mildest form of posterior aphasia, called *anomic aphasia*, the ability to name objects is the most severely impaired language skill, but comprehension is otherwise normal or nearly normal.

At worst, the speech of a posterior aphasic patient is filled with misused content words and nonsense words, run together very rapidly but with normal intonation, so that the speech sounds grammatical but is utterly meaningless. For example, the patient might say (Gardner 1974, p. 68):

> Boy, I'm sweating, I'm awfully nervous, you know, once in a while I get up, I can't mention the tarripoi, a month ago, quite a little, I've done a lot well, I impose a lot, while, on the other hand, you what I mean, I have to run around, look it over, trebbin and all that sort of stuff.

**Deficits in categorization.**    Posterior aphasic patients demonstrate little or no ability to comprehend anything. On all the systematic tests (word associations, similarity judgments, picture naming, etc.), posterior aphasic patients other than anomic aphasic patients exhibit poor overall performance. For example, we mentioned a study by Zurif *et al.* (1974) in which anterior aphasic patients grouped animal words somewhat differently than normal patients. In this same study a group of posterior aphasic patients did not appear to be sensitive to even the basic semantic distinction between humans and animals. Thus destruction of the semantic code seems to be the major component of posterior aphasia.

Sometimes, the semantic code can be damaged while lower language comprehension processes are left intact. In rare cases, called *transcortical aphasia,* sentences may be repeated correctly in the absence of comprehension or spontaneous production. In such cases, apparently, highly localized destruction of the semantic code blocks the construction of propositional representations (see Figure 13.1) but leaves intact the ability to identify words, form syntactic representations, and produce speech from them. Hence such patients do not merely echo at the phonetic level; in recoding to and from the syntactic level, they will correct a grammatical error in the original utterance during their repetition.

Since the categorical representation is central to concept learning (Chapter 5) and reasoning (Chapter 11), we would expect all thought to be disrupted, which is indeed the case. Not only do severe posterior aphasic patients perform very poorly on comprehension tests but unlike anterior aphasic patients, they also appear to be largely unaware of their disability. As a result, their responses to situations are frequently inappropriate. The moods of different patients vary from jovial to paranoid. Seemingly, Kurt Goldstein (1948) was correct to conclude that these symptoms suggest a disorder not only of language but of thought. After all, the surface manifestations of language—fluent, grammatical speech and writing—can still be produced. The speech is bizarre because it is meaningless, but meaninglessness seems to be due to a serious disturbance of the posterior aphasic patient's thought processes.

It is perhaps worth noting that at the most acute stages of their disorders schizophrenic patients and Korsakoff's patients (see Chapter 8) may utter speech that is virtually indistinguishable from that of a posterior aphasic patient. A comparison can also be made with children who suffer from *spina bifida,* a malformation of the spine in which the vertebrae fail to close. In one subgroup of the disorder (called *myelomeningocele*), some children also develop *hydrocephalus.* In this latter disorder fluid collects on the brain and damages it if the fluid is not drained off. Children with hydrocephalus sometimes develop semantically empty speech, similar to that of a posterior aphasic patient, as their intellects deteriorate (Schwartz 1974). If anterior aphasia seems to result in thought without language, posterior aphasia seems to result in language without thought.

## SUMMARY

In comprehending utterances, listeners attempt to construct a consistent interpretation as quickly as possible. *Lexical access* is typically extremely rapid. If an ambiguous word has multiple frequent meanings, all the meanings are accessed, and then the context is used to select the most appropriate interpretation. However, infrequent meanings are only accessed when the context is supportive. A variety of *wrap-up procedures* are performed at the ends of major *constituents.* Higher-order integration of the interpretation is performed, after which *verbatim representations* of the words in the closed constituent are allowed to deactivate. Comprehension is hindered by factors that overload active memory, such as long or center-embedded constituents or complex lexical items. Comprehension is heavily influenced by the ease with which the utterance can be integrated with prior knowledge stored in memory.

Skilled reading typically involves the direct activation of meaning by the visual representations of words, with relatively little dependency on auditory recoding. Extreme difficulty in learning to read is called *dyslexia.* Dyslexia appears to involve a general problem in language comprehension, but its causes remain elusive.

Damage to the left hemisphere commonly results in *aphasia,* the loss of facility with language. *Anterior aphasic patients* appear to maintain their general cognitive abilities, but they have great difficulty in speaking and some difficulty in comprehending language. Their syntactic knowledge appears to be particularly impaired. *Posterior aphasic patients* continue to speak in fluent and superficially grammatical sentences, but what they say is generally meaningless. Studies of aphasia suggest that language and thought can be independent of each other.

## RECOMMENDED READINGS

There are several fine introductions to language processing, and looking at more than one is worthwhile, because each is written from a different viewpoint. Among the best are Clark and Clark's *Psychology and Language* (1977), Fodor, Bever, and Garrett's *Psychology of Language* (1974), Foss and Hakes's *Psycholinguistics* (1978), Miller's *Language and Speech* (1981), and Paivio and Begg's *Psychology of Language* (1981).

# BIBLIOGRAPHY

Adams, J. A. (1967). *Human Memory.* New York: McGraw-Hill.

Adams, J. A. (1968). Response feedback and learning. *Psychological Bulletin, 70,* 486–504.

Adams, J. A. (1971). A closed-loop theory of motor learning. *Journal of Motor Behavior, 3,* 111–149.

Adams, J. A. (1976). *Learning and memory: An introduction.* Homewood, Ill.: Dorsey Press.

Adams, J. A., Goetz, E. T., & Marshall, P. H. (1972). Response feedback and motor learning. *Journal of Experimental Psychology, 92,* 391–397.

Adams, J. L. (1974). *Conceptual Blockbusting.* Stanford, Calif.: Stanford Alumni Association.

Adams, M. J. (1979). Models of word recognition. *Cognitive Psychology, 11,* 133–176.

Adamson, R. E., & Taylor, D. W. (1954). Functional fixedness as related to elapsed time and set. *Journal of Experimental Psychology, 47,*122–216.

Afifi, A. K., & Bergman, R. A. (1980). *Basic Neuroscience.* Baltimore: Urban & Schwarzenberg.

Ajzen, I. (1977). Intuitive theories of events and the effects of base-rate information on prediction. *Journal of Personality and Social Psychology, 35,* 303–314.

Albert, M. S., Butters, N., & Brandt, J. (1981a). Memory for remote events in alcoholics. *Journal of Studies on Alcohol, 41,* 1071–1081.

Albert, M. S., Butters, N., & Brandt, J. (1981b). Patterns of remote memory in amnesic and demented patients. *Archives of Neurology, 38,* 495–500.

Albert, M. S., Butters, N., & Levin, J. (1979). Temporal gradients in the retrograde amnesia of patients with alcoholic Korsakoff's disease. *Archives of Neurology, 36,* 211–216.

Anderson, J. R. (1976). *Language, Memory, and Thought.* Hillsdale, N. J.: Erlbaum.

Anderson, J. R. (1978). Arguments concerning representations for mental imagery. *Psychological Review, 85,* 249–277.

Anderson, J. R. (Ed.). (1981). *Cognitive Skills and Their Acquisition.* Hilldale, N.J.: Erlbaum.

Anderson, J. R. (1983). *The Architecture of Cognition.* Cambridge, Mass.: Harvard University Press.

Anderson, J. R., & Bower, G. H. (1973). *Human Associative Memory.* Washington, D.C.: Winston.

Anderson, J. R., Kline, P. J., & Beasley, C. M. (1979). A general learning theory and its application to schema abstraction. In G. H. Bower (Ed.), *The Psychology of Learning and Motivation* (Vol. 13). New York: Academic Press.

Anderson, R. C., & Pichert, J. W. (1978). Recall of previously unrecallable information following a shift in perspective. *Journal of Verbal Learning and Verbal Behavior, 17,* 1–12.

Annett, M. (1975). Hand preference and the laterality of cerebral speech. *Cortex, 11,* 305–328.

Arkes, H. R., & Harkness, A. R. (1980). Effect of making a diagnosis on subsequent recognition of symptoms. *Journal of Experimental Psychology: Human Learning and Memory, 6,* 568–575.

Arnett, J. L., & Di Lollo, V. (1979). Visual information processing in relation to age and to reading ability. *Journal of Experimental Child Psychology, 27,* 143–152.

Artes, J., & Hoops, R. (1976). Problems of aphasic and nonaphasic stroke patients as identified and evaluated by patients' wives. In Y. Lebrun & R. Hoops (Eds.), *Recovery in Aphasics.* Amsterdam: Swets and Zeitlinger. B.V.

Atkinson, R. C., Hermann, D. J., & Wescourt, K. T. (1974). Search processes in recognition memory. In R. L. Solso (Ed.), *Theories in Cognitive Psychology: The Loyola Symposium.* Hillsdale, N.J.: Erlbaum.

Atkinson, R. C., & Juola, J. F. (1974). Search and decision processes in recognition memory. In D. H. Krantz, R. C. Atkinson, & P. Suppes (Eds.), *Contemporary Developments in Mathematical Psychology.* San Francisco: Freeman.

Atkinson, R. C., & Raugh, M. R. (1975). An application of the mnemonic keyword method to the acquisition of a Russian vocabulary. *Journal of Experimental Psychology: Human Learning and Memory 104,* 126–133.

Atkinson, R. C., & Shiffrin, R. M. (1968). Human memory: A proposed system and its control processes. In K. W. Spence & J. T. Spence (Eds.), *The Psychology of Learning and Motivation* (Vol. 2). New York: Academic Press.

Attneave, A. (1957). Transfer of experience with a class schema to identification learning of patterns and shapes. *Journal of Experimental Psychology, 54,* 81–88.

Austin, J. L. (1962). *How to Do Things with Words.* Oxford: Oxford University Press.

Averbach, E., & Coriell, A. S. (1961). Short-term memory in vision. *Bell Systems Technical Journal, 40,* 309–328.

Baddeley, A. D. (1972). Selective attention and performance in dangerous environments. *British Journal of Psychology, 63,* 537–546.

Baddeley, A. D. (1976). *The Psychology of Memory.* New York: Basic Books.

Bahrick, H. P. (1970). Two-phase model for prompted recall. *Psychological Review, 77,* 215–222.

Bahrick, H. P. (1983). Memory and people. In J. Harris (Ed.), *Everyday Memory, Actions, and Absentmindedness.* New York: Academic Press.

Bahrick, H. P. (1984). Semantic memory content in permastore: Fifty years of memory for Spanish learned in school. *Journal of Experimental Psychology: General, 113,* 1–29.

Bahrick, H. P., Bahrick, P. O., & Wittlinger, R. P. (1975). Fifty years of memory for names and faces: A cross-sectional approach. *Journal of Experimental Psychology: General, 104,* 54–75.

Bakan, P. (1957). Vigilance, discussion III. *Advances in Science, 13,* 410.

Baker, L., & Santa, J. L. (1977). Context, integration, and retrieval. *Memory & Cognition, 5,* 308–314.

Bakker, D. J. (1970). Ear asymmetry with monaural stimulation: Relations to lateral dominance and lateral awareness. *Neuropsychologia, 8,* 103–117.

Ballard, P. B. (1913). Oblivescence and reminiscence. *British Journal of Psychology Monograph Supplement, 1,* No. 2.

Banks, W. P. (1970). Signal detection theory and human memory. *Psychological Bulletin, 74,* 81–99.

Banks, W. P., & Flora, J. (1977). Semantic and perceptual processes in symbolic comparisons. *Journal of Experimental*

*Psychology: Human Perception and Performance, 3,* 278–290.

Barber, T. X. (1969). *Hypnosis: A Scientific Approach.* New York: Van Nostrand Reinhold.

Barber, T. X., & Glass, L. B. (1962). Significant factors in hypnotic behavior. *Journal of Abnormal and Social Psychology, 64,* 222–228.

Barr, A., & Feigenbaum, E. A. (Eds.). (1981). *The Handbook of Artificial Intelligence.* Vol. 1. Los Altos, Calif.: Kaufmann.

Barr, A., & Feigenbaum, E. A. (Eds.). (1982). *The Handbook of Artificial Intelligence.* Vol. 2. Los Altos, Calif.: Kaufmann.

Barron, R. W., & Baron, J. (1977). How children get meaning from printed words. *Child Development, 48,* 587–594.

Barsalou, L. W. (1983). Ad hoc categories. *Memory & Cognition, 11,* 211–227.

Bartlett, F. C. (1932). *Remembering.* Cambridge: Cambridge University Press. (First paperback edition, 1967.)

Bartlett, J. C., Till, R. E., & Levy, J. C. (1980). Retrieval characteristics of complex pictures: Effects of verbal encoding. *Journal of Verbal Learning and Verbal Behavior, 19,* 430–449.

Bastian, J., Eimas, P. D., & Liberman, A. M. (1961). Identification and discrimination of a phonemic contrast induced by silent interval. *Journal of the Acoustical Society of America, 33,* 842.

Battig, W. F., & Montague, W. E. (1969). Category norms of verbal items in 56 categories: A replication and extension of the Connecticut category norms. *Journal of Experimental Psychology, 80,* 1–46.

Beck, J. (1966). Perceptual grouping produced by changes in orientation and shape. *Science, 154,* 538–540.

Beck, J. (1967). Perceptual grouping produced by line figures. *Perception & Psychophysics, 2,* 491–495.

Beck, J. (1972). Similarity grouping and peripheral discriminability under uncertainty. *American Journal of Psychology, 85,* 1–19.

Becker, C. A. (1980). Semantic context effects in visual word recognition: An analysis of semantic strategies. *Memory & Cognition, 6,* 493–512.

Becker, J. T., Butters, N., Hermann, A., & D'Angelo, N. (1983). A comparison of the effects of long-term alcohol abuse and aging on the performance of verbal and nonverbal divided attention tasks. *Alcoholism: Clinical and Experimental Research, 7,* 213–219.

Beecher, M. D., Peterson, M. R., Zoloth, S. R., Moody, D. B., & Stebbins, W. C. (1979). Perception of conspecific vocalizations by Japanese macaques. *Brain, Behavior and Evolution, 16,* 443–460.

Begg, I. (1978a). Similarity and contrast im memory for relations. *Memory & Cognition, 6,* 509–517.

Begg, I. (1978b). Imagery and organization in memory: Instructional effects. *Memory & Cognition, 6,* 174–183.

Begg, I. (1979). Trace loss and the recognition failure of unrecalled words. *Memory & Cognition, 7,* 113–123.

Bellezza, F. S. (1982). Updating memory using mnemonic devices. *Cognitive Psychology, 14,* 301–327.

Belmore, S. M. (1981). Imagery and semantic elaboration in hypermnesia for words. *Journal of Experimental Psychology: Human Learning and Memory, 7,* 191–203.

Bem, D. J., & McConnell, H. K. (1970). Testing the self-perception explanation of dissonance phenomena: On the salience of premanipulation attitudes. *Journal of Personality and Social Psychology, 14,* 23–31.

Ben-Shakhar, G., Lieblich, I., & Bar-Hillel, M. (1982). An evaluation of polygraphers' judgments: A review from a decision theoretic perspective. *Journal of Applied Psychology, 67,* 701–713.

Benson, D. F. (1967). Fluency in aphasia: Correlation with radioactive scan localization. *Cortex, 3,* 373–394.

Benson, D. F., & Greenberg, J. P. (1969). Visual form agnosia. *Archives of Neurology, 20,* 82–89.

Benton, A. L. (1968). Differential behavioral effects in frontal lobe disease. *Neuropsychologia, 6,* 53–60.

Benton, A. L. (1975). Developmental dyslexia: Neurological aspects. In W. J. Friedlander (Ed.), *Advances in Neurology.* (Vol. 7). New York: Raven Press.

Benton, A. L. (1980). The neuropsychology of facial recognition. *American Psychologist, 69,* 77–110.

Bergum, B. O., & Lehr, D. J. (1964). Monetary incentive and vigilance. *Journal of Experimental Psychology, 67,* 197–198.

Berlin, B., & Kay, P. (1969). *Basic Color Terms: Their Universality and Evolution.* Berkeley and Los Angeles: University of California Press.

Berlin, C. I. (1977). Hemispheric asymmetry in auditory tasks. In S. Harnad, R. W. Doty, L. Goldstein, J. Jaynes, & G. Krauthamer (Eds.), *Lateralization in the Nervous System.* New York: Academic Press.

Best, C. T., Morrongiello, B., & Robson, R. (1981). Perceptual equivalence of acoustic cues in speech and nonspeech perception. *Perception & Psychophysics, 29,* 191–211.

Bevan, W., & Steger, J. A. (1971). Free recall and abstractness of stimuli. *Science, 172,* 597–599.

Bever, T. G. (1975). Cerebral asymmetries in humans are due to the differentiation of two incompatible processes: Holistic and analytic. *Annals of the New York Academy of Science, 263,* 251–262.

Bever, T. G., & Chiarello, R. J. (1974). Cerebral dominance in musicians and nonmusicians. *Science, 185,* 137–139.

Biederman, I., & Checkosky, S. F. (1970). Processing redundant information. *Journal of Experimental Psychology, 83,* 486–490.

Biederman, I., Mezzanotte, R. J., & Rabinowitz, J. C. (1982). Scene perception: Detecting and judging objects undergoing relational violations. *Cognitive Psychology, 14,* 143–177.

Bisiach, E., Capitani, E., Luzzatti, C., & Perani, D. (1981). Brain and conscious representation of outside reality. *Neuropsychologia, 19,* 543–551.

Bjork, R. A., & Whitten, W. B. (1974). Recency-sensitive retrieval process in long-term free recall. *Cognitive Psychology, 6,* 173–189.

Black, J. B., & Bower, G. H. (1980). Story understanding as problem solving. *Poetics, 9,* 223–250.

Blaxton, T. A., & Neely, J. H. (1983). Inhibition from semantically related primes: Evidence of a category-specific inhibition. *Memory & Cognition, 11,* 500–510.

Block, N. (Ed.). (1981). *Imagery.* Cambridge, Mass.: MIT Press.

Boden, M. (1977). *Artificial Intelligence and Natural Man.* New York: Basic Books.

Bogen, J. E. (1969). The other side of the brain: An appositional mind. *Bulletin of the Los Angeles Neurological Societies, 34,* 135–162. Reprinted in R. E. Ornstein (Ed.), (1973), *Readings in the Nature of Human Consciousness.* San Francisco: Freeman.

Bogen, J. E., & Bogen, G. M. (1976). Wernicke's region—where is it? *Annals of the New York Academy of Sciences, 280,* 834–843.

Bohannon, J. N., & Baker-Ward, L. (1981). Right-ear advantage and delayed recall. *Memory & Cognition, 9,* 115–120.

Bornstein, M. H. (1976). Infants are trichromats. *Journal of Experimental Child Psychology, 21,* 425–445.

Bousfield, W. A., & Sedgewick, H. W. (1944). An analysis of sequences of restricted associative responses. *Journal of General Psychology, 30,* 149–165.

Bower, G. H. (1967). A multi-component theory of the memory trace. In K. W. Spence & J. T. Spence (Eds.), *The Psychology of Learning and Motivation: Advances in Research and Theory* (Vol. 1). New York: Academic Press.

Bower, G. H. (1970). Analysis of a mnemonic device. *American Scientist, 58,* 496–510.

Bower, G. H. (1972). Mental imagery and associative learning. In L. W. Gregg (Ed.), *Cognition in Learning and Memory.* New York: Wiley.

Bower, G. H. (1981). Mood and memory. *American Psychologist, 36,* 129–148.

Bower, G. H., & Clark, M. C. (1969). Narrative stories as mediators for serial learning. *Psychonomic Science, 14,* 181–182.

Bower, G. H., Clark, M. C., Lesgold, A. M., & Winzenz, D. (1969). Hierarchical retrieval schemes in recall of categorized word lists. *Journal of Verbal Learning and Verbal Behavior, 8,* 323–343.

Bower, G. H., Gilligan, S. G., & Monteiro, K. P. (1981). Selective learning caused by affective state. *Journal of Experimental Psychology: General, 110,* 451–473.

Bower, G. H., & Glass, A. L. (1976). Structural units and the reintegrative power of picture fragments. *Journal of Experimental Psychology: Human Learning and Memory, 2,* 456–466.

Bower, G. H., & Holyoak, K. J. (1973). Encoding and recognition memory for naturalistic sounds. *Journal of Experimental Psychology, 101,* 360–366.

Bower, G. H., Lesgold, A. M., & Tieman, D. (1969). Grouping operations in free recall. *Journal of Verbal Learning and Verbal Behavior, 8,* 481–493.

Bower, G. H., Monteiro, K. P., & Gilligan, S. G. (1978). Emotional mood as a context for learning and recall. *Journal of Verbal Learning and Verbal Behavior, 17,* 573–585.

Bower, G. H., & Reitman, J. S. (1972). Mnemonic elaboration in multilist learning. *Journal of Verbal Learning and Verbal Behavior, 11,* 478–485.

Bower, G. H., & Winzenz, D. (1969). Group structure, coding and memory for digit series. *Journal of Experimental Psychology Monograph, 80,* (2, Pt. 2).

Bower, G. H., & Winzenz, D. (1970). Comparison of associative learning strategies. *Psychonomic Science, 20,* 119–120.

Bradley, D. C., Garrett, M. F., & Zurif, E. B. (1980). Syntactic deficits in Broca's aphasia. In D. Caplan (Ed.), *Biological Studies of Mental Processes.* Cambridge, Mass.: MIT Press.

Brandt, J., Butters, N., Ryan, C., & Bayog, R. (1983). Cognitive loss and recovery in long-term alcohol abusers. *Archives of General Psychiatry, 40,* 435–442.

Bransford, J. D. (1979). *Human Cognition. Learning, Understanding and Remembering.* Belmont, Calif.: Wadsworth.

Bransford, J. D., & Johnson, M. K. (1972). Contextual prerequisites for understanding: Some investigations of comprehension and recall. *Journal of Verbal Learning and Verbal Behavior, 11,* 717–721.

Bransford, J. D., & Johnson, M. K. (1973). Consideration of some problems of comprehension. In W. G. Chase (Ed.), *Visual*

*Information Processing.* New York: Academic Press.

Bregman, A. S. (1981). Asking the "what for" question in auditory perception. In M. Kubovy & J. R. Pomerantz (Eds.), *Perceptual Organization.* Hillsdale, N.J.: Erlbaum.

Briggs, G. E. (1957). Retroactive inhibition as a function of the degree of original and interpolated learning. *Journal of Experimental Psychology, 53,* 60–67.

Britton, B. K., & Tesser, A. (1982). Effects of prior knowledge on use of cognitive capacity in three complex cognitive tasks. *Journal of Verbal Learning and Verbal Behavior, 21,* 421–436.

Broadbent, D. E. (1958). *Perception and Communication.* London: Pergamon Press.

Broadbent, D. E., & Broadbent, M. H. P. (1977). Effects of recognition on subsequent recall: Comments on "Determinants of recognition and recall: Accessibility and generation," by Rabinowitz, Mandler, and Patterson. *Journal of Experimental Psychology: General, 106,* 330–335.

Broen, P. (1972). The verbal environment of the language-learning child. *Monographs of the American Speech and Hearing Association, 17.*

Broen, W. E. (1973). Limiting the flood of stimulation: A protective deficit in chronic schizophrenia. In R. Solso (Ed.), *Contemporary Issues in Cognitive Psychology: The Loyola Symposium.* Washington, D.C.: Winston.

Brooks, L. R. (1978). Nonanalytic concept formation and memory for instances. In E. Rosch & B. B. Lloyd (Eds.), *Cognition and Categorization.* Hillsdale, N.J.: Erlbaum.

Brooks, L. R. (1968). Spatial and verbal components of the act of recall. *Canadian Journal of Psychology, 22,* 349–368.

Broughton, R. (1975). Biorhythmic varia-

tions in consciousness and psychological functions. *Canadian Psychological Review, 16,* 217–239.

Brown, A. L., & Scott, M. S. (1971). Recognition memory for pictures in preschool children. *Journal of Experimental Child Psychology, 11,* 401–412.

Brown, A. S. (1979). Priming effects in semantic memory retrieval processes. *Journal of Experimental Psychology: Human Learning and Memory, 5,* 65–77.

Brown, A. S. (1981). Inhibition in cued retrieval. *Journal of Experimental Psychology: Human Learning and Memory, 7,* 204–215.

Brown, H. B. (1935). An experience in identification testimony. *Journal of the American Institute of Criminal Law, 25,* 621–622.

Brown, J. (1958). Some tests of the decay theory of immediate memory. *Quarterly Journal of Experimental Psychology, 10,* 12–21.

Brown, J. (1968). Reciprocal facilitation and impairment of free recall. *Psychonomic Science, 10,* 41–42.

Brown, R., & Bellugi, U. (1964). Three processes in the child's acquisition of syntax. *Harvard Educational Review, 34,* 133–151.

Brown, R., & Herrnstein, R. J. (1975). *Psychology.* Boston: Little, Brown.

Brown, R., & Kulik, J. (1977). Flashbulb memories. *Cognition, 5,* 73–99.

Brown, R., and Lenneberg, E. H. (1954). A study in language and cognition. *Journal of Abnormal and Social Psychology, 49,* 454–462.

Brown, R., & McNeill, D. (1966). The "tip of the tongue" phenomenon. *Journal of Verbal Learning and Verbal Behavior, 5,* 325–337.

Brown, W. (1923). To what extent is memory measured by a single recall? *Journal of Experimental Psychology, 6,* 377–382.

Bruce, D. (1980). Single probes, double probes, and the structure of the memory traces. *Journal of Experimental Psychology: Human Learning and Memory*, 6, 276–292.

Bruner, J. S. (1983). *Child's Talk*. New York: Norton.

Bruner, J. S., Goodnow, J. J., & Austin, G. A. (1956). *A Study of Thinking*. New York: Wiley.

Bryan, W. L., & Harter, N. (1899). Studies on the telegraphic language: The acquisition of a hierarchy of habits. *Psychological Review*, 6, 345–375.

Bryden, M. P., & Allard, F. (1976). Visual hemifield differences depend on typeface. *Brain and Language*, 3, 191–200.

Buckhout, R. (1974). Eyewitness testimony. *Scientific American*, 231, 23–31.

Buffart, H. E., Leuwenberg, E., & Restle, F. (1981). A coding theory of visual pattern completion. *Journal of Experimental Psychology: Human Perception and Performance*, 7, 241–274.

Bugelski, B. R., & Alampay, D. A. (1961). The role of frequency in developing perceptual set. *Canadian Journal of Psychology*, 15, 205–211.

Burke, D. M., & Light, L. L. (1981). Memory and aging: The role of retrieval processes. *Psychological Bulletin*, 90, 513–546.

Buschke, H. (1973). Selective reminding for analysis of memory and learning. *Journal of Verbal Learning and Verbal Behavior*, 12, 543–550.

Buschke, H. (1974). Spontaneous remembering after recall failure. *Science*, 184, 579–581.

Buschke, H. (1976). Learning is organized by chunking. *Journal of Verbal Learning and Verbal Behavior*, 15, 313–324.

Buschke, H. (1977). Two-dimensional recall: Immediate identification of clusters in episodic and semantic memory. *Journal of Verbal Learning and Verbal Behavior*, 16, 201–215.

Buschke, H., & Schaier, A. H. (1979). Memory units, ideas, and propositions in semantic remembering. *Journal of Verbal Learning and Verbal Behavior*, 18, 549–563.

Butters, N. (1984). Alcoholic Korsakoff's syndrome: An update. *Seminars in Neurology*, 4, 226–244.

Butters, N., & Barton, M. (1970). Effect of parietal lobe damage on the performance of reversible operations in space. *Neuropsychologia*, 8, 205–214.

Butters, N., Barton, M., & Brody, B. A. (1970). Role of the right parietal lobe in the mediation of cross modal associations and reversible operations in space. *Cortex*, 6, 174–190.

Butters, N., & Cermak, L. S. (1980). *Alcoholic Korsakoff's Syndrome*. New York: Academic Press.

Butters, N., Miliotis, P., Albert, M. S., & Sax, D. S. (1983). Memory assessment: Evidence of the heterogeneity of amnesic symptoms. In G. Goldstein (Ed.), *Advances in Clinical Neuropsychology*. New York: Plenum.

Butters, N., Samuels, I., Goodglass, H., & Brody, B. (1970). Short-term visual and auditory memory disorders after parietal and frontal lobe damage. *Cortex*, 6, 440–459.

Byrne, B. (1974). Item concreteness vs. spatial organization as predictors of visual imagery. *Memory & Cognition*, 2, 53–59.

Calis, G., & Leuwenberg, E. (1981). Grounding the figure. *Journal of Experimental Psychology: Human Perception and Performance*, 7, 1386–1397.

Caplan, D. (1972). Clause boundaries and recognition latencies for words in sentences. *Perception & Psychophysics*, 12, 73–76.

Caramazza, A., & Berndt, R. S. (1978). Semantic and syntactic processes in aphasia: A review of the literature. *Psychological Bulletin, 85*, 898–918.

Caramazza, A., & Zurif, E. B. (1976). Dissociation of algorithmic and heuristic processes in language comprehension: Evidence from aphasia. *Brain and Language, 3*, 572–582.

Carlton, L. G. (1981). Processing visual feedback information for movement control. *Journal of Experimental Psychology: Human Perception and Performance, 7*, 1019–1030.

Carmichael, L., Hogan, H. P., & Walter, A. A. (1932). An experimental study of the effect of language on the reproduction of visually perceived form. *Journal of Experimental Psychology, 15*, 73–86.

Carpenter, P. A., & Daneman, M. (1981). Lexical retrieval and error recovery in reading: A model based on eye fixations. *Journal of Verbal Learning and Verbal Behavior, 20*, 137–160.

Carpenter, P. A., & Eisenberg, P. (1978). Mental rotation and the frame of reference in blind and sighted individuals. *Perception & Psychophysics, 23*, 117–124.

Carpenter, P. A., & Just, M. A. (1983). What your eyes do while your mind is reading. In K. Rayner (Ed.), *Eye Movements in Reading: Perceptual and Language Processes.* New York: Academic Press.

Carroll, J. B., & White, M. N. (1973). Word frequency and age of acquisition as determiners of picture-naming latency. *Quarterly Journal of Experimental Psychology, 25*, 85–95.

Carroll, J. D., & Arabie, P. (1980). Multidimensional scaling. *Annual Review of Psychology, 31*, 607–649.

Cattel, J. M. (1886). The inertia of the eye and brain. *Brain, 8*, 295–312.

Cavanaugh, J. P. (1972). Relation between the immediate memory span and the memory search rate. *Psychological Review, 79*, 525–530.

Cermak, L. S., Lewis, R., Butters, N., & Goodglass, H. (1973). The role of verbal mediation in performance of motor tasks by Korsakoff patients. *Perceptual and Motor Skills, 37*, 259–262.

Chapman, L. J., & Chapman, J. P. (1973). *Disordered Thought in Schizophrenia.* New York: Appleton-Century-Crofts.

Chase, S. (1938). *The Tyranny of Words.* New York: Harcourt, Brace and World.

Chase, W. G., & Ericsson, K. A. (1980). Skilled memory. In J. R. Anderson (Ed.), *Cognitive Skills and Their Acquisition.* Hillsdale, N.J.: Erlbaum.

Chase, W. G., & Ericsson, K. A. (1982). Skill and working memory. In G. H. Bower (Ed.), *The Psychology of Learning and Motivation* (Vol. 16). New York: Academic Press.

Chase, W. G., & Simon, H. A. (1973). The mind's eye in chess. In W. G. Chase (Ed.), *Visual Information Processing.* New York: Academic Press.

Chastain, G. (1977). Feature analysis and the growth of a percept. *Journal of Experimental Psychology: Human Perception and Performance, 3*, 291–298.

Cheng, P. W., & Holyoak, K. J. (1985). Pragmatic reasoning schemas. *Cognitive Psychology, 17*.

Cherry, E. C. (1953). Some experiments on the recognition of speech, with one and two ears. *Journal of the Acoustical Society of America, 25*, 975–979.

Chi, M. T. H., Feltovich, P. J., & Glaser, R. (1981). Categorization and representation of physics problems by experts and novices. *Cognitive Science, 5*, 121–152.

Chomsky, C. (1969). *The Acquisition of Syntax in Children from 5 to 10.* Cambridge, Mass.: MIT Press.

Chomsky, N. (1972). *Language and Mind.* New York: Harcourt Brace Jovanovich.

Chomsky, N. (1975). *Reflections on Language.* New York: Pantheon Books.

Christen, F., & Bjork, R. A. (1976). *On Updating the Loci in the Method of Loci.* Paper presented at the seventeenth annual meeting of the Psychonomic Society, St. Louis.

Christina, R. W., Lambert, P. J., Fischman, M. G., & Anson, J. G. (1982). Hand position as a variable determining the accuracy of aiming movements. *Journal of Experimental Psychology: Human Perception and Performance, 8,* 341–348.

Cirilo, R. K., & Foss, D. J. (1980). Text structure and reading time for sentences. *Journal of Verbal Learning and Verbal Behavior, 19,* 96–109.

Clark, E. V. (1973). What's in a word? On the child's acquisition of semantics in his first language. In T. E. Moore (Ed.), *Cognitive Development and the Acquisition of Language.* New York: Academic Press.

Clark, E. V. (1975). Knowledge, context, and strategy in the acquisition of meaning. In D. P. Dato (Ed.), *Georgetown University Round Table on Languages and Linguistics.* Washington, D.C.: Georgetown University Press.

Clark, H. H. (1969). Linguistic processes in deductive reasoning. *Psychological Review, 76,* 387–404.

Clark, H. H. (1974). Semantics and comprehension. In T. A. Sebeok (Ed.), *Current Trends in Linguistics.* Vol. 12, *Linguistics and Adjacent Arts and Sciences.* The Hague: Mouton.

Clark, H. H., & Chase, W. G. (1972). On the process of comparing sentences against pictures. *Cognitive Psychology, 3,* 472–517.

Clark, H. H., & Clark, E. V. (1977). *Psychology and Language.* New York: Harcourt Brace Jovanovich.

Clark, H. H., & Haviland, S. E. (1977). Comprehension and the given-new contract. In R. O. Freedle (Ed.), *Discourse Production and Comprehension.* Norwood, N.J.: Ablex.

Cohen, N. J., & Squire, L. R. (1981). Retrograde amnesia and remote memory impairment. *Neuropsychologia, 19,* 337–356.

Cohen, P. R., & Feigenbaum, E. A. (Eds.). (1982). *The Handbook of Artificial Intelligence.* Vol. 3. Los Altos, Calif.: Kaufmann.

Cohen, R. L., & Granström, K. (1970). Reproduction and recognition in short-term visual memory. *Quarterly Journal of Experimental Psychology, 22,* 450–457.

Colavita, F. B. (1974). Human sensory dominance. *Perception & Psychophysics, 16,* 409–412.

Cole, R. A., (1973). Listening for mispronunciations: A measure of what we hear during speech. *Perception & Psychophysics, 11,* 153–156.

Collins, A. M., & Loftus, E. F. (1975). A spreading-activation theory of semantic processing. *Psychological Review, 82,* 407–428.

Collins, A. M., & Quillian, M. R. (1969). Retrieval time from semantic memory. *Journal of Verbal Learning and Verbal Behavior, 8,* 240–248.

Collins, A. M., Warnock, E. H., Aiello, N., & Miller, M. L. (1975). Reasoning from incomplete knowledge. In D. G. Bobrow & A. Collins (Eds.), *Representation and Understanding.* New York: Academic Press.

Conrad, R. (1964). Acoustic confusion in immediate memory. *British Journal of Psychology, 55,* 75–84.

Conrad, R. (1972). Speech and reading. In J. F. Kavanagh & I. G. Mattingly (Eds.), *The Relationships Between Speech and Reading.* Cambridge, Mass.: MIT Press.

Coombs, C. H., Dawes, R. M., & Tversky, A. (1970). *Mathematical Psychology: An Elementary Introduction.* Englewood Cliffs, N.J.: Prentice-Hall.

Cooper, L. A., & Shepard, R. N. (1973). Chronometric studies of the rotation of mental images. In W. G. Chase (Ed.), *Visual Information Processing.* New York: Academic Press.

Corcoran, D. W. J., & Weening, W. J. (1968). Acoustic factors in visual search. *Quarterly Journal of Experimental Psychology, 20,* 83–85.

Corcoran, D. W. J. (1966). An acoustic factor in letter cancellation. *Nature, 210,* 658.

Corcoran, D. W. J. (1967). Acoustic factor in proofreading. *Nature, 214,* 851–852.

Corkin, S. (1968). Acquisition of motor skills after bilateral medial temporal-lobe excision. *Neuropsychologia, 6,* 255–265.

Cornell, E. H. (1980). Distributed study facilitates infants' delayed recognition memory. *Memory & Cognition, 8,* 539–542.

Corteen, R. S., & Dunn, D. (1974). Shock-associated words in a nonattended message: A test for momentary awareness. *Journal of Experimental Psychology, 102,* 1143–1144.

Corteen, R. S., & Wood, B. (1972). Autonomic responses to shock-associated words in an unattended channel. *Journal of Experimental Psychology, 94,* 308–313.

Craik, F. I. M. (1970). The fate of primary items in free recall. *Journal of Verbal Learning and Verbal Behavior, 9,* 143–148.

Craik, F. I. M. (1977). Age differences in human memory. In J. E. Birren & K. W. Schaie (Eds.), *Handbook of the Psychology of Aging.* New York: Van Nostrand Reinhold.

Craik, F. I. M., & Lockhart, R. S. (1972). Levels of processing: A framework for memory research. *Journal of Verbal Learning and Verbal Behavior, 11,* 671–684.

Craik, F. I. M., & Tulving, E. (1975). Depth of processing and the retention of words in episodic memory. *Journal of Experimental Psychology: General, 104,* 268–294.

Craik, F. I. M., & Watkins, M. J. (1973). The role of rehearsal in short-term memory. *Journal of Verbal Learning and Verbal Behavior, 12,* 599–607.

Crossman, E. R. F. W. (1959). A theory of the acquisition of speed-skill. *Ergonomics, 2,* 153–166.

Crovitz, H. F., & Quina-Holland, K. (1976). Proportion of episodic memories from early childhood by years of age. *Bulletin of the Psychonomic Society, 7,* 61–62.

Crovitz, H. F., & Schiffman, H. (1974). Frequency of episodic memories as a function of their age. *Bulletin of the Psychonomic Society, 4,* 517–518.

Crowder, R. G. (1976). *Principles of Learning and Memory.* Hillsdale, N.J.: Erlbaum.

Crowder, R. G. (1982). *The Psychology of Reading.* New York: Oxford University Press.

Cuddy, L. J., & Jacoby, L. L. (1982). When forgetting helps memory: An analysis of repetition effects. *Journal of Verbal Learning and Verbal Behavior, 21,* 451–467.

Curtiss, S. (1977). *Genie: A Psycholinguistic Study of a Modern-Day "Wild Child."* New York: Academic Press.

Curtiss, S., Fromkin, V., Krashen, S., Rigler, D., & Rigler, M. (1974). The linguistic development of Genie. *Language, 50,* 528–554.

Cutting, J. (1976). Auditory and linguistic processes in speech perception: Inferences from fusions in dichotic listening. *Psychological Review, 83,* 114–140.

D'Agostino, P. R., O'Neill, B. J., & Paivio, A. (1977). Memory for pictures and words as a function of level processing: Depth or dual coding? *Memory & Cognition, 5,* 252-256.

D'Amato, M. R. (1973). Delayed matching and short-term memory in monkeys. In G. H. Bower (Ed.), *The Psychology of Learning and Motivation: Advances in Theory and Research* (Vol. 7). New York: Academic Press.

Daneman, M., & Carpenter, P. A. (1983). Individual differences in integrating information between and within sentences. *Journal of Experimental Psychology: Learning, Memory and Cognition, 9,* 561-584.

Dark, V. J., & Loftus, G. R. (1976). The role of rehearsal in long-term memory performance. *Journal of Verbal Learning and Verbal Behavior, 15,* 479-490.

Darley, C. F., & Glass, A. L. (1975). Effects of rehearsal and serial list position on recall. *Journal of Experimental Psychology: Human Learning and Memory, 104,* 453-458.

Darwin, C. T., Turvey, M. T., & Crowder, R. G. (1972). An auditory analogue of the Sperling partial report procedure: Evidence for brief auditory storage. *Cognitive Psychology, 3,* 255-267.

Davies, D. R., & Krkovic, A. (1965). Skin conductance, alpha activity and vigilance. *American Journal of Psychology, 78,* 304-306.

Davies, D. R., & Tune, G. S. (1969). *Human Vigilance Performance.* New York: Elsevier.

Davis, R., Buchanan, B., & Shortliffe, E. (1977). Production rules as a representation for a knowledge-based consultation program. *Artificial Intelligence, 8,* 15-45.

Dawes, R. (1964). Cognitive distortion. *Psychological Reports, 14,* 443-459.

Dawson, M. E., & Schell, A. M. (1982). Electrodermal responses to attended and nonattended significant stimuli during dichotic listening. *Journal of Experimen-tal Psychology: Human Perception and Performance, 8,* 315-324.

DeBono, E. (1972). *Children Solve Problems.* New York: Harper & Row.

Deese, J. (1961). From the isolated verbal unit to connected discourse. In C. N. Cofer (Ed.), *Verbal Learning and Verbal Behavior.* New York: McGraw-Hill.

De Groot, A. D. (1965). *Thought and Choice in Chess.* The Hague: Mouton.

Denis, M. (1982). Imagine while reading text: A study of individual differences. *Memory & Cognition, 10,* 540-545.

Dennett, D. C. (1983). Intentional systems in cognitive ethology: The "Panglossian paradigm" defended. *Behavioral and Brain Sciences, 6,* 343-355.

Dennis, M. (1980). Capacity and strategy for syntactic comprehension after left or right hemi-decortication. *Brain and Language, 10,* 287-317.

Dennis, M., & Kohn, B. (1975). Comprehension of syntax in infantile hemiplegics after cerebral hemi-decortication: Left hemisphere superiority. *Brain and Language, 2,* 475-486.

Dennis, M., & Whitaker, H. A. (1976). Language acquisition following hemi-decortication: Linguistic superiority of the left over the right hemisphere. *Brain and Language, 3,* 404-433.

DeSoto, L. B., London, M., & Handel, L. S. (1965). Social reasoning and spatial paralogic. *Journal of Personality and Social Psychology, 2,* 513-521.

Detterman, D. K., & Ellis, N. R. (1972). Determinants of induced amnesia in short-term memory. *Journal of Experimental Psychology, 95,* 308-316.

Deutsch, W. (Ed.). (1981). *The Child's Construction of Language.* New York: Academic Press.

De Valois, R. L., & Jacobs, G. H. (1968). Primate color vision. *Science, 162,* 533-540.

Dewson, J. H., III. (1977). Preliminary evidence of hemispheric asymmetry of auditory function in monkeys. In S. Harnad, R. W. Doty, L. Goldstein, J. Jaynes, & G. Krauthamer (Eds.), *Lateralization in the Nervous System*. New York: Academic Press.

Di Lollo, V., Arnett, J. L., & Kruk, R. V. (1982). Age-related changes in rate of visual information processing. *Journal of Experimental Psychology: Human Perception and Performance, 8*, 225–237.

Dimond, S. J. (1977). Vigilance and split-brain research. In R. R. Mackie (Ed.), *Vigilance: Theory, Operational Performance and Physiological Correlates*. New York: Plenum.

Dooling, D. J., & Lachman, R. (1971). Effects of comprehension on retention of prose. *Journal of Experimental Psychology, 88*, 216–222.

Dorman, M. F., Raphael, L. J., & Liberman, A. M. (1979). Some experiments on the sound of silence in phonetic perception. *Journal of the Acoustical Society of America, 65*, 1518–1532.

Doty, R. W., & Overman, W. H., Jr. (1977). Mnemonic role of forebrain commissures in macaques. In S. Harnad, R. W. Doty, L. Goldstein, J. Jaynes, & G. Krauthamer (Eds.), *Lateralization in the Nervous System*. New York: Academic Press.

Drewnowski, A., & Murdock, B. B. (1980). The role of auditory features in memory span for words. *Journal of Experimental Psychology: Human Learning and Memory, 6*, 319–332.

Druker, J. F., & Hagen, J. W. (1969). Developmental trends in the processing of task-relevant and task-irrelevant information. *Child Development, 40*, 371–382.

Duda, R. O., & Shortliffe, E. H. (1983). Expert systems research. *Science, 220*, 261–268.

Dulaney, D. E., Carlson, R. A., & Dewey, G. I. (1984). A case of syntactical learning and judgment: How conscious and how abstract? *Journal of Experimental Psychology: General*.

Duncan, J. (1980). The locus of interference in the perception of simultaneous stimuli. *Psychological Review, 87*, 272–300.

Duncker, K. (1945). On problem solving. *Psychological Monographs, 58* (No. 270).

Dunlap, G. L., & Dunlap, L. L. (1979). Manipulating the word frequency effect in free recall. *Memory & Cognition, 7*, 420–425.

Durso, F. T., & Johnson, M. K. (1980). The effects of orienting tasks on recognition, recall, and modality confusion of pictures and words. *Journal of Verbal Learning and Verbal Behavior, 19*, 416–429.

Dyer, F. N. (1973). The Stroop phenomenon and its use in the study of perceptual, cognitive and response processes. *Memory & Cognition, 1*, 106–120.

Dykes, J. R. (1981). Perceptual encoding and decision strategies for integral dimensions. *Journal of Experimental Psychology: Human Perception and Performance, 7*, 56–70.

Easterbrook, J. A. (1959). The effect of emotion on cue utilization and the organization of behavior. *Psychological Review, 66*, 183–201.

Easton, R., & Moran, P. W. (1978). A quantitative confirmation of visual capture of curvature. *Journal of General Psychology, 98*, 105–112.

Efron, R., Bogen, J. E., & Yund, E. W. (1977). Perception of dichotic chords by normal and commissurotomized human subjects. *Cortex, 13*, 137–149.

Efron, R., & Yund, E. W. (1974). Dichotic competition of simultaneous tone bursts of different frequency. I. Dissociation of pitch from lateralization and loudness. *Neuropsychologia, 12*, 149–156.

Egan, D., & Greeno, J. (1974). Theory of inductive learning: Knowledge acquired in concept identification, serial pattern learning, and problem solving. In L. Gregg (Ed.), *Knowledge and Cognition*. Hillsdale, N.J.: Erlbaum.

Egeth, H. E., & Sager, L. C. (1977). On the locus of visual dominance. *Perception & Psychophysics, 22*, 77–86.

Ehrlich, S. F., & Rayner, K. (1981). Contextual effects on word perception and eye movements during reading. *Journal of Verbal Learning and Verbal Behavior, 20*, 641–655.

Eich, J. E. (1980). The cue-dependent nature of state dependent retrieval. *Memory & Cognition, 8*, 157–173.

Eijkman, E., & Vendrik, A. J. H. (1965). Can a sensory system be specified by its internal noise? *Journal of the Acoustical Society of America, 37*, 1102–1109.

Einstein, G. O., & Hunt, R. R. (1980). Levels of processing and organization: Additive effects of individual-item and relational processing. *Journal of Experimental Psychology: Human Learning and Memory, 6*, 588–598.

Elio, R., & Anderson, J. R. (1981). The effects of category generalizations and instance similarity on schema abstraction. *Journal of Experimental Psychology: Human Learning and Memory, 7*, 397–417.

Elliott, E. (1957). Auditory vigilance tasks. *Advancement of Science, 53*, 393–399.

Ellis, N. C., & Miles, T. R. (1978). Visual information processing in dyslexic children. In M. M. Gruneberg, P. E. Morris, & R. N. Sykes (Eds.), *Practical Aspects of Memory*. London: Academic Press.

Engen, T., & Ross, B. M. (1973). Long-term memory of odors with and without verbal descriptions. *Journal of Experimental Psychology, 100*, 221–227.

Erber, J. T. (1978). Age differences in a controlled-lag memory test. *Experimental Aging Research, 4*, 195–205.

Erdelyi, M. H. (1974). A new look at the new look: Perceptual defense and vigilance. *Psychological Review, 81*, 1–25.

Erdelyi, M. H., & Becker, J. (1974). Hypermnesia for pictures: Incremental memory for pictures but not words in multiple recall trials. *Cognitive Psychology, 6*, 159–171.

Erdelyi, M. H., Finkelstein, S., Herrell, N., Miller, B., & Thomas, J. (1976). Coding modality vs. input modality in hypermnesia: Is a rose a rose a rose? *Cognition, 4*, 311–319.

Erdelyi, M. H., & Kleinbard, J. (1978). Has Ebbinghaus decayed with time? The growth of recall (hypermnesia) over days. *Journal of Experimental Psychology: Human Learning and Memory, 4*, 275–289.

Ericsson, K. A., & Simon, H. A. (1980). Verbal reports as data. *Psychological Review, 87*, 215–251.

Erman, L. D., Hayes-Roth, F., Lesser, V. R., & Reddy, D. R. (1980). The Hearsay-II speech-understanding system: Integrating knowledge to resolve uncertainty. *Computing Surveys, 12*, 213–253.

Ernst, G. W., & Newell, A. (1969). *GPS: A Case Study in Generality and Problem Solving*. New York: Academic Press.

Ervin, S. (1964). Imitation and structural change in children's language. In E. H. Lenneberg (Ed.), *New Directions in the Study of Language*. Cambridge, Mass.: MIT Press.

Estes, W. K. (1972). Interactions of signal and background variables in visual processing. *Perception & Psychophysics, 12*, 278–282.

Estes, W. K. (1982). Similarity-related channel interactions in visual processing. *Journal of Experimental Psychology: Human Perception and Performance, 8*, 353–382.

Estes, W. K., Allmeyer, D. H., & Reder, S. M. (1976). Serial position functions for letter identification at brief and extended exposure durations. *Perception & Psychophysics, 19,* 1–15.

Evans, G. W., & Pezdek, K. (1980). Cognitive mapping: Knowledge of real-world distance and location information. *Journal of Experimental Psychology: Human Learning and Memory, 6,* 13–24.

Evans, J. St. B. T. (1982). *The Psychology of Deductive Reasoning.* London: Routledge & Kegan Paul.

Evans, J. St. B. T. (Ed.). (1983). *Thinking and Reasoning: Psychological Approaches.* London: Routledge & Kegan Paul.

Evans, J. St. B. T., Barston, J. L., & Pollard, P. (1983). On the conflict between logic and belief in syllogistic reasoning. *Memory & Cognition, 11,* 295–306.

Evans, S. H. (1967). A brief statement of schema theory. *Psychonomic Science, 8,* 87–88.

Fagan, J. F. (1970). Memory in the infant. *Journal of Experimental Child Psychology, 9,* 217–226.

Fagan, S. F. (1973). Infant's delayed recognition memory and forgetting. *Journal of Experimental Child Psychology, 16,* 424–450.

Fantz, R. L. (1964). Visual experience in infants: Decreased attention to familiar patterns relative to novel ones. *Science, 146,* 668–670.

Fedio, P., & Van Buren, J. M. (1975). Memory and perceptual deficits during electrical stimulation in the left and right thalamus and parietal subcortex. *Brain and Language, 2,* 78–100.

Feigenbaum, E. A., Buchanan, B. G., & Lederberg, J. (1971). On generality and problem solving: A case study using the DENDRAL program. In B. Meltzer & D. Michie (Eds.), *Machine Intelligence* (Vol. 6). Edinburgh: Edinburgh University Press.

Feldman, H., Goldin-Meadow, S., & Gleitman, L. (1979). Beyond Herodotus: The creation of language by linguistically deprived deaf children. In A. Lock (Ed.), *Action, Gesture, and Symbol: The Emergence of Language.* New York: McGraw-Hill.

Fillenbaum, S. (1975). If: Some uses. *Psychological Research, 37,* 245–260.

Finke, R. A. (1980). Levels of equivalence in imagery and perception. *Psychological Review, 87,* 113–132.

Fischhoff, B. (1975). Hindsight ≠ foresight: The effect of outcome knowledge on judgment under uncertainty. *Journal of Experimental Psychology: Human Perception and Performance, 1,* 288–299.

Fischler, I. (1977a). Semantic facilitation without association in a lexical decision task. *Memory & Cognition, 5,* 335–339.

Fischler, I. (1977b). Associative facilitation without expectancy in a lexical decision task. *Journal of Experimental Psychology: Human Perception and Performance, 3,* 18–26.

Fisher, C. B., & Bornstein, M. H. (1982). *Perception & Psychophysics, 32,* 443–448.

Fitch, H. L., Halwes, T., Erickson, D. M., & Liberman, A. M. (1980). Perceptual equivalence of two acoustic cues for stop-consonant manner. *Perception & Psychophysics, 27,* 343–350.

Fitts, P. M., & Posner, M. I. (1967). *Human Performance.* Belmont, Calif.: Brooks/Cole.

Flannagan, M. J., Fried, L. S., & Holyoak, K. J. (1985). Distributional expectations and the induction of category structure. *Journal of Experimental Psychology: Learning, Memory and Cognition, 11.*

Flavell, J. H. (1984). *Cognitive Development.* 2nd ed. Englewood Cliffs, N.J.: Prentice-Hall.

Flavell, J. H., Beach, D. H., & Chinsky, J. M. (1966). Spontaneous verbal rehearsal in a memory task as a function of age. *Child Development, 37,* 283–299.

Flavell, J. H., & Wellman, H. M. (1976). Metamemory. In R. V. Kail & J. W. Hagen (Eds.), *Memory in Cognitive Development.* Hillsdale, N.J.: Erlbaum.

Fleishman, E. A., & Parker, J. K. (1962). Factors in the retention and relearning of perceptual-motor skills. *Journal of Experimental Psychology, 64,* 215–226.

Flexser, A. J., & Tulving, E. (1978). Retrieval independence in recognition and recall. *Psychological Review, 85,* 153–171.

Flowers, J. H., Warner, J. L., & Polansky, M. L. (1979). Response and encoding factors in ignoring irrelevant information. *Memory & Cognition, 7,* 86–94.

Fodor, J. A., Bever, T. G., & Garrett, M. F. (1974). *The Psychology of Language.* New York: McGraw-Hill.

Folkard, S. (1979). Time of day and level of processing. *Memory & Cognition, 7,* 247–252.

Forster, P. M., & Govier, E. (1978). Discrimination without awareness? *Quarterly Journal of Experimental Psychology, 30,* 289–295.

Foss, D. J., & Hakes, D. T. (1978). *Psycholinguistics.* Englewood Cliffs, N.J.: Prentice-Hall.

Fowler, C. A., Wolford, G., Slade, R., & Tassinary, L. (1981). Lexical access with and without awareness. *Journal of Experimental Psychology: General, 110,* 341–362.

Fowles, J. (1969). *The French Lieutenant's Woman.* New York: New American Library.

Francis, W. N., & Kučera, M. (1982). *Frequency Analysis of English Usage.* Boston: Houghton Mifflin.

Franklin, H. C., & Holding, D. H. (1977). Personal memories at different ages. *Quarterly Journal of Experimental Psychology, 29,* 527–532.

Franklin, S. S., & Erickson, N. L. (1969). Perceived size of off-size familiar objects under normal and degraded viewing conditions. *Psychonomic Science, 15,* 312–313.

Freedman, J. L., & Landauer, T. K. (1966). Retrieval of long-term memory: "Tip-of-the-tongue" phenomenon. *Psychonomic Science, 4,* 309–310.

Freud, S. (1904). The psychopathology of everyday life. In A. A. Brill (Ed.), *The Basic Writings of Sigmund Freud.* New York: Random House. (Reprinted, 1938.)

Fried, L. S., & Holyoak, K. J. (1984). Induction of category distributions: A framework for classification learning. *Journal of Experimental Psychology: Learning, Memory, and Cognition, 10,* 234–257.

Friedland, R. P., & Weinstein, E. A. (Eds.). (1977). *Advances in Neurology.* Vol. 18; *Hemi-Inattention and Hemisphere Specialization.* New York: Raven Press.

Friedman, A., & Polson, M. C. (1981). Hemispheres as independent resources systems: Limited-capacity processing and cerebral specialization. *Journal of Experimental Psychology: Human Perception and Performance, 7,* 1031–1058.

Fromkin, V., & Rodman, R. (1978). *An Introduction to Language* (2nd ed.). New York: Holt, Rinehart and Winston.

Fuld, P. A., & Buschke, H. (1976). Stages of retrieval in verbal learning. *Journal of Verbal Learning and Verbal Behavior, 15,* 401–410.

Fulgosi, A., & Guilford, J. P. (1968). Short-term incubation in divergent production. *American Journal of Psychology, 81,* 241–246.

Galton, F. (1883). *Inquiries into Human Faculty and Its Development.* London: Macmillan.

Ganong, W. F. (1980). Phonetic categorization in auditory word perception. *Journal of Experimental Psychology:*

*Human Perception and Performance, 6,* 110–125.

Gardiner, J. M., Craik, F. I. M., & Birtwistle, J. (1972). Retrieval cues and release from proactive inhibition. *Journal of Verbal Learning and Verbal Behavior, 11,* 778–783.

Gardner, B. T., & Gardner, R. A. (1975). Evidence for sentence constituents in the early utterances of child and chimpanzee. *Journal of Experimental Psychology: General, 104,* 244–267.

Gardner, H. (1976). *The Shattered Mind.* New York: Vintage Books. (Copyright, 1974.)

Gardner, H. (1980). *Artful Scribbles: The Significance of Children's Drawings.* New York: Basic Books.

Gardner, R. A., & Gardner, B. T. (1969). Teaching sign language to a chimpanzee. *Science, 165,* 664–672.

Garner, W. R. (1970). The stimulus in information processing. *American Psychologist, 25,* 350–358.

Gates, A., & Bradshaw, J. L. (1977). The role of the cerebral hemispheres in music. *Brain and Language, 4,* 403–431.

Gazzaniga, M. S. (1970). *The Bisected Brain.* New York: Appleton-Century-Crofts.

Gazzaniga, M. S. (1977). Consistency and diversity in brain organization. *Annals of the New York Academy of Sciences, 299,* 415–423.

Gazzaniga, M. S. (1983). Right hemisphere language following brain bisection. *American Psychologist, 38,* 525–537.

Gazzaniga, M. S., & Hillyard, S. A. (1971). Language and speech capacity of the right hemisphere. *Neuropsychologia, 9,* 273–280.

Geiss, M. C., & Zwicky, A. M. (1971). On invited inferences. *Linguistic Inquiry, 2,* 561–566.

Gelman, S. A., & Markman, E. M. (1983). *Natural Kind Terms and Children's Ability to Draw Inferences.* Paper presented at the meeting of the Western Psychological Association, San Francisco.

Gentner, D., & Gentner, D. R. (1983). Flowing waters or teeming crowds: Mental models of electricity. In D. Gentner & A. L. Stevens (Eds.), *Mental Models.* Hillsdale, N.J.: Erlbaum.

Gescheider, G. A., Sager, L. C., & Ruffolo, L. J. (1975). Simultaneous auditory and tactile information processing. *Perception & Psychophysics, 18,* 209–216.

Geschwind, N. (1965). Disconnection syndromes in animals and man. *Brain, 88,* 237–294, 585–644.

Geschwind, N. (1970). The organization of language and the brain. *Science, 170,* 940–944.

Geschwind, N., & Levitsky, W. (1968). Human brain: Left-right asymmetries in temporal speech region. *Science, 161,* 186–187.

Gibson, E. J. (1969). *Principles of Perceptual Learning and Development.* New York: Appleton-Century-Crofts.

Gibson, J. J. (1957). Optimal motions and transformations as stimuli for visual perception. *Psychological Review, 64,* 288–295.

Gibson, J. J. (1966). *The Senses Considered as Perceptual Systems.* Boston: Houghton Mifflin.

Gick, M. L., & Holyoak, K. J. (1980). Analogical problem solving. *Cognitive Psychology, 12,* 306–355.

Gick, M. L., & Holyoak, K. J. (1983). Schema induction and analogical transfer. *Cognitive Psychology, 15,* 1–38.

Gilovich, T. (1981). Seeing the past in the present: The effect of associations to familiar events on judgments and decisions. *Journal of Personality and Social Psychology, 40,* 797–808.

Gilson, E. Q., and Baddeley, A. D. (1969). Tactile short-term memory. *Quarterly Journal of Experimental Psychology, 21,* 180–184.

Glanzer, M., & Cunitz, A. R. (1966). Two storage mechanisms in free recall. *Journal of Verbal Learning and Verbal Behavior, 5,* 351–360.

Glaser, R. (1984). Education and thinking: The role of knowledge. *American Psychologist, 39,* 93–104.

Glass, A. L. (1984). The effect of memory set on reaction time. In J. R. Anderson & S. M. Kosslyn (Eds.), *Tutorials in Learning and Memory: Essays in Honor of Gordon Bower.* San Francisco: Freeman.

Glass, A. L., Eddy, J. E., & Schwanenflugel, P. J. (1980). The verification of high and low imagery sentences. *Journal of Experimental Psychology: Human Learning and Memory, 6,* 692–704.

Glass, A. L., & Holyoak, K. J. (1975). Alternative conceptions of semantic memory. *Cognition, 3,* 313–339.

Glass, A. L., Holyoak, K. J., & Kiger, J. I. (1979). Role of antonymy relations in semantic judgments. *Journal of Experimental Psychology: Human Learning and Memory, 5,* 598–606.

Glass, A. L., Holyoak, K. J., & O'Dell, C. (1974). Production frequency and the verification of quantified statements. *Journal of Verbal Learning and Verbal Behavior, 13,* 237–254.

Glenberg, A., & Adams, F. (1978). Type I rehearsal and recognition. *Journal of Verbal Learning and Verbal Behavior, 17,* 455–463.

Glenberg, A., Smith, S. M., & Green, C. (1977). Type I rehearsal: Maintenance and more. *Journal of Verbal Learning and Verbal Behavior, 16,* 339–352.

Glenberg, A. M. (1979). Component-levels theory of the effects of spacing of repetitions on recall and recognition. *Memory & Cognition, 7,* 95–112.

Gloning, K. (1977). Handedness and aphasia. *Neuropsychologia, 15,* 355–358.

Glucksberg, S., & Cowen, G. N., Jr. (1970). Memory for nonattended auditory material. *Cognitive Psychology, 1,* 149–156.

Glucksberg, S., & Danks, J. (1968). Effects of discriminative labels and of nonsense labels upon availability of novel function. *Journal of Verbal Learning and Verbal Behavior, 7,* 72–76.

Glucksberg, S., & King, L. J. (1967). Motivated forgetting mediated by implicit verbal chaining: A laboratory analog of repression. *Science, 158,* 517–519.

Glucksberg, S., & Weisberg, R. W. (1966). Verbal behavior and problem solving: Some effects of labeling in a functional fixedness problem. *Journal of Experimental Psychology, 71,* 659–664.

Godden, D. R., & Baddeley, A. D. (1975). Context-dependent memory in two natural environments: On land and underwater. *British Journal of Psychology, 66,* 325–332.

Goldberg, E., Antin, S. P., Bilder, R. M., Gerstman, L. J., Hughes, J. E. D., & Mattis, S. (1981). Retrograde amnesia: Possible role of mesencephalic reticular activation in long-term memory. *Science, 213,* 1392–1394.

Goldberg, M. E., & Wurtz, R. H. (1972). Activity of superior colliculus in behaving monkeys. II. Effects of attention on neuronal responses. *Journal of Neurophysiology, 35,* 560–574.

Golding, E. (1981). *The Effect of Past Experience on Problem Solving.* Paper presented at the Annual Conference of the British Psychological Society, Surrey University.

Goldstein, K. (1948). *Language and Language Disturbances.* New York: Grune & Stratton.

Goodglass, H. (1968). Studies on the grammar of aphasics. In S. Rosenberg & J. Kaplin (Eds.), *Developments in Applied*

*Psycholinguistic Research.* New York: Macmillan.

Goodglass, H. (1976). Agrammatism. In H. Whitaker & M. A. Whitaker (Eds.), *Perspectives in Neurolinguistics and Psycholinguistics.* New York: Academic Press.

Goodglass, H., & Berko, J. (1960). Aphasia and inflectional morphology in English. *Journal of Speech and Hearing Research,* 10, 257–262.

Goodglass, H., Fodor, I., & Schulhoff, S. (1967). Prosodic factors in grammar—evidence from aphasia. *Journal of Speech and Hearing Research,* 10, 5–20.

Goodglass, H., & Geschwind, N. (1976). Language disorders (aphasia). In E. C. Carterette & M. Friedman (Eds.), *Handbook of Perception* (Vol. 8). New York: Academic Press.

Goodglass, H., & Hunt, J. (1958). Grammatical complexity and aphasic speech. *Word,* 14, 197–207.

Goodglass, H., & Kaplan, E. (1972). *The Assessment of Aphasia and Related Disorders.* Philadelphia: Lea & Febiger.

Goodglass, H., Quadfasel, F. A., & Timberlake, W. H. (1964). Phrase length and the type and severity of aphasia. *Cortex,* 1, 133–158.

Goodwin, C. J. (1976). Changes in primacy and recency with practice in single-trial free recall. *Journal of Verbal Learning and Verbal Behavior,* 15, 119–132.

Gordon, H. W. (1970). Hemispheric asymmetries in the perception of musical chords. *Cortex,* 6, 387–398.

Gordon, H. W. (1974). Hemispheric asymmetry and musical performance. *Science,* 189, 68–69.

Gordon, H. W. (1980). Degree of ear asymmetries for perception of dichotic chords and for illustory chord localization in musicians of different levels of competence. *Journal of Experimental Psychology: Human Perception and Performance,* 6, 516–527.

Gorman, A. M. (1961). Recognition memory for nouns as a function of abstractness and frequency. *Journal of Experimental Psychology,* 61, 23–29.

Graesser, A., & Mandler, G. (1978). Limited processing capacity constrains the storage of unrelated sets of words and retrieval from natural categories. *Journal of Experimental Psychology: Human Learning and Memory,* 4, 86–100.

Graham, K. R. (1977). Perceptual processes and hypnosis: Support for a cognitive-state theory based on laterality. *Annals of the New York Academy of Sciences,* 296, 274–283.

Grasselli, A. (Ed.). (1969). *Automatic Interpretation and Classification of Images.* New York: Academic Press.

Gray, C. R., & Gummerman, K. (1975). The enigmatic eidetic image: A critical examination of methods, data, and theories. *Psychological Bulletin,* 82, 383–407.

Greenberg, J. H. (1963). Some universals of grammar with particular reference to the order of meaningful elements. In J. H. Greenberg (Ed.), *Universals of Language.* Cambridge, Mass.: MIT Press.

Greene, R. L. (1984). Incidental learning of event frequency. *Memory & Cognition,* 12, 90–95.

Greeno, J. G. (1974). Hobbits and orcs: Acquisition of a sequential concept. *Cognitive Psychology,* 6, 270–292.

Greenwald, A. G. (1980). The totalitarian ego: Fabrication and revision of personal history. *American Psychologist,* 35, 603–618.

Griggs, R. A. (1983). The role of problem content in the selection task and in the THOG problem. In J. St. B. T. Evans (Ed.), *Thinking and Reasoning: Psychological Approaches.* London: Routledge & Kegan Paul.

Griggs, R. A., & Cox, J. R. (1982). The elusive thematic-materials effect in Wason's selection task. *British Journal of Psychology, 73,* 407–420.

Groves, P. M., & Thompson, R. F. (1970). Habituation: A dual-process theory. *Psychological Review, 77,* 419–450.

Gruber, H. E. (1974). *Darwin on Man: A Psychological Study of Scientific Creativity.* New York: Dutton.

Gruenewald, P. J., & Lockhead, G. R. (1980). The free recall of category examples. *Journal of Experimental Psychology: Human Learning and Memory, 6,* 225–240.

Gruneberg, M. M., & Monks, J. (1974). Feeling of knowing and cued recall. *Acta Psychologica, 38,* 257–265.

Gur, R., & Gur, R. (1977). Correlates of conjugate lateral eye movements in man. In S. Harnad, R. W. Doty, L. Goldstein, J. Jaynes, & G. Krauthamer (Eds.), *Lateralization in the Nervous System.* New York: Academic Press.

Guttman, N., & Julesz, B. (1963). Lower limits of auditory periodicity analysis. *Journal of the Acoustical Society of America, 35,* 610.

Guzman, A. (1968). *Computer Recognition of Three-Dimensional Objects in a Visual Scene* (AI–TR–228). Cambridge, Mass.: MIT AI Laboratory.

Haber, R. N. (1983). The impending demise of the icon: A critique of the concept of iconic storage in visual information processing. *Behavioral and Brain Sciences, 6,* 1–54.

Haber, R. N., & Hershenson, M. (1965). The effects of repeated brief exposures on the growth of a percept. *Journal of Experimental Psychology, 69,* 40–46.

Haber, R. N., & Schindler, R. M. (1981). Error in proofreading: Evidence of syntactic control of letter processing? *Journal of Experimental Psychology: Human Perception and Performance, 7,* 573–579.

Haberlandt, K., Berian, C., & Sandson, J. (1980). The episodic schema in story processing. *Journal of Verbal Learning and Verbal Behavior, 19,* 635–650.

Hagen, J. W., Meacham, J. A., & Mesibov, G. (1970). Verbal labeling, rehearsal, and short-term memory. *Cognitive Psychology, 1,* 47–58.

Hall, J. F. (1954). Learning as a function of word frequency. *American Journal of Psychology, 67,* 138–140.

Hamilton, C. R. (1977). An assessment of hemispheric specialization in monkeys. *Annals of the New York Academy of Sciences, 299,* 222–232.

Hammerton, M. (1963). Retention of learning in a difficult tracking task. *Journal of Experimental Psychology, 66,* 108–110.

Hanson, A. R., & Riseman, E. M. (1978). VISIONS: A computer system for interpreting scenes. In A. R. Hanson & E. M. Riseman (Eds.), *Computer Vision Systems.* New York: Academic Press.

Hardyck, C. D., & Petrinovich, I. F. (1970). Subvocal speech and comprehension level as a function of the difficulty level of the reading material. *Journal of Verbal Learning and Verbal Behavior, 9,* 647–652.

Harris, G., Begg, I., & Mitterer, J. (1980). On the relation between frequency estimates and recognition memory. *Memory & Cognition, 8,* 99–104.

Hart, J. T. (1965). Memory and the feeling of knowing experience. *Journal of Educational Psychology, 56,* 208–216.

Hartley, J. T., Birnbaum, I. M., & Parker, E. S. (1978). Alcohol and storage deficits: Kind of processing? *Journal of Verbal Learning and Verbal Behavior, 17,* 635–647.

Hasher, L., & Chromiak, W. (1977). The processing of frequency information: An automatic mechanism? *Journal of Verbal*

Learning and Verbal Behavior, 16, 173–184.

Hasher, L., & Zacks, R. T. (1979). Automatic and effortful processes in memory. *Journal of Experimental Psychology: General, 108*, 356–388.

Hay, J. C., Pick, H. L., & Ikeda, K. (1965). Visual capture produced by prism spectacles. *Psychometric Science, 2*, 215–216.

Hayes, C. (1951). *The Ape in Our House.* New York: Harper & Row.

Hayes-Roth, B., & Hayes-Roth, F. (1977). Concept learning and the recognition and classification of exemplars. *Journal of Verbal Learning and Verbal Behavior, 16*, 321–338.

Healy, A. F. (1976). Detection errors on the word *the:* Evidence for reading units larger than letters. *Journal of Experimental Psychology: Human Perception and Performance, 2*, 235–242.

Healy, A. F. (1980). Proofreading errors on the word *the:* New evidence on reading units. *Journal of Experimental Psychology: Human Perception and Performance, 6*, 45–57.

Healy, A. F. (1981). The effects of visual similarity on proofreading for misspellings. *Memory & Cognition, 9*, 453–460.

Hearst, E. (1977). Man and machine: Chess achievements and chess thinking. In P. W. Frey (Ed.), *Chess Skill in Man and Machine.* New York: Springer-Verlag.

Hebb, D. O. (1961). Distinctive features of learning in the higher animal. In J. F. Delafresnaye (Ed.), *Brain Mechanisms and Learning.* London: Blackwell.

Heider, E. R. (1972). Universals in color naming and memory. *Journal of Experimental Psychology, 93*, 10–20.

Heider, E. R., & Olivier, D. (1972). The structure of the color space in naming and memory for two languages. *Cognitive Psychology, 3*, 337–354.

Heilman, K. M., & Watson, R. T. (1977). The neglect syndrome—a unilateral defect of the orienting response. In S. Harnad, R. W. Doty, L. Goldstein, J. Jaynes, & G. Krauthamer (Eds.), *Lateralization in the Nervous System.* New York: Academic Press.

Hellige, J. B. (1980). Effects of perceptual quality and visual field of probe stimulus presentation on memory search for letters. *Journal of Experimental Psychology: Human Perception and Performance, 6*, 639–651.

Hellige, J. B., Cox, P. J., & Litvac, L. (1979). Information processing in the cerebral hemispheres: Selective hemisphere activation and capacity limitations. *Journal of Experimental Psychology: General, 108*, 251–279.

Helmick, J., Watamori, T., & Palmer, J. (1976). Spouses' understanding of the communication disabilities of aphasic patients. *Journal of Speech and Hearing Disorders, 41*, 238–243.

Henle, M. (1962). On the relation between logic and thinking. *Psychological Review, 69*, 366–378.

Hering, E. (1964). *Outlines of a Theory of the Light Sense.* Cambridge, Mass.: Harvard University Press. (Originally published, 1920.)

Herrmann, D. J., & Kay, B. E. (1977). Familiarity and organization of category terms in semantic memory. *Memory & Cognition, 5*, 139–145.

Herrnstein, R. J., & de Villiers, P. A. (1980). Fish as a natural category for people and pigeons. In G. H. Bower (Ed.), *The Psychology of Learning and Motivation* (Vol. 14). New York: Academic Press.

Hilgard, E. R., & Hilgard, J. R. (1975). *Hypnosis in the Relief of Pain.* Los Altos, Calif.: Kaufmann.

Hinrichs, J., & Craft, J. L. (1971). Stimulus and response factors in discrete choice reaction time. *Journal of Experimental Psychology, 91,* 305–309.

Hintzman, D. L. (1974). Theoretical implications of the spacing effect. In R. L. Solso (Ed.), *Theories in Cognitive Psychology: The Loyola Symposium.* Hillsdale, N.J.: Erlbaum.

Hintzman, D. L., & Block, R. A. (1971). Repetition and memory: Evidence for a multiple trace hypothesis. *Journal of Experimental Psychology, 88,* 297–306.

Hochberg, J. E. (1970). Attention, organization, and consciousness. In D. I. Mostofsky (Ed.), *Attention: Contemporary Theory and Analysis.* New York: Appleton-Century-Crofts.

Hochberg, J. E. (1971). Perception II. Space and movement. In J. W. Kling & L. A. Riggs (Eds.), *Experimental Psychology.* New York: Holt, Rinehart and Winston.

Hockett, C. F. (1960). The origin of speech. *Scientific American, 203,* 89–96.

Hockey, G. R. (1970). Effect of loud noise on attentional selectivity. *Quarterly Journal of Experimental Psychology, 22,* 28–36.

Hoff-Ginsberg, E., & Shatz, M. (1982). Linguistic input and the child's acquisition of language. *Psychological Bulletin, 92,* 3–26.

Hoffman, J. E. (1978). Search through a sequentially presented visual display. *Perception & Psychophysics, 23,* 1–11.

Hoffman, J. E. (1979). A two-stage model of visual search. *Perception & Psychophysics, 25,* 319–327.

Hoffman, J. E., & Nelson, B. (1981). Spatial selectivity in visual search. *Perception & Psychophysics, 30,* 283–290.

Holbrook, M. B. (1978). Effect of subjective interletter similarity, perceived word similarity, and contextual variables on the recognition of letter substitutions in a proofreading task. *Perceptual and Motor Skills, 47,* 251–258.

Holmes, D. S. (1984). Meditation and somatic arousal reduction: A review of the experimental evidence. *American Psychologist, 39,* 1–10.

Holyoak, K. J., & Glass, A. L. (1975). The role of contradictions and counterexamples in the rejection of false sentences. *Journal of Verbal Learning and Verbal Behavior, 14,* 215–239.

Holyoak, K. J., & Patterson, K. K. (1981). A positional discriminability model of linear-order judgments. *Journal of Experimental Psychology: Human Perception and Performance, 7,* 1283–1302.

Holyoak, K. J., & Walker, J. H. (1976). Subjective magnitude information in semantic orderings. *Journal of Verbal Learning and Verbal Behavior, 15,* 287–299.

Homa, D., & Vosburgh, R. (1976). Category breadth and the abstraction of prototypical information. *Journal of Experimental Psychology: Human Learning and Memory, 2,* 322–330.

Howard, D. V. (1980). Category norms: A comparison of the Battig and Montague (1969) norms with the responses of adults between the ages of 20 and 80. *Journal of Gerontology, 35,* 225–231.

Howes, D. H. (1967). Some experimental investigations of language in aphasia. In K. Salzinger & S. Salzinger (Eds.), *Research in Verbal Behavior and Some Neuropsychological Implications.* New York: Academic Press.

Hulicka, I. M., & Grossman, J. L. (1967). Age-group comparisons for the use of mediators in paired-associate learning. *Journal of Gerontology, 22,* 46–51.

Hulicka, I. M., Sterns, H., & Grossman, J. (1967). Age-group comparisons of paired-associate learning as a function of paced and self-paced association and response times. *Journal of Gerontology, 22,* 274–280.

Hulicka, I. M., & Wheeler, D. (1976). Recall scores of old and young people as function of registration intervals. *Educational Gerontology, 1,* 361–372.

Hultsch, D. F. (1971). Adult age differences in free classification and free recall. *Developmental Psychology, 4,* 338–342.

Hunt, E., & Love, T. (1972). How good can memory be? In A. W. Melton & E. Martin (Eds.), *Coding Processes in Human Memory.* Washington, D.C.: Winston/Wiley.

Hunt, M. (1982). *The Universe Within.* New York: Simon & Schuster.

Hunt, R. R., & Einstein, G. O. (1981). Relational and item-specific information in memory. *Journal of Verbal Learning and Verbal Behavior, 20,* 497–514.

Hunt, R. R., Elliott, J. M., & Spence, M. J. (1979). Independent effects of process and structure on encoding. *Journal of Experimental Psychology: Human Learning and Memory, 5,* 339–347.

Hunt, R. R., & Ellis, H. D. (1974). Recognition memory and degree of semantic contextual change. *Journal of Experimental Psychology, 103,* 1153–1159.

Hunter, I. M. L. (1962). An exceptional talent for calculative thinking. *British Journal of Psychology, 53,* 243–258.

Hunter, I. M. L. (1977). Mental calculation. In P. N. Johnson-Laird & P. C. Wason (Eds.), *Thinking.* New York: Cambridge University Press. (Originally published, 1966.)

Hupert, F., & Piercy, M. (1977). Recognition memory in amnesic patients: A defect of acquisition? *Neuropsychologia, 15,* 643–652.

Huppert, F. A., & Piercy, M. (1979). Normal and abnormal forgetting in organic amnesia: Effect of locus of lesion. *Cortex, 15,* 385–390.

Huttenlocher, J. (1968). Constructing spatial images: A strategy in reasoning. *Psychological Review, 75,* 286–298.

Huttenlocher, J. (1974). The origins of language comprehension. In R. L. Solso (Ed.), *Theories in Cognitive Psychology.* Hillsdale, N.J.: Erlbaum.

Intons-Peterson, M. J. (1983). Imagery paradigms: How susceptible are they to experimenters' expectations? *Journal of Experimental Psychology: Human Perception and Performance, 9,* 394–412.

Intraub, H. (1980). Presentation rate and the representation of briefly glimpsed pictures in memory. *Journal of Experimental Psychology: Human Learning and Memory, 6,* 1–12.

Intraub, H. (1981). Rapid conceptual identification of sequentially presented pictures. *Journal of Experimental Psychology: Human Perception and Performance, 7,* 604–610.

Jacoby, L. L. (1972). Effects of organization on recognition memory. *Journal of Experimental Psychology, 92,* 325–331.

Jacoby, L. L., Craik, F. I. M., & Begg, I. (1979). Effects of decision difficulty on recognition and recall. *Journal of Verbal Learning and Verbal Behavior, 18,* 585–616.

Jacoby, L. L., & Dallas, M. (1981). On the relationship between autobiographical memory and perceptual learning. *Journal of Experimental Psychology: General, 110,* 306–340.

Jacoby, L. L., & Hendricks, R. L. (1973). Recognition effects of study organization and test context. *Journal of Experimental Psychology, 100,* 73–82.

Jakobson, R. (1968). *Child Language, Aphasia, and Phonological Universals.* The Hague: Mouton.

James, W. (1950). *The Principles of Psychology.* New York: Dover. (Originally published, 1890.)

Jameson, D., & Hurvich, L. M. (1955). Some quantitative aspects of an opponent-colors theory. Chromatic responses and spectral saturation. *Journal of* the *Optical Society of America, 45,* 546–552.

Jamieson, D. G., & Petrusic, W. M. (1975). Relational judgments with remembered stimuli. *Perception & Psychophysics, 18,* 373–378.

Jarvella, R. J. (1970). Effects of syntax on running memory span for connected discourse. *Psychonomic Science, 19,* 235–236.

Jarvella, R. J. (1971). Syntactic processing of connected speech. *Journal of Verbal Learning and Verbal Behavior, 10,* 409–416.

Jeffries, R., Polson, P., Razran, L., & Atwood, M. (1977). A process model for missionaries-cannibals and other river-crossing problems. *Cognitive Psychology, 9,* 412–440.

Jerison, H. J. (1977). Vigilance: Biology, psychology, theory, and practice. In R. R. Mackie (Ed.), *Vigilance: Theory, Operational Performance, and Physiological Correlates.* New York: Plenum.

Johnson, L. C., Slye, E., & Dement, W. C. (1965). EEG and autonomic activity during and after prolonged sleep deprivation. *Psychonomic Medicine, 27,* 415–423.

Johnson, M. K., & Foley, M. E. (1984). Differentiating fact from fantasy: The reliability of children's memory. *Journal of Social Issues, 40,* 33–50.

Johnson, M. K., & Raye, C. L. (1981). Reality monitoring. *Psychological Review, 88,* 67–85.

Johnson-Laird, P. N., Gibbs, G., & deMowbray, J. (1978). Meaning, amount of processing, and memory for words. *Memory & Cognition, 6,* 372–375.

Johnson-Laird, P. N., Legrenzi, P., & Legrenzi, M. (1972). Reasoning and a sense of reality. *British Journal of Psychology, 63,* 395–400.

Johnson-Laird, P. N., & Wason, P. C. (Eds.). (1978). *Thinking.* Cambridge: Cambridge University Press.

Johnston, J. C., & McClelland, J. L. (1973). Visual factors in word perception. *Perception & Psychophysics, 14,* 365–370.

Johnston, J. C., & McClelland, J. C. (1980). Experimental tests of a hierarchical model of word identification. *Journal of Verbal Learning and Verbal Behavior, 19,* 503–524.

Johnston, W. A., & Heintz, S. P. (1979). Depth of nontarget processing in an attention task. *Journal of Experimental Psychology: Human Perception and Performance, 5,* 168–175.

Johnston, W. A., & Uhl, C. N. (1976). The contributions of encoding effort and variability to the spacing effect on free recall. *Journal of Experimental Psychology: Human Learning and Memory, 2,* 153–160.

Johnston, W. A., & Wilson, J. (1980). Perceptual processing of nontargets in an attention task. *Memory & Cognition, 8,* 372–377.

Jolicoeur, P., Gluck, M., & Kosslyn, S. M. (1984). Pictures and names: Making the connection. *Cognitive Psychology, 16,* 243–275.

Jones, B. (1980). Sex and handedness factors in visual field organization for a categorization task. *Journal of Experimental Psychology: Human Perception and Performance, 6,* 494–500.

Jones, B. M., & Parsons, O. A. (1972). Specific vs. generalized deficits of abstracting ability in chronic alcoholics. *Archives of General Psychiatry, 26,* 380–384.

Jones, G. V. (1978). Recognition failure and dual mechanisms in recall. *Psychological Review, 85,* 464–469.

Jones, G. V. (1980). On the dual-mechanism theory of recognition failure: A reply to Begg. *Memory & Cognition, 8,* 180–181.

Jones, M. R., & Zamostny, K. P. (1975). Memory and rule structure in the prediction of serial patterns. *Journal of Experi-*

*mental Psychology: Human Learning and Memory, 104,* 295–306.

Jorg, S., & Hormann, H. (1978). The influence of general and specific verbal labels on the recognition of labeled and unlabeled parts of pictures. *Journal of Verbal Learning and Verbal Behavior, 17,* 445–454.

Jorgerson, W. S. (1965). Multidimensional scaling of similarity. *Psychometrika, 30,* 379–393.

Julesz, B. (1975). Experiments in the visual perception of texture. *Scientific American, 232,* 34–43.

Julesz, B. (1981). Figure and ground perception in briefly presented isodipole textures. In M. Kubovy & J. R. Pomerantz (Eds.), *Perceptual Organization.* Hillsdale, N.J.: Erlbaum.

Juola, J. F., Taylor, G. A., & Young, M. E. (1974). Stimulus encoding and decision processes in recognition memory. *Journal of Experimental Psychology, 102,* 1108–1115.

Just, M. A., & Carpenter, P. A. (1980). A theory of reading: From eye fixations to comprehension. *Psychological Review, 87,* 329–354.

Kahneman, D. (1973). *Attention and Effort.* Englewood Cliffs, N.J.: Prentice-Hall.

Kahneman, D., Slovic, P., & Tversky, A. (Eds.). (1982). *Judgment Under Uncertainty: Heuristics and Biases.* Cambridge: Cambridge University Press.

Kahneman, D., & Tversky, A. (1972). Subjective probability: A judgment of representativeness. *Cognitive Psychology, 3,* 430–454.

Kahneman, D., & Tversky, A. (1973). On the psychology of prediction. *Psychological Review, 80,* 237–251.

Kahneman, D., & Tversky, A. (1982). The simulation heuristic. In D. Kahneman, P. Slovic, & A. Tversky (Eds.), *Judgment Under Uncertainty: Heuristics and Bi-* *ases.* Cambridge: Cambridge University Press.

Kasper, L. F. (1983). The effects of linking sentence and interactive picture mnemonics on the acquisition of Spanish nouns by middle school children. *Human Learning, 2,* 141–156.

Katz, J. J. (1972). *Semantic Theory.* New York: Harper & Row.

Kausler, D. H., & Klein, D. M. (1978). Age differences in processing relevant versus irrelevant stimuli in multiple-item recognition learning. *Journal of Gerontology, 33,* 87–93.

Kay, P., & McDaniel, C. K. (1978). The linguistic significance of the meanings of basic color terms. *Language, 54,* 610–646.

Keeney, T. J., Cannizzo, S. R., & Flavell, J. H. (1967). Spontaneous and induced verbal rehearsal in a recall task. *Child Development, 38,* 953–966.

Keil, F. C. (1979). *Semantic and Conceptual Development.* Cambridge, Mass.: Harvard University Press.

Keppel, G., Postman, L., & Zavortink, B. (1968). Studies of learning to learn. VIII. The influence of massive amounts of training upon the learning and retention of paired-associate lists. *Journal of Verbal Learning and Verbal Behavior, 7,* 790–796.

Keppel, G., & Underwood, B. J. (1962). Proactive inhibition in short-term retention of single terms. *Journal of Verbal Learning and Verbal Behavior, 1,* 153–161.

Kerr, N. H. (1983). The role of vision in "visual imagery" experiments: Evidence from the congenitally blind. *Journal of Experimental Psychology: General, 112,* 265–277.

Kiger, J. I., & Glass, A. L. (1983). The facilitation of lexical decisions by a prime occurring after the target. *Memory & Cognition, 11,* 356–365.

Kihlstrom, J. F. (1977). Models of posthypnotic amnesia. *Annals of the New York Academy of Sciences, 296,* 284–301.

Kimura, D. (1961). Cerebral dominance and the perception of verbal stimuli. *Canadian Journal of Psychology, 15,* 166–171.

Kimura, D. (1967). Functional asymmetry of the brain in dichotic listening. *Cortex, 3,* 163–178.

Kimura, D. (1974). Left-right differences in the perception of melodies. *Quarterly Journal of Experimental Psychology, 16,* 355–358.

Kinney, J. A. S., & Luria, D. M. (1970). Conflicting visual and tactual-kinesthetic stimulation. *Perception & Psychophysics, 8,* 189–192.

Kinsbourne, M. (1972). Eye and head turning indicates cerebral lateralization. *Science, 176,* 539–541.

Kinsbourne, M., & Cooke, J. (1971). Generalized and lateralized effects of concurrent verbalization on a unimanual skill. *Quarterly Journal of Experimental Psychology, 23,* 341–345.

Kinsbourne, M., & Wood, F. (1975). Short-term memory processes and the amnesic syndrome. In D. Deutsch & J. A. Deutsch (Eds.), *Short-term Memory.* New York: Academic Press.

Kintsch, W. (1974). *The Representation of Meaning in Memory.* Hillsdale, N.J.: Erlbaum.

Kintsch, W., Mandel, T. S., & Kozminsky, E. (1977). Summarizing scrambled stories. *Memory & Cognition, 5,* 547–552.

Klapp, S. T. (1979). Doing two things at once: The role of temporal compatibility. *Memory & Cognition, 7,* 375–381.

Klapp, S. T. (1981). Temporal compatibility in dual motor tasks. II. Simultaneous articulation and hand movements. *Memory & Cognition, 9,* 398–401.

Kleiman, G. M. (1975). Speech recoding in reading. *Journal of Verbal Learning and Verbal Behavior, 14,* 323–329.

Klein, G. S. (1964). Semantic power measured through the interference of words with color-naming. *American Journal of Psychology, 77,* 576–588.

Klein, R., & Armitage, R. (1979). Rhythms in human performance: 1 1/2-hour oscillations in cognitive style. *Science, 204,* 1326–1328.

Kleinmuntz, B., & Szucko, J. J. (1982). On fallibility of lie detection. *Law and Society Review, 17,* 85–104.

Kleitman, N. (1963). *Sleep and Wakefulness.* Chicago: University of Chicago Press.

Koestler, A. (1964). *The Act of Creation.* New York: Macmillan.

Köhler, W. (1925). *The Mentality of Apes.* London: Routledge & Kegan Paul.

Kolb, B., & Whishaw, I. Q. (1980). *Fundamentals of Human Neuropsychology.* San Francisco: Freeman.

Kolers, P. A. (1979). A pattern analysing basis of recognition. In L. S. Cermak & F. I. M. Craik (Eds.), *Levels of Processing in Human Memory.* Hillsdale, N.J.: Erlbaum.

Koriat, A., & Fischoff, B. (1974). What day is today? An inquiry into the process of time orientation. *Memory & Cognition, 2,* 201–205.

Kosslyn, S. M. (1975). Information representation in visual images. *Cognitive Psychology, 7,* 341–370.

Kosslyn, S. M. (1980). *Image and Mind.* Cambridge, Mass.: Harvard University Press.

Kosslyn, S. M. (1981). The medium and the message in mental imagery: A theory. *Psychological Review, 88,* 46–66.

Kosslyn, S. M., Ball, T. M., & Reiser, B. J. (1978). Visual images preserve metric spatial information: Evidence from studies of image scanning. *Journal of Experi-*

*mental Psychology: Human Perception and Performance, 4,* 47–60.

Kosslyn, S. M., Holyoak, K. J., & Huffman, C. S. (1976). A processing approach to the dual coding hypothesis. *Journal of Experimental Psychology: Human Learning and Memory, 2,* 223–233.

Kosslyn, S. M., & Pomerantz, J. R. (1977). Imagery, propositions, and the form of internal representations. *Cognitive Psychology, 9,* 52–76.

Kozlowski, L. T. (1977). Effects of distorted auditory and of rhyming cues on retrieval of tip-of-the-tongue words by poets and nonpoets. *Memory & Cognition, 5,* 477–481.

Kozminsky, E. (1977). Altering comprehension: The effect of biasing titles on text comprehension. *Memory & Cognition, 5,* 482–490.

Krashen, S. D. (1975). The critical period for language acquisition and its possible bases. *Annals of the New York Academy of Sciences, 263,* 211–224.

Kristofferson, A. B. (1967). Attention and psychophysical time. *Acta Psychologica, 27,* 93–100.

Kroll, N. E. A., Parks, T., Parkinson, S. P., Bieber, S. L., & Johnson, A. L. (1970). Short-term memory while shadowing: Recall of visually and aurally presented letters. *Journal of Experimental Psychology, 85,* 220–224.

Kruskal, J. B. (1964a). Multidimensional scaling by optimizing goodness of fit to a nonmetric hypothesis. *Psychometrika, 29,* 1–27.

Kruskal, J. B. (1964b). Nonmetric multidimensional scaling: A numerical method. *Psychometrika, 29,* 115–129.

Kubovy, M., & Howard, F. P. (1976). Persistence of a pitch segregating echoic memory. *Journal of Experimental Psychol-ogy: Human Perception and Performance, 2,* 531–537.

La Berge, D. (1973). Attention and the measurement of perceptual learning. *Memory & Cognition, 1,* 268–276.

Labov, W. (1973). The boundaries of words and their meanings. In C.-J. N. Bailey & R. W. Shuy (Eds.), *New Ways of Analysing Variation in English.* Washington, D.C.: Georgetown University Press.

Lachman, J. L., & Lachman, R. (1980). Age and the actualization of world knowledge. In L. W. Poon, J. R. Fozard, L. S. Cermak, D. Arenberg, & L. W. Thompson (Eds.), *New Directions in Memory and Aging: Proceedings of the George A. Talland Memorial Conference.* Hillsdale, N.J.: Erlbaum.

Lachman, R., Lachman, J. L., & Butterfield, E. C. (1979). *Cognitive Psychology and Information Processing: An Introduction.* Hillsdale, N.J.: Erlbaum.

Lachman, R., Shaffer, J. P., & Henrikus, D. (1974). Language and cognition: Effects of stimulus codability, name-frequency, and age of acquisition on lexical reaction-time. *Journal of Verbal Learning and Verbal Behavior, 13,* 613–625.

Lane, D. M. (1980). Incidental learning and the development of selective attention. *Psychological Review, 87,* 316–319.

Larkin, J. H., McDermott, J., Simon, D. P., & Simon, H. A. (1980). Expert and novice performance in solving physics problems. *Science, 208,* 1335–1342.

Lawless, H. T., & Cain, W. S. (1975). Recognition memory for odors. *Chemical Senses and Flavor, 1,* 331–337.

Lawrence, D. M. (1971). Two studies of visual search for word targets with controlled rates of presentation. *Perception & Psychophysics, 10,* 85–89.

Lawrence, D. M., & Banks, W. P. (1973). Accuracy of recognition memory for common sounds. *Bulletin of the Psychonomic Society, 1,* 298–300.

Lebrun, Y., & Hoops, R. (Eds.). (1976). *Recovery in Aphasics.* Amsterdam: Swets & Zeitlinger.

Lederman, S. J., & Abbott, S. G. (1981). Texture perception in studies of intersensory organization using a discrepancy paradigm and visual versus tactual psychophysics. *Journal of Experimental Psychology: Human Perception & Performance, 7,* 902–915.

Lee, W. (1971). *Decision Theory and Human Behavior.* New York: Wiley.

Leech, G. (1974). *Semantics.* Harmondsworth: Penguin.

Leeper, R. (1935). A study of a neglected portion of the field of learning—the development of sensory organization. *Journal of Genetic Psychology, 46,* 41–75.

Lenat, D. B. (1979). On automated scientific theory formation: A case study using the AM program. In J. Hayes, D. Michie, & L. I. Mikulich (Eds.), *Machine Intelligence, 9.* New York: Halstead.

Lenat, D. B. (1983). EURISKO: A program that learns new heuristics and domain concepts. *Artificial Intelligence, 21,* 61–98.

Lenneberg, E. (1967). *Biological Foundations of Language.* New York: Wiley.

Lester, O. P. (1932). Mental set in relation to retroactive inhibition. *Journal of Experimental Psychology, 15,* 681–699.

Levinthal, C. F. (1979). *The Physiological Approach to Psychology.* Englewood Cliffs, N.J.: Prentice-Hall.

Levitt, D. R., & Teitelbaum, P. (1975). Somnolence, akinesia, and sensory activation of motivated behavior in the lateral hypothalamic syndrome. *Proceedings of the National Academy of Sciences, 72,* 2819–2823.

Levy, B. A. (1978). Speech analysis during sentence processing: Reading versus listening. *Visible Language, 12,* 81–101.

Levy, J. (1976). Evolution of language lateralization and cognitive function. *Annals of the New York Academy of Sciences, 280,* 810–820.

Levy, J. (1977). The mammalian brain and the adaptive advantage of cerebral asymmetry. *Annals of the New York Academy of Sciences, 299,* 264–272.

Levy, J. (1983). Language, cognition and the right hemisphere. *American Psychologist, 8,* 538–541.

Levy, J., & Trevarthan, C. (1976). Metacontrol of hemispheric function in human split-brain patients. *Journal of Experimental Psychology: Human Perception and Performance, 2,* 299–312.

Levy, J., & Trevarthan, C. (1977). Perceptual, semantic and phonetic aspects of elementary language processes in split-brain patients. *Brain, 100,* 105–118.

Levy, J., Trevarthan, C., & Sperry, R. W. (1972). Perception of bilateral chimeric figures following hemispheric deconnexion. *Brain, 95,* 61–78.

Lewis, J. L. (1970). Semantic processing of unattended messages using dichotic listening. *Journal of Experimental Psychology, 85,* 225–228.

Liberman, A. M. (1982). On finding that speech is special. *American Psychologist, 37,* 148–167.

Liberman, A. M., Cooper, F. S., Shankweiler, D. P., & Studdert-Kennedy, M. (1967). Perception of the speech code. *Psychological Review, 74,* 431–461.

Liberman, A. M., Harris, K., Eimas, P., Lisker, L., & Bastian, J. (1961). An effect of learning on speech perception: The discrimination of durations of silence with and without phonemic significance. *Language and Speech, 4,* 175–195.

Liberman, A. M., Isenberg, D., & Rakerd, B. (1981). Duplex perception of cues for stop consonants: Evidence for a phonetic mode. *Perception & Psychophysics, 30,* 133–143.

Lichtenstein, S., Slovic, P., Fischhoff, B., Layman, M., & Combs, B. (1978). Judged frequency of lethal events. *Journal of Experimental Psychology: Human Learning and Memory, 4,* 551–578.

Light, L. L., & Carter-Sobell, L. (1970). Effects of changed semantic context on recognition memory. *Journal of Verbal Learning and Verbal Behavior, 9,* 1–11.

Light, L. L., Kayra-Stuart, F., & Hollander, S. (1979). Recognition memory for typical and unusual faces. *Journal of Experimental Psychology: Human Learning and Memory, 5,* 212–228.

Limber, J. (1977). Language in child and chimp? *American Psychologist, 32,* 280–295.

Loess, H. (1964). Proactive inhibition in short-term memory. *Journal of Verbal Learning and Verbal Behavior, 3,* 362–368.

Loftus, E. F. (1975). Leading questions and the eyewitness report. *Cognitive Psychology, 7,* 560–572.

Loftus, E. F. (1977). Shifting human color memory. *Memory & Cognition, 5,* 696–699.

Loftus, E. F. (1980). *Memory.* Reading, Mass.: Addison-Wesley.

Loftus, E. F., & Marburger, W. (1983). Since the eruption of Mt. St. Helens, has anyone beaten you up? Improving the accuracy of retrospective reports with landmark events. *Memory & Cognition, 11,* 114–120.

Loftus, E. F., & Palmer, J. C. (1974). Reconstruction of automobile destruction: An example of the interaction between language and memory. *Journal of Verbal Learning and Verbal Behavior, 13,* 585–589.

Loftus, G. R., & Kallman, H. J. (1979). Encoding and use of detail information in picture recognition. *Journal of Experimental Psychology: Human Learning and Memory, 5,* 197–211.

Loftus, G. R., & Patterson, K. K. (1975). Components of short-term proactive interference. *Journal of Verbal Learning and Verbal Behavior, 14,* 105–121.

Long, G. M. (1980). Iconic memory: A review and critique of the study of short-term visual storage. *Psychological Bulletin, 88,* 785–820.

Lorayne, H., & Lucas, J. (1974). *The Memory Book.* New York: Stein & Day.

Lorayne, M. (1975). *Remembering People.* New York: Warner Books.

Lorch, R. F., Jr. (1978). The role of two types of semantic information in the processing of false sentences. *Journal of Verbal Learning and Verbal Behavior, 17,* 523–437.

Lorch, R. F., Jr. (1981). Effects of relation strength and semantic overlap on retrieval and comparison processes during sentence verification. *Journal of Verbal Learning and Verbal Behavior, 20,* 593–610.

Lorch, R. F., Jr. (1982). Priming and search processes in semantic memory: A test of three models of spreading activation. *Journal of Verbal Learning and Verbal Behavior, 21,* 468–492.

Lord, C., Lepper, M. R., & Ross, L. (1978). Biased assimilation and attitude polarization: The effects of prior theories on subsequently considered evidence. *Journal of Personality and Social Psychology, 37,* 2098–2110.

Luchins, A. (1942). Mechanization in problem solving. *Psychological Monographs, 54*(No. 248).

Luchins, A., & Luchins, E. (1950). New experimental attempts at preventing mechanization in problem solving. *Journal of General Psychology, 42,* 279–297.

Lucy, J. A., & Schweder, R. A. (1979). Whorf and his critics: Linguistic and nonlinguistic influences on color memory. *American Anthropologist, 81,* 581–615.

Lupker, S. J. (1979). On the nature of perceptual information during letter perception. *Perception & Psychophysics, 25,* 303–312.

Lupker, S. J., & Katz, A. N. (1981). Input decision and response factors in picture-word interference. *Journal of Experimental Psychology: Human Learning and Memory, 1,* 269–282.

Luria, A. R. (1968). *The Mind of a Mnemonist.* New York: Basic Books.

Luria, A. R. (1972). *The Man with the Shattered World.* Chicago: Regney.

Lykken, D. T. (1981). *A Tremor in the Blood: Uses and Abuses of the Lie Detector.* New York: McGraw-Hill.

Lynch, S., & Yarnell, P. R. (1973). Retrograde amnesia: Delayed forgetting after concussion. *American Journal of Psychology, 86,* 643–645.

MacKay, D. G. (1968). Phonetic factors in the perception and recall of spelling errors. *Neuropsychologia, 6,* 321–325.

MacKay, D. G. (1973). Aspects of the theory of comprehension, memory, and attention. *Quarterly Journal of Experimental Psychology, 25,* 22–40.

Mackie, R. R. (Ed.). (1977). *Vigilance: Theory, Operational Performance, and Physiological Correlates.* New York: Plenum.

Mackworth, J. F. (1964). Performance decrement in vigilance, threshold, and high-speed perceptual motor tasks. *Canadian Journal of Psychology, 18,* 209–223.

Mackworth, N. H. (1948). The breakdown of vigilance during prolonged visual search. *Quarterly Journal of Experimental Psychology, 1,* 6–21.

Madigan, S. A. (1969). Intraserial repetition and coding processes in free recall.

*Journal of Verbal Learning and Verbal Behavior, 8,* 828–835.

Maki, R. H., & Schuler, J. (1980). Effects of rehearsal duration and level of processing on memory for words. *Journal of Verbal Learning and Verbal Behavior, 19,* 36–45.

Malpass, R. S., & Kravatz, J. (1969). Recognition for faces of own and other race. *Journal of Personality and Social Psychology, 13,* 330–334.

Mandler, G. (1967). Organization and memory. In K. W. Spence & J. T. Spence (Eds.), *The Psychology of Learning and Motivation* (Vol. 1). New York: Academic Press.

Mandler, G. (1972). Organization and recognition. In E. Tulving & W. Donaldson (Eds.), *Organization and Memory.* New York: Academic Press.

Mandler, G. (1980). Recognizing: The judgment of previous occurrence. *Psychological Review, 87,* 252–271.

Mandler, G., & Boeck, W. J. (1974). Retrieval processes in recognition. *Memory & Cognition, 2,* 613–615.

Mandler, G., & Pearlstone, Z. (1966). Free and constrained concept learning and subsequent recall. *Journal of Verbal Learning and Verbal Behavior, 5,* 126–131.

Mandler, J. M., & Johnson, N. S. (1977). Remembrance of things parsed: Story structure and recall. *Cognitive Psychology, 9,* 111–151.

Manktelow, K. I., & Evans, J. St. B. T. (1979). Facilitation of reasoning by realism: Effect or non-effect? *British Journal of Psychology, 70,* 477–488.

Maratsos, M., & Chalkley, A. (1980). The internal language of children's syntax: The ontogenesis and representation of syntactic categories. In K. E. Nelson (Ed.), *Children's Language* (Vol. 2). New York: Gardner Press.

Marcel, A. J. (1983). Conscious and unconscious perception: Experiments on visual masking and word recognition. *Cognitive Psychology, 15,* 197–237.

Markus, H. (1977). Self-schemata and processing information about the self. *Journal of Personality and Social Psychology, 35,* 63–78.

Marler, P. (1967). Animal communication signals. *Science, 157,* 769–774.

Marmor, G. S., & Zabeck, L. A. (1976). Mental rotation by the blind: Does mental rotation depend on visual imagery? *Journal of Experimental Psychology: Human Perception and Performance, 2,* 515–521.

Marslen-Wilson, W. D. (1975). Sentence perception as an interactive parallel process. *Science, 189,* 226–228.

Marslen-Wilson, W. D., & Welsh, A. (1978). Processing interactions and lexical access during word recognition in continuous speech. *Cognitive Psychology, 10,* 29–63.

Martone, M., Butters, N., Payne, M., Becker, J. T., & Sax, D. S. (1984). Dissociations between skill learning and verbal recognition in amnesia and dementia. *Archives of Neurology, 41,* 965–970.

Martz, R. L., & Harris, J. D. (1961). Signal presentation rate and auditory vigilance. *Journal of the Acoustical Society of America, 33,* 855.

Mattis, S., French, J. H., & Rapin, I. (1975). Dyslexia in children and young adults: Three independent neuropsychological syndromes. *Developmental Medicine and Child Neurology, 17,* 150–163.

Mazuryk, G. F., (1974). Positive recency in final free recall. *Journal of Experimental Psychology, 103,* 812–814.

McArthur, D. J. (1982). Computer vision and perceptual psychology. *Psychological Bulletin, 92,* 283–309.

McCauley, C., Parmelee, C. M., Sperber, R. D., & Carr, T. H. (1980). Early extraction of meaning from pictures and its relation to conscious identification. *Journal of Experimental Psychology: Human Perception and Performance, 6,* 265–276.

McClelland, J. L., & Rumelhart, D. E. (1981). An interactive model of context effects in letter perception. Part 1. An account of basic findings. *Psychological Review, 88,* 375–407.

McCloskey, M., & Glucksberg, S. (1979). Decision processes in verifying category membership statements: Implications for models of semantic memory. *Cognitive Psychology, 11,* 1–37.

McConkie, G. W., & Rayner, K. (1975). The span of the effective stimulus during a fixation in reading. *Perception & Psychophysics, 17,* 578–586.

McDaniel, M. A., Friedman, A., & Bourne, L. E., Jr. (1978). Remembering the levels of information in words. *Memory & Cognition, 6,* 156–164.

McDowell, J. (1979). Effects of encoding instructions and retrieval cuing on recall in Korsakoff patients. *Memory & Cognition, 7,* 232–239.

McFarland, C. E., Jr., Rhodes, D. D., & Frey, J. J. (1979). The spacing effect. *Journal of Verbal Learning and Verbal Behavior, 18,* 163–172.

McGaugh, J. L. (1983). Preserving the presence of the past: Hormonal influence on memory storage. *American Psychologist, 38,* 161–174.

McGeoch, J. A. (1936). Studies in retroactive inhibition. VIII. Retroactive inhibition as a function of the length and frequency of the interpolated lists. *Journal of Experimental Psychology, 19,* 674–693.

McGhie, A., & Chapman, J. (1961). Disorders of attention and perception in early schizophrenia. *British Journal of Medical Pathology, 34,* 103–116.

Medin, D. L., & Schaffer, M. M. (1978). A context theory of classification. *Psychological Review, 85,* 207–238.

Medin, D. L., & Smith, E. E. (1984). Concepts and concept formation. *Annual Review of Psychology, 35,* 113–138.

Melton, A. W. (1963). Implications of short-term memory for a general theory of memory. *Journal of Verbal Learning and Verbal Behavior, 63,* 81–97.

Melton, A. W. (1967). Repetition and retrieval from memory. *Science, 158,* 532.

Melton, A. W., & Irwin, J. M. (1940). The influence of degree of interpolated learning on retroactive inhibition and the overt transfer of specific responses. *American Journal of Psychology, 53,* 173–203.

*The Merck Manual (12th ed.).* (1972). Rahway, N.J.: Merck.

Mervis, C. B., & Roth, E. M. (1981). The internal structure of basic and non-basic color categories. *Language, 57,* 384–405.

Mewhort, D. J., Campbell, A. J., Marchetti, F. M., & Campbell, J. I. (1981). Identification, localization, and "iconic memory": An evaluation of the bar-probe task. *Memory & Cognition, 9,* 50–67.

Mewhort, D. J. K., & Campbell, A. J. (1980). The rate of word integration and the overprinting paradigm. *Memory and Cognition, 8,* 15–23.

Meyer, D. E., & Schvaneveldt, R. W. (1971). Facilitation in recognizing pairs of words: Evidence of a dependence between retrieval operations. *Journal of Experimental Psychology, 90,* 227–234.

Meyer, D. E., & Schvaneveldt, R. W. (1975). Meaning, memory structure, and mental processes. In C. N. Cofer (Ed.), *The Structure of Human Memory.* San Francisco: Freeman.

Michalski, R. S., Carbonell, J. G., & Mitchell, T. M. (Eds.). (1983). *Machine Learning.* Palo Alto, Calif.: Tioga Press.

Miller, E. A. (1972). Interaction of vision and touch in conflict and nonconflict form perception tasks. *Journal of Experimental Psychology, 96,* 114–123.

Miller, G. A. (1956). The magical number seven, plus or minus two: Some limits of our capacity for processing information. *Psychological Review, 63,* 81–97.

Miller, G. A. (1981). *Language and Speech.* San Francisco: Freeman.

Miller, G. A., Galanter, E., & Pribram, K. H. (1960). *Plans and the Structure of Behavior.* New York: Holt, Rinehart and Winston.

Miller, G. A., & Johnson-Laird, P. N. (1976). *Language and Perception.* Cambridge, Mass.: Belknap Press.

Miller, J. L. (1981). Some effects of speaking rate on phonetic perception. *Phonetica, 38,* 159–180.

Miller, J. L., & Grosjean, P. (1981). How the components of speaking rate influence perception of phonetic segments. *Journal of Experimental Psychology: Human Perception and Performance, 7,* 208–215.

Milner, B. (1971). Interhemispheric differences in the localization of psychological processes in man. *British Medical Bulletin, 27,* 272–277.

Milner, B. (1975). Psychological aspects of focal epilepsy and its neurological management. *Advances in Neurology, 8,* 299–321.

Milner, B., Corkin, S., & Teuber, H. L. (1968). Further analysis of the hippocampal amnesic syndrome: 14 year follow-up study of H. M. *Neuropsychologia, 6,* 215–234.

Milner, B., Taylor, L., & Sperry, R. W. (1968). Lateralized suppression of dichotically presented digits after commisural section in man. *Science, 161,* 184–185.

Minsky, M. A. (1975). A framework for representing knowledge. In P. H. Winston (Ed.), *The Psychology of Computer Vision.* New York: McGraw-Hill.

Mitchell, D. B., & Richman, C. L. (1980). Confirmed reservations: Mental travel.

Journal of Experimental Psychology: Human Perception and Performance, 6, 58–66.

Moar, I., & Bower, G. H. (1983). Inconsistency in spatial knowledge. Memory & Cognition, 11, 107–113.

Moates, D. R., & Schumacher, G. M. (1980). An Introduction to Cognitive Psychology. Belmont, Calif.: Wadsworth.

Modigliani, V. (1980). Immediate rehearsal and initial retention interval in free recall. Journal of Experimental Psychology: Human Learning and Memory, 6, 241–253.

Mohr, J. P. (1976). Broca's area and Broca's aphasia. In H. Whitaker & M. A. Whitaker (Eds.), Studies in Neurolinguistics (Vol. 1). New York: Academic Press.

Molfese, D. L., Nunez, V., Seibert, S. M., & Ramanaiah, N. V. (1976). Cerebral asymmetry: Changes in factors affecting its development. Annals of the New York Academy of Sciences, 280, 821–833.

Montague, W. E., Adams, J. A., & Kiess, H. O. (1966). Forgetting and natural language mediation. Journal of Experimental Psychology, 72, 829–833.

Moore, J. J., & Massaro, D. W. (1973). Attention and processing capacity in auditory recognition. Journal of Experimental Psychology, 99, 49–54.

Moray, N. (1959). Attention in dichotic listening: Affective cues and the influence of instructions. Quarterly Journal of Experimental Psychology, 11, 56–60.

Moray, N. (1970). Attention: Selective Processes in Vision and Hearing. New York: Academic Press.

Moray, N., Bates, A., & Barnett, T. (1965). Experiments on the four-eared man. Journal of the Acoustical Society of America, 38, 196–201.

Moray, N., & Fitter, M. (1973). A theory and the measurement of attention: Tutorial review. In S. Kornblum (Ed.), Attention and Performance IV. New York: Academic Press.

Moray, N., Fitter, M., Ostry, D., Favreau, D., & Nagy, V. (1976). Attention to pure tones. Quarterly Journal of Experimental Psychology, 28, 271–283.

Morton, J. (1969). Interaction of information in word recognition. Psychological Review, 76, 165–178.

Morton, J. (1979). Facilitation in word recognition: Experiments that cause changes in the logogen model. In P. A. Kolers, M. E. Wrolstad, & H. Bouma (Eds.), Processing of Visual Language (Vol. I). New York: Plenum.

Moscovitch, M., & Craik, F. I. M. (1976). Depth of processing, retrieval cues, and uniqueness of encoding as factors in recall. Journal of Verbal Learning and Verbal Behavior, 15, 447–458.

Moss, C. S. (1972). Recovery with Aphasia. Urbana, Ill.: University of Illinois Press.

Moyer, R. S. (1973). Comparing objects in memory: Evidence suggesting an internal psychophysics. Perception & Psychophysics, 13, 180–184.

Moyer, R. S., & Landauer, T. K. (1967). Time required for judgments of numerical inequality. Nature, 215, 1519–1520.

Müller, G. E. (1913). Zur Analyse der Gedächtnistätigkeit und des Vorstellungsverlautes, III. Teil. Zeitschrift für Psychologie, Ergänzungsband 8. Cited by Rabinowitz, Mandler, and Patterson (1977).

Murphy, G. L., & Smith, E. E. (1982). Basic-level superiority in picture categorization. Journal of Verbal Learning and Verbal Behavior, 21, 1–20.

Murray, H. G., & Denny, J. P. (1969). Interaction of ability level and interpolated activity (opportunity for incubation) in human problem solving. *Psychological Reports, 24,* 271–276.

Myers, J. J. (1984). Right hemisphere language: Science or fiction? *American Psychologist, 39,* 315–320.

Myerson, R., & Goodglass, H. (1972). Transformational grammars of three agrammatic patients. *Language and Speech, 15,* 40–50.

Nachreiner, F. (1977). Experiments on the validity of vigilance experiments. In R. R. Mackie (Ed.), *Vigilance: Theory, Operational Performance, and Physiological Correlates.* New York: Plenum.

Nagae, S. (1980). Nature of discriminating and categorizing functions of verbal labels on recognition memory for shape. *Journal of Experimental Psychology: Human Learning and Memory, 6,* 421–429.

Neely, J. H. (1977). Semantic priming and retrieval from lexical memory: Role of inhibitionless spreading activation and limited capacity attention. *Journal of Experimental Psychology: General, 106,* 226–254.

Neely, J. H., Schmidt, S. R., & Roediger, H. L. (1983). Inhibition from related primes in recognition memory. *Journal of Experimental Psychology: Learning, Memory, and Cognition, 9,* 196–211.

Neill, W. T. (1977). Inhibitory and facilitatory processes in selective attention. *Journal of Experimental Psychology: Human Perception and Performance, 3,* 444–450.

Neill, W. T. (1979). Switching attention within and between categories: Evidence for intracategory inhibition. *Memory & Cognition, 1,* 283–290.

Neisser, U. (1963). Decision-time without reaction-time: Experiments in visual scanning. *American Journal of Psychology, 76,* 376–385.

Neisser, U. (1967). *Cognitive Psychology.* Englewood Cliffs, N.J.: Prentice-Hall.

Neisser, U. (Ed.). (1982). *Memory Observed.* San Francisco: Freeman.

Nelson, D. L., & McEvoy, C. L. (1979). Encoding context and set size. *Journal of Experimental Psychology: Human Learning and Memory, 5,* 292–314.

Nelson, R. L., Walling, J. R., & McEvoy, C. L. (1979). Doubts about depth. *Journal of Experimental Psychology: Human Learning and Memory, 5,* 24–44.

Nelson, T. O. (1977). Repetition and depth of processing. *Journal of Verbal Learning and Verbal Behavior, 16,* 151–172.

Neumann, P. G. (1977). Visual prototype information with discontinuous representation of dimensions of variability. *Memory & Cognition, 5,* 187–197.

Newcomb, F. B., Oldfield, R. C., & Wingfield, A. (1965). Object-naming by dysphasic patients. *Nature, 207,* 1217–1218.

Newell, A. (1969). Heuristic programming: Ill-structured problems. In J. S. Aronofsky (Ed.), *Progress in Operations Research* (Vol. 3). New York: Wiley.

Newell, A., & Simon, H. (1972). *Human Problem Solving.* Englewood Cliffs, N.J.: Prentice-Hall.

Newman, S. E., & Saltz, E. (1958). Isolation effects: Stimulus and response generalization as explanatory concepts. *Journal of Experimental Psychology, 55,* 467–472.

Newport, E. L., Gleitman, H., & Gleitman, L. R. (1977). Mother, I'd rather do it myself: Some effects and noneffects of maternal speech style. In C. E. Snow & C. A. Ferguson (Eds.), *Talking to Children: Language Input and Acquisition.* Cambridge: Cambridge University Press.

Nickerson, R. A., & Adams, M. J. (1979). Long-term memory for a common object. *Cognitive Psychology, 11,* 287–307.

Nilsson, N. J. (1971). *Problem Solving Methods in Artificial Intelligence.* New York: McGraw-Hill.

Nilsson, T. H., & Nelson, T. M. (1981). Delayed monochromatic hue matches indicate characteristics of visual memory. *Journal of Experimental Psychology: Human Performance and Perception, 7,* 141–150.

Nisbett, R., & Ross, L. (1980). *Human Inference: Strategies and Shortcomings of Social Judgment.* Englewood Cliffs, N.J.: Prentice-Hall.

Nisbett, R. E., Krantz, D. H., Jepson, C., & Kunda, Z. (1983). The use of statistical heuristics in everyday inductive reasoning. *Psychological Review, 90,* 339–363.

Norman, D. A. (1969). Memory while shadowing. *Quarterly Journal of Experimental Psychology, 21,* 85–93.

Norman, D. A., & Bobrow, D. G. (1975). On data-limited and resource-limited processes. *Cognitive Psychology, 7,* 44–64.

Norman, D. A., Rumelhart, D. E., & the LNR Research Group. (1975). *Explorations in Cognition.* San Franciso: Freeman.

Nottebohm, F. (1977). Asymmetries in neural control of vocalization in the canary. In S. Harnad, R. W. Doty, L. Goldstein, J. Jaynes, & G. Krauthamer (Eds.), *Lateralization in the Nervous System.* New York: Academic Press.

Notterman, J. M., & Tufano, D. R. (1980). Variables influencing outflow-inflow interpretations of tracking performance: Predictability of target motion, transfer function, and practice. *Journal of Experimental Psychology: Human Perception and Performance, 6,* 85–88.

Obusek, C. J., & Warren, R. M. (1973). Relation of the verbal transformation and the phonemic restoration effects. *Cognitive Psychology, 5,* 97–107.

Ojemann, G. A. (1977). Asymmetric function of the thalamus in man. *Annals of the New York Academy of Sciences, 299,* 380–396.

Oldfield, R. C., & Wingfield, A. (1964). The time it takes to name an object. *Nature, 202,* 1031–1032.

Oldfield, R. C., & Wingfield, A. (1965). Response latencies in naming objects. *Quarterly Journal of Experimental Psychology, 17,* 273–281.

Olson, G. M. (1976). An information processing analysis of visual memory and habituation in infants. In T. Tighe & R. Leaton (Eds.), *Habituation: Perspectives from Child Development, Animal Behavior, and Neurophysiology.* Hillsdale, N.J.: Erlbaum.

Olson, G. M. (1984). Learning and memory in infants. In J. R. Anderson & S. M. Kosslyn (Eds.), *Tutorials in Learning and Memory: Essays in Honor of Gordon Bower.* San Francisco: Freeman.

Olson, R. K., & Attneave, F. (1970). What variables produce similarity groupings? *American Journal of Psychology, 83,* 1–21.

Oltmanns, T. F., & Neale, J. M. (1975). Schizophrenic performance when distractors are present: Attentional deficit or differential task difficulty? *Journal of Abnormal Psychology, 84,* 205–209.

Olton, D. S. (1977). Spatial memory. *Scientific American, 236,* 82–98.

Oppenheimer, J. R. (1956). Analogy in science. *American Psychologist, 11,* 127–135.

Orne, M. T. (1959). The nature of hypnosis: Artifact and essence. *Journal of Abnormal and Social Psychology, 58,* 277–299.

Orne, M. T. (1966). Hypnosis, motivation and compliance. *American Journal of Psychiatry, 122,* 721–726.

Orne, M. T. (1977). The construct of hypnosis: Implications of the definition for research and practice. *Annals of the New York Academy of Sciences, 296,* 14–33.

Ornstein, R. E. (1969). *On the Experience of Time.* Baltimore: Penguin Books.

Orwell, G. (1949). *1984.* New York: Harcourt, Brace & World.

Oscar-Berman, M., Weinstein, A., & Wysocki, D. (1983). Bimanual tactual discrimination in aging alcoholics. *Alcoholism: Clinical and Experimental Research, 1,* 398–403.

Overton, D. A. (1972). State dependent learning produced by alchohol and its relevance to alcoholism. In B. Kissen & H. Begleiter (Eds.), *The Biology of Alcoholism* (Vol. 2). New York: Plenum.

Owen, F. W. (1978). Dyslexia—genetic aspects. In A. L. Benton & D. Pearl (Eds.), *Dyslexia.* New York: Oxford University Press.

Packard, V. (1957). *The Hidden Persuaders.* New York: McKay.

Paivio, A. (1969). Mental imagery in associative learning and memory. *Psychological Review, 76,* 241–263.

Paivio, A. (1971). *Imagery and Verbal Processes.* New York: Holt, Rinehart and Winston.

Paivio, A. (1974). Spacing of repetitions in the incidental and intentional free recall of pictures and words. *Journal of Verbal Learning and Verbal Behavior, 13,* 497–511.

Paivio, A., & Begg, I. (1981). *Psychology of Language.* Englewood Cliffs, N.J.: Prentice-Hall.

Paivio, A., & Csapo, K. (1973). Picture superiority in free recall: Imagery or dual coding? *Cognitive Psychology, 5,* 176–206.

Paivio, A., Yuille, J. C., & Madigan, S. A. (1968). Concreteness, imagery, and meaningfulness values for 925 nouns. *Journal of Experimental Psychology Monograph Supplement, 76,* 1–25.

Palmer, S. F. (1978). Fundamental aspects of cognitive representation. In E. Rosch & B. B. Lloyd (Eds.), *Cognition and Categorization.* Hillsdale, N.J.: Erlbaum.

Parker, E. S., Birnbaum, I. M., & Noble, E. P. (1976). Alcohol and memory: Storage and state dependency. *Journal of Verbal Learning and Verbal Behavior, 15,* 691–702.

Pavlov, I. P. (1927). *Conditional Reflexes: An Investigation of the Physiological Activity of the Cerebral Cortex.* Oxford: Oxford University Press.

Perkins, D. N. (1981). *The Mind's Best Work.* Cambridge, Mass.: Harvard University Press.

Peterson, L. R., & Peterson, M. J. (1959). Short-term retention of individual items. *Journal of Experimental Psychology, 58,* 193–198.

Petrides, M., & Milner, B. (1982). Deficits on subject-ordered tasks after frontal and temporal lobe lesions in man. *Neuropsychologia, 20,* 249–262.

Phillips, J. R. (1973). Syntax and vocabulary of mothers' speech to young children: Age and sex comparisons. *Child Development, 44,* 182–185.

Pick, H., Warren, D., & Hay, I. (1969). Sensory conflict in judgments of spatial direction. *Perception & Psychophysics, 6,* 203–205.

Pinker, S. (1980). Mental imagery and the third dimension. *Journal of Experimental Psychology: General, 109,* 354–357.

Pinker, S., & Finke, R. A. (1980). Emergent two-dimensional patterns in images rotated in depth. *Journal of Experimental Psychology: Human Perception and Performance, 6,* 244–264.

Podgorny, P., & Shepard, R. N. (1978). Functional representations common to visual perception and imagination. *Journal of Experimental Psychology: Human Perception and Performance, 4,* 21–35.

Pohlmann, L. D., & Sorkin, R. D. (1976). Simultaneous three-channel signal detection: Performance and criterion as a function of order of report. *Perception & Psychophysics, 20,* 179–186.

Poincaré, H. (1913). In G. B. Halsted (Trans.), *The Foundations of Science.* New York: Science Press.

Poltrock, S. E., Lansman, M., & Hunt, E. (1982). Automatic and controlled attention processes in auditory target detection. *Journal of Experimental Psychology: Human Perception and Performance, 8,* 37–45.

Polya, G. (1957). *How to Solve It.* Garden City, N.Y.: Doubleday/Anchor.

Polya, G. (1973). *Mathematics and Plausible Reasoning.* Princeton, N.J.: Princeton University Press.

Pomerantz, J. R. (1981). Perceptual organization in information processing. In M. Kubovy & J. R. Pomerantz (Eds.), *Perceptual Organization.* Hillsdale, N.J.: Erlbaum.

Pomerantz, J. R., Sager, L. C., & Stoever, R. J. (1977). Perception of wholes and their component parts: Some configural superiority effects. *Journal of Experimental Psychology: Human Perception and Performance, 3,* 422–435.

Posner, M. I. (1969). Abstraction and the process of recognition. In G. H. Bower & J. T. Spence (Eds.), *The Psychology of Learning and Motivation* (Vol. 3). New York: Academic Press.

Posner, M. I. (1973). *Cognition: An Introduction.* Glenview, Ill.: Scott, Foresman.

Posner, M. I. (1980). Orienting of attention. *Quarterly Journal of Experimental Psychology, 32,* 3–25.

Posner, M. I. (1982). Cumulative development of attention theory. *American Psychologist, 37,* 168–179.

Posner, M. I., & Keele, S. W. (1968). On the genesis of abstract ideas. *Journal of Experimental Psychology, 77,* 353–363.

Posner, M. I., & Keele, S. W. (1970). Retention of abstract ideas. *Journal of Experimental Psychology, 83,* 304–308.

Posner, M. I., Nissen, M. J., & Klein, R. M. (1976). Visual dominance: An informa-tion-processing account of its origins and significance. *Psychological Review, 83,* 157–171.

Posner, M. I., & Snyder, C. R. R. (1975). Attention and cognitive control. In R. Solso (Ed.), *Information Processing and Cognition: The Loyola Symposium.* Hillsdale, N.J.: Erlbaum.

Postman, L., & Phillips, L. W. (1965). Short-term temporal changes in free recall. *Quarterly Journal of Experimental Psychology, 17,* 132–138.

Potter, M. C. (1975). Meaning in visual search. *Science, 187,* 965–966.

Potter, M. C. (1976). Short-term conceptual memory for pictures. *Journal of Experimental Psychology: Human Learning and Memory, 2,* 509–522.

Potts, G. R. (1972). Information processing strategies used in the encoding of linear orderings. *Journal of Verbal Learning and Verbal Behavior, 11,* 727–740.

Potts, G. R. (1974). Storing and retrieving information about ordered relationships. *Journal of Experimental Psychology, 103,* 431–439.

Poulton, E. C. (1977). Arousing stresses increase vigilance. In R. R. Mackie (Ed.), *Vigilance Theory: Operational Performance, and Physiological Correlates.* New York: Plenum.

Premack, A. J., & Premack, D. (1972). Teaching language to an ape. *Scientific American, 227,* 92–99.

Premack, D. (1971). Language in chimpanzee? *Science, 172,* 808–822.

Premack, D., & Woodruff, G. (1978). Does the chimpanzee have a theory of mind? *Behavioral and Brain Sciences, 1,* 515–526.

Pribram, K. H. (1977). Hemispheric specialization: Evolution or revolution. *Annals of the New York Academy of Sciences, 299,* 18–22.

Pribram, K. H., & McGuinness, D. (1975). Arousal, activation, and effort in the control of attention. *Psychological Review*, *82*, 116–149.

Proctor, R. W. (1981). A unified theory for matching-task phenomena. *Psychological Review*, *88*, 291–326.

Proctor, R. W., & Rao, V. (1983). Reinstating the original principles of Proctor's unified theory for matching-task phenomena: An evaluation of Krueger and Shapiro's reformulation. *Psychological Review*, *90*, 21–37.

Prytulak, L. S. (1971). Natural language mediation. *Cognitive Psychology*, *2*, 1–56.

Pullum, G. K. (1977). Word order universals and grammatical relations. In P. Cole & J. M. Sadock (Eds.), *Syntax and Semantics. Vol. 8, Grammatical Relations.* New York: Academic Press.

Pylyshyn, Z. W. (1973). What the mind's eye tells the mind's brain: A critique of mental imagery. *Psychological Bulletin*, *80*, 1–24.

Pylyshyn, Z. W. (1981). The imagery debate: Analogue media versus tacit knowledge. *Psychological Review*, *88*, 16–45.

Raaijmakers, J. G. W., & Shiffrin, R. M. (1981). Search of associative memory. *Psychological Review*, *88*, 93–134.

Rabbitt, P. M. A. (1967). Time to detect errors as a function of factors affecting choice-response time. *Acta Psychologica*, *27*, 131–142.

Rabbitt, P. M. A. (1968). Three kinds of error-signalling responses in a serial choice task. *Quarterly Journal of Experimental Psychology*, *20*, 179–188.

Rabin, M. D., & Cain, W. S. (1984). Odor recognition: Familiarity, identifiability, and encoding consistency. *Journal of Experimental Psychology: Learning, Memory, and Cognition*, *10*, 316–325.

Rabinowitz, J. C., Mandler, G., & Barsalou, L. W. (1979). Generation-recognition as an auxiliary retrieval strategy. *Journal of Verbal Learning and Verbal Behavior*, *18*, 57–72.

Rabinowitz, J. C., Mandler, G., & Patterson, K. E. (1977). Determinants of recognition and recall: Accessibility and generation. *Journal of Experimental Psychology: General*, *106*, 302–329.

Radtke, R. C., Grove, E. K., & Talasi, U. (1982). PI in short-term and delayed recall. *Journal of Experimental Psychology: Learning, Memory, and Cognition*, *8*, 117–125.

Rakover, S. S. (1977). Does interpolated interference affect only the short-term store in a free recall task? *Memory & Cognition*, *5*, 453–456.

Rand, T. C. (1974). Dichotic release from masking for speech. *Journal of the Acoustical Society of America*, *55*, 678–680.

Raphael, B. (1976). *The Thinking Computer.* San Francisco: Freeman.

Rasmussen, T., & Milner, B. (1977). The role of early left-brain injury in determining lateralization of cerebral speech functions. *Annals of the New York Academy of Sciences*, *299*, 355–369.

Raye, C. L., Johnson, M. K., & Taylor, J. H. (1980). Is there something special about memory for internally generated information? *Memory & Cognition*, *8*, 141–148.

Reber, A. S. (1967). Implicit learning of artificial grammars. *Journal of Verbal Learning and Verbal Behavior*, *5*, 855–863.

Reber, A. S. (1976). Implicit learning of synthetic languages: The role of instructional set. *Journal of Experimental Psychology: Human Learning and Memory*, *2*, 88–94.

Reber, A. S., & Allen, R. (1978). Analogy and abstraction strategies in synthetic grammar learning: A functional interpretation. *Cognition*, *6*, 189–221.

Reber, A. S., Kassin, S. M., Lewis, S., & Cantor, G. W. (1980). On the relationship between implicit and explicit modes in the learning of a complex rule structure. *Journal of Experimental Psycholo-*

gy: *Human Learning and Memory, 6,* 492–502.

Reder, L. M. (1982). Plausibility judgments versus fact retrieval: Alternative strategies for sentence verification. *Psychological Review, 89,* 250–280.

Reed, S. K. (1972). Pattern recognition and categorization. *Cognitive Psychology, 3,* 383–407.

Reese, H. W. (1965). Imagery in paired-associate learning in children. *Journal of Experimental Child Psychology, 2,* 290–296.

Reicher, G. M. (1969). Perceptual recognition as a function of meaningfulness of stimulus material. *Journal of Experimental Psychology, 81,* 275–280.

Reisberg, D., Baron, J., & Kemler, D. G. (1980). Overcoming Stroop interference: The effects of practice on distractor potency. *Journal of Experimental Psychology: Human Perception and Performance, 6,* 140–150.

Reitman, J. S. (1974). Without surreptitious rehearsal, information in short-term memory decays. *Journal of Verbal Learning and Verbal Behavior, 13,* 365–377.

Reitman, J. S. (1976). Skilled perception in Go: Deducing memory structures from inter-response times. *Cognitive Psychology, 8,* 336–356.

Reitman, J. S., & Bower, G. H. (1973). Storage and later recognition of exemplars of concepts. *Cognitive Psychology, 4,* 194–206.

Reitman, W. (1964). Heuristic decision procedures, open constraints, and the structure of ill-defined problems. In M. W. Shelley & G. L. Bryan (Eds.), *Human Judgments and Optimality.* New York: Wiley.

Remington, R. (1980). Attention and saccadic eye movements. *Journal of Experimental Psychology: Human Perception and Performance, 6,* 726–744.

Repp, B. H., Liberman, A. M., Eccardt, T., & Pesetsky, D. (1978). Perceptual integration of acoustic cues for stop, fricative, and affricate manner. *Journal of Experimental Psychology: Human Perception and Performance, 4,* 621–637.

Rescorla, L. A. (1980). Overextension in early language development. *Journal of Child Language, 7,* 321–335.

Reynolds, B. (1945). The acquisition of a trace conditioned response as a function of the magnitude of the stimulus trace. *Journal of Experimental Psychology, 35,* 15–30.

Rich, E. (1983). *Artificial Intelligence.* New York: McGraw-Hill.

Riggs, L. A. (1971). Vision. In J. W. Kling & L. A. Riggs (Eds.), *Experimental Psychology.* New York: Holt, Rinehart and Winston.

Rips, L. J. (1983). Cognitive processes in propositional reasoning. *Psychological Review, 90,* 38–71.

Rips, L. J., Shoben, E. J., & Smith, E. E. (1973). Semantic distance and the verification of semantic relations. *Journal of Verbal Learning and Verbal Behavior, 12,* 1–20.

Robbins, D., Barresi, J., Compton, P., Furst, A., Russo, M., & Smith, M. A. (1978). The genesis and use of exemplar vs. prototype knowledge in abstract category learning. *Memory & Cognition, 6,* 473–480.

Roberts, L. G. (1965). Machine perception of three-dimensional solids. In J. T. Tippett, D. A. Berkowitz, L. C. Clapp, C. J. Koester, & A. Vanderburgh (Eds.), *Electro-Optical Information Processing.* Cambridge, Mass.: MIT Press.

Robinson, G. M., & Solomon, D. J. (1974). Rhythm is processed in the speech hemisphere. *Journal of Experimental Psychology, 102,* 508–511.

Robinson, J. A. (1976). Sampling autobiographical memory. *Cognitive Psychology, 8*, 578–595.

Rochford, G., & Williams, M. (1962). Studies in the development and breakdown of the use of names. I. The relationship between nominal dysphasia and the acquisition of vocabulary in childhood. *Journal of Neurological and Neurosurgical Psychiatry, 25*, 222–223.

Rochford, G., & Williams, M. (1963). Studies in the development and breakdown of the use of names. III. Recovery from nominal dysphasia. *Journal of Neurological and Neurosurgical Psychiatry, 26*, 377–381.

Rock, I. (1983). *The Logic of Perception.* Cambridge, Mass.: MIT Press.

Rock, I. (1984). *Perception.* New York: Scientific American.

Rock, I., & Gutman, D. (1981). The effect of inattention on form perception. *Journal of Experimental Psychology: Human Perception and Performance, 7*, 275–285.

Rock, I., Halper, F., & Clayton, T. (1972). The perception and recognition of complex figures. *Cognitive Psychology, 3*, 655–673.

Rock, I., & Victor, J. (1964). Vision and touch: An experimentally created conflict between the two senses. *Science, 143*, 594–596.

Roediger, H. L. (1974). Inhibiting effects of recall. *Memory & Cognition, 2*, 261–269.

Roediger, H. L. (1978). Recall as a self-limiting process. *Memory & Cognition, 8*, 54–63.

Roediger, H. L. (1980). The effectiveness of four mnemonics in ordering recall. *Journal of Experimental Psychology: Human Learning and Memory, 6*, 558–567.

Roediger, H. L., & Neely, J. M. (1982). Retrieval blocks in episodic and semantic memory. *Canadian Journal of Psychology, 36*, 213–242.

Roediger, H. L., Neely, J. H., & Blaxton, T. A. (1983). Inhibition from related primes in semantic memory retrieval: A reappraisal of Brown's (1979) paradigm. *Journal of Experimental Psychology: Learning, Memory, and Cognition, 9*, 478–485.

Roediger, H. L., & Schmidt, S. R. (1980). Output interference in the recall of categorized and paired-associate lists. *Journal of Experimental Psychology: Human Learning and Memory, 6*, 91–105.

Roediger, H. L., & Thorpe, L. A. (1978). The role of recall time in producing hypermnesia. *Memory & Cognition, 6*, 296–305.

Rosch, E. (1973). On the internal structure of perceptual and semantic categories. In T. E. Moore (Ed.), *Cognitive Development and the Acquisition of Language.* New York: Academic Press.

Rosch, E. (1975). Cognitive representations of semantic categories. *Journal of Experimental Psychology: General, 104*, 192–233.

Rosch, E., & Lloyd, B. B. (Eds.). (1978). *Cognition and Categorization.* Hillsdale, N.J.: Erlbaum.

Rosch, E., & Mervis, C. B. (1975). Family resemblances: Studies in the internal structure of categories. *Cognitive Psychology, 7*, 573–605.

Rosch, E., Mervis, C. B., Gray, W., Johnson, D., & Boyes-Braem, P. (1976). Basic objects in natural categories. *Cognitive Psychology, 8*, 382–439.

Rosch, E., Simpson, C., & Miller, R. S. (1976). Structural bases of typicality effects. *Journal of Experimental Psychology: Human Perception and Performance, 2*, 491–502.

Rosenbaum, D. A. (1984). Planning and control of motor movements. In J. R. Anderson & S. M. Kosslyn (Eds.), *Tutorials in Learning and Memory: Essays in Honor of Gordon Bower.* San Francisco: Freeman.

Ross, B. H. (1981). The more the better? Number of decisions as a determinant of memorability. *Memory & Cognition, 9,* 23–33.

Ross, B. H., & Bower, G. H. (1981). Comparison of models of associative recall. *Memory & Cognition, 9,* 1–16.

Rotondo, J. A. (1979). Independence of trace storage and organized recall. *Journal of Verbal Learning and Verbal Behavior, 18,* 675–686.

Rourke, B. P. (1978). Neuropsychological research in reading retardation: A review. In A. L. Benton & D. Pearl (Eds.), *Dyslexia.* New York: Oxford University Press.

Rubin, D. C. (1982). On the retention function for autobiographical memory. *Journal of Verbal Learning and Verbal Behavior, 21,* 21–38.

Rubin, D. C., & Kontis, T. S. (1983). A schema for common cents. *Memory & Cognition, 11,* 335–341.

Rubin, E. (1915). *Synoplevede Figurer.* Copenhagen: Gyldendalska. Cited by Hochberg (1971).

Rumbaugh, D., Gill, T. V., & von Glaserfeld, E. C. (1973). Reading and sentence completion by a chimpanzee (Pan). *Science, 183,* 731–733.

Rumelhart, D. E. (1977). Understanding and summarizing brief stories. In D. Laberge & S. J. Samuels (Eds.), *Basic Processes in Reading: Perception and Comprehension.* Hillsdale, N.J.: Erlbaum.

Rumelhart, D. E. (1980). Schemata: The building blocks of cognition. In R. Spiro, B. Bruce, & W. Brewer (Eds.), *Theoretical Issues in Reading Comprehension.* Hillsdale, N.J.: Erlbaum.

Rumelhart, D. E., & McClelland, J. L. (1982). An interactive model of context effects in letter perception. Part 2. The contextual enhancement effect and some tests and extensions of the model. *Psychological Review, 89,* 60–94.

Rumelhart, D. E., & Norman, D. A. (1982). Simulating a skilled typist: A study of skilled cognitive-motor performance. *Cognitive Science, 6,* 1–36.

Rundus, D. (1971). Analysis of rehearsal processes in free recall. *Journal of Experimental Psychology, 89,* 63–77.

Rundus, D. (1973). Negative effects of using list items as recall cues. *Journal of Verbal Learning and Verbal Behavior, 12,* 43–50.

Rundus, D. (1980). Maintenance rehearsal and long-term recency. *Memory & Cognition, 8,* 226–230.

Rundus, D., & Atkinson, R. C. (1970). Rehearsal processes in free recall: A procedure for direct observation. *Journal of Verbal Learning and Verbal Behavior, 9,* 99–105.

Russell, W. R., & Espir, M. L. E. (1961). *Traumatic Aphasia—A Study of Aphasia in War Wounds of the Brain.* London: Oxford University Press.

Rutter, M. (1978). Prevalence and types of dyslexia. In A. L. Benton & D. Pearl (Eds.), *Dyslexia.* New York: Columbia University Press.

Ryan, C., & Butters, N. (1980). Learning and memory impairments in young and old alcoholics: Evidence for the premature-aging hypothesis. *Alcoholism, 4,* 288–293.

Ryan, C., & Butters, N. (1983). Cognitive deficits in alcoholics. In B. Kissin & H. Begleiter (Eds.), *The Pathogenesis of Alcoholism* (Vol. 7). New York: Plenum.

Ryan, C., & Butters, N. (1984). Alcohol consumption and premature aging: A critical review. In M. Galanter (Ed.), *Recent Developments in Alcoholism* (Vol. 1). New York: Plenum.

Sachs, J. S., Brown, R., & Salerno, R. A. (1976). Adults' speech to children. In W. van Raffler Engel & Y. Lebrun (Eds.), *Baby Talk and Infant Speech* (Neurolinguistics 5). Amsterdam: Swets & Zeitlinger.

Sachs, J. S., & Johnson, M. (1976). Language development in a hearing child of deaf parents. In W. van Raffler Engel & Y. Lebrun (Eds.), *Baby Talk and Infant Speech* (Neurolinguistics 5). Amsterdam: Swets & Zeitlinger.

Sadalla, E. K., Burroughs, W. J., & Staplin, L. J. (1980). Reference points in spatial cognition. *Journal of Experimental Psychology: Human Learning and Memory, 6,* 516–528.

Samuel, A. G. (1981). The role of bottom-up confirmation in the phonemic restoration illusion. *Journal of Experimental Psychology: Human Perception and Performance, 7,* 1124–1131.

Santa, J. L., Ruskin, A. B., Snuttjer, D., & Baker, L. (1975). Retrieval in cued recall. *Memory & Cognition, 3,* 341–348.

Sapir, E. (1944). Grading: A study in semantics. *Philosophy of Science, 11,* 93–116.

Sarbin, J. R., & Coe, W. C. (1972). *Hypnosis: A Social Psychological Analysis of Influence Communication.* New York: Holt, Rinehart and Winston.

Sarno, M. T. (1976). The status of research in recovery from aphasia. In Y. Lebrun & R. Hoops (Eds.), *Recovery in Aphasics.* Amsterdam: Swets & Zeitlinger.

Saugstad, P. (1955). Problem-solving as dependent on availability of functions. *British Journal of Psychology, 46,* 191–198.

Saugstad, P., & Raaheim, K. (1960). Problem-solving, past experience and availability of functions. *British Journal of Psychology, 51,* 97–104.

Savage-Rambaugh, E. S., Pate, J. L., Lawson, J., Smith, S. T., & Rosenbaum, S. (1983). Can a chimpanzee make a statement? *Journal of Experimental Psychology: General, 112,* 457–492.

Scarborough, D. L., Cortese, C., & Scarborough, H. S. (1977). Frequency and repetition effects in lexical memory. *Journal of Experimental Psychology: Human Perception and Performance, 3,* 1–17.

Scarborough, D. L., Gerard, L., & Cortese, C. (1979). Accessing lexical memory: The transfer of word repetition effects across task and modality. *Memory & Cognition, 7,* 3–12.

Scarborough, H. S. (1984). Continuity between childhood dyslexia and adult reading. *British Journal of Psychology, 75,* 329–348.

Schaeffer, B., & Wallace, R. (1969). Semantic similarity and the comparison of word meanings. *Journal of Experimental Psychology, 82,* 343–346.

Schaeffer, B., & Wallace, R. (1970). The comparison of word meanings. *Journal of Experimental Psychology, 86,* 144–152.

Schaie, K. W., & Parham, I. A. (1977). Cohort-sequential analyses of adult intellectual development. *Developmental Psychology, 13,* 649–653.

Schaie, K. W., & Strother, C. R. (1968). A cross-sequential study of age changes in cognitive behavior. *Psychological Bulletin, 70,* 671–680.

Schatz, C. D. (1954). The role of context in the perception of stops. *Language, 30,* 47–56.

Schiffman, H. R. (1967). Size estimation of familiar objects under informative and reduced conditions of viewing. *American Journal of Psychology, 80,* 229–235.

Schindler, R. M. (1978). The effect of prose context on visual search for letters. *Memory & Cognition, 6,* 124–130.

Schneider, W., & Shiffrin, R. M. (1977). Controlled and automatic human information processing. I. Detection, search, and attention. *Psychological Review, 84,* 1–66.

Schuell, H. (1974). *Aphasia Theory and Therapy: Selected Lectures and Papers of*

*Hildred Schuell.* Baltimore: University Park Press.

Schvaneveldt, R. W., Durso, F. T., & Mukerji, B. R. (1982). Semantic distance effects in categorization tasks. *Journal of Experimental Psychology: Human Learning and Memory, 18,* 1–15.

Schwartz, E. R. (1974). Characteristics of speech and language development in the child with myelomeningocele and hydrocephalus. *Journal of Speech and Hearing Disorders, 39,* 465–468.

Seamon, J. G. (1980). *Human Memory: Contemporary Readings.* New York: Oxford University Press.

Seamon, J. G., & Chumbley, J. I. (1977). Retrieval processes for serial order information. *Memory & Cognition, 5,* 709–715.

Searle, J. R. (1969). *Speech Acts.* Cambridge: Cambridge University Press.

Searleman, A. (1977). A review of right hemisphere linguistic capabilities. *Psychological Bulletin, 84,* 503–528.

Segal, S. J., & Fusella, V. (1970). Influence of imaged pictures and sounds in detection of visual and auditory signals. *Journal of Experimental Psychology, 83,* 458–474.

Seidenberg, M. S., Tanenhaus, M. K., Leiman, J. M., & Bienkowski, M. (1982). Automatic access of the meanings of ambiguous words in context: Some limitations of knowledge-based processing. *Cognitive Psychology, 14,* 489–537.

Selfe, L. (1977). *Nadia: A Case of Extraordinary Drawing Ability in an Autistic Child.* New York: Harcourt Brace Jovanovich.

Selfridge, O. G., & Neisser, U. (1960). Pattern recognition by machine. *Scientific American, 203,* 60–68.

Shaffer, W. O., & La Berge, D. (1979). Automatic semantic processing of unattended words. *Journal of Verbal Learning and Verbal Behavior, 18,* 413–426.

Shanon, B. (1978). Classification and identification in an aphasic patient. *Brain and Language, 5,* 188–194.

Shanon, B. (1979). Yesterday, today, and tomorrow. *Acta Psychologica, 43,* 469–476.

Shatz, M. (1983). Communication. In J. Flavell & E. Markman (Eds.), *Cognitive Development.* In P. Mussen (Gen. ed.), *Handbook of Child Psychology* (4th ed.). New York: Wiley.

Shatz, M., & Gelman, R. (1973). The development of communication skills: Modifications in the speech of young children as a function of listener. *Monographs of the Society for Research in Child Development, 38* (Serial No. 152).

Shean, G. (1978). *Schizophrenia.* Cambridge, Mass.: Winthrop.

Shepard, R. N. (1962a). The analysis of proximities: Multidimensional scaling with an unknown distance function. Part I. *Psychometrika, 27,* 125–140.

Shepard, R. N. (1962b). The analysis of proximities: Multidimensional scaling with an unknown distance function. Part II. *Psychometrika, 27,* 219–246.

Shepard, R. N. (1964). Attention and the metric structure of the stimulus space. *Journal of Mathematical Psychology, 1,* 54–87.

Shepard, R. N. (1967). Recognition memory for words, sentences, and pictures. *Journal of Verbal Learning and Verbal Behavior, 6,* 156–163.

Shepard, R. N. (1974). Representation of structure in similarity data: Problems and prospects. *Psychometrika, 39,* 373–421.

Shepard, R. N. (1980). Multidimensional scaling, tree-fitting, and clustering. *Science, 210,* 390–398.

Shepard, R. N., & Cooper, L. A. (1982). *Mental Images and Their Transformations.* Cambridge, Mass.: MIT Press.

Shepard, R. N., & Feng, C. (1972). A chronometric study of mental paper folding. *Cognitive Psychology, 3*, 228–243.

Shepard, R. N., & Metzler, J. (1971). Mental rotation of three-dimensional objects. *Science, 171*, 701–703.

Shepard, R. N., & Podgorny, P. (1978). Cognitive processes that resemble perceptual processes. In W. K. Estes (Ed.), *Handbook of Learning and Cognitive Processes* (Vol. 5). Hillsdale, N.J.: Erlbaum.

Shiffrin, R. M., & Gardner, G. T. (1972). Visual processing capacity and attentional control. *Journal of Experimental Psychology, 93*, 72–82.

Shiffrin, R. M., & Grantham, D. W. (1974). Can attention be allocated to sensory modalities? *Perception & Psychophysics, 15*, 460–474.

Shiffrin, R. M., & Schneider, W. (1977). Controlled and automatic human information processing. II. Perceptual learning, automatic attending, and a general theory. *Psychological Review, 84*, 127–190.

Shor, R. E., & Orne, E. C. (1962). *The Harvard Group Scale of Hypnotic Susceptibility: Form A.* Palo Alto, Calif.: Consulting Psychologists Press.

Silveira, J. (1971). *Incubation: The Effect of Interruption Timing and Length on Problem Solution and Quality of Problem Processing.* Unpublished doctoral dissertation, University of Oregon. (Cited in Posner 1973.)

Simon, H. (1973). The structure of ill-structured problems. *Artificial Intelligence, 4*, 181–201.

Simon, H., & Gilmartin, K. (1973). A simulation of memory for chess positions. *Cognitive Psychology, 5*, 29–46.

Simon, H., & Reed, S. (1976). Modeling strategy shifts in a problem-solving task. *Cognitive Psychology, 8*, 86–97.

Singer, G., & Day, R. N. (1969). Visual capture of haptically judged depth. *Perception & Psychophysics, 5*, 315–316.

Slack, C. W. (1956). Familiar size as a cue to size in the presence of conflicting cues. *Journal of Experimental Psychology, 52*, 194–198.

Slamecka, N. J. (1968). An examination of trace storage in free recall. *Journal of Experimental Psychology, 76*, 504–513.

Slamecka, N. J. (1969). Testing for associative storage in multitrial free recall. *Journal of Experimental Psychology, 81*, 557–560.

Slobin, D. I. (1966). Grammatical transformations and sentence comprehension in childhood and adulthood. *Journal of Verbal Learning and Verbal Behavior, 5*, 219–227.

Slobin, D. I. (1973). Cognitive prerequisites for the acquisition of grammar. In C. A. Ferguson & D. I. Slobin (Eds.), *Studies of Child Language Development.* New York: Holt, Rinehart and Winston.

Slobin, D. I. (1979). *Psycholinguistics.* Glenview, Ill.: Scott, Foresman.

Smith, E. E. (1968). Choice reaction time: An analysis of the major theoretical positions. *Psychological Bulletin, 69*, 77–110.

Smith, E. E. (1978). Theories of semantic memory. In W. K. Estes (Ed.), *Handbook of Learning and Cognitive Processes* (Vol. 6). Hillsdale, N.J.: Erlbaum.

Smith, E. E., Barresi, J., & Gross, A. E. (1971). Imaginal versus verbal coding and the primary-secondary memory distinction. *Journal of Verbal Learning and Verbal Behavior, 10*, 597–603.

Smith, E. E., & Medin, D. L. (1981). *Categories and Concepts.* Cambridge, Mass.: Harvard University Press.

Smith, E. E., Shoben, E. J., & Rips, L. J. (1974). Structure and process in semantic memory: A featural model for semantic decisions. *Psychological Review, 81*, 214–241.

Smith, M. C., & Magee, L. E. (1980). Tracing the time course of picture-word processing. *Journal of Experimental Psychology: General, 109*, 373–392.

Smith, S. B. (1983). *The Great Mental Calculators: The Psychology, Methods, and Lives of Calculating Prodigies, Past and Present.* New York: Columbia University Press.

Smith, S. M. (1979). Remembering in and out of context. *Journal of Experimental Psychology: Human Learning and Memory, 5*, 460–471.

Smith, S. M., Glenberg, A., & Bjork, R. A. (1978). Environmental context and human memory. *Memory & Cognition, 6*, 342–353.

Snow, C. E. (1972). Mothers' speech to children learning language. *Child Development, 43*, 549–565.

Snow, C. E. (1977). The development of conversation between mothers and babies. *Journal of Child Language, 4*, 1–22.

Snow, C. E., Arlman-Rupp, A., Hassing, Y., Jobse, J., Joosten, J., & Vorster, J. (1976). Mothers' speech in three social classes. *Journal of Psycholinguistic Research, 5*, 1–20.

Snyder, S. (1974). *Madness and the Brain.* New York: McGraw-Hill.

Sokolov, E. N. (1969). The modeling properties of the nervous system. In M. Cole & I. Maltzman (Eds.), *A Handbook of Contemporary Soviet Psychology.* New York: Basic Books.

Sorkin, R., Pohlman, L., & Gilliam, J. (1973). Simultaneous two-channel signal detection. III. 630 and 1400 Hz signals. *Journal of the Acoustical Society of America, 53*, 1045–1051.

Sowa, J. F. (1983). *Conceptual Structures: Information Processing in Mind and Machine.* Reading, Mass.: Addison-Wesley.

Sparks, R., & Geschwind, N. (1968). Dichotic listening in man after section of neocortical commissures. *Cortex, 4*, 3–16.

Sperling, G. (1960). The information available in brief visual presentations. *Psychological Monographs, 74*, 1–29.

Spiro, R. J. (1980). Accommodative reconstruction in prose recall. *Journal of Verbal Learning and Verbal Behavior, 19*, 84–95.

Squire, L. R. (1981). Two forms of human amnesia: An analysis of forgetting. *Journal of Neuroscience, 1*, 635–640.

Squire, L. R., & Slater, P. C. (1975). Forgetting in very long-term memory as assessed by an improved questionnaire technique. *Journal of Experimental Psychology: Human Learning and Memory, 1*, 50–54.

Squire, L. R., Slater, P. C., & Chace, P. M. (1975). Retrograde amnesia: Temporal gradient in very long-term memory following electroconvulsive therapy. *Science, 187*, 77–79.

Standing, L. (1973). Learning 10,000 pictures. *Quarterly Journal of Experimental Psychology, 25*, 207–222.

Standing, L., Conezio, J., & Haber, R. N. (1970). Perception and memory for pictures: Single-trial learning of 2560 visual stimuli. *Psychonomic Science, 19*, 73–74.

Sternberg, S. (1975). Memory scanning: New findings and current controversies. *Quarterly Journal of Experimental Psychology, 27*, 1–32.

Sternberg, S., Knoll, R. L., & Gates, B. A. (1971). *Prior Entry Reexamined: Effect of Attentional Bias on Order Perception.* Paper presented at the Psychonomic Society meeting, San Antonio.

Sternberg, S., Knoll, R. L., & Wright, C. E. (1978). Experiments on temporal aspects of keyboard entry. In J. P. Duncanson (Ed.), *Getting It Together: Research and Applications in Human Factors.* Santa Monica: Human Factors Society.

Stevens, A., & Coupe, P. (1978). Distortions in judged spatial relations. *Cognitive Psychology, 10*, 422–437.

Stigler, J. W. (1984). "Mental abacus": The effect of abacus training on Chinese children's mental calculation. *Cognitive Psychology, 16*, 145–176.

Stoke, S. M. (1929). Memory for onomatopes. *Journal of Genetic Psychology, 36*, 594–596.

Stratton, G. M. (1897). Vision without inversion of the retinal image. *Psychological Review, 4*, 341–360.

Stratton, G. M. (1917). The mnemonic feat of the "Shass Pollak." *Psychological Review, 24*, 244–247.

Stroh, C. M. (1971). *Vigilance: The Problem of Sustained Attention.* Oxford: Pergamon Press.

Stroop, J. R. (1935). Studies of interference in serial verbal reactions. *Journal of Experimental Psychology, 18*, 643–662.

Sugarman, S. (1983). Why talk? Comment on Savage-Rumbaugh *et al. Journal of Experimental Psychology: General, 112*, 493–497.

Sulin, R. A., & Dooling, D. J. (1974). Intrusions of a thematic idea in retention of prose. *Journal of Experimental Psychology, 103*, 255–262.

Swets, J. A., Tanner, W. P., & Birdsall, T. G. (1961). Decision processes in perception. *Psychological Review, 68*, 301–340.

Swinney, D. A. (1979). Lexical access during sentence comprehension: (Re)consideration of context effects. *Journal of Verbal Learning and Verbal Behavior, 18*, 645–659.

Taft, M. (1979). Lexical access via an orthographic code: The basic orthographic syllabic structure (boss). *Journal of Verbal Learning and Verbal Behavior, 18*, 21–29.

Talland, G. (1965). *Deranged Memory.* New York: Academic Press.

Tanenhaus, M. K., Leiman, J. M., & Seidenberg, M. S. (1979). Evidence for multiple stages in the processing of ambiguous words in syntactic contexts. *Journal of Verbal Learning and Verbal Behavior, 18*, 427–440.

Taplin, J. E. (1971). Reasoning with conditional sentences. *Journal of Verbal Learning and Verbal Behavior, 10*, 219–225.

Taplin, J. E., & Staudenmayer, H. (1973). Interpretation of abstract conditional sentences in deductive reasoning. *Journal of Verbal Learning and Verbal Behavior, 12*, 530–542.

Taubman, R. E. (1950). Studies in judged number. I. The judgment of auditory number. II. The judgment of visual number. *Journal of General Psychology, 43*, 167–219.

Taylor, I. (1976). *Introduction to Psycholinguistics.* New York: Holt, Rinehart and Winston.

Teghtsoonian, R., & Teghtsoonian, M. (1970). Two varieties of perceived length. *Perception & Psychophysics, 8*, 389–392.

Tenenbaum, J. M., & Barrow, H. G. (1977). Experiments in interpretation-guided segmentation. *Artificial Intelligence, 8*, 241–274.

Terrace, H. S. (1979). *Nim.* New York: Knopf.

Thomas, J. C., Jr. (1974). An analysis of behavior in the hobbits-orcs problem. *Cognitive Psychology, 6*, 257–269.

Thompson, R. K. R. (1980). *Auditory Cued Reversal and Matching-to-Sample Learning by Rhesus Monkeys.* Paper presented at the Eighth Congress of Primatology, Florence, Italy.

Thompson, R. K. R., & Herman, L. M. (1981). Auditory delayed discriminations by the dolphin: Nonequivalence with delayed-matching performance. *Animal Learning and Behavior, 9*, 9–15.

Thompson, J. R., & Chapman, R. S. (1977). Who is "Daddy" revisited: The status of two-year-olds' over-extended words in use and comprehension. *Journal of Child Language, 4,* 359–375.

Thorndyke, P. W. (1977). Cognitive structures in comprehension and memory of narrative discourse. *Cognitive Psychology, 9,* 77–110.

Thorndyke, P. W., & Hayes-Roth, B. (1982). Differences in spatial knowledge acquired from maps and navigation. *Cognitive Psychology, 14,* 560–589.

Titchener, E. B. (1908). *Lectures on the Elementary Psychology of Feeling and Attention.* New York: Macmillan.

Todd, J. T. (1982). Visual information about rigid and nonrigid motion: A geometric analysis. *Journal of Experimental Psychology: Human Perception and Performance, 8,* 238–252.

Tolman, E. C. (1948). Cognitive maps in rats and men. *Psychological Review, 55,* 189–208.

Trabasso, T., Riley, C. A., & Wilson, E. G. (1975). The representation of linear order and spatial strategies in reasoning: A developmental study. In R. Falmagne (Ed.), *Psychological Studies of Logic and Development.* Hillsdale, N.J.: Erlbaum.

Treat, N. J., & Reese, H. W. (1976). Age, pacing, and imagery in paired-associate learning. *Developmental Psychology, 12,* 119–124.

Treisman, A. M. (1977). Focused attention in the perception and retrieval of multidimensional stimuli. *Perception & Psychophysics, 22,* 1–11.

Treisman, A. M. (1982). Perceptual grouping and attention in visual search for features and for objects. *Journal of Experimental Psychology: Human Perception and Performance, 8,* 194–214.

Treisman, A. M., Squire, R., & Green, J. (1974). Semantic processing in dichotic listening? A replication. *Memory & Cognition, 2,* 641–646.

Treisman, A. M. (1964). Verbal cues, language, and meaning in selective attention. *American Journal of Psychology, 77,* 215–216.

Treisman, A. M., & Davis, A. (1973). Divided attention to ear and eye. In S. Kornblum (Ed.), *Attention and Performance IV.* New York: Academic Press.

Treisman, A. M., & Geffen, G. (1967). Selective attention: Perception or response? *Quarterly Journal of Experimental Psychology, 19,* 1–17.

Treisman, A. M., & Gelade, G. (1980). A feature-integration theory of attention. *Cognitive Psychology, 12,* 97–136.

Treisman, A. M., & Riley, J. G. A. (1969). Is selective attention selective perception or selective response? A further test. *Journal of Experimental Psychology, 79,* 27–34.

Tulving, E. (1962). Subjective organization in free recall of "unrelated" words. *Psychological Review, 69,* 344–354.

Tulving, E. (1967). The effects of presentation and recall of materials in free-recall learning. *Journal of Verbal Learning and Verbal Behavior, 6,* 175–184.

Tulving, E. (1968). When is recall higher than recognition? *Psychonomic Science, 10,* 53–54.

Tulving, E. (1972). Episodic and semantic memory. In E. Tulving & W. Donaldson (Eds.), *Organization and Memory.* New York: Academic Press.

Tulving, E. (1981). Similarity relations in recognition. *Journal of Verbal Learning and Verbal Behavior, 20,* 479–496.

Tulving, E., & Lindsay, P. H. (1967). Identification of simultaneously presented simple visual and auditory stimuli. In A. F. Sanders (Ed.), *Attention and Performance I.* Amsterdam: North-Holland.

Turkewitz, G., & Birch, H. G. (1971). Neurobehavioral organization of the human newborn. In J. Hellmuth (Ed.), *Exceptional Infant* (Vol. 2). New York: Brunner/Mazel.

Tversky, A. (1977). Features of similarity. *Psychological Review, 84*, 327–352.

Tversky, A., & Gati, I. (1978). Studies in similarity. In E. Rosch & B. B. Lloyd (Eds.), *Cognition and Categorization*. Hillsdale, N.J.: Erlbaum.

Tversky, A., & Kahneman, D. (1973). Availability: A heuristic for judging frequency and probability. *Cognitive Psychology, 5*, 207–232.

Tversky, A., & Kahneman, D. (1974). Judgments under uncertainty: Heuristics and biases. *Science, 185*, 1124–1131.

Tversky, A., & Kahneman, D. (1978). Causal schemata in judgments under uncertainty. In M. Fishbein (Ed.), *Progress in Social Psychology*. Hillsdale, N.J.: Erlbaum.

Tversky, A., & Kahneman, D. (1983). Extensional versus intuitive reasoning: The conjunction fallacy in probability judgment. *Psychological Review, 90*, 293–315.

Tversky, B. (1981). Distortions in memory for maps. *Cognitive Psychology, 13*, 407–433.

Tweney, R. D. (Ed.). (1981). *On Scientific Thinking*. New York: Columbia University Press.

Ullman, S. (1979). *The Interpretation of Visual Motion*. Cambridge, Mass.: MIT Press.

Underwood, B. J. (1957). Interference and forgetting. *Psychological Review, 64*, 49–60.

Underwood, G. (1976). Semantic interference from unattended printed words. *British Journal of Psychology, 67*, 327–338.

Unger, S. M. (1964). Habituation of the vasoconstrictive orienting reaction. *Journal of Experimental Psychology, 67*, 11–18.

Vellutino, F. R. (1979). *Dsylexia: Theory and Research*. Cambridge, Mass.: MIT Press.

Victor, M., Adams, R. D., & Collins, G. H. (1977). *The Wernicke-Korsakoff Syndrome*. Philadelphia: Davis.

Von Frisch, K. (1967). [*The Dance Language and Orientation of Bees*] (C. E. Chadwick, trans.). Cambridge, Mass.: Belknap Press.

Von Restorff, H. (1933). Uber die Wirkung von Bereichsbildungen im Spurenfeld. *Psychologisch Forschung, 18*, 299–342.

Wada, J. A. (1977). Prelanguage and fundamental asymmetry of the infant brain. *Annals of the New York Academy of Sciences, 299*, 370–379.

Wagner, D. A. (1974). The development of short-term and incidental memory: A cross-cultural study. *Child Development, 45*, 389–396.

Walker, J. T., & Scott, K. J. (1981). Auditory-visual conflicts in the perceived duration of lights, tones, and gaps. *Journal of Experimental Psychology: Human Perception and Performance, 7*, 1327–1339.

Wallace, B. (1984). Apparent equivalence between perception and imagery in the production of various visual illusions. *Memory & Cognition, 12*, 156–162.

Wallace, B., & Fisher, L. E. (1983). *Consciousness and Behavior*. Boston: Allyn and Bacon.

Wallas, G. (1926). *The Art of Thought*. New York: Harcourt, Brace.

Wallsten, T. S. (Ed.). (1980). *Cognitive Processes in Choice and Decision Behavior*. Hillsdale, N.J.: Erlbaum.

Waltz, D. L. (1975). Understanding line drawings of scenes with shadows. In P. H. Winston (Ed.), *The Psychology of Computer Vision*. New York: McGraw-Hill.

Wanner, E., & Gleitman, L. (Eds.). (1982). *Language Acquisition*. New York: Cambridge University Press.

Wardlaw, K. A., & Knoll, N. E. (1976). Autonomic responses to shock-associated words in a non-attended message: A failure to replicate. *Journal of Experimental Psychology: Human Perception and Performance, 2,* 357–360.

Warr, P. B. (1964). The relative importance of proactive inhibition and degree of learning in retention of paired-associate items. *British Journal of Psychology, 55,* 19–30.

Warren, D. H., & Cleaves, W. T. (1971). Visual-proprioceptive interaction under large amounts of conflict. *Journal of Experimental Psychology, 90,* 206–214.

Warren, D. H., & Pick, H. L. (1970). Intermodality relation in localization in blind and sighted people. *Perception & Psychophysics, 8,* 430–432.

Warren, J. M. (1977). Functional lateralization of the brain. *Annals of the New York Academy of Sciences, 299,* 273–280.

Warren, L. R., & Horn, J. W. (1982). What does naming a picture do? Effects of prior picture naming on recognition of identical and same-name alternatives. *Memory & Cognition, 10,* 167–175.

Warren, R. M. (1970). Perceptual restoration of missing speech sounds. *Science, 167,* 392–393.

Warren, R. M., & Obusek, C. J. (1971). Speech perception and phonemic restorations. *Perception & Psychophysics, 9,* 358–362.

Warren, R. M., & Warren, R. P. (1970). Auditory illusions and confusions. *Scientific American, 223,* 30–36.

Warrington, E. K., & Sanders, H. (1971). The fate of old memories. *Quarterly Journal of Experimental Psychology, 23,* 432–442.

Wason, P. C. (1966). Reasoning. In B. M. Foss (Ed.), *New Horizons in Psychology.* Harmondsworth: Penguin.

Wason, P. C. (1968). Reasoning about a rule. *Quarterly Journal of Experimental Psychology, 20,* 273–281.

Wason, P. C., & Johnson-Laird, P. N. (1972). *Psychology of Reasoning.* Cambridge, Mass.: Harvard University Press.

Wason, R. A. (1983). Realism and rationality in the selection task. In J. St. B. T. Evans (Ed.), *Thinking and Reasoning: Psychological Approaches.* London: Routledge & Kegan Paul.

Watkins, M. J., & Gardiner, J. M. (1979). An appreciation of generate-recognize theory of recall. *Journal of Verbal Learning and Verbal Behavior, 18,* 687–704.

Watkins, O. G., & Watkins, M. J. (1975). Buildup of proactive interference as a cue-overload effect. *Journal of Experimental Psychology: Human Learning and Memory, 104,* 442–452.

Waugh, N. C., & Norman, D. A. (1965). Primary memory. *Psychological Review, 72,* 89–104.

Wechsler, D. (1945). A standardized memory scale for clinical use. *Journal of Psychology, 19,* 87–95.

Weisberg, R. W., & Alba, J. W. (1981). An examination of the alleged role of "fixation" in the solution of several "insight" problems. *Journal of Experimental Psychology: General, 110,* 169–192.

Weisberg, R., & Suls, J. (1973). An information-processing model of Duncker's candle problem. *Cognitive Psychology, 4,* 255–276.

Weitzenhoffer, A. M., & Hilgard, E. R. (1959). *Stanford Hypnotic Susceptibility Scale: Forms A and B.* Palo Alto, Calif.: Consulting Psychologists Press.

Weitzenhoffer, A. M., & Hilgard, E. R. (1962). *Stanford Hypnotic Susceptibility Scale: Form C.* Palo Alto, Calif.: Consulting Psychologists Press.

Wellman, H. M. (1977). Tip-of-the-tongue and the feeling of knowing experience: A developmental study of memory monitoring. *Child Development, 48,* 13–21.

Wells, C. E. (1979). Pseudodementia. *American Journal of Psychiatry, 136,* 895–900.

Weltman, G., Smith, J. E., and Egstom, G. H. (1971). Perceptual narrowing during simulated pressure-chamber exposure. *Human Factors, 13,* 99–107.

Wertheimer, M. (1923). Untersuchungen zur Lehre von der Gestalt. II. *Psychologische Forschung, 4,* 301–350. [Principles of perceptual organization] (abridged translation by M. Wertheimer, 1958). In D. C. Beardslee & M. Wertheimer (Eds.), *Readings in Perception.* New York: Van Nostrand.

Wertheimer, M. (1959). *Productive Thinking.* New York: Harper & Row.

West, L. J. (1967). Vision and kinesthesis in the acquisition of typewriting skill. *Journal of Applied Psychology, 51,* 161–166.

Wheeler, D. D. (1970). Processes in word recognition. *Cognitive Psychology, 1,* 59–85.

Whitaker, M. A., & Ojemann, G. A. (1977). Lateralization of higher cortical functions: A critique. *Annals of the New York Academy of Sciences, 299,* 459–473.

Whitten, W. B., & Leonard, J. M. (1981). Directed search through autobiographical memory. *Memory & Cognition, 9,* 566–579.

Whorf, B. L. (1956). Science and linguistics. In J. B. Carroll (Ed.), *Language, Thought and Reality: Selected Writings of Benjamin Lee Whorf.* Cambridge, Mass.: MIT Press.

Wickelgren, W. A. (1974). *How to Solve Problems.* San Francisco: Freeman.

Wickelgren, W. A. (1975). More on the long and short of memory. In D. Deutsch & J. A. Deutsch (Eds.), *Short-term Memory.* New York: Academic Press.

Wickens, D. D. (1972). Characteristics of word encoding. In A. W. Melton & E. Martin (Eds.), *Coding Processes in Human Memory.* Washington, D.C.: Winston.

Wickens, D. D., Born, D. G., & Allen, C. K. (1963). Proactive inhibition and item similarity in short-term memory. *Journal of Verbal Learning and Verbal Behavior, 2,* 440–445.

Wilkins, A. T. (1971). Conjoint frequency, category size, and categorization time. *Journal of Verbal Learning and Verbal Behavior, 10,* 382–385.

Wilkins, M. C. (1928). The effect of changed material on the ability to do formal syllogistic reasoning. *Archives of Psychology, 16,* No. 102.

Wingfield, A., & Byrnes, D. L. (1981). *The Psychology of Human Memory.* New York: Academic Press.

Winocur, G., Kinsbourne, M., & Moscovitch, M. (1981). The effect of cuing on release from proactive interference in Korsakoff-amnesic patients. *Journal of Experimental Psychology: Human Learning and Memory, 7,* 56–65.

Winston, P. H. (1984). *Artificial Intelligence* (2nd ed.). Reading, Mass.: Addison-Wesley.

Witelson, S. F. (1977). Anatomic asymmetry in the temporal lobes: Its documentation, phylogenesis, and relationship to functional asymmetry. *Annals of the New York Academy of Sciences, 299,* 328–354.

Wittgenstein, L. (1953). *Philosophical Investigations.* New York: Macmillan.

Wixon, D. R., & Laird, J. D. (1976). Awareness and attitude change in the forced compliance paradigm: The importance of when. *Journal of Personality and Social Psychology, 34,* 376–384.

Wollen, K. A., Weber, A., & Lowry, D. (1972). Bizarreness versus interaction of mental images as determinants of learning. *Cognitive Psychology, 3,* 518–523.

Woocher, F. D., Glass, A. L., & Holyoak, K. J. (1978). Positional discriminability in linear orderings. *Memory & Cognition, 6,* 165–173.

Woodhead, M. M., & Baddeley, A. D. (1981). Individual differences and memory for faces, pictures, and words. *Memory & Cognition, 9,* 368–370.

Woods, B. T. (1980). The restricted effects of right hemisphere lesions after age one: Wechsler test data. *Neuropsychologia, 18,* 65–70.

Woods, B. T., & Teuber, H. L. (1978). Changing patterns of childhood aphasia. *Annals of Neurology, 3,* 273–280.

Woodward, A. E., Bjork, R. A., & Jongeward, R. H., Jr. (1973). Recall and recognition as a function of primary rehearsal. *Journal of Verbal Learning and Verbal Behavior, 12,* 608–617.

Woodworth, R. S. (1938). *Experimental Psychology.* New York: Holt, Rinehart and Winston.

Woodworth, R. S., & Schlosberg, H. (1954). *Experimental Psychology.* New York: Holt, Rinehart and Winston.

Woodworth, R. S., & Sells, S. B. (1935). An atmosphere effect in syllogistic reasoning. *Journal of Experimental Psychology, 18,* 451–460.

Yates, F. A. (1966). *The Art of Memory.* London: Routledge & Kegan Paul.

Yates, J. F. (1983). Anticipating the unknown: How and how well. (Review of *Judgment Under Uncertainty: Heuristics and Biases,* edited by D. Kahneman, P. Slovic, & A. Tversky.) *Contemporary Psychology, 28,* 181–182.

Zaidel, E. (1976). Auditory vocabulary of the right hemisphere following brain bisection or hemidecortication. *Cortex, 12,* 191–211.

Zaidel, E. (1978a). Lexical organization in the right hemisphere. In P. Buser & A. Rougel-Buser (Eds.), *Cerebral Correlates of Conscious Experience.* Amsterdam: North Holland.

Zaidel, E. (1978b). Concepts of cerebral dominance in the split brain. In P. Buser & A. Rougel-Buser (Eds.), *Cerebral Correlates of Conscious Experience.* Amsterdam: North Holland.

Zaidel, E. (1983). A response to Gazzaniga. Language in the right hemisphere, convergent perspectives. *American Psychologist, 38,* 542–546.

Zelaznik, H. N., Shapiro, D. C., & McColsky, D. (1981). Effects of a secondary task on the accuracy of single aiming movements. *Journal of Experimental Psychology: Human Perception and Performance, 7,* 1007–1018.

Zelniker, T. (1971). Perceptual attenuation of an irrelevant auditory verbal input as measured by an involuntary verbal response in a selective-attention task. *Journal of Experimental Psychology, 87,* 52–56.

Zimler, J., & Keenan, J. M. (1983). Imagery in the congenitally blind: How visual are visual images? *Journal of Experimental Psychology: Learning, Memory, and Cognition, 9,* 269–282.

Zola-Morgan, S. M., & Oberg, R. G. (1980). Recall of life experiences in an alcoholic Korsakoff patient: A naturalistic approach. *Neuropsychologia, 18,* 549–557.

Zurif, E. B., Caramazza, A., Meyerson, R., & Galvin, J. (1974). Semantic feature representations for normal and aphasic language. *Brain and Language, 1,* 167–187.

172    Reed, S. K., 1972. Pattern recognition and categorization. *Cognitive Psychology* 3: 383–407.

187    Bower, G. H., and A. L. Glass, 1976. Structural units and the reintegrative power of picture fragments. *Journal of Experimental Psychology: Human Learning and Memory* 2: 456–466. Copyright 1976 by the American Psychological Association. Reprinted by permission.

190    Tulving, E., 1981. Similarity relations in recognition. *Journal of Verbal Learning and Verbal Behavior* 20: 479–496.

192    Biederman, I., R. J. Mezzanotte, and J. C. Rabinowitz, 1982. Scene perception: Detecting and judging objects undergoing relational violations. *Cognitive Psychology* 14: 143–177.

195    Rubin, D. C., and T. S. Kontis, 1983. A schema for common cents. *Memory & Cognition* 11: 335–341.

213    Keppel, G., and B. J. Underwood, 1962. Proactive inhibition in short-term retention of single terms. *Journal of Verbal Learning and Verbal Behavior* 1: 153–161.

216    Wickens, D. D., 1972. Characteristics of work encoding. In A. W. Melton and E. Martin (eds.), *Coding Processes in Human Memory*. Washington, D.C.: Winston. Reprinted by permission of Hemisphere Publishing Corporation.

219, 220, 221    Gruenewald, P. J., and G. R. Lockhead, 1980. The free recall of category examples. *Journal of Experimental Psychology: Human Learning and Memory* 6: 225–240.

226    Godden, D. R., and A. D. Baddeley, 1975. Context-dependent memory in two natural environments: on land and underwater. *British Journal of Psychology* 66: 325–332. Reprinted by permission of the British Psychological Society and Cambridge University Press, publishers.

232    Erdelyi, M. H., and J. Kleinbard, 1978. Has Ebbinghaus decayed with time?: the growth of recall (hypermnesia) over days. *Journal of Experimental Psychology: Human Learning and Memory* 4: 275–289. Copyright by the American Psychological Association. Reprinted by permission.

238    Dawes, R., 1964. Cognitive distortion. *Psychological Reports* 14: 443–459. Thorndyke, P. W., 1977. Cognitive structures in comprehension and memory of narrative discourse. *Cognitive Psychology* 9: 77–110.

247    Shanon, B., 1979. Yesterday, today, and tomorrow. *Acta Psychologica* 43: 469–476.

250    Anderson, R. C., and J. W. Pichert, 1978. Recall of previously unrecallable information following a shift in perspective. *Journal of Verbal Learning and Verbal Behavior* 17: 1–12.

253    Squire, L. R., P. C. Slater, and P. M. Chace, 1975. Retrograde amnesia: Temporal gradient in very long-term memory following electroconvulsive therapy. *Science* 187: 77–79.

256 Albert, M. S., N. Butters, and J. Levin, 1979. Temporal gradients in the retrograde amnesia of patients with alcoholic Korsakoff's disease. *Archives of Neurology* 36: 211–216.

257, 258 Butters, N., 1984. Alcoholic Korsakoff's syndrome: An update. *Seminars in Neurology* 4: 226–244.

266 Reber, A. S., 1967. Implicit learning of artificial grammars. *Journal of Verbal Learning and Verbal Behavior* 5: 855–863.

270 Madigan, S. A., 1969. Intraserial repetition and coding processes in free recall. *Journal of Verbal Learning and Verbal Behavior.* 8: 828–835.

272 Johnston, W. A., and C. N Uhl, 1976. The contributions of encoding effort and variability to the spacing effect on free recall. *Journal of Experimental Psychology: Human Learning and Memory* 2: 153–160. Copyright by the American Psychological Association. Reprinted by permission.

275 Detterman, D. K., and N. R. Ellis, 1972. Determinants of induced amnesia in short-term memory. *Journal of Experimental Psychology* 95: 308–316.

276 Underwood, B. J., 1957. Interference and forgetting. *Psychological Review* 64: 49–60.

279 Bahrick, H. P., 1984. Sematic memory content in permastore: Fifty years of memory for Spanish learned in school. *Journal of Experimental Psychology: General* 113: 1–29.

284 D'Agostino, P. R., B. J. O'Neill, and A. Paivio, 1977. Memory for pictures and words as a function of level of processing: Depth or dual coding? *Memory & Cognition* 5: 252–256.

285, 286 Durso, F. T., and M. K. Johnson, 1980. The effects of orienting tasks on recognition, recall, and modality confusion of pictures and words. *Journal of Verbal Learning and Verbal Behavior* 19: 416–429.

292 Loftus, E. F., 1977. Shifting human color memory. *Memory & Cognition* 5: 696–699.

299 Butters, N., P. Miliotis, M. S. Albert, and D. S. Sax, 1983. Memory assessment: Evidence of the heterogeneity of amnesic symptoms. In G. Goldstein (ed.), *Advances in Clinical Neuropsychology.* New York: Plenum.

305 Rundus, D., 1971. Analysis of rehersal processes in free recall. *Journal of Experimental Psychology* 89: 63–77. Copyright 1971 by the American Psychological Association. Reprinted by permission.

308 Craik, F. I. M., and M. J. Watkins, 1973. The role of rehersal in short-term memory. *Journal of Verbal Learning and Verbal Behavior* 12: 599–607.

312, 324, 325 Bower, G. H., M. C. Clark, A. M. Lesgold, and D. Winzenz, 1969. Hierarchical retrieval schemes in recall of categorized word lists. *Journal of Verbal Learning and Verbal Behavior* 8: 323–343.

313 Mandler, G., 1967. Organization and memory. In K. W. Spence and J. T. Spence (eds.), *The Psychology of Learning and Motivation,* Vol. 1. New York: Academic Press.

316, 317   Chase, W. G., and K. A. Ericsson, 1982. Skill and working memory. In G. H. Bower (ed.), *The Psychology of Learning and Motivation* Vol. 16. New York: Academic Press.

322   Baker, L., and J. L. Santa, 1977. Context, integration and retrieval. *Memory & Cognition* 5: 308–314.

342   Holyoak, K. J., and J. H. Walker, 1976. Subjective magnitude information in semantic orderings. *Journal of Verbal Learning and Verbal Behavior* 15: 287–299.

344   Wason, P. C., and P. N. Johnson-Laird, 1972. *Psychology of Reasoning.* Cambridge, Mass.: Harvard University Press.

348   Tversky, A., 1977. Features of similarity. *Psychological Review* 84: 327–352. Copyright 1977 by the American Psychological Association. Reprinted by permission.

349   Tversky, A., and I. Gati, 1978. Studies of similarity. In E. Rosch and B. B. Lloyd (eds.), *Cognition and Categorization.* Hillsdale, N.J.: Erlbaum.

359   Gilovich, T., 1981. Seeing the past in the present: The effect of associations to familiar events on judgments and decision. *Journal of Personality and Social Psychology* 40: 797–808.

372   Figure from *The Mind of a Mnemonist: A Little Book about a Vast Memory,* by a A. R. Luria, translated from the Russian by Lynn Solotaroff, © 1968 by Basic Books, Inc., Publishers, New York.

385   Gick, M. L., and K. J. Holyoak, 1983. Schema induction and analogical transfer. *Cognitive Psychology* 15: 1–38.

388, 389, 391   Chase, W. G., and H. A. Simon, 1973. The mind's eye in chess. In W. G. Chase (ed.), *Visual Information Processing.* New York: Academic Press.

390   Reitman, J., 1976. Skilled perception in Go: Deducing memory structures from inter-response times. *Cognitive Psychology* 8: 336–356.

393   Chi, M. T. H., P. J. Feltovich, and R. Glaser, 1981. Categorization and representation of physics problems by experts and novices. *Cognitive Science* 5: 121–152.

395   Luchins, A., 1942. Mechanization in problem solving. *Psychological Monographs* 54: No. 248.

401, 402   Allen Newell, Herbert A. Simon, *Human Problem Solving,* © 1972. Reprinted by permission of Prentice-Hall, Inc., Englewood Cliffs, New Jersey.

414   "Human Design–6" (p. 163) from *Children Solve Problems,* by Edward DeBono. Copyright © 1972 by The Cognitive Trust. By permission of Harper & Row, Publishers, Inc.

425   Liberman, A. M., 1982. On finding that speech is special. *American Psychologist* 37: 148–167.

436   Levy, J., C. Trevarthan, and R. W. Sperry, 1972. Perception of bilateral chimeric figures following hemispheric deconnexion. *Brain* 95: 61–78.

439   Rasmussen, T., and B. Milner, 1977. The role of early left-brain injury in determining lateralization of cerebral speech functions. *Annals of the New York Academy of Sciences* 299: 355–369.

470 Haberlandt, K., C. Berian and J. Sandson, 1980. The episodic schema in story processing. *Journal of Verbal Learning and Verbal Behavior* 19: 635–650.

475 Just, M. A., and P. A. Carpenter, 1980. A theory of reading: From eye fixations to comprehension. *Psychological Review* 87: 329–354.

# INDEX